Stanley Gibbons
Commonwealth Stamps

New Zealand & Dependencies

7th edition 2022

STANLEY GIBBONS
THE HOME OF STAMP COLLECTING

By Appointment to
Her Majesty The Queen
Philatelists
Stanley Gibbons Ltd,
London

Published by Stanley Gibbons Ltd
Editorial, Publications Sales Offices
and Distribution Centre:
7 Parkside, Christchurch Road, Ringwood,
Hants BH24 3SH

© Stanley Gibbons Ltd 2022

Copyright Notice

The contents of this Catalogue, including the numbering system and illustrations, are fully protected by copyright. Except as permitted in law, no part of this publication may be reproduced, stored in a retrieval system, or transmitted in any form or by any means, electronic, mechanical, photocopying, recording or otherwise, without the prior permission of Stanley Gibbons Limited. Requests for such permission should be addressed to the Catalogue Editor. This Catalogue is sold on condition that it is not, by way of trade or otherwise, lent, re-sold, hired out, circulated or otherwise disposed of other than in its complete, original and unaltered form and without a similar condition including this condition being imposed on the subsequent purchaser.

British Library Cataloguing in
Publication Data.
A catalogue record for this book is available
from the British Library.

1st Edition - 2003, 2nd Edition - 2006
3rd Edition - 2009, 4th Edition - 2010
5th Edition - 2014, 6th Edition - 2016
7th Edition - 2022

Errors and omissions excepted
the colour reproduction of stamps is only as
accurate as the printing process will allow.

ISBN-13: 978-1-911304-92-0

Item No. R2876-22

Printed by
Sterling, Kettering

Contents

Stanley Gibbons Holdings Plc	iv
General Philatelic Information	v
Prices	v
Guarantee	vi
Condition Guide	viii
The Catalogue in General	ix
Contacting the Editor	x
Technical Matters	x
Acknowledgements	xx
Abbreviations	xxi
Features Listing	xxii
International Philatelic Glossary	xxiv
Guide to Entries	xxviii
New Zealand's 'Third Pictorials'	xxx
New Zealand	1
Machine Labels	117
Customised Advertising Labels (CALs)	117
Regional Postage Labels	117
Design Index	119
Stamp Booklets	125
Premium Booklets	140
Express Delivery Stamps	143
Official Stamps	143
Official Stamp Booklet	145
Police Department Provisionals	145
Life Insurance Department	145
Postage Due Stamps	147
Postal Fiscal Stamps	148
Antarctic Expeditions	152
Ross Dependency	152
Tokelau Islands	156
Cook Islands	171
British Protectorate	171
New Zealand Territory	171
Aitutaki	175
Penrhyn Island	176
Niue	177
Samoa	181
German Protectorate	184
New Zealand Occupation	185
League of Nations Mandate	185
United Nations Trust Territory	187
New Zealand Used Abroad	188
Gilbert and Ellice Islands	188
Pitcairn Islands	188

Stanley Gibbons Holdings Plc

Stanley Gibbons Limited,
Stanley Gibbons Auctions
399 Strand, London WC2R 0LX
Tel: +44 (0)207 836 8444
E-mail: support@stanleygibbons.com
Website: www.stanleygibbons.com
for all departments, Auction and Specialist Stamp Departments.
Open Monday–Friday 9.30 a.m. to 6 p.m.
Shop. Open Monday–Saturday 9.30 a.m. to 6 p.m.

Stanley Gibbons Publications,
Mail Order, Gibbons Stamp Monthly
and Philatelic Exporter
7 Parkside, Christchurch Road,
Ringwood, Hampshire BH24 3SH.
Tel: +44 (0)1425 472363
E-mail: support@stanleygibbons.com
Monday–Friday 8.30 a.m. to 5 p.m.

Stanley Gibbons Publications
Overseas Representation
Stanley Gibbons Publications are represented overseas by the following

Australia
Renniks Publications PTY LTD
Unit 6, 30 Perry St, Matraville,
NSW 2036, Australia
Tel: +612 9695 7055
Website: www.renniks.com

Canada
Unitrade Associates
99 Floral Parkway, Toronto,
Ontario M6L 2C4, Canada
Tel: +1 416 242 5900
Website: www.unitradeassoc.com

Canada
F.v.H. Stamps
102-340 West Cordova Street,
Vancouver, BC, V6B 1E8, Canada
Tel: +1 604 684 8408
Website: www.fvhstamps.com

Denmark
Nordfrim A/S
Kvindevadet 42,
Otterup DK-5450, Denmark
Tel: +45 64 82 1256
Website: www.nordfrim.com

Italy
Ernesto Marini S.R.L.
V. Struppa, 300, Genova, 16165, Italy
Tel: +39 010 802 186
Website: www.ernestomarini.it

Japan
Japan Philatelic
PO Box 2, Suginami-Minami,
Tokyo 168-8081, Japan
Tel: +81 3330 41641
Website: www.yushu.co.jp

Netherlands
Uitgeverij Davo BV
PO Box 411, Ak Deventer, 7400
Netherlands
Tel: +3188 0284300
Website: www.davo.nl

New Zealand
Mowbray Collectables
Private Bag 63000
Wellington
New Zealand

New Zealand
Philatelic Distributors
PO Box 863
15 Mount Edgecumbe Street
New Plymouth 4615, New Zealand
Tel: +6 46 758 65 68
Website: www.stampcollecta.com

Singapore
C S Philatelic Agency
Peninsula Shopping Centre #04-29
3 Coleman Street, 179804, Singapore
Tel: +65 6337-1859
Website: www.cs.com.sg

USA
Vidiforms Company Inc
115 North Route 9W, Congers,
New York NY 10920, United States
Tel: +1 845 268 4005
Website: www.showgard.com

USA
Amos Media Company
1660 Campbell Road,
Suite A, Door #9,
Sidney OH 453652480,
United States
Tel: +1 937 498 2111
Website: www.amosmedia.com

General Philatelic Information and Guidelines to the Scope of Stanley Gibbons Commonwealth Catalogues

These notes reflect current practice in compiling the Stanley Gibbons Commonwealth Catalogues.

The Stanley Gibbons Stamp Catalogue has a very long history and the vast quantity of information it contains has been carefully built up by successive generations through the work of countless individuals. Philately is never static and the Catalogue has evolved and developed over the years. These notes relate to the current criteria upon which a stamp may be listed or priced. These criteria have developed over time and may have differed somewhat in the early years of this catalogue. These notes are not intended to suggest that we plan to make wholesale changes to the listing of classic issues in order to bring them into line with today's listing policy, they are designed to inform catalogue users as to the policies currently in operation.

PRICES

The prices quoted in this Catalogue are the estimated selling prices of Stanley Gibbons Ltd at the time of publication. They are, unless it is specifically stated otherwise, for examples in fine condition for the issue concerned. Superb examples are worth more; those of a lower quality considerably less.

All prices are subject to change without prior notice and Stanley Gibbons Ltd may from time to time offer stamps below catalogue price. Individual low value stamps sold at 399 Strand are liable to an additional handling charge. Purchasers of new issues should note the prices charged for them contain an element for the service rendered and so may exceed the prices shown when the stamps are subsequently catalogued. Postage and handling charges are extra.

No guarantee is given to supply all stamps priced, since it is not possible to keep every catalogued item in stock. Commemorative issues may, at times, only be available in complete sets and not as individual values.

Quotation of prices. The prices in the left-hand column are for unused stamps and those in the right-hand column are for used.

A dagger (†) denotes that the item listed does not exist or has not been reported in that condition and a blank, or dash, that it exists, or may exist, but we are unable to quote a price.

We welcome information concerning items which are currently unpriced. Such assistance may lead to them being priced in future editions.

Prices are expressed in pounds and pence sterling. One pound comprises 100 pence (£1 = 100p).

The method of notation is as follows: pence in numerals (e.g. 10 denotes ten pence); pounds and pence, up to £100, in numerals (e.g. 4·25 denotes four pounds and twenty-five pence); prices above £100 are expressed in whole pounds with the '£' sign shown.

Unused stamps. Great Britain and Commonwealth: the prices for unused stamps of Queen Victoria to King George V are for lightly hinged examples. Unused prices for King Edward VIII, King George VI and Queen Elizabeth issues are for unmounted mint (MNH).

Some stamps from the King George VI period are often difficult to find in unmounted mint condition. In such instances we would expect that collectors would need to pay a high proportion of the price quoted to obtain mounted mint examples. Generally speaking lightly mounted mint stamps from this reign, issued before 1945, are in considerable demand.

Used stamps. The used prices are normally for fine postally used stamps, which for the vast majority of those issued since 1900 refers to cancellation with a clear circular or oval dated postmark. It may also include stamps cancelled-to-order where this practice exists or with commemorative or first day postmarks.

A pen-cancellation on early issues can sometimes correctly denote postal use.

Prices quoted for bisects on cover or large piece are for those dated during the period officially authorised.

Stamps not sold unused to the public (e.g. some official stamps) are priced used only.

The use of 'unified' designs, that is stamps inscribed for both postal and fiscal purposes, results in a number of stamps of very high face value. In some instances these may not have been primarily intended for postal purposes, but if they are so inscribed we include them. The used prices shown refer to stamps postally used, although fiscally used examples are sometimes priced in brackets. Collectors should be careful to avoid stamps with fiscal cancellations that have been cleaned and fraudulent postmarks added.

Cover prices. To assist collectors, cover prices are quoted for issues up to 1945 at the beginning of each country.

The system gives a general guide in the form of a factor by which the corresponding used price of the basic loose stamp should be multiplied when found in fine average condition on cover.

Care is needed in applying the factors and they relate to a cover which bears a single of the denomination listed; if more than one denomination is present the most highly priced attracts the multiplier and the remainder are priced at the simple figure for used singles in arriving at a total.

The cover should be of non-philatelic origin; bearing the correct postal rate for the period and distance involved and cancelled with the markings normal to the offices concerned. **Purely philatelic items have a cover value only slightly greater than the catalogue value for the corresponding used stamps**. This applies generally to those high-value stamps used philatelically rather than in the normal course of commerce. Low-value stamps, e.g. ¼d. and ½d., are desirable when used as a single rate on cover and merit an increase in 'multiplier' value.

First day covers in the period up to 1945 are not within the scope of the system and the multiplier should not be used. As a special category of philatelic usage, with wide variations in valuation according to scarcity, they require separate treatment.

Oversized covers, difficult to accommodate on an album page, should be reckoned as worth little more

Information and Guidelines

than the corresponding value of the used stamps. The condition of a cover also affects its value. Except for 'wreck covers', serious damage or soiling reduce the value where the postal markings and stamps are ordinary ones. Conversely, visual appeal adds to the value and this can include freshness of appearance, important addresses, old-fashioned but legible handwriting, historic town-names, etc.

The multipliers are a base on which further value would be added to take account of the cover's postal historical importance in demonstrating such things as unusual, scarce or emergency cancels, interesting routes, significant postal markings, combination usage, the development of postal rates, and so on.

Minimum price. The minimum catalogue price quoted is 10p. For individual stamps prices between 10p. and 95p. are provided as a guide for catalogue users. The lowest price charged for individual stamps or sets purchased from Stanley Gibbons Ltd is £1

Set prices. Set prices are generally for one of each value, excluding shades and varieties, but including major colour changes. Where there are alternative shades, etc., the cheapest is usually included. The number of stamps in the set is always stated for clarity. The prices for sets containing *se-tenant* pieces are based on the prices quoted for such combinations, and not on those for the individual stamps.

Varieties. Where plate or cylinder varieties are priced in used condition the price quoted is for a fine used example with the cancellation well clear of the listed flaw.

Specimen stamps. The pricing of these items is explained under that heading.

Stamp booklets. Prices are for complete assembled booklets in fine condition with those issued before 1945 showing normal wear and tear. Incomplete booklets and those which have been 'exploded' will, in general, be worth less than the figure quoted.

Repricing. Collectors will be aware that the market factors of supply and demand directly influence the prices quoted in this Catalogue. Whatever the scarcity of a particular stamp, if there is no one in the market who wishes to buy it cannot be expected to achieve a high price. Conversely, the same item actively sought by numerous potential buyers may cause the price to rise.

All the prices in this Catalogue are examined during the preparation of each new edition by the expert staff of Stanley Gibbons and repriced as necessary. They take many factors into account, including supply and demand, and are in close touch with the international stamp market and the auction world.

Commonwealth cover prices and advice on postal history material originally provided by Edward B Proud.

GUARANTEE

All stamps are guaranteed originals in the following terms:

If not as described, and returned by the purchaser, we undertake to refund the price paid to us in the original transaction. If any stamp is certified as genuine by the Expert Committee of the Royal Philatelic Society, London, or by BPA Expertising Ltd, the purchaser shall not be entitled to make any claim against us for any error, omission or mistake in such certificate.

Consumers' statutory rights are not affected by the above guarantee.

The recognised Expert Committees in this country are those of the Royal Philatelic Society, 15 Abchurch Lane, London EC4 7BW, and BPA Expertising Ltd, PO Box 1141, Guildford, Surrey GU5 0WR. They do not undertake valuations under any circumstances and fees are payable for their services.

Information and Guidelines

MARGINS ON IMPERFORATE STAMPS

| Superb | Very fine | Fine | Average | Poor |

GUM

| Unmounted | Very lightly mounted | Lightly mounted | Mounted/ large part original gum (o.g.). | Heavily mounted small part o.g. |

CENTRING

| Superb | Very fine | Fine | Average | Poor |

CANCELLATIONS

| Superb | Very fine | Fine | Average | Poor |

Superb   Very fine

Fine   Average   Poor

CONDITION GUIDE

To assist collectors in assessing the true value of items they are considering buying or in reviewing stamps already in their collections, we now offer a more detailed guide to the condition of stamps on which this catalogue's prices are based.

For a stamp to be described as 'Fine', it should be sound in all respects, without creases, bends, wrinkles, pin holes, thins or tears. If perforated, all perforation 'teeth' should be intact, it should not suffer from fading, rubbing or toning and it should be of clean, fresh appearance.

Margins on imperforate stamps: These should be even on all sides and should be at least as wide as half the distance between that stamp and the next. To have one or more margins of less than this width, would normally preclude a stamp from being described as 'Fine'. Some early stamps were positioned very close together on the printing plate and in such cases 'Fine' margins would necessarily be narrow. On the other hand, some plates were laid down to give a substantial gap between individual stamps and in such cases margins would be expected to be much wider.

An 'average' four-margin example would have a narrower margin on one or more sides and should be priced accordingly, while a stamp with wider, yet even, margins than 'Fine' would merit the description 'Very Fine' or 'Superb' and, if available, would command a price in excess of that quoted in the catalogue.

Gum: Since the prices for stamps of King Edward VIII, King George VI and Queen Elizabeth are for 'unmounted' or 'never hinged' mint, even stamps from these reigns which have been very lightly mounted should be available at a discount from catalogue price, the more obvious the hinge marks, the greater the discount.

Catalogue prices for stamps issued prior to King Edward VIII's reign are for mounted mint, so unmounted examples would be worth a premium. Hinge marks on 20th century stamps should not be too obtrusive, and should be at least in the lightly mounted category. For 19th century stamps more obvious hinging would be acceptable, but stamps should still carry a large part of their original gum—'Large part o.g.'—in order to be described as 'Fine'.

Centring: Ideally, the stamp's image should appear in the exact centre of the perforated area, giving equal margins on all sides. 'Fine' centring would be close to this ideal with any deviation having an effect on the value of the stamp. As in the case of the margins on imperforate stamps, it should be borne in mind that the space between some early stamps was very narrow, so it was very difficult to achieve accurate perforation, especially when the technology was in its infancy. Thus, poor centring would have a less damaging effect on the value of a 19th century stamp than on a 20th century example, but the premium put on a perfectly centred specimen would be greater.

Cancellations: Early cancellation devices were designed to 'obliterate' the stamp in order to prevent it being reused and this is still an important objective for today's postal administrations. Stamp collectors, on the other hand, prefer postmarks to be lightly applied, clear, and to leave as much as possible of the design visible. Dated, circular cancellations have long been 'the postmark of choice', but the definition of a 'Fine' cancellation will depend upon the types of cancellation in use at the time a stamp was current—it is clearly illogical to seek a circular datestamp on a Penny Black.

'Fine', by definition, will be superior to 'Average', so, in terms of cancellation quality, if one begins by identifying what 'Average' looks like, then one will be half way to identifying 'Fine'. The illustrations will give some guidance on mid-19th century and mid-20th century cancellations of Great Britain, but types of cancellation in general use in each country and in each period will determine the appearance of 'Fine'.

As for the factors discussed above, anything less than 'Fine' will result in a downgrading of the stamp concerned, while a very fine or superb cancellation will be worth a premium.

Combining the factors: To merit the description 'Fine', a stamp should be fine in every respect, but a small deficiency in one area might be made up for in another by a factor meriting an 'Extremely Fine' description.

Some early issues are so seldom found in what would normally be considered to be 'Fine' condition, the catalogue prices are for a slightly lower grade, with 'Fine' examples being worth a premium. In such cases a note to this effect is given in the catalogue, while elsewhere premiums are given for well-centred, lightly cancelled examples.

Stamps graded at less than fine remain collectable and, in the case of more highly priced stamps, will continue to hold a value. Nevertheless, buyers should always bear condition in mind.

The Catalogue in General

Contents. The Catalogue is confined to adhesive postage stamps, including miniature sheets. For particular categories the rules are:
(a) Revenue (fiscal) stamps are listed only where they have been expressly authorised for postal duty.
(b) Stamps issued only precancelled are included, but normally issued stamps available additionally with precancel have no separate precancel listing unless the face value is changed.
(c) Stamps prepared for use but not issued, hitherto accorded full listing, are nowadays foot-noted with a price (where possible).
(d) Bisects (trisects, etc.) are only listed where such usage was officially authorised.
(e) Stamps issued only on first day covers or in presentation packs and not available separately are not listed but may be priced in a footnote.
(f) New printings are only included in this Catalogue where they show a major philatelic variety, such as a change in shade, watermark or paper. Stamps which exist with or without imprint dates are listed separately; changes in imprint dates are mentioned in footnotes.
(g) Official and unofficial reprints are dealt with by footnote.
(h) Stamps from imperforate printings of modern issues which occur perforated are covered by footnotes, but are listed where widely available for postal use.

Exclusions. The following are excluded:
(a) non-postal revenue or fiscal stamps.
(b) postage stamps used fiscally (although prices are now given for some fiscally used high values).
(c) local carriage labels and private local issues.
(d) bogus or phantom stamps.
(e) railway or airline letter fee stamps, bus or road transport company labels or the stamps of private postal companies operating under licence from the national authority.
(f) cut-outs.
(g) all types of non-postal labels and souvenirs.
(h) documentary labels for the postal service, e.g. registration, recorded delivery, air-mail etiquettes, etc.
(i) privately applied embellishments to official issues and privately commissioned items generally.
(j) stamps for training postal officers.

Full listing. 'Full listing' confers our recognition and implies allotting a catalogue number and (wherever possible) a price quotation.

In judging status for inclusion in the catalogue broad considerations are applied to stamps. They must be issued by a legitimate postal authority, recognised by the government concerned, and must be adhesives valid for proper postal use in the class of service for which they are inscribed. Stamps, with the exception of such categories as postage dues and officials, must be available to the general public, at face value, in reasonable quantities without any artificial restrictions being imposed on their distribution.

For errors and varieties the criterion is legitimate (albeit inadvertent) sale through a postal administration in the normal course of business. Details of provenance are always important; printers' waste and deliberately manufactured material are excluded.

Certificates. In assessing unlisted items due weight is given to Certificates from recognised Expert Committees and, where appropriate, we will usually ask to see them.

Date of issue. Where local issue dates differ from dates of release by agencies, 'date of issue' is the local date. Fortuitous stray usage before the officially intended date is disregarded in listing.

Catalogue numbers. Stamps of each country are catalogued chronologically by date of issue. Subsidiary classes are placed at the end of the country, as separate lists, with a distinguishing letter prefix to the catalogue number, e.g. D for postage due, O for official and E for express delivery stamps.

The catalogue number appears in the extreme left-column. The boldface Type numbers in the next column are merely cross-references to illustrations.

A catalogue number with a suffix will normally relate to the main number, so 137a with be a variant of No. 137, unless the suffix appears as part of the number in the left-hand column such as Great Britain No. 20a, in which case that should be treated as the main number. A number with multiple suffixes will relate to the first letter or letters of that suffix, so 137ab will be a variant of 137a and 137aba a variant of 137ab. The exception is the 'aa' suffix, which will precede an 'a' and always refers to the main number, so 137aa relates to 137 not 137a.

Once published in the Catalogue, numbers are changed as little as possible; really serious renumbering is reserved for the occasions when a complete country or an entire issue is being rewritten. The edition first affected includes cross-reference tables of old and new numbers.

Our catalogue numbers are universally recognised in specifying stamps and as a hallmark of status.

'Missing' numbers. Following rewriting it is frequently the case that individual or series of numbers become redundant. Apparent gaps in the numbering, such as, New Zealand 472/543 or St Helena 102 do not indicate that a stamp or stamps are omitted, but that an earlier revision has been made to the listing.

Illustrations. Stamps are illustrated at three-quarters linear size. Stamps not illustrated are the same size and format as the value shown, unless otherwise indicated. Stamps issued only as miniature sheets have the stamp alone illustrated but sheet size is also quoted. Overprints, surcharges, watermarks and postmarks are normally actual size. Illustrations of varieties are often enlarged to show the detail. Stamp booklet covers are illustrated half-size, unless otherwise indicated.

The colour illustrations of stamps are intended as a guide only, they may differ in shade from the originals.

Designers. Designers' names are quoted where known, though space precludes naming every individual concerned in the production of a set. In particular, photographers supplying material are usually named only where they also make an active contribution in the design stage; posed photographs of reigning monarchs are, however, an exception to this rule.

CONTACTING THE CATALOGUE EDITOR

The editor is always interested in hearing from people who have new information which will improve or correct the Catalogue. As a general rule he must see and examine the actual stamps before they can be considered for listing; although a high-resolution scan particularly if supported by a certificate provided by a reliable authority may provide sufficient evidence. An initial email to thecatalogueeditor@stanleygibbons.com will determine whether or not an item is likely to be of interest.

Submissions should be made in writing to the Catalogue Editor, Stanley Gibbons Publications at the Ringwood office. The cost of return postage for items submitted is appreciated, and this should include the registration fee if required.

Where information is solicited purely for the benefit of the enquirer, the editor cannot undertake to reply if the answer is already contained in these published notes or if return postage is omitted. Written or email communications are greatly preferred to enquiries by telephone and the editor regrets that he or his staff cannot see personal callers without a prior appointment being made. Correspondence may be subject to delay during the production period of each new edition.

The editor welcomes close contact with study circles and is interested, too, in finding reliable local correspondents who will verify and supplement official information in countries where this is deficient.

We regret we do not give opinions as to the genuineness of stamps, nor do we identify stamps or number them by our Catalogue.

TECHNICAL MATTERS

The meanings of the technical terms used in the catalogue will be found in our *Philatelic Terms Illustrated*.

References below to (more specialised) listings are to be taken to indicate, as appropriate, the Stanley Gibbons *Great Britain Specialised Catalogue* or the *Great Britain Concise Catalogue*.

1. Printing

Printing errors. Errors in printing are of major interest to the Catalogue. Authenticated items meriting consideration would include: background, centre or frame inverted or omitted; centre or subject transposed; error of colour; error or omission of value; double prints and impressions; printed both sides; and so on.

Apparent 'double prints' including overprints, on stamps printed by offset litho arising from movement of the rubber 'blanket' involved in this process are however, outside the scope of this catalogue, although they may be included in more specialised listings.

Designs *tête-bêche*, whether intentionally or by accident, are listable. *Se-tenant* arrangements of stamps are recognised in the listings or footnotes. Gutter pairs (a pair of stamps separated by blank margin) are not included in this volume. Colours only partially omitted are not listed. Stamps with embossing omitted are reserved for our more specialised listings.

Printing varieties. Listing is accorded to major changes in the printing base which lead to completely new types. In recess-printing this could be a design re-engraved; in photogravure or photolithography a screen altered in whole or in part. It can also encompass flat-bed and rotary printing if the results are readily distinguishable.

To be considered at all, varieties must be constant.

Early stamps, produced by primitive methods, were prone to numerous imperfections; the lists reflect this, recognising re-entries, retouches, broken frames, misshapen letters, and so on. Printing technology has, however, radically improved over the years, during which time photogravure and lithography have become predominant. Varieties nowadays are more in the nature of flaws and these, being too specialised for this general catalogue, are almost always outside the scope.

In no catalogue, however, do we list such items as: dry prints, kiss prints, doctor-blade flaws, colour shifts or registration flaws (unless they lead to the complete omission of a colour from an individual stamp), lithographic ring flaws, and so on. Neither do we recognise fortuitous happenings like paper creases or confetti flaws.

Varieties of varieties. We no longer provide individual listings for combinations of two or more varieties; thus a plate variety or overprinting error will not be listed for different watermark orientations.

Overprints (and surcharges). Overprints of different types qualify for separate listing. These include overprints in different colours; overprints from different printing processes such as litho and typo; overprints in totally different typefaces, etc. Major errors in machine-printed overprints are important and listable. They include: overprint inverted or omitted; overprint double (treble, etc.); overprint diagonal; overprint double, one inverted; pairs with one overprint omitted, e.g. from a radical shift to an adjoining stamp; error of colour; error of type fount; letters inverted or omitted, etc. If the overprint is handstamped, few of these would qualify and a distinction is drawn. We continue, however, to list pairs of stamps where one has a handstamped overprint and the other has not, unless it is known that such items were created deliberately at the request of purchasers (see note below Zanzibar Nos. 394/413).

Albino prints or double prints, one of them being albino (i.e. showing an uninked impression of the printing plate) are listable unless they are particularly common in this form (see the note below Travancore No. 32fa, for example). We do not, however, normally list reversed albino overprints, caused by the accidental or deliberate folding of sheets prior to overprinting (British Levant Nos. 51/8).

Varieties occurring in overprints will often take the form of broken letters, slight differences in spacing, rising space's, etc. Only the most important would be considered for listing or footnote mention.

Sheet positions. If space permits we quote sheet positions of listed varieties and authenticated data is solicited for this purpose.

De La Rue plates. The Catalogue classifies the general plates used by De La Rue for printing British Colonial stamps as follows:

The Catalogue in General

VICTORIAN KEY TYPE

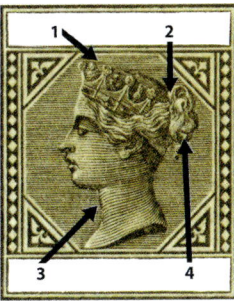

Die I

1. The ball of decoration on the second point of the crown appears as a dark mass of lines.
2. Dark vertical shading separates the front hair from the bun.
3. The vertical line of colour outlining the front of the throat stops at the sixth line of shading on the neck.
4. The white space in the coil of the hair above the curl is roughly the shape of a pin's head.

Die II

1. There are very few lines of colour in the ball and it appears almost white.
2. A white vertical strand of hair appears in place of the dark shading.
3. The line stops at the eighth line of shading.
4. The white space is oblong, with a line of colour partially dividing it at the left end.

Plates numbered 1 and 2 are both Die I. Plates 3 and 4 are Die II.

GEORGIAN KEY TYPE

Die I

A. The second (thick) line below the name of the country is cut slanting, conforming roughly to the shape of the crown on each side.
B. The labels of solid colour bearing the words 'POSTAGE' and '& REVENUE' are square at the inner top corners.
C. There is a projecting 'bud' on the outer spiral of the ornament in each of the lower corners.

Die II

A. The second line is cut vertically on each side of the crown.
B. The labels curve inwards at the top.
C. There is no 'bud' in this position.

Unless otherwise stated in the lists, all stamps with watermark Multiple Crown CA (w **8**) are Die I while those with watermark Multiple Script CA (w **9**) are Die II. The Georgian Die II was introduced in April 1921 and was used for Plates 10 to 22 and 26 to 28. Plates 23 to 25 were made from Die I by mistake.

2. Paper

All stamps listed are deemed to be on (ordinary) paper of the wove type and white in colour; only departures from this are normally mentioned.

Types. Where classification so requires we distinguish such other types of paper as, for example, vertically and horizontally laid; wove and laid bâtonné; card(board); carton; cartridge; glazed; granite; native; pelure; porous; quadrillé; ribbed; rice; and silk thread.

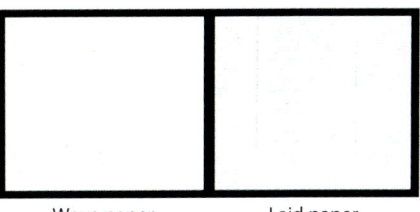

Wove paper   Laid paper

Granite paper   Quadrillé paper

The Catalogue in General

Burelé band

The various makeshifts for normal paper are listed as appropriate. The varieties of double paper and joined paper are recognised. The security device of a printed burelé band on the back of a stamp, as in early Queensland, qualifies for listing.

Descriptive terms. The fact that a paper is handmade (and thus probably of uneven thickness) is mentioned where necessary. Such descriptive terms as 'hard' and 'soft'; 'smooth' and 'rough'; 'thick', 'medium' and 'thin' are applied where there is philatelic merit in classifying papers.

Coloured, very white and toned papers. A coloured paper is one that is coloured right through (front and back of the stamp). In the Catalogue the colour of the paper is given in italics, thus:

black/*rose* = black design on rose paper.

Papers have been made specially white in recent years by, for example, a very heavy coating of chalk. We do not classify shades of whiteness of paper as distinct varieties. There does exist, however, a type of paper from early days called toned. This is off-white, often brownish or buffish, but it cannot be assigned any definite colour. A toning effect brought on by climate, incorrect storage or gum staining is disregarded here, as this was not the state of the paper when issued.

'Ordinary' and 'Chalk-surfaced' papers. The availability of many postage stamps for revenue purposes made necessary some safeguard against the illegitimate re-use of stamps with removable cancellations. This was at first secured by using fugitive inks and later by printing on paper surfaced by coatings containing either chalk or china clay, both of which made it difficult to remove any form of obliteration without damaging the stamp design.

This catalogue lists these chalk-surfaced paper varieties from their introduction in 1905. Where no indication is given, the paper is 'ordinary'.

The 'traditional' method of indentifying chalk-surfaced papers has been that, when touched with a silver wire, a black mark is left on the paper, and the listings in this catalogue are based on that test. However, the test itself is now largely discredited, for, although the mark can be removed by a soft rubber, some damage to the stamp will result from its use.

The difference between chalk-surfaced and pre-war ordinary papers is fairly clear: chalk-surfaced papers being smoother to the touch and showing a characteristic sheen when light is reflected off their surface. Under good magnification tiny bubbles or pock marks can be seen on the surface of the stamp and at the tips of the perforations the surfacing appears 'broken'. Traces of paper fibres are evident on the surface of ordinary paper and the ink shows a degree of absorption into it.

Initial chalk-surfaced paper printings by De La Rue had a thinner coating than subsequently became the norm. The characteristics described above are less pronounced in these printings.

During and after the Second World War, substitute papers replaced the chalk-surfaced papers, these do not react to the silver test and are therefore classed as 'ordinary', although differentiating them without recourse to it is more difficult, for, although the characteristics of the chalk-surfaced paper remained the same, some of the ordinary papers appear much smoother than earlier papers and many do not show the watermark clearly. Experience is the only solution to identifying these, and comparison with stamps whose paper type is without question will be of great help.

Another type of paper, known as 'thin striated' was used only for the Bahamas 1s. and 5s. (Nos. 155a, 156a, 171 and 174) and for several stamps of the Malayan states. Hitherto these have been described as 'chalk-surfaced' since they gave some reaction to the silver test, but they are much thinner than usual chalk-surfaced papers, with the watermark showing clearly. Stamps on this paper show a slightly 'ribbed' effect when the stamp is held up to the light. Again, comparison with a known striated paper stamp, such as the 1941 Straits Settlements Die II 2c. orange (No. 294) will prove invaluable in separating these papers.

Glazed paper. In 1969 the Crown Agents introduced a new general-purpose paper for use in conjunction with all current printing processes. It generally has a marked glossy surface but the degree varies according to the process used, being more marked in recess-printing stamps. As it does not respond to the silver test this represented a significant change where previous printings had been on chalk-surfaced paper. The glazed papers are separately listed, usually as 'a' numbers (e.g. British Solomon Islands Nos. 166a/175a).

Green and yellow papers. Issues of the First World War and immediate postwar period occur on green and yellow papers and these are given separate Catalogue listing. The original coloured papers (coloured throughout) gave way to surface-coloured papers, the stamps having 'white backs'; other stamps show one colour on the front and a different one at the back. Because of the numerous variations a grouping of colours is adopted as follows:

Yellow papers

(1) The original *yellow* paper (throughout), usually bright in colour. The gum is often sparse, of harsh consistency and dull-looking. Used 1912–1920.
(2) The *white-backs*. Used 1913–1914.
(3) A bright lemon paper. The colour must have a pronounced greenish tinge, different from the 'yellow' in (1). As a rule, the gum on stamps using this lemon paper is plentiful, smooth and shiny, and the watermark shows distinctly. Care is needed with stamps printed in green on yellow paper (1) as it may appear that the paper is this lemon. Used 1914–1916.
(4) An experimental *orange-buff* paper. The colour must have a distinct brownish tinge. It is not to be confused with a muddy yellow (1) nor the misleading appearance (on the surface) of stamps printed in red on yellow paper where an engraved plate has been insufficiently wiped. Used 1918–1921.
(5) An experimental *buff* paper. This lacks the brownish tinge of (4) and the brightness of the yellow shades. The gum is shiny when compared with the matt type used on (4). Used 1919–1920.
(6) A *pale yellow* paper that has a creamy tone to the yellow. Used from 1920 onwards.

Green papers

(7) The original 'green' paper, varying considerably through shades of blue-green and yellow-green, the front and back sometimes differing. Used 1912–1916.
(8) The *white backs*. Used 1913–1914.
(9) A paper blue-green on the surface with *pale olive* back. The back must be markedly paler than the front and this and the pronounced olive tinge to the back distinguish it from (7). Used 1916–1920.
(10) Paper with a vivid green surface, commonly called *emerald-green*; it has the olive back of (9). Used 1920.
(11) Paper with *emerald-green* both back and front. Used from 1920 onwards.

3. Perforation and Rouletting

Perforation gauge. The gauge of a perforation is the number of holes in a length of 2 cm. For correct classification the size of the holes (large or small) may need to be distinguished; in a few cases the actual number of holes on each edge of the stamp needs to be quoted.

Measurement. The Gibbons *Instanta* gauge is the standard for measuring perforations. The stamp is viewed against a dark background with the transparent gauge put on top of it. Though the gauge measures to decimal accuracy, perforations read from it are generally quoted in the Catalogue to the nearest half. For example:

Just over perf 12¾ to just under 13¼ = perf 13
Perf 13¼ exactly, rounded up = perf 13½
Just over perf 13¼ to just under 13¾ = perf 13½
Perf 13¾ exactly, rounded up = perf 14

However, where classification depends on it, actual quarter-perforations are quoted.

Notation. Where no perforation is quoted for an issue it is imperforate. Perforations are usually abbreviated (and spoken) as follows, though sometimes they may be spelled out for clarity. This notation for rectangular stamps (the majority) applies to diamond shapes if 'top' is read as the edge to the top right.

P 14: perforated alike on all sides (read: 'perf 14').
P 14×15: the first figure refers to top and bottom, the second to left and right sides (read: 'perf 14 by 15'). This is a compound perforation. For an upright triangular stamp the first figure refers to the two sloping sides and second to the base. In inverted triangulars the base is first and the second figure to the sloping sides.
P 14–15: perforation measuring anything between 14 and 15: the holes are irregularly spaced, thus the gauge may vary along a single line or even along a single edge of the stamp (read: 'perf 14 to 15').
P 14 *irregular*: perforated 14 from a worn perforator, giving badly aligned holes irregularly spaced (read: 'irregular perf 14').
P *comp(ound)* 14×15: two gauges in use but not necessarily on opposite sides of the stamp. It could be one side in one gauge and three in the other; or two adjacent sides with the same gauge. (Read: 'perf compound of 14 and 15'.) For three gauges or more, abbreviated as 'P 12, 14½, 15 *or compound*' for example.
P 14, 14½: perforated approximately 14¼ (read: 'perf 14 or 14½'). It does *not* mean two stamps, one perf 14 and the other perf 14½. This obsolescent notation is gradually being replaced in the Catalogue.
Imperf: imperforate (not perforated)
Imperf×P 14: imperforate at top ad bottom and perf 14 at sides.
P 14×*imperf*: perf 14 at top and bottom and imperforate at sides.

Imperf×perf

Such headings as 'P 13×14 (*vert*) and P 14×13 (*horiz*)' indicate which perforations apply to which stamp format—vertical or horizontal.

Some stamps are additionally perforated so that a label or tab is detachable; others have been perforated for use as two halves. Listings are normally for whole stamps, unless stated otherwise.

Other terms. Perforation almost always gives circular holes; where other shapes have been used they are specified, e.g. square holes; lozenge perf. Interrupted perfs are brought about by the omission of pins at regular intervals. Perforations merely simulated by being printed as part of the design are of course ignored. With few exceptions, privately applied perforations are not listed.

In the 19th century perforations are often described as clean cut (clean, sharply incised holes), intermediate or rough (rough holes, imperfectly cut, often the result of blunt pins).

Perforation errors and varieties. Authenticated errors, where a stamp normally perforated is accidentally issued imperforate, are listed provided no traces of perforation (blind holes or indentations) remain. They must be provided as pairs, both stamps wholly imperforate, and are only priced in that form.

Note that several postal administrations and their agencies are now deliberately releasing imperforate versions of issued stamps in restricted quantities and at premium prices. These are not listable, but, where possible, their existence will be noted.

In recent years a growing number of imperforates have been released from printers' archives. These are also not listable but they are so widespread that it is not practical to note all of them. Collectors are warned against confusing such releases with genuine errors.

Stamps imperforate between stamp and sheet margin are not listed in this catalogue, but such errors on Great Britain stamps will be found in the *Great Britain Specialised Catalogue*.

Pairs described as 'imperforate between' have the line of perforations between the two stamps omitted.

Imperf between (horiz pair): a horizontal pair of stamps with perfs all around the edges but none between the stamps.

Imperf between (vert pair): a vertical pair of stamps with perfs all around the edges but none between the stamps.

Where several of the rows have escaped perforation the resulting varieties are listable. Thus:

Imperf vert (horiz pair): a horizontal pair of stamps perforated top and bottom; all three vertical directions are imperf—the two outer edges and between the stamps.

Imperf horiz (vert pair): a vertical pair perforated at left and right edges; all three horizontal directions are imperf—the top, bottom and between the stamps.

The Catalogue in General

Imperf between (vertical pair) Imperf horizontally (vertical pair)

Straight edges. Large sheets cut up before issue to post offices can cause stamps with straight edges, i.e. imperf on one side or on two sides at right angles. They are not usually listable in this condition and are worth less than corresponding stamps properly perforated all round. This does not, however, apply to certain stamps, mainly from coils and booklets, where straight edges on various sides are the manufacturing norm affecting every stamp. The listings and notes make clear which sides are correctly imperf.

Malfunction. Varieties of double, misplaced or partial perforation caused by error or machine malfunction are not listable, neither are freaks, such as perforations placed diagonally from paper folds, nor missing holes caused by broken pins.

Types of perforating. Where necessary for classification, perforation types are distinguished.

These include:

Line perforation from one line of pins punching single rows of holes at a time.

Comb perforation from pins disposed across the sheet in comb formation, punching out holes at three sides of the stamp a row at a time.

Harrow perforation applied to a whole pane or sheet at one stroke.

Rotary perforation from toothed wheels operating across a sheet, then crosswise.

Sewing machine perforation. The resultant condition, clean-cut or rough, is distinguished where required.

Pin-perforation is the commonly applied term for pin-roulette in which, instead of being punched out, round holes are pricked by sharp-pointed pins and no paper is removed.

Mixed perforation occurs when stamps with defective perforations are re-perforated in a different gauge.

Punctured stamps. Perforation holes can be punched into the face of the stamp. Patterns of small holes, often in the shape of initial letters, are privately applied devices against pilferage. These (perfins) are outside the scope except for Australia, Canada, Cape of Good Hope, Papua and Sudan where they were used as official stamps by the national administration. Identification devices, when officially inspired, are listed or noted; they can be shapes, or letters or words formed from holes, sometimes converting one class of stamp into another.

Rouletting. In rouletting the paper is cut, for ease of separation, but none is removed. The gauge is measured, when needed, as for perforations. Traditional French terms descriptive of the type of cut are often used and types include:

Arc roulette (percé en arc). Cuts are minute, spaced arcs, each roughly a semicircle.

Cross roulette (percé en croix). Cuts are tiny diagonal crosses.

Line roulette (percé en ligne or en ligne droite). Short straight cuts parallel to the frame of the stamp. The commonest basic roulette. Where not further described, 'roulette' means this type.

Rouletted in colour or coloured roulette (percé en lignes colorées or en lignes de coleur). Cuts with coloured edges, arising from notched rule inked simultaneously with the printing plate.

Saw-tooth roulette (percé en scie). Cuts applied zigzag fashion to resemble the teeth of a saw.

Serpentine roulette (percé en serpentin). Cuts as sharply wavy lines.

Zigzag roulette (percé en zigzags). Short straight cuts at angles in alternate directions, producing sharp points on separation. US usage favours 'serrate(d) roulette' for this type.

Pin-roulette (originally *percé en points* and now *perforés trous d'epingle*) is commonly called pin-perforation in English.

4. Gum

All stamps listed are assumed to have gum of some kind; if they were issued without gum this is stated. Original gum (o.g.) means that which was present on the stamp as issued to the public. Deleterious climates and the presence of certain chemicals can cause gum to crack and, with early stamps, even make the paper deteriorate. Unscrupulous fakers are adept in removing it and regumming the stamp to meet the unreasoning demand often made for 'full o.g.' in cases where such a thing is virtually impossible.

The gum normally used on stamps has been gum arabic until the late 1960s when synthetic adhesives were introduced. Harrison and Sons Ltd for instance used *polyvinyl alcohol*, known to philatelists as PVA. This is almost invisible except for a slight yellowish tinge which was incorporated to make it possible to see that the stamps have been gummed. It has advantages in hot countries, as stamps do not curl and sheets are less likely to stick together. Gum arabic and PVA are not distinguished in the lists except that where a stamp exists with both forms this is indicated in footnotes. Our more specialised catalogues provide separate listing of gums for Great Britain.

Self-adhesive stamps are issued on backing paper, from which they are peeled before affixing to mail. Unused examples are priced as for backing paper intact, in which condition they are recommended to be kept. Used examples are best collected on cover or on piece.

5. Watermarks

Stamps are on unwatermarked paper except where the heading to the set says otherwise.

Detection. Watermarks are detected for Catalogue description by one of four methods: (1) holding stamps to the light; (2) laying stamps face down on a dark background; (3) adding a few drops of petroleum ether 40/60 to the stamp laid face down in a watermark tray; (4) by use of the Stanley Gibbons Detectamark Spectrum, or other equipment, which work by revealing the thinning of the paper at the watermark. (Note that petroleum ether is highly inflammable in use and can damage some photogravure stamps.)

Listable types. Stamps occurring on both watermarked and unwatermarked papers are different types and both receive full listing.

Single watermarks (devices occurring once on every stamp) can be modified in size and shape as between different issues; the types are noted but not usually separately listed. Fortuitous absence of watermark from a single stamp or its gross displacement would not be listable.

To overcome registration difficulties the device may be repeated at close intervals *(a multiple watermark)*, single stamps thus showing parts of several devices. Similarly, a *large sheet watermark* (or *all-over watermark*) covering numerous stamps can be used. We give informative notes and illustrations for them. The designs may be such that numbers of stamps in the sheet automatically lack watermark: this is not a listable variety. Multiple and all-over watermarks sometimes undergo modifications, but if the various types are difficult to distinguish from single stamps notes are given but not separate listings.

Papermakers' watermarks are noted where known but not listed separately, since most stamps in the sheet will lack them. Sheet watermarks which are nothing more than officially adopted papermakers' watermarks are, however, given normal listing.

Marginal watermarks, falling outside the pane of stamps, are ignored except where misplacement caused the adjoining row to be affected, in which case they may be footnoted. They usually consist of straight or angled lines and double-lined capital letters, they are particularly prevalent on some Crown CC and Crown CA watermarked stamps.

Watermark errors and varieties. Watermark errors are recognised as of major importance. They comprise stamps intended to be on unwatermarked paper but issued watermarked by mistake, or stamps printed on paper with the wrong watermark. Varieties showing letters omitted from the watermark are also included, but broken or deformed bits on the dandy roll are not listed unless they represent repairs.

Watermark positions. The diagram shows how watermark position is described in the Catalogue. Paper has a side intended for printing and watermarks are usually impressed so that they read normally when looked through from that printed side. However, since philatelists customarily detect watermarks by looking at the back of the stamp the watermark diagram also makes clear what is actually seen.

Illustrations in the Catalogue are of watermarks in normal positions (from the front of the stamps) and are actual size where possible.

Differences in watermark position are collectable varieties. This Catalogue now lists inverted, sideways inverted and reversed watermark varieties on Commonwealth stamps from the 1860s onwards, except where the watermark position is completely haphazard or, due to the method of printing, appear in equal quantities, upright and inverted (e.g. Papua Nos. 47/83). In such cases it should be assumed that the price is the same, either way.

Where a watermark comes indiscriminately in various positions our policy is to cover this by a general note: we do not give separate listings because the watermark position in these circumstances has no particular philatelic importance.

Sideways watermarks. A review of the sideways watermarks listed in this catalogue has shown that, while in Great Britain it is fair to say that the 'normal' sideways watermark shows the top of the device (as shown in its illustration) pointing to the left as seen from the front and to the right as seen from the back of the stamp, the opposite is very often the case on Crown Agents colonial issues.

We have therefore adopted the policy of clearly stating whether the normal sideways watermark points to the left or to the right for all issues up to 1970. Where the normal watermark is upright and the sideways variant constitutes a rare error it has not always been possible to confirm its orientation, so we welcome the assistance of collectors in 'filling in the gaps' in these cases.

We repeat here the watermark diagram which has appeared in these introductory notes for many years, with the caveat that, while valid for Great Britain, individual listings should be consulted for the normal orientation of other sideways watermark issues.

AS DESCRIBED (Read through front of stamp)		AS SEEN DURING WATERMARK DETECTION (Stamp face down and back examined
GvR	Normal	ЯvƆ
ЯʌƆ	Inverted	GʌR
ЯvƆ	Reversed	GvR
GʌR	Reversed and Inverted	ЯʌƆ
GvR (sideways)	Sideways	ƆʌR (sideways)
GvR (sideways)	Sideways Inverted	ЯvƆ (sideways)

Standard types of watermark. Some watermarks have been used generally for various British possessions rather than exclusively for a single colony. To avoid repetition the Catalogue classifies 11 general types, as under, with references in the headings throughout the listings being given either in words or in the form ('W w **9**') (meaning 'watermark type w **9**'). In those cases where watermark illustrations appear in the listings themselves, the respective reference reads, for example, W **153**, thus indicating that the watermark will be found in the normal sequence of illustrations as (type) **153**.

The general types are as follows, with an example of each quoted.

W	Description	Example
w **1**	Large Star	St. Helena No. 1
w **2**	Small Star	Turks Is. No. 4
w **2a**	Truncated Star	Queensland No. 59
w **3**	Broad (pointed) Star	Grenada No. 24
w **4**	Crown (over) CC, small stamp	Antigua No. 13
w **5**	Crown (over) CC, large stamp	Antigua No. 31
w **6**	Crown (over) CA, small stamp	Antigua No. 21
w **7**	Crown CA (CA over Crown), large stamp	Sierra Leone No. 54
w **8**	Multiple Crown CA	Antigua No. 41

The Catalogue in General

w **9** Multiple Script CA — Seychelles No. 158
w **9***a* do. Error — Seychelles No. 158a
w **9***b* do. Error — Seychelles No. 158b
w **10** V over Crown — Queensland No. 265
w **11** Crown over A — Queensland No. 282

CC in these watermarks is an abbreviation for 'Crown Colonies' and CA for 'Crown Agents'. Watermarks w **1**, w **2** and w **3** are on stamps printed by Perkins, Bacon; w **4** onwards on stamps from De La Rue and other printers.

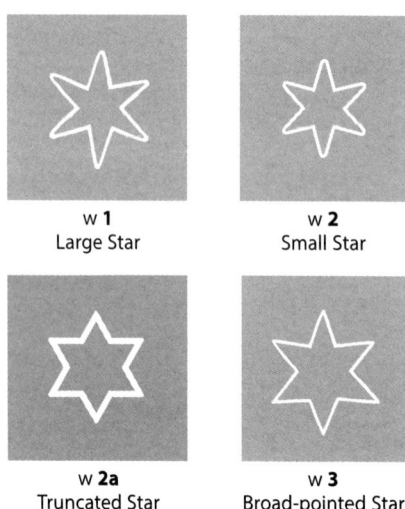

w **1** Large Star
w **2** Small Star
w **2a** Truncated Star
w **3** Broad-pointed Star

Watermark w **1**, *Large Star*, measures 15 to 16 mm across the star from point to point and about 27 mm from centre to centre vertically between stars in the sheet. It was made for long stamps like Ceylon 1857 and St. Helena 1856. Watermark w **2**, *Small Star* is of similar design but measures 12 to 13½mm from point to point and 24 mm from centre to centre vertically. It was for use with ordinary-size stamps such as Grenada 1863–71.

When the Large Star watermark was used with the smaller stamps it only occasionally comes in the centre of the paper. It is frequently so misplaced as to show portions of two stars above and below and this eccentricity will very often help in determining the watermark.

Watermark w **3**, *Broad-pointed Star*, resembles w **1** but the points are broader.

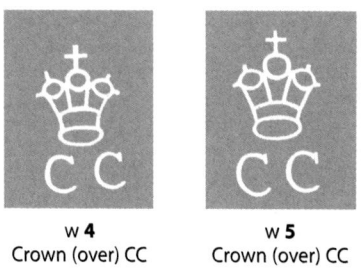

w **4** Crown (over) CC
w **5** Crown (over) CC

Two *Crown (over) CC* watermarks were used: w **4** was for stamps of ordinary size and w **5** for those of larger size. It is known that the latter was sometimes used for stamps of ordinary size, but since the differences are difficult to identify on single stamps, we do not list them separately.

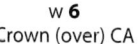

w **6** Crown (over) CA
w **7** CA over Crown

Two watermarks of *Crown CA* type were used, w **6** being for stamps of ordinary size. The other, w **7**, is properly described as *CA over Crown*. It was specially made for paper on which it was intended to print long fiscal stamps: that some were used postally accounts for the appearance of w **7** in the Catalogue. The watermark occupies twice the space of the ordinary Crown CA watermark, w **6**. Stamps of normal size printed on paper with w **7** watermark show it *sideways*; it takes a horizontal pair of stamps to show the entire watermark (e.g. Labuan Nos. 1/4).

w **8** Multiple Crown CA
w **9** Multiple Script CA

Multiple watermarks began in 1904 with w **8**, *Multiple Crown CA*, changed from 1921 to w **9**, *Multiple Script CA*. On stamps of ordinary size portions of two or three watermarks appear and on the large-sized stamps a greater number can be observed. The change to letters in script character with w **9** was accompanied by a Crown of distinctly different shape.

It seems likely that there were at least two dandy rolls for each Crown Agents watermark in use at any one time with a reserve roll being employed when the normal one was withdrawn for maintenance or repair.

Both the Mult Crown CA and the Mult Script CA types exist with one or other of the letters omitted from individual impressions. It is possible that most of these occur from the reserve rolls as they have only been found on certain issues. The MCA watermark experienced such problems during the early 1920s and the Script over a longer period from the early 1940s until 1951.

During the 1920s damage must also have occurred on one of the Crowns as a substituted Crown has been found on certain issues. This is smaller than the normal and consists of an oval base joined to two upright ovals with a circle positioned between their upper ends. The upper line of the Crown's base is omitted, as are the left and right-hand circles at the top and also the cross over the centre circle.

The Catalogue in General

Substituted Crown

w **12**
Multiple St. Edward's
Crown Block CA

w **13**
Multiple PTM

The *Multiple Script CA* watermark, w **9**, is known with two errors, recurring among the 1950–52 printings of several territories. In the first a crown has fallen away from the dandy-roll that impresses the watermark into the paper pulp. It gives w **9a**, *Crown missing*, but this omission has been found in both 'Crown only' (*illustrated*) and 'Crown CA' rows. The resulting faulty paper was used for Bahamas, Johore, Seychelles and the postage due stamps of nine colonies

The *Multiple St. Edward's Crown Block CA* watermark, w **12**, was introduced in 1957 and besides the change in the Crown (from that used in Multiple Script CA, w **9**) the letters reverted to block capitals. The new watermark began to appear sideways in 1966 and these stamps are generally listed as separate sets.

The watermark w **13**, *Multiple PTM*, was introduced for new Malaysian issues in November 1961.

w **9a**:
Error, Crown missing

w **14**
Multiple Crown CA Diagonal

w **9b**:
Error, St. Edward's Crown

When the omission was noticed a second mishap occurred, which was to insert a wrong crown in the space, giving w **9b**, St. Edward's Crown. This produced varieties in Bahamas, Perlis, St. Kitts-Nevis and Singapore and the incorrect crown likewise occurs in (Crown only) and (Crown CA) rows.

By 1974 the two dandy-rolls the 'upright' and the 'sideways' for w **12** were wearing out; the Crown Agents therefore discontinued using the sideways watermark one and retained the other only as a stand-by. A new dandy-roll with the pattern of w **14**, *Multiple Crown CA Diagonal*, was introduced and first saw use with some Churchill Centenary issues.

The new watermark had the design arranged in gradually spiralling rows. It is improved in design to allow smooth passage over the paper (the gaps between letters and rows had caused jolts in previous dandy-rolls) and the sharp corners and angles, where fibres used to accumulate, have been eliminated by rounding.

This watermark had no 'normal' sideways position amongst the different printers using it. To avoid confusion our more specialised listings do not rely on such terms as 'sideways inverted' but describe the direction in which the watermark points.

w **10**
V over Crown

w **11**
Crown over A

w **15**
Multiple POST OFFICE

Resuming the general types, two watermarks found in issues of several Australian States are: w **10**, *V over Crown*, and w **11**, *Crown over A*.

During 1981 w **15**, *Multiple POST OFFICE* was introduced for certain issues prepared by Philatelists Ltd, acting for various countries in the Indian Ocean, Pacific and West Indies.

w **16**
Multiple Crown Script CA Diagonal

A new Crown Agents watermark was introduced during 1985, w **16**, *Multiple Crown Script CA Diagonal*. This was very similar to the previous w **14**, but showed 'CA' in script rather than block letters. It was first used on the omnibus series of stamps commemorating the Life and Times of Queen Elizabeth the Queen Mother.

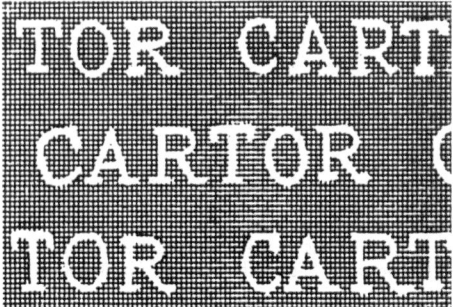

w **17**
Multiple CARTOR

Watermark w **17**, *Multiple CARTOR*, was used from 1985 for issues printed by this French firm for countries which did not normally use the Crown Agents watermark.

w **18**

In 2008, following the closure of the Crown Agents Stamp Bureau, a new Multiple Crowns watermark, w **18** was introduced

In recent years the use of watermarks has, to a small extent, been superseded by fluorescent security markings. These are often more visible from the reverse of the stamp (Cook Islands from 1970 onwards), but have occurred printed over the design (Hong Kong Nos. 415/30). In 1982 the Crown Agents introduced a new stock paper, without watermark, known as 'C-Kurity' on which a fluorescent pattern of blue rosettes is visible on the reverse, beneath the gum. This paper was used for issues from Gambia and Norfolk Island.

6. Colours

Stamps in two or three colours have these named in order of appearance, from the centre moving outwards. Four colours or more are usually listed as multicoloured.

In compound colour names the second is the predominant one, thus:

orange-red = a red tending towards orange;
red-orange = an orange containing more red than usual.

Standard colours used. The 200 colours most used for stamp identification are given in the Stanley Gibbons Stamp Colour Key. The Catalogue has used the Stamp Colour Key as standard for describing new issues for some years. The names are also introduced as lists are rewritten, though exceptions are made for those early issues where traditional names have become universally established.

Determining colours. When comparing actual stamps with colour samples in the Stamp Colour Key, view in a good north daylight (or its best substitute; fluorescent 'colour matching' light). Sunshine is not recommended. Choose a solid portion of the stamp design; if available, marginal markings such as solid bars of colour or colour check dots are helpful. Shading lines in the design can be misleading as they appear lighter than solid colour. Postmarked portions of a stamp appear darker than normal. If more than one colour is present, mask off the extraneous ones as the eye tends to mix them.

Errors of colour. Major colour errors in stamps or overprints which qualify for listing are: wrong colours; one colour inverted in relation to the rest; albinos (colourless impressions), where these have Expert Committee certificates; colours completely omitted, but only on unused stamps (if found on used stamps the information is footnoted) and with good credentials, missing colours being frequently faked.

Colours only partially omitted are not recognised, Colour shifts, however spectacular, are not listed.

Shades. Shades in philately refer to variations in the intensity of a colour or the presence of differing amounts of other colours. They are particularly significant when they can be linked to specific printings. In general, shades need to be quite marked to fall within the scope of this Catalogue; it does not nowadays favour listing the often numerous shades of a stamp, but chooses a single applicable colour name which will indicate particular groups of outstanding shades. Furthermore, the listings refer to colours as issued; they may deteriorate into something different through the passage of time. Collectors are warned against according any significance to colours which may have been altered by immersion in water or exposure to sunlight, but time, alone will sometimes cause colours to change, notably some of the letterpress De La Rue stamps of the late 19th and early 20th centuries.

Modern colour printing by lithography is prone to marked differences of shade, even within a single run, and variations can occur within the same sheet. Such shades are not listed.

Aniline colours. An aniline colour meant originally one derived from coal-tar; it now refers more widely to colour of a particular brightness suffused on the surface of a stamp and showing through clearly on the back.

Colours of overprints and surcharges. All overprints and surcharges are in black unless stated otherwise in the heading or after the description of the stamp.

7. Specimen Stamps

Originally, stamps overprinted SPECIMEN were circulated to postmasters or kept in official records, but after the establishment of the Universal Postal Union supplies were sent to Berne for distribution to the postal administrations of member countries.

During the period 1884 to 1928 most of the stamps of British Crown Colonies required for this purpose were overprinted SPECIMEN in various shapes and sizes by their printers from typeset formes. Some locally produced provisionals were handstamped locally, as were sets prepared for presentation. From 1928 stamps were punched with holes forming the word SPECIMEN, each firm of printers using a different machine or machines. From 1948 the stamps supplied for UPU distribution were no longer punctured, although receiving authorities sometimes applied SPECIMEN markings of their own.

Stamps of some other Commonwealth territories were overprinted or handstamped locally, while stamps of Great Britain and those overprinted for use in overseas postal agencies (mostly of the higher denominations) bore SPECIMEN overprints and handstamps applied by the Inland Revenue or the Post Office.

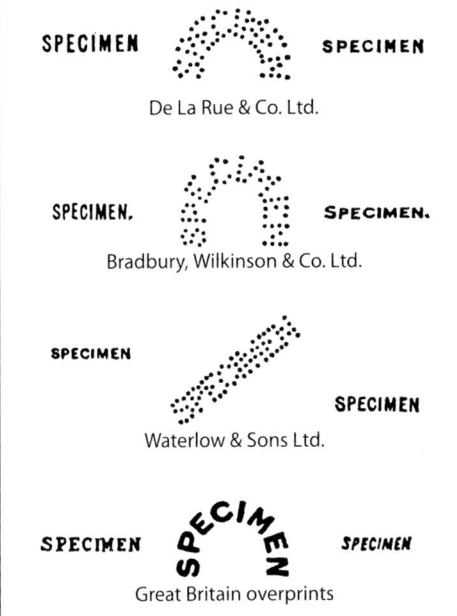

Some of the more common types of overprints or punctures are illustrated here. Collectors are warned that dangerous forgeries of the punctured types exist.

The *Stanley Gibbons Commonwealth Catalogues* record those Specimen overprints or perforations intended for distribution by the UPU to member countries and we are grateful to James Bendon, author and publisher of *UPU Specimen Stamps 1878 – 1961*, a much expanded edition of which was published in 2015, for his assistance with these listings. The Specimen overprints of Australia and its dependent territories, which were sold to collectors by the Post Office, are also included.

All other Specimens are outside the scope of this volume.

In specifying type of specimen for individual high-value stamps, 'H/S' means handstamped, 'Optd' is overprinted and 'Perf' is punctured. Some sets occur mixed, e.g. 'Optd/Perf'. If unspecified, the type is apparent from the date or it is the same as for the lower values quoted as a set. Note that the form of specimen overprints, i.e. Roman Capitals, italics or upper and lower case lettering is reflected in the listings and footnotes.

Prices. Prices for stamps up to £1 are quoted in sets; higher values are priced singly. Where specimens exist in more than one type the price quoted is for the cheapest. Specimen stamps have rarely survived even as pairs; these and strips of three, four or five are worth considerably more than singles.

Various Perkins Bacon issues exist obliterated with a 'CANCELLED' within an oval of bars handstamp.

Perkins Bacon 'CANCELLED' Handstamp

This was applied to six examples of those issues available in 1861 which were then given to members of Sir Rowland Hill's family. 75 different stamps (including four from Chile) are recorded with this handstamp although others may possibly exist. The unauthorised gift of these 'CANCELLED' stamps to the Hill family was a major factor in the loss of the Agent General for the Crown Colonies (the forerunner of the Crown Agents) contracts by Perkins Bacon in the following year. Where examples of these scarce items are known to be in private hands the catalogue provides a price.

For full details of these stamps see *CANCELLED by Perkins Bacon* by Peter Jaffé (published by Spink in 1998).

8. Luminescence

Machines which sort mail electronically have been introduced in recent years. In consequence some countries have issued stamps on fluorescent or phosphorescent papers, while others have marked their stamps with phosphor bands.

The various papers can only be distinguished by ultraviolet lamps emitting particular wavelengths. They are separately listed only when the stamps have some other means of distinguishing them, visible without the use of these lamps. Where this is not so, the papers are recorded in footnotes or headings.

For this catalogue we do not consider it appropriate that collectors be compelled to have the use of an ultraviolet lamp before being able to identify stamps by our listings. Some experience will also be found necessary in interpreting the results given by ultraviolet. Collectors using the lamps, nevertheless, should exercise great care in their use as exposure to their light is potentially dangerous to the eyes.

Phosphor bands are listable, since they are visible to the naked eye (by holding stamps at an angle to the light and looking along them, the bands appear dark). Stamps existing with or without phosphor bands or with differing numbers of bands are given separate listings. Varieties such as double bands, bands omitted, misplaced or printed on the back are not listed.

Detailed descriptions appear at appropriate places in the listings in explanation of luminescent papers; see, for example, Australia above No. 363, Canada above Nos. 472 and 611, Cook Islands above 249, etc.

For Great Britain, where since 1959 phosphors have played a prominent and intricate part in stamp issues, the main notes above Nos. 599 and 723 should be studied, as well as the footnotes to individual listings where appropriate. In general the classification is as follows.

Stamps with phosphor bands are those where a separate cylinder applies the phosphor after the stamps are printed. Issues with 'all-over' phosphor have the 'band' covering the entire stamp. Parts of the stamp covered by phosphor bands, or the entire surface for 'all-over' phosphor versions, appear matt. Stamps on phosphorised paper have the phosphor added to the paper coating before the stamps are printed. Issues on this paper have a completely shiny surface.

Further particularisation of phosphor – their methods of printing and the colours they exhibit under ultraviolet – is outside the scope. The more specialised listings should be consulted for this information.

9. Coil Stamps

Stamps issued only in coil form are given full listing. If stamps are issued in both sheets and coils the coil stamps are listed separately only where there is some feature (e.g. perforation or watermark sideways) by which singles can be distinguished. Coil stamps containing different stamps *se-tenant* are also listed.

Coil join pairs are too random and too easily faked to permit listing; similarly ignored are coil stamps which have accidentally suffered an extra row of perforations from the claw mechanism in a malfunctioning vending machine.

10. Stamp Booklets

Stamp booklets are now listed in this catalogue.

Single stamps from booklets are listed if they are distinguishable in some way (such as watermark or perforation) from similar sheet stamps.

Booklet panes are listed where they contain stamps of different denominations *se-tenant*, where stamp-size labels are included, or where such panes are otherwise identifiable. Booklet panes are placed in the listing under the lowest denomination present and are only priced in unused condition.

Particular perforations (straight edges) are covered by appropriate notes.

The majority of booklets were made up from normal sheets and panes may be bound upright or inverted and booklets may be stapled or stitched at either the left or right-hand side. Unless specifically mentioned in the listings, such variations do not command a price premium.

11. Miniature Sheets and Sheetlets

We distinguish between 'miniature sheets' and 'sheetlets' and this affects the catalogue numbering. An item in sheet form that is postally valid, containing a single stamp, pair, block or set of stamps, with wide, inscribed and/or decorative margins, is a miniature sheet if it is sold at post offices as an indivisible entity. As such the Catalogue allots a single **MS** number and describes what stamps make it up. The sheetlet or small sheet differs in that the individual stamps are intended to be purchased separately for postal purposes. For sheetlets, all the component postage stamps are numbered individually and the composition explained in a footnote. Note that the definitions refer to post office sale—not how items may be subsequently offered by stamp dealers.

12. Forgeries and Fakes

Forgeries. Where space permits, notes are considered if they can give a concise description that will permit unequivocal detection of a forgery. Generalised warnings, lacking detail, are not nowadays inserted, since their value to the collector is problematic.

Forged cancellations have also been applied to genuine stamps. This catalogue includes notes regarding those manufactured by 'Madame Joseph', together with the cancellation dates known to exist. It should be remembered that these dates also exist as genuine cancellations.

For full details of these see *Madame Joseph Forged Postmarks* by Derek Worboys (published by the Royal Philatelic Society London and the British Philatelic Trust in 1994) or *Madame Joseph Revisited* by Brian Cartwright (published by the Royal Philatelic Society London in 2005).

Fakes. Unwitting fakes are numerous, particularly 'new shades' which are colour changelings brought about by exposure to sunlight, soaking in water contaminated with dyes from adherent paper, contact with oil and dirt from a pocketbook, and so on. Fraudulent operators, in addition, can offer to arrange: removal of hinge marks; repairs of thins on white or coloured papers; replacement of missing margins or perforations; reperforating in true or false gauges; removal of fiscal cancellations; rejoining of severed pairs, strips and blocks; and (a major hazard) regumming. Collectors can only be urged to purchase from reputable sources and to insist upon Expert Committee certification where there is any kind of doubt.

The Catalogue can consider footnotes about fakes where these are specific enough to assist in detection.

ACKNOWLEDGEMENTS

We are grateful to individual collectors, members of the philatelic trade and specialist societies and study circles for their assistance in improving and extending the Stanley Gibbons range of catalogues. The address of the study circle relevant to this volume is:

New Zealand Society of Great Britain
Membership Secretary — Mr J. Stimson,
Mead Cottage, Boulters Lane,
Maidenhead SL6 8TJ

Royal Philatelic Society of New Zealand
Secretary — Mr P. McTaggart,
PO Box 33435, Wellington Mail Centre
Lower Hutt 5045, New Zealand

The Fellowship of Samoa Specialists
Membership Secretary — Mr S. Zirinsky,
PO Box 230049, Ansonia Station, New York
NY 10023, USA

Abbreviations

Printers

A.B.N. Co.	American Bank Note Co, New York.
B.A.B.N.	British American Bank Note Co. Ottawa
B.D.T.	B.D.T. International Security Printing Ltd, Dublin, Ireland
B.W.	Bradbury Wilkinson & Co, Ltd.
Cartor	Cartor S.A., La Loupe, France
C.B.N.	Canadian Bank Note Co, Ottawa.
Continental	Continental Bank Note Co. B.N. Co.
Courvoisier	Imprimerie Courvoisier S.A., La-Chaux-de-Fonds, Switzerland.
D.L.R.	De La Rue & Co, Ltd, London.
Enschedé	Joh. Enschedé en Zonen, Haarlem, Netherlands.
Format	Format International Security Printers Ltd., London
Harrison	Harrison & Sons, Ltd. London
J.W.	John Waddington Security Print Ltd., Leeds
P.B.	Perkins Bacon Ltd, London.
Questa	Questa Colour Security Printers Ltd, London
Walsall	Walsall Security Printers Ltd
Waterlow	Waterlow & Sons, Ltd, London.

General Abbreviations

Alph	Alphabet
Anniv	Anniversary
Comp	Compound (perforation)
Des	Designer; designed
Diag	Diagonal; diagonally
Eng	Engraver; engraved
F.C.	Fiscal Cancellation
H/S	Handstamped
Horiz	Horizontal; horizontally
Imp, Imperf	Imperforate
Inscr	Inscribed
L	Left
Litho	Lithographed
mm	Millimetres
MS	Miniature sheet
N.Y.	New York
Opt(d)	Overprint(ed)
P or P-c	Pen-cancelled
P, Pf or Perf	Perforated
Photo	Photogravure
Pl	Plate
Pr	Pair
Ptd	Printed
Ptg	Printing
R	Right
R.	Row
Recess	Recess-printed
Roto	Rotogravure
Roul	Rouletted
S	Specimen (overprint)
Surch	Surcharge(d)
T.C.	Telegraph Cancellation
T	Type
Typo	Typographed
Un	Unused
Us	Used
Vert	Vertical; vertically
W or wmk	Watermark
Wmk s	Watermark sideways

(†) = Does not exist
(–) (or blank price column) = Exists, or may exist, but no market price is known.
/ between colours means 'on' and the colour following is that of the paper on which the stamp is printed.

Colours of Stamps

Bl (blue); blk (black); brn (brown); car, carm (carmine); choc (chocolate); clar (claret); emer (emerald); grn (green); ind (indigo); mag (magenta); mar (maroon); mult (multicoloured); mve (mauve); ol (olive); orge (orange); pk (pink); pur (purple); scar (scarlet); sep (sepia); turq (turquoise); ultram (ultramarine); verm (vermilion); vio (violet); yell (yellow).

Colour of Overprints and Surcharges

(B.) = blue, (Blk.) = black, (Br.) = brown, (C.) = carmine, (G.) = green, (Mag.) = magenta, (Mve.) = mauve, (Ol.) = olive, (O.) = orange, (P.) = purple, (Pk.) = pink, (R.) = red, (Sil.) = silver, (V.) = violet, (Vm.) or (Verm.) = vermilion, (W.) = white, (Y.) = yellow.

Arabic Numerals

As in the case of European figures, the details of the Arabic numerals vary in different stamp designs, but they should be readily recognised with the aid of this illustration.

0   1   2   3   4   5   6   7   8   9

Features Listing

An at-a-glance guide to what's in the Stanley Gibbons catalogues

Area	Feature	Collect British Stamps	Stamps of the World	Thematic Catalogues	Stamps and country catalogues	Commonwealth and British Empire Catalogue, Parts 1-22 (including Comprehensive catalogues)	Great Britain Concise	Specialised catalogues
General	SG number	√	√	√		√	√	√
General	Specialised Catalogue number							√
General	Year of issue of first stamp in design	√	√	√		√	√	√
General	Exact date of issue of each design					√	√	√
General	Face value information	√	√	√		√	√	√
General	Historical and geographical information	√	√	√		√	√	√
General	General currency information, including dates used	√	√	√		√	√	√
General	Country name	√	√	√		√	√	√
General	Booklet panes					√	√	√
General	Coil stamps					√		√
General	First Day Covers	√					√	√
General	Brief footnotes on key areas of note	√	√	√		√	√	√
General	Detailed footnotes on key areas of note					√	√	√
General	Extra background information					√	√	√
General	Miniature sheet information (including size in mm)	√	√	√		√	√	√
General	Sheetlets					√		
General	Stamp booklets					√	√	√
General	Perkins Bacon "Cancelled"					√		
General	PHQ Cards	√					√	√
General	Post Office Label Sheets						√	
General	Post Office Yearbooks	√					√	√
General	Presentation and Souvenir Packs	√					√	√
General	Se-tenant pairs	√				√	√	√
General	Watermark details - errors, varieties, positions					√	√	√
General	Watermark illustrations	√				√	√	√
General	Watermark types	√				√	√	√
General	Forgeries noted					√		√
General	Surcharges and overprint information	√	√	√		√	√	√
Design and Description	Colour description, simplified			√	√			
Design and Description	Colour description, extended		√			√	√	√
Design and Description	Set design summary information	√	√	√		√	√	√
Design and Description	Designer name						√	√
Design and Description	Short design description	√	√	√		√	√	√

xxii

Features Listing

Area	Feature	Collect British Stamps	Stamps of the World	Thematic Catalogues	Stamps and country catalogues and British Empire and Commonwealth	Comprehensive Catalogue, Parts 1-22 (including Commonwealth and country catalogues)	Great Britain Concise	Specialised catalogues
Design and Description	Shade varieties					√	√	√
Design and Description	Type number	√	√			√	√	√
Illustrations	Multiple stamps from set illustrated	√				√	√	√
Illustrations	A Stamp from each set illustrated in full colour (where possible, otherwise mono)	√	√	√		√	√	√
Price	Catalogue used price	√	√	√		√	√	√
Price	Catalogue unused price	√	√	√		√	√	√
Price	Price - booklet panes					√	√	√
Price	Price - shade varieties					√	√	√
Price	On cover and on piece price					√	√	√
Price	Detailed GB pricing breakdown	√				√	√	√
Print and Paper	Basic printing process information	√	√	√		√	√	√
Print and Paper	Detailed printing process information, e.g. Mill sheets					√		√
Print and Paper	Paper information					√		√
Print and Paper	Detailed perforation information	√				√	√	√
Print and Paper	Details of research findings relating to printing processes and history							√
Print and Paper	Paper colour	√	√			√	√	√
Print and Paper	Paper description to aid identification					√	√	√
Print and Paper	Paper type					√	√	√
Print and Paper	Ordinary or chalk-surfaced paper					√	√	√
Print and Paper	Embossing omitted note							√
Print and Paper	Essays, Die Proofs, Plate Descriptions and Proofs, Colour Trials information							√
Print and Paper	Glazed paper					√	√	√
Print and Paper	Gum details					√		√
Print and Paper	Luminescence/Phosphor bands - general coverage	√				√	√	√
Print and Paper	Luminescence/Phosphor bands - specialised coverage							√
Print and Paper	Overprints and surcharges - including colour information	√	√	√		√	√	√
Print and Paper	Perforation/Imperforate information	√	√			√	√	√
Print and Paper	Perforation errors and varieties					√	√	√
Print and Paper	Print quantities							√
Print and Paper	Printing errors					√	√	√
Print and Paper	Printing flaws							√
Print and Paper	Printing varieties					√	√	√
Print and Paper	Punctured stamps - where official					√		
Print and Paper	Sheet positions					√	√	√
Print and Paper	Specialised plate number information							√
Print and Paper	Specimen overprints (only for Commonwealth & GB)					√	√	√
Print and Paper	Underprints						√	√
Print and Paper	Visible Plate numbers	√				√	√	√
Print and Paper	Yellow and Green paper listings					√		√
Index	Design index	√				√	√	

International Philatelic Glossary

English	French	German	Spanish	Italian
Agate	Agate	Achat	Agata	Agata
Air stamp	Timbre de la poste aérienne	Flugpostmarke	Sello de correo aéreo	Francobollo per posta aerea
Apple Green	Vert-pomme	Apfelgrün	Verde manzana	Verde mela
Barred	Annulé par barres	Balkenentwertung	Anulado con barras	Sbarrato
Bisected	Timbre coupé	Halbiert	Partido en dos	Frazionato
Bistre	Bistre	Bister	Bistre	Bistro
Bistre-brown	Brun-bistre	Bisterbraun	Castaño bistre	Bruno-bistro
Black	Noir	Schwarz	Negro	Nero
Blackish Brown	Brun-noir	Schwärzlichbraun	Castaño negruzco	Bruno nerastro
Blackish Green	Vert foncé	Schwärzlichgrün	Verde negruzco	Verde nerastro
Blackish Olive	Olive foncé	Schwärzlicholiv	Oliva negruzco	Oliva nerastro
Block of four	Bloc de quatre	Viererblock	Bloque de cuatro	Bloco di quattro
Blue	Bleu	Blau	Azul	Azzurro
Blue-green	Vert-bleu	Blaugrün	Verde azul	Verde azzuro
Bluish Violet	Violet bleuâtre	Bläulichviolett	Violeta azulado	Vioitto azzurrastro
Booklet	Carnet	Heft	Cuadernillo	Libretto
Bright Blue	Bleu vif	Lebhaftblau	Azul vivo	Azzurro vivo
Bright Green	Vert vif	Lebhaftgrün	Verde vivo	Verde vivo
Bright Purple	Mauve vif	Lebhaftpurpur	Púrpura vivo	Porpora vivo
Bronze Green	Vert-bronze	Bronzegrün	Verde bronce	Verde bronzo
Brown	Brun	Braun	Castaño	Bruno
Brown-lake	Carmin-brun	Braunlack	Laca castaño	Lacca bruno
Brown-purple	Pourpre-brun	Braunpurpur	Púrpura castaño	Porpora bruno
Brown-red	Rouge-brun	Braunrot	Rojo castaño	Rosso bruno
Buff	Chamois	Sämisch	Anteado	Camoscio
Cancellation	Oblitération	Entwertung	Cancelación	Annullamento
Cancelled	Annulé	Gestempelt	Cancelado	Annullato
Carmine	Carmin	Karmin	Carmín	Carminio
Carmine-red	Rouge-carmin	Karminrot	Rojo carmín	Rosso carminio
Centred	Centré	Zentriert	Centrado	Centrato
Cerise	Rouge-cerise	Kirschrot	Color de ceresa	Color Ciliegia
Chalk-surfaced paper	Papier couché	Kreidepapier	Papel estucado	Carta gessata
Chalky Blue	Bleu terne	Kreideblau	Azul turbio	Azzurro smorto
Charity stamp	Timbre de bienfaisance	Wohltätigkeitsmarke	Sello de beneficencia	Francobollo di beneficenza
Chestnut	Marron	Kastanienbraun	Castaño rojo	Marrone
Chocolate	Chocolat	Schokolade	Chocolate	Cioccolato
Cinnamon	Cannelle	Zimtbraun	Canela	Cannella
Claret	Grenat	Weinrot	Rojo vinoso	Vinaccia
Cobalt	Cobalt	Kobalt	Cobalto	Cobalto
Colour	Couleur	Farbe	Color	Colore
Comb-perforation	Dentelure en peigne	Kammzähnung, Reihenzähnung	Dentado de peine	Dentellatura e pettine
Commemorative stamp	Timbre commémoratif	Gedenkmarke	Sello conmemorativo	Francobollo commemorativo
Crimson	Cramoisi	Karmesin	Carmesí	Cremisi
Deep Blue	Blue foncé	Dunkelblau	Azul oscuro	Azzurro scuro
Deep bluish Green	Vert-bleu foncé	Dunkelbläulichgrün	Verde azulado oscuro	Verde azzurro scuro
Design	Dessin	Markenbild	Diseño	Disegno

International Philatelic Glossary

English	French	German	Spanish	Italian
Die	Matrice	Urstempel. Type, Platte	Cuño	Conio, Matrice
Double	Double	Doppelt	Doble	Doppio
Drab	Olive terne	Trüboliv	Oliva turbio	Oliva smorto
Dull Green	Vert terne	Trübgrün	Verde turbio	Verde smorto
Dull purple	Mauve terne	Trübpurpur	Púrpura turbio	Porpora smorto
Embossing	Impression en relief	Prägedruck	Impresión en relieve	Impressione a relievo
Emerald	Vert-eméraude	Smaragdgrün	Esmeralda	Smeraldo
Engraved	Gravé	Graviert	Grabado	Inciso
Error	Erreur	Fehler, Fehldruck	Error	Errore
Essay	Essai	Probedruck	Ensayo	Saggio
Express letter stamp	Timbre pour lettres par exprès	Eilmarke	Sello de urgencia	Francobollo per espresso
Fiscal stamp	Timbre fiscal	Stempelmarke	Sello fiscal	Francobollo fiscale
Flesh	Chair	Fleischfarben	Carne	Carnicino
Forgery	Faux, Falsification	Fälschung	Falsificación	Falso, Falsificazione
Frame	Cadre	Rahmen	Marco	Cornice
Granite paper	Papier avec fragments de fils de soie	Faserpapier	Papel con filamentos	Carto con fili di seta
Green	Vert	Grün	Verde	Verde
Greenish Blue	Bleu verdâtre	Grünlichblau	Azul verdoso	Azzurro verdastro
Greenish Yellow	Jaune-vert	Grünlichgelb	Amarillo verdoso	Giallo verdastro
Grey	Gris	Grau	Gris	Grigio
Grey-blue	Bleu-gris	Graublau	Azul gris	Azzurro grigio
Grey-green	Vert gris	Graugrün	Verde gris	Verde grigio
Gum	Gomme	Gummi	Goma	Gomma
Gutter	Interpanneau	Zwischensteg	Espacio blanco entre dos grupos	Ponte
Imperforate	Non-dentelé	Geschnitten	Sin dentar	Non dentellato
Indigo	Indigo	Indigo	Azul indigo	Indaco
Inscription	Inscription	Inschrift	Inscripción	Dicitura
Inverted	Renversé	Kopfstehend	Invertido	Capovolto
Issue	Émission	Ausgabe	Emisión	Emissione
Laid	Vergé	Gestreift	Listado	Vergato
Lake	Lie de vin	Lackfarbe	Laca	Lacca
Lake-brown	Brun-carmin	Lackbraun	Castaño laca	Bruno lacca
Lavender	Bleu-lavande	Lavendel	Color de alhucema	Lavanda
Lemon	Jaune-citron	Zitrongelb	Limón	Limone
Light Blue	Bleu clair	Hellblau	Azul claro	Azzurro chiaro
Lilac	Lilas	Lila	Lila	Lilla
Line perforation	Dentelure en lignes	Linienzähnung	Dentado en linea	Dentellatura lineare
Lithography	Lithographie	Steindruck	Litografía	Litografia
Local	Timbre de poste locale	Lokalpostmarke	Emisión local	Emissione locale
Lozenge roulette	Percé en losanges	Rautenförmiger Durchstich	Picadura en rombos	Perforazione a losanghe
Magenta	Magenta	Magentarot	Magenta	Magenta
Margin	Marge	Rand	Borde	Margine
Maroon	Marron pourpré	Dunkelrotpurpur	Púrpura rojo oscuro	Marrone rossastro
Mauve	Mauve	Malvenfarbe	Malva	Malva
Multicoloured	Polychrome	Mehrfarbig	Multicolores	Policromo
Myrtle Green	Vert myrte	Myrtengrün	Verde mirto	Verde mirto
New Blue	Bleu ciel vif	Neublau	Azul nuevo	Azzurro nuovo
Newspaper stamp	Timbre pour journaux	Zeitungsmarke	Sello para periódicos	Francobollo per giornali
Obliteration	Oblitération	Abstempelung	Matasello	Annullamento
Obsolete	Hors (de) cours	Ausser Kurs	Fuera de curso	Fuori corso

International Philatelic Glossary

English	French	German	Spanish	Italian
Ochre	Ocre	Ocker	Ocre	Ocra
Official stamp	Timbre de service	Dienstmarke	Sello de servicio	Francobollo di
Olive-brown	Brun-olive	Olivbraun	Castaño oliva	Bruno oliva
Olive-green	Vert-olive	Olivgrün	Verde oliva	Verde oliva
Olive-grey	Gris-olive	Olivgrau	Gris oliva	Grigio oliva
Olive-yellow	Jaune-olive	Olivgelb	Amarillo oliva	Giallo oliva
Orange	Orange	Orange	Naranja	Arancio
Orange-brown	Brun-orange	Orangebraun	Castaño naranja	Bruno arancio
Orange-red	Rouge-orange	Orangerot	Rojo naranja	Rosso arancio
Orange-yellow	Jaune-orange	Orangegelb	Amarillo naranja	Giallo arancio
Overprint	Surcharge	Aufdruck	Sobrecarga	Soprastampa
Pair	Paire	Paar	Pareja	Coppia
Pale	Pâle	Blass	Pálido	Pallido
Pane	Panneau	Gruppe	Grupo	Gruppo
Paper	Papier	Papier	Papel	Carta
Parcel post stamp	Timbre pour colis postaux	Paketmarke	Sello para paquete postal	Francobollo per pacchi postali
Pen-cancelled	Oblitéré à plume	Federzugentwertung	Cancelado a pluma	Annullato a penna
Percé en arc	Percé en arc	Bogenförmiger Durchstich	Picadura en forma de arco	Perforazione ad arco
Percé en scie	Percé en scie	Bogenförmiger Durchstich	Picado en sierra	Foratura a sega
Perforated	Dentelé	Gezähnt	Dentado	Dentellato
Perforation	Dentelure	Zähnung	Dentar	Dentellatura
Photogravure	Photogravure, Héliogravure	Rastertiefdruck	Fotograbado	Rotocalco
Pin perforation	Percé en points	In Punkten durchstochen	Horadado con alfileres	Perforato a punti
Plate	Planche	Platte	Plancha	Lastra, Tavola
Plum	Prune	Pflaumenfarbe	Color de ciruela	Prugna
Postage Due stamp	Timbre-taxe	Portomarke	Sello de tasa	Segnatasse
Postage stamp	Timbre-poste	Briefmarke, Freimarke, Postmarke	Sello de correos	Francobollo postale
Postal fiscal stamp	Timbre fiscal-postal	Stempelmarke als Postmarke verwendet	Sello fiscal-postal	Fiscale postale
Postmark	Oblitération postale	Poststempel	Matasello	Bollo
Printing	Impression, Tirage	Druck	Impresión	Stampa, Tiratura
Proof	Épreuve	Druckprobe	Prueba de impresión	Prova
Provisionals	Timbres provisoires	Provisorische Marken. Provisorien	Provisionales	Provvisori
Prussian Blue	Bleu de Prusse	Preussischblau	Azul de Prusia	Azzurro di Prussia
Purple	Pourpre	Purpur	Púrpura	Porpora
Purple-brown	Brun-pourpre	Purpurbraun	Castaño púrpura	Bruno porpora
Recess-printing	Impression en taille douce	Tiefdruck	Grabado	Incisione
Red	Rouge	Rot	Rojo	Rosso
Red-brown	Brun-rouge	Rotbraun	Castaño rojizo	Bruno rosso
Reddish Lilac	Lilas rougeâtre	Rötlichlila	Lila rojizo	Lilla rossastro
Reddish Purple	Poupre-rouge	Rötlichpurpur	Púrpura rojizo	Porpora rossastro
Reddish Violet	Violet rougeâtre	Rötlichviolett	Violeta rojizo	Violetto rossastro
Red-orange	Orange rougeâtre	Rotorange	Naranja rojizo	Arancio rosso
Registration stamp	Timbre pour lettre chargée (recommandée)	Einschreibemarke	Sello de certificado	Francobollo per raccomandate
Reprint	Réimpression	Neudruck	Reimpresión	Ristampa
Reversed	Retourné	Umgekehrt	Invertido	Rovesciato
Rose	Rose	Rosa	Rosa	Rosa
Rose-red	Rouge rosé	Rosarot	Rojo rosado	Rosso rosa
Rosine	Rose vif	Lebhaftrosa	Rosa vivo	Rosa vivo
Roulette	Percage	Durchstich	Picadura	Foratura
Rouletted	Percé	Durchstochen	Picado	Forato
Royal Blue	Bleu-roi	Königblau	Azul real	Azzurro reale

International Philatelic Glossary

English	French	German	Spanish	Italian
Sage green	Vert-sauge	Salbeigrün	Verde salvia	Verde salvia
Salmon	Saumon	Lachs	Salmón	Salmone
Scarlet	Écarlate	Scharlach	Escarlata	Scarlatto
Sepia	Sépia	Sepia	Sepia	Seppia
Serpentine roulette	Percé en serpentin	Schlangenliniger Durchstich	Picado a serpentina	Perforazione a serpentina
Shade	Nuance	Tönung	Tono	Gradazione de colore
Sheet	Feuille	Bogen	Hoja	Foglio
Slate	Ardoise	Schiefer	Pizarra	Ardesia
Slate-blue	Bleu-ardoise	Schieferblau	Azul pizarra	Azzurro ardesia
Slate-green	Vert-ardoise	Schiefergrün	Verde pizarra	Verde ardesia
Slate-lilac	Lilas-gris	Schierferlila	Lila pizarra	Lilla ardesia
Slate-purple	Mauve-gris	Schieferpurpur	Púrpura pizarra	Porpora ardesia
Slate-violet	Violet-gris	Schieferviolett	Violeta pizarra	Violetto ardesia
Special delivery stamp	Timbre pour exprès	Eilmarke	Sello de urgencia	Francobollo per espressi
Specimen	Spécimen	Muster	Muestra	Saggio
Steel Blue	Bleu acier	Stahlblau	Azul acero	Azzurro acciaio
Strip	Bande	Streifen	Tira	Striscia
Surcharge	Surcharge	Aufdruck	Sobrecarga	Soprastampa
Tête-bêche	Tête-bêche	Kehrdruck	Tête-bêche	Tête-bêche
Tinted paper	Papier teinté	Getöntes Papier	Papel coloreado	Carta tinta
Too-late stamp	Timbre pour lettres en retard	Verspätungsmarke	Sello para cartas retardadas	Francobollo per le lettere in ritardo
Turquoise-blue	Bleu-turquoise	Türkisblau	Azul turquesa	Azzurro turchese
Turquoise-green	Vert-turquoise	Türkisgrün	Verde turquesa	Verde turchese
Typography	Typographie	Buchdruck	Tipografia	Tipografia
Ultramarine	Outremer	Ultramarin	Ultramar	Oltremare
Unused	Neuf	Ungebraucht	Nuevo	Nuovo
Used	Oblitéré, Usé	Gebraucht	Usado	Usato
Venetian Red	Rouge-brun terne	Venezianischrot	Rojo veneciano	Rosso veneziano
Vermilion	Vermillon	Zinnober	Cinabrio	Vermiglione
Violet	Violet	Violett	Violeta	Violetto
Violet-blue	Bleu-violet	Violettblau	Azul violeta	Azzurro violetto
Watermark	Filigrane	Wasserzeichen	Filigrana	Filigrana
Watermark sideways	Filigrane couché	Wasserzeichen liegend	Filigrana acostado	Filigrana coricata
Wove paper	Papier ordinaire, Papier uni	Einfaches Papier	Papel avitelado	Carta unita
Yellow	Jaune	Gelb	Amarillo	Giallo
Yellow-brown	Brun-jaune	Gelbbraun	Castaño amarillo	Bruno giallo
Yellow-green	Vert-jaune	Gelbgrün	Verde amarillo	Verde giallo
Yellow-olive	Olive-jaunâtre	Gelboliv	Oliva amarillo	Oliva giallastro
Yellow-orange	Orange jaunâtre	Gelborange	Naranja amarillo	Arancio giallastro
Zig-zag roulette	Percé en zigzag	Sägezahnartiger Durchstich	Picado en zigzag	Perforazione a zigzag

Guide to Entries

A **Country of Issue** – When a country changes its name, the catalogue listing changes to reflect the name change, for example Namibia was formerly known as South West Africa, the stamps are all listed under Namibia, but split into South West Africa and then Namibia.

B **Country Information** – Brief geographical and historical details for the issuing country.

C **Currency** – Details of the currency, and dates of earliest use where applicable, on the face value of the stamps.

D **Illustration** – Generally, the first stamp in the set. Stamp illustrations are reduced to 75%, with overprints and surcharges shown actual size.

E **Illustration or Type Number** – These numbers are used to help identify stamps, either in the listing, type column, design line or footnote, usually the first value in the set. These type numbers are in a bold typeface – **123**; when bracketed (**123**) an overprint or a surcharge is indicated. Some type numbers include a lower-case letter – **123a**, this indicates they have been added to an existing set.

F **Date of issue** – This is the date that the stamp/set of stamps was issued by the post office and was available for purchase. When a set of definitive stamps has been issued over several years the Year Date given is for the earliest issue. Commemorative sets are listed in chronological order. Stamps of the same design, or issue are usually grouped together, for example some of the New Zealand landscapes definitive series were first issued in 2003 but the set includes stamps issued to May 2009.

G **Number Prefix** – Stamps other than definitives and commemoratives have a prefix letter before the catalogue number.
Their use is explained in the text: some examples are D for postage due and O for official stamps.

H **Footnote** – Further information on background or key facts on issues.

I **Stanley Gibbons Catalogue number** – This is a unique number for each stamp to help the collector identify stamps in the listing. The Stanley Gibbons numbering system is universally recognized as definitive.
Where insufficient numbers have been left to provide for additional stamps to a listing, some stamps will have a suffix letter after the catalogue number (for example 214a). If numbers have been left for additions to a set and not used they will be left vacant.
The separate type numbers (in bold) refer to illustrations (see **E**).

J **Colour** – If a stamp is printed in three or fewer colours then the colours are listed, working from the centre of the stamp outwards (see **R**).

K **Design line** – Further details on design variations

L **Key Type** – Indicates a design type on which the stamp is based. These are the bold figures found below each illustration, for example listed in Cameroon, in the West Africa catalogue, is the Key type A and B showing the ex-Kaiser's yacht *Hohenzollern*. The type numbers are also given in bold in the second column of figures alongside the stamp description to indicate the design of each stamp. Where an issue comprises stamps of similar design, the corresponding type number should be taken as indicating the general design. Where there are blanks in the type number column it means that the type of the corresponding stamp is that shown by the number in the type column of the same issue. A dash (–) in the type column means that the stamp is not illustrated. Where type numbers refer to stamps of another country, e.g. where stamps of one country are overprinted for use in another, this is always made clear in the text.

M **Coloured Papers** – Stamps printed on coloured paper are shown – e.g. "brown/*yellow*" indicates brown printed on yellow paper.

N **Surcharges and Overprints** – Stamps with the same overprints in different colours are listed separately. Numbers in brackets after the descriptions are the catalogue numbers of the non-overprinted stamps. The words 'inscribed' or 'inscription' refer to the wording incorporated in the design of a stamp and not surcharges or overprints.

O **Face value** – This refers to the value of each stamp and is the price it was sold for at the Post Office when issued. Some modern stamps do not have their values in figures but instead it is shown as a letter, for example Great Britain use 1st or 2nd on their stamps as opposed to the actual value.

P **Catalogue Value** – Mint/Unused. Prices quoted for Queen Victoria to King George V stamps are for lightly hinged examples.

Q **Catalogue Value** – Used. Prices generally refer to fine postally used examples. For certain issues they are for cancelled-to-order.

Prices
Prices are given in pence and pounds. Stamps worth £100 and over are shown in whole pounds:

Shown in Catalogue as	Explanation
10	10 pence
1·75	£1·75
15·00	£15
£150	£150
£2300	£2300

Prices assume stamps are in 'fine condition'; we may ask more for superb and less for those of lower quality. The minimum catalogue price quoted is 10p and is intended as a guide for catalogue users. The lowest price for individual stamps purchased from Stanley Gibbons is £1.
Prices quoted are for the cheapest variety of that particular stamp. Differences of watermark, perforation, or other details, often increase the value. Prices quoted for mint issues are for single examples, unless otherwise stated. Those in *se-tenant* pairs, strips, blocks or sheets may be worth more. Where no prices are listed it is either because the stamps are not known to exist (usually shown by a †) in that particular condition, or, more usually, because there is no reliable information on which to base their value.
All prices are subject to change without prior notice and we cannot guarantee to supply all stamps as priced. Prices quoted in advertisements are also subject to change without prior notice.

R **Multicoloured** – Nearly all modern stamps are multicoloured (more than three colours); this is indicated in the heading, with a description of the stamp given in the listing.

S **Perforations** – Please see page xiii for a detailed explanation of perforations.

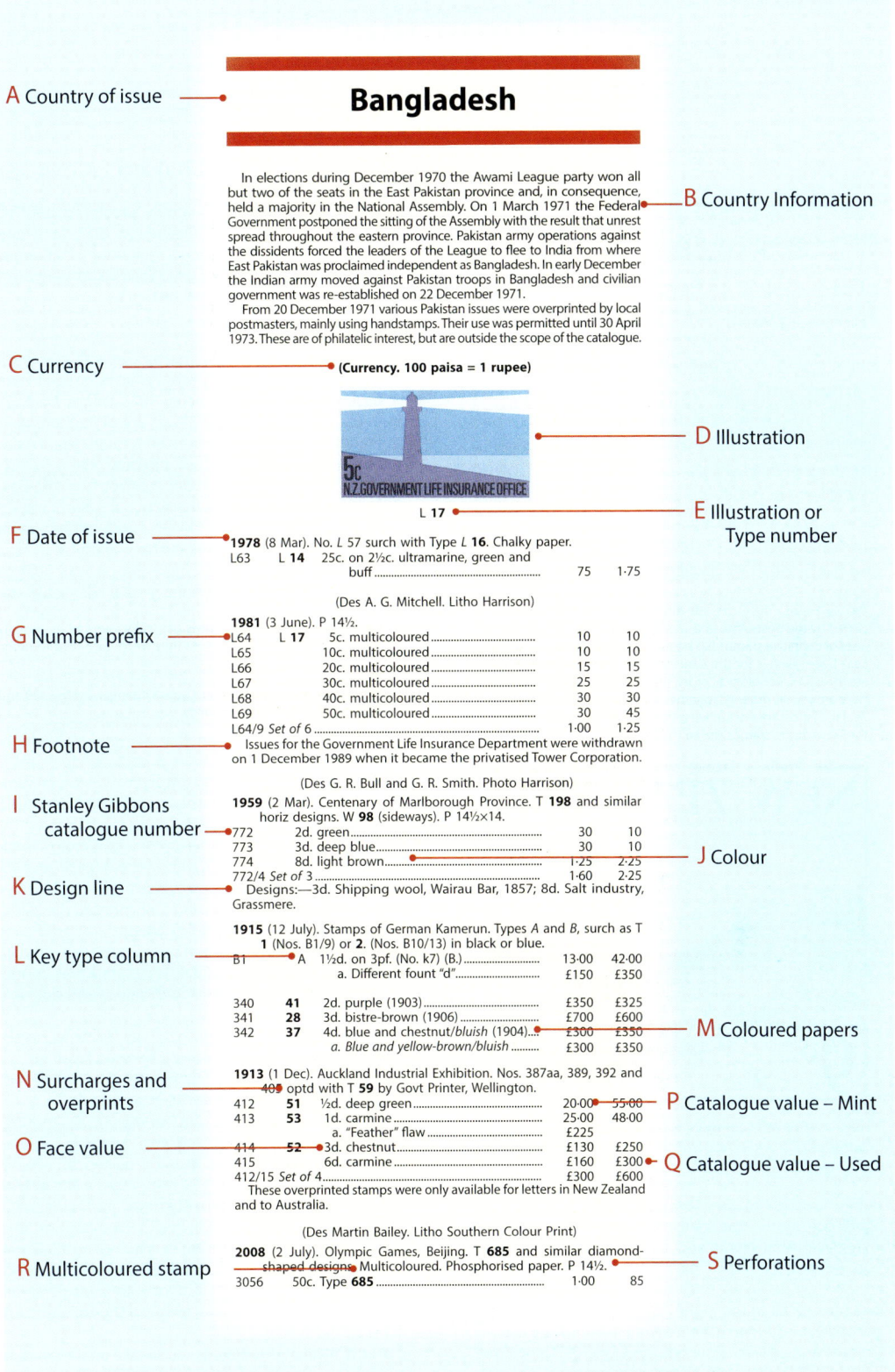

New Zealand's 'Third Pictorials'
By Paul Wreglesworth

2020 saw the 60th anniversary of one of New Zealand's most intriguing definitive issues. The country has a long tradition of showcasing its flora, fauna and natural beauty through the medium of postage stamps. In particular definitive issues have been used to great effect over the years, starting with the popular 'First Pictorials' issued in 1898 and followed by the 1935 'Second Pictorials'. Both relied on the skill of the engraver and high quality recess printing in order to produce series of stamps that have, over the years, amassed a significant fan base in the philatelic world. By the 1960s the technologies available to stamp printers, such as the photogravure process, should have enabled the New Zealand Post Office to create a high quality series with high visual impact, a perfect window to advertise the country's great natural assets.

1072 entries were received for the public competition, including this unadopted artwork for 'Aerial Topdressing'

Public reaction to the new series was mixed. While some considered the stamps, particularly the lower values featuring plants and flowers, to be simple and visually attractive, the Post Office came in for much criticism, in particular over poor colour selection and lack of contrast in the higher values. The £1 stamp was printed in pink for no other reason, it would seem, than the fact that all New Zealand's previous £1 stamps had been pink! Despite much negative reaction, the set, which remained in place largely unaltered until the introduction of decimal currency in 1967, (and even then the designs and colours remained unchanged) proved to be a gold mine for collectors as new errors and varieties came thick and fast.

THE STAMPS

In November 1958, the Postmaster General announced that a new set of pictorial stamps would be issued in 1960. A public competition attracted 1072 entries from 268 individuals. A selection panel was appointed and given guidance that values from 1d. to 8d. should depict native flora, the set should include subjects relating to the Maoris and that representations received from the Dairy Board, the Timber Industry, the National Parks Board and the Tourist Department should be considered favourably.

Because of the postal rates that would be in force at the time the set was to be issued, it was deemed necessary to add a ½d. value and a 9d. value was required to meet the airmail rate for postcards to North America. A design for the ½d., consistent with the required flora theme, was prepared by artists at Harrison and Sons Ltd, and artwork for the 9d., depicting New Zealand's national flag, was prepared by officers of the Post Office Publicity Department.

The decision was taken that all values should be produced by the photogravure process. De La Rue and Co Ltd were contracted to produce the lower value stamps (½d. to 8d.), which they printed on rotary web-fed presses perforating the sheets as the paper left the printing machine. The paper used was Wiggins Teape 50 per cent esparto paper with vertical mesh and the familiar Multiple NZ and Star watermark upright.

By comparison Harrison and Sons printed the values entrusted to them in sheet-fed presses and used a rag and sulphite paper with horizontal mesh supplied by Guard Bridge Mill. The Multiple watermark was upright on the 9d., 1s., 1s.9d., 2s., 5s. and £1 values and sideways on the other values.

The majority of the series (2d., 4d., 1s., 1s.3d., 1s.6d., 1s.9d., 2s., 2s.6d., 3s., 5s., 10s. and £1) were placed on sale on 11 July 1960 and the remaining values (½d., 1d., 3d., 6d., 8d. and 9d.) followed on 1 September 1960.

Inevitably, during the life of the issue, changes to postal rates necessitated the addition of new values with 2½d. and 5d. stamps placed on sale in November 1961 and May 1962 respectively. The airmail rate for 1st class letters to Australia and the surface letter rate to non-Commonwealth destinations rose to 7d. on 1 October 1964 yet it was not until March 1966 that a 7d. stamp was issued. This was little more than a year before decimalisation—as a result covers showing correct commercial usage of the 7d. stamp are particularly elusive.

Harrison and Sons were asked to take on the printing of all three of these additional values which they duly

New Zealand's 'Third Pictorials'

did using a 50:50 esparto and sulphite paper with chalk surfacing and horizontal mesh. The NZ and Star watermark was sideways on the 2½d. and 5d. values and upright on the 7d. The 2½d. was initially printed on a web-fed rotary press but later printings, in common with the other two values, were printed using sheet-fed presses.

These three values, together with the 1s.3d., 1s.9d. (multicolour) and 3s. (multicolour) are known with watermark inverted and the 2½d., 5d., 1s.3d., 1s.6d., 2s.6d., 3s. and 10s. values have been found with watermark sideways, suggesting that less attention was paid to this feature when printing using sheet-fed presses.

A change in the postal rates in October 1961 necessitated the addition of 2½d. and 5d. values. A 7d. value was placed on sale in March 1966

REISSUE OF THE 1s.9d. AND 3s.

The higher values of the series in particular had been much criticised for being printed in single colours, some even suggesting that they would have been better suited to the traditional engraved process. The 1s.9d. and 3s. values in their original monochrome colours of bistre-brown and sepia were not particularly attractive and certainly did not use the photogravure process to best advantage. One critic wrote, 'It looks as if the plane is pouring out smoke rather than topdressing material… the colour chosen for the stamp, khaki, would make it appear a waste of time topdressing such country as it would seem the hills have not seen any rain for several years.' [Ref 1]

A new 1s.9d. was placed on sale in November 1963 and 3s. in April 1964. Both were printed in bright colours on a chalk-surfaced paper. The design of the 1s.9d. was unchanged whilst minor modifications were made to the image for the 3s. value. Plate numbers were not printed in the margins of the reprinted stamps as had been the case with the original issue. Although available for more than three years the original printings received little attention from collectors, perhaps because they were so drab, and consequently they can be difficult to find today—particularly in plate blocks.

The 1s.9d. and 3s. values, with their drab colours, were not well received

The 2d., 4d., 1s., 1s.3d., 1s.6d., 1s.9d., 2s., 2s.6d., 3s., 5s., 10s. and £1 values were placed on sale on 11 July 1960. The ½d., 1d., 3d., 6d., 8d. and 9d values were released on 1 September 1960

The 1s.9d. and 3s. were finally reprinted in 'multicolour' in November 1963 and April 1964

xxxi

THE PLATES

Not surprisingly, the lower value stamps were printed in great numbers and the printers had to use several cylinders throughout the life of the issue. Some colours appeared to give more problems than others with six different green cylinders used in the printing of the 2d. value and seven different blue cylinders used in producing the 3d. value, giving 14 different plate number combinations. These are, in the main, still relatively easy to find. Less well known is that both printers used two cylinders with the same numbers during the initial printings of some values. Detailed study of the relevant plates has identified two green cylinders numbered 1 were used for the 2d. value, two black cylinders numbered 1A used for the 2½d., two dark blue cylinders numbered 1 for the 3d. and two blue cylinders numbered 1 for the 4d.. In most cases it is only study of the flaws and retouches that enables the cylinders to be distinguished, however for the 3d. value the font used for the dark blue cylinder number differs and plate blocks showing the 'small "1"' are worth searching out in dealer's stocks.

In 1965, without prior warning, sheets of the 1d., 3d., 4d. and 6d. values appeared printed on paper with heavy chalk surfacing. The quality of print was much improved, with less background 'grain'

Harrisons also introduced a chalk-surfaced paper whilst reprinting the 2s., 5s. and 10s. values in 1966. The new paper is much whiter than the original and there are strong shade variations in the printed stamps.

PERFORATIONS

Both De La Rue and Harrisons used comb heads for perforating the printed sheets and a range of single, double and even triple comb heads were used during the life of the issue. The original low values (½d., 1d., 2d., 3d., 4d., 6d. and 8d.) printed by De La Rue were perforated on the web as the paper left the printing machine and a single comb head gauging 14½×14 was used. Stamps printed by Harrisons were perforated using a double comb head gauging 14¾×14 for the 9d., 1s. and 1s.9d. values with the 1s.3d. and 1s.6d. values gauging 14×14¾. A triple comb head was used for the 2s.6d., 3s. (sepia) and 10s., which were perforated vertically 14¾×14 and 2s., 5s. and £1 perforated horizontally 14×14¾. Finally, a single comb head was used for a period to perforate sheets of the 2s. and 5s. on both original and chalk-surfaced paper. This same head was used latterly for sheets of the 2s.6d., 3s. (multicolour) and 10s. on chalk-surfaced paper.

Examples of partial or completely doubled strikes of the comb head can be found on many values and are, for those interested in such detail, a useful indicator as to the type of comb used and direction of movement through the sheet.

One of the most noteworthy aspects of the Third Pictorial issue was the use of an unusual comb perforating head supplied by Messrs Chambon and Sons. Although similar formats of comb were used to perforate stamps for other postal administrations (A number of Israeli issues for example were perforated using Chambon perforating heads) these were certainly unique in New Zealand philately.

De La Rue used this perforating head, in conjunction with their Chambon printing presses, for the ½d., 1d., 2d., 3d., 4d., 6d. and 8d. values. The gauge of the perforations remained 14½×14, however the special feature of the Chambon perforating head was the 'H' shaped comb. At one strike it perforated

De La Rue used two blue cylinders, both numbered '1', for early printings of the 3d. They can be distinguished by the size of the blue numeral

CHALK-SURFACED PAPER

With little or no prior warning, sheets of the 1d., 3d., 4d. and 6d. values were placed on sale during 1965, printed on paper with similar watermark characteristics but with heavy chalk surfacing. The quality of print was much improved with less 'grain' to the background. These are relatively easy to detect but caution should be exercised with the 4d. value. Whilst used copies can be found, generally postmarked from mid-1966 or later, mint copies are amongst the great rarities of this issue. Bright fluorescence, both front and back, under ultraviolet light is an additional although not, in itself, conclusive test. Purchase from a reputable source would be a strong recommendation if looking to acquire a mint copy of this rarity.

a complete horizontal row of stamps together with half of the vertical sides of all adjacent stamps in the rows immediately above and below. Its use is often evidenced by the presence of 'wide' or 'narrow' perforations half-way down both vertical sides of a stamp. It is often referred to as 'experimental' and blocks which show clear characteristics of the perforating head generally retail at a premium to examples with 'standard' comb characteristics, despite the fact that its use was far more extensive than any of the other comb heads.

Examples of the Chambon perfs are also to be found on booklet panes and coil stamps produced from printed sheets.

'Narrow' or 'wide' perforations down the vertical sides are characteristic of the 'Chambon' perforating head

Block of 1d. value showing 'narrow' perfs in top and bottom rows

Double comb perfs
A blind perf in every other row and two close perforation holes between the first and second rows are indicative of a double comb perforating head moving vertically

Block of 2d. value showing (top row) 'wide' perfs and (bottom row) 'narrow' perfs

1d. Booklet pane, from stapled booklet, showing 'narrow' perfs along centre of bottom row

BOOKLETS

The first issue of booklets, with a face value of 4s., was placed on sale on 1 September 1960. It contained 12x 1d. and 12 x 3d. stamps (each in panes of six), a page of airmail labels, waxed paper interleaving and a number of panes of advertising. A second issue of booklets was issued in June 1962 which had a number of changes to the advertising panes but also two panes of ½d. stamps, giving a face value of 4s.6d. Twelve x ½d. stamps far exceeded public requirement and in 1964 a third issue, containing just one pane of ½d. stamps, was placed on

A double strike of the single comb moving vertically through a sheet of 2½d. stamps

sale with a face value of 4s.3d. Further alterations were made to the advertisements and the book was stitched, whereas the first two issues had been stapled.

A separate printing plate was used to produce the stamps for booklet production and for the third printing the numbers 1 to 6 were inserted at six positions on the printing cylinder resulting in these numbers being printed on the binding selvedge adjacent to the top left stamp in each pane of six stamps.

Three booklet printings were produced. The first two stapled and the third stitched

Numbers, from 1 to 6, were inserted at six positions on the printing plate for the third issue of booklets

COIL STAMPS—VENDING MACHINE COILS

The 1d. Karaka and 3d. Kowhai were required for use in coin in the slot vending machines, replacing the previous Small Queen definitives, and the first were produced in September 1960 from sheets of stamps supplied by De La Rue. The Government Printer's Office prepared continuous coils of 480 or 960 stamps, wound horizontally, with a join every 12 stamps.

In late 1963 a new development in New Zealand coil stamps was the production of continuous rolls of stamps for vending machines. Printed on a continuous web, they are easily distinguishable from stamps produced in sheet form as the watermark is sideways and the perforations gauge 14½×13. The splitting of rolls into individual coils was still undertaken in New Zealand. Although web printed coils were the norm in most countries, the USA having used such a process since 1914, the New Zealand Post Office seemed bedevilled by practical problems with the coils. Occasionally the reels would split, necessitating repair with strips of stamp paper.

Late in the life of the issue, vending machine coils were once again produced by coiling standard sheets, although the stamps were printed on chalk-surfaced paper which had been introduced for the 1d. in 1965 and 3d. in 1966.

'LIGHTNING' COILS

Whilst many New Zealand businesses used metered mailing machines for their post, some preferred to use stamps and a number of stamp affixing machines were commercially available. One such was the 'Lightning Stamp Affixer'. Used in New Zealand as early as the 1930s, special coils were prepared by the Government Printer for use in these devices. Throughout the period of issue of the 1960 Pictorials rolls of 480 stamps were prepared, 2d., 2½d., 3d. and 4d. values were rolled reflecting the principal inland postal rate at various times. Because most collectors were largely unaware of these coils, few were saved and examples remain scarce. Prepared from standard sheets and rolled horizontally (as distinct from counter-coils that were rolled vertically) it is possible to find coil joins or possibly the 'lead papers' that were wrapped round the roll prior to use. These papers are inscribed 'Lightning Roll', together with the stamp value and total roll value, which included a 4d. surcharge as a rolling fee.

COUNTER COILS

An interesting facet of New Zealand philately is the, so called, 'counter coil'. As early as 1945 the Post Office introduced a counter-top dispenser which held strips of current definitive stamps in roll form which could be drawn off, on demand, by the counter clerk. The coils were not specially printed but were made up from sheets joined together by the selvedges. For accounting purposes a number was printed at each join, which, unlike other coil formats was not hidden, and pairs of stamps showing a numbered join are highly collectable. Counter coils remained in use until the late 1970s.

With the 1960 pictorials the coils were produced by joining sheets along the top and bottom selvedges or side selvedges and rolled vertically (low values and 1s.3d. and 1s.6d.) and horizontally for other values. The lower values, to 8d., were processed into rolls of 480 stamps with 24 sections of 20 stamps, whilst the others were in rolls of 320 stamps, 24 sections of 16 stamps.

New Zealand's 'Third Pictorials'

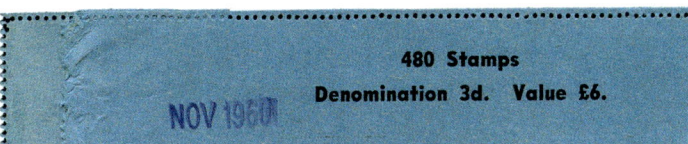

Vending machine coils.
Start papers for the initial issue showing the date of coiling

Only 1d. and 3d. values were made available for vending machines, prepared from standard sheets with a join every 12 stamps

In 1963 continuous rolls were produced. The watermark was now sideways and the perforations gauge 14½×13. The wrappers were not glued to the roll but formed a band round the finished roll

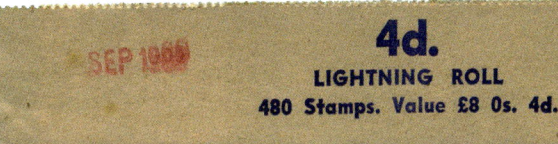   

Stamp rolls were produced for business customers to use with the 'Lightning' stamp applicator

Consequently numbers printed at the joins are from 1 to 23 for the lower values and 1 to 19 for all other values.

Before the rolling process began a sheet of coloured paper was attached to the first sheet of stamps. After 'slitting' into individual rolls this created an 'end paper'. A second sheet of paper, printed with details of the coil, was attached to the last sheet of stamps and in turn became the 'start paper' for the roll. The date of rolling was stamped on both start and end papers. A range of different coloured papers was used across the values.

The first counter coils produced were for 2d., 4d., 1s., 1s.6d. and 1s.9d. values and the numbers printed on the joins were in black. It soon became apparent that 'Sheet Value' markings in the selvedge of some values made it difficult to read the printed numbers. As a result these and all subsequent values were produced with the section numbers in red. In addition to the initial values prepared, coils of the 2½d., 3d., 6d., 8d., 1s.3d. and 1s.9d. (multicolour) were produced during the period of issue of the pictorials.

Naturally, any flaws and retouches found on the sheets used to produce the counter coil rolls are present in the finished roll and, where those varieties occur in the first or last row of the sheet (or first or last column where rolling was horizontal) they can be collected in counter coil pairs.

The 2d., 3d., 4d., 6d. and 8d. values can be found with evidence of the 'Chambon' perforations.

Initial supplies of 'counter coils' had the numbers printed in black.
It was claimed the black numbers could be difficult to read against the sheet selvedge markings and they were later changed to red

Around August 1966 the printers, De La Rue, processed another order for low value definitives. Part of the consignment was printed on chalk-surfaced paper and on receipt some of the 3d. and 6d. sheets were used to make counter rolls. Coil-join pairs with

xxxv

stamps printed on chalk-surfaced paper are quite scarce, however even more elusive are se-tenant coil-join pairs of the 3d. value printed on plain and chalk-surfaced paper. This combination arose when, during the rolling process, a mixture of sheets printed on the two papers was used. This resulted in all chalk-surfaced coil-join pairs numbered 1, 2, 3 and 18 and mixed pairs numbered 4, 17 and 19. These mixed coil-join pairs are particularly scarce.

Different coloured papers were used for the 'start' and 'end' papers

3d. counter coil-join (1) with both stamps on chalk-surfaced paper and (4) se-tenant pair with upper stamp on ordinary paper and lower stamp on chalky paper.

VARIETIES

The 1960 Third Pictorials present the collector with an almost endless range of varieties from minor 'flyspeck' to dramatic missing colours and much in between. Something to suit all pockets and all degrees of specialisation.

The nature of the photogravure process and the techniques used to convert the original artwork into a finished postage stamp provide a wealth of new errors and varieties not seen in the age of the engraved stamp. It is beyond the scope of this article to discuss these in detail, but constant flaws may be found on the stamps or, if it was deemed necessary to correct these before printing, stamps may be found with 'touching up'. If the flaw becomes apparent after printing, or it becomes more extensive, then the printing plate or cylinder may be retouched. In some cases this may happen several times, resulting in different 'states' of retouch. Introduction of a totally new cylinder may be required at which point early flaws and retouches may disappear and new ones appear. Those interested in more specialised information on this subject are referred to the series of Handbooks published by the Royal Philatelic Society of New Zealand. [Ref 2, 3]

In the photogravure printing process ink is applied to the revolving cylinder by an inking roller and surplus ink removed, by a wiper or 'doctor' blade, from the non-printing surface of the plate. Coloured or colourless lines can be found on stamps where the doctor blade has trapped dirt or foreign matter and dragged it across the plate surface, has been lifted on contact with foreign material or, at worst, has been damaged. Examples can vary from hairlines to wide bands of colour.

Examples of 'Doctor' blade flaws which can vary from a thin colourless line to a broad band of colour

MISSING COLOURS

Whilst misplaced colours may be of limited philatelic significance, they can, at times, be spectacular, as is the case with those found on the 2½d. value where misplacement of the red of the berries is sometimes referred to as 'fruit salad'. A number of sheets of the 1s.9d. multicolour were found with a major displacement of the red colour giving, in some cases two planes on one stamp!

Missing colours may occur, with sheet-fed printing, when two sheets pass through the printing machine simultaneously. With high-speed printing processes, and the introduction of printing on a continuous reel or web, colours may be missing from one or two rows or simply part of a row. Such an error is caused by a temporary loss of pressure on the paper against the printing cylinder, perhaps when the machine is stopped for adjustment or maintenance. Examples of missing, or partially missing, colours can be found on nearly every value in this series. Some, like the 2d. value with missing black, are quite spectacular as the country name is missing!

Another feature of modern continuous production processes, like newspaper printing, is the need to generate large rolls of paper either for printing directly on rotary web-fed presses or for production of sheets for sheet-fed presses. In the paper production or coating process, or during the printing process itself,

New Zealand's 'Third Pictorials'

if the web breaks, or a new roll needs to be connected to an old one then the two ends are overlapped and glued. A narrow strip of double thickness paper is created which may ultimately pass through the printing machine. Affected sheets are generally removed during post-production quality control checks but examples of the 1s. and 2s.6d. values are known with these characteristic reel joins. As both values were printed on sheet-fed presses the paper-join must have been created during the paper production process prior to guillotining into sheets for printing.

2s.—one sheet was found at the Auckland Post Office with the buff partially missing from the last vertical row of six stamps

A scarce example of a paper overlap where two rolls of paper have been joined together, this is less obvious from the front

CAVEAT EMPTOR!

Finally a few words of caution for those interested in major errors from this period. Some years ago pre-issue proof material from the De La Rue archives was sold into the philatelic market. This included a number of single-colour printings (often referred to as colour separations) in full sheet form.

Colour shifts can be quite spectacular

Examples of De La Rue proof material

2d.—imperf on gummed and watermarked paper taken from a series of progressive proofs

3d.—not 'three colours missing' but a single colour printing made by De La Rue prior to initial print runs

Missing Colours
2d.—black (including country name) progressively missing
1d.—upper stamp orange omitted
3d.—lower stamp yellow omitted

The 3d. value from the 1963 Railway Centenary Issue and the 2d., 3d.. and 6d. values of the 1960 pictorial definitives are found in this format. For each value a series of separated colours, and a final printing using all colours, exists. With the 2d. Kowhai-Ngutukaka and 3d. Kowhai each series is printed on watermarked paper. The 2d. printings were not perforated so any examples of the 2d. value, in the issued colours, offered imperforate should be considered with a degree of scepticism. Even more caution should be exercised with the 3d. value. The series of proofs for this particular value were printed on watermarked, gummed paper and perforated just as the issued stamps would have been. As a series these offer a fascinating insight into the printing process, however a number of examples of the blue-green colour separation, on its own, have been offered for sale in recent years and described as 'three colours missing'. Now, as we have seen, missing colours are quite common in this issue, but three colours missing on one stamp, passing unnoticed over a post office counter, is highly unlikely. Further confirmation that these stamps were originally from the De La Rue pre-issue trial printings is found in the shade which is a cold grey-blue colour. This shade is not recorded as having been used for any printing of the 3d. value sold through Post Offices.

REFERENCES
1. Laurie Franks, All the Stamps of New Zealand (A H & A W Reed, 1977) p.88
2. The Postage Stamps of New Zealand, Vol IV, (1964), Chapter XII
3. The Postage Stamps of New Zealand, Vol VI, (1977), Chapter X

Paul Wreglesworth is a member of the New Zealand Society of Great Britain and a Fellow of both the Royal Philatelic Society London and Royal Philatelic Society New Zealand. He currently edits *The Kiwi* journal of the New Zealand Society of Great Britain, published six times a year. The Society caters for all levels of collector with an interest in the stamps or postal history of New Zealand and its dependencies. Regular meetings are held in London, at the premises of the Royal Philatelic Society London, together with regional meetings in Scotland, the North of England and the Midlands. Members benefit from a circulating packet, annual auction and library facilities.

Membership details are available from the Society's website: www.nzstamps.org.uk/nzsgb

This article first appeared in the October 2010 issue of Gibbons Stamp Monthly.

The New Zealand Society of Great Britain

Celebrating our 70th Anniversary in 2022

Promoting the study of the stamps and postal history of New Zealand and its Dependencies

- 'The Kiwi' - award winning journal published six times a year in paper and electronic format
- London and regional meetings
- Additional on-line meetings
- Access to an extensive library held at the Royal Philatelic Society London
- Annual auction
- Circulating exchange packet
- Biennial residential weekend
- Website - all journal back issues, articles, research aids and links to other relevant sites

Visit our website for details of membership:
www.nzsgb.org.uk

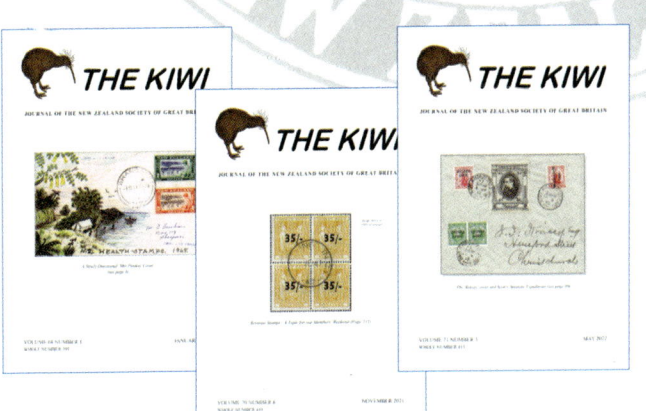

For a complimentary pdf copy of our award winning journal contact the editor:

kiwieditor@gmail.com

New Zealand's leading Auction House

MOWBRAY COLLECTABLES

We hold two Public Auctions, 12 monthly Postal Auctions, and several Fixed Price Lists each year.

Lots are fully described, and unconditionally guaranteed.

Your £ goes further with our favourable exchange rates

We also hold extensive stock of New Zealand and Tokelau stamps. Please send us your wants list.

Visit our website
www.mowbraycollectables.com

To join our mailing list please contact us:

MOWBRAY COLLECTABLES
Private Bag 63000 Wellington 6140, New Zealand
Phone +64 6 364 8270, Fax +64 6 364 8252
Email auctions@mowbrays.nz

NEW ZEALAND

New Zealand

From 1831 mail from New Zealand was sent to Sydney, New South Wales, routed through an unofficial postmaster at Kororareka.

The first official post office opened at Kororareka in January 1840 to be followed by others at Auckland, Britannia, Coromandel Harbour, Hokianga, Port Nicholson, Russell and Waimate during the same year. New South Wales relinquished control of the postal service when New Zealand became a separate colony on 3 May 1841.

The British GPO was responsible for the operation of the overseas mails from 11 October 1841 until the postal service once again passed under colonial control on 18 November 1848.

CC1   CC2

AUCKLAND
CROWNED-CIRCLE HANDSTAMPS

CC1	CC1	AUCKLAND NEW ZEALAND (R.) (31.10.1846)..............Price on cover	£400

NELSON
CROWNED-CIRCLE HANDSTAMPS

CC2	CC1	NELSON NEW ZEALAND (R.) (31.10.1846)..............Price on cover	£1100

NEW PLYMOUTH
CROWNED-CIRCLE HANDSTAMPS

CC3	CC1	NEW PLYMOUTH NEW ZEALAND (Red or Black) (31.10.1846) Price on cover	£3000
CC3a	CC2	NEW PLYMOUTH NEW ZEALAND (Red or Black) (1854). Price on cover	£3250

OTAGO
CROWNED-CIRCLE HANDSTAMPS

CC4	CC2	OTAGO NEW ZEALAND (R.) (1851) ....Price on cover	£1900

PETRE
CROWNED-CIRCLE HANDSTAMPS

CC5	CC1	PETRE NEW ZEALAND (R.) (31.10.1846)..............Price on cover	£1400

PORT VICTORIA
CROWNED-CIRCLE HANDSTAMPS

CC6	CC2	PORT VICTORIA NEW ZEALAND (R.) (1851)......................Price on cover	£1200

RUSSELL
CROWNED-CIRCLE HANDSTAMPS

CC7	CC1	RUSSELL NEW ZEALAND (R.) (31.10.1846)..............Price on cover	£8000

WELLINGTON
CROWNED-CIRCLE HANDSTAMPS

CC8	CC1	WELLINGTON NEW ZEALAND (R.) (31.10.1846)..............Price on cover	£350

A similar mark for Christchurch as T **CC2** is only known struck, in black, as a cancellation after the introduction of adhesive stamps.

No. CC3a is a locally-cut replacement with the office name around the circumference, but a straight 'PAID AT' in the centre.

PRICES FOR STAMPS ON COVER TO 1945

Nos.	1/125	from × 2
Nos.	126/136	from × 4
Nos.	137/139	from × 4

PRICES FOR STAMPS ON COVER TO 1945

No.	140	—
No.	141	from × 8
No.	142	—
Nos.	143/148	from × 2
Nos.	149/151	from × 10
Nos.	152/184	from × 2
Nos.	185/186	—
Nos.	187/203	from × 3
Nos.	205/207e	—
Nos.	208/213	from × 2
Nos.	214/216j	—
Nos.	217/258	from × 3
No.	259	—
Nos.	260/269	from × 3
No.	270	—
Nos.	271/276	from × 3
Nos.	277/307	from × 2
Nos.	308/316	from × 3
No.	317	—
Nos.	318/328	from × 3
Nos.	329/348	—
No.	349	from × 5
Nos.	350/351	—
No.	352	from × 5
Nos.	353/369	—
Nos.	370/386	from × 2
No.	387	from × 4
Nos.	388/399	from × 3
Nos.	400/666	from × 2
Nos.	E1/E5	from × 5
No.	E6	from × 10
Nos.	O1/O34	from × 5
Nos.	O59/O66	from × 4
Nos.	O67/O68	—
Nos.	O69/O81	from × 5
Nos.	O82/O87	—
Nos.	O88/O93	from × 20
Nos.	O94/O99	from × 12
Nos.	O100/O111	from × 5
Nos.	O112/O113	—
Nos.	O115/O119	from × 15
Nos.	O120/O133	from × 10
Nos.	O134/O151	from × 4
Nos.	P1/P7	from × 8
Nos.	L1/L9	from × 10
Nos.	L9a/L12	—
Nos.	L13/L20	from × 15
Nos.	L21/L23	—
Nos.	L24/L41	from × 12
Nos.	D1/D8	from × 3
Nos.	D9/D16	from × 5
Nos.	D17/D20	from × 3
Nos.	D21/D47	from × 6
No.	F1	—
No.	F2	from × 5
Nos.	F3/F144	—
Nos.	F145/F158	from × 3
Nos.	F159/F168	—
Nos.	F169/F179	from × 3
Nos.	F180/F186	—
Nos.	F187/F190	from × 2
Nos.	F191/F203	from × 3
Nos.	F204/F211	—
Nos.	F212/F218	from × 2
Nos.	A1/A3	from × 2

CROWN COLONY

PERKINS BACON 'CANCELLED'. For notes on these handstamps, showing 'CANCELLED' between horizontal bars forming an oval, see Catalogue Introduction.

NEW ZEALAND

1 **2**

(Eng by Humphreys. Recess P.B.)

1855 (20 July*)–**57**. Wmk Large Star, W w **1**. Imperf.

1	**1**	1d. dull carmine *(white paper)* (H/S 'CANCELLED' in oval £32000)	£80000	£20000
2		2d. dull blue *(blued paper)* (H/S 'CANCELLED' in oval £32000)	£35000	£700
3		1s. pale yellow-green *(blued paper)* (H/S 'CANCELLED' in oval £26000)	£60000	£6000
		a. Bisected (6d.) *(on cover)* (1857)	†	£50000

* The stamps went on sale in Auckland on 20 July 1855, but were not available elsewhere until later. The earliest date known for Wellington is 19 September 1855.

The 2d. and 1s. on white paper formerly listed are now known to be stamps printed on blued paper which have had the bluing washed out. Nos. 3a and 6a were used at Port Chalmers between March 1857, when the rate for ½ oz. letters to Great Britain was reduced to 6d., and August 1859. All known examples are bisected vertically.

(Printed by J. Richardson, Auckland, NZ)

1855 (Dec). First printing. White paper. Wmk Large Star. Imperf.

3b	**1**	1d. orange		£32000

1855 (Nov)–**58**. Blue paper. No wmk. Imperf.

4	**1**	1d. red	£14000	£2500
5		2d. blue (3.56)	£4000	£325
6		1s. green (9.57)	£50000	£4000
		a. Bisected (6d.) *(on cover)* (1858)	†	£30000

These stamps on blue paper may occasionally be found watermarked with the names of the manufacturers. Four such watermarks are known: 'SANDS & McDOUGALL MELBOURNE', 'CHARLES SKIPPER & EAST LONDON' and 'SANDS & KENNY' all in uppercase double-lined letters, or 'IPM Co 1852' in upper case script lettering.

1857 (Jan). White paper similar to the issue of July 1855. Wmk Large Star.

7	**1**	1d. dull orange	†	£30000

This stamp is in the precise shade of the 1d. of the 1858 printing by Richardson on no wmk white paper. An unsevered pair is known with Dunedin cancellation on a cover front showing an Auckland arrival postmark of 19.1.1857.

The paper employed for the local printings was often too small to cover the full printing plate, a problem which was overcome by overlapping two sheets on the press. Depending on how accurately the sheets were overlapped, stamps may be found with portions of the design missing (including a unique example of the 2d. value in the Royal Philatelic Collection with the value tablet missing, formerly listed as No. 5a), or may resemble marginal copies, in spite of coming from the middle of the plate.

1857–63. Hard or soft white paper. No wmk.

(a) Imperf.

8	**1**	1d. dull orange (1858)	£4250	£900
8a		2d. deep ultramarine (1858)	£4500	£1200
9		2d. pale blue	£1600	£180
10		2d. blue (12.57)	£1600	£180
11		2d. dull deep blue	£2250	£325
12		6d. bistre-brown (8.59)	£4500	£600
13		6d. brown	£3500	£350
14		6d. pale brown	£3500	£350
15		6d. chestnut	£5000	£750
16		1s. dull emerald-green (1858)	£25000	£1800
17		1s. blue-green	£20000	£1800

(b) Pin-roulette, about 10 at Nelson (1860).

18	**1**	1d. dull orange	†	£6000
19		2d. blue	†	£4250
20		6d. brown	†	£5500
20a		1s. dull emerald-green	†	£8000
21		1s. blue-green	†	£9000

(c) Serrated perf about 16 or 18 at Nelson (1862).

22	**1**	1d. dull orange	†	£5500
23		2d. blue	†	£4500
24		6d. brown	†	£4500
25		6d. chestnut	†	£8500
26		1s. blue-green	†	£8000

(d) Rouletted 7 at Auckland (April 1859).

27	**1**	1d. dull orange	£10000	£6000
		a. Imperf between (horiz pair)		
28		2d. blue	£9500	£4000
29		6d. brown	£8500	£3250
		a. Imperf between (pair)	£35000	£15000
30		1s. dull emerald-green	†	£5500
31		1s. blue-green	†	£6000

(e) Perf 13 at Dunedin (1863).

31a	**1**	1d. dull orange	†	£7500
31b		2d. pale blue	£10000	£5000
32		6d. pale brown	†	£8000

(f) 'H' roulette 16 at Nelson.

32a	**1**	2d. blue	†	£6000
32b		6d. brown	†	£6250

(g) 'Y' roulette 18 at Nelson.

32c	**1**	1d. dull orange	†	£6000
32d		2d. blue	†	£4500
32e		6d. brown	†	£5500
32f		6d. chestnut	†	£6250
32g		1s. blue-green	†	£9000

(h) Oblique roulette 13 at Wellington.

32h	**1**	1d. dull orange	†	£6500

The various separations detailed above were all applied by hand to imperforate sheets. The results were often poorly cut and badly aligned and examples showing separations on all sides are rare. Nos. 32a/32b and 32c/32g were produced using roulette wheels fitted with cutting edges in the shape of 'H' or 'Y', and cannot readily be distinguished from Nos. 22/26 unless the separations are well-preserved.

The separation type described as 'Serrated perf' in these listings is technically a form of roulette.

(Printed by John Davies at the GPO, Auckland, NZ)

1862 (Feb)–**64**. Wmk Large Star.

(a) Imperf.

33	**1**	1d. orange-vermilion	£1000	£350
34		1d. vermilion (9.62)	£1000	£350
35		1d. carmine-vermilion (10.63)	£1000	£400
36		2d. deep blue (Plate I)	£1000	£120
		a. Double print	—	£5000
37		2d. slate-blue (Plate I)	£2250	£300
37a		2d. milky blue (Plate I, worn) (1863)	—	£350
38		2d. pale blue (Plate I, worn)	£850	£110
39		2d. blue *(to deep)* (Plate I, very worn) (1864)	£850	£110
40		3d. brown-lilac (1.63)	£750	£225
41		6d. black-brown	£2500	£180
42		6d. brown	£2750	£180
43		6d. red-brown (1863)	£2000	£150
44		1s. green	£3000	£500
45		1s. yellow-green	£3000	£450
46		1s. deep green	£3500	£500

The 2d. in a distinctive deep bright blue on white paper wmkd. Large Star is believed by experts to have been printed by Richardson in 1861 or 1862. This also exists doubly printed and with serrated perf.

No. 37 shows traces of plate wear to the right of the Queen's head. This is more pronounced on Nos. 37a/38 and quite extensive on No. 39.

(b) Rouletted 7 at Auckland (5.62).

47	**1**	1d. orange-vermilion	£5000	£1000
48		1d. vermilion	£4000	£800
48a		1d. carmine-vermilion	£7500	£1000
49		2d. deep blue	£4500	£600
50		2d. slate-blue	£5000	£1000
51		2d. pale blue	£3750	£750
52		3d. brown-lilac	£7500	£900
53		6d. black-brown	£4000	£700
54		6d. brown	£4000	£700
55		6d. red-brown	£3750	£600
56		1s. green	£4500	£950
57		1s. yellow-green	£4500	£950
58		1s. deep green	£6000	£1200

(c) Serrated perf 16 or 18 at Nelson (7.62).

59	**1**	1d. orange-vermilion	£10000	£2500
60		2d. deep blue	†	£2500
61		2d. slate-blue		
62		3d. brown-lilac	£7500	£2000
63		6d. black-brown	†	£2500
64		6d. brown	†	£2750
65		1s. yellow-green	†	£4750

(d) Pin-perf 10 at Nelson (8.62).

66	**1**	2d. deep blue	†	£3500
67		6d. black-brown	†	£5000

(e) 'H' roulette 16 at Nelson.

67a	**1**	2d. deep blue (Plate I)	†	£2500
67b		6d. black-brown	†	£2500
67c		1s. green	†	£4750

(f) 'Y' roulette 18 at Nelson (6.62).

67d	**1**	1d. orange-vermilion	†	£2500
67e		2d. deep blue (Plate I)	†	£2250
		a. Imperf between (horiz pair)	†	£10000
67f		2d. slate-blue (Plate I)	†	£2750
67g		3d. brown-lilac	†	£3000
67h		6d. black-brown	†	£2500
67i		6d. brown	†	£2500
67j		1s. yellow-green	†	£4750

(g) Oblique roulette 13 at Wellington.

67k	**1**	2d. deep blue (Plate I)	†	£3000
67l		2d. slate-blue (Plate I)		
67m		3d. brown-lilac	†	£3750
67n		6d. brown	†	£3000

NEW ZEALAND

(h) Square roulette 14 at Auckland.

67o	1	1d. orange-vermilion	†	£2500
67p		2d. deep blue (Plate I)	†	£2500
67q		3d. brown-lilac	†	£4000
67r		6d. red-brown	†	£3250

(i) Serrated perf 13 at Dunedin.

67s	1	1d. orange-vermilion	†	£3000
67t		2d. deep blue (Plate I)	†	£2500
67u		3d. brown-lilac	£5500	£2500
67v		6d. brown	†	£3500
67w		1s. yellow-green	†	£5000

The dates put to the above varieties are the earliest recorded.

1862 (Dec)–**64**. Wmk Large Star. Perf 13 (at Dunedin by Ferguson & Mitchell).

68	1	1d. orange-vermilion	£3250	£400
		a. Imperf between (horiz pair)	†	£11000
69		1d. carmine-vermilion	£3250	£400
70		2d. deep blue (Plate I)	£1800	£200
71		2d. slate-blue (Plate I)	†	£1100
72		2d. blue (Plate I)	£1000	£100
72a		2d. milky blue (Plate I)	£1500	£500
73		2d. pale blue (Plate I)	£1500	£100
74		3d. brown-lilac	£4000	£600
75		6d. black-brown	£3250	£225
		a. Imperf between (horiz pair)	£2000	£180
76		6d. brown	£2000	£180
77		6d. red-brown	£1800	£130
78		1s. dull green	£3500	£500
79		1s. deep green	£3750	£500
80		1s. yellow-green	£4250	£500

See also Nos. 110/125 and the note that follows these.

1862 (Aug)–**63**. Pelure paper. No wmk.

(a) Imperf.

81	1	1d. orange-vermilion (1863)	£12000	£2750
82		2d. ultramarine (10.62)	£10000	£1200
83		2d. pale ultramarine	£9000	£1200
84		3d. lilac (1863)	£50000	†
85		6d. black-brown	£4250	£350
86		1s. deep green	£18000	£1200

The 3d. is known only unused.

(b) Rouletted 7 at Auckland.

87	1	1d. orange-vermilion	†	£8000
88		6d. black-brown	£4500	£750
89		1s. deep green	£18000	£2000

(c) Perf 13 at Dunedin.

90	1	1d. orange-vermilion	£18000	£4500
91		2d. ultramarine	£11000	£1200
92		2d. pale ultramarine	£10000	£1400
93		6d. black-brown	£10000	£500
94		1s. deep green	£16000	£2500

(d) Serrated perf 16 at Nelson.

95	1	6d. black-brown	—	£6500

(e) Serrated perf 13 at Dunedin.

95a	1	1d. orange-vermilion	†	£10000

1863 (early). Thick soft white paper. No wmk.

(a) Imperf.

96	1	2d. dull deep blue (shades)	£5000	£1300

(b) Perf 13.

96a	1	2d. dull deep blue (shades)	£3500	£750

These stamps show slight beginnings of wear of the printing plate in the background to right of the Queen's ear, as one looks at the stamps. By the early part of 1864, the wear of the plate had spread, more or less, all over the background of the circle containing the head. The major portion of the stamps of this printing appears to have been consigned to Dunedin and to have been there perforated 13.

1864. Wmk 'N Z', W **2**.

(a) Imperf.

97	1	1d. carmine-vermilion	£950	£350
98		2d. pale blue (Plate I worn)	£2000	£350
99		6d. red-brown	£6000	£900
100		1s. green	£3500	£450

(b) Rouletted 7 at Auckland.

101	1	1d. carmine-vermilion	£7500	£3000
102		2d. pale blue (Plate I worn)	£3500	£1100
103		6d. red-brown	£8000	£3250
104		1s. green	£5500	£1200

(c) Perf 13 (line) at Dunedin.

104a	1	1d. carmine-vermilion	£15000	£5500
105		2d. pale blue (Plate I worn)	£1600	£225
106		1s. green	£3250	£750
		a. Imperf between (horiz pair)	†	£45000
		aa. Perf 6½×13	†	£4250

(d) 'Y' roulette 18 at Nelson.

106b	1	1d. carmine-vermilion	†	£6500

(e) Perf 12½ (comb) at Auckland.

106c	1	1d. carmine-vermilion	£15000	£5500
107		2d. pale blue (Plate I worn)	£500	£100

108		6d. red-brown	£750	65·00
109		1s. yellow-green	£10000	£4500

The 'NZ' watermark is frequently found inverted.

1864–71. Wmk Large Star. Perf 12½ (comb or line)* (at Auckland).

110	1	1d. carmine-vermilion (1865)	£275	50·00
111		1d. pale orange-vermilion (1866)	£300	50·00
		a. Imperf (pair)	£6000	£3500
		b. Imperf between (vert pair)	†	—
112		1d. orange (1871)	£750	£100
113		2d. pale blue (Plate I worn)	£400	40·00
114		2d. deep blue (Plate II) (7.65)	£250	30·00
		a. Imperf vert (horiz pair)	†	£6000
115		2d. blue (Plate II)	£250	30·00
		a. Retouched (Plate II) (1867)	£400	75·00
		c. Imperf (pair) (Plate II)	£5000	£3500
		d. Retouched Imperf (pair)	£5500	£5000
116		3d. brown-lilac	£3750	£750
117		3d. lilac (1867)	£180	45·00
		a. Imperf (pair)	£5500	£2250
		b. Imperf between (horiz pair)	†	—
118		3d. deep mauve (1867)	£1200	£100
		a. Imperf (pair)	£6000	£2250
119		4d. deep rose (1.6.65)	£3500	£300
120		4d. yellow (1866)	£300	£200
121		4d. orange (1869)	£3000	£1200
122		6d. red-brown	£350	30·00
122a		6d. brown (1867)	£450	50·00
		b. Imperf (pair)	£3250	£3250
123		1s. deep green	£1500	£600
124		1s. green	£1000	£180
125		1s. yellow-green	£400	£150

* Until late 1866 two comb perforating heads were in use. These were then converted to single-line heads, and all subsequent printings were line perforated. Some stamps (such as Nos. 110, 113, 116 and 119) only exist with the early comb perforation, while others (such as Nos. 112, 117/118, 121 and 122a) are always line perforated. The above issue is sometimes difficult to distinguish from Nos. 68/80 because the vertical perforations usually gauge 12¾ and sometimes a full 13. However, stamps of this issue invariably gauge 12½ horizontally, whereas the 1862 stamps measure a full 13.

Nos. 111a, 115c/115d, 117a, 118a and 122ab were issued during problems with the perforation machine which occurred in 1866–1867, 1869–1870 and 1871–1873. Imperforate sheets of the 1s. were also released, but these stamps are very similar to Nos. 44/46.

The new plate of the 2d. showed signs of deterioration during 1866 and 30 positions in rows 13 and 16 to 20 were retouched by a local engraver.

The 1d., 2d. and 6d. were officially reprinted imperforate, without gum, in 1884 for presentation purposes. They can be distinguished from the errors listed by their shades which are pale orange, dull blue and dull chocolate-brown respectively, and by the worn state of the plates from which they were printed (*Prices £100 each unused*).

1871 (1 Oct)–**73**. Wmk Large Star. New colours (except No. 129/129a).

(a) Perf 10.

126	1	1d. brown	£1500	£150

(b) Perf 12½×10.

127	1	1d. deep brown	†	£5500

(c) Perf 10×12½.

128	1	1d. brown	£425	60·00
		a. Perf 12½ comp 10 (1 side)	£850	£250
129		2d. deep blue (Plate II)	†	£20000
		a. Perf 10*	†	£40000
130		2d. vermilion	£350	50·00
		a. Retouched	£475	75·00
		b. Perf 12½ comp 10 (1 side)	£2250	£550
		c. Perf 10*	†	£30000
131		6d. deep blue	£4000	£1100
		a. Blue	£2250	£750
		b. Imperf between (vert pair)		
		c. Perf 12½ comp 10 (1 side)	£2000	£750
		ca. Imperf vert (horiz pair)	†	—

(d) Perf 12½ (1872–1873).

132	1	1d. red-brown	£300	60·00
		a. Brown (shades, worn plate) (1873)	£275	55·00
		b. Imperf horiz (vert pair)	—	£6500
133		2d. orange	£180	35·00
		a. Retouched	£300	60·00
134		2d. vermilion	£225	35·00
		a. Retouched	£350	65·00
135		6d. blue	£350	75·00
136		6d. pale blue	£250	75·00

* Only one used copy of No. 129a and two of No. 130c have been reported.

1873 (Aug–Sept). No wmk. Perf 12½.

137	1	1d. brown	£2000	£400
		a. Watermarked (script letters)*	£5500	£2500
		b. Watermarked (double-lined capitals)*	£2500	£850
138		2d. vermilion	£200	60·00
		a. Retouched	£300	90·00
		b. Watermarked (script letters)*	£4500	£1800
		c. Watermarked (double-lined capitals)*	£2250	£1100
139		4d. orange-yellow	£300	£1200
		a. Watermarked (double-lined capitals)*	£500	£2500

* 1d., 2d. and 4d. stamps were printed on paper showing sheet watermarks of either 'W. T. & Co.' (Wiggins Teape & Co.) in script letters or 'T. H. Saunders' in double-lined capitals (the former appearing once, at the top or bottom of the sheet, may be found either inverted or reversed, while the latter occurs twice in the sheet); portions of these letters are occasionally found on stamps. A third, as yet unidentified script watermark has also been reported on the 1d. and 2d. values, while a fourth watermark consisting of small separate lozenges, approximately 10 mm tall has been certified on two examples of the 2d. vermilion.

It seems likely that Nos. 137/139 were printed and issued after Nos. 140/142.

1873 (July?). Wmk 'N Z', W **2**. Perf 12½.

140	**1**	1d. brown	†	£12000
141		2d. vermilion	£2500	£500
		a. Retouched	£3000	£600

The 'NZ' watermark may be found inverted or inverted and reversed.

1873 (Aug). Wmk Lozenges, with 'INVICTA' reading upwards in double-lined capitals four times in the sheet. Perf 12½.

142	**1**	2d. vermilion	£3750	£600
		a. Retouched	£5000	£900

The Lozenge watermark is made up of diamond-shaped units of approximately stamp height, alternately plain and vertically lined and arranged in chequerboard fashion, either side of a separate vertical panel containing the word 'INVICTA' in double-lined capitals. The 'INVICTA' panel occurs four times in a sheet.

3

4

(Des John Davies. Die eng on wood in Melbourne. Printed from electrotypes at Govt Ptg Office, Wellington)

1873 (1 Jan).

*(a) Wmk 'NZ', W **F5**.*

143	**3**	½d. pale dull rose (Perf 10)	£180	60·00
144		½d. pale dull rose (Perf 12½)	£200	95·00
145		½d. pale dull rose (Perf 12½×10)	£225	95·00
		a. Perf 10×12½	£500	£180

(b) No wmk.

146	**3**	½d. pale dull rose (Perf 10)	£450	£100
147		½d. pale dull rose (Perf 12½)	£500	£200
148		½d. pale dull rose (Perf 12½×10)	£600	£200
		a. Perf 10×12½	£600	£225

As the paper used for Nos. 143/145 was originally intended for fiscal stamps which were more than twice as large, about one-third of the impressions fall on portions of the sheet showing no watermark, giving rise to varieties Nos. 146/148. In later printings of No. 151 a few stamps in each sheet are without watermark. These can be distinguished from No. 147 by the shade.

1875 (Jan). Wmk Star, W **4**.

149	**3**	½d. pale dull rose (Perf 12½)	32·00	4·00
		a. Imperf horiz (vert pair)	£1000	£750
		b. Imperf between (horiz pair)	£1500	£850
		c. Perf compound of 12½ and 10	†	£1000
150		½d. dull pale rose (Perf *nearly* 12)	75·00	14·00

1892 (May). Wmk 'NZ and Star'. W **12b**. Perf 12½.

151	**3**	½d. bright rose (*shades*)	15·00	2·00
		a. No wmk	75·00	30·00
		w. Wmk inverted	80·00	60·00
		x. Wmk reversed	—	£200

5

6

7

8

9

10

11

12

12a (6 mm)

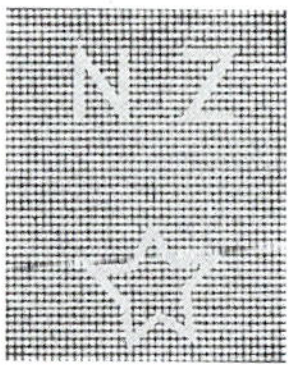
12b (7 mm)

12c (4 mm)

Description of Watermarks

W **12a**. 6 mm between 'N Z' and star; broad irregular star; comparatively wide 'N'; 'N Z' 11½ mm wide.

W **12b**. 7 mm between 'N Z' and star; narrower star; narrow 'N'; 'N Z' 10 mm wide.

W **12c**. 4 mm between 'N Z' and star; narrow star; wide 'N'; 'N Z' 11½ mm wide.

(Types **5/10** eng De La Rue. Types **11** and **12** des, eng and plates by W. R. Bock. Typo Govt Ptg Office, Wellington)

1874 (2 Jan)–**78**.

*A. White paper. W **12a***

(a) Perf 12½.

152	**5**	1d. lilac	£130	20·00
		a. Imperf (pair)	£2500	£2500
		w. Wmk inverted	†	£120
		x. Wmk reversed	†	£500
		y. Wmk inverted and reversed	†	£1000
153	**6**	2d. rose	£200	10·00
		w. Wmk inverted	—	£250
154	**7**	3d. brown	£250	£100
155	**8**	4d. maroon	£400	85·00
		w. Wmk inverted	£1000	£300
156	**9**	6d. blue	£350	15·00
		w. Wmk inverted	—	£120
		x. Wmk reversed	†	£500
157	**10**	1s. green	£750	55·00
		w. Wmk inverted	£2000	£350

(b) Perf nearly 12 (line).

158	**5**	1d. lilac	†	—
158*a*	**6**	2d. rose (1878)	£1500	£250

(c) Perf compound of 12½ and 10.

159	**5**	1d. lilac	£190	50·00
		w. Wmk inverted	—	£150
160	**6**	2d. rose	£300	£120
		w. Wmk inverted	£750	£170
161	**7**	3d. brown	£250	£100
		w. Wmk inverted	†	—
162	**8**	4d. maroon	£1000	£200
163	**9**	6d. blue	£400	55·00
		w. Wmk inverted	—	£140
164	**10**	1s. green	£1000	£200
		a. Imperf between (vert pair)	†	£8500
		bw. Wmk inverted	†	£500

(d) Perf nearly 12×12½.

164*c*	**5**	1d. lilac (1878)	—	£450
165	**6**	2d. rose (1878)	£1200	£350

B. Blued paper

(a) Perf 12½.

166	**5**	1d. lilac	£300	40·00
167	**6**	2d. rose	£350	42·00
		w. Wmk inverted	£500	£150
		x. Wmk reversed	†	£250
168	**7**	3d. brown	£600	£150
169	**8**	4d. maroon	£800	£130
170	**9**	6d. blue	£750	60·00
171	**10**	1s. green	£1200	£225

(b) Perf compound of 12½ and 10.

172	**5**	1d. lilac	£350	65·00
173	**6**	2d. rose	£600	£150
174	**7**	3d. brown	£600	£130
175	**8**	4d. maroon	£1200	£200
176	**9**	6d. blue	£750	£100
177	**10**	1s. green	£1600	£300

1875. Wmk Large Star, W w **1**. Perf 12½.

178	**5**	1d. deep lilac	£2250	£500
179	**6**	2d. rose	£1000	50·00

NEW ZEALAND

1878. W **12a**. Perf 12×11½ (comb.)

180	5	1d. mauve-lilac	75·00	10·00
181	6	2d. rose	80·00	12·00
182	8	4d. maroon	£350	75·00
183	9	6d. blue	£225	15·00
184	10	1s. green	£325	75·00
		w. Wmk inverted	†	£500
185	11	2s. deep rose (1.7)	£600	£325
186	12	5s. grey (1.7)	£550	£325

This perforation is made by a horizontal 'comb' machine, giving a gauge of 12 horizontally and about 11¾ vertically. Single examples can be found apparently gauging 11½ all round or 12 all round, but these are all from the same machine.

The perforation described above as 'nearly 12' was from a single-line machine. Identification of Nos. 158/158*a* can be confirmed by their having 14 perforation holes on the vertical sides, while the comb perf stamps have only 13.

Descriptions of Papers

1882–1888. Smooth paper with horizontal mesh. W **12a**.
1888–1898. Smooth paper with vertical mesh. W **12b**.
1890–1891. Smooth paper with vertical mesh. W **12c**.
1898. Thin yellowish toned, coarse paper with clear vertical mesh. W **12b**. Perf 11 only.

In 1899–1900 stamps appeared on medium to thick white coarse paper but we do not differentiate these (except where identifiable by shade) as they are more difficult to distinguish.

> **PAPER MESH.** This shows on the back of the stamp as a series of parallel grooves, either vertical or horizontal. It is caused by the use of wire gauze conveyor belt during papermaking.

Descriptions of Dies

1d.

Die 1

Die 2

Die 3

1882.	Die 1. Background shading complete and heavy.
1886.	Die 2. Background lines thinner. Two lines of shading weak or missing left of Queen's forehead.
1889.	Die 3. Shading on head reduced; ornament in crown left of chignon clearer, with the vertical line on the band of the crown appearing as a bold '1'.

2d.

Die 1

Die 2

Die 3

1882.	Die 1. Background shading complete and heavy.
1886.	Die 2. Weak line of shading left of forehead and missing shading lines below 'TA'.
1889.	Die 3. As Die 2 but with comma-like white notch in hair below '&'.

6d.

Die 1

Die 2

NEW ZEALAND

1882. Die 1. Shading heavy. Top of head merges into shading. Second ornament from the right on the crown shows a line in its left portion.

1892. Die 2. Background lines thinner. Shading on head more regular with clear line of demarcation between head and background shading. Second ornament from the right in the crown has small dots in its left portion. Most examples also show a break in the back line of the neck immediately above its base.

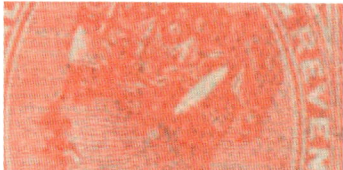

1d. 'Ellipse' flaw (Die 3, lower left pane, R. 9/2)

1d. 'Chisel' flaw (Die 3, upper left pane, R. 4/6) (a smaller break occurs in the lower right frame of this stamp)

'2' and '1' joined (Upper right pane, R. 9/1)

1s. 'Bulbous nose' (Lower right pane, R. 1/1)

HIGH VALUES. From 1882 to 1931 postal requirements for higher value stamps were met by the Queen Victoria 'Stamp Duty' adhesives (Nos. F5/F144).

Truebridge Miller

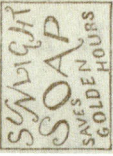
Sunlight Soap

STAMPS WITH ADVERTISEMENTS. During November 1891 the New Zealand Post Office invited tenders for the printing of advertisements on the reverse of the current 1d. to 1s. stamps. The contract was awarded to Messrs Miller, Truebridge & Reich and the first sheets with advertisements on the reverse appeared in February 1893. Different advertisements were applied to the backs of the individual stamps within the sheets of 240 (four panes of 60).

On the first setting those in a vertical format were inverted in relation to the stamps and each of the horizontal advertisements had its base at the left-hand side of the stamp *when seen from the back*. For the second and third settings the vertical advertisements were the same way up as the stamps and the bases of those in the horizontal format were at the right *as seen from the back*. The third setting only differs from the second in the order of the individual advertisements.

Examples of the advertisements being printed double are known, but we do not list them.

The experiment was not, however, a success and the contract was cancelled at the end of 1893.

(Des F. W. Sears (½d.), A. E. Cousins (2½d.), A. W. Jones (5d.); others adapted from 1874 issue by W. H. Norris. Dies eng A. E. Cousins (½d., 2½d., 5d.), W. R. Bock (others). Typo Govt Ptg Office)

1882–1900. Inscr 'POSTAGE & REVENUE'.

A. Paper with horiz mesh (1.4.1882–1886). W **12a**
(a) Perf 12×11½

187	14	1d. rose *to* rose-red (Die 1)	50·00	7·00
		a. Imperf (pair)	£1200	
		b. Imperf between (vert pair)	£1300	
		cw. Wmk inverted	£500	£250
		d. Die 2. Pale rose to carmine-rose (1886)	75·00	9·00
		dw. Wmk inverted	†	£250
		dx. Wmk reversed	£250	£200
188	15	2d. lilac *to* lilac-purple (Die 1)	65·00	4·00
		a. Imperf (pair)	£1200	
		b. Imperf between (vert pair)	£1300	
		cw. Wmk inverted	£225	£200
		d. Die 2. *Lilac* (1886)	75·00	20·00
189	17	3d. yellow	85·00	22·00
190	18	4d. blue-green	90·00	12·00
191	20	6d. brown (Die 1)	£120	4·00
		w. Wmk inverted	£425	£150
192	21	8d. blue	£110	75·00
193	22	1s. red-brown	£160	22·00

(b) Perf 12½ (1884?).

193a	14	1d. rose *to* rose-red (Die 1)	£750	£500

B. Paper with vert mesh (1888–1895). W **12b**
(a) Perf 12×11½ (1888–1895).

194	13	½d. black (1.4.95)	42·00	£130
195	14	1d. rose *to* rosine (Die 2)	55·00	5·50
		aw. Wmk inverted	£250	£100
		b. Die 3. *Rose to carmine* (1889)	55·00	4·50
		bb. Red-brown advert (1st setting) (2.93)	£250	85·00
		bc. Red advert (1st setting) (3.93)	£250	85·00
		bd. Blue advert (2nd setting) (4.93)	£500	£200
		be. Mauve advert (2nd setting) (5.93)	£250	70·00
		bf. Green advert (2nd setting) (6.93)	†	£1000
		bg. Brown-red advert (3rd setting) (9.93)	£250	65·00
		bh. 'Ellipse' flaw	£150	32·00
		bi. 'Chisel' flaw	£150	32·00
		bw. Wmk inverted	£200	£100
		bx. Wmk reversed	£250	£150
196	15	2d. lilac (Die 2)	75·00	5·50
		a. Die 3. *Lilac to purple* (1889)	75·00	6·50
		ab. Red advert (1st setting) (3.93)	£350	60·00
		ac. Mauve advert (2nd setting) (5.93)	£350	60·00
		ad. Sepia advert (2nd setting) (5.93)	£350	60·00
		ae. Green advert (2nd setting) (6.93)	—	£170
		af. Brown-red advert (3rd setting) (9.93)	£350	60·00
		aw. Wmk inverted	£300	50·00
197	16	2½d. pale blue (1891)	80·00	8·00
		a. Brown-red advert (2nd setting) (4.93)	£650	£250
		ax. Wmk reversed	£750	£300
		b. Ultramarine (green advert. 2nd setting) (6.93)	£650	£250
198	17	3d. yellow	75·00	24·00
		a. Brown-red advert (2nd setting) (4.93)	£650	£275
		b. Sepia advert (2nd setting) (5.93)	£850	£475
199	18	4d. green *to* bluish green	80·00	5·00
		a. Sepia advert (2nd setting) (5.93)	£375	£250
		aw. Wmk inverted	†	£300
200	19	5d. olive-black (1.2.91)	£120	25·00
		a. Imperf (pair)	£1200	
		b. Brown-purple advert (3rd setting) (9.93)	£750	£200
201	20	6d. brown (Die 1)	£110	6·50
		a. Die 2 (1892)	£200	£250
		ab. Sepia advert (2nd setting) (5.93)	—	£1200
		ac. Brown-red advert (3rd setting) (9.93)	—	£600
		ax. Wmk reversed	£750	£400
202	21	8d. blue	90·00	60·00
203	22	1s. red-brown	£140	10·00
		a. Black advert (2nd setting) (5.93)	£1000	£500
		b. Brown-purple advert (3rd setting) (9.93)	£500	90·00
		w. Wmk inverted	£750	£180

NEW ZEALAND

(b) Perf 12×12½ (1888–1891).

No.	Type	Description	Unused	Used
204	14	1d. rose (Die 2)	£500	£750
		a. Die 3 (1889)	†	—

(c) Perf 12½ (1888–1889).

No.	Type	Description	Unused	Used
205	14	1d. rose (Die 3) (1889)	£750	£500
		a. Mauve advert (3rd setting) (5.93)	†	£1100
		x. Wmk reversed	†	£1200
206	15	2d. lilac (Die 2)	£750	£750
		a. Die 3. Deep lilac (1889)	£475	£550
		ab. Brown-red advert (3rd setting) (9.93)	£1100	£1000
207	16	2½d. blue (1891)	£800	£550

(d) Mixed perfs 12×11½ and 12½ (1891–1893).

No.	Type	Description	Unused	Used
207a	14	1d. rose (Die 3) (brown-red advert. 3rd setting)	£375	£225
207b	15	2d. lilac (Die 3)	†	£600
		ba. Brown-red advert (3rd setting) (9.93)	†	—
207c	18	4d. green	†	£375
207d	19	5d. olive-black	†	£450
207e	20	6d. brown (Die 1)	†	£250
		ea. Die 2	†	£300

C. Paper with vert mesh (1890). W 12c
(a) Perf 12×11½.

No.	Type	Description	Unused	Used
208	14	1d. rose (Die 3)	£400	45·00
		a. 'Ellipse' flaw	£1000	£150
		b. 'Chisel' flaw	£1000	£150
209	15	2d. purple (Die 3)	£110	20·00
		x. Wmk reversed	†	£225
210	16	2½d. ultramarine (27.12)	65·00	15·00
		x. Wmk reversed	†	£225
211	17	3d. yellow	£120	85·00
		a. Lemon-yellow	£120	85·00
212	20	6d. brown (Die 1)	£190	60·00
213	22	1s. deep red-brown	£300	£350

(b) Perf 12½.

No.	Type	Description	Unused	Used
214	14	1d. rose (Die 3)	£800	£600
215	15	2d. purple (Die 3)	£750	£1000
216	16	2½d. ultramarine	£1000	£600

(c) Perf 12×12½.

No.	Type	Description	Unused	Used
216a	20	6d. brown (Die 1)	£800	£750

D. Paper with vert mesh (1891–1900). Continuation of W 12b
(a) Perf 10×12½ (1891–1894).

No.	Type	Description	Unused	Used
216b	14	1d. rose (Die 3)	£325	£550
		ba. Perf 12½×10	£700	£600
		bb. Red-brown advert (1st setting) (2.93)	£1200	£1000
		bc. Brown-red advert (2nd setting) (4.93)	£1200	£1000
		bd. Mauve advert (2nd setting) (5.93)	£1200	£1000
		be. Green advert (2nd setting) (6.93)	£1200	£1000
		bf. 'Ellipse' flaw	£750	
		bg. 'Chisel' flaw	£750	
216c	15	2d. lilac (Die 3)	£750	£750
		ca. Perf 12½×10	£1500	£1000
216d	16	2½d. blue (1893)	£550	£500
		da. Perf 12½×10	£1200	£750
		dab. Mauve advert (2nd setting)	†	£400
216e	17	3d. yellow	£600	£850
		ea. Perf 12½×10	£1500	£1000
216f	18	4d. green	£700	£850
		fa. Perf 12½×10, brown-purple advert (3rd setting)	†	£1200
216g	19	5d. olive-black (1894)	£300	£400
		ga. Perf 12½×10	£600	£425
		gb. Brown-purple advert (3rd setting) (6.93)	£1200	£500
216h	20	6d. brown (Die 1)	£800	£1000
		i. Die 2 (1892)	£700	£850
		ia. Brown-purple advert (3rd setting) (9.93)		
216j	22	1s. red-brown	£275	£375
		ja. Perf 12½×10	£650	£500

(b) Perf 10 (1891–1895).

No.	Type	Description	Unused	Used
217	13	½d. black (1895)	10·00	2·25
		x. Wmk reversed	†	£120
218	14	1d. rose (Die 3)	16·00	1·00
		a. Carmine	16·00	1·50
		b. Imperf (pair)	£1100	£1100
		c. Imperf between (pair)	£1200	
		d. Imperf horiz (vert pair)	£1100	
		e. Mixed perfs 10 and 12½	£400	£275
		f. Red-brown advert (1st setting) (2.93)	60·00	10·00
		g. Red advert (1st setting) (3.93)	60·00	12·00
		h. Brown-red advert (2nd and 3rd settings) (4.93)	60·00	4·00
		i. Blue advert (2nd setting) (4.93)	£130	55·00
		j. Mauve advert (2nd setting) (5.93)	60·00	4·00
		k. Green advert (2nd setting) (6.93)	£100	32·00
		l. Brown-purple advert (3rd setting) (9.93)	60·00	5·50
		m. 'Ellipse' flaw	48·00	12·00
		n. 'Chisel' flaw	48·00	12·00
		w. Wmk inverted	£200	£250
		x. Wmk reversed	£300	£200
219	15	2d. lilac (Die 3)	23·00	1·75
		a. Purple	23·00	1·75
		b. Imperf between (pair)	£1200	
		c. Mixed perfs 10 and 12½	£750	£600
		d. Red-brown advert (1st setting) (2.93)	55·00	14·00
		e. Red advert (1st setting) (3.93)	55·00	12·00
		f. Brown-red advert (2nd and 3rd settings) (4.93)	55·00	6·00
		g. Sepia advert (2nd setting) (5.93)	55·00	7·50
		h. Green advert (2nd setting) (6.93)	80·00	15·00
		l. Brown-purple advert (3rd setting) (9.93)	55·00	4·50
		x. Wmk reversed	£180	£150
220	16	2½d. blue (1892)	65·00	4·50
		a. Ultramarine	65·00	4·50
		b. Mixed perfs 10 and 12½	£450	£250
		c. Mauve advert (2nd setting) (5.93)	£200	16·00
		d. Green advert (2nd setting) (6.93)	£225	25·00
		e. Brown-purple advert (3rd setting) (9.93)	£200	16·00
		ex. Wmk reversed	£300	£120
221	17	3d. pale orange-yellow	70·00	19·00
		a. Orange	70·00	25·00
		b. Lemon-yellow	70·00	25·00
		c. Mixed perfs 10 and 12½	£1300	£1200
		d. Brown-red advert (2nd and 3rd settings) (4.93)	£200	32·00
		e. Sepia advert (2nd setting) (5.93)	£200	50·00
		f. Brown-purple advert (3rd setting) (9.93)	£200	30·00
222	18	4d. green (1892)	75·00	8·50
		a. Blue-green	75·00	8·50
		b. Mixed perfs 10 and 12½	£300	£250
		c. Brown-red advert (2nd setting) (4.93)	£225	16·00
		d. Brown-purple advert (3rd setting) (9.93)	£225	16·00
223	19	5d. olive-black (1893)	70·00	30·00
		a. Brown-purple advert (3rd setting) (9.93)	£200	60·00
		ab. Mixed perfs 10 and 12½	£450	£425
224	20	6d. brown (Die 1)	£200	70·00
		a. Mixed perfs 10 and 12½	£100	9·00
		b. Die 2 (1892)	£100	9·00
		ba. Black-brown	£1500	
		bb. Imperf (pair)	£450	£225
		bc. Mixed perfs 10 and 12½	£400	22·00
		bd. Sepia advert (2nd setting) (4.93)	£400	22·00
		be. Brown-red advert (3rd setting) (9.93)	£400	22·00
		bf. Brown-purple advert (3rd setting) (9.93)	†	£140
		bx. Wmk reversed (with brown-purple advert)	£100	85·00
225	21	8d. blue (brown-purple advert. 3rd setting) (9.93)	£130	24·00
226	22	1s. red-brown	£3000	
		a. Imperf between (pair)	£600	£375
		b. Mixed perfs 10 and 12½	£375	90·00
		c. Sepia advert (2nd setting) (5.93)	£400	£180
		d. Black advert (2nd setting) (5.93)	£375	75·00
		e. Brown-red advert (3rd setting) (9.93)	£375	75·00
		f. Brown-purple advert (3rd setting) (9.93)	£650	£140
		g. 'Bulbous nose'		

(c) Perf 10×11 (1895–1897).

No.	Type	Description	Unused	Used
227	13	½d. black (1896)	6·00	60
		a. Mixed perfs 10 and 11	£170	£150
		b. Perf 11×10 (11.95)	42·00	18·00
228	14	1d. rose (Die 3)	20·00	15
		a. Mixed perfs 10 and 11	£250	£120
		b. Perf 11×10 (10.95)	90·00	13·00
		c. 'Ellipse' flaw	50·00	15·00
		d. 'Chisel' flaw	50·00	15·00
		x. Wmk reversed	£120	85·00
229	15	2d. purple (Die 3)	25·00	30
		a. Mixed perfs 10 and 11	£120	80·00
230	16	2½d. blue (1896)	65·00	4·50
		a. Ultramarine	65·00	4·50
		b. Mixed perfs 10 and 11	£350	£150
		c. '2' and '1' joined	£275	£160
231	17	3d. lemon-yellow (1896)	75·00	24·00
232	18	4d. pale green (1896)	95·00	12·00
		a. Mixed perfs 10 and 11	—	£200
233	19	5d. olive-black (1897)	70·00	18·00
234	20	6d. deep brown (Die 2) (1896)	£100	20·00
		a. Mixed perfs 10 and 11	£500	£375
		b. Perf 11×10	£325	£275
235	22	1s. red-brown (1896)	£130	15·00
		a. Mixed perfs 10 and 11	£325	£200
		b. 'Bulbous nose'	£500	£160

(d) Perf 11 (1895–1900).

No.	Type	Description	Unused	Used
236	13	½d. black (1896)	9·50	15
		aw. Wmk inverted	£100	75·00

NEW ZEALAND

		ax. Wmk reversed	£180	£100
		b. Thin coarse toned paper (1898)	40·00	7·50
		ba. Wmk sideways	£3750	£3000
237	14	1d. rose (Die 3) (6.95)	7·50	20
		a. Deep carmine	7·50	1·50
		b. Imperf between (pair)	£1100	
		c. Deep carmine/thin coarse toned (1898)	35·00	5·00
		ca. Wmk sideways	†	£3000
		d. 'Ellipse' flaw	35·00	10·00
		e. 'Chisel' flaw	35·00	10·00
		w. Wmk inverted	£110	£100
		x. Wmk reversed	£110	60·00
		y. Wmk inverted and reversed	£180	£150
238	15	2d. mauve (Die 3)	18·00	1·00
		a. Purple	18·00	1·00
		b. Deep purple/thin coarse toned (1898)	40·00	7·50
		ba. Wmk sideways	†	£3000
		w. Wmk inverted	£110	75·00
		x. Wmk reversed	£190	£200
239	16	2½d. blue (1897)	55·00	4·50
		a. Thin coarse toned paper (1898)	£150	30·00
		b. '2' and '1' joined	£275	£160
240	17	3d. pale yellow (1897)	55·00	10·00
		a. Pale dull yellow/thin coarse toned (1898)	£150	40·00
		b. Orange (1899)	55·00	18·00
		c. Dull orange-yellow (1900)	55·00	30·00
241	18	4d. yellowish green (7.96)	60·00	5·00
		a. Bluish green (1897)	55·00	4·50
		w. Wmk inverted	£250	£225
242	19	5d. olive-black/thin coarse toned (1899)	75·00	40·00
243	20	6d. brown (Die 2) (1897)	£100	7·50
		a. Black-brown	£100	7·50
		b. Brown/thin coarse toned (1898)	£300	28·00
		x. Wmk reversed	†	£225
244	21	8d. blue (1898)	85·00	60·00
245	22	1s. red-brown (1897)	£120	15·00
		a. Imperf between (vert pair)	£3000	
		b. 'Bulbous nose'	£500	£160

Only the more prominent shades have been included.
Stamps perf compound of 10×11 and 12½ and 11 and 12½ exist.
For the ½d. and 2d. with double-lined watermark, see Nos. 271/272.

34 Kea and Kaka   **35** Milford Sound   **36** Mount Cook

(Des H. Young (½d.), J. Gaut (1d.), W. Bock (2d., 3d., 9d., 1s.), E. Howard (4d., 6d., 8d.), E. Luke (others). Eng A. Hill (2½d., 1s.), J. A. C. Harrison (5d.), Rapkin (others). Recess Waterlow)

1898 (5 Apr). No wmk. Perf 12 to 16.

246	23	½d. purple-brown	7·00	1·50
		a. Imperf between (pair)	£1700	£1400
		b. Purple-slate	7·50	1·50
		c. Purple-black	12·00	2·75
247	24	1d. blue and yellow-brown	6·00	60
		a. Imperf between (horiz pair)	£1500	£1300
		b. Imperf vert (horiz pair)	£900	£1000
		c. Imperf horiz (vert pair)	£900	£1000
		d. Blue and brown	7·00	1·00
		da. Imperf between (vert pair)	£1500	£1300
248	25	2d. lake	50·00	25
		a. Imperf vert (horiz pair)	£1300	£1000
		b. Rosy lake	50·00	25
		ba. Imperf between (vert pair)	£1400	
		bb. Imperf vert (horiz pair)	£1300	
249	26	2½d. sky-blue (inscr 'WAKITIPU')	13·00	50·00
		a. Blue	13·00	50·00
250	27	2½d. blue (inscr 'WAKITIPU')	60·00	10·00
		a. Deep blue	60·00	10·00
251	28	3d. yellow-brown	35·00	9·50
252	29	4d. bright rose	25·00	23·00
		a. Lake-rose	25·00	23·00
		b. Dull rose	25·00	23·00
253	30	5d. sepia	£130	£200
		a. Purple-brown	95·00	25·00
254	31	6d. green (to deep green)	95·00	50·00
		a. Grass-green	£300	£350
255	32	8d. indigo	£100	50·00
		a. Prussian blue	£100	50·00
256	33	9d. purple	£130	65·00
257	34	1s. vermilion	£110	32·00
		a. Dull red	£110	32·00
		ab. Imperf between (pair)	£5500	
258	35	2s. grey-green	£225	£150
		a. Imperf between (vert pair)	£5500	£5500
259	36	5s. vermilion	£350	£550
246/259		*Set of* 13	£1100	£850

Collectors are warned against faked examples of the imperforate between errors, made from imperforate plate proofs.

23 Mount Cook or Aorangi   **24** Lake Taupo and Mount Ruapehu   **25** Pembroke Peak, Milford Sound

26 Lake Wakatipu and Mount Earnslaw, Inscribed 'WAKITIPU'   **27** Lake Wakatipu and Mount Earnslaw, Inscribed 'WAKATIPU'

28 Huia   **29** White Terrace, Rotomahana   **30** Otira Gorge and Mount Ruapehu

37 Lake Taupo and Mount Ruapehu   **38**

(Recess Govt Printer, Wellington)

1899 (May)–**1903**. Thick, soft Pirie paper. No wmk. Perf 11.

260	27	2½d. blue (6.99)	26·00	7·50
		a. Imperf between (horiz pair)	£1500	
		b. Imperf horiz (vert pair)	£750	
		c. Deep blue	26·00	7·50
261	28	3d. yellow-brown (5.1900)	32·00	2·50
		a. Imperf between (pair)	£1500	
		b. Imperf vert (horiz pair)	£750	
		c. Deep brown	32·00	2·50
		ca. Imperf between (horiz pair)	£1500	
262	37	4d. indigo and brown (8.99)	9·50	5·00
		a. Bright blue and chestnut	9·50	5·00
		b. Deep blue and bistre-brown	9·50	5·00
263	30	5d. purple-brown (6.99)	55·00	6·50
		a. Deep purple-brown	55·00	6·50
		ab. Imperf between (pair)	£3250	
264	31	6d. deep green	£100	85·00
		a. Yellow-green	£150	£180
265		6d. pale rose (5.5.1900)	50·00	10·00
		a. Imperf vert (horiz pair)	£750	
		b. Imperf between (horiz pair)	£1300	
		c. Rose-red	50·00	10·00

31 Brown Kiwi   **32** Maori War Canoe   **33** Pink Terrace, Rotomahana

NEW ZEALAND

		ca. Printed double	£1000	£850
		cb. Imperf between (vert pair)	£1600	
		cc. Imperf vert (horiz pair)	£750	
		cd. Showing part of sheet wmk (7.02)*	£100	£120
		d. Scarlet	80·00	27·00
		da. Imperf vert (horiz pair)	£750	
266	32	8d. indigo	75·00	28·00
		a. Prussian blue	75·00	28·00
267	33	9d. deep purple (8.99)	£100	40·00
		a. Rosy purple	£100	30·00
268	34	1s. red (5.1900)	95·00	15·00
		a. Dull orange-red	95·00	12·00
		b. Dull brown-red	95·00	22·00
		c. Bright red	£100	42·00
269	35	2s. blue-green (7.99)	£225	75·00
		a. Laid paper (1.03)	£500	£250
		b. Grey-green	£225	75·00
270	36	5s. vermilion (7.99)	£400	£500
		a. Carmine-red	£400	£500
260/270		Set of 11	£1000	£650

* No. 265cd is on paper without general watermark, but showing the words 'LISBON SUPERFINE' wmkd once in the sheet; the paper was obtained from Parsons Bros, an American firm with a branch at Auckland.

1900. Thick, soft Pirie paper. Wmk double-lined 'NZ' and Star, W **38** (sideways*). Perf 11.

271	13	½d. black	12·00	20·00
		x. Wmk sideways reversed	£400	£275
272	15	2d. bright purple	32·00	25·00
		w. Wmk sideways inverted	£150	£130
		y. Wmk sideways inverted and reversed	£750	£350

* The normal sideways wmk on Nos. 271/272 shows the top of the star pointing to the left, *as seen from the back of the stamp*.

39 White Terrace, Rotomahana
40 Commemorative of the New Zealand Contingent in the South African War
41

1½d. Major re-entry (R. 2/12)

(Des J. Nairn (1½d.). Recess Govt Printer, Wellington)

1900 (Mar–Dec). Thick, soft Pirie paper. W **38**. Perf 11.

273	23	½d. pale yellow-green (7.3.1900)	20·00	7·00
		a. Yellow-green	12·00	2·25
		b. Green	11·00	2·00
		ba. Imperf between (pair)	£600	
		c. Deep green	11·00	2·00
		w. Wmk inverted	60·00	30·00
		y. Wmk inverted and reversed	£110	50·00
274	39	1d. crimson (7.3.1900)	18·00	50
		a. Rose-red	18·00	50
		ab. Imperf between (pair)	£1600	£1800
		ac. Imperf vert (horiz pair)	£650	
		b. Lake	50·00	10·00
		w. Wmk inverted	†	£350
		x. Wmk reversed	†	£250
		y. Wmk inverted and reversed	†	£400
275	40	1½d. khaki (7.12.1900)	£2000	£1000
		a. Brown	75·00	65·00
		ab. Imperf vert (horiz pair)	£1200	
		ac. Imperf (pair)	£1300	
		b. Chestnut	15·00	9·50
		ba. Imperf vert (horiz pair)	£1200	
		bb. Imperf horiz (vert pair)	£1800	
		c. Pale chestnut	15·00	9·50
		ca. Imperf (pair)	£1300	
		d. Major re-entry	£300	£180
276	41	2d. dull violet (3.1900)	21·00	1·00
		a. Imperf between (pair)	£1500	
		b. Mauve	26·00	2·50
		c. Purple	20·00	1·00
		ca. Imperf between (pair)	£1500	

The above ½d. stamps are slightly smaller than those of the previous printing. A new plate was made to print 240 stamps instead of 120 as previously, and to make these fit the watermarked paper, the border design was redrawn and contracted, the centre vignette remaining as before. The 2d. stamp is also from a new plate providing smaller designs.

42

(Des G. Bach and G. Drummond. Eng J. A. C. Harrison. Recess Waterlow)

1901 (1 Jan). Universal Penny Postage. No wmk. Perf 12 to 16.

277	42	1d. carmine	4·00	4·50

All examples of No. 277 show a minute dot above the upper left corner of the value tablet which is not present on later printings.

(Recess Govt Printer, Wellington)

1901 (Feb–Dec). Thick, soft Pirie paper with vertical mesh. W **38**.

(a) Perf 11.

278	42	1d. carmine	6·00	25
		a. Imperf vert (horiz pair)	£500	
		b. Deep carmine	6·00	25
		ba. Imperf vert (horiz pair)	£500	
		c. Carmine-lake	28·00	15·00
		x. Wmk reversed	†	£100
		y. Wmk inverted and reversed	£500	£150

(b) Perf 14.

279	23	½d. green (11.01)	25·00	15·00
280	42	1d. carmine	75·00	25·00
		a. Imperf vert (horiz pair)	£500	
		y. Wmk inverted and reversed	£250	£100

(c) Perf 14×11.

281	23	½d. green	13·00	17·00
		a. Deep green	13·00	17·00
		b. Perf 11×14	15·00	28·00
282	42	1d. carmine	£400	£150
		a. Perf 11×14	£3000	£1300

(d) Perf 11 and 14 mixed.*

283	23	½d. green	55·00	95·00
284	42	1d. carmine	£400	£140

* The term 'mixed' is applied to stamps from sheets which were at first perforated 14, or 14×11, and either incompletely or defectively perforated. These sheets were patched on the back with strips of paper, and re-perforated 11 in those parts where the original perforation was defective.

Nos. 278/284 were printed from new plates supplied by Waterlow. These were subsequently used for Nos. 285/307 with later printings on Cowan paper showing considerable plate wear.

WATERMARK VARIETIES. The watermark on the Basted Mills version of the W **38** paper used for Nos. 285/292 occurs indiscriminately normal, reversed, inverted etc.

(Recess Govt Printer, Wellington)

1901 (Dec). Thin, hard Basted Mills paper with vertical mesh. W **38**.

(a) Perf 11.

285	23	½d. green	£100	£150
286	42	1d. carmine	£225	£200

(b) Perf 14.

287	23	½d. green	48·00	48·00
		a. Imperf vert (horiz pair)	£450	
288	42	1d. carmine	21·00	10·00
		a. Imperf vert (horiz pair)	£450	
		b. Imperf horiz (vert pair)	£350	

(c) Perf 14×11.

289	23	½d. green	50·00	70·00
		a. Deep green	50·00	70·00
		b. Perf 11×14	29·00	50·00
290	42	1d. carmine	38·00	20·00
		a. Perf 11×14	12·00	5·50

(d) Mixed perfs.

291	23	½d. green	70·00	£150
292	42	1d. carmine	90·00	85·00

(Recess Govt Printer, Wellington)

1902 (Jan). Thin, hard Cowan paper with horizontal mesh. No wmk.

(a) Perf 11.

293	23	½d. green	£250	£300

NEW ZEALAND

		(b) Perf 14.		
294	23	½d. green	38·00	9·50
295	42	1d. carmine	14·00	4·50

		(c) Perf 14×11.		
296	23	½d. green	£150	£250
		a. Perf 11×14	£250	£425
297	42	1d. carmine	£130	£160
		a. Perf 11×14	£170	£225

		(d) Mixed perfs.		
298	23	½d. green	£200	£300
299	42	1d. carmine	£130	£180

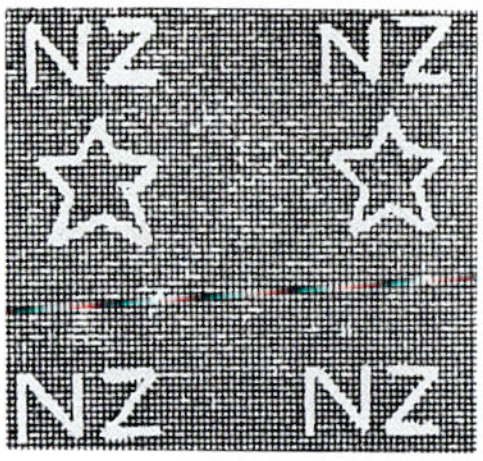

43 'Single' Wmk

SIDEWAYS WATERMARKS ON LOCALLY PRINTED STAMPS. In its sideways format the single NZ and Star watermark W **43**, exists indiscriminately sideways, sideways inverted, sideways reversed and sideways inverted plus reversed.

(Recess Govt Printer, Wellington)

1902 (Apr). Thin, hard Cowan paper. W **43**.

		(a) Perf 11.		
300	23	½d. green	85·00	£150
301	42	1d. carmine	£1500	£1000

		(b) Perf 14.		
302	23	½d. green	10·00	1·50
		a. Imperf vert (horiz pair)	£400	
		b. Deep green	10·00	1·50
		ba. Imperf vert (horiz pair)	£400	
		c. Yellow green	12·00	1·50
		d. Pale yellow-green	22·00	4·50
		w. Wmk inverted	55·00	24·00
		x. Wmk reversed	55·00	32·00
		y. Wmk inverted and reversed	90·00	45·00
303	42	1d. carmine	4·00	10
		a. Imperf horiz (vert pair)	£250	
		b. Booklet pane of 6 (21.8.02)	£275	
		c. Pale carmine	4·00	10
		ca. Imperf horiz (vert pair)	£250	
		cb. Booklet pane of 6	£275	
		d. Deep carmine*	32·00	4·25
		w. Wmk inverted	£100	50·00
		x. Wmk reversed	£100	50·00
		y. Wmk inverted and reversed	£120	50·00

		(c) Perf 14×11.		
304	23	½d. green	32·00	£150
		a. Deep green	35·00	£150
		b. Perf 11×14	32·00	£120
305	42	1d. carmine	£120	£150
		a. Perf 11×14	£225	£200
		ab. Deep carmine*	£600	£600

		(d) Mixed perfs.		
306	23	½d. green	42·00	75·00
		a. Deep green	50·00	75·00
307	42	1d. carmine	38·00	60·00
		a. Pale carmine	38·00	60·00
		b. Deep carmine*	£350	£350
		y. Wmk inverted and reversed	£750	£500

* Nos. 303*d*, 305*ab* and 307*b* were printed from a plate made by Waterlow & Sons, known as the 'Reserve' plate. The stamps do not show evidence of wearing and the area surrounding the upper part of the figure is more deeply shaded. This plate was subsequently used to produce Nos. 362, 364 and 366/369.

A special plate, made by W. R. Royle & Sons, showing a minute dot between the horizontal rows, was introduced in 1902 to print the booklet pane, No. 303b. A special characteristic of the booklet pane was that the pearl in the top left-hand corner was large. Some panes exist with the outer edges imperforate.

(Recess Govt Printer, Wellington)

1902 (28 Aug)–**07**. Thin, hard Cowan paper. W **43** (sideways on 3d., 5d., 6d., 8d., 1s. and 5s.).

		(a) Perf 11.		
308	27	2½d. blue (5.03)	40·00	15·00
		a. Deep blue	40·00	15·00
		w. Wmk inverted	£250	£100
		x. Wmk reversed	£275	65·00
		y. Wmk inverted and reversed	£450	£100
309	28	3d. yellow-brown	50·00	3·75
		a. Bistre-brown	50·00	3·75
		b. Pale bistre	55·00	6·00
310	37	4d. deep blue and deep brown/*bluish* (27.11.02)	10·00	95·00
		a. Imperf vert (horiz pair)	£650	
311	30	5d. red-brown (4.03)	55·00	10·00
		a. Deep brown	55·00	8·50
		b. Sepia	60·00	22·00
312	31	6d. rose (9.02)	42·00	7·50
		a. Rose-red	42·00	7·50
		ab. Wmk upright (?1.03)	£3500	£2500
		b. Rose-carmine	50·00	7·50
		ba. Imperf vert (horiz pair)	£1000	
		bb. Imperf horiz (vert pair)		
		c. Bright carmine-pink	65·00	10·00
		d. Scarlet	85·00	20·00
313	32	8d. blue (2.03)	75·00	14·00
		a. Steel-blue	75·00	14·00
		ab. Imperf vert (horiz pair)	£2000	
		ac. Imperf horiz (vert pair)	£2000	
314	33	9d. purple (5.03)	80·00	15·00
		w. Wmk inverted	£350	£160
		x. Wmk reversed	£375	£250
		y. Wmk inverted and reversed	£425	£300
315	34	1s. brown-red (11.02)	90·00	17·00
		a. Bright red	90·00	17·00
		b. Orange-red	90·00	10·00
		ba. Error. Wmk W **12b** (inverted)	—	£2000
		c. Orange-brown	80·00	24·00
316	35	2s. green (4.03)	£225	75·00
		a. Blue-green	£225	50·00
		x. Wmk reversed	£1000	
		w. Wmk inverted	£850	£225
317	36	5s. deep red (6.03)	£400	£425
		a. Wmk upright	£400	£425
		b. Vermilion	£350	£400
		ba. Wmk upright	£400	£425
		w. Wmk inverted	£1700	£850

		(b) Perf 14.		
318	40	1½d. chestnut (2.07)	27·00	75·00
		a. Major re-entry	£350	
319	41	2d. grey-purple (12.02)	7·50	2·00
		a. Purple	7·50	2·00
		ab. Imperf vert (horiz pair)	£550	£950
		ac. Imperf horiz (vert pair)	£800	
		b. Bright reddish purple	6·50	3·00
320	27	2½d. blue (1906)	28·00	5·00
		a. Deep blue	28·00	5·00
		w. Wmk inverted	£180	£150
		x. Wmk reversed	†	£350
		y. Wmk inverted and reversed	£475	£250
321	28	3d. bistre-brown (1906)	35·00	3·50
		a. Imperf vert (horiz pair)	£1000	
		b. Bistre	35·00	3·50
		c. Pale yellow-bistre	75·00	20·00
322	37	4d. deep blue and deep brown/*bluish* (1903)	8·50	3·50
		a. Imperf vert (horiz pair)	£900	
		b. Imperf horiz (vert pair)	£650	
		c. Centre inverted	†	
		d. Blue and chestnut/*bluish*	8·50	2·75
		e. Blue and ochre-brown/*bluish*	8·50	2·75
		w. Wmk inverted	£100	50·00
		x. Wmk reversed	£250	£160
		y. Wmk inverted and reversed	£275	£250
323	30	5d. black-brown (1906)	60·00	38·00
		a. Red-brown	45·00	16·00
324	31	6d. bright carmine-pink (1906)	75·00	12·00
		a. Imperf vert (horiz pair)	£1000	
		b. Rose-carmine	80·00	12·00
325	32	8d. steel-blue (1907)	50·00	12·00
326	33	9d. purple (1906)	55·00	14·00
		w. Wmk inverted	£500	£400
327	34	1s. orange-brown (1906)	80·00	12·00
		a. Orange-red	75·00	12·00
		b. Pale red	£325	£120
328	35	2s. green (1.06)	£225	35·00
		a. Blue-green	£225	42·00
		aw. Wmk inverted	£1000	£300
		ax. Wmk reversed	†	—
		ay. Wmk inverted and reversed	£1000	£300
329	36	5s. deep red (1906)	£400	£375
		a. Wmk upright	£400	£375
		b. Dull red	£400	£375
		ba. Wmk upright	£400	£375

		(c) Perf compound of 11 and 14.		
330	40	1½d. chestnut (1907)	£1600	
331	41	2d. purple (1903)	£750	£600
332	28	3d. bistre-brown (1906)	£1000	£950
333	37	4d. blue and yellow-brown (1903)	£600	£850
		x. Wmk reversed	—	£1000
334	30	5d. red-brown (1906)	£1700	£1400
335	31	6d. rose-carmine (1907)	£600	£750
336	32	8d. steel-blue (1907)	£1500	£1800
337	33	9d. purple (1906)	£1700	£1600
338	36	5s. deep red (wmk sideways)(1906)	£3750	£4000

NEW ZEALAND

(d) Mixed perfs.

339	40	1½d. chestnut (1907)	£1600	
340	41	2d. purple (1903)	£750	£650
341	28	3d. bistre-brown (1906)	£1000	£950
342	37	4d. blue and chestnut/*bluish* (1904)	£600	£850
		a. Blue and yellow-brown/*bluish*	£600	£850
		w. Wmk inverted	£1200	£1000
		x. Wmk reversed	£1200	£1000
343	30	5d. red-brown (1906)	£1600	£1300
344	31	6d. rose-carmine (1907)	£500	£750
		a. Bright carmine-pink	£500	£750
345	32	8d. steel-blue (1907)	£1500	£1800
346	33	9d. purple (1906)	£1500	£1600
347	35	2s. blue-green (1906)	£1700	£1800
348	36	5s. vermilion (Wmk upright) (1906)	£3000	£3500
		w. Wmk inverted		

Two sizes of paper were used for the above stamps:

(1). A sheet containing 240 wmks, with a space of 9 mm between each.
(2). A sheet containing 120 wmks, with a space of 24 mm between each vertical row.

Size (1) was used for the ½d., 1d., 2d. and 4d., and size (2) for 2½d., 5d., 9d. and 2s. The paper in each case exactly fitted the plates, and had the watermark in register, though in the case of the 4d., the plate of which contained only 80 stamps, the paper was cut up to print it. The 3d., 6d., 8d. and 1s. were printed on variety (1), but with watermark sideways: by reason of this, examples from the margins of the sheets show parts of the words 'NEW ZEALAND POSTAGE' in large letters, and some have no watermark at all. For the 1½d. and 5s. stamps variety (1) was also used, but two watermarks appear on each stamp.

* The only known example of No. 322c, postmarked at Picton on 21 March 1904, was purchased for the New Zealand Post archive collection in 1998.

(Recess Govt Printer, Wellington)

1904 (Feb). Printed from new 'dot' plates made by W. R. Royle & Sons. Thin, hard Cowan paper. W **43**.

(a) Perf 14.

349	42	1d. rose-carmine	11·00	50
		a. Pale carmine	11·00	50
		w. Wmk inverted	£150	45·00
		y. Wmk inverted and reversed	£150	45·00

(b) Perf 11×14.

350	42	1d. rose-carmine	£250	£180

(c) Mixed perfs.

351	42	1d. rose-carmine	42·00	55·00
		a. Pale carmine	42·00	55·00

These plates have a dot in the margins between stamps, level with the small pearls at the side of the design, but it is frequently cut out by the perforations. However, they can be further distinguished by the notes below.

In 1906 fresh printings were made from four new plates, two of which, marked in the margin 'W1' and 'W2', were supplied by Waterlow Bros and Layton, and the other two, marked 'R1' and 'R2', by W. R. Royle & Son. The intention was to note which pair of plates wore the best and produced the best results. They can be distinguished as follows:

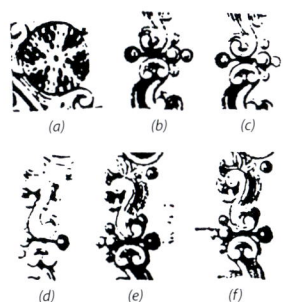

(a) Four o'clock flaw in rosette at top right corner. Occurs in all these plates but not in the original Waterlow plates.
(b) Pearl at right strong.
(c) Pearl at right weak.
(d) Dot at left and S-shaped ornament unshaded.
(e) S-shaped ornament with one line of shading within.
(f) As (e) but with line from left pearl to edge of stamp.

'Dot' plates comprise (a) and (d).
Waterlow plates comprise (a), (b) and (e).
Royle plates comprise (a), (c) and (e) and the line in (f) on many stamps but not all.

(Recess Govt Printer, Wellington)

1906. Thin, hard Cowan paper. W **43**.

(a) Printed from new Waterlow plates
(i) Perf 14.

352	42	1d. deep rose-carmine	55·00	4·00
		a. Imperf horiz (vert pair)	£400	
		b. Aniline carmine	55·00	4·00
		ba. Imperf vert (horiz pair)	£400	
		c. Rose-carmine	55·00	4·00
		y. Wmk inverted and reversed	£1200	£500

(ii) Perf 11.

353	42	1d. aniline carmine	£750	£1100

(iii) Perf 11×14.

354	42	1d. rose-carmine	£500	£1500
		a. Perf 14×11	£600	£1300

(iv) Mixed perfs.

355	42	1d. deep rose-carmine	£500	£850

(b) Printed from new Royle plates
(i) Perf 14.

356	42	1d. rose-carmine	12·00	1·50
		a. Imperf horiz (vert pair)	£400	£550
		b. Bright rose-carmine	13·00	1·50
		w. Wmk inverted	£1000	£600
		y. Wmk inverted and reversed	£750	£350

(ii) Perf 11.

357	42	1d. bright rose-carmine	£110	£250

(iii) Perf 11×14.

358	42	1d. rose-carmine	£120	£275
		a. Perf 14×11	£225	£300

(iv) Mixed perfs.

359	42	1d. rose-carmine	£250	£350

(v) Perf 14×14½ (comb).

360	42	1d. bright rose-carmine	£100	60·00
		a. Rose-carmine	£100	60·00

Nos. 360/360a are known both with and without the small dot. See also No. 386.

1905 (15 June)–06. Stamps supplied to penny-in-the-slot machines.
(i) 'Dot' plates of 1904
(ii) Waterlow 'reserve' plate of 1902

(a) Imperf top and bottom; zigzag roulette 9½ on one or both sides, two large holes at sides.

361	42	1d. rose-carmine (i)	£200	£300
362		1d. deep carmine (ii)	£225	

(b) As last but rouletted 14½ (8.7.05).

363	42	1d. rose-carmine (i)	£200	£300
364		1d. deep carmine (ii)	£500	

(c) Imperf all round, two large holes each side (6.3.06).

365	42	1d. rose-carmine (i)	£160	
366		1d. deep carmine (ii)	£170	£300

(d) Imperf all round (21.6.06).

367	42	1d. deep carmine (ii)	£180	£300

(e) Imperf all round. Two small indentations on back of stamp (1.06).

368	42	1d. deep carmine (ii)	£225	£300

(f) Imperf all round; two small pin-holes in stamp (21.6.06).

369	42	1d. deep carmine (ii)	£200	£300

No. 365 only exists from strips of Nos. 361 or 363 (resulting from the use of successive coins) which have been separated by scissors. Similarly strips of Nos. 362 and 364 can produce single copies of No. 366 but this also exists in singles from a different machine.

Most used copies of Nos. 361/367 are forgeries and they should only be collected *on cover*.

44 Maori Canoe, *Te Arawa*

45 Maori Art

46 Landing of Cook

46a Annexation of New Zealand

NEW ZEALAND

3d. White flaw behind Chieftain
(Left pane, R. 4/2)

(Des L. J. Steele. Eng W. R. Bock. Typo Govt Printer, Wellington)

1906 (1–17 Nov). New Zealand Exhibition, Christchurch. W **43** (sideways). Perf 14.

370	**44**	½d. emerald-green	40·00	30·00
371	**45**	1d. vermilion	16·00	18·00
		a. Claret	£12500	£20000
372	**46**	3d. brown and blue	55·00	90·00
		a. Flaw behind Chieftain	£350	£450
373	**46a**	6d. pink and olive-green (17.11)	£200	£300
370/373 Set of 4			£275	£375

The 1d. in claret was the original printing, which was considered unsatisfactory.

47 (T **28** reduced) **48** (T **31** reduced) **49** (T **34** reduced)

(New plates (except 4d.), supplied by Perkins Bacon. Recess Govt Printer, Wellington)

1907–08. Thin, hard Cowan paper. W **43**.

(a) Perf 14 (line).

374	**23**	½d. green (1907)	45·00	16·00
		a. Imperf (pair)	£400	
		b. Yellow-green	38·00	7·50
		c. Deep yellow-green	38·00	7·50
375	**47**	3d. brown (6.07)	95·00	30·00
376	**48**	6d. carmine-pink (3.07)	55·00	15·00
		a. Red	65·00	40·00

(b) Perf 14×13, 13½ (comb).

377	**23**	½d. green (1907)	17·00	17·00
		a. Yellow-green	11·00	8·50
		b. Imperf three sides (top stamp of vert pair)	£500	
378	**47**	3d. brown (2.08)	60·00	50·00
		a. Yellow-brown	60·00	50·00
379	**37**	4d. blue and yellow-brown/*bluish* (6.08)	42·00	65·00
380	**48**	6d. pink (2.08)	£550	£170
381	**49**	1s. orange-red (12.07)	£225	65·00

(c) Perf 14×15 (comb).

382	**23**	½d. yellow-green (1907)	8·50	1·00
		a. Imperf three sides (top stamp of vert pair)	£450	
		y. Wmk inverted and reversed	—	£325
383	**47**	3d. brown (8.08)	50·00	18·00
		a. Yellow-brown	50·00	18·00
384	**48**	6d. carmine-pink (8.08)	55·00	12·00
385	**49**	1s. orange-red (8.08)	£225	35·00
		a. Deep orange-brown	£500	£1800

The ½d. stamps of this 1907–1908 issue have a minute dot in the margin between the stamps, where not removed by the perforation. (See note after No. 351a). Those perforated 14 can be distinguished from the earlier stamps, Nos. 302/302d, by the absence of plate wear. This is most noticeable on the 1902 printings as a white patch at far left, level with the bottom of the 'P' in 'POSTAGE'. Such damage is not present on the new plates used for Nos. 374/374c.

Stamps of Types **47**, **48** and **49** also have a small dot as described in note after No. 351a.

TYPOGRAPHY PAPERS.

1908–1930. **De La Rue paper** is chalk-surfaced and has a smooth finish. The watermark is as illustrated. The gum is toned and strongly resistant to soaking.

Jones paper is chalk-surfaced and has a coarser texture, is poorly surfaced and the ink tends to peel. The outline of the watermark commonly shows on the surface of the stamp. The gum is colourless or only slightly toned and washes off readily.

Cowan paper is chalk-surfaced and is white and opaque. The watermark is usually smaller than in the Jones paper and is often barely visible.

Wiggins Teape paper is chalk-surfaced and is thin and hard. It has a vertical mesh with a narrow watermark, whereas the other papers have a horizontal mesh and a wider watermark.

50

(Typo Govt Printer, Wellington, from Perkins Bacon plate).

1908 (1 Dec). De La Rue chalk-surfaced paper. W **43**. Perf 14×15 (comb).

386	**50**	1d. carmine	25·00	2·00
		w. Wmk inverted	—	£200

The design of T **50** differs from T **42** by alterations in the corner rosettes and by the lines on the globe which are diagonal instead of vertical.

51 **52** **53**

(Eng. P.B. Typo Govt Printer, Wellington)

1909 (8 Nov)–**12**. De La Rue chalk-surfaced paper with toned gum. W **43**. Perf 14×15 (comb).

387	**51**	½d. yellow-green	6·00	50
		aa. Deep green	6·00	50
		a. Imperf (pair)	£300	
		b. Booklet pane. 5 stamps plus label in position 1 (4.10)	£800	
		c. Ditto, but label in position 6 (4.10)	£800	
		d. Booklet pane of 6 (4.10)	£250	
		e. Ditto, but with coloured bars on selvedge (5.12)	£225	
		w. Wmk inverted	†	£1000

Stamps with blurred and heavy appearance are from booklets.

(Eng W. R. Royle & Son, London. Recess Govt Printer, Wellington)

1909 (8 Nov)–**16**. T **52** and similar portraits.

*(a) W **43**. Perf 14×14½ (comb).*

388		2d. mauve	15·00	6·50
		a. Deep mauve	18·00	6·50
		w. Wmk inverted	†	£1200
389		3d. chestnut	23·00	1·40
390		4d. orange-red	28·00	27·00
390a		4d. yellow (1912)	7·50	12·00
		aw. Wmk inverted	£600	£250
391		5d. brown (1910)	20·00	5·00
		a. Red-brown	20·00	5·00
		w. Wmk inverted	—	—
392		6d. carmine (1910)	45·00	2·25
		a. Deep carmine (29.10.13)	50·00	3·50
393		8d. indigo-blue	14·00	3·75
		a. Deep bright blue	14·00	3·75
		w. Wmk inverted	£100	55·00
394		1s. vermilion (1910)	75·00	8·00
		w. Wmk inverted	£475	£170
388/394 Set of 8			£200	60·00

*(b) W **43**. Perf 14 (line)*.*

395		3d. chestnut (1910)	50·00	22·00
396		4d. orange (1910)	23·00	18·00
397		5d. brown	26·00	5·00
		a. Red-brown (15.9.11)	26·00	5·00
		w. Wmk inverted	—	—
398		6d. carmine	55·00	15·00
399		1s. vermilion	75·00	18·00
395/399 Set of 5			£200	70·00

*(c) W **43** (sideways) (paper with widely spaced wmk as used for Nos. 308 and 320, see note below No. 348). Perf 14 (line)*.*

400		8d. indigo-blue (8.16)	75·00	£130
		a. No wmk	£180	£275

*(d) W **43**. Perf 14×13½ (comb)†.*

401		3d. chestnut (1915)	£100	£180
		a. Vert pair. Perf 14×13½ and 14×14½	£325	£650
		w. Wmk inverted	£500	£500
402		5d. red-brown (1916)	22·00	3·50
		a. Vert pair. Perf 14×13½ and 14×14½	£100	£275
403		6d. carmine (1915)	£120	£225
		a. Vert pair. Perf 14×13½ and 14×14½	£400	£950
404		8d. indigo-blue (3.16)	£100	3·50
		a. Vert pair. Perf 14×13½ and 14×14½	£150	£250
		b. Deep bright blue	£100	3·50
		ba. Vert pair. Perf 14×13½ and 14×14½	£150	£250
		w. Wmk inverted	£300	60·00
401/404 Set of 4			£300	£350

* In addition to showing the usual characteristics of a line perforation, these stamps may be distinguished by their vertical perforation which measures 13.8. Nos. 388/394 generally measure vertically 14 to 14.3. An exception is 13.8 one vertical side but 14 the other.

NEW ZEALAND

† The 3d. and 6d. come in full sheets perf 14×13½.
The 3d., 5d. and 6d. values also exist in two combinations: (a) five top rows perf 14×13½ with five bottom rows perf 14×14½ and (b) four top rows perf 14×13½ with six bottom rows perf 14×14½.
The 8d. perf 14×13½ only exists from combination (b).

1d. 'Feather' flaw (Plate 12, R. 3/1)

1d. 'Globe' flaw (Plate 12, R. 5/24)

1d. 'Q' flaw (Plate 13, R. 10/19)

1d. 'N' flaw (Plate 12, R. 9/23, printings from 1925)

(Eng P.B. Typo Govt Printer, Wellington)

1909 (8 Nov)–**27**. Perf 14×15 (comb).
*(a) W **43**. De La Rue chalk-surfaced paper with toned gum.*

405	53	1d. carmine	1·75	10
		a. Imperf (pair)	£500	
		b. Booklet pane of 6 (4.10)	£200	
		c. Ditto, but with coloured bars on selvedge (5.12)	£160	
		d. 'Feather' flaw	32·00	10·00
		e. 'Globe' flaw	32·00	10·00
		f. 'Q' flaw	70·00	30·00
		w. Wmk inverted	£150	£120
		y. Wmk inverted and reversed		

*(b) W **43**. Jones chalk-surfaced paper with white gum.*

406	53	1d. deep carmine (6.24)	22·00	6·00
		a. On unsurfaced paper. *Pale carmine*	£750	
		b. Booklet pane of 6 with bars on selvedge (1.12.24)	£160	
		c. 'Feather' flaw	£100	60·00
		d. 'Globe' flaw	£100	55·00
		w. Wmk inverted	£140	70·00

*(c) W **43**. De La Rue unsurfaced medium paper with toned gum.*

407	53	1d. rose-carmine (4.25)	75·00	£180
		a. 'Feather' flaw	£450	
		b. 'Globe' flaw	£450	

*(d) W **43** (sideways). De La Rue chalk-surfaced paper with toned gum.*

408	53	1d. bright carmine (4.25)	10·00	35·00
		a. No wmk	35·00	80·00
		b. Imperf (pair)	£350	
		c. 'Feather' flaw	£100	
		d. 'Globe' flaw	£100	

(e) No wmk, but bluish 'NZ' and Star lithographed on back. Art paper.

409	53	1d. rose-carmine (7.25)	2·00	5·00
		a. 'NZ' and Star in black	24·00	
		b. 'NZ' and Star colourless	25·00	
		c. 'Feather' flaw	70·00	95·00
		d. 'Globe' flaw	70·00	95·00

*(f) W **43**. Cowan thick, opaque, chalk-surfaced paper with white gum.*

410	53	1d. deep carmine (8.25)	12·00	50
		a. Imperf (pair)	£250	£250
		b. Booklet pane of 6 with bars and adverts on selvedge	£190	
		c. 'Feather' flaw	75·00	50·00
		d. 'Globe' flaw	75·00	50·00
		e. 'N' flaw	£130	£130
		w. Wmk inverted	£150	60·00
		x. Wmk reversed (1926)	16·00	3·00
		xa. Booklet pane of 6 with bars and adverts on selvedge (1927)	£180	
		xc. 'Feather' flaw	£140	70·00
		xd. 'Globe' flaw	£140	70·00
		xe. 'N' flaw	£180	£110
		y. Wmk inverted and reversed (1926)	£200	£150

*(g) W **43**. Wiggins Teape thin, hard, chalk-surfaced paper with white gum.*

411	53	1d. rose-carmine (6.26)	35·00	20·00
		a. 'Feather' flaw	£180	75·00
		b. 'Globe' flaw	£180	75·00
		c. 'N' flaw	£200	£100
		w. Wmk inverted	£110	60·00

Examples of No. 405 with a blurred and heavy appearance are from booklets.

No. 406a comes from a sheet on which the paper coating was missing from the right-hand half.

Many stamps from the sheets of No. 408 were without watermark or showed portions of 'NEW ZEALAND POSTAGE' in double-lined capitals.

AUCKLAND EXHIBITION, 1913.
(59)   60

1913 (1 Dec). Auckland Industrial Exhibition. Nos. 387aa, 389, 392 and 405 optd with T **59** by Govt Printer, Wellington.

412	51	½d. deep green	23·00	45·00
413	53	1d. carmine	30·00	40·00
		a. 'Feather' flaw	£325	£425
		b. 'Globe' flaw	£325	£425
414	52	3d. chestnut	£180	£300
415		6d. carmine	£225	£400
412/415	Set of 4		£400	£700

These overprinted stamps were only available for letters in New Zealand and to Australia.

(Des H. L. Richardson. Recess Govt Printer, Wellington, from plates made in London by P.B.)

1915 (30 July)–**30**. W **43**. Perf 14×13½ (comb) (see notes below).
(a) Cowan unsurfaced paper.

416	60	1½d. grey-slate	3·25	1·50
		a. Perf 14×14½ (1915)	5·00	1·50
		aw. Wmk inverted	£500	£500
		b. Vert pair. Nos. 416/416a	35·00	£130
417		2d. bright violet	12·00	40·00
		a. Perf 14×14½	8·50	32·00
		b. Vert pair. Nos. 417/417a	35·00	£200
418		2d. yellow (15.1.16)	7·50	28·00
		a. Perf 14×14½	7·50	28·00
		b. Vert pair. Nos. 418/418a	30·00	£400
419		2½d. blue	4·50	6·00
		a. Perf 14×14½ (1916)	10·00	19·00
		b. Vert pair. Nos. 419/419a	50·00	£250
420		3d. chocolate	22·00	1·50
		aw. Wmk inverted	£250	£150
		ax. Wmk reversed	£500	£250
		b. Perf 14×14½	15·00	2·25
		bw. Wmk inverted	£600	£250
		bx. Wmk reversed	£800	£350
		c. Vert pair. Nos. 420 and 420b	£100	£200
		cw. Wmk inverted	£950	
		cx. Wmk reversed	£1500	
421		4d. yellow	5·50	60·00
		a. Re-entry (Pl 20 R. 1/6)	75·00	
		b. Re-entry (Pl 20 R. 4/10)	£100	
		c. Perf 14×14½	5·50	60·00
		d. Vert pair. Nos. 421 and 421c	28·00	£250
422		4d. bright violet (7.4.16)	11·00	50
		a. Imperf three sides (top stamp of vertical pair)	£1800	
		b. Re-entry (Pl 20 R. 1/6)	75·00	40·00
		c. Re-entry (Pl 20 R. 4/10)	95·00	45·00
		dx. Wmk reversed	£450	£350
		e. Perf 14×14½	4·50	50
		ex. Wmk reversed	£750	£450
		f. Vert pair. Nos. 422 and 422e	75·00	£225

NEW ZEALAND

	fx. Wmk reversed	£1500	
	g. Deep purple (7.26)	£120	20·00
	h. Ditto. Perf 14×14½	10·00	75
	ha. Imperf three sides (top stamp of vertical pair)	£1800	
	hb. Vert pair. Nos. 422g/422h	£3500	£2250
	hw. Wmk inverted	†	£2500
423	4½d. deep green	20·00	25·00
	a. Perf 14×14½ (1915)	18·00	40·00
	b. Vert pair. Nos. 423/423a	75·00	£225
424	5d. light blue (4.22)	8·00	1·00
	a. Imperf (pair)	£500	£500
	aa. Imperf (top stamp of vertical pair)	£850	
	bw. Wmk inverted	—	£300
	c. Perf 14×14½	15·00	40·00
	d. Pale ultramarine (5.30)	17·00	13·00
	da. Perf 14×14½	32·00	45·00
	db. Vert pair. Nos. 424d/424da	80·00	£350
425	6d. carmine	9·00	50
	a. Imperf three sides (top stamp of vert pair)	£2000	
	bw. Wmk inverted	£250	£250
	bx. Wmk reversed	—	£250
	by. Wmk inverted and reversed	£3000	£2500
	c. Carmine-lake (11.27)	£750	£950
	d. Perf 14×14½ (1915)	20·00	1·25
	dw. Wmk inverted	£300	£100
	e. Vert pair. Nos. 425 and 425d	£100	£150
426	7½d. red-brown	18·00	35·00
	a. Perf 14×14½ (10.20)	16·00	£100
	b. Vert pair. Nos. 426/426a	50·00	£250
427	8d. indigo-blue (19.4.21)	15·00	40·00
	a. Perf 14×14½	10·00	40·00
	b. Vert pair. Nos. 427/427a	38·00	£250
428	8d. red-brown (3.22)	32·00	2·00
429	9d. sage-green	22·00	3·50
	a. Imperf (pair)	£1500	
	b. Imperf three sides (top stamp of vert pair)	£2000	
	c. Yellowish olive (12.25)	22·00	24·00
	dw. Wmk inverted	†	£1900
	e. Perf 14×14½	20·00	35·00
	f. Vert pair. Nos. 429 and 429e	95·00	£350
430	1s. vermilion	25·00	3·00
	a. Imperf (pair)	£2250	
	aa. Imperf (top stamp of vertical pair)	£2500	
	bw. Wmk inverted	£500	£500
	c. Perf 14×14½ (1915)	20·00	50
	ca. Pale orange-red (4.24)	40·00	25·00
	cb. Imperf (pair)	£550	
	cba. Imperf (top stamp of vertical pair)	£1000	
	cc. Orange-brown (20.1.28)	£950	£900
	cw. Wmk inverted	£300	£250
	d. Vert pair. Nos. 430 and 430c	£140	£400
	dw. Wmk inverted		
416/430c	Set of 15	£160	£225

(b) W **43** *(sideways on 2d., 3d. and 6d.). Thin paper with widely spaced watermark as used for Nos. 308 and 320 (see note below No. 348). Perf 14×13½ (comb) (see notes below) (1½d.) or Perf 14 (line) (others).*

431	**60**	1½d. grey-slate (3.16)	3·00	11·00
		a. No wmk	5·50	23·00
		b. Perf 14×14½	3·00	11·00
		ba. No wmk	5·50	23·00
		by. Wmk inverted and reversed	£500	£550
		c. Vert pair. Nos. 431 and 431b	26·00	£180
		ca. Vert pair. Nos. 431a and 431ba	75·00	£225
432		2d. yellow (6.16)	6·00	75·00
		a. No wmk	75·00	£160
433		3d. chocolate (6.16)	7·50	50·00
		a. No wmk	75·00	£160
434		6d. carmine (6.16)	11·00	£150
		a. No wmk	£100	£250
431/434	Set of 4		25·00	£200

The 1½d., 2½d., 4½d. and 7½d. have value tablets as shown in T **60** For the other values the tablets are shortened and the ornamental border each side of the crown correspondingly extended.

With the exception of Nos. 432/434 stamps in this issue were comb-perforated 14×13½, 14×14½ or a combination of the two.

The 1½d. (No. 416), 2½d., 4d. (both), 4½d., 5d., 6d., 7½d., 8d. red-brown, 9d. and 1s. are known to have been produced in sheets perforated 14×13½ throughout with the 4d. bright violet, 5d., 6d. and 1s. known perforated 14×14½ throughout.

On the sheets showing the two perforations combined, the top four rows are usually perforated 14×13½ and the bottom six 14×14½. Combination sheets are known to have been produced in this form for the 1½d. (Nos. 416 and 431), 2d. (both), 2½d., 3d., 4d. (both), 4½d., 6d., 7½d., 8d. indigo-blue, 9d. and 1s. On a late printing of the 4d. deep purple and 5d. pale ultramarine the arrangement is different with the top five rows perforated 14×14½ and the bottom five 14×13½.

With the exception of Nos. 432/434 any with perforations measuring 14×14 or nearly must be classed as 14×14½, this being an irregularity of the comb machine, and not a product of the 14-line machine.

4d. Re-entry (Plate 20, R. 1/6)    **4d.** Re-entry (Plate 20, R. 4/10)

During the laying-down of plate 20 for the 4d., from the roller-die which also contained dies of other values, an impression of the 4½d. value was placed on R. 1/6 and of the 2½d. on R. 4/10. These errors were subsequently corrected by re-entries of the 4d. impression, but on R. 1/6 traces of the original impression can be found in the right-hand value tablet and above the top frame line, while on R. 4/10 the foot of the '2' is visible in the left-hand value tablet with traces of '½' to its right.

 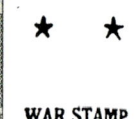

61   **62**   **WAR STAMP (63)**

T **62** (from local plates) can be identified from T **61** (prepared by Perkins Bacon) by the shading on the portrait. This is diagonal on T **62** and horizontal on T **61**.

*(Die eng W. R. Bock. Typo Govt Printer, Wellington, from plates made by P.B. (T **61**) or locally (T **62**))*

1915 (30 July)–**33**. W **43**. Perf 14×15.

(a) De La Rue chalk-surfaced paper with toned gum.

435	**61**	½d. green	1·50	20
		a. Booklet pane of 6 with bars on selvedge	£170	
		b. Yellow-green	5·00	1·50
		ba. Booklet pane of 6 with bars on selvedge	£150	
		c. Very thick, hard, highly surfaced paper with white gum (12.15)	14·00	60·00
		w. Wmk inverted	£110	£150
		x. Wmk reversed	—	£180
		y. Wmk inverted and reversed	—	£225
436	**62**	1½d. grey-black (4.16)	13·00	1·25
		a. Black	13·00	2·00
		x. Wmk reversed	†	£450
		y. Wmk inverted and reversed	—	£400
437	**61**	1½d. slate (5.9.16)	9·00	20
		w. Wmk inverted	—	£400
438		1½d. orange-brown (9.18)	2·25	20
		w. Wmk inverted	£225	£200
		x. Wmk reversed	†	£500
		y. Wmk inverted and reversed	£375	£350
439		2d. yellow (9.16)	2·25	20
		a. Pale yellow	7·50	1·25
		w. Wmk inverted	£160	£100
		y. Wmk inverted and reversed	†	£450
440		3d. chocolate (5.19)	9·50	1·50
435/440	Set of 6		35·00	3·50

*(b) W **43**. Jones chalk-surfaced paper with white gum.*

441	**61**	½d. green (10.24)	12·00	15·00
		a. Booklet pane of 6 with bars on selvedge (1.12.24)	£160	
		w. Wmk inverted	£150	£150
442		2d. dull yellow (7.24)	15·00	75·00
		w. Wmk inverted	£170	£225
443		3d. deep chocolate (3.25)	30·00	35·00
441/443	Set of 3		50·00	£100

(c) No wmk, but bluish 'NZ' and Star lithographed on back. Art paper.

444	**61**	½d. apple-green (4.25)	2·75	10·00
		a. 'NZ' and Star almost colourless	10·00	
445		2d. yellow (7.25)	12·00	£100

*(d) W **43**. Cowan thick, opaque, chalk-surfaced paper with white gum.*

446	**61**	½d. green (8.25)	1·75	20
		aa. Imperf 3 sides (top stamp of vertical pair)	£1500	
		a. Booklet pane of 6 with bars and adverts on selvedge	£180	
		ab. Booklet pane of 6 with bars on selvedge (1928)	£425	
		bw. Wmk inverted	£140	£130
		bx. Wmk reversed (1926)	15·00	4·00
		bxa. Booklet pane of 6 with bars and adverts on selvedge (1927)	£150	
		by. Wmk inverted and reversed (1926)	£200	£180
		c. Perf 14 (1927)	3·00	35
		ca. Booklet pane of 6 with bars on selvedge (1928)	£140	
		cb. Booklet pane of 6 with bars and adverts on selvedge (1928)	£140	

NEW ZEALAND

447		cw. Wmk inverted	£200	£170
		1½d. orange-brown (Perf 14) (8.29)	9·50	45·00
		a. Perf 14×15 (7.33)	50·00	£100
448		2d. yellow (8.25)	11·00	1·50
		ax. Wmk reversed (1927)	50·00	£180
		ay. Wmk inverted and reversed (1927)	£375	£750
		b. Perf 14 (1929)	2·75	20
		bw. Wmk inverted	£160	60·00
449		3d. chocolate (8.25)	10·00	2·00
		aw. Wmk inverted	£130	£100
		b. Perf 14 (1929)	10·00	4·50
446/449	Set of 4		21·00	45·00

*(e) W **43**. Wiggins Teape thin, hard, chalk-surfaced paper.*

450	61	1½d. orange-brown (Perf 14) (1930)	45·00	£130
451		2d. yellow (5.26)	15·00	20·00
		aw. Wmk inverted	£100	£100
		b. Perf 14 (10.27)	15·00	15·00
		bw. Wmk inverted	£130	55·00

The designs of these stamps also differ as described beneath No. 434. Stamps from booklet panes often have blurred, heavy impressions. Different advertisements can be found on the listed booklet panes. Examples of No. 446aa, which occur in booklet panes, show the stamps perforated at top.

The ½d. and 2d. (Nos. 446c and 448b) are known showing ½d. and 1d. local surcharges from 1932 applied diagonally in blue to stamps previously stuck on to envelopes or cards at Christchurch (½d.) or Wellington (1d.).

1915 (24 Sept). No. 435 optd with T **63**.

452	61	½d. green	2·25	50

64 Peace and Lion

65 Peace and Lion

66

66a

67

67a

(Des and typo D.L.R. from plates by P.B., Waterlow and D.L.R.)

1920 (27 Jan). Victory. De La Rue chalk-surfaced paper. W **43** (sideways on ½d., 1½d., 3d. and 1s.). Perf 14.

453	64	½d. green	3·50	2·00
		a. Pale yellow-green	30·00	28·00
454	65	1d. carmine-red	5·00	60
		a. Bright carmine	7·50	70
		w. Wmk inverted	45·00	24·00
		x. Wmk reversed	£200	£100
455	66	1½d. brown-orange	3·00	50
456	66a	3d. chocolate	16·00	15·00
457	67	6d. violet	18·00	21·00
		a. Wmk sideways	†	£1500
		w. Wmk inverted	£1000	£600
458	67a	1s. orange-red	32·00	45·00
453/458	Set of 6		70·00	75·00

The above stamps were placed on sale in London in November, 1919.

2d. **2d.**

TWOPENCE
(**68**)

69

1922 (Mar). No. 453 surch with T **68**.

459	64	2d. on ½d. green (R.)	6·50	1·40

(Des and eng W. R. Bock, Typo Govt Printer, Wellington)

1923 (1 Oct)–**25**. Restoration of Penny Postage. W **43**. Perf 14×15.

(a) De La Rue chalk-surfaced paper with toned gum.

460	69	1d. carmine	5·00	60

(b) Jones chalk-surfaced paper with white gum.

461	69	1d. carmine (3.24)	14·00	6·50
		a. Wmk sideways	†	£700
		w. Wmk inverted	80·00	75·00

(c) Cowan unsurfaced paper with very shiny gum.

462	69	1d. carmine-pink (4.25)	48·00	22·00

The paper used for No. 462 is similar to that of Nos. 416/430.

70 Exhibition Buildings

(Des H. L. Richardson. Eng and typo Govt Printer, Wellington)

1925 (17 Nov). Dunedin Exhibition. Cowan chalk-surfaced paper. W **43**. Perf 14×15.

463	70	½d. yellow-green/*green*	3·00	12·00
		w. Wmk inverted	£250	£180
464		1d. carmine/*rose*	4·25	6·00
		w. Wmk inverted	£500	£375
465		4d. mauve/*pale mauve*	30·00	75·00
		a. 'POSTAGF' at right (R. 10/1)	£120	£180
463/465	Set of 3		32·00	85·00

There is a similar variety to No. 465a at R. 1/2 showing 'POSTAGF.', with a full stop after the 'F'.

71 King George V as Field-Marshal

72 King George V as Admiral

(Des H. L. Richardson; plates by B.W. (1d. from sheets), P.B. (1d. from booklets), Royal Mint, London (others). Typo Govt Printer, Wellington)

1926 (12 July)–**34**. W **43**. Perf 14.

(a) Jones chalk-surfaced paper with white gum.

466	72	2s. deep blue	80·00	70·00
		w. Wmk inverted	£100	95·00
467		3s. mauve	£140	£200
		w. Wmk inverted	£180	£275

(b) Cowan thick, opaque, chalk-surfaced paper with white gum.

468	71	1d. rose-carmine (15.11.26)	1·00	20
		a. Imperf (pair)	£300	
		ab. Imperf three sides (horiz pair)	£400	£500
		b. Booklet pane of 6 with bars on selvedge (1928)	£150	
		c. Booklet pane of 6 with bars and adverts on selvedge (1928)	£130	
		dw. Wmk inverted	£120	60·00
		e. Perf 14×15 (3.27)	75	50
		ea. Booklet pane of 6 with bars and adverts on selvedge (1934)	£140	
		ew. Wmk inverted	£150	75·00
		ex. Wmk reversed	15·00	£350
469	72	2s. light blue (5.27)	75·00	30·00
470		3s. pale mauve (9.27)	£150	£200
468/470	Set of 3		£200	£200

(c) Wiggins Teape thin, hard, chalk-surfaced paper with white gum.

471	71	1d. rose-carmine (6.30)	50·00	13·00
		w. Wmk inverted	£250	£120

No. 468ex exists in a range of colours including scarlet and deep carmine to magenta but we have insufficient evidence to show that these were issued.

NEW ZEALAND

Following the reduction of the postage rate to ½d. on 1 June 1932 the firm of R. H. White & Co. Ltd. of Stratford returned a quantity of envelopes stamped with 1d. stamps (No. 468) to the New Plymouth post office who surcharged the stamps 'HALFPENNY' in purple using a handstamp. The covers were then returned to the firm for normal use. Similar local surcharges were applied diagonally to 1d. stamps stuck onto postcards or lettercards at Dunedin, Greymouth and Invercargill in blue or at Palmerston North in purple. With the exception of the Greymouth provisional, where 40 mint examples were acquired by a stamp dealer, these local surcharges are only found unused, no gum, or used.

Nos. 472/543 are vacant.

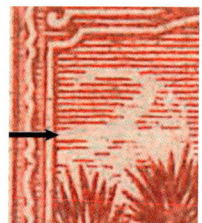

Cloud flaw (R. 2/1)

(Des J. Berry. Eng H. T. Peat. Recess Govt Printing Office, Wellington)

1933 (8 Nov). Health Stamp. W **43**. Perf 14.
553	**78**	1d.+1d. carmine	18·00	19·00
		a. Cloud flaw	85·00	85·00
		w. Wmk inverted	£325	£200

73 Nurse   **74** Smiling Boy

(Typo Govt Printing Office, Wellington)

1929–30. Anti-Tuberculosis Fund. T **73** and similar design. W **43**. Perf 14.
(a) Inscribed 'HELP STAMP OUT TUBERCULOSIS'.
544		1d.+1d. scarlet (11.12.29)	12·00	17·00
		w. Wmk inverted	£375	£275

(b) Inscribed 'HELP PROMOTE HEALTH'.
545		1d.+1d. scarlet (29.10.30)	22·00	40·00

HIGH VALUES. From 1931 postal requirements for higher values were met by the Arms 'Stamp Duty' adhesives (No. F145 etc.).

(Des L. C. Mitchell. Dies eng and plates made Royal Mint, London (1d.), Govt Ptg Office, Wellington from W. R. Bock die (2d.). Typo Govt Ptg Office, Wellington)

1931 (31 Oct). Health Stamps. W **43** (sideways). Perf 14½×14.
546	**74**	1d.+1d. scarlet	80·00	85·00
547		2d.+1d. blue	80·00	75·00

TRANS-TASMAN AIR MAIL "FAITH IN AUSTRALIA."
(79)   **80** Crusader

1934 (17 Jan). Air. T **75** in new colour optd with T **79**. W **43**. Perf 14×14½.
554	**75**	7d. light blue (B.)	35·00	45·00

(Des J. Berry. Recess D.L.R.)

1934 (25 Oct). Health Stamp. W **43** (sideways). Perf 14×13½.
555	**80**	1d.+1d. carmine	12·00	15·00

25 October 1934 was the first day of issue in Wellington. Most other offices put the stamp on sale a dew days later

75 New Zealand Lake Scenery   **FIVE PENCE** (76)

(Des L. C. Mitchell. Plates Royal Mint, London. Typo Govt Printing Office)

1931 (10 Nov)–**35**. Air. W **43**. Perf 14×14½.
548	**75**	3d. chocolate	20·00	13·00
		a. Perf 14×15 (4.35)	£130	£450
549		4d. blackish purple	20·00	20·00
550		7d. brown-orange	20·00	15·00
548/550	Set of 3		55·00	42·00

1931 (18 Dec). Air. Surch with T **76**. W **43**. Perf 14×14½.
551	**75**	5d. on 3d. green (R.)	12·00	12·00

81 Collared Grey Fantail   **82** Brown Kiwi   **83** Maori Woman

84 Maori Carved House   **85** Mount Cook   **86** Maori Girl

87 Mitre Peak   **88** Striped Marlin

77 Hygeia, Goddess of Health   **78** The Path to Health

(Des R. E. Tripe and W. J. Cooch. Eng H. T. Peat. Recess Govt Printing Office, Wellington)

1932 (18 Nov). Health Stamp. W **43**. Perf 14.
552	**77**	1d.+1d. carmine	26·00	26·00
		w. Wmk inverted	£450	£250
		x. Wmk reversed	†	£600

89 Harvesting   **90** Tuatara Lizard   **91** Maori Panel

NEW ZEALAND

92 Parson Bird   **93** Captain Cook at Poverty Bay

94 Mount Egmont

Die I (left) and Die II (right)

2s. 'CAPTAIN COQK' (R. 1/4)

(Des J. Fitzgerald (½d., 4d.), C. H. and R. J. G. Collins (1d.) M. Matthews (1½d.), H. W. Young (2d.), L. C. Mitchell (2½d., 3d., 8d., 1s., 3s.), W. J. Cooch and R. E. Tripe (5d.), T. I. Archer (6d.), I. F. Calder (9d.) and I. H. Jenkins (2s.). Litho Waterlow (9d.). Recess D.L.R. (remainder))

1935 (1 May)**–36**. W **43** (sideways on. 8d.*).

556	81	½d. bright green, Perf 14×13½	3·50	1·50
		w. Wmk inverted (12.35)	7·00	8·50
557	82	1d. scarlet (Die I), Perf 14×13½	3·50	1·50
		aw. Wmk inverted (2.36)	10·00	15·00
		b. Perf 13½×14 (1936)	85·00	65·00
		c. Die II. Perf 14×13½ (18.11.35)	14·00	3·75
		ca. Booklet pane of 6 with adverts on selvedge	65·00	
		cw. Wmk inverted	18·00	7·50
558	83	1½d. red-brown, Perf 14×13½	16·00	16·00
		a. Perf 13½×14 (11.35)	7·00	11·00
		ay. Wmk inverted and reversed (2.36)	22·00	35·00
559	84	2d. orange, Perf 14×13½	3·75	2·00
		w. Wmk inverted	£1500	£700
560	85	2½d. chocolate and slate, Perf 13–14×13½	14·00	35·00
		aw. Wmk inverted	40·00	95·00
		b. Perf 13½×14 (11.35)	12·00	24·00
		bx. Wmk reversed	†	£4500
561	86	3d. brown, Perf 14×13½	18·00	3·00
		w. Wmk inverted	£1200	£500
562	87	4d. black and sepia, Perf 14	5·50	3·00
		w. Wmk inverted	£1000	£600
563	88	5d. ultramarine, Perf 13–14×13½	25·00	30·00
		a. Double print, one albino	—	—
		bw. Wmk inverted	†	£1000
		c. Perf 13½×14	50·00	40·00
564	89	6d. scarlet, Perf 13½×14	12·00	8·00
		w. Wmk inverted	£950	£550
565	90	8d. chocolate, Perf 14×13½	13·00	15·00
		w. Wmk sideways inverted	£750	£500
566	91	9d. scarlet and black, Perf 14×14½	22·00	5·00
567	92	1s. deep green, Perf 14×13½	24·00	20·00
		w. Wmk inverted	—	£1200
568	93	2s. olive-green, Perf 13–14×13½	50·00	45·00
		a. 'CAPTAIN COQK'	£225	£160
		bw. Wmk inverted	£180	95·00
		c. Perf 13½×14 (1935)	65·00	60·00
		ca. 'CAPTAIN COQK'	£250	£170
569	94	3s. chocolate and yellow-brown, Perf 13–14×13½	25·00	55·00
		a. Perf 13½×14 (11.35)	25·00	60·00
		aw. Wmk inverted	†	£2500
		ay. Wmk inverted and reversed (1936)	£500	£500
556/569 Set of 14			£170	£190

* The normal sideways watermark on No. 565 shows the top of the star pointing to the right, *as seen from the back of the stamp*.
Some stamps from sheets perforated 14×13½ by De La Rue sometimes show the horizontal perforations nearer 13½.
In the 2½d., 5d., 2s. and 3s. perf 13–14×13½ the horizontal perforations of each stamp are in two sizes, one half of each horizontal side measuring 13 and the other 14.
See also Nos. 577/590 and 630/631.

95 Bell Block Aerodrome   **96** King George V and Queen Mary

(Des J. Berry. Eng Stamp Printing Office, Melbourne. Recess Govt Printing Office, Wellington)

1935 (4 May). Air. W **43**. Perf 14.

570	95	1d. carmine	1·00	70
		w. Wmk inverted	£200	£110
571		3d. violet	4·50	3·00
		w. Wmk inverted	£250	£120
572		6d. blue	7·50	3·00
		w. Wmk inverted	£300	£130
570/572 Set of 3			11·00	6·00

(Frame by J. Berry. Recess B.W.)

1935 (7 May). Silver Jubilee. W **43**. Perf 11×11½.

573	96	½d. green	75	50
574		1d. carmine	1·00	50
575		6d. red-orange	20·00	32·00
573/575 Set of 3			20·00	32·00

97 The Key to Health   **98** Multiple Wmk

(Des S. Hall. Recess John Ash, Melbourne)

1935 (30 Sept). Health Stamp. W **43**. Perf 11.

576	97	1d.+1d. scarlet	2·50	3·25

WATERMARKS. In W **43** the wmk units are in vertical columns widely spaced and the sheet margins are unwatermarked or wkmd 'NEW ZEALAND POSTAGE' in large letters. In W **98** the wmk units are arranged alternately in horizontal rows closely spaced and are continued into the sheet margins. Stamps with W **98** sideways show the top of the star pointing to the right, *as seen from the back of the stamp*. Sideways inverted varieties have the top of the star to left *as seen from the back of the stamp*.

2½d. Line across flower (R. 8/6)

(Litho Govt Ptg Office, Wellington (9d). Recess Waterlow or D.L.R. (others))

1936–42. W **98**.

577	81	½d. bright green, Perf 14×13½	2·50	10
		w. Wmk inverted	7·50	11·00
578	82	1d. scarlet (Die II), Perf 14×13½ (4.36)	3·00	10
		w. Wmk inverted	12·00	10·00
579	83	1½d. red-brown, Perf 14×13½ (6.36)	18·00	7·50
580	84	2d. orange, Perf 14×13½ (3.36)	50	10
		aw. Wmk inverted	£750	£500
		b. Perf 12½† (6.41)	5·00	20

NEW ZEALAND

		bw. Wmk inverted	†	
		c. Perf 14 (6.41)	30·00	1·50
		d. Perf 14×15 (6.41)	35·00	26·00
581	85	2½d. chocolate and slate, Perf 13–14×13½	10·00	26·00
		aw. Wmk inverted	90·00	£225
		b. Perf 14 (11.36)	5·00	1·50
		bw. Wmk inverted	65·00	£120
		c. Perf 14×13½ (11.42)	1·50	6·00
		ca. Line across flower	£100	
		cw. Wmk inverted	†	£4500
582	86	3d. brown, Perf 14×13½	40·00	1·50
		w. Wmk inverted	£100	90·00
583	87	4d. black and sepia, Perf 14×13½	7·50	1·00
		aw. Wmk inverted	30·00	45·00
		b. Perf 12½* (8.41)	40·00	20·00
		bw. Wmk inverted	†	—
		c. Perf 14, line (11.41)	£100	£130
		d. Perf 14×14½ comb (7.42)	2·00	20
		dw. Wmk inverted	£900	£400
584	88	5d. ultramarine, Perf 13–14×13½ (8.36)	25·00	3·50
		aw. Wmk inverted	95·00	80·00
		b. Perf 12½*† (7.41)	25·00	10·00
		c. Perf 14×13½ (11.42)	3·00	2·25
		ca. Double print, one albino	£950	
		cw. Wmk inverted	£750	£500
585	89	6d. scarlet, Perf 13½×14 (8.36)	20·00	1·00
		aw. Wmk inverted	£100	£120
		b. Perf 12½* (10.41)	3·50	4·00
		c. Perf 14½×14 (6.42)	2·00	20
		cw. Wmk inverted	£1000	£1000
586	90	8d. chocolate, Perf 14×13½ (wmk sideways)	15·00	4·00
		aw. Wmk sideways inverted	60·00	£180
		b. Wmk upright (7.39)	4·50	5·00
		bw. Wmk inverted	†	
		c. Perf 12½* (wmk sideways) (7.41)	4·50	1·25
		d. Perf 14×14½ (wmk sideways) (7.42)	3·75	1·25
		dw. Wmk sideways inverted	—	£500
587	91	9d. red and grey, Perf 14×15 (wmk sideways)	60·00	4·50
		ay. Wmk sideways inverted and reversed	—	£1500
		b. Wmk upright. Red and grey-black, Perf 14×14½ (1.3.38)	70·00	6·50
		bw. Wmk inverted	£225	£180
588	92	1s. deep green, Perf 14×13½	4·00	1·00
		aw. Wmk inverted	£120	£350
		b. Perf 12½* (11.41)	80·00	25·00
589	93	2s. olive-green, Perf 13–14×13½ (8.36)	55·00	11·00
		a. 'CAPTAIN COQK'	£110	42·00
		bw. Wmk inverted	£1000	£750
		c. Perf 13½×14 (3.39)	£400	4·00
		ca. 'CAPTAIN COQK'	£450	65·00
		d. Perf 12½*† (7.41)	20·00	7·50
		da. 'CAPTAIN COQK'	80·00	38·00
		e. Perf 14×13½ (9.42)	6·50	1·50
		ea. 'CAPTAIN COQK'	£200	£100
		ew. Wmk inverted	—	£1300
590	94	3s. chocolate and yellow-brown, Perf 13–14×13½	50·00	11·00
		aw. Wmk inverted	£200	£150
		b. Perf 12½* (1941)	85·00	50·00
		c. Perf 14×13½ (9.42)	10·00	2·75
577/590c		Set of 14	£130	21·00

*† Stamps indicated with an asterisk were printed and perforated by Waterlow; those having a dagger were printed by D.L.R. and perforated by Waterlow. No. 580d was printed by D.L.R. and perforated by Harrison and No. 583c was printed by Waterlow and perforated by D.L.R. These are all known as 'Blitz perfs' because De La Rue were unable to maintain supplies after their works were damaged by enemy action. All the rest, except the 9d., were printed and perforated by D.L.R.

On stamps printed and perforated by De La Rue the perf 14×13½ varies in the sheet and is sometimes nearer 13½. 2d. perf 14×15 is sometimes nearer 14×14½.

2½d., 5d., 2s. and 3s. In perf 13–14×13½ one half the length of each horizontal perforation measures 13 and the other 14. In perf 14×13½ the horizontal perforation is regular.

4d. No. 583c. is line-perf measuring 14 exactly and has a blackish sepia frame. No. 583d is a comb-perf measuring 14×14.3 or 14×14.2 and the frame is a warmer shade.

2s. No. 589c is comb-perf and measures 13.5×13.75.

For 9d. typographed, see Nos. 630/631.

Counter Coil Pairs. To facilitate the dispensing of stamps to customers by post office clerks, rolls of stamps were created from normal sheets. The rolls were prepared in either horizontal or vertical format and between each row or column of stamps a section of sheet margin was left, on to which numbers were applied as a aid to accounting. The numbers were initially handstamped in either purple or red, but subsequently they were machine-printed in black (after 1960 in red).

The first rolls were introduced in 1945 using 2d., 5d., 6d., 8d. and 1s. values from the 1936–1942 Pictorial series on Multiple NZ and Star watermarked paper, as well as the current 1d. and 3d. King George VI definitives. Subsequently, other values in the King George VI 'Head' series were also provided in this form.

From Nos. 577/590c the following stamps were used to make up counter coils: Nos. 580, 584c, 585c, 586d and 588.

99 NZ Soldier at Anzac Cove   **100** Wool

101 Butter   **102** Sheep

103 Apples   **104** Exports

(Des L. C. Mitchell. Recess John Ash, Melbourne)

1936 (27 Apr). Charity. 21st Anniversary of Anzac Landing at Gallipoli. W **43**. Perf 11.

591	**99**	½d.+½d. green	75	1·40
592		1d.+1d. scarlet	1·00	1·10

(Des L. C. Mitchell. Recess John Ash, Melbourne)

1936 (1 Oct). Congress of British Empire Chambers of Commerce, Wellington. Industries Issue. Types **100/104**. W **43** (sideways). Perf 11½.

593	**100**	½d. emerald-green	30	30
594	**101**	1d. scarlet	30	20
595	**102**	2½d. blue	1·50	5·00
596	**103**	4d. violet	1·25	4·00
597	**104**	6d. red-brown	4·00	5·00
593/597		Set of 5	6·50	13·00

105 Otaki Health Camp   **106** King George VI and Queen Elizabeth

(Des J. Berry. Recess John Ash, Melbourne)

1936 (2 Nov). Health Stamp. W **43** (sideways). Perf 11.

598	**105**	1d.+1d. scarlet	2·75	3·00

NEW ZEALAND

(Recess B.W.)

1937 (13 May). Coronation. W **98**. Perf 14×13½.

599	**106**	1d. carmine	30	10
600		2½d. Prussian blue	60	1·50
601		6d. red-orange	80	1·50
599/601 Set of 3			1·50	2·75

107 Rock climbing **108** King George VI **108a**

(Des G. Bull and J. Berry. Recess John Ash, Melbourne)

1937 (1 Oct). Health Stamp. W **43**. Perf 11.

602	**107**	1d.+1d. scarlet	3·75	3·50

Broken ribbon flaw (R. 6/6 of Pl 8)

(Des W. J. Cooch. Recess B.W.)

1938–44. W **98**. Perf 14×13½.

603	**108**	½d. green (1.3.38)	5·00	10
		w. Wmk inverted (from booklets)	30·00	7·00
604		½d. orange-brown (10.7.41)	20	40
		w. Wmk inverted		
605		1d. scarlet (1.7.38)	5·00	10
		a. Broken ribbon	£120	
		w. Wmk inverted (from booklets)	24·00	4·75
606		1d. green (21.7.41)	20	10
		w. Wmk inverted	£110	75·00
607	**108a**	1½d. purple-brown (26.7.38)	20·00	3·25
		w. Wmk inverted (from booklets)	45·00	13·00
608		1½d. scarlet (1.2.44)	20	80
		w. Wmk inverted	—	£225
609		3d. blue (26.9.41)	20	10
		w. Wmk inverted	—	£275
603/609 Set of 7			32·00	4·00

Counter Coil Pairs. Nos. 606 and 609 were used to make up counter coils, both in horizontal format. No. 606 is only known with handstamped numbers, while No. 609 exists with either handstamped or machine-printed numbers.

For other values see Nos. 680/689.

109 Children Playing **110** Beach Ball

(Des J. Berry. Recess B.W.)

1938 (1 Oct). Health Stamp. W **98**. Perf 14×13½.

610	**109**	1d.+1d. scarlet	4·50	2·75

(Des S. Hall. Recess Note Printing Branch, Commonwealth Bank of Australia, Melbourne)

1939 (16 Oct). Health Stamps. Surcharged with new value. W **43**. Perf 11.

611	**110**	1d. on ½d.+½d. green	4·50	5·00
612		2d. on 1d.+1d. scarlet	5·00	5·00

111 Arrival of the Maoris, 1350 **112** *Endeavour*, Chart of NZ and Captain Cook

113 British Monarchs **114** Tasman with his Ship and Chart

115 Signing Treaty of Waitangi, 1840 **116** Landing of Immigrants, 1840

117 Road, Rail, Sea and Air Transport **118** HMS *Britomart* at Akaroa, 1840

119 *Dunedin* and Frozen Mutton Route to London **120** Maori Council

121 Gold Mining in 1861 and 1940 **122** Giant Kauri Tree

(Des L. C. Mitchell (½d., 3d., 4d.); J. Berry (others). Recess B.W.)

1940 (2 Jan–8 Mar). Centenary of Proclamation of British Sovereignty. Types **111/122**. W **98**. Perf 14×13½ (2½d.), 13½×14 (5d.) or 13½ (others).

613	**111**	½d. blue-green	60	10
614	**112**	1d. chocolate and scarlet	3·00	10
615	**113**	1½d. light blue and mauve	30	10
616	**114**	2d. blue-green and chocolate	1·50	10
617	**115**	2½d. blue-green and blue	1·50	60
618	**116**	3d. purple and carmine	4·00	75
619	**117**	4d. chocolate and lake	8·00	1·50
620	**118**	5d. pale blue and brown	7·00	3·00
621	**119**	6d. emerald-green and violet	9·50	1·00
622	**120**	7d. black and red	5·00	4·25
623		8d. black and red (8.3)	9·00	4·00
624	**121**	9d. olive-green and orange	15·00	3·50
625	**122**	1s. sage-green and deep green	20·00	3·00
613/625 Set of 13			75·00	20·00

1940 (1 Oct). Health Stamps. As T **110**, but without extra surcharge. W **43**. Perf 11.

626	**110**	1d.+½d. blue-green	9·00	9·00
627		2d.+1d. brown-orange	9·00	9·00

19

NEW ZEALAND

1ᴰ   1ᴰ   2ᴰ

■   ■   ■ 1941
(123)   (123a)   (124)

1941. Nos. 603 and 607 surch as Types **123/123a**.
628	**108**	1d. on ½d. green (1.5.41)............	1·25	10
629	**108a**	2d. on 1½d. purple-brown (4.41)......	1·25	10
		a. Inserted '2'............	£650	£450

The variety 'Inserted 2' occurs on the tenth stamp, tenth row. It is identified by the presence of remnants of the damaged '2', and by the spacing of '2' and 'D' which is variable and different from the normal.

(Typo Govt Printing Office, Wellington)

1941. As T **91**, but smaller (17½×20½ mm). Chalk-surfaced paper. Perf 14×15.

(a) W **43**.
630	**91**	9d. scarlet and black (5.41)............	£125	35·00
		w. Wmk Inverted............	†	£750

(b) W **98**.
631	**91**	9d. scarlet and black (29.9.41)......	3·00	5·00
		w. Wmk inverted............	£750	£650

1941 (4 Oct). Health Stamps. Nos. 626/627 optd with T **124**.
632	**110**	1d.+½d. blue-green............	90	1·75
633		2d.+1d. brown-orange............	90	1·75

129 Queen Elizabeth II as Princess and Princess Margaret   **130** Statue of Peter Pan, Kensington Gardens

(Recess B.W.)

1944 (9 Oct). Health Stamps. W **98**. Perf 13½.
663	**129**	1d.+½d. green............	30	40
664		2d.+1d. blue............	30	30

(Des J. Berry. Recess B.W.)

1945 (1 Oct). Health Stamps. W **98**. Perf 13½.
665	**130**	1d.+½d. green and buff............	15	20
		w. Wmk inverted............	£110	£140
666		2d.+1d. carmine and buff............	15	20
		w. Wmk inverted............	£350	£225

125 Boy and Girl on Swing   **126** Princess Margaret

131 Lake Matheson   **132** King George VI and Parliament House, Wellington

127 Queen Elizabeth II as Princess

(Des S. Hall. Recess Note Printing Branch, Commonwealth Bank of Australia, Melbourne)

1942 (1 Oct). Health Stamps. W **43**. Perf 11.
634	**125**	1d.+½d. blue-green............	30	90
635		2d.+1d. orange-red............	30	90

(Des J. Berry. Recess B.W.)

1943 (1 Oct). Health Stamps. Types **126/127**. W **98**. Perf 12.
636	**126**	1d.+½d. green............	30	1·25
		a. Imperf between (vert pair)......	£15000	
637	**127**	2d.+1d. red-brown............	30	25
		a. Imperf between (vert pair)......	£18000	£18000

The watermark is at an angle in relation to the design on single stamps.

133 St Paul's Cathedral   **134** The Royal Family

135 RNZAF Badge and Aircraft   **136** Army Badge, Tank and Plough

✠ **TENPENCE** ✠
(128)

1944 (1 May). No. 615 surch with T **128**.
662		10d. on 1½d. light blue and mauve......	15	30

137 Navy Badge, HMNZS *Achilles* (cruiser) and *Dominion Monarch* (liner)   **138** NZ Coat of Arms, Foundry and Farm

NEW ZEALAND

139 St George (Wellington College War Memorial Window)

140 Southern Alps and Franz Joseph Glacier

(Des J. Berry. Photo Harrison (1½d. and 1s.). Recess B.W. (1d. and 2d.) and Waterlow (others))

1946 (1 Apr). Peace issue. Types **131/141**. W **98** (sideways on 1½d.). Perf 13 (1d., 2d.), 14×14½ (1½d., 1s.), 13½ (others).

667	**131**	½d. green and brown	20	65
		a. Printer's guide mark	25·00	38·00
		w. Wmk inverted	£150	£100
668	**132**	1d. green	10	10
		w. Wmk inverted	£110	75·00
669	**133**	1½d. scarlet	10	35
		w. Wmk sideways inverted	10	35
670	**134**	2d. purple	15	10
671	**135**	3d. ultramarine and grey	45	15
		a. Completed rudder	20·00	22·00
		b. Ultramarine omitted	£17000	
672	**136**	4d. bronze-green and orange	50	35
		w. Wmk inverted	£225	£110
673	**137**	5d. green and ultramarine	1·25	1·75
		a. Trailing aerial	40·00	50·00
674	**138**	6d. chocolate and vermilion	20	30
675	**139**	8d. black and carmine	20	30
676	**140**	9d. blue and black	20	30
		a. Guide mark	35·00	42·00
677	**141**	1s. grey-black	1·00	40
667/677 *Set* of 11			3·50	4·00

Only one example of No. 671b is known. It was caused by a paper fold.

141 National Memorial Campanile

½d. Printer's guide mark (R. 12/3)

3d. Completed rudder (R. 3/2 of Pl 42796 and R. 2/4 of Pl 42883, the latter also showing retouching in the sky around the wing tip at left, as illustrated)

142 Soldier Helping Child over Stile

2d.+1d. Feathers in hat (R. 8/8 of Pl 43010)

(Des J. Berry. Recess Waterlow)

1946 (24 Oct). Health Stamps. W **98**. Perf 13½.

678	**142**	1d.+½d. green and orange-brown	15	15
		a. Yellow-green and orange-brown	6·00	12·00
		w. Wmk inverted	80·00	85·00
679		2d.+1d. chocolate and orange-brown	15	15
		a. Feathers in hat	35·00	35·00

5d. Trailing aerial (R. 8/1 of Pl 42794)

 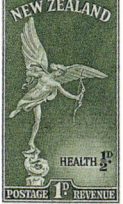

144 King George VI

145 Statue of Eros

9d. Guide mark (R. 3/3 of Pl 42723)

Plate 1

Plate 2

NEW ZEALAND

(Des W. J. Cooch. Recess T **108a**, B.W.; T **144**, D.L.R.)

1947 (1 May)–**52**. W **98** (sideways on shilling values).

(a) Perf 14×13½.

680	**108a**	2d. orange	30	10
		w. Wmk inverted	£250	£350
681		4d. bright purple	80	1·00
682		5d. slate	1·00	1·00
683		6d. carmine	1·00	10
		w. Wmk inverted	£325	£225
684		8d. violet	1·25	1·25
685		9d. purple-brown	2·00	60
		w. Wmk inverted	£110	95·00

(b) Perf 14.

686	**144**	1s. red-brown and carmine (Plate 1)	2·00	1·50
		aw. Wmk sideways inverted	28·00	48·00
		b. Wmk upright (Plate 1)	60	80
		c. Wmk upright (Plate 2) (1950)	2·25	1·25
		cw. Wmk inverted	£180	£100
687		1s.3d. red-brown and blue (Plate 2)	2·75	1·25
		aw. Wmk sideways inverted	22·00	48·00
		b. Wmk upright (14.1.52)	2·25	4·50
		bw. Wmk inverted	†	—
688		2s. brown-orange and green (Plate 1)	9·00	2·50
		aw. Wmk sideways inverted	38·00	95·00
		b. Wmk upright (Plate 1)	11·00	18·00
689		3s. red-brown and grey (Plate 2)	5·00	3·50
		w. Wmk sideways inverted	60·00	55·00
680/689 *Set of 10*			20·00	11·00

In head-plate 2 the diagonal lines of the background have been strengthened and result in the upper corners and sides appearing more deeply shaded.

For details of the sideways watermarks, see above No. 577.

Counter Coil Pairs. All values to the 1s.3d. were made up into counter coils; the 2d. to 9d. in horizontal coils and the 1s. (Nos. 686 and 686b) and 1s.3d. in vertical coils. The 2d. and 6d. exist with either handstamped or machine-printed numbers, the 8d. to 1s.3d. with machine-printed numbers only.

(Des J. Berry. Recess Waterlow)

1947 (1 Oct). Health Stamps. W **98** (sideways). Perf 13½.

690	**145**	1d.+½d. green	15	15
		w. Wmk sideways inverted	£120	£120
691		2d.+1d. carmine	15	15
		w. Wmk sideways inverted	£150	£180

150 Boy Sunbathing and Children Playing

151 Nurse and Child

(Des E. Linzell. Recess B.W.)

1948 (1 Oct). Health Stamps. W **98**. Perf 13½.

696	**150**	1d.+½d. blue and green	15	20
		w. Wmk inverted	£130	£100
697		2d.+1d. purple and scarlet	15	20

1949 ROYAL VISIT ISSUE. Four stamps were prepared to commemorate this event: 2d. Treaty House, Waitangi; 3d. HMS *Vanguard*; 5d. Royal portraits; 6d. Crown and sceptre. The visit did not take place and the stamps were destroyed, although a few examples of the 3d. later appeared on the market. A similar set was prepared in 1952, but was, likewise, not issued.

(Des J. Berry. Photo Harrison)

1949 (3 Oct). Health Stamps. W **98**. Perf 14×14½.

698	**151**	1d.+½d. green	25	20
699		2d.+1d. ultramarine	25	20
		a. No stop below 'D' of '1D.' (R. 1/2)	10·00	21·00

146 Port Chalmers, 1848

147 Cromwell, Otago

1½d.

POSTAGE

(152)

153 Queen Elizabeth II as Princess and Prince Charles

1950 (28 July). As T **F6**, but without value, surch with T **152**. Chalk-surfaced paper. W **98** (inverted). Perf 14.

700	F6	1½d. carmine	40	30
		w. Wmk upright	7·50	8·50

(Des J. Berry and R. S. Phillips. Photo Harrison)

1950 (2 Oct). Health Stamps. W **98**. Perf 14×14½.

701	**153**	1d.+½d. green	25	20
		w. Wmk inverted	9·00	13·00
702		2d.+1d. plum	25	20
		w. Wmk inverted	£110	£110

148 First Church, Dunedin

149 University of Otago

(Des J. Berry. Recess B.W.)

1948 (23 Feb). Centennial of Otago. Types **146/149**. W **98** (sideways inverted on 3d.). Perf 13½.

692	**146**	1d. blue and green	25	35
		w. Wmk inverted	£100	£100
693	**147**	2d. green and brown	25	35
694	**148**	3d. purple	30	60
695	**149**	6d. black and rose	30	60
		w. Wmk inverted	—	£450
692/695 *Set of 4*			1·00	1·75

154 Christchurch Cathedral

155 Cairn on Lyttelton Hills

NEW ZEALAND

156 John Robert Godley **157** Canterbury University College

158 Aerial View of Timaru

(Des L. C. Mitchell (2d.), J. A. Johnstone (3d.) and J. Berry (others). Recess B.W.)

1950 (20 Nov). Centennial of Canterbury, NZ Types **154/158**. W **98** (sideways inverted on 1d. and 3d.). Perf 13½.

703	154	1d. green and blue	40	85
704	155	2d. carmine and orange	40	1·00
705	156	3d. dark blue and blue	45	1·25
706	157	6d. brown and blue	50	1·00
707	158	1s. reddish purple and blue	50	1·60
703/707 Set of 5			2·00	5·00

159 Takapuna Class Yachts

(Des J. Berry and R. S. Phillips. Recess B.W.)

1951 (1 Nov). Health Stamps. W **98**. Perf 13½.

708	159	1½d.+½d. scarlet and yellow	50	1·00
709		2d.+1d. deep green and yellow	50	25
		w. Wmk inverted	£110	£120

160 Princess Anne **161** Prince Charles **(162)**

(From photographs by Marcus Adams. Photo Harrison)

1952 (1 Oct). Health Stamps. W **98**. Perf 14×14½.

710	160	1½d.+½d. carmine-red	15	30
711	161	2d.+1d. brown	15	20

1952–53. Nos. 604 and 606 surch as T **162**.

712	108	1d. on ½d. brown-orange (11.9.53)	60	70
		a. 'D' omitted	†	£5000
713		3d. on 1d. green (12.12.52)	10	10

163 Buckingham Palace **164** Queen Elizabeth II

165 Coronation State Coach **166** Westminster Abbey

167 St Edward's Crown and Royal Sceptre

(Des L. C. Mitchell (1s.6d.), J. Berry (others). Recess D.L.R. (2d., 4d.), Waterlow (1s.6d.) Photo Harrison (3d., 8d.))

1953 (25 May). Coronation. Types **163/167**. W **98**. Perf 13 (2d., 4d.), 13½ (1s.6d.) or 14×14½ (3d., 8d.).

714	163	2d. deep bright blue	40	30
715	164	3d. brown	50	10
716	165	4d. carmine	1·75	2·00
717	166	8d. slate-grey	1·50	1·25
718	167	1s.6d. purple and ultramarine	3·00	2·75
714/718 Set of 5			6·50	5·75

168 Girl Guides **169** Boy Scouts

(Des J. Berry. Photo Harrison)

1953 (7 Oct). Health Stamps. W **98**. Perf 14×14½.

719	168	1½d.+½d. blue	15	10
720	169	2d.+1d. deep yellow-green	15	40
		a. Imperf 3 sides (block of 4)	£3500	

No. 720a shows the left-hand vertical pair imperforate at right and the right-hand pair imperforate at left, top and bottom.

170 Queen Elizabeth II **171** Queen Elizabeth II and Duke of Edinburgh

(Des L. C. Mitchell. Recess Waterlow)

1953 (9 Dec). Royal Visit. W **98**. Perf 13×14 (3d.) or 13½ (4d.).

721	170	3d. dull purple	15	10
		w. Wmk inverted	—	£225
722	171	4d. deep ultramarine	15	60

172 **173** Queen Elizabeth II **174**

NEW ZEALAND

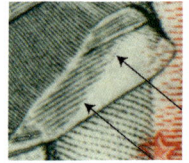 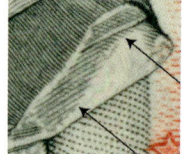

Die I   Die II

(Des L. C. Mitchell (Types **172**/**173**), J. Berry (T **174**). Recess D.L.R. (T **173**), B.W. (others))

1953 (15 Dec)–**59**. W **98**. Perf 14×13½ (T **172**), 14 (T **173**) or 13½ (T **174**).

723	**172**	½d. slate-black (1.3.54)	15	30
724		1d. orange (1.3.54)	15	10
		w. Wmk inverted	50	2·25
725		1½d. brown-lake	20	10
		w. Wmk inverted	†	£600
726		2d. bluish green (1.3.54)	20	10
		w. Wmk inverted	†	£600
727		3d. vermilion (1.3.54)	20	10
		w. Wmk inverted (from booklets)	50	2·50
728		4d. blue (1.3.54)	40	50
		w. Wmk inverted	†	£750
729		6d. purple (1.3.54)	70	2·00
		w. Wmk inverted	£550	£350
730		8d. carmine (1.3.54)	60	60
		w. Wmk inverted	£950	£700
731	**173**	9d. brown and bright green (1.3.54)	60	60
		w. Wmk inverted	£550	£375
732		1s. black and carmine-red (Die I) (1.3.54)	65	10
		aw. Wmk inverted	£550	£425
		b. Die II (1958)	£225	20·00
733		1s.6d. black and bright blue (1.3.54)	2·00	60
		aw. Wmk inverted	£475	£375
733b		1s.9d. black and red-orange (1.7.57)	5·50	1·50
		bw. Wmk inverted	£750	£450
		c. White opaque paper (2.2.59)	3·75	1·50
733d	**174**	2s.6d. brown (1.7.57)	15·00	3·25
734		3s. bluish green (1.3.54)	15·00	75
		w. Wmk inverted	£800	£500
735		5s. carmine (1.3.54)	32·00	3·50
736		10s. deep ultramarine (1.3.54)	65·00	20·00
723/736 Set of 16			£120	30·00

1s. Dies I and II. The two dies of the Queen's portrait differ in the shading on the sleeve at right. The long lines running upwards from left to right are strong in Die I and weaker in Die II. In the upper part of the shading the fine cross-hatching is visible in Die I only between the middle two of the four long lines, but in Die II it extends clearly across all four lines.

In the lower part of the shading the strength of the long lines in Die I makes the cross-hatching appear subdued, whereas in Die II the weaker long lines make the cross-hatching more prominent.

Centre plates 1A, 1B and 2B are Die I; 3A and 3B are Die II.

For stamps as T **172** but with larger figures of value see Nos. 745/751.

Counter Coil Pairs. All values from 2d. to 1s.9d. were made up into counter coils, the 9d., 1s. and 1s.6d. in either vertical or horizontal coils, the 1s.9d. in vertical coils only and the lower values in horizontal coils. All coil numbers were machine-printed in black.

> WHITE OPAQUE PAPER. A new white opaque paper first came into use in August 1958. It is slightly thicker than the paper previously used, but obviously different in colour (white, against cream) and opacity (the previous paper being relatively transparent).

175 Young Climber and Mount Aspiring and Mount Everest

(Des J. Berry. Recess; vignette litho B.W.)

1954 (4 Oct). Health Stamps. W **98**. Perf 13½.

737	**175**	1½d.+½d. sepia and deep violet	15	30
738		2d.+1d. sepia and blue-black	15	30

176 Maori Mail Carrier   **177** Queen Elizabeth II

178 Douglas DC-3 Airliner

(Des R. M. Conly (2d.), J. Berry (3d.), A. G. Mitchell (4d.). Recess D.L.R.)

1955 (18 July). Centenary of First New Zealand Postage Stamps. W **98**. Perf 14 (2d.) 14×14½ (3d.) or 13 (4d.).

739	**176**	2d. sepia and deep green	10	10
		w. Wmk inverted	—	£325
740	**177**	3d. brown-red	10	10
741	**178**	4d. black and bright blue	70	1·00
739/741 Set of 3			80	1·00

179 Children's Health Camps Federation Emblem   **180**

(Des E. M. Taylor. Recess B.W.)

1955 (3 Oct). Health Stamps. W **98** (sideways). Perf 13½×13.

742	**179**	1½d.+½d. sepia and orange-brown	10	60
743		2d.+1d. red-brown and green	10	35
744		3d.+1d. sepia and deep rose-red	15	15
		a. Centre omitted	£15000	
742/744 Set of 3			30	1·00

Only one example of No. 744a is known. It was caused by a paper fold.

1955–59. As Nos. 724/730 but larger figures of value with stars omitted from lower right corner and new colour (8d.).

745	**180**	1d. orange (12.7.56)	50	10
		aw. Wmk inverted	1·75	3·50
		b. White opaque paper (2.6.59)	50	75
		bw. Wmk inverted	1·75	4·25
746		1½d. brown-lake (1.12.55)	60	60
747		2d. bluish green (19.3.56)	40	10
		a. White opaque paper (10.11.59)	40	10
748		3d. vermilion (1.5.56)	50	50
		aw. Wmk inverted	1·50	2·50
		b. White opaque paper (20.6.59)	30	10
		bw. Wmk inverted	2·00	5·00
749		4d. blue (3.2.58)	1·00	80
		a. White opaque paper (9.9.59)	1·00	2·50
750		6d. purple (20.10.55)	5·00	20
751		8d. chestnut (*white opaque paper*) (1.12.59)	2·75	4·25
745/751 Set of 7			9·50	5·50

See note re white opaque paper after No. 736.

Counter Coil Pairs. All values from 2d. to 8d. were made up into horizontal counter coils with numbers machine-printed in black.

181 'The Whalers of Foveaux Strait'   **182** Farming

NEW ZEALAND

183 Takahe

(Des E. R. Leeming (2d.), L. C. Mitchell (3d.), M. R. Smith (8d.). Recess D.L.R.)

1956 (16 Jan). Southland Centennial. Types **181**/**183**. W **98**. Perf 13½×13 (8d.) or 13×12½ (others).
752	**181**	2d. deep blue-green	30	15
753	**182**	3d. sepia	10	10
		w. Wmk inverted	—	£300
754	**183**	8d. slate-violet and rose-red	1·25	1·50
752/754 Set of 3			1·50	1·50

184 Children Picking Apples

(Des L. C. Mitchell, after photo by J. F. Louden. Recess B.W.)

1956 (24 Sept). Health Stamps. W **98**. Perf 13×13½.
755	**184**	1½d.+½d. purple-brown	15	70
		a. Blackish brown	2·00	7·00
756		2d.+1d. blue-green	15	55
757		3d.+1d. claret	15	15
755/757 Set of 3			40	1·25

185 New Zealand Lamb and Map   **186** Lamb, *Dunedin* and *Port Brisbane* (refrigerated freighter)

(Des M. Goaman. Photo Harrison)

1957 (15 Feb). 75th Anniversary of First Export of New Zealand Lamb. W **98** (sideways inverted on 4d.). Perf 14×14½ (4d.) or 14½×14 (8d.).
758	**185**	4d. blue	75	1·00
		w. Wmk sideways	15·00	22·00
759	**186**	8d. deep orange-red	1·00	1·00

187 Sir Truby King

(Des M. R. Smith. Recess B.W.)

1957 (14 May). 50th Anniversary of Plunket Society. W **98**. Perf 13.
760	**187**	3d. bright carmine-red	10	10
		w. Wmk inverted		£180

188 Lifesavers in Action   **189** Children on Seashore

(Des L. Cutten (2d.), L. C. Mitchell (3d.). Recess Waterlow)

1957 (25 Sept). Health Stamps. W **98** (sideways). Perf 13½.
761	**188**	2d.+1d. black and emerald	15	70
762	**189**	3d.+1d. ultramarine and rose-red	15	10
MS762b Two sheets each 112×96 mm with Nos. 761 and 762 in blocks of 6 (2×3)		*Per pair*	5·00	23·00
MS762c As last but with wmk upright		*Per pair*	7·00	48·00

2d

(190)

1958 (6 Jan–Mar). No. 746 surch as T **190**.
763	**180**	2d. on 1½d. brown-lake	70	10
		a. Smaller dot in surch	15	10
		b. Error. Surch on No. 725 (3.58)	£130	£170

Diameter of dot on No. 763 is 4¼ mm; on No. 763a 3¾ mm.
Forgeries of No. 763b are known.
Almost all examples of No. 763b have the 4¼ mm dot, but examples with the smaller dot are known.

191 Girls' Life Brigade Cadet   **192** Boys' Brigade Bugler

(Des J. Berry. Photo Harrison)

1958 (20 Aug). Health Stamps. W **98**. Perf 14×14½.
764	**191**	2d.+1d. green	20	40
765	**192**	3d.+1d. blue	20	40
MS765a Two sheets each 104×124 mm with Nos. 764/765 in blocks of 6 (3×2)		*Per pair*	7·00	20·00

193 Sir Charles Kingsford-Smith and Fokker F.VIIa/3m Southern Cross   **194** Seal of Nelson

(Des J. E. Lyle. Eng F. D. Manley. Recess Commonwealth Bank of Australia Note Ptg Branch)

1958 (27 Aug). 30th Anniversary of First Air Crossing of the Tasman Sea. W **98** (sideways). Perf 14×14½.
766	**193**	6d. deep ultramarine	50	75

(Des M. J. Macdonald. Recess B.W.)

1958 (29 Sept). Centenary of City of Nelson. W **98**. Perf 13½×13.
767	**194**	3d. carmine	10	10

195 Pania Statue, Napier   **196** Australian Gannets on Cape Kidnappers

NEW ZEALAND

(Des M. R. Smith (2d.), J. Berry (3d.), L. C. Mitchell (8d.). Photo Harrison)

1958 (3 Nov). Centenary of Hawke's Bay Province. Types **195/196** and similar design. W **98** (sideways inverted on 3d.). Perf 14½×14 (3d.) or 13½×14½ (others).

768	195	2d. yellow-green	10	10
769	196	3d. blue	30	10
770	-	8d. red-brown	70	1·00
768/770 Set of 3			1·00	1·00

Design: Vert—8d. Maori Sheep Shearer.

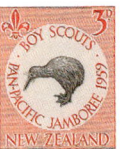
197 'Kiwi' Jamboree Badge

198 Careening HMS *Endeavour* at Ship Cove

(Des Mrs S. M. Collins. Recess B.W.)

1959 (5 Jan). Pan-Pacific Scout Jamboree, Auckland. W **98**. Perf 13½×13.

771	**197**	3d. sepia and carmine	30	10

(Des G. R. Bull and G. R. Smith. Photo Harrison)

1959 (2 Mar). Centenary of Marlborough Province. T **198** and similar horiz designs. W **98** (sideways). Perf 14½×14.

772	**198**	2d. green	30	10
773	-	3d. deep blue	30	10
774	-	8d. light brown	1·10	1·00
772/774 Set of 3			1·40	1·00

Designs: 3d. Shipping wool, Wairau Bar, 1857; 8d. Salt industry, Grassmere.

201 Red Cross Flag

(Photo Harrison)

1959 (3 June). Red Cross Commemoration. W **98** (sideways). Perf 14½×14.

775	**201**	3d.+1d. red and ultramarine	20	10
		a. Red Cross omitted	£3750	

202 Grey Teal

203 New Zealand Stilt

(Des Display Section, GPO. Photo Harrison)

1959 (16 Sept). Health Stamps. W **98** (sideways). Perf 14×14½.

776	**202**	2d.+1d. greenish yellow, olive and rose-red	50	65
777	**203**	3d.+1d. black, pink and light blue	50	65
		a. Pink omitted	£180	£120
		bw. Wmk sideways inverted	20·00	32·00
MS777c Two sheets, each 95×109 mm with Nos. 776/777 in blocks of 6 (3×2) .... *Per Pair*			8·00	24·00

204 'The Explorer'

205 'The Gold Digger'

206 'The Pioneer Woman'

(Des G. R. Bull and G. R. Smith. Photo Harrison)

1960 (16 May). Centenary of Westland Province. Types **204/206**. W **98**. Perf 14×14½.

778	**204**	2d. deep dull green	15	10
779	**205**	3d. orange-red	25	10
780	**206**	8d. grey-black	70	1·50
778/780 Set of 3			1·00	1·50

207 Manuka (Tea Tree)

208 Karaka

209 Kowhai Ngutu-kaka (Kaka-Beak)

209a Titoki

210 Kowhai

211 Puarangi (Hibiscus)

211a Matua Tikumu (Mountain Daisy)

212 Pikiarero

212a Koromiko

213 Rata

214 National Flag

215 Timber Industry

216 Rainbow Trout

217 Tiki

218 Aerial Top Dressing

218a Aerial Top Dressing

219 Taniwha (Maori Rock Drawing)

220 Butter Making

221 Tongariro National Park and Château

NEW ZEALAND

221a Tongariro National Park and Château

222 Sutherland Falls

223 Tasman Glacier

224 Pohutu Geyser

2d. 'F' for 'E' in 'ZEALAND', (R. 3/1, black Pl. 2)

(Des Harrison (½d.), G. F. Fuller (1d., 3d., 6d.), A. G. Mitchell (2d., 4d., 5d., 8d., 3s., 10s., £1), PO Public Relations Division (7d.), PO Publicity Section (9d.), J. Berry (1s., 1s.6d.), R. E. Barwick (1s.3d.), J. C. Boyd (1s.9d.), D. F. Kee (2s.), L. C. Mitchell (2s.6d., 5s.). Photo D.L.R. (½d., 1d., 2d., 3d., 4d., 6d., 8d.) or Harrison (others))

1960 (11 July)–**66**. Types **207/224**. Chalk-surfaced paper (2½d., 5d., 7d., 1s.9d. (No. 795), 3s. (No. 799). W **98** (sideways on 5d., 1s.3d., 1s.6d., 2s.6d., 3s. and 10s. or sideways inverted (2½d.)). Perf 14×14½ (1s.3d., 1s.6d., 2s., 5s., £1) or 14½×14 (others).

781	207	½d. pale blue, green and cerise (1.9.60)	10	10
		a. Pale blue omitted	£325	£250
		b. Green omitted	£450	
782	208	1d. orange, green, lake and brown (1.9.60)	10	10
		a. Orange omitted	£650	£375
		b. Coil. Perf 14½×13. Wmk sideways (11.63)	1·40	2·75
		ba. Orange omitted	£2500	£1000
		c. Chalk-surfaced paper (1965?)	10	2·00
783	209	2d. carmine, black, yellow and green	10	10
		a. Black omitted	£550	£400
		b. Yellow omitted	£600	
		c. 'ZFALAND'	85·00	
784	209a	2½d. red, brown, black and green (1.11.61)	65	10
		a. Red omitted	£850	£600
		b. Brown omitted	£325	
		c. Green omitted	£400	£225
		d. Red and green omitted	£1100	
		w. Wmk sideways	£300	£150
785	210	3d. yellow, green, yellow-brown and deep greenish blue (1.9.60)	30	10
		a. Yellow omitted	£225	£170
		b. Green omitted	£325	£225
		c. Yellow-brown omitted	£250	
		e. Coil. Perf 14½×13. Wmk sideways (3.10.63)	1·40	2·75
		f. Chalk-surfaced paper (1965?)	30	2·25
		fa. Yellow-brown omitted	£750	
786	211	4d. purple, buff, yellow-green and light blue	40	10
		a. Purple omitted	£450	£300
		b. Buff omitted	£900	
		d. Chalk-surfaced paper (6.65)	£950	18·00
787	211a	5d. yellow, deep green, black and violet (14.5.62)	65	10
		a. Yellow omitted	£425	£425
		w. Wmk sideways inverted	£225	£140
788	212	6d. lilac, green and deep bluish green (1.9.60)	50	10
		a. No wmk	55·00	
		b. Lilac omitted	£425	
		c. Green omitted	£500	£425
		d. Chalk-surfaced paper (1966?)	65	4·50
788e	212a	7d. red, green, yellow and pale red (16.3.66)	65	75
		ew. Wmk inverted	4·50	12·00
789	213	8d. rose-red, yellow, green and grey (1.9.60)	40	10
790	214	9d. red and ultramarine (1.9.60)	40	10
		a. Red omitted	£550	
791	215	1s. brown and deep green	30	10
792	216	1s.3d. carmine, sepia and bright blue	2·50	70
		a. Carmine omitted	£850	£450
		b. Carmine, sepia and greyish blue	1·50	25
		w. Wmk sideways inverted	£250	£200
793	217	1s.6d. olive-green and orange-brown	80	10
794	218	1s.9d. bistre-brown	10·00	15
795	218a	1s.9d. orange-red, blue, green and yellow (4.11.63)	2·00	1·00
		a. Wmk sideways	£1000	
		w. Wmk inverted	£800	£900
796	219	2s. black and orange-buff	2·00	10
		a. Chalk-surfaced paper (1966)	1·00	2·75
797	220	2s.6d. yellow and light brown	2·00	1·00
		a. Yellow omitted	£1400	£850
798	221	3s. blackish brown	20·00	1·00
799	221a	3s. bistre, blue and green (1.4.64)	4·00	2·00
		w. Wmk sideways inverted	90·00	90·00
800	222	5s. blackish green	2·50	40
		a. Chalk-surfaced paper (1966)	2·50	5·50
801	223	10s. steel-blue	7·50	2·00
		a. Chalk-surfaced paper (1966)	5·00	10·00
802	224	£1 deep magenta	15·00	6·00
781/802		Set of 23	60·00	13·50

Nos. 782b and 785e were replaced by coils with upright watermark perf 14½×14 in 1966.

Examples of the 3d., perf 14×14½ with watermark sideways inverted (top of star pointing to the left, *as seen from the back of the stamp*) are known. They are believed to come from a trial printing.

Counter Coil Pairs. All values from 2d. to 1s.9d. were made up into counter coils, apart from the 5d., 7d. and 9d. The 1s. and 1s.9d. (both Nos. 794 and 795) were horizontal, the remaining values vertical. The 2d., 4d., 1s., 1s.6d. and 1s.9d. (No. 794) have numbers machine-printed in black or red, the remainder in red only.

> **CHALK-SURFACED PAPER.** The chalk-surfaced paper is not only whiter but also thicker, making the watermark difficult to see. Examples of the 4d. value can be found on a thick surfaced paper. These should not be confused with the rare chalk-surfaced printing, No. 786d, which can be identified by its positive reaction to the silver test and fluoresces brightly, both front and back, under ultraviolet light.

225 Sacred Kingfisher

226 New Zealand Pigeon

(Des Display Section, GPO. Recess B.W.)

1960 (10 Aug). Health Stamps. W **98**. Perf 13½.
803	225	2d.+1d. sepia and turquoise-blue	50	75
804	226	3d.+1d. deep purple-brown and orange	50	75
MS804b		Two sheets each 95×107 mm with Nos. 803/804 in blocks of 6. Perf 11½×11............ *Per pair*	18·00	45·00

227 The Adoration of the Shepherds (Rembrandt)

(Photo Harrison)

1960 (1 Nov). Christmas. W **98**. Perf 12.
805	227	2d. red and deep brown/*cream*	15	10
		a. Red omitted	£425	£425

NEW ZEALAND

228 Great Egret   **229** New Zealand Falcon   **235** Red-fronted Parakeet   **236** Tieke Saddleback

(Des Display Section, GPO. Recess B.W.)

1961 (2 Aug). Health Stamps. W **98**. Perf 13½.
806	**228**	2d.+1d. black and purple	50	70
807	**229**	3d.+1d. deep sepia and yellow-green	50	70

MS807*a* Two sheets each 97×121 mm with Nos. 806/807 in blocks of 6 (3×2)............. *Per pair* 22·00 45·00

(Des Display Section, GPO. Photo D.L.R.)

1962 (3 Oct). Health Stamps. W **98**. Perf 15×14.
812	**235**	2½d.+1d. multicoloured	50	70
		a. Orange omitted	£2250	£1200
		b. Printed on the gummed side	£1500	
		w. Wmk inverted	£160	£150
813	**236**	3d.+1d. multicoloured	50	70
		a. Orange omitted	£2750	

MS813*b* Two sheets each 96×101 mm with Nos. 812/813 in blocks of 6 (3×2)............. *Per pair* 28·00 50·00

No. 812*b* comes from a miniature sheet.

(230)   (231)   **232** Adoration of the Magi (Dürer)   **237** Madonna in Prayer (Sassoferrato)

1961 (1 Sept). No. 748 surch with T **230** (wide setting).
808	**180**	2½d. on 3d. vermilion	25	30
		a. Narrow setting (Type **231**)	15	30
		b. Pair, wide and narrow	16·00	35·00

The difference in the settings is in the overall width of the new value, caused by two different spacings between the '2', '½' and 'd'.

(Photo Harrison)

1961 (16 Oct). Christmas. W **98** (sideways). Perf 14½×14.
809	**232**	2½d. multicoloured	10	10
		a. Yellow omitted	£500	
		w. Wmk sideways inverted	80·00	48·00

(Photo Harrison)

1962 (15 Oct). Christmas. W **98**. Perf 14½×14.
814	**237**	2½d. multicoloured	10	10

 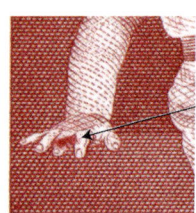

238 Prince Andrew   **239**   **3d.+1d.** A prominent flaw on the middle finger of the Prince's right hand appears as a bloodstain. Later attempts to remove the flaw met with only partial success (Pl. 1B, R. 3/5)

(Design after photographs by Studio Lisa, London. Recess D.L.R.)

1963 (7 Aug). Health Stamps. W **98**. Perf 14.
815	**238**	2½d.+1d. dull ultramarine	30	70
		a. Ultramarine	40	80
		b. Deep blue	30	40
816	**239**	3d.+1d. carmine	30	10
		a. Bloodstained finger	90·00	50·00

MS816*b* Two sheets each 93×100 mm with Nos. 815/816 in blocks of 6 (3×2)............. *Per pair* 20·00 35·00

The price for No. 816*a* is for the flaw in its original state, as illustrated. Examples with the flaw partially removed are worth less.

 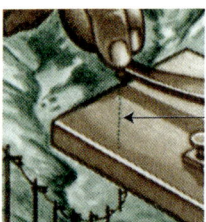

233 Morse Key and Port Hills, Lyttelton

3d. Damage to the plate resulted in a vertical green dotted line below the fingers (R. 14/1)

(Des A. G. Mitchell (3d.) and L. C. Mitchell (8d.). Photo Harrison)

1962 (1 June). Telegraph Centenary. T **233** and similar horiz design. W **98** (sideways). Perf 14½×14.
810		3d. sepia and bluish green	10	10
		a. Bluish green omitted	£3000	
		b. Dotted line flaw	15·00	
811		8d. black and brown-red	90	90
		a. Imperf (pair)	£2500	
		b. Black omitted	£2750	

Design: 3d. T **233**; 8d. Modern teleprinter.

No. 811*a* comes from a sheet with the two top rows imperforate and the third row imperforate on three sides.

240 The Holy Family (Titian)

NEW ZEALAND

An orange flaw over the Donkey's nose appears as a nosebag (Pl. 1B, R. 3/8)

(Photo Harrison)

1963 (14 Oct). Christmas. W **98** (sideways). Perf 12½.
817	**240**	2½d. multicoloured	10	10
		a. Imperf (pair)	£275	
		b. Yellow omitted	£300	
		c. Nosebag flaw	5·00	2·00
		w. Wmk sideways inverted	40	40

241 Steam Locomotive *Pilgrim* (1863) and Class DG Diesel Locomotive

242 Diesel Express and Mount Ruapehu

(Des Commercial Art Section, NZ Railways. Photo D.L.R.)

1963 (25 Nov). Railway Centenary. W **98** (sideways on 3d., sideways inverted on 1s.9d). Perf 14.
818	**241**	3d. multicoloured	40	10
		a. Blue (sky) omitted	£750	
819	**242**	1s.9d. multicoloured	1·75	1·25
		a. Red (value) omitted	£2750	

243 'Commonwealth Cable'

(Des P. Morriss. Photo Note Printing Branch, Reserve Bank of Australia)

1963 (3 Dec). Opening of COMPAC (Trans-Pacific Telephone Cable). No wmk. Perf 13½.
820	**243**	8d. red, blue and yellow	50	1·00

244 Road Map and Car Steering Wheel

245 Silver Gulls

3d. Flaw between 'W' and 'Z' of 'NEW ZEALAND' resembling an apostrophe (R. 3/2)

(Des L. C. Mitchell. Photo Harrison)

1964 (1 May). Road Safety Campaign. W **98**. Perf 15×14.
821	**244**	3d. black, ochre-yellow and blue	30	10
		a. 'Apostrophe' flaw	15·00	14·00

(Des Display Section GPO, after Miss T. Kelly. Photo Harrison)

1964 (5 Aug). Health Stamps. T **245** and similar horiz design. Multicoloured. W **98**. Perf 14½.
822		2½d.+1d. Type **245**	40	50
		a. Red (beak and legs) omitted	£350	£250
		w. Wmk inverted	†	£475
823		3d.+1d. Little Penguin	40	50
		aw. Wmk inverted	£225	

MS823b Two sheets each 171×84 mm with Nos.
822/823 in blocks of 8 (4×2) .... *Per pair* 30·00 65·00
bw. Wmk inverted (No. 823 only) ....

246 Reverend S. Marsden Taking First Christian Service at Rangihoua Bay, 1814

(247)

(Des L. C. Mitchell. Photo Harrison)

1964 (12 Oct). Christmas. W **98** (sideways). Perf 14×13½.
824	**246**	2½d. multicoloured	10	10
		a. Red omitted	£1500	—

1964 (14 Dec). As T **F6**, but without value, surch with T **247**. W **98**. Unsurfaced paper. Perf 14×13½.
825	**F6**	7d. carmine-red	50	1·00

248 Anzac Cove

(Des R. M. Conly. Photo Harrison)

1965 (14 Apr). 50th Anniversary of Gallipoli Landing. T **248** and similar horiz design. W **98**. Perf 12½.
826	**248**	4d. yellow-brown	10	10
827	—	5d. green and red	10	60

Design: 5d. Anzac Cove and Poppy.

249 ITU Emblem and Symbols

250 Sir Winston Churchill

(Photo Harrison)

1965 (17 May). ITU Centenary. W **98**. Perf 14½×14.
828	**249**	9d. blue and pale chocolate	55	35

(Des P. Morriss from photograph by Karsh. Photo Note Ptg Branch, Reserve Bank of Australia)

1965 (24 May). Churchill Commemoration. Perf 13½.
829	**250**	7d. black, pale grey and light blue	30	50

251 Wellington Provincial Council Building

(Des from painting by L. B. Temple (1867). Photo Harrison)

1965 (26 July). Centenary of Government in Wellington. W **98** (sideways). Perf 14½×14.
830	**251**	4d. multicoloured	10	10

NEW ZEALAND

252 Kaka   **253** Collared Grey Fantail (after Miss T. Kelly)

(Des Display Section, GPO. Photo Harrison)

1965 (4 Aug). Health Stamps. W **98**. Perf 14×14½.
831	**252**	3d.+1d. multicoloured	40	65
		w. Wmk inverted	†	£110
832	**253**	4d.+1d. multicoloured	40	65
		a. Green ('POSTAGE HEALTH' and on leaves) omitted	£2250	£1200
		bw. Wmk inverted	90·00	£140
MS832c		Two sheets each 100×109 mm with Nos. 831/832 in blocks of 6 (3×2)............ *Per pair*	28·00	48·00
		cw. Wmk inverted (No. 831 only)	†	—

254 ICY Emblem   **255** The Two Trinities (Murillo)

(Litho D.L.R.)

1965 (28 Sept). International Co-operation Year. W **98** (sideways inverted). Perf 14.
833	**254**	4d. carmine-red and light yellow-olive	20	10
		w. Wmk sideways	4·25	4·75

(Photo Harrison)

1965 (11 Oct). Christmas. W **98**. Perf 13½×14.
834	**255**	3d. multicoloured	10	10
		a. Gold (frame) omitted	£1500	
		b. Red omitted	£750	
		c. Yellow omitted	£750	

256 Arms of New Zealand   **259** 'Progress' Arrowhead

(Des Display Section, GPO. Photo D.L.R.)

1965 (30 Nov). 11th Commonwealth Parliamentary Conference. T **256** and similar horiz designs. Multicoloured. Perf 14.
835		4d. Type **256**	15	10
		a. Blue (incl value) omitted	£1300	
		b. Printed on the gummed side	£1300	
836		9d. Parliament House, Wellington and Badge	30	35
837		2s. Wellington from Mount Victoria	1·40	2·50
		a. Carmine omitted	£1400	
835/837		*Set of 3*	1·60	2·50

There is invariably a faint impression of the crossed regalia at upper left on No. 837a.

(Des Display Section, GPO. Photo Harrison)

1966 (5 Jan). Fourth National Scout Jamboree, Trentham. W **98**. Perf 14×15.
838	**259**	4d. gold and myrtle-green	15	10
		a. Gold (arrowhead) omitted	£1200	£1100

260 New Zealand Bellbird   **262** The Virgin with Child (Maratta)

(Des Display Section, GPO. Photo Harrison)

1966 (3 Aug). Health Stamps. T **260** and similar vert design. Multicoloured. W **98** (sideways). Perf 14×14½.
839		3d.+1d. Type **260**	40	65
		w. Wmk sideways inverted	£130	
840		4d.+1d. Weka Rail	40	65
		a. Deep brown (values and date) omitted	£2750	
		w. Wmk sideways inverted	£130	
MS841		Two sheets each 107×91 mm. Nos. 839/840 in blocks of 6 (3×2)............ *Per pair*	11·00	50·00

In No. 840a besides the value, '1966' and 'Weka' are also omitted and the bird, etc. appears as light brown.

(Photo Harrison)

1966 (3 Oct). Christmas. W **98** (sideways). Perf 14½.
842	**262**	3d. multicoloured	10	10
		a. Red omitted	£350	

263 Queen Victoria and Queen Elizabeth II   **264** Half-sovereign of 1867 and Commemorative Dollar Coin

(Des Display Section, GPO. Photo Harrison)

1967 (3 Feb). Centenary of New Zealand Post Office Savings Bank. W **98** (sideways on 4d.). Perf 14×14½.
843	**263**	4d. black, gold and maroon	10	10
		w. Wmk sideways inverted	£110	35·00
844	**264**	9d. gold, silver, black, light blue and deep green	10	20
		w. Wmk inverted	£600	

(New Currency. 100 cents = 1 New Zealand Dollar)

265 Manuka (Tea Tree)   **266** Pohutu Geyser

NEW ZEALAND

(Photo D.L.R. (½c. to 3c., 5c. and 7c.) or Harrison (others))

1967 (10 July). Decimal Currency. Designs as 1960–1966 issue, but with values inscr in decimal currency as Types **265/266**. Chalk-surfaced paper. W **98** (sideways on 8c., 10c., 20c., 50c. and $2). Perf 13½×14 (½c. to 3c., 5c. and 7c.), 14½×14 (4c., 6c., 8c., 10c., 25c. and $1) or 14×14½ (15c., 20c., 50c. and $2).

845	265	½c. pale blue, yellow-green and cerise	10	10
846	208	1c. yellow, carmine, green and light brown (as 1d.)	10	10
		a. Booklet pane. Five stamps plus one printed label	2·25	
847	209	2c. carmine, black, yellow and green (as 2d.)	10	10
848	210	2½c. yellow, green, yellow-brown and deep bluish green (as 3d.)	10	10
		a. Deep bluish green omitted*	£3750	
		b. Imperf (pair)†	£150	
849	211	3c. purple, buff, yellow-green and light greenish blue (as 4d.)	10	10
850	211a	4c. yellow, deep green, black and violet (as 5d.)	30	10
851	212	5c. lilac, yellow-olive and bluish green (as 6d.)	50	1·00
852	212a	6c. red, green, yellow and light pink (as 7d.)	50	1·00
853	213	7c. rose-red, yellow, green and grey (as 8d.)	60	1·50
		w. Wmk inverted		£750
854	214	8c. red and ultramarine	60	60
		a. Red omitted	£1200	
855	215	10c. brown and deep green (as 1s.)	75	1·00
		w. Wmk sideways inverted	£750	£550
856	217	15c. olive-green and orange-brown (as 1s.6d.)	1·00	2·25
		w. Wmk inverted	2·75	10·00
857	219	20c. black and buff	2·00	20
858	220	25c. yellow and light brown	2·00	2·00
859	221a	30c. olive-yellow, green and greenish blue	3·00	25
		w. Wmk inverted	£130	85·00
860	222	50c. blackish green (as 5s.)	3·50	35
861	223	$1 Prussian blue (as 10s.)	7·00	1·00
		w. Wmk inverted	£375	£200
862	266	$2 deep magenta	9·00	6·00
845/862		Set of 18	26·00	15·00

* This occurred on one horizontal row of ten, affecting the background colour so that the value is also missing. In the row above and the row below, the colour was partially omitted. The price is for a vertical strip.

† This comes from a sheet of which the six right-hand vertical rows were completely imperforate and the top, bottom and left-hand margins had been removed.

The 2½c. value has been seen with the yellow omitted, but only on a used example.

The 4c., 30c. and 50c. exist with PVA gum as well as gum arabic.

Counter Coil Pairs. All values from 2½c. to 20c., apart from the 5c., 7c., 10c. and 15c., were made up into coils, the 2½c., 3c. and 20c. being vertical and the remainder horizontal. The numbers were machine-printed in red.

For $4 to $10 in the Arms type, see under Postal Fiscal stamps.

For other versions of 15c., 30c. and $2 see Nos. 870/879.

268 Running with Ball

(Des L. C. Mitchell. Photo Harrison)

1967 (2 Aug). Health Stamps. Rugby Football. T **268** and similar multicoloured design. W **98** (sideways on 2½c.). Perf 14½×14 (2½c.) or 14×14½ (3c.)

867		2½c.+1c. Type **268**	15	15
868		3c.+1c. Positioning for a place-kick (horiz)	15	15
MS869		Two sheets. (a) 76×130 mm (No. 867). (b) 130×76 mm (No. 868). Containing blocks of six......Per pair	12·00	32·00

270 Kaita (trawler) and Catch

271 Brown Trout

272 Apples and Orchard

273 Forest and Timber

274 Sheep and the Woolmark

275 Consignments of Beef and Herd of Cattle

276 Dairy Farm, Mount Egmont and Butter Consignment

277 Fox Glacier, Westland National Park

(Des Display Section, GPO (7c., 8c., 10c., 18c., 20c., 25c. and 28c. from photo), R. M. Conly (7½c.). Litho B.W. (7c., 8c., 18c., 20c.) or photo D.L.R. (7½c.) and Harrison (10c., 25c., 28c.). Others (15c., 30c., $2) as before)

1967–70. Types **270/277**. Chalk-surfaced paper (except 7c., 8c., 18c., 20c.). No wmk (7c., 8c., 20c., 30c.) or W **98** (sideways inverted on 7½c., sideways on 10c., 15c., 25c., upright on 18c., 28c., $2). Perf 13½ (7c., 7½c.), 13×13½ (8c., 18c., 20c.), 14½×14 (10c., 25c., 30c.) or 14×14½ (15c., 28c., $2).

870	270	7c. multicoloured (3.12.69)	60	1·00
871	271	7½c. multicoloured* (29.8.67)	50	70
		a. Wmk upright (10.68)	50	1·00
872	272	8c. multicoloured (8.7.69)	75	70
873	273	10c. multicoloured (2.4.68)	50	10
		a. Green (background) omitted	£1250	
		w. Wmk sideways inverted	†	£1100
874	217	15c. apple-green, myrtle-green and carmine (as No. 856†) (19.3.68)	60	1·00
		w. Wmk sideways inverted	†	£180
875	274	18c. multicoloured (8.7.69)	60	55
		a. Printed on the gummed side	£1000	
876	275	20c. multicoloured (8.7.69)	1·00	20
877	276	25c. multicoloured (10.12.68)	1·00	1·50
878	277	28c. multicoloured (30.7.68)	75	10
		a. Yellow omitted	£3000	
		bw. Wmk inverted	†	£1200
878c	221a	30c. olive-green, green and greenish blue (as No. 859) (2.6.70)	4·00	5·00
879	266	$2 black, ochre and pale blue (as No. 862) (10.12.68)	12·00	13·00
870/879		Set of 11	20·00	22·00

* No. 871 was originally issued to commemorate the introduction of the Brown Trout into New Zealand.

† No. 874 is slightly larger than No. 856, measuring 21×25 mm and the inscriptions and numerals differ in size.

No. 873a was made up into counter coils and thus have trimmed perforations.

Counter Coil Pairs. The 10c. and 20c. were made up into horizontal coils and the 15c. into vertical coils. All counter coil numbers were machine-printed in red.

278 The Adoration of the Shepherds (Poussin)

279 Mount Aspiring, Aurora Australis and Southern Cross

280 Sir James Hector (founder)

NEW ZEALAND

(Photo Harrison)

1967 (3 Oct). Christmas. W **98** (sideways). Perf 13½×14.
880   **278**   2½c. multicoloured   10   10

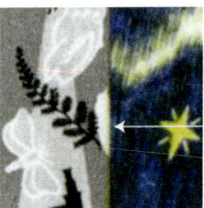

4c. A large white flaw to the right of the fern (a multipositive flaw affecting all plates R. 1/10)

(Des J. Berry. Litho D.L.R.)

1967 (10 Oct). Centenary of the Royal Society of New Zealand. W **98** (sideways on 4c.). Perf 14 (4c.) or 13×14 (8c.).
881   **279**   4c. multicoloured   25   20
            a. Fern flaw ....   6·00
            w. Wmk sideways inverted ....   8·00   9·00
882   **280**   8c. multicoloured   25   80

281 Open Bible   **282** Soldiers and Tank

(Des Display Section, GPO. Litho D.L.R.)

1968 (23 Apr). Centenary of Maori Bible. W **98**. Perf 13½.
883   **281**   3c. multicoloured   10   10
            a. Gold (inscr etc.) omitted £160   £130
            w. Wmk inverted ....   45·00   38·00

(Des L. C. Mitchell. Litho D.L.R.)

1968 (7 May). New Zealand Armed Forces. T **282** and similar horiz designs. Multicoloured. W **98** (sideways). Perf 14×13½.
884   4c. Type **282**   25   10
            w. Wmk sideways inverted ....   9·50   14·00
885   10c. Airmen, Fairey Firefly and English Electric Canberra aircraft.............   40   50
886   28c. Sailors and HMNZS *Achilles*, 1939, and HMNZS *Waikato*, 1968   70   1·60
            w. Wmk sideways inverted ....   1·50   5·00
884/886 Set of 3................................   1·25   2·00

285 Boy Breasting Tape, and Olympic Rings   **287** Placing Votes in Ballot Box

(Des L. C. Mitchell. Photo Harrison)

1968 (7 Aug). Health Stamps. T **285** and similar horiz design. Multicoloured. Perf 14½×14.
887   2½c.+1c. Type **285**   20   15
888   3c.+1c. Girl swimming and Olympic rings.......   20   15
            a. Red (ring) omitted £3500
            b. Blue (ring) omitted £2250
MS889 Two sheets each 145×95 mm. Nos. 887/888 in blocks of 6....................*Per pair*   12·00   40·00

No. 888a occurred in one miniature sheet. Six examples are known, one being used.
No. 888b occurred from a second miniature sheet.

(Des J. Berry. Photo Japanese Govt Ptg Bureau, Tokyo)

1968 (19 Sept). 75th Anniversary of Universal Suffrage in New Zealand. Perf 13.
890   **287**   3c. ochre, olive-green and light blue ..   10   10

288 Human Rights Emblem   **289** *Adoration of the Holy Child* (G. van Honthorst)

(Photo Japanese Govt Ptg Bureau, Tokyo)

1968 (19 Sept). Human Rights Year. Perf 13.
891   **288**   10c. scarlet, yellow and deep green.......   10   30

(Photo Harrison)

1968 (1 Oct). Christmas. W **98** (sideways inverted). Perf 14×14½.
892   **289**   2½c. multicoloured   10   10

290 ILO Emblem

(Photo Harrison)

1969 (11 Feb). 50th Anniversary of International Labour Organisation. W **98** (sideways). Perf 14½×14.
893   **290**   7c. black and carmine-red...............   15   30

 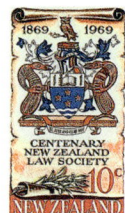

291 Supreme Court Building, Auckland   **292** Law Society's Coat of Arms

(Des R. M. Conly. Litho B.W.)

1969 (8 Apr). Centenary of New Zealand Law Society. Types **291**/**292** and similar design. Perf 13½×13 (3c.) or 13×13½ (others).
894   **291**   3c. multicoloured (*shades*)   10   10
895   **292**   10c. multicoloured   20   35
896   –   18c. multicoloured (*shades*)   30   95
894/896 Set of 3................................   55   1·25

Design: Vert—18c. Justice (from Memorial Window in University of Canterbury, Christchurch).

295 Student being Conferred with Degree

(Des R. M. Conly. Litho B.W.)

1969 (3 June). Centenary of Otago University. T **295** and similar multicoloured design. Perf 13×13½ (3c.) or 13½×13 (10c.).
897   3c. Otago University (*vert*)...............   15   10
898   10c. Type **295**................................   30   25

NEW ZEALAND

296 Boys Playing Cricket   **298** Dr Elizabeth Gunn (Founder of First Children's Health Camp)

306 Girl, Wheat Field and CORSO Emblem   **307** Mother Feeding her Child, Dairy Herd and CORSO Emblem

(Des R. M. Conly (4c.); L. C. Mitchell (others). Litho B.W.)

1969 (6 Aug). Health Stamps. T **296** and similar horiz design and T **298**. Perf 12½×13 (No. 901) or 13×12½ (others).

899	**296**	2½c.+1c. multicoloured	40	65
900	–	3c.+1c. multicoloured	40	65
901	**298**	4c.+1c. brown and ultramarine	40	1·50
899/901		Set of 3	1·10	2·50
MS902		Two sheets each 144×84 mm. Nos. 899/900 in blocks of 6........ *Per pair*	14·00	50·00

Design: 3c. Girls playing cricket.

(Des L. C. Mitchell. Photo Japanese Govt Printing Bureau, Tokyo)

1969 (18 Nov). 25th Anniversary of CORSO (Council of Organisations for Relief Services Overseas). Perf 13.

911	**306**	7c. multicoloured	35	85
912	**307**	8c. multicoloured	35	90

308 Cardigan Bay (champion trotter)

(Des L. C. Mitchell. Photo Courvoisier)

1970 (28 Jan). Return of Cardigan Bay to New Zealand. Perf 11½.

913	**308**	10c. multicoloured	30	30

299 Oldest Existing House in New Zealand, and Old Stone Mission Store, Kerikeri

(Litho D.L.R.)

1969 (18 Aug). Early European Settlement in New Zealand, and 150th Anniversary of Kerikeri. T **299** and similar horiz design. Multicoloured. W **98** (sideways inverted). Perf 13×13½.

903		4c. Type **299**	20	25
904		6c. View of Bay of Islands	30	1·75

309 *Vanessa gonerilla* (Red Admiral)   **310** Queen Elizabeth II and New Zealand Coat of Arms

(Des Enid Hunter (½c., 1c., 2c., 18c., 20c.), Eileen Mayo (2½c. to 7c.), D. B. Stevenson (7½c., 8c.), M. Cleverley (10c., 15c., 25c., 30c., $1, $2), M. V. Askew (23c., 50c.). Photo Harrison (½c. to 20c.), Enschedé (23c., 50c.), Courvoisier ($1, $2) or Litho B.W. (25c., 30c.))

1970 (12 Mar)–**76**. Various designs as Types **309/310**. W **98** (sideways on 10c., or sideways inverted on 15c., 20c.) or No wmk (23c. to $2).

*(a) Size as T **309**. Perf 13½×13.*

914	½c. multicoloured (2.9.70)	10	20
	w. Wmk inverted	£450	£200
915	1c. multicoloured (2.9.70)	10	10
	aw. Wmk inverted	35·00	35·00
	b. Wmk sideways inverted (booklets) (6.7.71)	80	2·50
	ba. Booklet pane. No. 915b×3 with 3 *se-tenant* printed labels	2·25	
	bb. Red omitted	£275	
	bc. Blue omitted (booklets)	£250	£200
	bw. Wmk sideways	£130	£100
916	2c. multicoloured (2.9.70)	10	10
	a. Black (inscr, etc) omitted	£425	
	w. Wmk inverted	4·00	1·50
917	2½c. multicoloured (2.9.70)	30	20
918	3c. black, brown and orange (2.9.70)	15	10
	aw. Wmk inverted	2·50	2·75
	b. Wmk sideways inverted (booklets) (6.7.71)	55	1·50
	bw. Wmk sideways	32·00	32·00
919	4c. multicoloured (2.9.70)	15	10
	aw. Wmk inverted	3·00	1·75
	b. Wmk sideways inverted (booklets) (6.7.71)	55	1·75
	ba. Bright green (wing veins) omitted	£250	£110
	bw. Wmk sideways	95·00	75·00
	c. Bright green (wing veins) omitted	†	£250
920	5c. multicoloured (4.11.70)	30	10
	w. Wmk inverted	†	£450
921	6c. blackish green, yellow-green and carmine (4.11.70)	30	75
	w. Wmk inverted	†	£350
922	7c. multicoloured (4.11.70)	50	1·00
	w. Wmk inverted	—	£300
923	7½c. multicoloured (4.11.70)	50	2·00
	w. Wmk inverted	†	£450
924	8c. multicoloured (4.11.70)	50	1·00
	w. Wmk inverted	†	£250

301 *The Nativity* (Federico Fiori (Barocci))   **302** Captain Cook, Transit of Venus and 'Octant'

(Photo Harrison)

1969 (1 Oct). Christmas. W **98**. Perf 13×14.

905	**301**	2½c. multicoloured	10	10
		a. No wmk	10	15

(Des Eileen Mayo. Photo; portraits embossed Harrison)

1969 (9 Oct). Bicentenary of Captain Cook's Landing in New Zealand. T **302** and similar horiz designs. Perf 14½×14.

906		4c. black, cerise and blue	30	15
		a. Imperf (pair)	£425	
907		6c. slate-green, purple-brown and black	40	1·00
908		18c. purple-brown, slate-green and black	60	40
909		28c. cerise, black and blue	1·00	1·25
906/909		Set of 4	2·10	2·50
MS910		109×90 mm. Nos. 906/909	11·00	25·00

Designs: 4c. T **302**; 6c. Sir Joseph Banks (naturalist) and outline of HMS *Endeavour*; 18c. Dr Daniel Solander (botanist) and his plant; 28c. Queen Elizabeth II and Cook's chart 1769.

The miniature sheet exists additionally inscribed on the selvedge at bottom. 'A SOUVENIR FROM NEW ZEALAND STAMP EXHIBITION, NEW PLYMOUTH 6TH–11TH OCTOBER. 1969'. These were not sold from Post Offices.

Scott Starling Stamps
www.scottstarling.com.au
Australia | Great Britain | Europe | British Commonwealth

Dr. Scott Starling, PO Box 625, Epping, NSW, 1710. Australia.

The Stanley Gibbons Auction House has been operating philatelic auctions since 1901.

STANLEY GIBBONS AUCTIONS

The Stanley Gibbons Auction House has been operating philatelic auctions since 1901. Following the refurbishment of our auction room, and the continuing increase of instructions from third parties, we are looking for national and international agents who may be interested in working with our recognised and trusted brand as we continue to expand our global reach.

We offer uncapped commission, and our un-rivalled team of in-house experts ensure maximum realisation from our lots.

If you would be interested in working with us please email our Head of Auctions, Tom Hazell at thazell@stanleygibbons.com

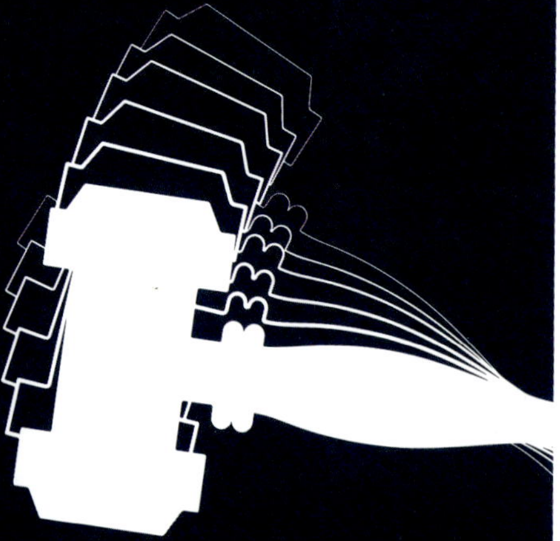

@StanleyGibbons   /StanleyGibbonsGroup   @StanleyGibbons

*(b) Size as T **310**. Various perfs.*

925	10c. multicoloured (Perf 14½×14)	50	10
	w. Wmk sideways inverted	8·00	3·75
926	15c. black, flesh and pale brown (Perf 13½×13) (20.1.71)	55	15
	a. Pale brown omitted	£700	
	w. Wmk sideways	50·00	45·00
927	18c. chestnut, black and apple-green (Perf 13×13½) (20.1.71)	55	20
	w. Wmk inverted	55·00	45·00
928	20c. black and yellow-brown (Perf 13½×13) (20.1.71)	55	10
929	23c. multicoloured (Perf 13½×12½) (1.12.71)	45	10
930	25c. multicoloured (Perf 13×13½) (1.9.71)	70	25
	a. Printed on the gummed side	£750	
	b. Perf 14 (11.76?)	40	55
931	30c. multicoloured (Perf 13×13½) (1.9.71)	35	15
	a. Perf 14 (9.76?)	1·00	1·75
932	50c. multicoloured (Perf 13½×12½) (1.9.71)	35	15
	a. Apple-green (hill on right) omitted	28·00	24·00
	b. Buff (shore) omitted	45·00	
	c. Dark green (hill on left) omitted	£350	
933	$1 multicoloured (Perf 11½) (14.4.71)	1·00	70
934	$2 multicoloured (Perf 11½) (14.4.71)	2·50	1·00
914/934 *Set of 21*		9·00	7·00

Designs: Vert—½c. *Lycaena salustius* (Glade Copper Butterfly); 1c. T **309**; 2c. *Argyrophenga antipodum* (Tussock Butterfly); 2½c. *Nyctemera annulata* (Magpie Moth); 3c. *Detunda egregia* (Lichen Moth); 4c. *Charagia virescens* (Puriri Moth); 5c. Scarlet Wrasse ('Scarlet Parrot Fish'); 6c. Big-bellied Sea Horses; 7c. Leatherjacket (fish); 7½c. Intermediate Halfbeak ('Garfish'); 8c. John Dory (fish); 18c. Maori club; 25c. Hauraki Gulf Maritime Park; 30c. Mount Cook National Park. Horiz—10c. T **310**: 15c. Maori fish hook; 20c. Maori tattoo Pattern, 23c. Egmont National Park; 50c. Abel Tasman National Park; $1 Geothermal Power; $2 Agricultural Technology.

Although issued as a definitive No. 925 was put on sale on the occasion of the Royal Visit to New Zealand.

Used examples of No. 931 are known showing the sky in light blue instead of the normal stone colour. It was suggested by the printer involved that this was caused by a residue of ink used for another stamp remaining in the ink ducts when a printing of the 30c. commenced. Most authorities, however, agree that the 'blue sky' stamps are colour changelings.

Counter Coil Pairs. All values from 3c. to 20c. were made up into counter coils with the exception of the 7c., 7½c., 15c. and 18c. All were in horizontal format with red machine-printed numbers.

See also Nos. 1008/1020.

311 Geyser Restaurant

312 UN HQ Building

(Des M. Cleverley. Photo Japanese Govt Printing Bureau, Tokyo)

1970 (8 Apr). World Fair, Osaka. T **311** and similar horiz designs. Multicoloured. Perf 13.

935	7c. Type **311**	20	55
936	8c. New Zealand Pavilion	20	55
937	18c. Bush Walk	40	55
935/937 *Set of 3*		70	1·50

(Des R. M. Conly (3c.), L. C. Mitchell (10c.). Litho D.L.R.)

1970 (24 June). 25th Anniversary of United Nations. T **312** and similar vert design. Perf 13½.

938	3c. multicoloured	10	10
939	10c. scarlet and yellow	20	20

Design: 3c. T **312**; 10c. Tractor on horizon.

313 Soccer

(Des L. C. Mitchell. Litho D.L.R.)

1970 (5 Aug). Health Stamps. T **313** and similar multicoloured design. Perf 13½.

940	2½c.+1c. Netball (*vert*)	25	70
941	3c.+1c. Type **313**	25	70
MS942	Two sheets: (a) 102×125 mm (No. 940). (b) 125×102 mm (No. 941), containing blocks of 6 *Per pair*	11·00	50·00

314 *The Virgin adoring the Child* (Correggio)

315 The Holy Family (stained glass window, Invercargill Presbyterian Church)

(Litho D.L.R.)

1970 (1 Oct). Christmas. Types **314/315** and similar design. Perf 12½.

943	2½c. multicoloured	10	10
944	3c. multicoloured	10	10
	a. Green (inscr and value) omitted	£300	£200
945	10c. black, orange and silver	30	75
943/945 *Set of 3*		35	75

Design: Vert—2½c. T **314**; 3c. T **315**. Horiz—10c. Tower of Roman Catholic Church, Sockburn.

Nos. 943/945 exist as imperforate proofs with the country inscription and face value omitted.

316 Chatham Islands Lily

317 Country Women's Institute Emblem

(Des Eileen Mayo. Photo Japanese Govt Printing Bureau, Tokyo)

1970 (2 Dec). Chatham Islands. T **316** and similar horiz design. Multicoloured. Perf 13.

946	1c. Type **316**	10	35
947	2c. Shy Albatross	30	40

(Des L. C. Mitchell. Photo Japanese Govt Ptg Bureau, Tokyo)

1971 (10 Feb). 50th Anniversaries of Country Women's Institutes and Rotary International in New Zealand. T **317** and similar horiz design. Multicoloured. Perf 13.

948	4c. Type **317**	10	10
949	10c. Rotary emblem and map of New Zealand	20	60

318 *Rainbow II* (yacht)

319 Civic Arms of Palmerston North

(Des J. Berry (5c.), G. F. Fuller (8c.). Litho B.W.)

1971 (3 Mar). One Ton Cup Racing Trophy. T **318** and similar horiz design. Multicoloured. Perf 13½×13.

950	5c. Type **318**	25	25
951	8c. One Ton Cup	25	1·50

(Des R. M. Conly. Photo Japanese Govt Ptg Bureau, Tokyo)

1971 (12 May). City Centenaries. T **319** and similar horiz designs. Multicoloured. Perf 13.

952	3c. Type **319**	15	15
953	4c. Arms of Auckland	15	15
954	5c. Arms of Invercargill	15	1·10
952/954 *Set of 3*		40	1·25

NEW ZEALAND

320 Antarctica on Globe   **321** Child on Swing

(Des Eileen Mayo. Photo Japanese Govt Ptg Bureau, Tokyo)

1971 (9 June). Tenth Anniversary of Antarctic Treaty. Perf 13.
955	**320**	6c. multicoloured	1·00	1·75

(Des Eileen Mayo. Photo Japanese Govt Ptg Bureau, Tokyo)

1971 (9 June). 25th Anniversary of UNICEF. Perf 13.
956	**321**	7c. multicoloured	50	1·40

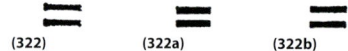

(322)   (322a)   (322b)

T **322**: Photo, showing screening dots; thin bars, wide apart.
T **322a**: Typo, without screening dots; thick bars, closer together.
T **322b**: Typo, bars similar to T **322**.

1971–73. No. 917 surcharged

(a) In photogravure, by Harrison (23.6.71*).
957	**322**	4c. on 2½c. multicoloured	15	10
		a. Red omitted	£1500	
		b. Pair, one without surcharge	£350	

(b) Typographically, by Harrison (13.7.72*).
957c	**322a**	4c. on 2½c. multicoloured	45	10
		ca. Albino surch	90·00	
		cb. Surch double, one albino	50·00	
		cc. Pair, one without surch	£450	
		cd. Red omitted	£1500	
		ce. Surch inverted on back		
		cf. Surch double	£250	

(c) Typographically, locally (18.6.73*).
957d	**322b**	4c. on 2½c. multicoloured	15	10

* Earliest known postmarks.
No. 957ce was caused by a paper fold.

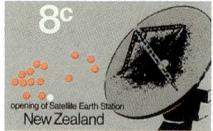 

323 Satellite-tracking Aerial   **324** Girls playing Hockey

(Des M. Cleverley. Photo Courvoisier)

1971 (14 July). Opening of Satellite Earth Station. T **323** and similar horiz design. Perf 11½.
958	8c. black, drab-grey and vermilion	50	1·50
959	10c. black, turquoise-green and pale bluish violet	50	1·00

Designs: 8c. T **323**; 10c. Satellite.

(Des L. C. Mitchell. Litho Harrison)

1971 (4 Aug). Health Stamps. T **324** and similar horiz designs. Multicoloured. W **98** (sideways on 5c.). Perf 13½×13.
960	3c.+1c. Type **324**	40	65
961	4c.+1c. Boys playing hockey	40	65
962	5c.+1c. Dental Health	60	2·00
960/962 Set of 3		1·25	3·00
MS963 Two sheets each 122×96 mm. Nos. 960/961 in blocks of six .... Per pair		16·00	38·00

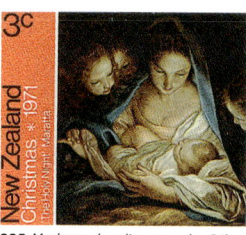 

325 Madonna bending over the Crib (Maratta)   **326** Tiffany Rose

(Des Enid Hunter (10c.), D. A. Hatcher (others). Photo Harrison)

1971 (6 Oct). Christmas. T **325** and similar vert designs. Multicoloured. Perf 13×13½.
964	3c. Type **325**	10	10
965	4c. The Annunciation (stained glass window) (21½×38 mm)	10	10
966	10c. The Three Kings (21½×38 mm)	50	1·25
964/966 Set of 3		60	1·25

(Des A. G. Mitchell. Photo Courvoisier)

1971 (3 Nov). First World Rose Convention, Hamilton. T **326** and similar vert designs showing roses. Multicoloured. Perf 11½.
967	2c. Type **326**	15	90
968	5c. Peace	35	25
969	8c. Chrysler Imperial	60	1·10
967/969 Set of 3		1·00	2·00

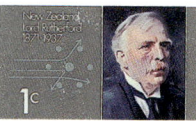

327 Lord Rutherford and Alpha Particles   **328** Benz (1895)

(Des M. Cleverley. Litho B.D.T.)

1971 (1 Dec). Birth Centenary of Lord Rutherford (scientist). T **327** and similar horiz design. Multicoloured. Perf 13½×13.
970	1c. Type **327**	20	50
971	7c. Lord Rutherford and formula	55	1·75

(Des A. G. Mitchell. Litho B.D.T.)

1972 (2 Feb). International Vintage Car Rally. T **328** and similar horiz designs. Multicoloured. Perf 14.
972	3c. Type **328**	15	10
973	4c. Oldsmobile (1904)	15	10
974	5c. Ford Model T (1914)	15	10
975	6c. Cadillac Service car (1915)	15	45
976	8c. Chrysler (1924)	25	1·25
977	10c. Austin 7 (1923)	25	1·00
972/977 Set of 6		1·00	2·50

329 Coat of Arms of Wanganui   **330** Black Scree Cotula

(Des M. Cleverley. Litho Harrison)

1972 (5 Apr). Anniversaries. T **329** and similar designs. Perf 13×13½ (3c., 5c. and 8c.) or 13½×13 (others).
978	3c. multicoloured	10	10
979	4c. red-orange, brown-bistre and black	15	10
980	5c. multicoloured	25	10
981	8c. multicoloured	30	1·50
982	10c. multicoloured	30	1·00
978/982 Set of 5		1·00	2·50

NEW ZEALAND

Designs and Events: Vert—3c. T **329** (centenary of Wanganui Council government); 5c. de Havilland DH.89 Dragon Rapide and Boeing 737 (25th anniversary of National Airways Corp); 8c. French frigate and Maori palisade (bicentenary of landing by Marion du Fresne). Horiz—4c. Postal Union symbol (tenth anniversary of Asian-Oceanic Postal Union); 10c. Stone cairn (150th anniversary of New Zealand Methodist Church).

(Des Eileen Mayo. Litho Harrison)

1972 (7 June). Alpine Plants. T **330** and similar vert designs. Multicoloured. Perf 13½.

983	4c. Type **330**	20	10
984	6c. North Island Edelweiss	25	35
985	8c. Haast's Buttercup	35	70
986	10c. Brown Mountain Daisy	45	1·10
983/986	Set of 4	1·10	2·00

331 Boy playing Tennis   **332** *Madonna with Child* (Murillo)

(Des L. C. Mitchell. Litho Harrison)

1972 (2 Aug). Health Stamps. T **331** and similar vert design. Perf 13×13½.

987	3c.+1c. light grey and chestnut	30	65
988	4c.+1c. light red-brown, grey and lemon	30	65
MS989	Two sheets each 107×123 mm. Nos. 987/988 in blocks of six *Per pair*	15·00	35·00

Designs: No. 987 T **331**; No. 988, Girl playing tennis.

(Des D. A. Hatcher. Photo Courvoisier)

1972 (4 Oct). Christmas. T **332** and similar vert designs. Multicoloured. Perf 11½.

990	3c. Type **332**	10	10
991	5c. The Last Supper (stained glass window, St John's Church, Levin)	15	10
992	10c. Pohutukawa flower	35	70
990/992	Set of 3	50	70

333 Lake Waikaremoana   **334** Old Pollen Street

(Des D. A. Hatcher. Photo Courvoisier)

1972 (6 Dec). Lake Scenes. T **333** and similar vert designs. Multicoloured. Perf 11½.

993	6c. Type **333**	40	1·25
994	8c. Lake Hayes	50	1·25
995	18c. Lake Wakatipu	60	1·50
996	23c. Lake Rotomahana	70	2·00
993/996	Set of 4	2·00	5·50

No. 995 is inscribed 'Lake Wakatipu', but actually shows Kawarau River, which flows out of the Lake.

(Des Miss V. Jepsen (3c.), B. Langford (others). Litho Harrison)

1973 (7 Feb). Commemorations. T **334** and similar horiz designs. Multicoloured (except 8c.). Perf 13½×13.

997	3c. Type **334**	10	10
998	4c. Coal mining and pasture	15	10
999	5c. Cloister	10	15
1000	6c. Forest, birds and lake	35	50
1001	8c. Rowers (light grey, indigo and gold)	15	50
1002	10c. Graph and people	25	80
997/1002	Set of 6	1·00	1·90

Events: 3c. Centennial of Thames Borough; 4c. Centennial of Westport Borough; 5c. Centennial of Canterbury University; 6c. 50th Anniversary of Royal Forest and Bird Protection Society; 8c. Success of NZ Rowers in 1972 Olympics; 10c. 25th Anniversary of ECAFE.

335 Class W Locomotive   **336** *Maori Woman and Child*

(Des R. M. Conly. Litho Harrison)

1973 (4 Apr). New Zealand Steam Locomotives. T **335** and similar horiz designs. Multicoloured. Perf 14×14½.

1003	3c. Type **335**	20	10
1004	4c. Class X	20	10
1005	5c. Class Ab	20	10
1006	10c. Class Ja No. 1274	75	1·40
1003/1006	Set of 4	1·25	1·50

1973–76. As Nos. 915 etc., but no wmk.

1008	1c. multicoloured (7.9.73)	60	1·25
	a. Booklet pane. No. 1008×3 with three se-tenant printed labels (8.74)	2·40	
	b. Red (wing markings) omitted	£250	
	c. Blue (spots on wings) omitted	£160	
1009	2c. multicoloured (6.73?)	30	10
	a. Purple and yellow omitted	£8500	
	b. Black (inscr, etc) omitted	£400	
1010	3c. black, light brown and orange (1974)	1·75	1·50
	a. Orange omitted	£450	
1011	4c. multicoloured (7.9.73)	45	10
	a. Bright green (wing veins) inverted	£950	
	b. Purple-brown omitted	£200	
	c. Orange-yellow omitted	£300	
	d. Greenish blue (background) omitted	£350	
	e. Bright green (wing veins) omitted	6·00	
	f. Apple-green (wings) omitted	£300	
	g. Orange-yellow, bright green and apple-green omitted	£6000	
	h. Imperf (pair)	£200	
1012	5c. multicoloured (1973)	3·00	2·00
1013	6c. blackish green, yellow-green and rose-carmine (7.9.73)	60	1·00
	a. Yellow-green (part of Seahorse) omitted	£225	
	b. Rose-carmine omitted	£1200	
1014	7c. multicoloured (1974)	7·00	3·50
	a. Black omitted	£350	
1015	8c. multicoloured (1974)	7·00	2·50
	a. Blue-green (background) omitted	£375	
1017	10c. multicoloured, Perf 13½×13 (6.73?)	75	10
	a. Silver (Arms) omitted	£200	
	b. Imperf (pair)	£250	
	c. Deep blue (Queen's head, face value etc.) omitted	£350	
	d. Red (hair ribbon) omitted	40·00	
	e. Blue (country name) omitted	£450	
1018	15c. black, flesh and pale brown, Perf 13½×13 (2.8.76)	75	20
1019	18c. chestnut, black and apple-green (1974)	1·25	1·00
	a. Black (inscr, etc) omitted	£400	
1020	20c. black and yellow-brown (1974)	80	40
	a. Black omitted	£1500	
1008/1020	Set of 12	22·00	12·00

Nos. 1009a and 1011g both result from paper folds.

(Des and photo Courvoisier)

1973 (6 June). Paintings by Frances Hodgkins. T **336** and similar vert designs. Multicoloured. Perf 11½.

1027	5c. Type **336**	20	15
1028	8c. *Hilltop*	30	80
1029	10c. *Barn in Picardy*	30	65
1030	18c. *Self Portrait Still Life*	70	1·75
1027/1030	Set of 4	1·40	3·00

NEW ZEALAND

337 Prince Edward   **338** *Tempi Madonna* (Raphael)

(Des and litho Harrison)

1973 (1 Aug). Health Stamps. Perf 13×13½.
1031	**337** 3c.+1c. dull yellowish green and reddish brown	30	50
1032	4c.+1c. rose-red and blackish brown	30	50
MS1033 Two sheets each 96×121 mm with Nos. 1031/1032 in blocks of 6 (3×2)............. *Per pair*		14·00	35·00

(Des A. G. Mitchell. Photo Enschedé)

1973 (3 Oct). Christmas. T **338** and similar vert designs. Multicoloured. Perf 12½×13½.
1034	3c. Type **338**	10	10
1035	5c. Three Kings (stained glass window, St Therese's Church, Auckland)	10	10
1036	10c. Family entering church	25	50
1034/1036 Set of 3		40	50

339 Mitre Peak   **340** Hurdling

(Des D. A. Hatcher. Photo Enschedé)

1973 (5 Dec). Mountain Scenery. T **339** and similar multicoloured designs. Perf 13×13½ (6c., 8c.) or 13½×13 (others).
1037	6c. Type **339**	25	70
1038	8c. Mount Ngauruhoe	30	1·00
1039	18c. Mount Sefton (*horiz*)	50	1·75
1040	23c. Burnett Range (*horiz*)	60	2·25
1037/1040 Set of 4		1·50	5·00

(Des M. Cleverley. Litho Harrison)

1974 (9 Jan). Tenth British Commonwealth Games, Christchurch. T **340** and similar vert designs. 5c. black and violet-blue, others multicoloured. Perf 13×14.
1041	4c. Type **340**	10	10
1042	5c. Ball player	10	10
1043	10c. Cycling	60	15
1044	18c. Rifle shooting	15	50
1045	23c. Bowls	20	80
1041/1045 Set of 5		1·00	1·50

No. 1042 does not show the Games emblem, and commemorates the Fourth Paraplegic Games, held at Dunedin.

 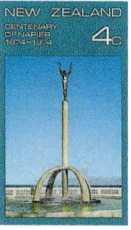

341 Queen Elizabeth II   **342** *Spirit of Napier* Fountain

(Des D. A. Hatcher and A. G. Mitchell. Litho Harrison)

1974 (5 Feb). New Zealand Day. Sheet 131×74 mm. containing T **341** and similar horiz designs, size 37×20 mm. Multicoloured. Perf 13.
MS1046 4c.×5 Treaty House, Waitangi; Signing Waitangi Treaty; Type **341**; Parliament Buildings Extensions; Children in Class	70	2·50

(Des Miss V. Jepsen. Photo Courvoisier)

1974 (3 Apr). Centenaries of Napier and UPU. T **342** and similar vert designs. Multicoloured. Perf 11½.
1047	4c. Type **342**	10	10
1048	5c. Clock Tower, Bern	20	30
1049	8c. UPU Monument, Bern	55	1·60
1047/1049 Set of 3		75	1·75

343 Boeing Seaplane, 1919   **344** Children, Cat and Dog

(Des R. M. Conly. Litho Harrison)

1974 (5 June). History of New Zealand Airmail Transport. T **343** and similar horiz designs. Multicoloured. Perf 14×13.
1050	3c. Type **343**	20	10
1051	4c. Lockheed 10 Electra *Kauha*, 1937	20	10
1052	5c. Bristol Type 170 Freighter Mk 31, 1958.	20	30
1053	23c. Short S.30 modified G Class flying boat *Aotearoa*, 1940	50	2·00
1050/1053 Set of 4		1·00	2·25

(Des B. Langford. Litho Harrison)

1974 (7 Aug). Health Stamps. Perf 13×13½.
1054	**344** 3c.+1c. multicoloured	20	50
1055	– 4c.+1c. multicoloured	25	50
1056	– 5c.+1c. multicoloured	70	1·50
1054/1056 Set of 3		1·00	2·25
MS1057 145×123 mm. No. 1055 in block of ten		14·00	35·00

Nos. 1055/1056 are as T **344**, showing children and pets.

345 *The Adoration of the Magi* (Konrad Witz)   **346** Great Barrier Island

(Des Eileen Mayo. Photo Courvoisier)

1974 (2 Oct). Christmas. T **345** and similar horiz designs. Multicoloured. Perf 11½.
1058	3c. Type **345**	10	10
1059	5c. The Angel Window (stained glass window, Old St Pauls Church, Wellington)	10	10
1060	10c. Madonna Lily	30	90
1058/1060 Set of 3		40	1·00

(Des D. A. Hatcher. Photo Enschedé)

1974 (4 Dec). Off-shore Islands. T **346** and similar horiz designs. Multicoloured. Perf 13½×13.
1061	6c. Type **346**	15	30
1062	8c. Stewart Island	25	80
1063	18c. White Island	30	80
1064	23c. The Brothers	40	90
1061/1064 Set of 4		1·00	2·50

347 Disabled Child   **348** Scow *Lake Erie*

NEW ZEALAND

(Des Miss V. Jepsen (3c, 5c.), A. G. Mitchell (10c., 18c.). Litho Harrison)

1975 (5 Feb). Anniversaries and Events. T **347** and similar horiz designs. Multicoloured. Perf 13½.

1065	3c. Type **347**	10	10
1066	5c. Farming family	10	10
1067	10c. IWY symbols	15	60
1068	18c. Medical School Building, Otago University	40	1·25
1065/1068	Set of 4	65	1·75

Commemorations: 3c. 40th Anniversary of NZ Crippled Children Society; 5c. 50th Anniversary of Women's Division, Federated Farmers of NZ; 10c. International Women's Year; 18c. Centenary of Otago Medical School.

(Des R. M. Conly. Litho Harrison)

1975 (2 Apr). Historic Sailing Ships. T **348** and similar horiz designs. Perf 13½×13.

1069	4c. black and red	20	10
1070	5c. black and turquoise-blue	20	10
1071	8c. black and yellow	25	50
1072	10c. black and olive-yellow	25	50
1073	18c. black and light brown	30	1·50
1074	23c. black and slate-lilac	40	1·50
1069/1074	Set of 6	1·40	3·75

Ships: 4c. T **348**; 5c. Schooner *Herald*; 8c. Brigantine *New Zealander*; 10c. Topsail schooner *Jessie Kelly*; 18c. Barque *Tory*; 23c. Full rigged clipper *Rangitiki*.

349 Lake Sumner Forest Park

(Des and photo Enschedé)

1975 (4 June). Forest Park Scenes. T **349** and similar horiz designs. Multicoloured. Perf 13.

1075	6c. Type **349**	20	40
1076	8c. North-west Nelson	25	70
1077	18c. Kaweka	40	1·25
	a. Blue omitted	£200	
1078	23c. Coromandel	50	1·40
1075/1078	Set of 4	1·25	3·25

350 Girl feeding Lamb **351** *Virgin and Child* (Zanobi Machiavelli)

(Des Margaret Chapman. Litho Harrison)

1975 (6 Aug). Health Stamps. T **350** and similar horiz designs. Multicoloured. Perf 13½×13.

1079	3c.+1c. Type **350**	15	30
1080	4c.+1c. Boy with Hen and Chicks	15	30
1081	5c.+1c. Boy with Duck and Duckling	40	1·50
1079/1081	Set of 3	65	1·90
MS1082	123×146 mm. No. 1080×10	9·00	35·00

(Des Enid Hunter. Photo Harrison)

1975 (1 Oct). Christmas. T **351** and similar horiz designs. Multicoloured. Perf 13×13½ (3c.) or 13½×13 (others).

1083	3c. Type **351**	10	10
	a. Red omitted*	£800	
	b. Black omitted	£1200	
1084	5c. Cross in Landscape (stained glass window, Greendale Church)	10	10
	a. Brown (face value) omitted	£180	
1085	10c. *I saw three ships. . .* (carol)	35	65
1083/1085	Set of 3	45	65

* This occurred in the last two vertical rows of the sheet with the red partially omitted on the previous row.

Used copies of No. 1083 have been seen with the orange ('Christmas 1975') omitted.

352 Sterling Silver   **353** Queen Elizabeth II (photograph by W. Harrison)   **353a** Maripi (knife)

353b Rainbow Abalone or Paua   **353c** 'Beehive' (section of Parliamentary Buildings, Wellington)

(Des A. G. Mitchell (1c. to 14c.), I. Hulse (20c. to $2), R. Conly ($5). Photo Harrison (1c. to 10c.), Courvoisier (11c. to 14c.), Heraclio Fournier (20c. to $5))

1975 (26 Nov)–**81**

(a) Vert designs as T **352** showing garden roses. Multicoloured. Perf 14½ (6c. to 8c.) or 14½×14 (others).

1086	1c. Type. **352**	10	10
1087	2c. Lilli Marlene	10	20
1088	3c. Queen Elizabeth	60	10
	a. Perf 14½ (8.79)	1·00	10
	b. Imperf (pair)	£150	—
1089	4c. Super Star	10	60
1090	5c. Diamond Jubilee	10	10
1091	6c. Cresset	40	1·00
	a. Perf 14½×14 (8.76)	40	1·00
1092	7c. Michele Meilland	85	1·40
	a. Perf 14½×14 (5.76)	40	10
1093	8c. Josephine Bruce	85	1·25
	aa. Yellow (frame) omitted	£1500	—
	a. Perf 14½×14 (8.76)	25	10
	b. Imperf (pair)	£125	—
1094	9c. Iceberg	40	60

(b) T **353**. Perf 14½×14 (7.12.77).

1094a	10c. multicoloured	45	20
	ab. Perf 14½ (1.79)	30	10
	c. Blue omitted	£350	—

(c) Vert designs as T **353a** showing Maori artefacts. Granite paper. Perf 11½ (24.11.76).

1095	11c. reddish brown, lemon and blackish brown	30	70
1096	12c. reddish brown, lemon and blackish brown	30	35
1097	13c. reddish brown, greenish blue and blackish brown	40	1·00
1098	14c. reddish brown, lemon and blackish brown	30	10

Designs: 11c. T **353a**; 12c. Putorino (flute); 13c. Wahaika (club); 14c. Kotiate (club).

(d) Horiz designs as T **353b** showing sea shells. Multicoloured. Perf 13.

1099	20c. Type **353b** (29.11.78)	15	10
1100	30c. Toheroa Clam (29.11.78)	25	40
1101	40c. Old Woman or Coarse Dosinia (29.11.78)	30	30
1102	50c. New Zealand or Spiny Murex (29.11.78)	30	35
1103	$1 New Zealand Scallop (26.11.79)	55	80
	a. Imperf between (vert pair)	£400	
1104	$2 Circular Saw (26.11.79)	70	1·25

(e) T **353c**. Perf 13 (2.12.81).

1105	$5 multicoloured	1·50	1·50
	a. Imperf (vert pair)	£900	
1086/1105	Set of 21	6·75	8·25

Faked 'missing colour errors' exist of No. 1094a, involving parts of the portrait.

Used examples of No. 1099 exist with the black colour omitted so that the body of the shell appears in blue instead of green.

No. 1103a occurs on the top two rows of the sheet; the lower stamp being imperforate on three edges except for two perforation holes at the foot of each vertical side.

39

NEW ZEALAND

354 Family and League of Mothers Badge

(Des A. P. Derrick. Litho J.W.)

1976 (4 Feb). Anniversaries and Metrication. T **354** and similar horiz designs. Multicoloured. Perf 13½×14.
1110	6c. Type **354**	10	10
1111	7c. Weight, temperature, linear measure and capacity	10	10
1112	8c. *William Bryan* (immigrant ship), mountain and New Plymouth	15	10
1113	10c. Two women shaking hands and YWCA badge	15	60
1114	25c. Map of the world showing cable links	30	1·25
1110/1114	Set of 5	70	1·90

Anniversaries: 6c. League of Mothers, 50th Anniversary; 7c. Metrication; 8c. Centenary of New Plymouth; 10c. 50th Anniversary of New Zealand YWCA; 25c. Centenary of link with International Telecommunications Network.

355 Gig **356** Purakaunui Falls

(Des G. F. Fuller. Litho Harrison)

1976 (7 Apr). Vintage Farm Transport. T **355** and similar horiz designs. Multicoloured. Perf 13½×13.
1115	6c. Type **355**	15	40
1116	7c. Thornycroft lorry	15	10
1117	8c. Scandi wagon	20	15
1118	9c. Traction engine	15	30
1119	10c. Wool wagon	15	30
1120	25c. Cart	40	1·75
1115/1120	Set of 6	1·10	2·75

(Des and photo Courvoisier)

1976 (2 June). Waterfalls. T **356** and similar vert designs. Multicoloured. Perf 11½.
1121	10c. Type **356**	20	10
1122	14c. Marakopa Falls	30	75
1123	15c. Bridal Veil Falls	30	80
1124	16c. Papakorito Falls	30	1·00
1121/1124	Set of 4	1·00	2·50

357 Boy and Pony **358** Nativity (Spanish carving)

(Des Margaret Chapman. Litho Harrison)

1976 (4 Aug). Health Stamps. T **357** and similar vert designs. Multicoloured. Perf 13×13½.
1125	7c.+1c. Type **357**	20	40
1126	8c.+1c. Girl and Calf	20	40
1127	10c.+1c. Girls and Bird	40	1·00
1125/1127	Set of 3	70	1·60
MS1128	96×121 mm. Nos. 1125/1127×2	1·75	6·00

(Des Margaret Chapman (18c.), D. A. Hatcher (others). Photo Harrison)

1976 (6 Oct). Christmas. T **358** and similar horiz designs. Multicoloured. Perf 14×14½ (7c.) or 14½×14 (others).
1129	7c. Type **358**	15	10
1130	11c. Resurrection (stained glass window, St Joseph's Catholic Church, Grey Lynn)	25	30
1131	18c. Angels	40	1·00
1129/1131	Set of 3	70	1·25

359 Arms of Hamilton **360** Queen Elizabeth II

(Des P. L. Blackie. Litho Harrison)

1977 (19 Jan). Anniversaries. T **359** and similar vert designs. Multicoloured. Perf 13×13½.
1132	8c. Type **359**	15	35
	a. Horiz strip of 3, Nos. 1132/1134	40	1·00
1133	8c. Arms of Gisborne	15	35
1134	8c. Arms of Masterton	15	35
1135	10c. AA emblem	15	50
	a. Horiz pair. Nos. 1135/1136	30	1·00
	b. Grey omitted	£500	
1136	10c. Arms of the College of Surgeons	15	50
1132/1136	Set of 5	70	1·75

Events: Nos. 1132/1134, City Centenaries; No. 1135, 75th Anniversary of the Automobile Association in New Zealand; No. 1136, 50th Anniversary of Royal Australasian College of Surgeons.

Designs of each value were printed in the same sheet horizontally *se-tenant*.

(Des and photo Harrison from photographs by Warren Harrison)

1977 (23 Feb). Silver Jubilee. Sheet 178×82 mm containing T **360** and similar vert designs showing different portraits. Perf 14×14½.
MS1137	8c.×5 multicoloured	50	1·25
	a. Imperf	£1800	
	ab. Imperf and silver omitted	£4500	
	b. Silver omitted	£1500	
	c. Indian red omitted	£550	

361 Physical Education and Maori Culture **(362)**

(Des A. G. Mitchell. Litho Harrison)

1977 (6 Apr). Education. T **361** and similar vert designs. Multicoloured. Perf 13×13½.
1138	8c. Type **361**	25	40
	a. Horiz strip of 5, Nos. 1138/1142	1·10	1·75
1139	8c. Geography, science and woodwork	25	40
1140	8c. Teaching the deaf, kindergarten and woodwork	25	40
1141	8c. Tertiary and language classes	25	40
1142	8c. Home science, correspondence school and teacher training	25	40
1138/1142	Set of 5	1·10	1·75

Nos. 1138/1142 were printed horizontally *se-tenant* throughout the sheet.

1977 (Apr). Coil stamps for use in stamp-fixing machines. Nos. 1010/1011 surch as T **362** by Government Printer, Wellington.
1143	7c. on 3c. *Detunda egregia* (Moth) (18.4)	25	50
1144	8c. on 4c. *Charagia virescens* (Moth) (20.4)	25	50
	a. Bright green (wing veins) omitted	£325	£250

Forged 7c. surcharges, similar to No. 1143, but in smaller type, are known applied to Nos. 918 and 1010.

NEW ZEALAND

1162	12c. Early telephone	15	15
1163	20c. Bay of Islands (*horiz*)	20	30
1160/1163	Set of 4	60	85

Centenaries commemorated are those of the towns of Ashburton and Stratford, of the telephone in New Zealand, and of the Bay of Islands County.

The 10c. values were printed together, *se-tenant*, in horizontal pairs throughout the sheet.

363 Karitane Beach   **364** Girl with Pigeon

(Des D. A. Hatcher. Photo Heraclio Fournier)

1977 (1 June). Seascapes. T **363** and similar horiz designs. Multicoloured. Perf 14½.

1145	10c. Type **363**	15	10
1146	16c. Ocean Beach, Mount Maunganui	20	30
1147	18c. Piha Beach	20	30
1148	30c. Kaikoura Coast	25	40
1145/1148	Set of 4	70	1·00

(Des A. P. Derrick. Litho Harrison)

1977 (3 Aug). Health Stamps. T **364** and similar vert designs. Multicoloured. Perf 13×13½.

1149	7c.+2c. Type **364**	20	50
1150	8c.+2c. Boy with Frog	20	55
1151	10c.+2c. Girl with Butterfly	40	1·00
1149/1151	Set of 3	70	1·90
MS1152	97×120 mm. Nos. 1149/1151×2	1·10	5·50

Stamps from the miniature sheet are without white border and together form a composite design.

365 The Holy Family (Correggio)

(Des Margaret Chapman (23c.), graphics for all values produced by printer. Photo Courvoisier)

1977 (5 Oct). Christmas. T **365** and similar vert designs. Multicoloured. Perf 11½.

1153	7c. Type **365**	15	10
1154	16c. Madonna and Child (stained glass window, St Michael's and All Angels, Dunedin)	25	25
1155	23c. Partridge in a Pear Tree	40	1·25
1153/1155	Set of 3	70	1·40

366 Merryweather Manual Pump, 1860   **367** Town Clock and Coat of Arms, Ashburton

(Des R. M. Conly. Litho Harrison)

1977 (7 Dec). Firefighting Appliances. T **366** and similar horiz designs. Multicoloured. Perf 14×13.

1156	10c. Type **366**	15	10
1157	11c. 2-wheel hose, reel and ladder, 1880	15	25
1158	12c. Shand Mason steam fire engine, 1873	20	30
1159	23c. Chemical fire engine, 1888	30	90
1156/1159	Set of 4	70	1·40

(Des P. L. Blackie (No. 1162), Harrison (No. 1163), P. J. Durrant (others),. Litho Harrison)

1978 (8 Mar). Centenaries. T **367** and similar multicoloured designs. Perf 14.

1160	10c. Type **367**	15	25
	a. Horiz pair. Nos. 1160/1161	30	50
1161	10c. Stratford and Mount Egmont	15	25

368 Students and Ivey Hall, Lincoln College   **369**   **370** Maui Gas Drilling Platform

(Des A. P. Derrick. Litho Harrison)

1978 (26 Apr). Land Resources and Centenary of Lincoln College of Agriculture. T **368** and similar vert designs. Multicoloured. Perf 14½.

1164	10c. Type **368**	15	10
1165	12c. Sheep grazing	15	30
1166	15c. Fertiliser ground spreading	15	30
1167	16c. Agricultural Field Days	15	60
1168	20c. Harvesting grain	20	40
1169	30c. Dairy farming	30	70
1164/1169	Set of 6	1·00	2·25

(Photo Harrison)

1978 (3 May–13 June). Coil Stamps. Perf 14½×14 (10c.) or 14×13 (others)

1170	**369**	1c. bright purple (13.6)	10	50
1171		2c. bright orange (13.6)	10	50
1172		5c. red-brown (13.6)	10	50
1173		10c. bright blue	30	60
1170/1173		Set of 4	45	1·90

(Des R. M. Conly. Litho Harrison)

1978 (7 June). Resources of the Sea. T **370** and similar vert designs. Multicoloured. Perf 13×14.

1174	12c. Type **370**	15	15
1175	15c. Trawler	15	20
1176	20c. Map of 200 mile fishing limit	20	30
1177	23c. Humpback Whale and Bottlenose Dolphins	25	35
1178	35c. Kingfish, Snapper, Grouper and Squid	40	60
1174/1178	Set of 5	1·00	1·40

371 First Health Charity Stamp   **372** The Holy Family (El Greco)   **373** Sir Julius Vogel

(Des A. G. Mitchell. Litho Harrison)

1978 (2 Aug). Health Stamps. Health Services Commemorations. T **371** and similar vert design. Perf 13×14.

1179	10c.+2c. black, red and gold	20	35
1180	12c.+2c. multicoloured	20	40
	a. Chestnut omitted		
MS1181	97×124 mm. Nos. 1179/1180×3	1·00	4·00
	a. Imprint centred	2·00	8·00

Designs and commemorations: 10c. T **371** (50th anniversary of health charity stamps); 12c. Heart operation (National Heart Foundation).

No. 1180a omits the shadow on the surgeons' faces and hands.

On No. **MS**1181 the printer's imprint falls below the two left-hand stamps. On No. **MS**1181a the imprint is 8 mm to the right, resulting in the second 'N' of 'LONDON' falling below the right-hand stamp.

41

NEW ZEALAND

(Des R. M. Conly. Photo Courvoisier)

1978 (4 Oct). Christmas. T **372** and similar multicoloured designs. Perf 11½.
1182	7c. Type **372**	10	10
1183	16c. All Saints' Church, Howick (horiz)	25	35
1184	23c. Beach scene (horiz)	30	50
1182/1184 Set of 3		60	85

(Des A. G. Mitchell. Litho J.W.)

1979 (7 Feb). Statesmen. T **373** and similar vert designs in sepia and drab. Perf 13×13½.
1185	10c. Type **373**	20	50
	a. Horiz strip of 3, Nos. 1185/1187	55	1·40
1186	10c. Sir George Grey	20	50
1187	10c. Richard John Seddon	20	50
1185/1187 Set of 3		55	1·40

Nos. 1185/1187 were printed together, se-tenant, in horizontal strips of three throughout the sheet.

Nos. 1185/1187 have matt, almost invisible, gum.

374 Riverlands Cottage, Blenheim

375 Whangaroa Harbour

(Des P. Leitch. Litho Enschedé)

1979 (4 Apr). Architecture (1st series). T **374** and similar horiz designs. Perf 13½×13.
1188	10c. black, new blue and deep blue	10	10
1189	12c. black, pale green and bottle green	10	40
1190	15c. black and grey	15	45
1191	20c. black, yellow-brown and sepia	20	45
1188/1191 Set of 4		50	1·25

Designs: 10c. T **374**; 12c. The Mission House, Waimate North; 15c. The Elms, Tauranga; 20c. Provincial Council Buildings, Christchurch.

See also Nos. 1217/1220 and 1262/1265.

(Photo Heraclio Fournier)

1979 (6 June). Small Harbours. T **375** and similar multicoloured designs. Perf 13.
1192	15c. Type **375**	15	10
1193	20c. Kawau Island	20	40
1194	23c. Akaroa Harbour (vert)	20	65
1195	35c. Picton Harbour (vert)	30	85
1192/1195 Set of 4		75	1·75

376 Children with Building Bricks

377 Two-spotted Chromis

(Des W. Kelsall. Litho J.W.)

1979 (6 June). International Year of the Child. Perf 14.
1196	**376**	10c. multicoloured	15	10

(Des P. Blackie (12c.), G. Fuller (others). Litho Harrison)

1979 (25 July). Health Stamps. Marine Life. T **377** and similar multicoloured designs. Perf 13×13½ (12c.) or 13½×13 (others).
1197	10c.+2c. Type **377**	20	50
	a. Horiz pair. Nos. 1197/1198	40	1·00
1198	10c.+2c. Sea Urchin	20	50
1199	12c.+2c. Red Goatfish and underwater cameraman (vert)	20	50
1197/1199 Set of 3		55	1·40
MS1200 144×72 mm. Nos. 1197/1199, each×2. Perf 14×14½ (12c.) or 14½×14 (others)		1·00	2·75

Nos. 1197/1198 were printed together, se-tenant, in horizontal pairs throughout the sheet.

4c
(378)

1979 (31 Aug)–**80**. Nos. 1091a, 1092a, 1093a and 1094aab surch as T **378** by Government Printer, Wellington.
1201	4c. on 8c. Josephine Bruce (24.9.79)	10	50
	a. Surch double	45·00	
	b. Black omitted	£1300	
1202	14c. on 10c. Type **353**	15	10
	a. Surch double, one albino	£150	
	b. Surch inverted	£400	
	c. Pair, one without surch	£300	
	d. Orange omitted	£150	
1203	17c. on 6c. Cresset (8.10.79)	20	1·00
	a. Surch double, one albino	£150	
1203b	20c. on 7c. Michele Meilland (29.9.80)	20	10
1201/1203b Set of 4		55	1·40

Neither of the impressions of the surcharge on No. 1201a is properly inked.

379 Madonna and Child (sculpture by Ghiberti)

380 Chamber, House of Representatives

(Des D. Hatcher. Photo Courvoisier)

1979 (3 Oct). Christmas. T **379** and similar vert designs. Multicoloured. Perf 11½.
1204	10c. Type **379**	10	10
1205	25c. Christ Church, Russell	20	50
1206	35c. Pohutukawa (tree)	30	70
1204/1206 Set of 3		55	1·10

(Des D. Hatcher. Litho J.W.)

1979 (26 Nov). 25th Commonwealth Parliamentary Conference, Wellington. T **380** and similar vert designs. Multicoloured. Perf 13½.
1207	14c. Type **380**	10	10
1208	20c. Mace and Black Rod	15	30
1209	30c. Wall hanging from the 'Beehive'	20	75
1207/1209 Set of 3		40	1·00

381 1855 1d. Stamp

(Des D. Hatcher (14c. (all designs)), R. M. Conly (others). Litho Harrison)

1980 (7 Feb). Anniversaries and Events. T **381** and similar designs. Perf 13½×13 (14c. (all designs)) or 14 (others).
1210	14c. black, brown-red and yellow	10	20
	a. Horiz strip of 3. Nos. 1210/1212	25	70
	ab. Black (inscription) omitted (strip of 3)	£375	
1211	14c. black, deep turquoise-blue and yellow	10	20
1212	14c. black, dull yellowish green and yellow	10	20
1213	17c. multicoloured	15	25
1214	25c. multicoloured	15	25
1215	30c. multicoloured	15	30
1210/1215 Set of 6		70	1·25
MS1216 146×96 mm. Nos. 1210/1212 (as horiz strip). Perf 14½×14 (sold at 52c.)		1·00	3·50

Designs and commemorations: (38×22 mm)—No. 1210, T **381**; No. 1211, 1855 2d. stamp; No. 1212, 1855 1s. stamp (125th anniversary of New Zealand stamps). (40×23 mm)—No. 1213, Geyser, wood carving and building (centenary of Rotorua (town)); No. 1214, Earina autumnalis and thelymitra venosa (International Orchid Conference, Auckland); No. 1215, Ploughing and Golden Plough Trophy (World Ploughing Championships, Christchurch).

The premium on No. **MS**1216 was used to help finance the Zeapex 80 International Stamp Exhibition, Auckland.

Nos. 1210/1212 were printed together, se-tenant, in horizontal strips of three throughout the sheet.

382 Ewelme Cottage, Parnell

383 Auckland Harbour

NEW ZEALAND

(Des P. Leitch. Litho Enschedé)

1980 (2 Apr). Architecture (2nd series). T **382** and similar horiz designs. Multicoloured. Perf 13½×12½.

1217	14c. Type **382**	15	10
1218	17c. Broadgreen, Nelson	15	25
1219	25c. Courthouse, Oamaru	20	35
1220	30c. Government Buildings, Wellington	25	40
1217/1220	Set of 4	65	1·00

(Des D. Hatcher. Photo Heraclio Fournier)

1980 (4 June). Large Harbours. T **383** and similar horiz designs. Multicoloured. Perf 13.

1221	25c. Type **383**	20	20
1222	30c. Wellington Harbour	25	30
1223	35c. Lyttelton Harbour	25	35
1224	50c. Port Chalmers	40	90
1221/1224	Set of 4	1·00	1·50

384 Surf Fishing

385 *Madonna and Child with Cherubim* (sculpture by Andrea della Robbia)

(Des Margaret Chapman. Litho Enschedé)

1980 (6 Aug). Health Stamps. Fishing. T **384** and similar horiz designs. Multicoloured. Perf 13×12½.

1225	14c.+2c. Type **384**	20	65
	a. Horiz pair. Nos. 1225/1226	40	1·25
1226	14c.+2c. Wharf fishing	20	65
1227	17c.+2c. Spear fishing	20	50
1225/1227	Set of 3	55	1·60
MS1228	148×75 mm. Nos. 1225/1227 each×2. Perf 13½×13	1·00	2·50

Nos. 1225/1226 were printed together, *se-tenant*, in horizontal pairs throughout the sheet.

(Des P. Durrant. Photo Courvoisier)

1980 (1 Oct). Christmas. T **385** and similar vert designs. Multicoloured. Perf 11½.

1229	10c. Type **385**	10	10
1230	25c. St Mary's Church, New Plymouth	20	25
1231	35c. Picnic scene	30	80
1229/1231	Set of 3	55	1·00

386 Te Heu Heu (chief)

387 Lieutenant colonel the Honourable W. H. A. Feilding and Borough of Feilding Crest

(Des R. M. Conly. Litho Heraclio Fournier)

1980 (26 Nov). Maori Personalities. Vert designs as T **386**. Multicoloured. Perf 12½×13.

1232	15c. Type **386**	10	10
1233	25c. Te Hau (chief)	10	15
1234	35c. Te Puea (princess)	15	10
1235	45c. Ngata (politician)	20	15
1236	60c. Te Ata-O-Tu (warrior)	30	30
1232/1236	Set of 5	70	70

(Des R. M. Conly. Litho Harrison)

1981 (4 Feb). Commemorations. T **387** and similar horiz design. Perf 14½.

1237	20c. multicoloured	20	20
1238	25c. black and brown-ochre	25	20

Designs and Commemorations: 20c. T **387** (Centenary of Feilding (town)); 25c. IYD emblem and cupped hands (International Year of the Disabled).

388 The Family at Play

389 Kaiauai River

(Des A. Derrick. Litho J.W.)

1981 (1 Apr). Family Life. T **388** and similar vert designs. Multicoloured. Perf 13½×13.

1239	20c. Type **388**	10	10
1240	25c. The family, young and old	15	20
1241	30c. The family at home	15	35
1242	35c. The family at church	20	45
1239/1242	Set of 4	55	1·00

(Des D. Hatcher. Photo Heraclio Fournier)

1981 (3 June). River Scenes. T **389** and similar multicoloured designs. Perf 13½×13 (30c., 35c.) or 13×13½ (others).

1243	30c. Type **389**	20	25
1244	35c. Mangahao	20	30
1245	40c. Shotover (*horiz*)	25	35
1246	60c. Cleddau (*horiz*)	45	50
1243/1246	Set of 4	1·00	1·25

390 St Paul's Cathedral

(Des and litho Harrison)

1981 (29 July). Royal Wedding. T **390** and similar horiz design. Multicoloured. Perf 14½.

1247	20c. Type **390**	30	20
	a. Pair. Nos. 1247/1248	60	45
	ab. Deep grey (inscriptions and date) omitted	£750	
1248	20c. Prince Charles and Lady Diana Spencer	30	20

Nos. 1247/1248 were printed together, *se-tenant*, in horizontal and vertical pairs throughout the sheet.

391 Girl with Starfish

(Des PO. Litho Harrison)

1981 (5 Aug). Health Stamps. Children playing by the Sea. T **391** and similar vert designs. Multicoloured. Perf 14½.

1249	20c.+2c. Type **391**	20	65
	a. Horiz pair. Nos. 1249/1250	40	1·25
1250	20c.+2c. Boy fishing	20	65
1251	25c.+2c. Children exploring rock pool	20	35
1249/1251	Set of 3	55	1·50
MS1252	100×125 mm. Nos. 1249/1251, each×2	1·00	2·50

The 20c. values were printed together, *se-tenant*, in horizontal pairs throughout the sheet.

The stamps from No. **MS**1252 were printed together, *se-tenant*, in two horizontal strips of three, each forming a composite design.

NEW ZEALAND

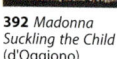

392 *Madonna Suckling the Child* (d'Oggiono)

393 Tauranga Mission House

(Des Margaret Chapman. Photo Courvoisier)

1981 (7 Oct). Christmas. T **392** and similar vert designs. Multicoloured. Perf 11½.

1253	14c. Type **392**	15	10
1254	30c. St John's Church, Wakefield	20	25
1255	40c. Golden Tainui (flower)	35	35
1253/1255	Set of 3	65	60

(Des A. Derrick. Litho Walsall)

1982 (3 Feb). Commemorations. T **393** and similar vert designs. Multicoloured. Perf 14½.

1256	20c. Type **393**	20	10
	a. Horiz pair. Nos. 1256/1257	40	30
1257	20c. Water tower, Hawera	20	10
1258	25c. Cat	25	30
1259	30c. *Dunedin* (refrigerated sailing ship)	25	30
1260	35c. Scientific research equipment	25	30
1256/1260	Set of 5	1·00	1·10

Commemorations: No. 1256, Centenary of Tauranga (town); No. 1257, Centenary of Hawera (town); No. 1258, Centenary of SPCA (Society for the Prevention of Cruelty to Animals in New Zealand); No. 1259, Centenary of Frozen Meat Exports; No. 1260, International Year of Science.

The 20c. values were printed together, *se-tenant*, in horizontal pairs throughout the sheet.

394 Map of New Zealand

395 Alberton, Auckland

(Des A. G. Mitchell. Litho Leigh-Mardon Ltd, Melbourne)

1982 (1 Apr–13 Dec). Perf 12½.

1261	**394**	24c. pale yellowish green and ultramarine	30	10
		a. Perf 14½×14 (13.12.82)	35	20

(Des P. Leitch. Litho Walsall)

1982 (7 Apr). Architecture (3rd series). T **395** and similar horiz designs. Multicoloured. Perf 14×14½.

1262	20c. Type **395**	10	20
1263	25c. Caccia Birch, Palmerston North	10	30
1264	30c. Railway station, Dunedin	30	40
1265	35c. Post Office, Ophir	15	45
1262/1265	Set of 4	60	1·25

396 Kaiteriteri Beach, Nelson (Summer)

397 Labrador

(Des D. Hatcher. Photo Heraclio Fournier)

1982 (2 June). The Four Seasons. New Zealand Scenes. T **396** and similar horiz designs. Multicoloured. Perf 13×13½.

1266	35c. Type **396**	20	25
1267	40c. St Omer Park, Queenstown (Autumn)	25	30
1268	45c. Mount Ngauruhoe, Tongariro National Park (Winter)	25	30
1269	70c. Wairarapa farm (Spring)	40	50
1266/1269	Set of 4	1·00	1·25

(Des R. M. Conly. Litho Enschedé)

1982 (4 Aug). Health Stamps. Dogs. T **397** and similar vert designs. Multicoloured. Perf 13×13½.

1270	24c.+2c. Type **397**	50	1·00
	a. Horiz pair. Nos. 1270/1271	1·00	2·00
1271	24c.+2c. Border Collie	50	1·00
1272	30c.+2c. Cocker Spaniel	50	1·00
1270/1272	Set of 3	1·40	2·75
MS1273	98×125 mm. Nos. 1270/1272, each×2. Perf 14×13½	2·00	5·00

The 24c. values were printed together, *se-tenant*, in horizontal pairs throughout the sheet.

398 *Madonna with Child and Two Angels* (Piero di Cosimo)

(Des Margaret Chapman. Photo Heraclio Fournier)

1982 (6 Oct). Christmas. T **398** and similar vert designs. Multicoloured. Perf 14×13½.

1274	18c. Type **398**	15	10
1275	35c. Rangiatea Maori Church, Otaki	25	30
1276	45c. Surf lifesaving	40	40
1274/1276	Set of 3	70	65

399 Nephrite **399a** Grapes **399b** Kokako

(Des P. Durrant (Nos. 1277/1282), D. Little (Nos. 1283/1287), Janet Marshall (Nos. 1288/1297). Litho Leigh-Mardon Ltd. Melbourne)

1982 (1 Dec)–**89**. Multicoloured. Perf 14½×14 (Nos. 1277/1287) or 14½ (Nos. 1288/1297)

(a) Minerals. T **399** *and similar vert designs.*

1277	1c. Type **399**	10	10
	a. Perf 12½	30	20
1278	2c. Agate	10	10
	a. Perf 12½	70	2·00
1279	3c. Iron Pyrites	10	10
1280	4c. Amethyst	15	10
1281	5c. Carnelian	15	10
1282	9c. Native Sulphur	20	10

(b) Fruits. T **399a** *and similar vert designs.*

1283	10c. Type **399a** (7.12.83)	20	10
1284	20c. Citrus Fruit (7.12.83)	20	10
1285	30c. Nectarines (7.12.83)	20	10
1286	40c. Apples (7.12.83)	25	10
1287	50c. Kiwifruit (7.12.83)	25	10

(c) Native Birds. T **399b**, *and similar vert designs. Phosphorised paper ($1, $2).*

1288	30c. Kakapo (1.5.86)	50	15
1289	40c. Mountain ('Blue') Duck (2.2.87)	50	20
1290	45c. New Zealand Falcon (1.5.86)	1·00	25
1291	60c. New Zealand Teal (2.2.87)	1·50	1·50
1292	$1 Type **399b**, (24.4.85)	1·00	15
1293	$2 Chatham Island Robin (24.4.85)	1·00	50
1294	$3 Stitchbird (23.4.86)	1·25	1·40
1295	$4 Saddleback (23.4.86)	1·50	1·50
1296	$5 Takahe (20.4.88)	3·25	3·00
1297	$10 Little Spotted Kiwi (19.4.89)	3·50	5·00
1277/1297	Set of 21	15·00	12·50
1292/1297	Optd 'Specimen' Set of 6	6·50	

Nos. 1292/1297 overprinted 'Specimen' come from a special NEW ZEALAND 1990 Presentation Pack issued on 19 April 1989.

NEW ZEALAND

A miniature sheet containing No. 1293 was only available from the New Zealand stand at PHILEXFRANCE '89 International Stamp Exhibition or the Philatelic Bureau at Wanganui.

Versions of the $3 with narrow face value and of the $4 in horizontal format were prepared, as was No. 1288 with a face value of 25c., but none were issued for postal purposes.

For No. 1297 in a miniature sheet for POST X 95 Postal History Exhibition see No. **MS**1854.

400 Old Arts Building, Auckland University   **401** Queen Elizabeth II

(Des G. Emery (35c.), P. Durrant (others). Litho Cambec Press, Melbourne (35c.), J.W. (others))

1983 (2 Feb). Commemorations. T **400** and similar vert designs. Multicoloured. Perf 13×13½ (35c.) or 14×13½ (others).

1303	24c. Salvation Army Centenary logo	20	10
1304	30c. Type **400**	20	40
1305	35c. Stylised Kangaroo and Kiwi	20	40
1306	40c. Rainbow Trout	25	55
1307	45c. Satellite over Earth	25	55
1303/1307	Set of 5	1·00	1·75

Commemorations: 24c. Centenary of Salvation Army; 30c. Centenary of Auckland University; 35c. Closer Economic Relationship agreement with Australia; 40c. Centenary of introduction of Rainbow Trout into New Zealand; 45c. World Communications Year.

(Des P. Durrant. Litho Harrison)

1983 (14 Mar). Commonwealth Day. T **401** and similar horiz designs. Multicoloured. Perf 13½.

1308	24c. Type **401**	20	10
1309	35c. Maori rock drawing	30	50
1310	40c. Woolmark and wool-scouring symbols	30	80
1311	45c. Coat of Arms	30	80
1308/1311	Set of 4	1·00	2·00

402 Boats, Island Bay (Rita Angus)   **403** Mount Egmont

(Des D. Hatcher. Litho Leigh-Mardon Ltd, Melbourne)

1983 (6 Apr). Paintings by Rita Angus. T **402** and similar vert designs. Multicoloured. Perf 14½.

1312	24c. Type **402**	20	10
1313	30c. *Central Otago Landscape*	25	45
1314	35c. *Wanaka Landscape*	30	50
1315	45c. *Tree*	35	70
1312/1315	Set of 4	1·00	1·60

(Des P. Durrant. Photo Heraclio Fournier)

1983 (1 June). Beautiful New Zealand. T **403** and similar multicoloured designs. Perf 13.

1316	35c. Type **403**	20	30
1317	40c. Cooks Bay	25	30
1318	45c. Lake Matheson (*horiz*)	25	40
1319	70c. Lake Alexandrina (*horiz*)	40	60
1316/1319	Set of 4	1·00	1·50

404 Tabby   **405** *The Family of the Holy Oak Tree* (Raphael)

(Des R. M. Conly. Litho Harrison)

1983 (3 Aug). Health Stamps. Cats. T **404** and similar vert designs. Multicoloured. Perf 14.

1320	24c.+2c. Type **404**	25	70
	a. Horiz pair. Nos. 1320/1321	50	1·40
1321	24c.+2c. Siamese	25	70
1322	30c.+2c. Persian	40	80
1320/1322	Set of 3	80	2·00
MS1323	100×126 mm. Nos. 1320/1322, each×2	1·40	2·50

The 24c. values were printed together, *se-tenant*, in horizontal pairs throughout the sheet.

(Des R. M. Conly (45c.), M. Wyatt (others). Photo Courvoisier)

1983 (5 Oct). Christmas. T **405** and similar vert designs. Multicoloured. Perf 12×11½.

1324	18c. Type **405**	15	10
1325	35c. St Patrick's Church, Greymouth	30	45
1326	45c. 'The Glory of Christmas' (star and flowers)	35	80
1324/1326	Set of 3	70	1·25

406 Geology

(Des R. M. Conly. Litho Cambec Press, Melbourne)

1984 (1 Feb). Antarctic Research. T **406** and similar horiz designs. Multicoloured. Perf 13½×13.

1327	24c. Type **406**	20	10
1328	40c. Biology	25	40
1329	58c. Glaciology	30	1·60
1330	70c. Meteorology	35	90
1327/1330	Set of 4	1·00	2·75
MS1331	126×110 mm. Nos. 1327/1330	1·00	2·75

407 *Mountaineer*, Lake Wakatipu   **408** Mount Hutt

(Des M. Wyatt. Litho Cambec Press, Melbourne)

1984 (4 Apr). New Zealand Ferry Boats. T **407** and similar horiz designs. Multicoloured. Perf 13½×13.

1332	24c. Type **407**	20	10
1333	40c. *Waikana*, Otago	25	45
1334	58c. *Britannia*, Waitemata	30	1·60
1335	70c. *Wakatere*, Firth of Thames	45	85
1332/1335	Set of 4	1·10	2·75

(Des D. Little. Litho Cambec Press, Melbourne)

1984 (6 June). Ski Slope Scenery. T **408** and similar horiz designs. Multicoloured. Perf 13½×13.

1336	35c. Type **408**	15	25
1337	40c. Coronet Peak	20	30
1338	45c. Turoa	20	30
1339	70c. Whakapapa	30	50
1336/1339	Set of 4	75	1·25

NEW ZEALAND

409 Hamilton's Frog   **410** Clydesdales ploughing Field

(Des A. G. Mitchell. Litho Cambec Press, Melbourne)

1984 (11 July). Amphibians and Reptiles. T **409** and similar horiz designs. Multicoloured. Perf 13½.

1340	24c. Type **409**	15	45
	a. Horiz pair. Nos. 1340/1341	30	90
1341	24c. Great Barrier Skink	15	45
1342	30c. Harlequin Gecko	15	35
1343	58c. Otago Skink	25	80
1344	70c. Gold-striped Gecko	30	75
1340/1344 Set of 5		80	2·50

Nos. 1340/1341 were printed together, *se-tenant*, in horizontal pairs throughout the sheet.

(Des Margaret Chapman. Litho Harrison)

1984 (1 Aug). Health Stamps. Horses. T **410** and similar horiz designs. Multicoloured. Perf 14½.

1345	24c.+2c. Type **410**	40	70
	a. Horiz pair. Nos. 1345/1346	80	1·40
1346	24c.+2c. Shetland Ponies	40	70
1347	30c.+2c. Thoroughbreds	40	70
1345/1347 Set of 3		1·10	1·90
MS1348 148×75 mm. Nos. 1345/1347, each×2		1·50	3·25

Nos. 1345/1346 were printed together, *se-tenant*, in horizontal pairs throughout the sheet.

411 Adoration of the Shepherds (Lorenzo di Credi)   **412** Mounted Riflemen, South Africa, 1901

(Des R. M. Conly (45c.), P. Durrant (others). Photo Heraclio Fournier)

1984 (26 Sept). Christmas. T **411** and similar multicoloured designs. Perf 13½×14 (18c.) or 14×13½ (others).

1349	18c. Type **411**	15	10
1350	35c. Old St Paul's, Wellington (*vert*)	20	30
1351	45c. The Joy of Christmas (*vert*)	30	70
1349/1351 Set of 3		60	1·00

(Des R. M. Conly. Litho Harrison)

1984 (7 Nov). New Zealand Military History. T **412** and similar horiz designs. Multicoloured. Perf 15×14.

1352	24c. Type **412**	20	10
1353	40c. Engineers, France, 1917	25	40
1354	58c. Tanks of 2nd NZ Divisional Cavalry, North Africa, 1942	30	1·25
1355	70c. Infantryman in jungle kit, and 25-pounder gun, Korea and South-East Asia, 1950–1972	35	75
1352/1355 Set of 4		1·00	2·25
MS1356 122×106 mm. Nos. 1352/1355		1·00	2·25

413 St John Ambulance Badge

(Des Lindy Fisher. Litho J.W.)

1985 (16 Jan). Centenary of St John Ambulance in New Zealand. Perf 14.

1357	**413**	24c. black, gold and bright rosine	20	10
1358		30c. black, silver and bright ultramarine	25	40
1359		40c. black and grey	30	70
1357/1359 Set of 3			65	1·00

The colours of the badge depicted are those for Bailiffs and Dames Grand Cross (24c.), Knights and Dames of Grace (30c.) and Officer Brothers and Sisters (40c.).

414 Nelson Horse Tram, 1862   **415** Shotover Bridge

(Des R. M. Conly. Litho Cambec Press, Melbourne)

1985 (6 Mar). Vintage Trams. T **414** and similar horiz designs. Multicoloured. Perf 13½.

1360	24c. Type **414**	15	10
1361	30c. Graham's Town steam tram, 1871	20	50
1362	35c. Dunedin cable car, 1881	20	55
1363	40c. Auckland electric tram, 1902	20	55
1364	45c. Wellington electric tram, 1904	20	65
1365	58c. Christchurch electric tram, 1905	30	1·75
1360/1365 Set of 6		1·10	3·50

TARAPEX '86. To support this National Philatelic Exhibition the New Zealand Post Office co-operated with the organisers in the production of a set of postage imprint labels. Five of the designs showed drawings of Maoris, taken from originals by Arthur Herbert Messenger and the sixth the Exhibition logo.

The sheetlets of six gummed and perforated labels were released by the Exhibition organisers on 3 April 1985. Although such labels were valid for postage, and could be so used by the general public, the sheetlets were not available from any New Zealand post office or from the Philatelic Bureau.

(Des R. Freeman. Photo Courvoisier)

1985 (12 June). Bridges of New Zealand. T **415** and similar multicoloured designs. Granite paper. Perf 11½.

1366	35c. Type **415**	25	45
1367	40c. Alexandra Bridge	25	45
1368	45c. South Rangitikei Railway Bridge (*vert*)	30	1·00
1369	70c. Twin Bridges (*vert*)	40	1·00
1366/1369 Set of 4		1·10	2·50

416 Queen Elizabeth II (from photo by Camera Press)

(Des B. Clinton. Litho Leigh-Mardon Ltd, Melbourne)

1985 (1 July). Multicoloured, background colours given. Perf 14½×14.

1370	**416**	25c. rosine	25	10
1371		35c. new blue	35	10

Examples of the 25c. value exist with the orders on the sash omitted. These are believed to originate from unissued sheets sent for destruction in March 1986.

417 Princess of Wales and Prince William

(Des D. Little. Litho Cambec Press, Melbourne)

1985 (31 July). Health Stamps. T **417** and similar vert designs showing photographs by Lord Snowdon. Multicoloured. Perf 13½.

1372	25c.+2c. Type **417**	75	1·25
	a. Horiz pair. Nos. 1372/1373	1·50	2·50
1373	25c.+2c. Princess of Wales and Prince Henry	75	1·25
1374	35c.+2c. Prince and Princess of Wales with Princes William and Henry	75	1·25
1372/1374 Set of 3		2·00	3·25
MS1375 118×84 mm. Nos. 1372/1374, each×2		3·25	4·50

Nos. 1372/1373 were printed together, *se-tenant*, in horizontal pairs throughout the sheet.

NEW ZEALAND

418 The Holy Family in the Stable   419 HMNZS *Philomel* (1914–1947)

(Des Eileen Mayo. Photo Enschedé)

1985 (18 Sept). Christmas. T **418** and similar vert designs. Multicoloured. Perf 13½×12½.
1376	18c. Type **418**	20	10
1377	40c. The shepherds	45	85
1378	50c. The Angels	45	1·00
1376/1378	Set of 3	1·00	1·75

Examples of the 18c. and 50c. stamps exist showing the spelling error 'CRISTMAS'. These are believed to originate from unissued sheets sent for destruction in March 1986. The New Zealand Post Office has stated that no such stamps were issued and that existing examples were removed unlawfully during the destruction process.

(Des P. Durrant. Litho Cambec Press, Melbourne)

1985 (6 Nov). New Zealand Naval History. T **419** and similar horiz designs. Multicoloured. Perf 13½.
1379	25c. Type **419**	40	15
1380	45c. HMNZS *Achilles* (1936–1946)	55	1·10
1381	60c. HMNZS *Rotoiti* (1949–1965)	70	1·50
1382	75c. HMNZS *Canterbury* (from 1971)	85	1·50
1379/1382	Set of 4	2·25	3·75
MS1383	124×108 mm. Nos. 1379/1382	2·25	3·75

420 Police Computer Operator   421 Indian Power Plus 1000 cc Motorcycle (1920)

(Des A. Mitchell. Litho Leigh-Mardon Ltd, Melbourne)

1986 (15 Jan). Centenary of New Zealand Police. T **420** and similar vert designs, each showing historical aspects above modern police activities. Multicoloured. Perf 14½×14.
1384	25c. Type **420**	30	55
	a. Horiz strip of 5. Nos. 1384/1388	1·40	2·50
1385	25c. Detective and mobile control room	30	55
1386	25c. Policewoman and badge	30	55
1387	25c. Forensic scientist, patrol car and policeman with child	30	55
1388	25c. Police College, Porirua, Patrol boat *Lady Elizabeth II* and dog handler	30	55
1384/1388	Set of 5	1·40	2·50

Nos. 1384/1388 were printed together, *se-tenant*, in horizontal strips of five throughout the sheet.

(Des M. Wyatt. Litho J.W.)

1986 (5 Mar). Vintage Motorcycles. T **421** and similar horiz designs. Multicoloured. Perf 13×12½.
1389	35c. Type **421**	25	35
1390	45c. Norton CS1 500 cc (1927)	25	50
1391	60c. BSA Sloper 500 cc (1930)	30	1·50
1392	75c. Triumph Model H 550 cc (1915)	40	1·60
1389/1392	Set of 4	1·10	3·50

422 Tree of Life   423 Knights Point

(Des Margaret Clarkson. Litho J.W.)

1986 (5 Mar). International Peace Year. T **422** and similar horiz design. Multicoloured. Perf 13×12½.
1393	25c. Type **422**	20	30
	a. Horiz pair. Nos. 1393/1394	40	60
1394	25c. Peace Dove	20	30

Nos. 1393/1394 were printed together, *se-tenant*, in horizontal pairs throughout the sheet.

(Des P. Durrant. Photo Heraclio Fournier)

1986 (11 June). Coastal Scenery. T **423** and similar horiz designs. Multicoloured. Perf 14.
1395	55c. Type **423**	35	55
1396	60c. Reeks Bay	35	70
1397	65c. Doubtless Bay	40	1·00
1398	80c. Wainui Bay	50	1·00
1395/1398	Set of 4	1·75	3·00
MS1399	124×99 mm. No. 1398 (sold at $1.20)	1·00	1·25

The 40c. premium on No. **MS**1399 was to support New Zealand 1990 International Stamp Exhibition, Auckland.

No. **MS**1399 exists overprinted for Stockholmia. Such miniature sheets were only available at this International Stamp Exhibition in Stockholm and were not placed on sale in New Zealand.

424 Football (Kylie Epapara)   425 A Partridge in a Pear Tree

(Litho Leigh-Mardon Ltd, Melbourne)

1986 (30 July). Health Stamps. Children's Paintings (1st series). T **424** and similar multicoloured designs. Perf 14½×14 (30c.) or 14×14½ (45c.).
1400	30c.+3c. Type **424**	40	75
	a. Horiz pair. Nos. 1400/1401	80	1·50
1401	30c.+3c. Children at Play (Philip Kata)	40	75
1402	45c.+3c. Children Skipping (Mia Flannery) (*horiz*)	50	75
1400/1402	Set of 3	1·10	1·75
MS1403	144×81 mm. Nos. 1400/1402, each×2	1·40	2·00

Nos. 1400/1401 were printed together, *se-tenant*, in horizontal pairs throughout the sheet.

No. **MS**1403 exists overprinted for Stockholmia. Such miniature sheets were only available at this International Stamp Exhibition in Stockholm and were not placed on sale in New Zealand.

See also Nos. 1433/**MS**1436.

(Des Margaret Halcrow-Cross. Photo Heraclio Fournier)

1986 (17 Sept). Christmas. *The Twelve Days of Christmas* (carol). T **425** and similar vert designs. Multicoloured. Perf 14½.
1404	25c. Type **425**	20	10
1405	55c. Two turtle doves	45	40
1406	65c. Three French hens	50	70
1404/1406	Set of 3	1·00	1·10

426 Conductor and Orchestra   427 Jet Boating

(Des R. Freeman. Litho Leigh-Mardon Ltd, Melbourne)

1986 (5 Nov). Music in New Zealand. T **426** and similar vert designs. Perf 14½×14.
1407	30c. multicoloured	15	10
	a. Imperf (pair)	£225	
1408	60c. black, new blue and yellow-orange	25	60
1409	80c. multicoloured	35	1·50
1410	$1 multicoloured	45	1·00
1407/1410	Set of 4	1·10	2·75

Designs: 30c. T **426**; 60c. Cornet and brass band; 80c. Piper and Highland pipe band; $1 Guitar and country music group.

NEW ZEALAND

(Des M. Wyatt. Litho Leigh-Mardon Ltd, Melbourne)

1987 (14 Jan). Tourism. T **427** and similar vert designs. Multicoloured. Perf 14½×14.

1411	60c. Type **427**	30	50
1412	70c. Sightseeing flights	40	75
1413	80c. Camping	45	75
1414	85c. Windsurfing	45	1·00
1415	$1.05 Mountaineering	50	1·40
1416	$1.30 River rafting	65	1·50
1411/1416	Set of 6	2·50	5·50

428 Southern Cross Cup

429 Hand writing Letter and Postal Transport

(Des R. Proud. Litho Leigh-Mardon Ltd, Melbourne)

1987 (2 Feb). Yachting Events. T **428** and similar horiz designs showing yachts. Multicoloured. Perf 14×14½.

1417	40c. Type **428**	15	15
1418	80c. Admiral's Cup	25	60
1419	$1.05 Kenwood Cup	35	1·00
1420	$1.30 America's Cup	40	1·00
1417/1420	Set of 4	1·00	2·50

(Des Communication Arts Ltd. Litho C.P.E. Australia Ltd, Melbourne)

1987 (1 Apr). New Zealand Post Ltd Vesting Day. T **429** and similar horiz design. Multicoloured. Perf 13½.

1421	40c. Type **429**	70	1·25
	a. Horiz pair. Nos. 1421/1422	1·40	2·50
1422	40c. Posting letter, train and mail box	70	1·25

Nos. 1421/1422 were printed together, *se-tenant*, in horizontal pairs throughout the sheet.

430 Avro Type 626 and Wigram Airfield, 1937

431 Urewera National Park and Fern Leaf

(Des P. Leitch. Litho Leigh-Mardon Ltd, Melbourne)

1987 (15 Apr). 50th Anniversary of Royal New Zealand Air Force. T **430** and similar horiz designs. Multicoloured. Perf 14×14½.

1423	40c. Type **430**	55	15
1424	70c. Curtiss P-40E Kittyhawk I over World War II Pacific airstrip	80	1·75
1425	80c. Short S.25 Sunderland flying boat and Pacific lagoon	90	1·75
1426	85c. Douglas A-4F Skyhawk and Mount Ruapehu	90	1·60
1423/1426	Set of 4	2·75	4·75
MS1427	115×105 mm. Nos. 1423/1426	5·50	6·50

No. **MS**1427 overprinted on the selvedge with the CAPEX logo was only available from the New Zealand stand at this International Philatelic Exhibition in Toronto.

(Des Tracey Purkis. Litho Leigh-Mardon Ltd, Melbourne)

1987 (17 June). Centenary of National Parks Movement. T **431** and similar vert designs. Multicoloured. Perf 14½.

1428	70c. Type **431**	25	40
1429	80c. Mount Cook and Buttercup	25	40
1430	85c. Fiordland and Pineapple shrub	25	40
1431	$1.30 Tongariro and tussock	40	60
1428/1431	Set of 4	1·00	1·60
MS1432	123×99 mm. No. 1431 (sold at $1.70)	70	1·25

The 40c. premium on No. **MS**1432 was to support New Zealand 1990 International Stamp Exhibition, Auckland.

No. **MS**1432 overprinted on the selvedge with the CAPEX logo was only available from the New Zealand stand at this International Philatelic Exhibition in Toronto.

432 Kite Flying (Lauren Baldwin)

433 Hark the Herald Angels Sing

(Adapted D. Little. Litho Leigh-Mardon Ltd, Melbourne)

1987 (29 July). Health Stamps. Children's Paintings (2nd series). T **432** and similar multicoloured designs. Perf 14½.

1433	40c.+3c. Type **432**	70	1·50
	a. Horiz pair. Nos. 1433/1434	1·40	3·00
1434	40c.+3c. Swimming (Ineke Schoneveld)	70	1·50
1435	60c.+3c. Horse Riding (Aaron Tylee) (*vert*)	1·00	1·50
1433/1435	Set of 3	2·25	4·00
MS1436	100×117 mm. Nos. 1433/1435, each×2	3·50	5·50

Nos. 1433/1434 were printed together, *se-tenant*, in horizontal pairs throughout the sheet.

(Des Ellen Giggenbach. Litho Leigh-Mardon Ltd, Melbourne)

1987 (16 Sept). Christmas. T **433** and similar vert designs. Multicoloured. Perf 14½.

1437	35c. Type **433**	30	10
1438	70c. *Away in a Manger*	65	70
1439	85c. *We Three Kings of Orient Are*	80	85
1437/1439	Set of 3	1·60	1·50

434 Knot (Pona)   **435** 'Geothermal'

(Des Nga Puna Waihanga. Litho Security Printers (M), Malaysia)

1987 (4 Nov). Maori Fibre Work. T **434** and similar vert designs. Multicoloured. W **138** of Malaysia. Perf 12.

1440	40c. Type **434**	20	10
1441	60c. Binding (Herehere)	30	50
1442	80c. Plait (Whiri)	40	80
1443	85c. Cloak weaving (Korowai) with flax fibre (Whitau)	40	90
1440/1443	Set of 4	1·10	2·10

(Des Fay McAlpine. Litho Leigh-Mardon Ltd, Melbourne)

1988 (13 Jan). Centenary of Electricity. T **435** and similar horiz designs, each showing radiating concentric circles representing energy generation. Perf 14×14½.

1444	40c. multicoloured	20	10
1445	60c. black, rosine and brownish black	30	30
1446	70c. multicoloured	30	60
1447	80c. multicoloured	30	50
1444/1447	Set of 4	1·00	1·40

Designs: 40c. T **435**; 60c. 'Thermal'; 70c. 'Gas'; 80c. 'Hydro'.

436 Queen Elizabeth II and 1882 Queen Victoria 1d. Stamp   **437** Mangopare

(Des A. G. Mitchell (40c.), R. M. Conly and M. Stanley ($1). Litho Leigh-Mardon Ltd, Melbourne)

1988 (13 Jan). Centenary of Royal Philatelic Society of New Zealand. T **436** and similar multicoloured designs. Perf 14×14½.

1448	40c. Type **436**	35	75
	a. Horiz pair. Nos. 1448/1449	70	1·50
1449	40c. As Type **436**, but 1882 Queen Victoria 2d.	35	75
MS1450	107×160 mm. $1 *Queen Victoria* (Chalon) (*vert*). Perf 14½×14	3·00	3·25

NEW ZEALAND

Nos. 1448/1449 were printed together, *se-tenant*, in horizontal pairs throughout the sheet.

No. **MS**1450 overprinted on the selvedge with the SYDPEX logo was only available from the New Zealand stand at this International Philatelic Exhibition in Sydney and from the Philatelic Bureau at Wanganui.

(Des S. Adsett. Litho Leigh-Mardon Ltd, Melbourne)

1988 (2 Mar). Maori Rafter Paintings. T **437** and similar vert designs. Multicoloured. Perf 14½.

1451	40c. Type **437**	25	45
1452	40c. *Koru*	25	45
1453	40c. *Raupunga*	25	45
1454	60c. *Koiri*	35	75
1451/1454	*Set of 4*	1·00	1·90

440 Milford Track   **441** Kiwi and Koala at Campfire

(Des H. Thompson. Litho Leigh-Mardon Ltd, Melbourne)

1988 (8 June). Scenic Walking Trails. T **440** and similar vert designs. Multicoloured. Perf 14½.

1469	70c. Type **440**	20	50
1470	80c. Heaphy Track	25	55
1471	85c. Copland Track	25	65
1472	$1.30 Routeburn Track	40	1·00
1469/1472	*Set of 4*	1·00	2·40
MS1473	124×99 mm. No. 1472 (sold at $1.70)	1·25	2·50

The 40c. premium on No. **MS**1473 was to support New Zealand 1990 International Stamp Exhibition, Auckland.

(Des R. Harvey. Litho Leigh-Mardon Ltd, Melbourne)

1988 (21 June). Bicentenary of Australian Settlement. Perf 14½.

1474	**441**	40c. multicoloured	40	50

A stamp in a similar design was also issued by Australia.

438 'Good Luck'   **439** Paradise Shelduck

(Des Communication Arts Ltd. Litho CPE Australia Ltd, Melbourne)

1988 (18 May). Greetings Stamps. T **438** and similar multicoloured designs. Perf 13½.

1455	40c. Type **438**	55	1·00
	a. Booklet pane. Nos. 1455/1459	2·50	4·50
1456	40c. 'Keeping in touch'	55	1·00
1457	40c. 'Happy birthday'	55	1·00
1458	40c. 'Congratulations' (41×27 mm)	55	1·00
1459	40c. 'Get well soon' (41×27 mm)	55	1·00
1455/1459	*Set of 5*	2·50	4·50

Nos. 1455/1459 were only issued in $2 stamp booklets.

442 Swimming   **443** O Come All Ye Faithful

(Des R. Proud. Litho Leigh-Mardon Ltd, Melbourne)

1988 (27 July). Health Stamps. Olympic Games, Seoul. T **442** and similar horiz designs. Multicoloured. Perf 14½.

1475	40c.+3c. Type **442**	40	75
1476	60c.+3c. Athletics	60	1·25
1477	70c.+3c. Canoeing	70	1·25
1478	80c.+3c. Show jumping	90	1·40
1475/1478	*Set of 4*	2·40	3·75
MS1479	120×90 mm. Nos. 1475/1478	3·25	4·25

(Des Fay McAlpine. Litho Leigh-Mardon Ltd, Melbourne)

1988 (14 Sept). Christmas. Carols. T **443** and similar vert designs, each showing illuminated verses. Multicoloured. Perf 14½.

1480	35c. Type **443**	30	15
1481	70c. *Hark the Herald Angels Sing*	50	65
1482	80c. *Ding Dong Merrily on High*	50	90
1483	85c. *The First Nowell*	55	1·10
1480/1483	*Set of 4*	1·75	2·50

(Des Pauline Morse. Litho Southern Colour Print, Dunedin (Nos. 1467aab/1467aac) or Leigh-Mardon Ltd, Melbourne (others))

1988 (7 June)–**95**. Native Birds. T **439** and similar vert designs. Multicoloured. Phosphorised paper (5c., 45c.). Perf 14½×14

1459a	5c. Sooty Crake (1.7.91)	15	65
1460	10c. Double-banded Plover ('Banded Dotterel') (2.11.88)	20	40
1461	20c. Yellowhead (2.11.88)	30	40
	a. Perf 13½ (22.9.95)	2·25	3·00
1462	30c. Grey-backed White-eye ('Silvereye') (2.11.88)	40	30
1463	40c. Brown Kiwi (2.11.88)	45	20
	a. Perf 13½×13 (8.11.89)	1·25	2·25
	ab. Pack pane. No. 1463a×10 with margins all round	12·00	
1463b	45c. Rock Wren (1.7.91)	50	60
	ba. Booklet pane. No. 1463b×10 with horiz sides of pane imperf (1.10.91)	4·00	
1464	50c. Sacred Kingfisher (2.11.88)	60	70
1465	60c. Spotted Cormorant ('Spotted Shag') (2.11.88)	60	80
	a. Perf 13½ (22.9.95)	3·00	5·00
1466	70c. Type **439**	1·00	1·50
1467	80c. Victoria Penguin ('Fiordland Crested Penguin') (2.11.88)	1·00	1·50
1467a	80c. New Zealand Falcon (31.3.93)	2·25	2·00
	ab. Perf 12 (7.94)	1·50	2·25
	ac. Booklet pane. No. 1467aab×10	13·00	
1468	90c. New Zealand Robin (2.11.88)	1·25	1·50
1459a/1468	*Set of 12*	7·00	9·50

No. 1463a was only issued in panes of ten with margins on all four sides. These panes were initially included in Stamp Pads of 50 such panes, but subsequently appeared in $4 stamp packs.

A miniature sheet containing No. 1466 was only available from the New Zealand stand at WORLD STAMP EXPO '89 International Stamp Exhibition or the Philatelic Bureau, Wanganui. It was subsequently overprinted with the New Zealand 1990 emblem.

No. 1467a was originally issued in $8 booklets on 31 March 1993, but appeared in sheets on 18 February 1994.

No. 1467aab was only issued in $8 stamp booklets and shows the vertical edges of the pane imperforate.

For 40c. and 45c. stamps in similar designs, but self-adhesive, see Nos. 1589/1589a.

For Nos. 1459a/1465 in miniature sheet for the Philakorea '94 International Stamp Exhibition see No. **MS**1830.

444 Lake Pukaki (John Gully)   **445** Brown Kiwi

(Litho Leigh-Mardon Ltd, Melbourne)

1988 (5 Oct). New Zealand Heritage (1st issue). The Land. T **444** and similar horiz designs showing 19th-century paintings. Multicoloured. Perf 14×14½.

1484	40c. Type **444**	15	10
1485	60c. *On the Grass Plain below Lake Arthur* (William Fox)	25	35
1486	70c. *View of Auckland* (John Hoyte)	30	65
1487	80c. *Mount Egmont from the Southward* (Charles Heaphy)	35	65
1488	$1.05 *Anakiwa, Queen Charlotte Sound* (John Kinder)	40	1·75
1489	$1.30 *White Terraces, Lake Rotomahana* (Charles Barraud)	45	1·40
1484/1489	*Set of 6*	1·75	4·25

NEW ZEALAND

See also Nos. 1505/1510, 1524/1529, 1541/1546, 1548/1553 and 1562/1567.

(Des A. Mitchell. Eng. G. Prosser of B.A.B.N. Recess Leigh-Mardon Ltd, Melbourne)

1988 (19 Oct)–**93**. Phosphorised paper (No. 1490*b*). Perf 14½ (and 13 around design)

1490	**445**	$1 bronze-green	1·75	3·75
		a. Booklet pane. No. 1490×6	9·00	
1490*b*		$1 bright scarlet (17.4.91)	2·25	2·75
1490*c*		$1 blue (9.6.93)	1·50	2·50
1490/1490*c* Set of 3			5·00	8·00

Nos. 1490/1490*c* were each printed within a square margin, perforated vertically for No. 1490 and on all four sides for Nos. 1490*b*/1490*c*, and with a further circular perforation around the design.

No. 1490 was only issued in $6 stamp booklets with the horizontal edges of the booklet pane imperforate.

Nos. 1490*b*/1490*c* were printed in sheets of 24 (6×4).

For miniature sheets containing similar stamps, some printed in lithography, see Nos. **MS**1745, **MS**1786 and **MS**2342.

For $1 violet, $1.10 and $1.50 see Nos. 2090/2090*b*.

See also Nos. 3308/3310.

446 Humpback Whale and Calf   **447** Clover

(Des Lindy Fisher. Litho Govt Ptg Office, Wellington)

1988 (2 Nov). Whales. T **446** and similar horiz designs. Multicoloured. Perf 13½.

1491	60c. Type **446**	40	70
1492	70c. Killer Whales	45	90
1493	80c. Southern Right Whale	45	1·00
1494	85c. Blue Whale	45	1·50
1495	$1.05 Southern Bottlenose Whale and Calf	60	2·00
1496	$1.30 Sperm Whale	70	2·00
1491/1496 Set of 6		2·75	7·25

Although inscribed 'ROSS DEPENDENCY' Nos. 1491/1496 were available from post offices throughout New Zealand.

(Des Heather Arnold. Litho Leigh-Mardon Ltd, Melbourne)

1989 (18 Jan). Wild Flowers. T **447** and similar horiz designs. Multicoloured. Perf 14½.

1497	40c. Type **447**	25	20
1498	60c. Lotus	30	65
1499	70c. Montbretia	35	1·25
1500	80c. Wild Ginger	40	1·25
1497/1500 Set of 4		1·10	3·00

448 Katherine Mansfield   **449** Moriori Man and Map of Chatham Islands

(Des A. G. Mitchell. Litho Harrison)

1989 (1 Mar). New Zealand Authors. T **448** and similar vert designs. Multicoloured. Perf 12½.

1501	40c. Type **448**	20	15
1502	60c. James K. Baxter	30	40
1503	70c. Bruce Mason	30	60
1504	80c. Ngaio Marsh	30	65
1501/1504 Set of 4		1·00	1·60

(Des D. Gunson. Litho Leigh-Mardon Ltd, Melbourne)

1989 (17 May). New Zealand Heritage (2nd issue). The People. T **449** and similar horiz designs. Perf 14×14½.

1505	40c. multicoloured	75	20
1506	60c. orange-brown, brownish grey and reddish brown	1·25	1·00
1507	70c. yellow-green, brownish grey and deep olive	60	1·25
1508	80c. bright greenish blue, brownish grey and deep dull blue	1·50	90
1509	$1.05 grey, brownish grey and grey-black	55	1·75
1510	$1.30 bright rose-red, brownish grey and lake-brown	70	1·75
1505/1510 Set of 6		4·75	6·00

Designs: 40c. T **449**; 60c. Gold prospector; 70c. Settler ploughing; 80c. Whaling; $1.05 Missionary preaching to Maoris; $1.30 Maori village.

450 White Pine (Kahikatea)   **451** Duke and Duchess of York with Princess Beatrice

(Des D. Gunson. Litho Questa)

1989 (7 June). Native Trees. T **450** and similar vert designs. Multicoloured. Perf 14×14½.

1511	80c. Type **450**	25	45
1512	85c. Red Pine (Rimu)	25	45
1513	$1.05 Totara	30	80
1514	$1.30 Kauri	30	80
1511/1514 Set of 4		1·00	2·25
MS1515 102×125 mm. No. 1514 (*sold at* $1.80)		1·25	1·75

The 50c. premium on No. **MS**1515 was to support New Zealand 1990 International Stamp Exhibition, Auckland.

(Des and litho Leigh-Mardon Ltd, Melbourne)

1989 (26 July). Health Stamps. T **451** and similar vert designs. Multicoloured. Perf 14½.

1516	40c.+3c. Type **451**	60	1·25
	a. Horiz pair. Nos. 1516/1517	1·10	2·50
1517	40c.+3c. Duchess of York with Princess Beatrice	60	1·25
1518	80c.+3c. Princess Beatrice	1·00	1·75
1516/1518 Set of 3		2·00	3·75
MS1519 120×89 mm. Nos. 1516/1518, each×2		3·50	6·00

Nos. 1516/1517 were printed together, *se-tenant*, in horizontal pairs throughout the sheet.

No. **MS**1519 overprinted on the selvedge with the WORLD STAMP EXPO '89 logo was only available from the New Zealand stand at this International Stamp Exhibition and from the Philatelic Bureau at Wanganui.

452 One Tree Hill, Auckland, through Bedroom Window   **453** Windsurfing

(Des H. Chapman. Litho Leigh-Mardon Ltd, Melbourne)

1989 (13 Sept). Christmas. T **452** and similar vert designs showing Star of Bethlehem. Multicoloured. Perf 14½.

1520	35c. Type **452**	20	10
1521	65c. Shepherd and Dog in mountain valley	40	50
1522	80c. Star over harbour	45	65
1523	$1 Star over globe	60	80
1520/1523 Set of 4		1·50	1·75

(Des M. Bailey. Litho Leigh-Mardon Ltd, Melbourne)

1989 (11 Oct). New Zealand Heritage (3rd issue). The Sea. T **453** and similar horiz designs. Multicoloured. Perf 14×14½.

1524	40c. Type **453**	50	20
1525	60c. Fish of many species	85	90
1526	65c. Striped Marlin and game fishing launch	90	1·00
1527	80c. Rowing boat and yachts in harbour	1·00	1·00
1528	$1 Coastal scene	1·25	1·10
1529	$1.50 *Rotoiti* (container ship) and tug	1·90	3·25
1524/1529 Set of 6		5·75	6·75

NEW ZEALAND

454 Games Logo

(Des Heather Arnold. Litho Leigh-Mardon Ltd, Melbourne)

1989 (8 Nov)–**90**. 14th Commonwealth Games. Auckland. T **454** and similar horiz designs. Multicoloured. Perf 14½.

1530	40c. Type **454**	15	30
1531	40c. Goldie (games kiwi mascot)	15	30
1532	40c. Gymnastics	15	30
1533	50c. Weightlifting	20	30
1534	65c. Swimming	25	45
1535	80c. Cycling	55	60
1536	$1 Lawn bowling	35	60
1537	$1.80 Hurdling	60	1·00
1530/1537	Set of 8	2·25	3·50

MS1538 Two sheets, each 105×92 mm. with different margin designs. (a) Nos. 1530/1531 (*horiz pair*). (b) Nos. 1530/1531 (*vert pair*) (24.1.90). Set of 2 sheets... 3·75 4·50

455 Short S.30 Modified G Class Flying Boat *Aotearoa* and Boeing 747-200

456 Chief Kawiti signing Treaty

(Des R. Proud. Litho Enschedé)

1990 (17 Jan). 50th Anniversary of Air New Zealand. Perf 13×14½.
1539 **455** 80c. multicoloured............ 1·40 1·10

(Des A. G. Mitchell from painting by L. C. Mitchell. Litho Enschedé)

1990 (17 Jan). 150th Anniversary of Treaty of Waitangi. Sheet 80×118 mm, containing T **456** and similar multicoloured design. Perf 13½.
MS1540 40c. Type **456**; 40c. Chief Hone Heke (first signatory) and Lieutenant-Governor Hobson (*horiz*)............ 1·00 2·75

457 Maori Voyaging Canoe

458 *Thelymitra pulchella*

(Des G. Fuller. Litho Leigh-Mardon Ltd, Melbourne)

1990 (7 Mar). New Zealand Heritage (4th issue). The Ships. T **457** and similar horiz designs. Multicoloured. Perf 14×14½.

1541	40c. Type **457**	60	15
1542	50c. HMS *Endeavour* (Cook), 1769	1·00	80
1543	60c. *Tory* (barque), 1839	1·00	1·00
1544	80c. *Crusader* (full-rigged immigrant ship), 1871	1·50	1·50
1545	$1 *Edwin Fox* (full-rigged immigrant ship), 1873	1·75	1·50
1546	$1.50 *Arawa* (steamer), 1884	2·00	3·25
1541/1546	Set of 6	7·00	7·50

A miniature sheet containing No. 1542 was only available from the New Zealand stand at Stamp World London '90 International Stamp Exhibition or from the Philatelic Bureau, Wanganui.

(Des Lindy Fisher. Litho Leigh-Mardon Ltd, Melbourne)

1990 (18 Apr). New Zealand 1990 International Stamp Exhibition, Auckland. Native Orchids. Sheet 179×80 mm, containing T **458** and similar vert designs. Multicoloured. Perf 14½.
MS1547 40c. Type **458**; 40c. *Corybas macranthus*; 40c. *Dendrobium cunninghamii*; 40c. *Pterostylis banksii*; 80c. *Aporostylis bifolia* (sold at $4.90)........... 2·50 4·50

The stamps in No. **MS**1547 form a composite design.
The $2.50 premium on No. **MS**1547 was used to support the Exhibition. Miniature sheets as No. **MS**1547, but imperforate, are from a limited printing distributed to those purchasing season tickets for the exhibition.

459 Grace Neill (social reformer) and Maternity Hospital, Wellington

460 Akaroa

(Des Elspeth Williamson. Litho Leigh-Mardon Ltd, Melbourne)

1990 (16 May). New Zealand Heritage (5th issue). Famous New Zealanders. T **459** and similar horiz designs. Multicoloured. Perf 14×14½.

1548	40c. Type **459**	45	10
1549	50c. Jean Batten (pilot) and Percival P.3 Gull Six aircraft	65	85
1550	60c. Katherine Sheppard (suffragette) and 19th-century women	50	1·00
1551	80c. Richard Pearse (inventor) and early flying machine	75	1·25
1552	$1 Lieutenant-General Freyberg and tank	80	1·25
1553	$1.50 Peter Buck (politician) and Maori pattern	70	2·25
1548/1553	Set of 6	3·25	6·00

(Des Lindy Fisher. Litho Leigh-Mardon Ltd, Melbourne)

1990 (13 June). 150th Anniversary of European Settlements. T **460** and similar vert designs. Multicoloured. Perf 14½.

1554	80c. Type **460**	35	60
1555	$1 Wanganui	40	60
1556	$1.50 Wellington	65	2·00
1557	$1.80 Takapuna Beach, Auckland	80	1·00
1554/1557	Set of 4	2·00	3·75

MS1558 125×100 mm. No. 1557 (sold at $2.30)............ 2·00 3·25

The 50c. premium on No. **MS**1558 was to support New Zealand 1990 International Stamp Exhibition, Auckland.

461 Jack Lovelock (athlete) and Race

462 Creation Legend of Rangi and Papa

(Des T. Crilley. Litho Questa)

1990 (25 July). Health Stamps. Sportsmen (1st series). T **461** and similar horiz design. Multicoloured. Perf 14½×13½.

1559	40c.+5c. Type **461**	70	1·00
1560	80c.+5c. George Nepia (rugby player) and match	90	1·75
MS1561	115×96 mm. Nos. 1559/1560, each×2	2·25	4·00

See also Nos. 1687/**MS**1689.

(Des K. Hall. Litho Leigh-Mardon Ltd, Melbourne)

1990 (24 Aug). New Zealand Heritage (6th issue). The Maori. T **462** and similar horiz designs. Multicoloured. Perf 14×14½.

1562	40c. Type **462**	15	10
	a. Violet-blue (face value) omitted	£250	£225
1563	50c. Pattern from Maori feather cloak	20	55
1564	60c. Maori women's choir	25	60
1565	80c. Maori facial tattoos	30	80
1566	$1 War canoe prow (detail)	35	1·00
1567	$1.50 Maori haka	45	1·75
1562/1567	Set of 6	1·50	4·25

NEW ZEALAND

463 Queen Victoria   **464** Angel

(Des A. G. Mitchell. Recess Leigh-Mardon Ltd, Melbourne)

1990 (29 Aug). 150th Anniversary of the Penny Black. Sheet 169×70 mm containing T **463** and similar vert designs. Perf 14½×14.
MS1568 40c.×6 indigo (Type **463**, King Edward VII, King George V, King Edward VIII, King George VI, Queen Elizabeth II).. 4·50   5·50

(Des Sally Simons. Litho Leigh-Mardon Ltd, Melbourne)

1990 (12 Sept). Christmas. T **464** and similar vert designs showing Angels. Perf 14½.
1569	40c. purple, deep greenish blue and deep yellow-brown	15	10
1570	$1 purple, blue-green and deep yellow-brown	40	30
1571	$1.50 purple, bright crimson and deep yellow-brown	60	2·25
1572	$1.80 purple, red and deep yellow-brown	65	1·00
1569/1572	*Set of 4*	1·60	3·25

465 Antarctic Petrel   **466** Coopworth Ewe and Lambs

(Des Janet Luxton. Litho Heraclio Fournier)

1990 (7 Nov). Antarctic Birds. T **465** and similar vert designs. Multicoloured. Perf 13½×13.
1573	40c. Type **465**	55	30
1574	50c. Wilson's Petrel	60	75
1575	60c. Snow Petrel	70	1·25
1576	80c. Southern Fulmar	80	1·25
1577	$1 Bearded Penguin ('Chinstrap Penguin')	90	1·25
1578	$1.50 Emperor Penguin	1·00	3·00
1573/1578	*Set of 6*	4·00	7·00

Although inscribed 'Ross Dependency' Nos. 1573/1578 were available from post offices throughout New Zealand.

(Des Lindy Fisher. Litho Leigh-Mardon Ltd, Melbourne)

1991 (23 Jan). New Zealand Farming and Agriculture. Sheep Breeds. T **466** and similar vert designs. Multicoloured. Perf 14½×14.
1579	40c. Type **466**	20	20
1580	60c. Perendale	30	60
1581	80c. Corriedale	40	70
1582	$1 Drysdale	50	75
1583	$1.50 South Suffolk	70	1·50
1584	$1.80 Romney	90	1·75
1579/1584	*Set of 6*	2·75	5·00

467 Moriori, Royal Albatross, Nikau Palm and Artefacts   **468** Goal and Footballers

(Des K. Hall. Litho Southern Colour Print Ltd, Dunedin)

1991 (6 Mar). Bicentenary of Discovery of Chatham Islands. T **467** and similar vert design. Multicoloured. Perf 13½.
1585	40c. Type **467**	75	50
1586	80c. Carvings, HMS *Chatham*, Moriori house of 1870, and Tommy Solomon	1·25	2·00

(Des T. Crilley. Litho Southern Colour Print Ltd, Dunedin)

1991 (6 Mar). Centenary of New Zealand Football Association. T **468** and similar horiz design. Multicoloured. Perf 13½.
1587	80c. Type **468**	60	1·60
	a. Horiz pair. Nos. 1587/1588	1·10	3·25
1588	80c. Five footballers and referee	60	1·60

Nos. 1587/1588 were printed together, *se-tenant*, in horizontal pairs throughout the sheet, each pair forming a composite design.

(Des Pauline Morse. Litho Printset-Cambec Pty Ltd, Melbourne (40c., 45c. (No. 1589)) or Leigh-Mardon Ltd, Melbourne (45c. (No. 1589*a*ab))

1991 (17 Apr–Dec). As Nos. 1463/1463*b*, but self-adhesive. Phosphorised paper. Perf 11½
1589	40c. Brown Kiwi	70	1·25
1589*a*	45c. Rock Wren (1.07)	50	1·25
	ab. Perf 11 (12.91)	50	70

Nos. 1589/1589*a* were only available in coils of 100, each stamp, with die-cut perforations, being separate on the imperforate backing paper. Initially the 45c. showed the surplus surface paper removed, but from December 1991 supplies of No. 1589*a*ab had the stamps surrounded by white selvedge. The format was changed again in March 1992 when the coils again appeared without the white selvedge. Part of the March 1992 printing, and all subsequent supplies, had the stamps interlocked with no backing paper visible between them.

A limited quantity of the 45c. (No. 1589*a*) in sheets of 200 (8×25) was produced for use on official first day covers. It is reported that a small number of such sheets were subsequently sold by a few post offices.

 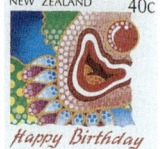

469 Tuatara on Rocks   **470** Clown

(Des Pauline Morse. Litho Leigh-Mardon Ltd, Melbourne)

1991 (17 Apr). Endangered Species. The Tuatara. T **469** and similar horiz designs. Multicoloured. Perf 14½.
1590	40c. Type **469**	30	60
1591	40c. Tuatara in crevice	30	60
1592	40c. Tuatara with foliage	30	60
1593	40c. Tuatara in dead leaves	30	60
1590/1593	*Set of 4*	1·00	2·25

(Des Helen Crawford. Litho Leigh-Mardon Ltd, Melbourne)

1991 (15 May–1 July). Happy Birthday. T **470** and similar multicoloured designs. Perf 13½
1594	40c. Type **470**	75	85
	a. Booklet pane. Nos. 1594/1598	3·25	3·75
1595	40c. Balloons	75	85
1596	40c. Party hat	75	85
1597	40c. Birthday present (41×27 mm)	75	85
1598	40c. Birthday cake (41×27 mm)	75	85
1599	45c. Type **470** (1.07)	75	85
	a. Booklet pane. Nos. 1599/1603	3·25	3·75
1600	45c. As No. 1595 (1.07)	75	85
1601	45c. As No. 1596 (1.07)	75	85
1602	45c. As No. 1597 (1.07)	75	85
1603	45c. As No. 1598 (1.07)	75	85
1594/1603	*Set of 10*	6·50	7·50

The above were only issued in $2 (Nos. 1594/1598) or $2.25 (Nos. 1599/1603) stamp booklets, Nos. SB54 and SB57.

471 Cat at Window   **472** Punakaiki Rocks

(Des Jennifer Lautusi. Litho Leigh-Mardon Ltd, Melbourne)

1991 (15 May–1 July). Thinking of You. T **471** and similar multicoloured designs. Perf 13½
1604	40c. Type **471**	75	95
	a. Booklet pane. Nos. 1604/1608	3·25	4·25
1605	40c. Cat playing with slippers	75	95

NEW ZEALAND

1606	40c. Cat with alarm clock		75	95
1607	40c. Cat in window (41×27 mm)		75	95
1608	40c. Cat at door (41×27 mm)		75	95
1609	45c. Type **471** (1.07)		75	85
	a. Booklet pane. Nos. 1609/1613		3·25	3·75
1610	45c. As No. 1605 (1.07)		75	85
1611	45c. As No. 1606 (1.07)		75	85
1612	45c. As No. 1607 (1.07)		75	85
1613	45c. As No. 1608 (1.07)		75	85
1604/1613 Set of 10			6·50	8·00

The above were only issued in $2 (Nos. 1604/1608) or $2.25 (Nos. 1609/1613) stamp booklets, Nos. SB55 and SB58.

(Des H. Thompson. Litho Leigh-Mardon Ltd, Melbourne)

1991 (12 June). Scenic Landmarks. T **472** and similar horiz designs. Multicoloured. Perf 14½.

1614	40c. Type **472**		30	10
1615	50c. Moeraki Boulders		35	35
1616	80c. Organ Pipes		55	80
1617	$1 Castle Hill		60	70
1618	$1.50 Te Kaukau Point		1·00	1·25
1619	$1.80 Ahuriri River Clay Cliffs		1·25	1·25
1614/1619 Set of 6			3·50	4·00

473 Dolphins Underwater   **474** Children's Rugby

(Des Heather Arnold. Litho Leigh-Mardon Ltd, Melbourne)

1991 (24 July). Health Stamps. Hector's Dolphin. T **473** and similar horiz design. Multicoloured. Perf 14½.

1620	45c.+5c. Type **473**		90	1·25
1621	80c.+5c. Dolphins leaping		1·25	2·00
MS1622 115×100 mm. Nos. 1620/1621, each×2			4·00	6·00

(Des A. G. Mitchell. Litho Leigh-Mardon Ltd, Melbourne)

1991 (21 Aug). World Cup Rugby Championship. T **474** and similar vert designs. Multicoloured. Perf 14½×14.

1623	80c. Type **474**		35	80
1624	$1 Women's rugby		40	90
1625	$1.50 Senior rugby		60	1·75
1626	$1.80 All Blacks (National Team)		75	1·50
1623/1626 Set of 4			1·90	4·50
MS1627 113×90 mm. No. 1626 (sold at $2.40)			1·75	3·50

No. **MS**1627 additionally inscribed PHILA NIPPON '91 was available, at $1.80, from the New Zealand stand at this International Stamp Exhibition in Tokyo and from the Philatelic Bureau at Wanganui.

475 Three Shepherds   **476** Dodonidia helmsii

(Des Designworks Communications. Litho Southern Colour Print, Dunedin)

1991 (18 Sept). Christmas. T **475** and similar vert designs. Multicoloured. Perf 13½.

1628	45c. Type **475**		30	80
	a. Block of four. Nos 1628/1631		1·10	2·50
1629	45c. Two Kings on Camels		30	80
1630	45c. Mary and Baby Jesus		30	80
1631	45c. King with gift		30	80
1632	65c. Star of Bethlehem		40	60
1633	$1 Crown		50	80
1634	$1.50 Angel		70	1·50
1628/1634 Set of 7			2·50	4·75

Nos. 1628/1631 were printed together, *se-tenant*, in blocks of four throughout the sheet.

(Des Pauline Morse)

1991 (6 Nov)–**2008**. Butterflies. T **476** and similar vert designs. Multicoloured.

(a) Litho Leigh-Mardon Ltd, Melbourne. Phosphorised paper ($4, $5). Perf 14½.

1635	$1 Type **476**		1·00	60
1636	$2 Zizina otis oxleyi		2·75	1·50
1637	$3 Vanessa itea		5·00	2·50
1638	$4 Lycaena salustius (25.1.95)		4·00	4·50
1639	$5 Bassaris gonerilla (25.1.95)		4·75	5·50
1635/1639 Set of 5			16·00	13·00

(b) Litho Southern Colour Print (No. 1643a) or Questa (others). Perf 13½×14.

1640	$1 As Type **476** (6.11.96)		1·75	2·00
1641	$2 As No. 1636 (6.11.96)		2·50	4·50
1642	$3 As No. 1637 (8.96)		3·25	6·00
	a. Grey (inscrs) and apple-green (frame) omitted		£600	
1643	$4 As No. 1638 (10.97)		2·50	4·50
	a. Perf 14 (3.4.08)		7·50	7·50
1644	$5 As No. 1639 (9.10.96)		8·50	7·00
1640/1644 Set of 5			17·00	22·00

(c) Booklet stamps. Litho Southern Colour Print, Dunedin. Perf 14×14½.

1645	$1 Type **476** (1.9.95)		3·75	6·50
	a. Booklet pane. No. 1645×5 and five air POST labels		17·00	

Nos. 1640/1642 are from the three kiwi printings, Nos. 1643/1644 from the one kiwi and No. 1643a from the two kiwi. The designs of Nos. 1640/1641 and 1643a are redrawn.

No. 1645 only exists imperforate at foot and was issued in $5 stamp booklets in which the airmail labels were vertically *se-tenant* with the stamps (No. SB74).

A miniature sheet containing No. 1637 was only available from the New Zealand stand at PHILA NIPPON '91 International Stamp Exhibition, Tokyo, or the Philatelic Bureau, Wanganui.

PRINTINGS. The initial printings of this and subsequent definitive sets had no Kiwi symbols in the sheet margins. Later printings had one, two, three or four Kiwis in the margin, to represent the first, second, third and fourth reprints.

479 Yacht *Kiwi Magic*, 1987   **480** Heemskerk

(Des R. Proud. Litho Leigh-Mardon Ltd, Melbourne)

1992 (22 Jan). New Zealand Challenge for America's Cup. T **479** and similar horiz designs. Multicoloured. Perf 14.

1655	45c. Type **479**		25	10
1656	80c. Yacht *New Zealand*, 1988		40	70
1657	$1 Yacht *America*, 1851		50	85
1658	$1.50 America's Cup Class yacht, 1992		75	1·75
1655/1658 Set of 4			1·75	3·00

(Des G. Fuller. Litho Enschedé)

1992 (12 Mar). Great Voyages of Discovery. T **480** and similar horiz designs. Multicoloured. Perf 13×14.

1659	45c. Type **480**		55	25
1660	80c. *Zeehan*		90	1·10
1661	$1 *Santa Maria*		1·25	1·10
1662	$1.50 *Pinta* and *Nina*		1·50	2·50
1659/1662 Set of 4			3·75	4·50

Nos. 1659/1660 commemorate the 350th anniversary of Tasman's discovery of New Zealand and Nos. 1661/1662 the 500th anniversary of discovery of America by Columbus.

A miniature sheet containing stamps as Nos. 1661/1662, but perforated 14, was only available from the New Zealand stand at World Columbian Stamp Expo '92, Chicago, and from the Philatelic Bureau at Wanganui.

481 Sprinters   **482** Weddell Seal and Pup

(Des Sheryl McCammon. Litho Southern Colour Print, Dunedin)

1992 (3 Apr). Olympic Games, Barcelona (1st issue). Perf 13½.

1663	**481**	45c. multicoloured	50	50

See also Nos. 1670/**MS**1674.

NEW ZEALAND

(Des Lindy Fisher. Litho Southern Colour Print, Dunedin)

1992 (8 Apr). Antarctic Seals. T **482** and similar horiz designs. Multicoloured. Perf 13½.

1664	45c. Type **482**	60	15
1665	50c. Crabeater Seals swimming	70	60
1666	65c. Leopard Seal and Adélie Penguins	90	1·50
1667	80c. Ross Seal	1·00	1·25
1668	$1 Southern Elephant Seal and harem	1·10	1·25
1669	$1.80 Hooker's Sea Lion and pup	1·75	4·25
1664/1669 Set of 6		5·50	8·00

Although inscribed 'ROSS DEPENDENCY' Nos. 1664/1669 were available from post offices throughout New Zealand.

483 Cycling   **484** Ice Pinnacles, Franz Josef Glacier

(Des M. Bailey. Litho Southern Colour Print, Dunedin)

1992 (13 May). Olympic Games, Barcelona (2nd issue). T **483** and similar horiz designs. Perf 13½.

1670	45c. Type **483**	65	20
1671	80c. Archery	60	70
1672	$1 Equestrian three-day eventing	65	85
1673	$1.50 Sailboarding	80	1·60
1670/1673 Set of 4		2·40	3·00
MS1674 125×100 mm. Nos. 1670/1673. Perf 14×14½		4·00	5·00

No. **MS**1674 exists overprinted with the emblem of the World Columbian, Stamp Expo '92 and was only available from the New Zealand stand at this International Stamp Exhibition in Chicago and from the Philatelic Bureau at Wanganui.

(Des A. Hollows. Litho Southern Colour Print, Dunedin)

1992 (12 June). Glaciers. T **484** and similar horiz designs. Multicoloured. Perf 13½.

1675	45c. Type **484**	30	10
1676	50c. Tasman Glacier	40	35
1677	80c. Snowball Glacier, Marion Plateau	50	50
1678	$1 Brewster Glacier	60	85
1679	$1.50 Fox Glacier	85	1·25
1680	$1.80 Franz Josef Glacier	95	1·25
1675/1680 Set of 6		3·25	3·75

485 Grand Finale, Camellia   **486** Tree and Hills

(Des Patricia Altman. Litho Leigh-Mardon Ltd, Melbourne)

1992 (8 July). Camellias. T **485** and similar vert designs. Multicoloured. Perf 14½.

1681	45c. Type **485**	35	10
1682	50c. Shows-No-Sakae	40	40
1683	80c. Sugar Dream	55	60
1684	$1 Night Rider	60	70
1685	$1.50 E. G. Waterhouse	85	2·75
1686	$1.80 Dr Clifford Parks	95	2·50
1681/1686 Set of 6		3·25	6·25

(Des T. Crilley. Litho Southern Colour Print, Dunedin)

1992 (12 Aug). Health Stamps. Sportsmen (2nd series). Horiz designs as T **461**. Multicoloured. Perf 13½.

1687	45c.+5c. Anthony Wilding (tennis player) and match	1·00	1·25
1688	80c.+5c. Stewie Dempster (cricketer) and batsman	1·25	1·75
MS1689 115×96 mm. Nos. 1687/1688, each×2. Perf 14		5·00	6·50

(Des Van de Roer Design. Litho Leigh-Mardon Ltd, Melbourne)

1992 (1 Sept). Landscapes. T **486** and similar horiz designs. Multicoloured. Perf 14×14½.

1690	45c. Type **486**	50	65
	a. Booklet pane. Nos. 1690/1699	4·50	6·00
1691	45c. River and hills	50	65
1692	45c. Hills and mountain	50	65
1693	45c. Glacier	50	65
1694	45c. Hills and waterfall	50	65
1695	45c. Tree and beach	50	65
1696	45c. Estuary and cliffs	50	65
1697	45c. Fjord	50	65
1698	45c. River delta	50	65
1699	45c. Ferns and beach	50	65
1690/1699 Set of 10		4·50	6·00

Nos. 1690/1699 were only issued in $4.50 stamp booklets with the pane forming a composite design.

487 Reindeer over Houses   **488** 1920s Fashions

(Des K. Hall. Litho Leigh-Mardon Ltd, Melbourne)

1992 (16 Sept). Christmas. T **487** and similar vert designs. Multicoloured. Perf 14½.

1700	45c. Type **487**	90	1·25
	a. Block of 4. Nos. 1700/1703	3·25	4·50
1701	45c. Santa Claus on sleigh over houses	90	1·25
1702	45c. Christmas tree in window	90	1·25
1703	45c. Christmas wreath and children at window	90	1·25
1704	65c. Candles and fireplace	1·10	90
1705	$1 Family going to church	1·40	1·00
1706	$1.50 Picnic under Pohutukawa tree	2·00	3·50
1700/1706 Set of 7		7·25	9·25

Nos. 1700/1703 were printed together, *se-tenant*, in blocks of four throughout the sheet.

(Des T. Crilley. Litho Southern Colour Print, Dunedin)

1992 (4 Nov). New Zealand in the 1920s. T **488** and similar vert designs. Multicoloured. Perf 13½.

1707	45c. Type **488**	50	15
1708	50c. Dr Robert Jack and early radio announcer	55	65
1709	80c. All Blacks rugby player, 1924	85	1·00
1710	$1 Swaggie and dog	95	1·00
1711	$1.50 Ford Model A car and young couple	1·75	2·25
1712	$1.80 Amateur aviators and biplane	2·00	2·75
1707/1712 Set of 6		6·00	7·00

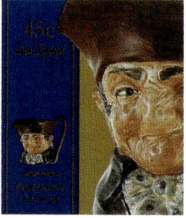 

489 'Old Charley' Toby Jug   **490** Women's Fashions of the 1930s

(Des Brand New Ltd. Litho Leigh-Mardon Ltd, Melbourne)

1993 (20 Jan). Royal Doulton Ceramics Exhibition, New Zealand. T **489** and similar vert designs. Multicoloured. Perf 13.

1713	45c. Type **489**	20	10
1714	50c. 'Bunnykins' nursery plate	25	35
1715	80c. 'Maori Art' tea set	40	60
1716	$1 'Ophelia' handpainted plate	50	75
1717	$1.50 'St George' figurine	65	2·00
1718	$1.80 'Lambeth' saltglazed stoneware vase	70	2·00
1713/1718 Set of 6		2·40	5·00
MS1719 125×100 mm. No. 1718		1·25	2·25

(Des R. Jones. Litho Leigh-Mardon Ltd, Melbourne)

1993 (17 Feb). New Zealand in the 1930s. T **490** and similar vert designs. Multicoloured. Perf 14½×14.

1720	45c. Type **490**	40	15
1721	50c. Unemployed protest march	45	60
1722	80c. Phar Lap (racehorse)	85	1·00
1723	$1 State housing project	65	1·00
1724	$1.50 Boys drinking free school milk	1·00	3·00
1725	$1.80 Cinema queue	1·00	2·50
1720/1725 Set of 6		3·75	7·50

NEW ZEALAND

491 Women signing Petition **492** Champagne Pool

(Des Lindy Fisher. Litho Southern Colour Print, Dunedin)

1993 (31 Mar). Centenary of Women's Suffrage. T **491** and similar vert designs. Multicoloured. Perf 13½.

1726	45c. Type **491**	20	10
1727	80c. Aircraft propeller and woman on tractor	40	75
1728	$1 Housewife with children	45	75
1729	$1.50 Modern women	60	2·00
1726/1729	Set of 4	1·50	3·25

(Des A. Hollows. Litho Southern Colour Print, Dunedin)

1993 (5 May). Thermal Wonders, Rotorua. T **492** and similar square designs. Multicoloured. Perf 12.

1730	45c. Type **492**	40	10
1731	50c. Boiling mud	40	40
1732	80c. Emerald Pool	55	70
1733	$1 Hakereteke Falls	60	80
1734	$1.50 Warbrick Terrace	1·00	1·75
1735	$1.80 Pohutu Geyser	1·00	1·75
1730/1735	Set of 6	3·50	5·00

For miniature sheet containing $1.80 see No. **MS**1770.

493 Yellow-eyed Penguin, Hector's Dolphin and New Zealand Fur Seal **494** Boy with Puppy

(Des Donna McKenna. Litho Southern Colour Print, Dunedin (No. 1740) or Leigh-Mardon Ltd, Melbourne (others))

1993 (9 June). Endangered Species Conservation. T **493** and similar horiz designs. Multicoloured. Perf 13½ (No. 1740) or 14×14½ (others).

1736	45c. Type **493**	85	1·25
	a. Block of 4. Nos. 1736/1739	3·00	4·50
1737	45c. Taiko (bird), Mount Cook Lily and Mountain Duck ('Blue Duck')	85	1·25
1738	45c. Giant Snail, Rock Wren and Hamilton's Frog	85	1·25
1739	45c. Kaka (bird), New Zealand Pigeon and Giant Weta	85	1·25
1740	45c. Tusked Weta (23×28 mm)	85	1·00
1736/1740	Set of 5	3·75	5·50

Nos. 1736/1739 were issued either in sheets of one design or in sheets containing *se-tenant* blocks of four, as No. 1736a, each forming a composite design.

No. 1740 was only issued in $4.50 stamp booklet, No. SB74.

(Des Karen Odiam. Litho Southern Colour Print, Dunedin)

1993 (21 July). Health Stamps. Children's Pets. T **494** and similar vert design. Multicoloured. Perf 13½.

1741	45c.+5c. Type **494**	60	90
1742	80c.+5c. Girl with Kitten	90	1·50
MS1743	115×96 mm. Nos. 1741/1742, each×2. Perf 14½	3·00	4·50

No. **MS**1743 exists surcharged 'STAMPEX '93 NATIONAL YOUTH PHILATELIC EXHIBITION CHRISTCHURCH 19TH–21ST AUGUST 1993 $6·00' in ultramarine. Such miniature sheets were prepared by the organisers and sold at the Exhibition PO philatelic counter.

(Recess and litho Leigh-Mardon Ltd, Melbourne (No. **MS**1745))

1993 (14 Aug). Taipei '93 Asian International Stamp Exhibition, Taiwan.

(a) No. **MS**1743 optd 'TAIPEI '93' and emblem on sheet margin.
MS1744 Nos. 1741/1742, each×2 .... 18·00 22·00

(b) Sheet 125×100 mm containing No. 1490c (recess) and two similar designs as Nos. 1490/1490b, but litho. Perf 13 (around design).
MS1745 **445** $1 deep green, $1 blue, $1 rosine .... 6·50 8·50

Unlike previous miniature sheets produced by New Zealand Post for international stamp exhibitions overseas Nos. **MS**1744/**MS**1745, and all subsequent issues of this type, were supplied to collectors in New Zealand and abroad by standing order.

495 Christmas Decorations (value at left) **496** Rainbow Abalone or Paua

(Des Kristine Cotton. Litho Southern Colour Print, Dunedin (Nos. 1746b/1749a) or Leigh-Mardon Ltd, Melbourne (others))

1993 (1 Sept–3 Nov). Christmas. T **495** and similar vert designs. Multicoloured. Perf 14½×14.

1746	45c. Type **495**	45	85
	a. Block of 4. Nos. 1746/1749	1·60	4·00
	b. Perf 12 (3.11)	1·40	1·60
	ba. Booklet pane. Nos. 1746b/1747a, each×3, and 1748a/1749a, each×2	8·00	
1747	45c. Christmas decorations (value at right)	45	85
	a. Perf 12 (3.11)	1·40	1·60
1748	45c. Sailboards, gifts and Christmas pudding (value at left)	45	85
	a. Perf 12 (3.11)	1·40	1·60
1749	45c. Sailboards, gifts and Christmas pudding (value at right)	45	85
	a. Perf 12 (3.11)	1·40	1·60
1750	$1 Sailboards, baubles and Christmas cracker	75	1·00
1751	$1.50 Sailboards, present and wreath	1·25	3·00
1746/1751	Set of 6	3·50	6·75

Nos. 1746/1749 were printed together, *se-tenant*, in blocks of four throughout the sheet.

Booklet pane No. 1746ba contains two *se-tenant* blocks of four and a horizontal pair.

(Des R. Youmans. Litho Southern Colour Print, Dunedin)

1993 (1 Sept). Marine Life. T **496** and similar horiz designs. Multicoloured. Perf 13½.

1752	45c. Type **498**	90	90
	a. Booklet pane. Nos. 1752/1761 and two stamp-size labels	8·00	8·00
1753	45c. Green Mussels	90	90
1754	45c. Tarakihi	90	90
1755	45c. Salmon	90	90
1756	45c. Southern Blue-finned Tuna, Yellow finned Tuna and Kahawai	90	90
1757	45c. Rock Lobster	90	90
1758	45c. Snapper	90	90
1759	45c. Grouper	90	90
1760	45c. Orange Roughy	90	90
1761	45c. Squid, Hoki and Black Oreo	90	90
1752/1761	Set of 10	8·00	8·00

Nos. 1752/1761 were only issued in $4.50 stamp booklets with the *se-tenant* pane, which includes two inscribed labels at left, forming a composite design.

497 Sauropod **498** Soldiers, National Flag and Pyramids

(Des G. Cox. Litho Southern Colour Print, Dunedin)

1993 (1 Oct). Prehistoric Animals. T **497** and similar multicoloured designs.

(a) Perf 14.

1762	45c. Type **497**	50	15
1763	80c. Pterosaur	75·00	85·00
1764	$1 Ankylosaur	80·00	95·00
1765	$1.20 Mauisaurus	1·10	2·50
1766	$1.50 Carnosaur	1·25	2·50
1762/1766	Set of 5	4·00	6·25
MS1768	125×100 mm. $1.50, As No. 1766. Perf 14½×14.	2·00	2·00

NEW ZEALAND

(b) Smaller Design, 30×25 mm. Perf 12.
1767	45c. Carnosaur and Sauropod	50	85
	a. Booklet pane of 10 and two labels	4·50	

No. 1767 was only issued in $4.50 stamp booklet, No. SB66.
A used example of No. 1762 is known with the yellow omitted.

(Des A. Hollows (No. 1770). Litho Southern Colour Print, Dunedin)

1993 (1 Oct). Bangkok '93 International Stamp Exhibition, Thailand.
(a) No. **MS***1768 optd 'BANGKOK '93' and emblem on sheet margin.*
MS1769 $1.50 As No. 1767.................... 1·60 2·00

(b) Sheet 115×100 mm, containing No. 1735.
MS1770 $1.80 multicoloured.................. 1·75 3·00

(Des P. Andrews. Litho Questa)

1993 (3 Nov). New Zealand in the 1940s. T **498** and similar vert designs.
Multicoloured. Perf 14.
1771	45c. Type **498**	70	25
1772	50c. Aerial crop spraying	75	75
1773	80c. Hydroelectric scheme	80	80
1774	$1 Marching majorettes	1·25	1·00
1775	$1.50 American troops	1·60	2·75
1776	$1.80 Crowd celebrating victory	1·75	2·75
1771/1776	Set of 6	6·25	7·50

499 Bungy Jumping **500** *New Zealand Endeavour* (yacht)

(Des G. Taylor. Litho Southern Colour Print, Dunedin)

1994 (19 Jan). Tourism. T **499** and similar multicoloured designs. Perf 12.
(a) As T **499***.*
1777	45c. Type **499**	25	10
1778	80c. Trout fishing	45	50
1779	$1 Jet boating (*horiz*)	50	80
1780	$1.50 Tramping	75	1·50
1781	$1.80 Heli-skiing	85	2·00
1777/1781	Set of 5	2·50	4·50

(b) Smaller design, 25×25 mm.
1782	45c. White-water rafting	30	65
	a. Booklet pane of 10 plus 4 half stamp-size greetings labels	2·75	5·50

No. 1782 was only issued in $4.50 stamp booklet, No. SB68.
For miniature sheet containing the $1.80 see No. **MS**1785.

(Des B. Hall. Litho Leigh-Mardon Ltd, Melbourne)

1994 (19 Jan). Round the World Yacht Race. Perf 14½ (and 13 around design).
1783	**500** $1 multicoloured	1·00	1·75

No. 1783 was printed in sheets of 24 (6×4) with each stamp within a square perforated margin and with a further circular perforation around the design.

501 Mount Cook and New Zealand Symbols

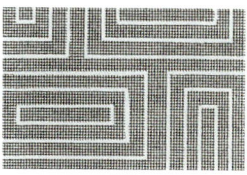

502

(Des Heather Arnold. Engraved C. Slania. Recess and die-stamped (gold) Leigh-Mardon Ltd, Melbourne)

1994 (18 Feb). W **502**. Phosphorised paper. Perf 14½×15.
1784	**501** $20 deep violet-blue and gold	15·00	16·00

No. 1784 shows a fluorescent security pattern of New Zealand Post printed beneath the design.

(Des G. Taylor (No. **MS**1785), Karen Odiam (No. **MS**1786). Litho Southern Colour Print, Dunedin (No. **MS**1785) or Leigh-Mardon Ltd, Melbourne (No. **MS**1786))

1994 (18 Feb). Hong Kong '94 International Stamp Exhibition. Perf 12 (No. **MS**1785) or 13 (No. **MS**1786).
MS1785 95×115 mm. $1.80, multicoloured (No. 1781).... 4·00 3·50
MS1786 100×125 mm. $1 deep green, $1 rosine, $1 blue (As Nos. 1490/1490c, but all printed litho)........ 5·50 6·00

503 Rock and Roll Dancers **504** Mount Cook and Mount Cook Lily ('Winter')

(Des Karen Odiam. Litho Leigh-Mardon Ltd, Melbourne)

1994 (23 Mar). New Zealand in the 1950s. T **503** and similar vert designs.
Multicoloured. Perf 14½×14.
1787	45c. Type **503**	25	10
1788	80c. Sir Edmund Hillary on Mount Everest	65	55
1789	$1 Aunt Daisy (radio personality)	50	65
1790	$1.20 Queen Elizabeth II during 1953 royal visit	1·00	1·25
1791	$1.50 Children playing with Opo the dolphin	1·00	1·75
1792	$1.80 Auckland Harbour Bridge	1·10	1·75
1787/1792	Set of 6	4·00	5·50

(Des R. Youmans. Litho Southern Colour Print, Dunedin)

1994 (27 Apr). The Four Seasons. T **504** and similar horiz designs. Multicoloured. Perf 12.
1793	45c. Type **504**	30	10
	a. Horiz strip of 4. Nos. 1793/1796	2·75	4·25
1794	70c. Lake Hawea and Kowhai ('Spring')	45	45
1795	$1.50 Opononi Beach and Pohutukawa ('Summer')	80	1·00
1796	$1.80 Lake Pukaki and Puriri ('Autumn')	1·10	1·25
1793/1796	Set of 4	2·40	2·50

In addition to separate sheets of 100 (10×10) Nos. 1793/1796 were also printed together, *se-tenant*, in horizontal strips of four throughout sheets of 80 (8×10).

 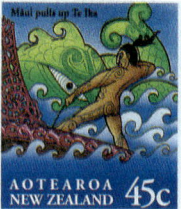

505 Rainbow Abalone or Paua Shell **506** Maui pulls up Te Ika

(Des D. Gunson. Litho Southern Colour Print, Dunedin)

1994 (27 Apr). New Zealand Life (1st series). T **505** and similar multicoloured designs. Perf 12.
1797	45c. Type **505** (25×20 mm)	30	45
	a. Booklet pane. Nos. 1797/1806	2·75	4·00

NEW ZEALAND

1798	45c. Pavlova dessert (35×20 mm)		30	45
1799	45c. Hokey pokey ice cream (35×20 mm)		30	45
1800	45c. Fish and chips (35×20 mm)		30	45
1801	45c. Jandals (30×20 mm)		30	45
1802	45c. Bush shirt (25×30½ mm)		30	45
1803	45c. Buzzy Bee (toy) (35×30½ mm)		30	45
1804	45c. Gumboots and black singlet (25×30½ mm)		30	45
1805	45c. Rugby boots and ball (35×30½ mm)		30	45
1806	45c. Kiwifruit (30×30½ mm)		30	45
1797/1806 Set of 10			2·75	4·00

Nos. 1797/1806 were only issued in $4.50 stamp booklet, No. SB69. See also Nos. 2318/2327.

(Des Manu Kopere Society. Litho Leigh-Mardon Ltd, Melbourne)

1994 (8 June). Maori Myths. T **506** and similar vert designs. Multicoloured. Perf 13.

1807	45c. Type **506**	25	10
1808	80c. Rona snatched up by Marama	40	40
1809	$1 Maui attacking Tuna	45	50
1810	$1.20 Tane separating Rangi and Papa	60	1·50
1811	$1.50 Matakauri slaying the Giant of Wakatipu	70	1·50
1812	$1.80 Panenehu showing crayfish to Tangaroa	80	1·50
1807/1812 Set of 6		3·00	5·00

 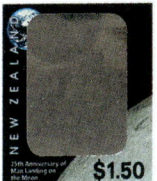

507 1939 2d. on 1d.+1d. Health Stamp and Children playing with Ball

508 Astronaut on Moon (hologram)

(Des D. Gunson. Litho Leigh-Mardon Ltd, Melbourne)

1994 (20 July). Health Stamps. 75th Anniversary of Children's Health Camps. T **507** and similar vert designs. Multicoloured. Perf 14½.

1813	45c.+5c. Type **507**	30	80
1814	45c.+5c. 1949 1d.+½d. stamp and nurse holding child	30	80
1815	45c.+5c. 1969 4c.+1c. stamp and children reading	30	80
1816	80c.+5c. 1931 2d.+1d. stamp and child in cap	50	1·00
1813/16 Set of 4		1·25	3·00
MS1817 130×90 mm. Nos. 1813/1816		1·25	3·25

(Des Brand New Ltd, Wellington. Litho Southern Colour Print, Dunedin (hologram by Woodmansterne. Ltd, Watford))

1994 (20 July). 25th Anniversary of First Moon Landing. Perf 12.

1818	**508**	$1.50 multicoloured	2·25	2·75
		aa. Hologram omitted	£750	—

509 'people reaching people'

510 African Elephants

Two types of T **509**:
Type I: 'w' of 'new' partly in blue. 'i' of 'reaching' without dot.
Type II: 'w' of 'new' all in magenta. 'i' of 'reaching' with dot.

(Des Van de Roer Designs. Litho Leigh-Mardon Ltd, Melbourne (Nos. 1818, 1819) or SNP Cambec (Nos. 1818aab, 1819a))

1994 (20 July)–95. Self-adhesive. Phosphorised paper (Nos. 1818aab, 1819a). Perf 11

1818a	**509**	40c. multicoloured (I) (2.10.95)	1·50	1·50
		ab. Perf 11½. Type II (11.95)	75	75
1819		45c. multicoloured (I)	1·00	65
		a. Perf 11½. Type II (8.95)	1·50	1·75

Nos. 1818a/1819a were each available in coils of 100.
On Nos. 1818a and 1819 the vertical die-cut perforations interlock, but on Nos. 1818aab and 1819a the stamps are separate on the backing paper.

(Des Denise Durkin. Litho Leigh-Mardon Ltd, Melbourne)

1994 (16 Aug). Stamp Month. Wild Animals. T **510** and similar horiz designs. Multicoloured. Perf 14×14½.

1820	45c. Type **510**	90	1·10
	a. Block of 10. Nos. 1820/1829	8·00	10·00
1821	45c. White Rhinoceros	90	1·10
1822	45c. Lions	90	1·10
1823	45c. Common Zebras	90	1·10
1824	45c. Giraffe and Calf	90	1·10
1825	45c. Siberian Tiger	90	1·10
1826	45c. Hippopotami	90	1·10
1827	45c. Spider Monkey	90	1·10
1828	45c. Giant Panda	90	1·10
1829	45c. Polar Bear and Cub	90	1·10
1820/1829 Set of 10		8·00	10·00

Nos. 1820/1829 were printed together, se-tenant, in sheets of 100 so arranged as to provide horizontal or vertical strips of ten or blocks of ten (5×2) showing all the designs.

(Des Pauline Morse (No. **MS**1830), Denise Durkin (No. **MS**1831). Litho Leigh-Mardon Ltd, Melbourne)

1994 (16 Aug). Philakorea '94 International Stamp Exhibition, Seoul. Multicoloured. Perf 14½×14 (No. **MS**1830) or 14×14½ (No. **MS**1831).

MS1830	125×100 mm. Nos. 1459a/1465	6·50	6·00
MS1831	125×100 mm. Nos. 1820, 1822, 1824/1825 and 1828/1829	3·25	4·50

511 Children with Crib

512 Batsman

(Des Karen Odiam. Litho Southern Colour Print, Dunedin (No. 1832) or Leigh-Mardon Ltd, Melbourne (others))

1994 (21 Sept). Christmas. T **511** and similar horiz designs. Multicoloured. Perf 12 (No. 1832) or 14½ (others).

1832	45c. Father Christmas and children (30×25 mm)	30	40
1833	45c. Type **511**	20	10
1834	70c. Men and toddler with crib	30	60
1835	80c. Three carol singers	35	65
1836	$1 Five carol singers	40	65
1837	$1.50 Children and candles	65	2·25
1838	$1.80 Parents with child	80	1·75
1832/1838 Set of 7		2·40	5·75
MS1839 125×100 mm. Nos. 1833/1836		1·50	2·50

No. 1832 was only issued in $4.50 stamp booklet, No. SB70.

(Des M. Bailey (Nos. 1840/1849), P. Andrews (others). Litho Southern Colour Print, Dunedin)

1994 (2 Nov). Centenary of New Zealand Cricket Council.

(a) Horiz designs, each 30×25 mm. Multicoloured. Perf 12.

1840	45c. Bathers catching balls	75	90
	a. Booklet pane of 10. Nos. 1840/1849	6·50	8·00
1841	45c. Child on surfboard at top	75	90
1842	45c. Young child with rubber ring at top	75	90
1843	45c. Man with beach ball at top	75	90
1844	45c. Woman with cricket bat at right	75	90
1845	45c. Boy in green cap with bat	75	90
1846	45c. Man in spotted shirt running	75	90
1847	45c. Woman in striped shorts with bat	75	90
1848	45c. Boy in wetsuit with surfboard at right	75	90
1849	45c. Sunbather with newspaper at right	75	90

(b) T **512** and similar vert designs. Multicoloured. Perf 13½.

1850	45c. Type **512**	85	40
1851	80c. Bowler	1·50	1·00
1852	$1 Wicket-keeper	1·75	1·00
1853	$1.80 Fielder	2·75	3·00
1840/1853 Set of 14		13·00	13·00

Nos. 1840/1849 were only issued in $4.50 stamp booklet, No. SB71.

(Litho Leigh-Mardon Ltd, Melbourne)

1995 (3 Feb). POST X '95 Postal History Exhibition, Auckland. Sheet 130×90 mm, containing No. 1297 and a reproduction of No. 557 optd 'SPECIMEN'. Perf 14½.

MS1854 $10 multicoloured	18·00	19·00

NEW ZEALAND

513 Auckland   **514** The 15th Hole, Waitangi

(Des Red Cactus Design. Litho Southern Colour Print, Dunedin)

1995 (22 Feb). New Zealand by Night. T **513** and similar horiz designs. Multicoloured. Perf 12.

1855	45c. Type **513**	30	10
1856	80c. Wellington	50	45
1857	$1 Christchurch	55	60
1858	$1.20 Dunedin	60	1·50
1859	$1.50 Rotorua	75	1·90
1860	$1.80 Queenstown	85	1·90
1855/1860	Set of 6	3·25	5·75

See also No. **MS**1915.

(Des R. Jones. Litho Leigh-Mardon Ltd, Melbourne)

1995 (22 Mar). New Zealand Golf Courses. T **514** and similar vert designs. Multicoloured. Perf 14½×14.

1861	45c. Type **514**	55	30
1862	80c. The 6th hole, New Plymouth	80	90
1863	$1.20 The 9th hole, Rotorua	1·25	2·50
1864	$1.80 The 5th hole, Queenstown	1·75	3·00
1861/1864	Set of 4	4·00	6·00

515 New Zealand Pigeon and Nest   **516** Teacher with Guitar and Children

(Des Niki Hill. Litho Southern Colour Print, Dunedin)

1995 (22 Mar). Environment. T **515** and similar horiz designs. Multicoloured. Perf 12.

1865	45c. Type **515**	65	65
	a. Booklet pane. Nos. 1865/1874	6·00	6·00
1866	45c. Planting sapling	65	65
1867	45c. Dolphins and Whales	65	65
1868	45c. Thunderstorm	65	65
1869	45c. Backpackers	65	65
1870	45c. Animal pests	65	65
1871	45c. Noxious plants	65	65
1872	45c. Undersized fish and shellfish	65	65
1873	45c. Pollution from factories	65	65
1874	45c. Family at picnic site	65	65
1865/1874	Set of 10	6·00	6·00

Nos. 1865/1874 were only issued in $4.50 stamp booklet, No. SB72, with the vertical edges of the pane imperforate.

Each vertical pair forms a composite design.

(Des M. Kopere. Litho Southern Colour Print, Dunedin)

1995 (3 May). Maori Language Year. T **516** and similar vert designs. Multicoloured. Perf 13½.

1875	45c. Type **516**	20	10
1876	70c. Singing group	30	55
1877	80c. Mother and baby	35	60
1878	$1 Women performing traditional welcome	40	75
1879	$1.50 Grandfather reciting family genealogy	60	1·75
1880	$1.80 Tribal orator	70	1·75
1875/1880	Set of 6	2·25	5·00

In addition to sheets containing stamps of one value Nos. 1875/1880 also exist in sheetlets of 24 containing four of each value *se-tenant*. These sheetlets were only available from Limited Edition Collectors Packs costing NZ$135.

 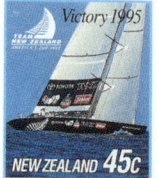

517 Map of Australasia and Asia   **518** *Black Magic* (yacht)

(Des Cue Design. Litho Southern Colour Print, Dunedin)

1995 (3 May). Meetings of Asian Development Bank Board of Governors and International Pacific Basin Economic Council, Auckland. T **517** and similar horiz design. Multicoloured. Perf 13½.

1881	$1 Type **517**	1·00	1·00
1882	$1.50 Map of Australasia and Pacific	1·50	2·75

(Des A. Hollows. Litho Southern Colour Print, Dunedin)

1995 (16 May). New Zealand's Victory in 1995 America's Cup. Perf 12.
1883	**518** 45c. multicoloured	40	55

No. 1883 was issued in small sheets of ten with a seascape printed on the margins. This sheetlet also exists numbered and overprinted in gold foil from a Limited Edition Collectors Pack costing NZ$25.

519 Boy on Skateboard   **520** Lion Red Cup and Players

(Des P. Martinson. Litho Leigh-Mardon Ltd, Melbourne)

1995 (21 June). Health Stamps. Children's Sports. T **519** and similar triangular design. Multicoloured. Perf 14½.

1884	45c.+5c. Type **519**	75	1·50
	a. Tête-bêche (pair)	1·50	3·00
1885	80c.+5c. Girl on bicycle	1·75	2·00
	a. Tête-bêche (pair)	3·50	4·00
MS1886 130×90 mm. Nos. 1884/1885, each×2		5·00	6·50

Nos. 1884/1885 were each printed in sheets with the horizontal rows made up of *tête-bêche* pairs.

1995 (1 July). Stampex '95 National Stamp Exhibition, Wellington. No. **MS**1886 additionally inscr with 'Stampex '95' and emblem on sheet margin.

MS1887 130×90 mm. Nos. 1884/1885, each×2 .... 6·00   8·00

(Des Heather Arnold. Litho Southern Colour Print, Dunedin (No. 1888) or Enschedé (others))

1995 (26 July). Centenary of Rugby League. T **520** and similar horiz designs. Multicoloured.

(a) As T **520**. *Perf 14×14½.*

1888	45c. Type **520**	25	10·00
1889	$1 Children's rugby and mascot	50	80
1890	$1.50 George Smith, Albert Baskerville and early match	70	2·00
1891	$1.80 Courtney Goodwill Trophy and match against Great Britain	85	1·75
1888/1891 Set of 4		2·10	4·25
MS1892 125×100 mm. No. 1891		1·50	2·50

(b) Smaller design, 30×25 mm. Perf 12.

1893	45c. Trans Tasman test match	35	50
	a. Booklet pane. No. 1893×10	3·00	4·50

No. 1893 was only issued in $4.50 stamp booklet, No. SB73, and has the vertical edges of the pane imperforate.

No. **MS**1892 imperforate comes from a Limited Edition Collectors Pack costing NZ$135.

521 Sheep and Lamb   **522** Archangel Gabriel

NEW ZEALAND

(Des Joanne Kreyl. Litho Southern Colour Print, Dunedin)

1995 (1 Sept–2 Oct). Farmyard Animals. T **521** and similar horiz designs. Multicoloured. Perf 14×14½

1894	40c. Type **521** (2.10)		60	75
	a. Booklet pane. Nos. 1894/1903		5·50	7·00
1895	40c. Deer (2.10)		60	75
1896	40c. Mare and Foal (2.10)		60	75
1897	40c. Cow with Calf (2.10)		60	75
1898	40c. Goats and Kid (2.10)		60	75
1899	40c. Common Turkey (2.10)		60	75
1900	40c. Ducks (2.10)		60	75
1901	40c. Red Jungle fowl (2.10)		60	75
1902	40c. Sow with Piglets (2.10)		60	75
1903	40c. Border Collie (2.10)		60	75
1904	45c. Type **521**		60	75
	a. Booklet pane. Nos. 1904/1913		5·50	7·00
1905	45c. As No. 1895		60	75
1906	45c. As No. 1896		60	75
1907	45c. As No. 1897		70	75
1908	45c. As No. 1898		60	75
1909	45c. As No. 1899		60	75
1910	45c. As No. 1900		60	75
1911	45c. As No. 1901		60	75
1912	45c. As No. 1902		60	75
1913	45c. As No. 1903		60	75
1894/1913 Set of 20			11·00	14·00

Nos. 1894/1903 and 1904/1913 were only issued in $4 (Nos. 1894/1903) and $4.50 (Nos. 1904/1913) stamp booklets in which the horizontal edges of the booklet panes are imperforate, Nos. SB75 and SB76.

(Des Joanne Kreyl (No. **MS**1914), Red Cactus Design (No. **MS**1915). Litho Southern Colour Print, Dunedin)

1995 (1 Sept). Singapore '95 International Stamp Exhibition. Perf 12.

MS1914	170×70 mm. Nos. 1909/1913	3·25	4·00
MS1915	148×210 mm. Nos. 1855/1860	11·00	16·00

No. **MS**1915 also includes the JAKARTA '95 logo.

(Des K. Hall. Litho Southern Colour Print, Dunedin)

1995 (1 Sept–9 Nov). Christmas. Stained Glass Windows from St Mary's Anglican Church, Merivale (Nos. 1916/1918), The Lady Chapel of St Luke's Anglican Church, Christchurch (Nos. 1919/1922) or St John the Evangelist Church, Cheviot (No. 1923). Multicoloured. Perf 12

(a) As T **522**.

1916	40c. Type **522** (2.10)	50	25
1917	45c. Type **522**	50	25
1918	70c. Virgin Mary	80	90
1919	80c. Shepherds	80	1·00
1920	$1 Virgin and Child	1·00	1·10
1921	$1.50 Two Wise Men	1·75	2·75
1922	$1.80 Wise Man kneeling	2·00	2·75
1916/1922 Set of 7		6·50	8·00

(b) Smaller design, 25×30 mm. Perf 14½×14.

1923	40c. Angel with Trumpet (9.11)	45	50
	a. Booklet pane. No. 1923×10	4·00	

No. 1923 was only issued in $4 stamp booklets which show the outer edges of the pane imperforate, No. SB77.

Nos. 1916 and 1918/1922 also exist as a miniature sheet, only available as part of a joint Phone Card and Stamp Collectors Pack produced in a limited quantity and costing NZ$115.

A used imperf pair of No. 1923 has been reported.

523 Face and Nuclear Disarmament Symbol

524 Mount Cook

(Des C. Martin. Litho Southern Colour Print, Dunedin)

1995 (1 Sept). Nuclear Disarmament. Perf 13½.

1924	**523**	$1 multicoloured	1·00	1·25

(Des Comm Arts Design (90c.), S. Fuller ($1.30, $2), Red Cactus Design (others). Litho Enschedé ($10) or Southern Colour Print, Dunedin (others))

1995 (2 Oct)–**2002**. New Zealand Scenery. T **524** and similar multicoloured designs. Ordinary or phosphorised paper (5c., $2), phosphorised paper (others). Perf 13½×14 ($10) or 13½ (others)

1925	5c. Type **524** (27.3.96)	10	50
1926	10c. Champagne Pool (27.3.96)	10	20
1927	20c. Cape Reinga (27.3.96)	15	50
1928	30c. Mackenzie Country (27.3.96)	20	25
1929	40c. Mitre Peak (*vert*)	30	35
	a. Yellow foliage frame and pink clouds (5.02)	1·00	50
	b. Olive-brown foliage frame	1·00	50
1930	50c. Mount Ngauruhoe (27.3.96)	35	40
1931	60c. Lake Wanaka (*vert*) (27.3.96)	45	1·00
1932	70c. Giant Kauri tree (*vert*) (27.3.96)	50	1·00
1933	80c. Doubtful Sound (*vert*) (27.3.96)	60	65
1934	90c. Waitomo Limestone Cave (*vert*) (27.3.96)	65	70
1934a	90c. Rangitoto Island (27×22 mm) (11.10.00)	3·50	70
1934b	$1 Taiaroa Head (27×22 mm) (6.3.00)	1·00	80
1934c	$1.10 Kaikoura Coast (27×22 mm) (6.3.00)	1·00	85
1934d	$1.30 Lake Camp, South Canterbury (27×22 mm) (11.10.00)	5·50	3·50
1934e	$2 Great Barrier Island (27×22 mm) (6.3.00)	1·25	1·60
1934f	$3 Cape Kidnappers (27×22 mm) (6.3.00)	1·75	2·40
1935	$10 Mount Ruapehu (38×32 mm) (12.2.97)	4·75	7·75
1925/1935 Set of 17		£220	21·00

On No. 1929 the foliage frame is predominantly green and the clouds white.

No. 1929a is from the two kiwi printing.

For similar self-adhesive designs see Nos. 1983*a*/1991*b*.

For miniature sheets containing some of these designs see Nos. **MS**1978, **MS**1998, **MS**2005, **MS**2328 and **MS**2401.

525 Dame Kiri te Kanawa (opera singer)

(Des Karen Odium. Litho Southern Colour Print, Dunedin)

1995 (4 Oct). Famous New Zealanders. T **525** and similar horiz designs. Multicoloured. Perf 12.

1936	40c. Type **525**	1·00	50
1937	80c. Charles Upham, VC (war hero)	1·00	1·25
1938	$1 Barry Crump (author)	1·25	1·25
1939	$1.20 Sir Brian Barratt-Boyes (surgeon)	1·75	1·75
1940	$1.50 Dame Whina Cooper (Maori leader)	1·75	2·50
1941	$1.80 Sir Richard Hadlee (cricketer)	3·00	2·25
1936/1941 Set of 6		8·75	8·50

Nos. 1936/1941 were issued in sheets with each stamp *se-tenant* horizontally with a 10×30 mm label inscribed 'STAMP MONTH October 1995'.

526 National Flags, Peace Dove and '50'

(Des S. Fuller. Litho Leigh-Mardon Ltd, Melbourne)

1995 (4 Oct). 50th Anniversary of United Nations. Perf 15.

1942	**526**	$1.80 multicoloured	2·25	3·00

527 Fern and Globe

(Des Red Cactus Design. Litho Leigh-Mardon Ltd, Melbourne)

1995 (9 Nov). Commonwealth Heads of Government Meeting, Auckland. T **527** and similar horiz design. Multicoloured. Perf 14.

1943	40c. Type **527**	40	25
1944	$1.80 Fern and New Zealand flag	1·75	3·00

NEW ZEALAND

528 Kiwi   **529** Kete (basket)

(Des Communication Arts Ltd. Litho Enschedé)

1996 (24 Jan). Famous Racehorses. T **528** and similar horiz designs. Multicoloured. Perf 14×14½.

1945	40c. Type **528**	45	10
1946	80c. Rough Habit	75	55
1947	$1 Blossom Lady	85	65
1948	$1.20 Il Vicolo	1·00	1·25
1949	$1.50 Horlicks	1·25	1·75
1950	$1.80 Bonecrusher	1·40	2·00
1945/1950 Set of 6		5·00	5·50
MS1951 Seven sheets, each 162×110 mm. (a) No. 1945. (b) No. 1946. (c) No. 1947. (d) No. 1948. (e) No. 1949. (f) No. 1950. (g) Nos. 1945/1950		16·00	19·00

Nos. **MS**1951(a)/**MS**1951(g) were only available from $13.70 stamp booklet, No. SB78, with each miniature sheet showing a line of roulettes at left.

An overprinted and numbered miniature sheet containing Nos. 1945/1950 comes from a Limited Edition Collectors Pack costing NZ$135.

(Des G. Hubbard. Litho Enschedé)

1996 (21 Feb). Maori Crafts. T **529** and similar vert designs. Multicoloured. Perf 14×13½.

1952	40c. Type **529**	15	10
1953	80c. Head of Taiaha (spear)	30	30
1954	$1 Taniko (embroidery)	35	40
1955	$1.20 Pounamu (greenstone)	45	80
1956	$1.50 Hue (gourd)	55	1·25
1957	$1.80 Korowai (feather cloak)	65	1·25
1952/1957 Set of 6		2·25	3·50

For miniature sheet containing some of these designs see No. **MS**2049.

530 Black-backed Gulls   **531** Fire and Ambulance Services

(Des Sue Wickison)

1996 (21 Feb–7 Aug). Seaside Environment. T **530** and similar horiz designs. Multicoloured.

(a) Litho Southern Colour Print, Dunedin. Perf 14×14½.

1958	40c. Type **530**	55	80
	a. Booklet pane of 10. Nos. 1958/1967	5·00	7·00
1959	40c. Children, Sea Cucumber and Spiny Starfish	55	80
1960	40c. Yacht, Gull and Common Shrimps	55	80
1961	40c. Gaudy Nudibranch	55	80
1962	40c. Large Rock Crab and Clingfish	55	80
1963	40c. Snake Skin Chiton and Red Rock Crab	55	80
1964	40c. Estuarine Triplefin and Cat's-eye shell	55	80
1965	40c. Cushion Star and Seahorses	55	80
1966	40c. Blue-eyed Triplefin and Yaldwyn's Triplefin	55	80
1967	40c. Common Octopus	55	80
1958/1967 Set of 10		5·00	7·00

Nos. 1958/1967 were only issued in $4 stamp booklets in which the horizontal edges of the pane are imperforate.

(b) Litho SNP Cambec, Australia. Self-adhesive. Phosphor frame. Perf 11½ (7 August).

1968	40c. Type **530**	50	60
	a. Booklet pane of 10. Nos. 1968/1977	4·50	5·50
1969	40c. Children, Sea Cucumber and Spiny Starfish	50	60
1970	40c. Yacht, Gull and Common Shrimps	50	60
1971	40c. Gaudy Nudibranch	50	60
1972	40c. Large Rock Crab and Clingfish	50	60
1973	40c. Snake Skin Chiton and Red Rock Crab	50	60
1974	40c. Estuarine Triplefin and Cat's-eye shell	50	60
1975	40c. Cushion Star and Seahorses	50	60
1976	40c. Blue-eyed Triplefin and Yaldwyn's Triplefin	50	60
1977	40c. Common Octopus	50	60
1968/1977 Set of 10		4·50	5·50

Nos. 1968/1977 were only issued in $4 self-adhesive stamp booklet, No. SB80, containing No. 1968a on which the surplus self-adhesive paper around each stamp was retained.

The phosphor, which shows pink under UV light, forms an irregular frame on two sides of each design.

(Litho Southern Colour Print, Dunedin)

1996 (15 Mar). SOUTHPEX '96 Stamp Show, Invercargill. Sheet 100×215 mm, containing No. 1929×10. Perf 12.

MS1978	40c.×10 multicoloured	6·50	7·50

(Des Dave Clark Design Associates. Litho Southern Colour Print, Dunedin)

1996 (27 Mar). Rescue Services. T **531** and similar vert designs. Multicoloured. Perf 14½×15.

1979	40c. Type **531**	50	20
1980	80c. Civil Defence	90	90
1981	$1 Air-sea rescue	1·10	1·10
1982	$1.50 Air ambulance and rescue helicopter	1·60	2·75
	a. Yellow value and background		
1983	$1.80 Mountain rescue and Red Cross	2·25	2·50
1979/1983 Set of 5		5·75	6·75

No. 1982a shows the value and background in yellow instead of green.

532 Mount Egmont, Taranaki   **533** Yellow-eyed Penguin

(Des Comm Arts Design (90c.), S. Fuller ($1.10) or Red Cactus Design (others). Litho Southern Colour Print, Dunedin (Nos. 1983, 1984b/1989, 1990 and 1991) or SNP Cambec, Australia (others))

1996 (1 May)–2004. New Zealand Scenery. Self-adhesive. T **532** and similar multicoloured designs. Phosphor frame. Perf 10 (10c., 90c., $1.10) or 11½ (others)

1983a	10c. Champagne Pool (28.1.04)	1·00	1·25
	ab. Booklet pane. Nos. 1983a×4 and 1986b×10	6·00	
1984	40c. Type **532**	55	55
	a. Sheetlet of 10. Nos. 1984/1989 (one each of two designs and two each of the remainder)	20·00	
	b. Perf 10 (14.1.98)	35	40
	ba. Booklet pane. Nos. 1984b×2, 1985b, 1986b×2, 1987b and 1988b/1989b, each×2	3·25	
	bab. Booklet pane. Printed on the backing paper	60·00	
	bb. On phosphorised paper (4.2000)	1·00	1·50
1985	40c. Piercy Island, Bay of Islands	55	55
	b. Perf 10 (14.1.98)	75	1·00
	bb. On phosphorised paper (4.2000)	1·00	1·50
1986	40c. Tory Channel, Marlborough Sounds	55	55
	b. Perf 10 (14.1.98)	35	40
	ba. 'Marlborough Sounds' inscr omitted	40·00	
	bb. On phosphorised paper (4.2000)	1·00	1·50
1987	40c. *Earnslaw* (ferry), Lake Wakatipu	55	55
	b. Perf 10 (14.1.98)	75	1·00
	bb. On phosphorised paper (4.2000)	1·00	1·50
1988	40c. Lake Matheson	55	55
	b. Perf 10 (14.1.98)	35	40
	bb. On phosphorised paper (4.2000)	1·00	1·50
1989	40c. Fox Glacier	55	55
	b. Perf 10 (14.1.98)	35	40
	bb. On phosphorised paper (4.2000)	1·00	1·50
1990	80c. Doubtful Sound (as No. 1933) (vert) (13.11.96)	90	90
	a. Booklet pane. No. 1990b×10	8·00	
1990b	90c. Rangitoto Island (5.4.04)	90	1·00
	ba. Booklet pane. No. 1990b×10	8·00	
1991	$1 Pohutukawa tree (33×22 mm) (7.8.96)	1·00	1·00
	a. Booklet pane. No. 1991×5	4·50	
1991b	$1.10 Kaikoura Coast (3.4.2000)	1·00	1·50

	ba. Booklet pane. No. 1991b×5 plus 5 airmail labels	4·50	
1983a/1991b Set of 11		6·50	7·50

The phosphor, which shows pink under UV light, appears as an irregular frame on the initial printing of Nos. 1984/1989, but further supplies released in November 1997 showed a regular phosphor frame as do Nos. 1983a, 1984b/1989b and 1990/1991b.

Nos. 1984/1989 and 1984bb/1989bb occur in rolls of 100, with the surplus self-adhesive paper around each stamp removed.

No. 1984a comes from the residue of special sheet stock used to prepare first day covers and subsequently sold as $4 hang-sell sheetlets.

Nos. 1984b/1989b come from $4 stamp booklet, No. SB89, containing No. 1984ba, on which the surplus self-adhesive paper was retained.

No. 1984bab occurred when the self-adhesive paper 'sandwich' became reversed so that the designs were printed on what should have been the back of the booklet. This results in the gum being attached to the backing paper instead of the stamps. Normal versions of the booklet show the paper around the stamps, outside the phosphor frames, as white with a strong fluorescent content. On the error this paper is off-white and non-fluorescent.

No. 1986ba occurs on one of the examples of this design in 2% of the original printing of booklet pane No. 1984ba.

Nos. 1983a, 1990 and 1991/1991b all come from separate stamp booklets on which the surplus self-adhesive paper around each stamp was retained.

No. 1990b was issued in sheets of 50 and in $4.50 booklets, both with the surplus paper retained.

(Des Sea Sky Design. Litho Southern Colour Print, Dunedin)

1996 (1 May). Marine Wildlife. T **533** and similar multicoloured designs. Perf 14.

1992	40c. Type **533**	35	25
	a. Block of 6. Nos. 1992/1997	3·75	6·25
1993	80c. Royal Albatross (horiz)	70	60
1994	$1 White Herons (horiz)	75	70
1995	$1.20 Flukes of Sperm Whale (horiz)	75	1·25
1996	$1.50 Fur Seals	80	1·50
1997	$1.80 Bottlenose Dolphin	90	1·50
1992/1997 Set of 6		3·75	5·25

In addition to separate sheets of 100 Nos. 1992/1997 were also issued in se-tenant blocks of six which also contained two irregular-shaped labels.

For miniature sheets containing these designs see Nos. MS1999 and MS2037.

(Des Diane Prosser (No. **MS**1998), Sea Sky Design (No. **MS**1999). Litho Southern Colour Print, Dunedin)

1996 (18 May). CHINA '96 Ninth International Stamp Exhibition, Peking. Multicoloured. Perf 13½ (No. **MS**1998) or 14 (No. **MS**1999).

MS1998 180×80 mm. Nos. 1926/1928 and 1930	1·75	2·25
MS1999 140×90 mm. Nos. 1994 and 1996	2·50	3·00
a. $1.50 value imperf at foot		

No. **MS**1999 also shows designs as Nos. 1992/1993, 1995 and 1997, but without face values.

534 Baby in Car Seat

(Des Helen Casey)

1996 (5 June). Health Stamps. Child Safety. T **534** and similar vert design. Multicoloured.

(a) Litho Southern Colour Print, Dunedin (No. 2000), Enschedé (Nos. 2000a, 2001) or SNP Cambec (No. **MS**2002). Perf 13½.

2000	40c.+5c. Type **534**	40	75
	a. As Type **534**, but teddy bear at top right and face value at bottom left	£800	£900
2001	80c.+5c. Child and adult on zebra crossing	60	1·50
MS2002 130×90 mm. Nos. 2000/2001, each×2. Perf 14×14½		2·25	2·75

(b) Litho SNP Cambec. Self-adhesive. Phosphor frame on three sides. Perf 11½.

2003	40c.+5c. Type **534**	50	75
	a. As Type **534**, but teddy bear at top right and face value at bottom left	£1000	£1300

The original versions (Nos. 2000a and 2003a) of the 40c.+5c. showed a teddy bear at top right and the face value above the inscription at bottom left. As depicted the design breached New Zealand safety guidelines and both versions were redrawn and replaced by T **534**. All the original versions should have been withdrawn from post office stocks before the release date, but examples were sold from at least two New Zealand Post outlets at Royal Oak (Auckland) and Te Ngae (Rotorua) and used for postal purposes.

Two examples of the miniature sheet, one with the CAPEX '96 overprint, including the teddy bear, were sold in the Netherlands during 1997. There is no evidence to link these two miniature sheets with New Zealand.

Stamps from No. **MS**2002 are slightly larger with 'NEW ZEALAND' and the face values redrawn.

No. 2003 is smaller, 21½×38 mm, and occurs in rolls of 100 with the surplus self-adhesive paper around each stamp removed. The phosphor shows pink under UV light.

(Des Diane Prosser (No. **MS**2005). Litho SNP Cambec (No. **MS**2004) or Southern Colour Print, Dunedin (No. **MS**2005))

1996 (8 June). CAPEX '96 International Stamp Exhibition, Toronto.

(a) No. **MS**2002 optd 'CAPEX '96' and emblem on sheet margin.

MS2004 Nos. 2000/2001, each×2	2·75	2·75

(b) Sheet 180×80 mm, containing Nos. 1931/1934. Perf 13½.

MS2005 $3 multicoloured	2·75	3·25

535 Violin

(Des M. Bailey. Litho and gold die-stamped Southern Colour Print, Dunedin)

1996 (10 July). 50th Anniversary of New Zealand Symphony Orchestra. T **535** and similar horiz design. Multicoloured. Perf 15×14½.

2006	40c. Type **535**	30	50
2007	80c. French horn	80	1·50

536 Swimming   **537** Hinemoa

(Des S. Fuller. Litho Southern Colour Print, Dunedin)

1996 (10 July). Centennial Olympic Games, Atlanta. T **536** and similar circular designs. Multicoloured. Perf 14½ (and 14 around bands).

2008	40c. Type **536**	30	15
2009	80c. Cycling	1·25	80
2010	$1 Running	60	80
2011	$1.50 Rowing	80	2·00
2012	$1.80 Dinghy sailing	80	2·00
2008/2012 Set of 5		3·25	5·25
MS2013 120×80 mm. Nos. 2008/2012		3·25	5·25

A miniature sheet containing Nos. 2008/2012 both perforated and imperforate comes from a Limited Edition Collectors Pack costing NZ$135.

(Des Eyework Design and Production. Litho Southern Colour Print, Dunedin (prize labels printed by Sabre Print))

1996 (7 Aug). Centenary of New Zealand Cinema. T **537** and similar vert designs. Multicoloured. Perf 14½.

2014	40c. Type **537**	25	15
2015	80c. Broken Barrier	50	60
2016	$1.50 Goodbye Pork Pie	80	2·25
2017	$1.80 Once Were Warriors	90	2·25
2014/2017 Set of 4		2·25	4·75

Nos. 2014/2017 were printed in sheets of 25, each stamp being se-tenant with a Scratch and Win stamp-size label.

NEW ZEALAND

538 Danyon Loader (swimmer) and Blyth Tait (horseman) **539** Beehive Ballot Box

(Des Red Cactus Design. Litho Southern Colour Print, Dunedin)

1996 (28 Aug). New Zealand Olympic Gold Medal Winners, Atlanta. Perf 14½ (and 14 around design).
2018 **538** 40c. multicoloured 50 50

No. 2018 was printed in sheets of 36 (6×6) with each stamp within a square perforated margin showing a pattern of Olympic rings and fern leaves.

(Des Gatehaus Design. Litho Southern Colour Print, Dunedin)

1996 (4 Sept). New Zealand's First Mixed Member Proportional Representation Election. Perf 12.
2019 **539** 40c. black, scarlet and pale yellow 30 40

No. 2019 was printed in sheets of ten (2×5) with decorated margins.

540 King following Star   **541** Adzebill

(Des Lindy Fisher)

1996 (4 Sept). Christmas. T **540** and similar horiz designs. Multicoloured.
(a) Litho Questa. Designs 35×35 mm. Perf 14.
2020	40c. Type **540**	30	10
2021	70c. Shepherd and Baby Jesus	50	40
2022	80c. Angel and shepherd	50	40
2023	$1 Mary, Joseph and Baby Jesus	65	50
2024	$1.50 Mary and Joseph with Donkey	1·00	2·75
2025	$1.80 The Annunciation	1·00	2·50
2020/2025	Set of 6	3·50	6·00

(b) Litho SNP Cambec, Australia. Smaller designs, 30×24 mm. Self-adhesive. Phosphor frame. Perf 11½.
2026	40c. Angels with trumpets	50	75
2027	40c. King with gift	50	50
	a. Booklet pane. No. 2027×10	4·25	4·25

No. 2026 comes from rolls of 100, on which the surplus self-adhesive paper around each stamp was removed.
No. 2027 from $4 booklet, No. SB82, containing No. 2027a on which the surplus paper was retained.
The phosphor, which shows pink under UV light, appears as a three-sided frame on stamps from both rolls and booklets.

(Des G. Cox)

1996 (2 Oct). Extinct Birds. T **541** and similar horiz designs. Multicoloured.
(a) Litho Southern Colour Print, Dunedin. Designs 40×28 mm. Perf 13½.
2028	40c. Type **541**	50	40
2029	80c. South Island Whekau ('Laughing Owl')	1·00	1·25
2030	$1 Piopio	1·00	1·40
2031	$1.20 Huia	1·25	1·75
2032	$1.50 Giant Eagle	1·50	2·25
2033	$1.80 Giant Moa	1·75	2·25
2028/2033	Set of 6	6·25	8·50
MS2034	105×92 mm. No. 2033. Perf 14	2·00	2·00

(b) Litho SNP Cambec, Australia. Smaller design, 30×24 mm. Self-adhesive. Perf 11½.
2035	40c. Stout-legged Wren	60	60
	a. Booklet pane. No. 2035×10	4·75	4·75

No. 2035 comes from $4 booklet, No. SB83, containing No. 2035a on which the surplus self-adhesive paper was retained.
The phosphor, which shows orange under UV light, appears as a vertical band at the right of the stamp.

(Des G. Cox (No. **MS**2036), Sea Sky Design (No. **MS**2037). Litho Southern Colour Print, Dunedin)

1996 (21 Oct). TAIPEI '96 Tenth Asian International Stamp Exhibition, Taiwan.
*(a) No. **MS**2034 overprinted with TAIPEI '96 logo on sheet margin.*
MS2036 105×92 mm. No. 2033.................................. 2·50 2·75

(b) Sheet 140×90 mm containing Nos. 1993 and 1997. Phosphor frame. Multicoloured. Perf 14.
MS2037 Nos. 1993 and 1997................................ 2·50 2·75

No. **MS**2037 also shows designs as Nos. 1992 and 1994/1996, but without face values.

542 Seymour Square, Blenheim   **543** Holstein Friesian Cattle

(Des H. Thompson. Litho Walsall)

1996 (13 Nov). Scenic Gardens. T **542** and similar vert designs. Multicoloured. Perf 13½.
2038	40c. Type **542**	30	10
2039	80c. Pukekura Park, New Plymouth	60	60
2040	$1 Wintergarden, Auckland	70	70
2041	$1.50 Botanic Garden, Christchurch	1·10	2·50
2042	$1.80 Marine Parade Gardens, Napier	1·25	2·50
2038/2042	Set of 5	3·50	5·75

BEST OF '96. Sets of three miniature sheets with this inscription and containing Nos. 1950, 1957, 1983, 1997, 2012, 2017, 2025, 2033 and 2042 were distributed by the Philatelic Bureau to customers who had purchased a certain amount of philatelic material from them during the year. These miniature sheets were printed in lithography by Southern Colour Print, Dunedin, and a number of the stamps they contain show different perforations from the examples in normal sheets. They could not be purchased by the general public at post offices.

(Des Lindy Fisher. Litho Questa)

1997 (15 Jan). Cattle Breeds. T **543** and similar vert designs. Multicoloured. Perf 14×14½.
2043	40c. Type **543**	30	10
2044	80c. Jersey	60	70
2045	$1 Simmental	70	75
2046	$1.20 Ayrshire	90	1·60
2047	$1.50 Angus	1·10	1·75
2048	$1.80 Hereford	1·25	1·75
2043/2048	Set of 6	4·25	6·00

(Des Red Cactus Design (No. **MS**2049), Lindy Fisher (No. **MS**2050). Litho Southern Colour Print, Dunedin (No. **MS**2049) or Questa (No. **MS**2050))

1997 (12 Feb). HONG KONG '97 International Stamp Exhibition. Perf 13 (No. **MS**2049) or 14×14½ (No. **MS**2050).
MS2049 130×110 mm. Nos. 1952/1953 and 1956........... 2·00 2·50
MS2050 101×134 mm. Nos. 2044/2045 and 2047........... 2·25 3·25

No. **MS**2050 is also inscribed for the Chinese New Year. Year of the Ox.

544 James Cook and Sextant

(Des Red Cactus Design. Litho Southern Colour Print, Dunedin)

1997 (12 Feb). Millennium Series (1st issue). Discoverers of New Zealand. T **544** and similar multicoloured designs. Perf 14½×14 ($1, $1.20) or 14×14½ (others).
2051	40c. Type **544**	80	45
2052	80c. Kupe and ocean-going canoe	60	90
2053	$1 Carved panel depicting Maui (*vert*)	75	1·00
2054	$1.20 Anchor and Jean de Surville's *St Jean Baptiste* (*vert*)	1·75	1·60
2055	$1.50 Dumont d'Urville, Crab and *l'Astrolabe*	1·75	2·00
2056	$1.80 Abel Tasman and illustration from journal	1·75	2·00
2051/2056	Set of 6	6·75	7·25

A miniature sheet containing Nos. 2051/2056 comes from a Limited Edition Millennium Collection costing NZ$129.
See also Nos. 2140/2145, 2216/2221, 2239/2244, 2304/2309 and 2310.

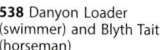

NEW ZEALAND

545 Rippon Vineyard, Central Otago   **546** Cottage Letter Box

(Des Dianne Prosser from paintings by Nancy Tichborne. Litho Southern Colour Print, Dunedin)

1997 (19 Mar). New Zealand Vineyards. T **545** and similar horiz designs. Multicoloured. Perf 14.

2057	40c. Type **545**	25	10
2058	80c. Te Mata Estate, Hawke's Bay	50	60
2059	$1 Cloudy Bay Vineyard, Marlborough	60	70
2060	$1.20 Pegasus Bay Vineyard, Waipara	75	1·75
2061	$1.50 Milton Vineyard, Gisborne	1·00	2·50
2062	$1.80 Goldwater Estate, Waiheke Island	1·10	2·25
2057/2062 Set of 6		3·75	7·00

MS2063 Seven sheets, each 150×110 mm. (a) No. 2057; (b) No. 2058; (c) No. 2059; (d) No. 2060; (e) No. 2061; (f) No. 2062; (g) Nos. 2057/2062 Set of 7 sheets... 11·00 17·00

Nos. **MS**2063(a)/**MS**2063(g) were only available from $13.40 stamp booklet, No. SB85 with each miniature sheet showing a line of roulettes at left.

An overprinted and numbered miniature sheet containing Nos. 2057/2062 comes from a Limited Edition Collectors Pack costing NZ$135.

For a further miniature sheet containing Nos. 2057, 2059 and 2061 see No. **MS**2081.

(Des Communication Arts. Litho SNP Cambec, Australia)

1997 (19 Mar). Curious Letter Boxes. T **546** and similar vert designs. Multicoloured. Self-adhesive. Phosphor frame. Perf 11½.

2064	40c. Type **546**	50	50
	a. Booklet pane of 10. Nos. 2064/2073	4·50	4·50
	b. Sheetlet of 10. Nos. 2064/2073	11·00	
2065	40c. Owl letter box	50	50
2066	40c. Blue Whale letter box	50	50
2067	40c. 'Kilroy is Back' letter box	50	50
2068	40c. Nesting box letter box	50	50
2069	40c. Piper letter box	50	50
2070	40c. Diver's helmet letter box	50	50
2071	40c. Aircraft letter box	50	50
2072	40c. Water tap letter box	50	50
2073	40c. Indian palace letter box	50	50
2064/2073 Set of 10		4·50	4·50

The phosphor, which appears orange under UV light, appears as a frame on two adjacent sides of each design.

Nos. 2064/2073 were only issued in $4 stamp booklet, No. SB86, in which the booklet pane, No. 2064a, shows the surplus self-adhesive paper around each stamp retained.

No. 2064b comes from the residue of special sheet stock used to prepare first day covers and subsequently sold as $4 hang-sell sheetlets. The stamps are on plain backing paper with the surplus self-adhesive paper around each stamp removed.

547 *The Promised Land*, 1948 (Colin McCahon)   **548** Carrier Pigeon (based on 1899 Pigeon-gram local stamp)

(Des H. Thompson. Litho Southern Colour Print, Dunedin)

1997 (7 May). Contemporary Paintings by Colin McCahon. T **547** and similar horiz designs. Multicoloured. Perf 14.

2074	40c. Type **547**	25	10
2075	$1 *Six Days in Nelson and Canterbury*, 1950	55	60
2076	$1.50 *Northland Panels* (detail), 1958	80	1·75
2077	$1.80 *Moby Dick is sighted off Muriwai Beach*, 1972	90	1·60
2074/2077 Set of 4		2·25	3·50

(Des S. Fuller. Litho Southern Colour Print, Dunedin)

1997 (7 May). Centenary of Great Barrier Island Pigeon Post. Perf 14×13½.

2078	**548**	40c. scarlet	50	80
		a. *Tête-bêche* pair	1·00	1·60
2079		80c. deep dull blue	90	1·10
		a. *Tête-bêche* pair	1·75	2·10

Nos. 2078/2079 were each issued in sheets of 50 on which the stamps were arranged both horizontally and vertically *tête bêche*.

For these stamps in miniature sheets see Nos. **MS**2080 and **MS**2122.

(Des S. Fuller (No. **MS**2080), Dianne Prosser (No. **MS**2081). Litho Southern Colour Print, Dunedin)

1997 (29 May). Pacific '97 International Stamp Exhibition, San Francisco. Perf 14×13½ (No. **MS**2080) or 14 (No. **MS**2081).

MS2080 137×120 mm. Nos. 2078/2079, each×2	2·50	3·00
MS2081 140×100 mm. Nos. 2057, 2059 and 2061	2·50	3·50

No. **MS**2080 is in a triangular format.

549 Rainbow Trout and Red Setter Fly   **550** Beach Scene (Fern Petrie)

(Des Joanne Kreyl. Litho Southern Colour Print, Dunedin)

1997 (18 June). Fly Fishing. T **549** and similar horiz designs. Multicoloured. Perf 13.

2082	40c. Type **549**	25	10
2083	$1 Sea-run Brown Trout and Grey Ghost fly	55	60
2084	$1.50 Brook Charr and Twilight Beauty fly	80	2·00
2085	$1.80 Brown Trout and Hare and Cooper fly	90	2·00
2082/2085 Set of 4		2·25	4·25

For miniature sheet containing Nos. 2082 and 2085 see No. **MS**2172.

(Adapted Communication Arts Ltd. Litho Southern Colour Print, Dunedin)

1997 (18 June). Children's Health. T **550** and similar multicoloured designs showing children's paintings.

(a) Perf 14.

2086	40c.+5c. Type **550**	45	75
2087	80c.+5c. Horse riding on the Waterfront (Georgia Dumergue)	80	1·50

MS2088 130×90 mm. Nos. 2086/2087 and 40c.+5c. As No. 2089 (25×36 mm). Perf 14½ (as No. 2089) or 14 (others) .... 1·75 2·00

(b) Self-adhesive. P 10×10½.

2089	40c.+5c. Picking Fruit (Anita Pitcher)	70	60
2086/2089 Set of 3		1·75	2·40

No. 2089 comes from rolls of 100 on which the surplus self-adhesive paper around each stamp was removed. This design with traditional gum was only available as part of No. **MS**2088.

(Des A. Mitchell. Litho Southern Colour Print, Dunedin)

1997 (6 Aug)–**2002**. Perf 14½ (and 14 around design)

2090	**445**	$1 violet	1·00	1·25
2090a		$1.10 gold (6.3.2000)	1·00	2·25
2090b		$1.50 purple-brown (5.6.02)	1·10	2·00

Nos. 2090/2090b were printed in sheets of 36 with each stamp within a square margin perforated on all four sides and with a further circular perforation around the design.

On Nos. 2090/2090*b* the border pattern continues around the top of the stamp, in place of the ONE DOLLAR inscription in T **445**.

Sheets of No. 2090 were re-issued on 31 December 1999 with a pattern of gold suns overprinted on the margins around each stamp to mark the Millennium.

For miniature sheet containing Nos. 2090/2090*a* see No. **MS**2342. See aslo Nos. 3308/3310.

551 The Overlander at Paremata, Wellington   **552** Samuel Marsden's *Active*, Bay of Islands

(Des R. Jones. Litho Southern Colour Print, Dunedin)

1997 (6 Aug). Scenic Railway Services. T **551** and similar horiz designs. Multicoloured. Perf 14×14½.

2091	40c. Type **551**	50	20
2092	80c. The Tranz Alpine in the Southern Alps	90	80

NEW ZEALAND

2093	$1 The Southerner at Canterbury		1·00	90
2094	$1.20 The Coastal Pacific on the Kaikoura Coast		1·40	2·00
2095	$1.50 The Bay Express at Central Hawke's Bay		1·60	2·50
2096	$1.80 The Kaimai Express at Tauranga Harbour		1·75	2·25
2091/2096 Set of 6			6·50	7·75

For miniature sheet containing Nos. 2092/2093 and 2095 see No. **MS**2173.

A miniature sheet containing Nos. 2091/2096 comes from a Limited Edition Collectors Pack costing NZ$135.

(Des Fifi Colston. Litho Southern Colour Print, Dunedin)

1997 (3 Sept.). Christmas. T **552** and similar vert designs. Multicoloured.

(a) Perf 14.

2097	40c. Type **552**	25	10
	a. Block of 6. Nos. 2097/2102	3·00	5·00
2098	70c. Reverend Marsden preaching	40	50
2099	80c. Marsden and Maori chiefs	50	50
2100	$1 Maori family	60	70
2101	$1.50 Handshake and cross	80	1·75
2102	$1.80 Pohutukawa (flower) and Rangihoua Bay	90	1·75

(b) Self-adhesive. Smaller design, 29×24 mm. Perf 10.

2103	40c. Memorial cross, Pohutukawa and Bay of Islands	30	40
	a. Booklet pane of 10	2·75	4·00
2097/2103 Set of 7		3·25	5·00

In addition to separate sheets Nos. 2097/2102 were also issued as *se-tenant* blocks of six.

No. 2103 comes from either rolls of 100, on which the surplus adhesive paper was removed, or from the $4 booklet, No. SB87, on which the surplus paper was retained.

553 Huhu Beetle   **554** *Rosa rugosa*

(Des D. Gunson. Litho SNP Cambec, Australia)

1997 (1 Oct). Insects. T **553** and similar horiz designs. Multicoloured. Self-adhesive. Two phosphor bands. Perf 11½.

2104	40c. Type **553**	40	50
	a. Booklet pane. Nos. 2104/2113	3·50	4·50
	b. Sheetlet of 10. Nos. 2104/2113	8·00	
2105	40c. Giant Land Snail	40	50
2106	40c. Giant Weta	40	50
2107	40c. Giant Dragonfly	40	50
2108	40c. Peripatus	40	50
2109	40c. Cicada	40	50
2110	40c. Puriri Moth	40	50
2111	40c. Veined Slug	40	50
2112	40c. Katipo	40	50
2113	40c. Flax Weevil	40	50
2104/2113 Set of 10		3·50	4·50

The phosphor, which shows pink under UV light, appears as horizontal bands across the top and bottom of each design.

Nos. 2104/2113 were only issued in the $4 stamp booklet, No. SB88 in which the booklet pane, No. 2104a, shows the surplus self-adhesive paper around each stamp retained.

No. 2104b comes from the residue of special sheet stock used to prepare first day covers and subsequently sold as $4 hang-sell sheetlets. The stamps are on plain backing paper, with the surplus self-adhesive paper around each stamp removed.

(Des Z. Guizheng. Litho Southern Colour Print, Dunedin)

1997 (9 Oct). New Zealand–China. Joint Issue. Roses. T **554** and similar vert design. Multicoloured. Perf 14.

2114	40c. Type **554**	50	50
	a. Horiz pair. Nos. 2114/2115	1·00	1·00
2115	40c. *Aotearoa*	50	50
MS2116 115×90 mm. 80c. Nos. 2114/2115		1·00	1·00

Nos. 2114/2115 were printed together, *se-tenant*, in horizontal pairs throughout the sheet.

Stamps in similar designs were also issued by China.

555 Queen Elizabeth II and Prince Philip   **556** Cartoon Kiwi on Busy-bee

(Des Red Cactus Design. Litho Southern Colour Print, Dunedin)

1997 (12 Nov). Golden Wedding of Queen Elizabeth and Prince Philip. Perf 12.

2117	**555**	40c. multicoloured	50	75

No. 2117 was printed in sheets of ten (2×5) with decorated margins. A limited quantity were also distributed imperforate.

(Des G. Tremain (40c.), J. Hubbard ($1), E. Heath ($1.50); B. Silver ($1.80). Litho Southern Colour Print, Dunedin)

1997 (12 Nov). New Zealand Cartoons. Kiwis taking on the World. T **556** and similar horiz designs. Multicoloured. Perf 14.

2118	40c. Type **556**	30	10
2119	$1 'Let's have 'em for Breakfast'	55	55
2120	$1.50 Kiwi dinghy winning race	80	1·25
2121	$1.80 CND emblem cut in forest	90	1·25
2118/2121 Set of 4		2·25	2·75

(Des S. Fuller. Litho Southern Colour Print, Dunedin)

1997 (13 Nov). Aupex '97 National Stamp Exhibition, Auckland. Sheet 140×120 mm. Perf 14×13½.

MS2122 Nos. 2078/2079, each×2		2·10	2·75

No. **MS**2122 is in a triangular format.

1997 (19 Nov). International Stamp and Coin Exhibition, 1997, Shanghai. Sheet as No. **MS**2116 but redrawn to include 'Issued by New Zealand Post to commemorate the International Stamp and Coin Expo. Shanghai, China. 19-23: November 1997' inscr in English and Chinese with additional die-stamped gold frame and logo.

MS2123 115×95 mm. Nos. 2114/2115		1·00	1·00

BEST OF '97. A further set of three miniature sheets, as described below No. 2042, was distributed by the Philatelic Bureau in 1997 to customers purchasing a certain amount of philatelic material. The stamps shown for 1997 were Nos. 2048, 2056, 2062, 2077, 2085, 2090, 2096, 2102 and 2121.

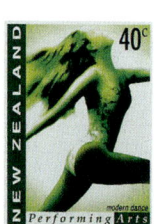 

557 Modern Dancer   **558** Museum of New Zealand

(Des N. Childs. Litho Southern Colour Print, Dunedin)

1998 (14 Jan). Performing Arts. T **557** and similar vert designs. Multicoloured. Perf 13½.

2124	40c. Type **557**	20	10
2125	80c. Trombone player	40	55
	a. Perf 14	1·75	3·00
2126	$1 Opera singer	1·00	75
2127	$1.20 Actor	50	1·25
2128	$1.50 Singer	75	2·00
2129	$1.80 Ballet dancer	85	2·00
	a. Perf 14	3·50	6·00
2124/2129 Set of 6		3·25	6·00
MS2130 Seven sheets, each 150×110 mm. (a) No. 2124; (b) No. 2125; (c) No. 2126; (d) No. 2127; (e) No. 2128; (f) No. 2129; (g) Nos. 2124/2129. Perf 12 (Nos. **MS**2130(c), **MS**2130(g)) or 13½ (others) *Set of 7 sheets*		10·00	13·00

Nos. **MS**2130(a)/**MS**2130(g) were only available from $13.40 stamp booklet, No. SB90, with each miniature sheet showing a line of roulettes at left.

The $1 value exists in a different design showing the performer wearing a four-cornered hat. It is only known on a New Zealand Post first day cover with the other five values.

NEW ZEALAND

(Des Joanne Kreyl. Litho Southern Colour Print, Dunedin)

1998 (11 Feb). Opening of Museum of New Zealand, Wellington. T **558** and similar diamond-shaped design. Multicoloured. Perf 14½.
2131	40c. Type **558**	30	35
2132	$1.80 Museum and Spotted Cormorant and Silver Gull	1·40	1·40

559 Domestic Cat   **560** Maoris and Canoe

(Des Julie Grieg. Litho Southern Colour Print, Dunedin)

1998 (11 Feb). Cats. T **559** and similar vert designs. Multicoloured. Perf 13½.
2133	40c. Type **559**	30	10
2134	80c. Burmese	60	60
2135	$1 Birman	65	65
2136	$1.20 British Blue	70	1·25
2137	$1.50 Persian	90	2·25
2138	$1.80 Siamese	1·10	2·00
2133/2138	Set of 6	3·75	6·00

(Des Julie Grieg. Litho Southern Colour Print, Dunedin)

1998 (11 Feb). Chinese New Year. Year of the Tiger. Perf 13½.
MS2139	100×135 mm. Nos. 2133, 2135 and 2138	1·75	2·50

(Des T. Crilley. Litho Southern Colour Print, Dunedin)

1998 (18 Mar). Millennium Series (2nd issue). Immigrants. T **560** and similar vert designs. Multicoloured. Perf 14½×14.
2140	40c. Type **560**	35	15
2141	80c. 19th-century European settlers and immigrant ship	75	65
2142	$1 Gold miners and mine	1·00	80
2143	$1.20 Post 1945 European migrants and liner	1·25	1·10
2144	$1.50 Pacific islanders and church	1·40	1·75
2145	$1.80 Asian migrant and jumbo jet	1·60	1·60
2140/2145	Set of 6	5·75	5·50

Miniature sheets containing Nos. 2140/2145 come from a Limited Edition Collectors Pack costing NZ$135 or a Limited Edition Millennium Collection costing NZ$129.

561 With Great Respect to the Mehmetcik Statue, Gallipoli   **562** Mother and Son hugging

(Des Dianne Prosser. Litho Southern Colour Print, Dunedin)

1998 (18 Mar). Joint Issue New Zealand–Turkey. Memorial Statues. T **561** and similar vert design. Multicoloured. Perf 13½.
2146	40c. Type **561**	30	35
2147	$1.80 Mother with Children, National War Memorial, Wellington	1·10	1·40

(Des Colenso Communications Ltd. Litho Southern Colour Print, Dunedin)

1998 (15 Apr). Stay in Touch Greetings Stamps. T **562** and similar multicoloured designs. Self-adhesive. Phosphorised paper. Perf 10½×10 (horiz) or 10×10½ (vert).
2148	40c. Type **562**	30	35
	a. Booklet pane. Nos. 2148/2157	2·75	3·25
	b. Sheetlet of 4. Nos. 2148/2151	2·50	4·25
2149	40c. Couple on beach	30	35
2150	40c. Boys striking hands	30	35
2151	40c. Grandmother and grandson	30	35
2152	40c. Young boys in pool (horiz)	30	35
	b. Sheetlet of 6. Nos. 2152/2157	3·75	6·50
2153	40c. 'I'LL MISS YOU... PLEASE WRITE' (horiz)	30	35
2154	40c. Symbolic couple and clouds (horiz)	30	35
2155	40c. Young couple kissing (horiz)	30	35
2156	40c. Couple sat on sofa (horiz)	30	35
2157	40c. Maoris rubbing noses (horiz)	30	35
2148/2157	Set of 10	2·75	3·25

Nos. 2148/2157 were only available from $4 stamp booklet, No. SB91, containing No. 2148a on which the surplus self-adhesive paper was retained.

Nos. 2148b and 2152b come from the residue of special sheet stock used to prepare first day covers and subsequently sold as $4 hang-sell packs containing the two sheetlets. The stamps are on plain backing paper, with the surplus self-adhesive paper around each stamp removed.

563 Mount Cook or Aorangi   **564** Wounded at Cassino

(Adapted R. Jones. Litho Southern Colour Print, Dunedin)

1998 (20 May). Centenary of 1898 Pictorial Stamps. Designs as Types **23**/**36** with modern face values as T **563**. Perf 14×14½ (Nos. 2158/2165) or 14½ (others).
2158	**563**	40c. purple-brown	25	50
2159	**24**	40c. deep blue and orange-brown	25	50
2160	**25**	40c. lake-brown	25	50
2161	**28**	40c. chestnut	25	50
2162	**29**	40c. deep rose-red	25	50
2163	**31**	40c. deep green	25	50
2164	**32**	40c. indigo	25	50
2165	**34**	40c. red-orange	25	50
2166	**26**	80c. steel-blue (inscr 'LAKE WAKITIPU') (35×23 mm)	50	1·00
2167	**27**	80c. steel-blue (inscr 'LAKE WAKATIPU') (35×23 mm)	50	1·00
2168	**30**	$1 reddish brown (23×35 mm)	60	1·25
2169	**33**	$1.20 purple-brown (35×23 mm)	85	1·60
2170	**35**	$1.50 deep blue-green (35×23 mm)	1·00	2·50
2171	**36**	$1.80 dull vermilion (23×35 mm)	1·25	2·00
2158/2171		Set of 14	6·00	12·00

For miniature sheets containing Nos. 2166/2167 and 2170 see Nos. **MS**2188 and **MS**2214.

Sheets of Nos. 2158/2171 numbered and with the margins decorated in gold come from special Centenary Collections.

(Des Joanne Kreyl (No. **MS**2172), R. Jones (No. **MS**2173). Litho Southern Colour Print, Dunedin)

1998 (20 May). Israel '98 World Stamp Exhibition, Tel Aviv. Perf 13 (No. **MS**2172) or 14×14½ (No. **MS**2173).
MS2172	112×90 mm. Nos. 2082 and 2085	2·50	2·75
MS2173	125×100 mm. Nos. 2092/2093 and 2095	4·00	4·50

(Des H. Thompson. Litho Southern Colour Print, Dunedin)

1998 (24 June). Paintings by Peter McIntyre. T **564** and similar horiz designs. Multicoloured. Perf 13½.
2174	40c. Type **564**	20	10
2175	$1 The Cliffs of Rangitikei	60	1·00
2176	$1.50 Maori Children, King Country	80	1·40
2177	$1.80 The Anglican Church, Kakahi	1·00	1·25
2174/2177	Set of 4	2·40	3·25

For Nos. 2176/2177 in miniature sheet for Italia '98 see No. **MS**2215.

A similar miniature sheet, but with the exhibition logo replaced by the Limited Edition symbol at bottom right, comes from Limited Edition Collectors Packs costing NZ$135.

565 Girl wearing Lifejacket

NEW ZEALAND

(Des Sea Sky Design)

1998 (24 June). Children's Health. Water Safety. T **565** and similar vert design. Multicoloured.

(a) Litho Southern Colour Print, Dunedin. Perf 13½.

2178	40c.+5c. Type **565**	40	75
2179	80c.+5c. Boy learning to swim	60	1·25
MS2180	125×90 mm. Nos. 2178/2179, each×2. Perf 14½×14	1·60	2·00

(b) Litho SNP Cambec. Smaller design, 25×37 mm. Self-adhesive. Phosphor on inscr panel and background. Perf 11½.

2181	40c.+5c. Type **565**	30	50

No. 2181, on which the phosphor shows pink under UV light, comes from rolls of 100 on which the surplus self-adhesive paper around each stamp was removed.

Examples without printer's imprint on the reverse come from $4.35 hang-sell packs containing Nos. 2178/2181.

566 Sunrise near Cambridge

(Des Cato Design. Litho Southern Colour Print, Dunedin)

1998 (29 July). Scenic Skies. T **566** and similar horiz designs. Multicoloured. Perf 15×14½.

2182	40c. Type **566**	30	10
2183	80c. Clouds over Lake Wanaka	60	50
2184	$1 Sunset over Mount Maunganui	70	55
2185	$1.20 Rain clouds over South Bay, Kaikoura	80	1·10
2186	$1.50 Sunset near Statue of Wairaka, Whakatane Harbour	1·10	1·25
2187	$1.80 Cloud formation above Lindis Pass	1·25	1·50
2182/2187 Set of 6		4·25	4·50

For Nos. 2182 and 2187 in miniature sheet for Australia '99 see No. **MS**2245.

(Des R. Jones. Litho Southern Colour Print, Dunedin)

1998 (7 Aug). TARAPEX '98 National Stamp Exhibition, New Plymouth. Perf 14½.

MS2188 90×80 mm. Nos. 2166/2167	1·25	1·75

567 Virgin Mary and Christ Child

568 Lemon and Mineral Water Bottle, Paeroa

(Des Sally Simons)

1998 (2 Sept). Christmas. T **567** and similar vert designs. Multicoloured.

(a) Litho Southern Colour Print, Dunedin. Perf 13½.

2189	40c. Type **567**	20	10
2190	70c. Shepherds approaching the stable	35	30
2191	80c. Virgin Mary, Joseph and Christ Child	40	35
2192	$1 Magi with gift of gold	50	40
2193	$1.50 Three magi	80	1·50
2194	$1.80 Angel and shepherds	90	1·50
2189/2194 Set of 6		2·75	3·50

(b) Litho SNP Cambec, Australia. Smaller design, 24×29 mm. Self adhesive. Phosphor frame. Perf 11½.

2195	40c. Type **567**	30	30
	a. Booklet pane of 10	2·75	3·50

No. 2195, which shows a broad band of pink phosphor over both the right-hand part of the centre design and 'NEW ZEALAND', comes from either rolls of 100, on which the surplus adhesive paper was removed, or from the $4 booklet, No. SB92, on which the surplus paper was retained.

(Des Donna McKenna. Litho SNP Cambec, Melbourne)

1998 (7 Oct). Town Icons. T **568** and similar vert designs. Multicoloured. Self-adhesive. Phosphor backgrounds. Perf 11 (Nos. 2202/2205) or 11½ (others).

2196	40c. Type **568**	30	40
	a. Booklet pane of 10. Nos. 2196/2205	2·75	3·75
	ab. Imperf	£750	
	b. Sheetlet of 10. Nos. 2196/2205	30	
2197	40c. Carrot, Ohakune	30	40
2198	40c. Brown Trout, Gore (25×36 mm)	30	40
2199	40c. Crayfish, Kaikoura (25×36 mm)	30	40
2200	40c. Sheepshearer, Te Kuiti (25×36 mm)	30	40
2201	40c. *Pania of the Reef* (Maori legend), Napier (25×36 mm)	30	40
2202	40c. Paua Shell, Riverton (24×29 mm)	30	40
2203	40c. Kiwifruit, Te Puke (24×29 mm)	30	40
2204	40c. Border Collie, Lake Tekapo (24×29 mm)	30	40
2205	40c. Big Cow, Hawera (24×29 mm)	30	40
2196/2205 Set of 10		2·75	3·75

Nos. 2196/2205 were only issued in $4 self-adhesive stamp booklet, No. SB93, containing No. 2196a on which the surplus self-adhesive paper was retained.

The phosphor, which shows pink under UV light, covers most of the background on each design.

No. 2196b comes from the residue of special sheet stock used to prepare first day covers and subsequently sold as $4 hang-sell sheetlets. The stamps are on plain backing paper with the surplus self-adhesive paper around each stamp removed.

Similar hang-sell packs, selling at $9.60, were prepared containing blocks or pairs of the individual designs for sale at the towns depicted. On these blocks or pairs the surplus self-adhesive paper was retained.

569 Moonfish   **570** Wellington in 1841 and 1998

(Des G. Cox. Litho Southern Colour Print, Dunedin)

1998 (7 Oct). International Year of the Ocean. T **569** and similar vert designs. Multicoloured. Perf 14.

2206	40c. Type **569**	20	50
	a. Block of 4. Nos. 2206/2209	70	2·00
2207	40c. Mako Shark	20	50
2208	40c. Yellowfin Tuna	20	50
2209	40c. Giant Squid	20	50
2210	80c. Striped Marlin	30	70
	a. Block of 4. Nos. 2210/2213	1·10	2·50
2211	80c. Porcupinefish	30	70
2212	80c. Eagle Ray	30	70
2213	80c. Sandager's Wrasse	30	70
2206/2213 Set of 8		1·75	4·25

Nos. 2206/2209 and 2210/2213 were each printed together, *se-tenant*, in blocks of four, forming composite designs.

A miniature sheet containing Nos. 2206/2213 comes from a Limited Edition Collectors Pack costing NZ$135.

For Nos. 2206/2207 and 2210/2211 in miniature sheet for Australia '99 see No. **MS**2246.

For Nos. 2208/2209 and 2212/2213 in a miniature sheet for PhilexFrance 99 see No. **MS**2277.

(Adapted R. Jones. Litho Southern Colour Print, Dunedin)

1998 (23 Oct). Italia '98 International Philatelic Exhibition, Milan. Perf 14½ (No. **MS**2214) or 14 (No. **MS**2215).

MS2214 90×80 mm. Nos. 2167 and 2170	2·00	3·25
MS2215 112×90 mm. Nos. 2176/2177	1·60	2·25

(Des Niki Hill. Litho Southern Colour Print, Dunedin)

1998 (11 Nov). Millennium Series (3rd issue). Urban Transformations. T **570** and similar horiz designs. Multicoloured. Perf 14×14½.

2216	40c. Type **570**	30	10
2217	80c. Auckland in 1852 and 1998	50	40
2218	$1 Christchurch in 1851 and 1998	55	50
2219	$1.20 Westport in 1919 and 1998	70	1·25
2220	$1.50 Tauranga in 1880 and 1998	80	1·50
2221	$1.80 Dunedin in 1862 and 1998	1·00	1·50
2216/2221 Set of 6		3·50	4·75

A miniature sheet containing Nos. 2216/2221 comes from a Limited Edition Millennium Collection costing NZ$129.

NEW ZEALAND

BEST OF '98. A further set of three miniature sheets, as described below No. 2042, was distributed by the Philatelic Bureau in 1998 to customers purchasing a certain amount of philatelic material. The stamps shown for 1998 were Nos. 2129, 2132, 2138, 2147, 2171, 2177, 2187, 2194 and 2221.

 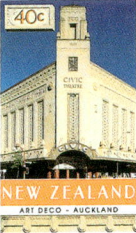

571 *Fuchsia excorticata* **572** Civic Theatre, Auckland

(Des Sue Wickison. Litho Southern Colour Print, Dunedin)

1999 (13 Jan). Flowering Trees of New Zealand. T **571** and similar vert designs. Multicoloured. Perf 14½×14.

2222	40c. Type **571**	20	10
2223	80c. *Solanum laciniatum*	35	35
2224	$1 *Sophora tetraptera*	40	50
2225	$1.20 *Carmichaelia stevensonii*	50	1·00
2226	$1.50 *Olearia angustifolia*	70	1·50
2227	$1.80 *Metrosideros umbellata*	80	1·50
2222/2227 Set of 6		2·75	4·50

A miniature sheet containing Nos. 2226/2227 comes from a Limited Edition Collectors Pack costing NZ$135.

For Nos. 2222/2223 in miniature sheet for China '99 see No. **MS**2286.

(Des Donna McKenna. Litho Southern Colour Print, Dunedin)

1999 (10 Feb). Art Deco Architecture. T **572** and similar vert designs. Multicoloured. Perf 14½×14.

2228	40c. Type **572**	20	10
2229	$1 Masonic Hotel, Napier	1·75	80
2230	$1.50 Medical and Dental Chambers, Hastings	65	1·40
2231	$1.80 Buller County Chambers, Westport	75	1·40
2228/2231 Set of 4		3·00	3·25

573 Labrador Puppy and Netherland Dwarf Rabbit **574** Toy Fire Engine and Marbles

(Des Lindy Fisher. Litho Southern Colour Print, Dunedin)

1999 (10 Feb). Popular Pets. T **573** and similar vert designs. Multicoloured. Perf 14.

2232	40c. Type **573**	30	20
2233	80c. Netherland Dwarf Rabbit	50	40
2234	$1 Tabby Kitten and Netherland Dwarf Rabbit	60	50
2235	$1.20 Lamb	75	1·25
2236	$1.50 Welsh Pony	1·00	1·50
2237	$1.80 Two Budgerigars	1·00	1·50
2232/2237 Set of 6		3·75	4·75
MS2238 100×135 mm. Nos. 2232/2234		1·75	1·75

No. **MS**2238 also commemorates the Chinese New Year. Year of the Rabbit.

For Nos. 2232 and 2234 in miniature sheet for China '99 see No. **MS**2287.

(Des Siren Communications Ltd. Litho Southern Colour Print, Dunedin)

1999 (10 Mar). Millennium Series (4th issue). Nostalgia. T **574** and similar horiz designs. Multicoloured. Perf 14×14½.

2239	40c. Type **574**	30	10
2240	80c. Commemorative tin of biscuits and cereal packet	40	40
2241	$1 Tram, tickets and railway crockery	60	50
2242	$1.20 Radio and *Woman's Weekly* magazine	70	1·25
2243	$1.50 Coins, postcards and stamps	80	1·60
2244	$1.80 Lawn mower and seed packets	90	1·60
2239/2244 Set of 6		3·25	4·75

A miniature sheet containing Nos. 2239/2244 comes from a Limited Edition Millennium Collection costing NZ$129.

(Des Cato Design (No. **MS**2245), G. Cox (No. **MS**2246). Litho Southern Colour Print, Dunedin)

1999 (19 Mar). Australia '99 World Stamp Exhibition, Melbourne. Perf 15×14½ (No. **MS**2245) or 14 (No. **MS**2246).

MS2245 130×70 mm. Nos. 2182 and 2187	1·90	1·90
MS2246 130×90 mm. Nos. 2206/2207 and 2210/2211	2·00	2·00

 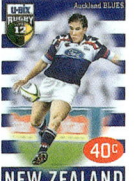

575 Hunter Building, Victoria University **576** Auckland Blue Player kicking Ball

(Litho Southern Colour Print)

1999 (7 Apr). Centenary of Victoria University, Wellington. Perf 14×14½.

2247	**575**	40c. multicoloured	30	30

(Des P. Martinson and Diane Prosser)

1999 (7 Apr). New Zealand U-Bix Rugby Super 12 Championship. T **576** and similar vert designs. Multicoloured.

(a) Litho Southern Colour Print. Perf 14½.

2248	40c. Type **576**	25	40
	a. Sheetlet of 10. Nos. 2248/2257	2·25	3·50
2249	40c. Auckland Blues player being tackled	25	40
2250	40c. Chiefs player being tackled	25	40
2251	40c. Chiefs lineout jump	25	40
2252	40c. Wellington Hurricanes player being tackled	25	40
2253	40c. Wellington Hurricanes player passing ball	25	40
2254	40c. Canterbury Crusaders lineout jump	25	40
2255	40c. Canterbury Crusaders player kicking ball	25	40
2256	40c. Otago Highlanders player diving for try	25	40
2257	40c. Otago Highlanders player running with ball	25	40
2248/2257 Set of 10		2·25	3·50

(b) Litho SNP Ausprint. Self-adhesive. Phosphor frame. Perf 11½.

2258	40c. Type **576**	25	40
	a. Booklet pane. Nos. 2258/2259, each×5	2·25	
2259	40c. Auckland Blues player being tackled	25	40
2260	40c. Chiefs player being tackled	25	40
	a. Booklet pane. Nos. 2260/2261, each×5	2·25	
2261	40c. Chiefs lineout jump	25	40
2262	40c. Wellington Hurricanes player being tackled	25	40
	a. Booklet pane. Nos. 2262/2263, each×5	2·25	
2263	40c. Wellington Hurricanes player passing ball	25	40
2264	40c. Canterbury Crusaders lineout jump	25	40
	a. Booklet pane. Nos. 2264/2265, each×5	2·25	
2265	40c. Canterbury Crusaders player kicking ball	25	40
2266	40c. Otago Highlanders player diving for try	25	40
	a. Booklet pane. Nos. 2266/2267, each×5	2·25	
2267	40c. Otago Highlanders player running with ball	25	40
2258/2267 Set of 10		2·25	3·50

Nos. 2248/2257 were printed together, *se-tenant*, in sheetlets of ten (2×5).

Nos. 2258/2267, on which the phosphor shows pink under UV light, were only issued in $4 booklets, Nos. SB94/SB98, (one for each team) on which the surplus self-adhesive paper was retained.

Examples on plain backing paper with the surplus self-adhesive paper around each stamp removed come from the residue of special sheet stock used to prepare first day covers and subsequently sold as $4 hang-sell packs containing five separate panes.

577 The Lake, Tuai

NEW ZEALAND

(Des H. Thompson. Litho Southern Colour Print, Dunedin)

1999 (16 June). Paintings by Doris Lusk. T **577** and similar horiz designs. Multicoloured. Perf 14.

2268	40c. Type **577**	25	10
2269	$1 The Pumping Station	60	50
2270	$1.50 *Arcade Awning, St Mark's Square, Venice (2)*	80	1·60
2271	$1.80 *Tuam St. 11*	90	1·40
2268/2271	Set of 4	2·25	3·25

For Nos. 2268 and 2271 in miniature sheet for PhilexFrance '99 see No. **MS**2276.

578 *A Lion in the Meadow* (Margaret Mahy) **579** 'APEC'

(Des Ann Adams from book illustrations. Litho Southern Colour Print, Dunedin)

1999 (16 June). Children's Health. Children's Books. T **578** and similar horiz designs. Multicoloured. Phosphorised paper.

(a) Perf 14.

2272	40c.+5c. Type **578**	55	55
2273	80c.+5c. *Greedy Cat* (Joy Cowley)	70	70
MS2274	130×90 mm. 40c.+5c. Type **578**; 40c.+5c. As No. 2275 (37×25 mm); 80c.+5c. No. 2273	1·40	1·40

(b) Self-adhesive. Perf 10.

| 2275 | 40c.+5c. *Hairy Maclary's Bone* (Lynley Dodd) (37×25 mm) | 50 | 50 |

No. 2275 comes only in rolls of 100 on which the surplus self-adhesive paper around each stamp was removed.

(Des G. Cox (No. **MS**2276), H. Thompson (No. **MS**2277). Litho Southern Colour Print, Dunedin)

1999 (2 July). PhilexFrance '99 International Stamp Exhibition, Paris. Perf 14.

MS2276	112×90 mm. Nos. 2268 and 2271	1·75	2·00
MS2277	130×90 mm. Nos. 2208/2209 and 2212/2213	1·75	2·00

(Des S. Fuller. Litho Southern Colour Print, Dunedin)

1999 (21 July). 10th Asia-Pacific Economic Co-operation Meeting, New Zealand. Perf 14.

| 2278 | **579** | 40c. multicoloured | 30 | 30 |

580 West Ruggedy Beach, Stewart Island

(Des Ocean Design. Litho Southern Colour Print, Dunedin)

1999 (28 July). Scenic Walks. T **580** and similar horiz designs. Multicoloured. Perf 14.

2279	40c. Type **580**	25	10
2280	80c. Ice lake, Butler Valley, Westland	45	40
2281	$1 Tonga Bay, Abel Tasman National Park	55	65
2282	$1.20 East Matakitaki Valley, Nelson Lakes National Park	65	90
2283	$1.50 Great Barrier Island	75	1·60
2284	$1.80 Mount Egmont, Taranaki	85	1·40
2279/2284	Set of 6	3·25	4·50
MS2285	Seven sheets, each 150×110 mm. (a) No. 2279. (b) No. 2280. (c) No. 2281. (d) No. 2282. (e) No. 2283. (f) No. 2284. (g) Nos. 2279/2284. *Set of 7 sheets*	10·00	13·00

Nos **MS**2285(a)/**MS**2285(g) were only available from the $13.40 stamp booklet, No. SB99, with each miniature sheet showing a line of roulettes at left.

For No. 2284 in miniature sheet for Palmpex '99 see No. **MS**2295.

No. **MS**2285(g) numbered and with logo in silver comes from a Limited Edition Collectors Pack costing NZ$135.

(Des Lindy Fisher (No. **MS**2286), Sue Wickison (No. **MS**2287). Litho Southern Colour Print, Dunedin)

1999 (21 Aug). China '99 International Stamp Exhibition, Peking. Perf 14½×14 (No. **MS**2286) or 14 (No. **MS**2287).

MS2286	112×90 mm. Nos. 2222/2223	1·00	1·50
MS2287	100×135 mm. Nos. 2232 and 2234	1·00	1·50

581 Baby Jesus with Animals **582** P Class Dinghy

(Des Lindy Fisher. Litho Southern Colour Print, Dunedin)

1999 (8 Sept–1 Nov). Christmas

*(a) T **581** and similar square designs. Multicoloured. Perf 13.*

2288	40c. Type **581**	20	10
2289	80c. Virgin Mary praying	40	30
2290	$1.10 Mary and Joseph on way to Bethlehem	55	50
2291	$1.20 Angel playing harp	60	80
2292	$1.50 Three shepherds	75	1·25
2293	$1.80 Three wise men with gifts	90	1·25
2288/2293	Set of 6	3·00	3·75

(b) Smaller multicoloured design, 23×28 mm. Self-adhesive. Phosphor frame. Perf 9½.

2294	40c. Type **581**	25	30
	a. Booklet pane. No. 2294×10 (1.11)	2·25	3·00

No. 2294, on which the phosphor shows pink under UV light, comes from rolls of 100 on which the surplus self-adhesive paper around each stamp was removed or from booklet No. SB101 where the surplus paper was retained. Examples on plain backing paper come from a hang-sell pack.

(Des Ocean Design. Litho Southern Colour Print, Dunedin)

1999 (1 Oct). Palmpex '99 National Stamp Exhibition, Palmerston North. Sheet 130×90 mm containing No. 2284. Multicoloured. Perf 14.

| **MS**2295 | $1.80 Mount Egmont, Taranaki | 1·50 | 2·00 |

(Des BNA Design,. Litho Southern Colour Print, Dunedin)

1999 (20 Oct). Yachting. T **582** and similar vert designs. Phosphorised paper. Multicoloured.

(a) Size 28×39 mm. Perf 14.

2296	40c. Type **582**	20	10
2297	80c. Laser dinghy	35	35
2298	$1.10 18' skiff	40	60
2299	$1.20 Hobie catamaran	40	75
2300	$1.50 Racing yacht	50	1·25
2301	$1.80 Cruising yacht	60	1·25
2296/2301	Set of 6	2·25	4·25
MS2302	125×100 mm. Nos. 2296/2301	2·25	3·75

(b) Self-adhesive. Size 23×28 mm. Perf 9½.

2303	40c. Optimist dinghy	25	30
	a. Booklet pane. No. 2303×10	2·25	3·00

No. **MS**2302 imperforate comes from a Limited Edition Collectors Pack costing NZ$135.

No. 2303 was only issued in the $4 stamp booklet, No. SB100, containing No. 2303a, on which the surplus self-adhesive paper was retained.

583 Group of Victorian Women (female suffrage, 1893)

(Des Deirdre Cassell. Litho Southern Colour Print, Dunedin)

1999 (17 Nov). Millennium Series (5th issue). New Zealand Achievements. T **583** and similar horiz designs. Phosphorised paper. Multicoloured. Perf 14×14½.

2304	40c. Type **583**	30	15
2305	80c. Richard Pearse's aircraft (powered flight, 1903)	70	55
2306	$1.10 Lord Rutherford (splitting the atom, 1919)	70	85
2307	$1.20 Boat on lake (invention of jet boat, 1953)	70	90

NEW ZEALAND

2308	$1.50 Sir Edmund Hillary (conquest of Everest 1953)	80	1·50
2309	$1.80 Protesters and warship (nuclear free zone, 1987)	90	1·60
2304/2309	Set of 6	3·50	5·00

A miniature sheet containing Nos. 2304/2309 comes from a Limited Edition Millennium Collection costing NZ$129.

BEST OF '99. A further set of three miniature sheets, as described below No. 2042, was distributed by the Philatelic Bureau to customers purchasing a certain amount of philatelic material. The stamps shown for 1999 were Nos. 2227, 2230, 2237, 2244, 2271, 2284, 2293, 2301 and 2309.

584 Sunrise and World Map   585 Araiteuru (North Island sea guardian)

(Des Diane Prosser. Litho Southern Colour Print, Dunedin)

2000. Millennium Series (6th issue). Phosphorised paper. Perf 14×14½.

2310	584	40c. multicoloured	65	30
		a. Sheetlet. No. 2310×10		6·00
		b. New Zealand Millennium logo missing from bottom left (sheetlet R. 3/1)		3·25

No. 2310 was printed in sheets of 50 (5×10) and in sheetlets of ten (2×5) with an enlarged right margin separated from the block of stamps by a line of roulettes.

No. 2310b, which shows the map of New Zealand and rays omitted from beside the time at bottom left, occurs on R. 3/1 of the sheetlet only.

A miniature sheet containing six examples of No. 2310 comes from a Limited Edition Millennium Collection costing NZ$129.

(Des M. Smith. Litho Southern Colour Print, Dunedin)

2000 (9 Feb). Chinese New Year. Year of the Dragon. Maori Spirits and Guardians. T **585** and similar vert designs. Multicoloured. Perf 14.

2311	40c. Type **585**	20	10
2312	80c. Kurangaituku (giant bird woman)	35	25
2313	$1.10 Te Hoata and Te Pupu (volcanic taniwha sisters)	50	45
2314	$1.20 Patupaiarehe (mountain fairy tribe)	55	70
2315	$1.50 Te Ngarara-huarau (giant first lizard)	60	1·00
2316	$1.80 Tuhirangi (South Island sea guardian)	70	1·00
2311/2316	Set of 6	2·50	3·00
MS2317	125×90 mm. Nos. 2315/2316	2·00	2·00

A further miniature sheet, containing Nos. 2313/2314, comes from a Limited Edition Collectors Pack costing NZ$135.

586 Chilly Bin (cool box)   587 Volkswagen Beetle

(Des B. Gagnon. Litho Southern Colour Print, Dunedin)

2000 (3 Apr). New Zealand Life (2nd series). T **586** and similar vert designs each including a cartoon kiwi. Multicoloured. Phosphorised paper. Self-adhesive. Perf 10.

2318	40c. Type **586**	30	40
	a. Booklet pane. Nos. 2318/2327	2·75	3·50
	b. Sheetlet of 10. Nos. 2318/2327	10·00	
2319	40c. Pipis (seafood delicacy)	30	40
2320	40c. 'Lilo'	30	40
2321	40c. Chocolate fish	30	40
2322	40c. Bach or Crib (holiday home)	30	40
2323	40c. Barbeque	30	40
2324	40c. Ug (fur-lined) boots	30	40
2325	40c. Anzac biscuits	30	40
2326	40c. Hot dog	30	40
2327	40c. Meat pie	30	40
2318/2327	Set of 10	2·75	3·50

No. 2318/2327 were normally issued in the $4 stamp booklet, No. SB102, with the surplus self-adhesive paper retained.

No. 2318b comes from the residue of special sheet stock used to prepare first day covers and subsequently sold as $4 hang-sell sheetlets. Philatelic Bureau customers with a standing order for stamps, rather than stamp booklets, also received this item, which has plain backing paper and the surplus self-adhesive paper removed.

(Des Red Cactus Design. Litho Southern Colour Print, Dunedin)

2000 (27 May). The Stamp Show 2000 International Stamp Exhibition, London. Sheet 110×80 mm, containing Nos. 1934b and 1934e/1934f. Multicoloured. Phosphorised paper. Perf 13½.

MS2328	$1 Taiaroa Head; $2 Great Barrier Island; $3 Cape Kidnappers	3·50	4·50

(Des Cato Partners. Litho Southern Colour Print, Dunedin)

2000 (1 June). On the Road. Motor Cars. T **587** and similar square designs. Phosphorised paper. Perf 14.

2329	40c. red-brown and black	25	10
2330	80c. grey-blue and black	45	35
2331	$1.10 light brown and black	65	60
2332	$1.20 green and black	70	75
2333	$1.50 olive-brown and black	80	1·25
2334	$1.80 slate-lilac and black	90	1·25
2329/2334	Set of 6	3·25	3·75

Designs: 40c. T **587**; 80c., Ford Zephyr MK I; $1.10, Morris Mini Mk II; $1.20, Holden HQ Kingswood; $1.50, Honda Civic; $1.80, Toyota Corolla.

The stamps also exist in seven miniature sheets, each 150×110 mm with a line of roulettes at left. Six of the miniature sheets contain Nos. 2329/2334 as single stamps and the seventh sheet contains all six designs. These miniature sheets were only available from a booklet, No. SP1, containing stamps with a face value of $13.60, but sold at $14.95.

A further miniature sheet, containing Nos. 2329/2334, both perforated and imperforate, comes from a Limited Edition Collectors Pack costing NZ$135.

588 Lake Lyndon, Canterbury

(Des Donna McKenna. Litho Southern Colour Print, Dunedin)

2000 (7 July). Scenic Reflections. T **588** and similar horiz designs. Multicoloured. Perf 14.

2336	40c. Type **588**	40	20
2337	80c. *Lion* (cruising launch) on Lake Wakatipu	70	40
2338	$1.10 Eruption of Mount Ruapehu	80	70
2339	$1.20 Rainbow Mountain Scenic Reserve, Rotorua	80	1·90
2340	$1.50 Tairua Harbour, Coromandel Peninsula	85	1·75
2341	$1.80 Lake Alexandrina	1·00	1·60
2336/2341	Set of 6	4·00	5·25

For miniature sheet containing Nos. 2336 and 2341 see No. **MS**2368.

(Des Donna McKenna. Litho Southern Colour Print, Dunedin)

2000 (7 July). EXPO 2000 World Stamp Exhibition, Anaheim, USA. Sheet 132×78 mm, containing circular designs as Nos. 1490, 1490b/1490c and 2090/2090a, but all now litho. Perf 14.

MS2342	$1 bright scarlet; $1 blue; $1 violet; $1 bronze-green; $1.10 gold	2·75	4·00

589 Lady Elizabeth Bowes-Lyon and Glamis Castle, 1907   590 Rowing

(Des Comm Arts Design. Litho Southern Colour Print, Dunedin)

2000 (4 Aug). Queen Elizabeth the Queen Mother's 100th Birthday. T **589** and similar horiz designs. Multicoloured. Perf 14.

2343	40c. Type **589**	45	30
2344	$1.10 Fishing in Lake Wanaka, New Zealand, 1966	80	70
2345	$1.80 With racehorse and holding bunch of daisies, 1997	1·25	1·60
2343/2345	Set of 3	2·25	2·40
MS2346	115×60 mm. Nos. 2343/2345	2·00	2·75

Nos. 2343/2345 with commemorative inscriptions on the sheet selvedge and No. **MS**2346 in imperforate vertical strip of three miniature sheets come from a limited edition book costing NZ$99.

NEW ZEALAND

(Des M. Bailey. Litho Southern Colour Print, Dunedin)

2000 (4 Aug). Olympic Games, Sydney, and Other Sporting Events. T **590** and similar horiz designs. Multicoloured. Perf 14×14½.

2347	40c. Type **590**	25	10
	a. New Zealand and 40c omitted	£275	
2348	80c. Show jumping	50	40
2349	$1.10 Cycling	1·00	80
2350	$1.20 Triathlon	60	85
2351	$1.50 Bowling	75	1·40
2352	$1.80 Netball	80	1·40
2347/2352	Set of 6	3·50	4·25

No. 2347a occurs on the bottom row of the sheet and was caused by a perforation shift.

Nos. 2351/2352 omit the Olympic logo.

591 Virgin Mary and Baby Jesus

(Des Joanne Kreyl)

2000 (6 Sept–1 Nov). Christmas

*(a) Litho Southern Colour Print, Dunedin. T **591** and similar horiz designs. Multicoloured. Phosphorised paper. Perf 14.*

2353	40c. Type **591**	25	10
2354	80c. Mary and Joseph on way to Bethlehem	40	25
2355	$1.10 Baby Jesus in manger	60	60
2356	$1.20 Archangel Gabriel	65	90
2357	$1.50 Shepherd with Lamb	75	1·90
2358	$1.80 Three Wise Men	80	1·75
2353/2358	Set of 6	3·00	5·00

(b) Litho SNP Ausprint. Self-adhesive. Multicoloured design 30×25 mm. Phosphor frame. Perf 11.

2359	40c. Type **591**	25	30
	a. Booklet pane. No. 2359×10 (1.11)	2·25	3·00

No. 2359 was issued in rolls of 100 on which the surplus self-adhesive paper around each stamp was removed, or in booklets of ten, No. SB105, on which the surplus paper was retained. The phosphor frame on three sides of the stamp appears pink under UV light.

592 Geronimo (teddy bear)

2000 (5 Oct). Children's Health. Teddy Bears and Dolls. T **592** and similar horiz designs. Multicoloured.

(a) Litho Southern Colour Print, Dunedin. Phosphorised paper. Perf 14½.

2360	40c.+5c. Type **592**	35	50
	a. Block of 6. Nos. 2360/2365	3·00	4·00
2361	80c.+5c. Antique French doll and wooden Schoenhut doll	45	70
2362	$1.10 Chad Valley bear	50	50
2363	$1.20 Poppy (doll)	55	80
2364	$1.50 Swanni (large bear) and Dear John (small bear)	60	1·00
2365	$1.80 Lia (doll) and bear	80	1·00
2360/2365	Set of 6	3·00	4·00
MS2366	100×60 mm. 40c.+5c. Type **592**; 80c.+5c. As No. 2361	1·00	1·00

(b) Litho SNP Ausprint. Self-adhesive. Size 29×24 mm. Phosphor on bear. Perf 11.

| 2367 | 40c.+5c. Type **592** | 35 | 40 |

Nos. 2360/2365 were either printed in individual sheets of 50 or together as *se-tenant* blocks of six.

No. 2367 was issued in rolls of 100 on which the surplus self-adhesive paper was removed. The phosphor, which shows pink under UV light, covers the bear.

(Litho Southern Colour Print, Dunedin)

2000 (5 Oct). CANPEX 2000 National Stamp Exhibition, Christchurch. Sheet 95×80 mm, containing Nos. 2336 and 2341. Phosphorised paper. Perf 14.

| **MS**2368 | 40c. Type **588**; $1.80 Lake Alexandrina | 1·60 | 1·75 |

593 Lesser Kestrel

594 *Sonoma* (mail ship) at Quay

(Des P. Martinson. Litho Southern Colour Print, Dunedin)

2000 (4 Nov). Threatened Birds. T **593** and similar horiz designs. Multicoloured. Phosphorised paper. Perf 14.

2369	40c. Type **593**	50	30
	a. Pair. Nos. 2369/2370	1·25	1·00
2370	40c. Yellow-fronted Parakeet	50	30
2371	80c. New Zealand Stilt ('Black Stilt')	70	55
2372	$1.10 Fernbird ('Stewart Island Fernbird')	1·00	70
2373	$1.20 Kakapo	1·00	1·00
2374	$1.50 Weka Rail ('North Island Weka')	1·25	1·25
2375	$1.80 Brown Kiwi ('Okarito Brown Kiwi')	1·50	1·25
2369/2375	Set of 7	6·25	5·25

Nos. 2369/2375 are printed in sheets of 25. The 40c. values exist either in separate sheets or with the two designs horizontally and vertically *se-tenant*.

Nos. 2369 and 2375 form a joint issue with France.

For miniature sheet containing Nos. 2374/2375 see No. **MS**2393.

BEST OF 2000. A further set of three miniature sheets as described below No. 2042, was distributed by the Philatelic Bureau to customers purchasing a certain amount of philatelic material during 2000. The stamps shown for 2000 were Nos. 1934e, 2090a, 2316, 2334, 2341, 2345, 2352, 2358 and 2375.

(Des Designworks. Litho Southern Colour Print, Dunedin)

2001. Moving the Mail in the 20th Century. T **594** and similar square designs. Phosphorised paper. Perf 14.

2376	40c. brown-purple and scarlet	35	35
	a. Sheetlet of 10. Nos. 2376/2385	3·25	3·25
2377	40c. grey-green	35	35
2378	40c. agate	35	35
2379	40c. violet-blue	35	35
2380	40c. olive-brown	35	35
2381	40c. blackish purple	35	35
2382	40c. black and cinnamon	35	35
2383	40c. multicoloured	35	35
2384	40c. maroon	35	35
2385	40c. multicoloured	35	35
2376/2385	Set of 10	3·25	3·25

Designs: No. 2376, T **594**; No. 2377, Stagecoach crossing river; No. 2378, Early postal lorry; No. 2379, Paddle-steamer on River Wanganui; No. 2380, Railway TPO; No. 2381, Loading mail through nose door of aircraft; No. 2382, Postwoman with bicycle; No. 2383, Loading lorry by forklift truck; No. 2384, Aircraft at night; No. 2385, Computer mouse.

Nos. 2376/2385 were printed together, *se-tenant*, in sheetlets of ten. Each design carries a description on the reverse over the gum.

For miniature sheet containing Nos. 2376/2385 without inscription on reverse see No. **MS**2424.

595 Green Turtle

596 Camellia

(Des Veda Austin. Litho Southern Colour Print, Dunedin)

2001 (1 Feb). Chinese New Year. Year of the Snake. Marine Reptiles. T **595** and similar vert designs. Multicoloured. Phosphorised paper. Perf 14.

2386	40c. Type **595**	25	10
2387	80c. Leathery Turtle	40	30
2388	90c. Loggerhead Turtle	45	50
2389	$1.30 Hawksbill Turtle	60	1·10
2390	$1.50 Banded Sea snake	70	1·40
2391	$2 Yellow-bellied Sea snake	85	1·40
2386/2391	Set of 6	3·00	4·25
MS2392	125×90 mm. Nos. 2390/2391	1·75	3·00

NEW ZEALAND

(Des P. Martinson. Litho Southern Colour Print, Dunedin)

2001 (1 Feb). Hong Kong 2001 Stamp Exhibition. Sheet 100×80 mm, containing Nos. 2374/2375. Phosphorised paper. Perf 14.
MS2393 $1.50, North Island Weka; $1.80, Okarito Brown Kiwi .... 2·50 3·00

(Des Lindy Fisher. Litho Southern Colour Print, Dunedin)

2001 (16 Mar). Garden Flowers. T **596** and similar horiz designs. Multicoloured. Phosphorised paper. Perf 14.

2394	40c. Type **596**	20	10
2395	80c. Siberian Iris	40	30
2396	90c. Daffodil	45	50
2397	$1.30 Chrysanthemum	60	1·10
2398	$1.50 Sweet Pea	70	1·25
2399	$2 Petunia	85	1·25
2394/2399 Set of 6		3·00	4·00
MS2400 95×125 mm. Nos. 2394/2399		3·00	4·50

An imperforate version of No. **MS**2400 comes from a Limited Edition Collectors Pack costing NZ$135.

(Des S. Fuller. Litho Southern Colour Print, Dunedin)

2001 (16 Mar). Invercargill Stamp Odyssey 2001 National Stamp Exhibition. Sheet 133×81 mm, containing Nos. 1934a/1934d. Phosphorised paper. Perf 13½.
MS2401 90c. Rangitoto Island; $1 Taiaroa Head; $1.10, Kaikoura Coast; $1.30, Lake Camp, South Canterbury .... 2·75 3·50

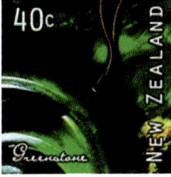 

597 Greenstone Amulet   **598** Douglas DC-3

(Des Cato Partners. Litho Southern Colour Print, Dunedin)

2001 (4 Apr). Art from Nature. T **597** and similar square designs. Multicoloured. Phosphorised paper. Perf 14.

2402	40c. Type **597**	20	10
2403	80c. Oamaru Stone sculpture	40	30
2404	90c. Paua ornament	50	50
2405	$1.30 Kauri ornament	60	1·10
2406	$1.50 Flax basket	70	1·25
2407	$2 Silver-dipped Fern frond	85	1·25
2402/2407 Set of 6		3·00	4·00

Nos. 2402/2407 were each printed in sheets of 25 (5×5) in which the stamps were included in four different orientations so that four blocks of four in each sheet showed the complete work of art.

(Des R. Poulton. Litho Southern Colour Print, Dunedin)

2001 (2 May). Aircraft. T **598** and similar horiz designs. Multicoloured. Perf 14.

2408	40c. Type **598**	35	15
2409	80c. Fletcher FU24 Topdresser	65	35
2410	90c. de Havilland DH.82A Tiger Moth ...	70	60
2411	$1.30 Fokker FVIIb/3m *Southern Cross* ...	90	1·10
2412	$1.50 de Havilland DH.100 Vampire	1·00	1·40
2413	$2 Boeing & Westervelt Seaplane	1·25	1·40
2408/2413 Set of 6		4·50	4·50

Nos. 2408/2413 also exist as seven miniature sheets, each 164×110 mm containing single examples of each value or the complete set. These come from a miniature sheet booklet, No. SP2, containing stamps with a face value of $13.80, which was sold for $19.95.

599 Parcel   **600** Bungy Jumping, Queenstown

(Des Esther Bunning. Litho SNP Ausprint)

2001 (6 June). Greetings Stamps. T **599** and similar square designs. Multicoloured. Perf 14½×14.

2414	40c. Type **599**	30	45
	a. Vert strip of 5. Nos. 2414/2418	1·40	2·00
2415	40c. Trumpet	30	45
2416	40c. Heart and ribbon	30	45
2417	40c. Balloons	30	45
2418	40c. Flower	30	45
2419	90c. Photo frame	50	80
	a. Vert strip of 5. Nos. 2419/2423	2·25	3·50
2420	90c. Fountain pen and letter	50	80
2421	90c. Candles on cake	50	80
2422	90c. Star biscuits	50	80
2423	90c. Candle and flowers	50	80
2414/2423 Set of 10		3·50	5·50

Nos. 2414/2418 and 2419/2423 were printed together, *se-tenant*, as vertical strips of five in sheets of 20, each stamp with a *se-tenant* label inscribed with the greetings.
Examples could also be personalised by the addition of a photograph in place of the inscriptions on the label.

(Des Comm Arts Design, Wellington. Litho Southern Colour Print, Dunedin)

2001 (9 June). Belgica 2001 International Stamp Exhibition, Brussels. Sheet 180×90 mm, containing Nos. 2376/2385 but with blue border and without inscriptions on reverse. Perf 14.
MS2424 40c.×10, Nos. 2376/2385 .... 4·75 5·50

(Des Designworks)

2001 (4 July). Tourism Centenary. T **600** and similar horiz designs. Multicoloured.

(a) Litho Southern Colour Print, Dunedin. Designs 38×32 mm. Ordinary or phosphorised paper ($1.50), phosphorised paper (others). Perf 14½.

2425	40c. Type **600**	20	10
2426	80c. Maori Canoe on Lake Rotoiti	40	30
2427	90c. Sightseeing from Mount Alfred ...	45	60
2428	$1.30 Fishing on Rees River	60	80
2429	$1.50 Sea kayaking in Abel Tasman National Park	75	1·25
2430	$2 Fiordland National Park	95	1·40
2425/2430 Set of 6		3·00	4·00

(b) Litho SNP Ausprint (also Southern Colour Print, Dunedin 40c., Nos. 2431c/2431ca). Designs 27×22 mm (Nos. 2431c/2431ca), 26×21 mm (others). Phosphor frame. Self-adhesive. Perf 11.

2431	40c. Type **600**	35	50
	a. Horiz strip of 3. Nos. 2431/2433 ...	1·75	3·00
	b. Booklet pane. No. 2431×10	3·00	4·00
	c. Perf 10	1·50	2·00
	ca. Phosphorised paper	45	60
2432	90c. Sightseeing from Mount Alfred ...	60	1·25
	a. Booklet pane. No. 2432×10	5·00	8·50
2433	$1.50 Sea kayaking in Abel Tasman Park	90	1·50
	a. Booklet pane. No. 2433×5 plus 5 air post international labels	4·00	6·50

Nos. 2431/2433 were printed by SNP Ausprint in booklets of five or ten, Nos. SB106/SB108, and as a strip of three. The 40c. perf 10 comes from rolls of 100 printed by Southern Colour Print. The strip of three and the roll have the surplus self-adhesive paper removed, but this is retained for the three booklet panes.

All self-adhesive stamps from booklets and the *se-tenant* strip have a phosphor frame which reacts pink under UV light. The rolls of a 100 have a similar frame which stops short of the black panel at the foot of the stamps. Some coils comprise 16 stamps (at right-hand end) with phosphor frames and 84 on phosphorised paper, the two sections being separated by a coil-join.

For miniature sheet containing Nos. 2429/2430 see **MS**2434.

(Des Designworks. Litho Southern Colour Print, Dunedin)

2001 (1 Aug). Philanippon 01 International Stamp Exhibition, Tokyo. Sheet 90×82 mm, containing Nos. 2429/2430. Phosphorised paper. Perf 14.
MS2434 $1.50 Sea kayaking in Abel Tasman National Park; $2 Fiordland National Park .... 2·50 3·50

601 Family cycling   **602** *When Christ was born of Mary free*

(Des Comm Arts Design. Litho Southern Colour Print, Dunedin)

2001 (1 Aug). Children's Health. Cycling. T **601** and similar horiz designs. Multicoloured.

(a) Size 39×29 mm. Ordinary gum. Phosphorised paper. Perf 14.

2435	40c.+5c. Type **601**	50	35
2436	90c.+5c. Stunt bike	85	75
MS2437 circular 100 mm diameter. Nos. 2435/2436		1·25	1·50

(b) Size 29×23½. Self-adhesive. Phosphor frame. Perf 10.

2438	40c.+5c. Boy on bike	40	30

No. 2435 was issued in sheets of 50 or in small sheets of ten (2×5) with red margins.

NEW ZEALAND

No. 2438 was issued in rolls of 100 on which the surplus self-adhesive paper was removed. The phosphor, which appears orange under UV light, is a three-sided frame with no markings along the top of the stamp.

(Des Comm Arts Design and R. Jones. Litho Southern Colour Print, Dunedin)

2001 (5 Sept–7 Nov). Christmas. Carols. T **602** and similar vert designs. Multicoloured.

(a) Size 29×34 mm. Ordinary gum. Phosphorised paper. Perf 13×14.

2439	40c. Type **602**	25	10
2440	80c. Away in a manger	45	35
2441	90c. Joy to the world	50	50
2442	$1.30 Angels we have heard on high	75	1·00
2443	$1.50 O holy night	85	1·25
2444	$2 While shepherds watched	1·10	1·75
2439/2444	Set of 6	3·50	4·50

(b) Size 21×26 mm. Self-adhesive. Phosphor frame. Perf 10.

2445	40c. Type **602**	35	30
	a. Phosphorised paper (7.11)	45	40
	b. Booklet pane No. 2445a×10	3·00	

No. 2445, on which the phosphor appears pink under UV light, was issued in rolls of 100 on which the surplus self-adhesive paper was removed.

Booklet pane No 2445b, No. SB109, retains the surplus self-adhesive paper around each stamp.

603 Queen Elizabeth II at State Opening of Parliament, 1954

604 Rockhopper Penguins

(Des Ann Adams. Litho Southern Colour Print, Dunedin)

2001 (3 Oct). Queen Elizabeth II's 75th Birthday. T **603** and similar vert designs. Multicoloured. Phosphorised paper. Perf 14.

2446	40c. Type **603** (black and silver)	40	30
	a. Horiz strip of 6. Nos. 2446/2451	4·25	4·75
2447	80c. Queen Elizabeth II on walkabout, 1970	60	50
2448	90c. Queen Elizabeth II wearing Maori cloak, 1977	70	55
2449	$1.30 Queen Elizabeth II with bouquet, 1986	90	80
2450	$1.50 Queen Elizabeth II at Commonwealth Games, 1990	1·00	90
2451	$2 Queen Elizabeth II, 1997	1·25	1·25
2446/2451	Set of 6	4·25	4·75

Nos. 2446/2451 were printed in sheets of one value or together, *se-tenant*, as horizontal strips of six.

Imperforate sheets of Nos. 2446/2451 and *se-tenant* strips of the six values were distributed by the Philatelic Bureau to customers who had purchased a certain amount of material from them during 2001.

(Des Communication Arts Ltd. Litho Southern Colour Print, Dunedin)

2001 (7 Nov). New Zealand Penguins. T **604** and similar horiz designs. Multicoloured. Perf 14½.

2452	40c. Type **604**	50	30
2453	80c. Little Blue Penguin	75	50
2454	90c. Snares Crested Penguins	85	60
2455	$1.30 Erect-crested Penguins	1·10	85
2456	$1.50 Fiordland Crested Penguins	1·25	1·10
2457	$2 Yellow-eyed Penguins	1·60	1·40
2452/2457	Set of 6	5·50	4·25

605 Gandalf (Sir Ian McKellen) and Saruman (Christopher Lee)

606 Christian Cullen (harness racing)

(Des Sacha Lees. Litho Southern Colour Print, Dunedin)

2001 (4 Dec). Making of *The Lord of the Rings* Film Trilogy (1st issue). *The Fellowship of the Ring*. T **605** and similar multicoloured designs.

(a) Designs 24×50 mm or 50×24 mm. Phosphorised paper. Perf 14½×14 (vert designs) or 14×14½ (horiz designs).

2458	40c. Type **605**	60	30
2459	80c. The Lady Galadriel (Cate Blanchett)	1·10	1·00
2460	90c. Sam Gamgee (Sean Austin) and Frodo Baggins (Elijah Wood) (*horiz*)	1·10	1·00
2461	$1.30 Guardian of Rivendell	1·60	2·50
2462	$1.50 Strider (Viggo Mortensen)	1·75	2·50
2463	$2 Boromir (Sean Bean) (*horiz*)	2·25	3·50
2458/2463	Set of 6	7·75	9·75

(b) Designs 26×37 mm or 37×26 mm. Self-adhesive. Phosphor frame. Perf 10½.

2464	40c. Type **605**	40	50
	a. Horiz strip of 6. Nos. 2464/2469	5·50	9·00
	b. Booklet pane. Nos. 2464×4, 2465, 2466×2 and 2467/2469	7·00	
2465	80c. The Lady Galadriel (Cate Blanchett)	60	1·00
2466	90c. Sam Gamgee (Sean Austin) and Frodo Baggins (Elijah Wood) (*horiz*)	75	1·25
2467	$1.30 Guardian of Rivendell	1·25	2·25
2468	$1.50 Strider (Viggo Mortensen)	1·50	2·50
2469	$2 Boromir (Sean Bean) (*horiz*)	1·60	2·75
2464/2469	Set of 6	5·50	9·00

Nos. 2458/2463 were each printed in sheets of 25 with the 40c. also available as a sheetlet of ten (5×2). They also exist as a set of six miniature sheets, each containing a single stamp, which were only available at a premium of $3 over the face value of the stamps.

Nos. 2464/2469, on which the phosphor shows pink under UV light, were issued as strips of six, on which the surplus self-adhesive paper around each stamp was either retained or removed, or as a $9 booklet, No. SB110, containing pane No. 2464b on which the surplus paper was retained.

For miniature sheets containing Nos. 2458, 2461, 2463 and 2462/2463, see **MS**2490 and **MS**2523.

See also Nos. 2550/2561, 2652/2663 and 2714/2726.

BEST OF 2001. The Stamp Rewards distributed by the Philatelic Bureau to customers purchasing a certain amount of material during 2001 were imperforate sheets of Nos. 2446/2451, and an imperforate *se-tenant* strip and imperforate *se-tenant* block of the same six stamps.

(Des K. Dunkley. Litho Southern Colour Print, Dunedin)

2002 (7 Feb). Chinese New Year. Year of the Horse. New Zealand Racehorses. T **606** and similar horiz designs. Phosphorised paper. Multicoloured. Perf 14.

2470	40c. Type **606**	25	15
2471	80c. Lyell Creek (harness racing)	40	25
2472	90c. Yulestar (harness racing)	45	50
2473	$1.30 Sunline	70	40
2474	$1.50 Ethereal	75	1·40
2475	$2 Zabeel	90	1·40
2470/2475	Set of 6	3·00	4·00
MS2476	127×90 mm. Nos. 2473/2474	3·75	4·50

Nos. 2470/2475 were each printed in sheets of 25 containing panes of 15 (3×5) and ten (2×5) separated by a vertical gutter showing Year of the Horse symbols.

607 *Hygrocybe rubrocarnosa*

608 War Memorial Museum, Auckland

(Des DNA Design. Litho Southern Colour Print, Dunedin)

2002 (6 Mar). Fungi. T **607** and similar vert designs. Multicoloured. Phosphorised paper. Perf 14.

2477	40c. Type **607**	30	10
2478	80c. *Entoloma hochstetteri*	45	30
2479	90c. *Aseroe rubra*	55	50
2480	$1.30 *Hericium coralloides*	70	1·10
2481	$1.50 *Thaxterogaster porphyreus*	80	1·40
2482	$2 *Ramaria aureoriza*	1·00	1·60
2477/2482	Set of 6	3·50	4·50
MS2483	114×104 mm. Nos. 2477/2482	3·50	5·50

NEW ZEALAND

(Des Mission Hall Design. Litho Southern Colour Print, Dunedin)

2002 (3 Apr). Architectural Heritage. T **608** and similar multicoloured designs. Phosphorised paper. Perf 14½×14.

2484	40c. Type **608**	25	10
	a. Block of 6. Nos. 2484/2489	3·25	4·50
2485	80c. Stone Store, Kerikeri (25×30 mm)	45	40
2486	90c. Arts Centre, Christchurch (50×30 mm)	50	50
2487	$1.30 Government Buildings, Wellington (50×30 mm)	75	80
2488	$1.50 Dunedin Railway Station (25×30 mm)	80	1·00
2489	$2 Sky Tower, Auckland	1·00	1·25
2484/2489	Set of 6	3·25	3·50

Nos. 2484/2489 were printed in sheets of one value or together, *se-tenant*, as blocks of six.

Nos. 2484/2489 also exist as seven miniature sheets, each 150×110 mm, containing single examples of each value or the complete set. These come from a miniature sheet booklet, No. SP3, containing stamps with a face value of $13.80, which was sold for $16.95.

(Des Sacha Lees. Litho Southern Colour Print, Dunedin)

2002 (5 Apr). Northpex 2002 Stamp Exhibition. Sheet, 130×95 mm, containing Nos. 2458, 2461 and 2463. Phosphorised paper. Perf 14×14½ ($2) or comp 14½×14 (others)*.

MS2490 40c. Gandalf (Sir Ian McKellen) and Saruman (Christopher Lee); $1.30, Guardian of Rivendell; $2 Boromir (Sean Bean) (*horiz*) .... 8·00 10·00

* The 40c. and $1.30 values in the miniature sheet are perforated 14½ at top and 14 on the other three sides.

No. **MS**2490 was sold at face value.

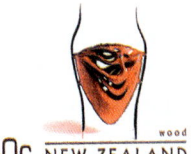

609 *Starfish Vessel* (wood sculpture)

610 Brodie (Anna Poland, Cardinal Priddle)

(Des Gardyne Design. Litho and recess Swedish Stamp Ptg Office (Nos. 2492, 2497) or Litho Southern Colour Print, Dunedin (others))

2002 (1 May). Artistic Crafts. Joint Issue with Sweden. T **609** and similar horiz designs. Multicoloured. Phosphorised paper. Perf 12½ (Nos. 2492, 2497) or 14 (others).

2491	40c. Type **609**	20	25
2492	40c. Flax basket (Willa Rogers) (37×29 mm)	20	25
2493	80c. *Catch II* (clay bowl) (Raewyn Atkinson)	35	40
2494	90c. *Vessel Form* (silver brooch) (Gavin Hitchings)	40	50
2495	$1.30 Glass towers from Immigration series (Emma Camden)	60	85
2496	$1.50 *Pacific Rim* (clay vessel) (Merilyn Wiseman)	65	1·40
2497	$2 Glass vase (Ola and Maria Höglund) (37×29 mm)	80	1·40
2491/2497	Set of 7	3·00	4·50

Nos. 2492 and 2497 are additionally inscribed 'JOINT ISSUE WITH SWEDEN'.

(Des CommArts Design. Litho Southern Colour Print, Dunedin)

2002 (5 June). Children's Book Festival. Stamp Design Competition. T **610** and similar horiz designs illustrating books. Multicoloured. Perf 14.

2498	40c. Type **610**	30	45
	a. Block of 10. Nos. 2498/2507	2·75	4·00
2499	40c. The Last Whale (Hee Su Kim)	30	45
2500	40c. Scarface Claw (Jayne Bruce)	30	45
2501	40c. Which New Zealand Bird? (Teigan Stafford-Bush)	30	45
2502	40c. Which New Zealand Bird? (Hazel Gilbert)	30	45
2503	40c. The Plight of the Penguin (Gerard Mackle)	30	45
2504	40c. Scarface Claw (Maria Rodgers)	30	45
2505	40c. Knocked for Six (Paul Read)	30	45
2506	40c. Grandpa's Shorts (Jessica Hitchings, Ashleigh Bree, Malyna Sengdara and Aniva Kini)	30	45
2507	40c. Which New Zealand Bird? (Olivia Duncan)	30	45
2498/2507	Set of 10	2·75	4·00
MS2508	230×90 mm. Nos. 2498/2507	3·50	4·50

Nos. 2498/2507 were printed together, *se-tenant*, as blocks of ten throughout the sheets of 50.

611 Queen Elizabeth the Queen Mother, 1992

612 Tongaporutu Cliffs, Taranaki

(Des Red Cactus Design. Litho Southern Colour Print, Dunedin)

2002 (5 June). Queen Elizabeth the Queen Mother Commemoration. Perf 14.

2509	**611**	$2 multicoloured	2·00	1·60

(Des The Bureau Interactive. Litho Pemara (No. 2516c) or Southern Colour Print, Dunedin) (others)

2002 (3 July)–**2003**. Coastlines. T **612** and similar horiz designs. Multicoloured.

(a) Size 38×29 mm. Ordinary gum. Phosphorised paper. Perf 14.

2510	40c. Type **612**	20	20
2511	80c. Lottin Point, East Cape	40	55
2512	90c. Curio Bay, Catlins	50	65
2513	$1.30 Kaikoura Coast	65	1·50
2514	$1.50 Meybille Bay, West Coast	75	1·75
2515	$2 Papanui Point, Raglan	95	1·75
2510/2515	Set of 6	3·00	5·75

(b) Size 28×21 mm. Self-adhesive. Phosphor frame. Perf 10.

2516	40c. Type **612**	20	50
	a. Horiz strip of 3. Nos. 2516/2518	1·25	3·00
	b. Booklet pane. No. 2516c×10	1·75	
	c. Perf 11 (27.5.03)	35	50
	ca. Booklet pane. No. 2516c×10	3·25	
	d. Perf 12½×13	30	50
2517	90c. Curio Bay, Catlins	50	80
	b. Booklet pane. No. 2517×10	4·50	
2518	$1.50 Meybille Bay, West Coast	75	1·75
	b. Booklet pane. No. 2518×5	3·25	

Nos. 2516/2518, on which the phosphor shows pink under UV light with a break in the frame corresponding to the design overlap on to the margin, were either issued together as strips of three, on which the surplus self-adhesive paper around each stamp was removed, or in booklets, Nos. SB111/SB113, each containing one value, on which it was retained.

No. 2516 was issued in rolls of 100 with surplus self-adhesive paper around each stamp removed.

For a cancelled *se-tenant* strip comprising Nos. 2510/2515 see note below No. 2561.

613 Basket of Fruit

(Des R. Jones. Litho Southern Colour Print, Dunedin)

2002 (7 Aug). Children's Health. Healthy Eating. T **613** and similar multicoloured designs. Phosphorised paper.

(a) Ordinary gum. Perf 14.

2519	40c.+5c. Type **613**	50	55
2520	90c.+5c. Selection of vegetables	75	80
MS2521	90×75 mm. Nos. 2519/2520 and as No. 2522 (22×26 mm)	1·75	2·00

(b) Self-adhesive. Perf 10.

2522	40c.+5c. Fruit and vegetables (22×26 mm)	30	35

No. 2522 was issued in rolls of 100 on which the surplus self-adhesive paper was removed.

(Des Sacha Lees/Comm Arts Design, Litho Southern Colour Print, Dunedin)

2002 (30 Aug). Amphilex 2002, International Stamp Exhibition, Amsterdam. Sheet 130×95 mm, containing Nos. 2462/2463. Phosphorised paper. Perf 14½×14 ($1.50) or comp 14×14½ ($2)*.

MS2523 $1.50 Strider (Viggo Mortensen); $2 Boromir (Sean Bean) (*horiz*) .... 2·50 3·25

* The $2 value in the miniature sheet is perforated 14 at top and left and 14½ at bottom and right.

No. **MS**2523 was sold at face value.

NEW ZEALAND

614 St Werenfried, Tokaanu

(Des Comm Arts Design. Litho Southern Colour Print, Dunedin)

2002 (4 Sept). Christmas. Church Interiors. T **614** and similar multicoloured designs.

(a) Size 35×35 mm. Phosphorised paper. Ordinary gum. Perf 14½.
2524	40c. Type **614**	20	10
2525	80c. St David's, Christchurch	40	25
2526	90c. Orthodox Church of Transfiguration of Our Lord, Masterton	45	50
2527	$1.30 Cathedral of the Holy Spirit, Palmerston North	70	75
2528	$1.50 St Paul's Cathedral, Wellington	80	1·10
2529	$2 Cathedral of the Blessed Sacrament, Christchurch	95	1·60
2524/2529 Set of 6		3·25	3·75

(b) Size 25×30 mm. Self-adhesive. Phosphor frame. Perf 13×12½.
2530	40c. St Werenfried, Tokaanu	30	30
	a. Perf 10	35	30
	ab. Booklet pane. No. 2530a×10	3·00	

No. 2530 was printed in rolls of 100 on which the surplus self-adhesive paper around each stamp was removed.
On Nos. 2530/2530a the phosphor shows pink under UV light.
No. 2530a was only available from the $4 stamp booklet, No. SB114, with the surplus self-adhesive paper around each stamp retained.

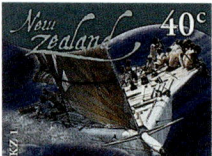 

615 *KZ 1* (racing yacht) **616** *Black Magic* (New Zealand) and *Luna Rossa* (Italy)

(Des Capiche Design. Litho Southern Colour Print, Dunedin)

2002 (2 Oct). Racing and Leisure Craft. T **615** and similar horiz designs. Multicoloured. Phosphorised paper. Perf 14.
2531	40c. Type **615**	25	30
2532	80c. *High 5* (ocean racing yacht)	40	55
2533	90c. *Gentle Spirit* (sports fishing and diving boat)	45	70
2534	$1.30 *North Star* (luxury motor cruiser)	70	1·00
2535	$1.50 *Ocean Runner* (powerboat)	80	1·40
2536	$2 *Salperton* (ocean-going yacht)	90	1·60
2531/2536 Set of 6		3·25	5·00
MS2537 140×80 mm. Nos. 2531/2536		3·25	5·00

(Des CommArts Design. Litho Southern Colour Print, Dunedin)

2002 (2 Oct). America's Cup, 2003 (1st issue). T **616** and similar horiz designs showing scenes from 2000 final, between New Zealand and Italy. Multicoloured. Phosphorised paper. Perf 14.
2538	$1.30 Type **616**	70	90
2539	$1.50 Aerial view of race	80	1·00
2540	$2 Yachts turning	95	1·60
2538/2540 Set of 3		2·25	3·25
MS2541 140×80 mm. Nos. 2538/2540		2·25	4·00

See also Nos. 2562/**MS**2565.

(Litho Southern Colour Print, Dunedin)

2002 (4 Oct). Stampshow 02, International Stamp Exhibition, Melbourne. No. **MS**2541 with Stampshow 02 emblem and inscription on the margin. Multicoloured. Phosphorised paper. Perf 14.
MS2542 140×80 mm. Nos. 2538/2540 .... 2·25 3·50

617 Green-roofed Holiday Cottage and Paua Shell

(Des Cato Partners. Litho Southern Colour Print, Dunedin)

2002 (6 Nov). Holiday Homes. T **617** and similar horiz designs. Multicoloured. Perf 14.
2543	40c. Type **617**	30	35
2544	40c. Red-roofed cottage and Sunflower	30	35
2545	40c. White-roofed cottage and lifebelt	30	35
2546	40c. Cottage with orange door, boat and fishing fly	30	35
2547	40c. Blue-roofed cottage and fish	30	35
2548	40c. Cottage and caravan	30	35
2543/2548 Set of 6		1·60	1·90

618 The Nativity (15th-century painting in style of di Baldese)

(Des CommArts Design. Litho Southern Colour Print, Dunedin)

2002 (21 Nov). New Zealand–Vatican City Joint Issue. Phosphorised paper. Perf 14.
2549 **618** $1.50 multicoloured .... 1·00 1·40

No. 2549 was printed in sheets of ten.

(Des Sacha Lees. Litho Southern Colour Print, Dunedin)

2002 (4 Dec). Making of *The Lord of the Rings* Film Trilogy (2nd issue). *The Two Towers*. Multicoloured designs as T **605**.

(a) Designs 50×24 mm or 24×50 mm. Phosphorised paper. Perf 14×14½ (horiz) or 14½×14 (vert).
2550	40c. Aragorn (Viggo Mortenson) and Eowyn (Miranda Otto) (*horiz*)	60	20
2551	80c. Orc raider (*horiz*)	1·00	40
2552	90c. Gandalf the White (Sir Ian McKellen)	1·10	70
2553	$1.30 Easterling warriors (*horiz*)	1·40	2·00
2554	$1.50 Frodo (Elijah Wood)	1·60	2·25
2555	$2 Eowyn, Shield Maiden of Rohan (Miranda Otto) (*horiz*)	1·90	2·25
2550/2555 Set of 6		7·00	7·00

(b) Designs 37×26 mm or 26×37 mm. Self-adhesive. Phosphor frame. Perf 10½.
2556	40c. Aragorn (Viggo Mortenson) and Eowyn (Miranda Otto) (*horiz*)	25	50
	a. Block of 6. Nos. 2556/2561	5·00	8·50
	b. Booklet pane. Nos. 2556×4, 2557, 2558×2 and 2559/2561	6·50	
2557	80c. Orc raider (*horiz*)	80	90
2558	90c. Gandalf the White (Sir Ian McKellen) (*horiz*)	70	1·00
2559	$1.30 Easterling warriors (*horiz*)	1·10	2·00
2560	$1.50 Frodo (Elijah Wood)	1·25	2·50
2561	$2 Eowyn, Shield Maiden of Rohan (Miranda Otto) (*horiz*)	1·40	2·50
2556/2561 Set of 6		5·00	8·50

Nos. 2550/2555 were each printed in sheets of 25. They also exist as a set of six miniature sheets, each containing a single stamp, which were only available at a premium of $3 over the face value of the stamps.

Nos. 2556/2561, on which the phosphor shows pink under UV light, were either issued as blocks of six, or as a $9 booklet, No. SB115, containing pane No. 2556b, with the surplus paper retained in both instances.

BEST OF 2002. A further set of miniature sheets as described below No. 2042 was distributed by the Philatelic Bureau to customers purchasing a certain amount of philatelic material during 2002. The stamps shown for 2002 were Nos. 2090b, 2475, 2482, 2489, 2496, 2515, 2520, 2529 and 2545.

In addition, a cancelled *se-tenant* strip was distributed comprising Nos. 2510/2515.

(Des CommArts Design. Litho Southern Colour Print, Dunedin)

2003 (8 Jan). America's Cup (2nd issue). The Defence. Horiz designs as T **616**. Multicoloured. Perf 14.
2562	40c. Aerial view of *Team New Zealand* yacht	25	30
2563	80c. Two *Team New Zealand* yachts	50	55
2564	90c. *Team New Zealand* yacht tacking	60	65
2562/2564 Set of 3		1·25	1·40
MS2565 140×80 mm. Nos. 2562/2564		1·25	1·75

NEW ZEALAND

619 Shepherd with Flock in High Country
620 Jon Trimmer in *Carmina Burana*

(Des Denise Durkin. Litho Southern Colour Print, Dunedin)

2003 (5 Feb). Chinese New Year. Year of the Sheep. Sheep Farming. T **619** and similar horiz designs. Multicoloured. Perf 14.

2566	40c. Type **619**	30	15
2567	90c. Mustering the Sheep	50	70
2568	$1.30 Sheep in pen with Sheep Dog	70	1·25
2569	$1.50 Sheep shearing	80	1·50
2570	$2 Sheep shearing (*different*)	1·00	1·60
2566/2570 Set of 5		3·00	4·75
MS2571 125×85 mm. Nos. 2568 and 2570		2·25	3·25

(Des CommArts Design. Litho Southern Colour Print, Dunedin)

2003 (5 Mar). 50th Anniversary of Royal New Zealand Ballet. T **620** and similar multicoloured designs showing scenes from past productions. Perf 14.

2572	40c. Type **620**	20	15
2573	90c. *Papillon* (horiz)	40	35
2574	$1.30 *Cinderella*	60	1·00
2575	$1.50 *FrENZy*	70	1·25
2576	$2 *Swan Lake* (horiz)	90	1·40
2572/2576 Set of 5		2·50	3·75

621 Officer, Forest Rangers, 1860s
622 Ailsa Mountains

(Des R. Jones. Litho Southern Colour Print, Dunedin)

2003 (2 Apr). New Zealand Military Uniforms. T **621** and similar vert designs. Multicoloured. Perf 14.

2577	40c. Type **621**	50	75
	a. Sheetlet of 20. Nos. 2577/2596	9·00	13·00
2578	40c. Lieutenant, Napier Naval Artillery Volunteers, 1890s	50	75
2579	40c. Officer, 2nd Regiment, North Canterbury Mounted Rifles, 1900–1910	50	75
2580	40c. Mounted Trooper, New Zealand Mounted Rifles, South Africa, 1899–1902	50	75
2581	40c. Staff Officer, New Zealand Division, France, 1918	50	75
2582	40c. Petty Officer, Royal New Zealand Navy, 1914–1918	50	75
2583	40c. Rifleman, New Zealand Rifle Brigade, France, 1916–1918	50	75
2584	40c. Sergeant, New Zealand Engineers, 1939–1945	50	75
2585	40c. Matron, Royal New Zealand Navy Hospital, 1940s	50	75
2586	40c. Private, New Zealand Women's Auxiliary Army Corps, Egypt, 1942	50	75
2587	40c. Pilot serving with RAF Bomber Command, Europe, 1943	50	75
2588	40c. Fighter Pilot, No. 1 (Islands) Group, Royal New Zealand Air Force, Pacific, 1943	50	75
2589	40c. Driver, Women's Auxiliary Air Force, 1943	50	75
2590	40c. Gunner, 16th Field Regiment, Royal New Zealand Artillery, Korea, 1950–1953	50	75
2591	40c. Acting Petty Officer, HMNZS Tamaki, 1957	50	75
2592	40c. Scouts, New Zealand Special Air Service, Malaya, 1955–1957	50	75
2593	40c. Canberra Pilot serving with RAF Far East Command, Malaya, 1960	50	75
2594	40c. Infantrymen, 1st Battalion, Royal New Zealand Infantry Regiment, South Vietnam, 1960s	50	75
2595	40c. Infantryman, New Zealand Battalion, UNTAET, East Timor, 2000	50	75
2596	40c. Monitor, Peace Monitoring Group, Bougainville, 2001	50	75
2577/2596 Set of 20		9·00	13·00

Nos. 2577/2596 were printed together, *se-tenant*, in sheetlets of 20 with detailed descriptions of the designs printed on the reverse.

The stamps also exist in five miniature sheets, each 150×110 mm, containing two examples each of Nos. 2577/2580, 2581/2584, 2585/2588, 2589/2592 and 2593/2596. These come from a miniature sheet booklet, No. SP4, containing stamps with a face value of $16, which was sold for $19.95.

Two Types of 45c.:

Two Types of $1.50:

Type I. Empty doorway
Type II. Figure in doorway

(Des CommArts Design. (Nos. 2600/2601, 2603, 2605/2607, 2610/2611, 2614 or Stamps Business (others). Litho Walsall (No. 2605), SNP Sprint, Australia (No. 2611) or Southern Colour Print, Dunedin (others))

2003 (9 May)–**2009**. New Zealand Landscapes (1st series). T **622** and similar horiz designs, each including the fern symbol after the country inscr. Multicoloured.

(a) Ordinary gum. Phosphorised paper. Perf 14×14½ ($1.35) or 13½ (others).

2597	5c. Geyser, Whakarewarewa, Rotorua (9.5.07)	10	50
2598	10c. Central Otago (9.5.07)	15	40
2599	20c. Rainbow Falls, Northland (9.5.07)	25	40
2600	45c. Kaikoura (Type I) (22.3.04)	55	50
2601	50c. Type **622**	55	60
2602	50c. Lake Coleridge, Canterbury (9.5.07)	55	50
2603	$1 Coromandel	1·00	75
2604	$1 Rangitoto Island, Auckland (9.5.07)	1·60	1·50
2605	$1.35 Church of the Good Shepherd Lake Tekapo (22.3.04)	1·75	3·00
	a. Perf 13½ (8.2006)	3·00	3·75
2606	$1.50 Arrowtown (Type I)	2·00	1·00
2607	$2 Tongariro National Park	2·25	1·50
2608	$2.50 Abel Tasman National Park (9.5.07)	2·50	2·25
2609	$3 Tongaporutu, Taranaki (9.5.07)	3·00	3·25
2610	$5 Castlepoint Lighthouse	5·50	6·50
2597/2610 Set of 14		19·00	20·00

(b) Self-adhesive. Phosphor frame. Perf 11½×11 (45c.) or 10 (others).

2611	45c. Kaikoura (Type I) (22.3.04)	55	35
	a. Booklet pane. No. 2611×10	5·50	
	b. Type II	55	55
2612	50c. As No. 2602 (9.5.07)	65	65
	a. Booklet pane. No. 2612×10	6·25	
	b. Horiz pair. Nos. 2612/2613	1·90	1·90
2613	$1 As No. 2604 (6.5.07)	1·25	1·75
	a. Booklet pane: No. 2613×10	12·50	
2614	$1.50 Arrowtown (Type I)	1·40	2·25
	a. Booklet pane. No. 2614×5	7·50	
	b. Type II (27.3.07)	2·00	2·25
	ba. Booklet pane. No. 2614b×5, 5 International Economy labels and 5 International Air labels (27.03.07)	10·00	
	c. Ordinary paper (Type II)	2·00	2·25
	ca. Booklet pane. No. 2614c×5 (2.3.09)	10·00	
	d. Booklet pane. No. 2614×5 and 2 International Air labels (18.5.09)	10·00	
	e. Booklet pane. No. 2614b×5 (30.10.09)	7·50	

Nos. 2601, 2603, 2606/2607 and 2610 were sold in limited quantities (and only in complete numbered sheets), with the black fern frond overprinted in silver foil. On all values the silver matches the black, with the fern frond segmented on its underside. An initial printing of the 50c. with the larger unsegmented fern frond was distributed by the New Zealand Post, who subsequently attempted to have them recalled for replacement.

No. 2611 was issued in sheets of 100 and $4.50 stamp booklet, No. SB122, both with the surplus self-adhesive paper retained.

No. 2611b was issued in rolls of 100 with the surplus self-adhesive paper around each stamp removed.

No. 2612 was issued in rolls of 100 and $5 stamp booklet, No. SB135.

No. 2613 was issued in $10 booklet No. SB137.

NEW ZEALAND

No. 2614 was issued in $7.50 stamp booklet (No. SB116). No. 2614b, which incorporates a number of other minor design changes, first appeared in booklet No. SB135. Both have phosphor showing pink under UV light. No. 2614c comes from booklet No. SB135a, but could also be purchased individually from the philatelic bureau. All versions have the self-adhesive backing paper retained.

See also Nos. 3150/3156, 3227/3233b, 3363/3367, 3556/3561 and 3773/3780.

623 Sir Edmund Hillary and Mount Everest

(Des S. Fuller. Litho Southern Colour Print, Dunedin)

2003 (29 May). 50th Anniversary of Conquest of Everest. T **623** and similar horiz design. Multicoloured. Phosphorised paper. Perf 14.

2616	40c. Type **623**	75	1·25
	a. Pair. Nos. 2616/2617	1·50	2·50
2617	40c. Climbers reaching summit and Tenzing Norgay	75	1·25

Nos. 2616/2617 were printed together, *se-tenant*, in horizontal and vertical pairs and were available in sheets of 50 and in sheetlets of ten with enlarged illustrated left-hand margins.

624 Buckingham Palace   **625** New Zealand v South Africa Match, 1937

(Des L. C. Mitchell ($2), J. Berry (others), adapted CommArts Design, Wellington. Litho Southern Colour Print, Dunedin)

2003 (4 June). 50th Anniversary of Coronation. As Types **163**/**164** (Coronation issue of 1953) but face values in decimal currency as T **624**. Phosphorised paper. Perf 14×14½ (40c., $1.30, $2) or 14½×14 (90c., $1.50).

2618	40c. deep ultramarine	35	25
2619	90c. reddish brown	65	1·00
2620	$1.30 carmine-red	1·00	1·50
2621	$1.50 deep blue	1·10	1·75
2622	$2 reddish violet and dull ultramarine	1·25	2·00
2618/2622 Set of 5		4·00	6·00

Designs: Vert (as T **164**)—90c. Queen Elizabeth II; $1.50, Westminster Abbey. Horiz (as T **624**)—40c. T **624**; $1.30, Coronation State Coach; $2 St Edward's Crown and Royal Sceptre.

(Des DNA Design. Litho Southern Colour Print, Dunedin)

2003 (2 July). Centenary of New Zealand Test Rugby. T **625** and similar horiz designs. Multicoloured. Phosphorised paper. Perf 14.

2623	40c. Type **625**	25	15
2624	90c. New Zealand v Wales match, 1963	45	45
2625	$1.30 New Zealand v Australia, 1985	60	70
2626	$1.50 New Zealand v France, 1986	65	1·40
2627	$1.50 All Black jersey	65	1·40
2628	$2 New Zealand v England, 1997	85	1·50
2623/2628 Set of 6		3·00	5·00
MS2629 100×180 mm. Nos. 2623/2628		3·00	5·00

626 Papaaroha, Coromandel Peninsula   **627** Boy on Swing

(Des Capiche Design. Litho Southern Colour Print, Dunedin)

2003 (6 Aug). New Zealand Waterways. T **626** and similar horiz designs. Multicoloured. Phosphorised paper. Perf 14½.

2630	40c. Type **626**	45	25
2631	90c. Waimahana Creek, Chatham Islands	75	85
2632	$1.30 Blue Lake, Central Otago	1·25	1·40
2633	$1.50 Waikato River	1·40	1·75
2634	$2 Hooker River, Canterbury	1·60	2·25
2630/2634 Set of 5		5·00	6·00

(Des G. Taylor. Litho Southern Colour Print, Dunedin)

2003 (6 Aug). Children's Health. Playgrounds. T **627** and similar multicoloured designs. Phosphorised paper.

(a) Size 39×29 mm. Ordinary gum. Perf 14.

2635	40c.+5c. Type **627**	50	60
2636	90c.+5c. Girls playing hopscotch	90	1·00
MS2637 88×90 mm. Nos. 2635/2636 (Perf 14) and 40c.+5c. Girl on climbing frame (Perf 14½×14)		2·00	2·00

(b) Size 24×29 mm. Self-adhesive. Perf 9½×10.

2638	40c.+5c. Girl on climbing frame	60	60

No. 2638 was available as single stamps or in rolls of 100, both with the surplus self-adhesive paper around each stamp retained.

628 Benz Velo (1895)   **629** Christ Child in Crib

(Des S. Fuller. Litho Cartor)

2003 (3 Sept). Veteran Vehicles. T **628** and similar horiz designs. Multicoloured. Phosphorised paper. Perf 13×13½.

2639	40c. Type **628**	35	25
2640	90c. Oldsmobile (1903)	60	70
2641	$1.30 Wolseley (1911)	90	1·25
2642	$1.50 Talbot (1915)	1·10	1·50
2643	$2 Model T Ford (1915)	1·25	1·75
2640/2643 Set of 5		3·75	5·00

(Des Lindy Fisher)

2003 (1 Oct). Christmas Decorations. T **629** and similar square designs. Multicoloured. Phosphorised paper.

(a) Size 30×30 mm. Ordinary gum. Litho Cartor. Perf 13½.

2644	40c. Type **629**	35	10
2645	90c. Silver and gold bird	65	50
2646	$1.30 Silver candle	90	1·25
2647	$1.50 Bells	1·00	1·50
2648	$2 Angel	1·25	1·60
2644/2648 Set of 5		3·75	4·50

(b) Size 21×26 mm. Self-adhesive. Litho Southern Colour Print, Dunedin. Perf 9½×10.

2649	40c. Type **629**	45	35
	a. Black 'Silver Fern' omitted	£350	£250
	b. Booklet pane. No. 2649×10	4·00	
2650	$1 Filigree metalwork decoration with baubles	1·00	1·00
	a. Booklet pane. No. 2650×8	7·00	

Nos. 2644/2648 were each printed in sheets of 50 (5×10) in which the stamps were included in four different orientations to make ten blocks of four and five pairs in each sheet.

No. 2649 was issued in rolls of 100 and $4 booklet, No. SB117. No. 2649a comes from rolls.

No. 2650 was issued as self-adhesive stamps or $8 booklet, No. SB118.

(Des CommArts Designs. Litho Southern Colour Print, Dunedin)

2003 (4 Oct). Bangkok 2003 World Philatelic Exhibition. Sheet 110×80 mm containing Nos. 2572/2573 and 2576. Phosphorised paper. Perf 14.
MS2651 40c. Type **620**; 90c. *Papillon* (horiz); $2 Swan Lake (horiz) .... 3·00 3·00

(Des F. Lenzen. Litho Southern Colour Print, Dunedin)

2003 (5 Nov). Making of *The Lord of the Rings* Film Trilogy (3rd issue). *The Return of the King*. Multicoloured designs as T **605**.

(a) Designs 24×49 mm or 49×24 mm. Phosphorised paper. Perf 14½×14 (vert designs) or 14×14½ (horiz designs).

2652	40c. Legolas	50	35
2653	80c. Frodo Baggins	85	1·00
2654	90c. Merry and Pippin (horiz)	95	1·00
2655	$1.30 Aragorn	1·25	1·50
2656	$1.50 Gandalf the White	1·50	1·75
2657	$2 Gollum (horiz)	2·00	2·75
2652/2657 Set of 6		6·25	7·50

(b) Designs 24×35 mm or 35×24 mm. Self-adhesive. Phosphor frame. Perf 10×10½ (vert designs) or 10½×10 (horiz designs).

2658	40c. Legolas	40	55
	a. Horiz strip of 6. Nos. 2658/2663	4·75	7·50
	b. Booklet pane. No. 2658×4, 2659, 2660×2 and 2661/2663	9·50	
2659	80c. Frodo Baggins	65	1·00
2660	90c. Merry and Pippin (horiz)	70	1·00
2661	$1.30 Aragorn	1·00	1·50

NEW ZEALAND

2662	$1.50 Gandalf the White	1·10	1·75
2663	$2 Gollum (horiz)	1·50	2·50
2658/2663	Set of 6	4·75	7·50

Nos. 2652/2657 were each printed in sheets of 25.

Nos. 2652/2657 also exist as a set of six miniature sheets, each containing a single stamp, which were only available at a premium of $3 over the face value of the stamps.

Nos. 2658/2663 were either issued as strips of six, or as a $9 booklet, No. SB119, containing pane No. 2658b, with the surplus paper retained in both circumstances.

2003 (7 Nov). Welpex 2003 National Stamp Exhibition, Wellington. Sheet 120×100 mm containing Nos. 2626/2628. Perf 14.

MS2664 $1.50 New Zealand v France, 1986; $1.50 All Blacks jersey; $2 New Zealand v England, 1997........ 4·25 6·50

BEST OF 2003. A further miniature sheet as described below No. 2042 was distributed by the Philatelic Bureau to customers purchasing a certain amount of material during 2003. The sheet comprised Nos. 2570, 2576 and 2602.

Imperforate sheets of Nos. 2618/2622 and a *se-tenant* strip comprising Nos. 2639/2643 were also distributed.

630 Hamadryas Baboon

631 New Zealand Team

(Des Donna McKenna (Nos. 2665/2669) or Lindy Fisher (No. **MS**2670))

2004 (28 Jan). New Zealand Zoo Animals. T **630** and similar vert designs. Multicoloured.

(a) Litho Cartor. Ordinary gum. Size 29×39 mm. Phosphorised paper. Perf 13½×13.

2665	40c. Type **630**	45	25
2666	90c. Malayan Sun Bear	85	1·00
2667	$1.30 Red Panda	1·25	1·50
2668	$1.50 Ring-tailed Lemur	1·40	1·50
2669	$2 Spider Monkey	1·60	1·75
2665/2669	Set of 5	5·00	5·50
MS2670	125×90 mm. Nos. 2668/2669	3·00	3·50

(b) Litho Pemara (No. 2671) or SNP Sprint (No. 2671a). Self-adhesive. Size 24×29 mm. Phosphor frame. Perf 13½×12½.

2671	40c. Type **630**	45	35
	a. Perf 11×11½	50	45
	ab. Booklet pane. No. 2671a×10	5·00	

No. **MS**2670 commemorates Chinese New Year. Year of the Monkey.

No. 2671 was printed in rolls of 100 and has the surplus self-adhesive paper around each stamp removed.

No. 2671a comes from $4 booklet, No. SB120, and has the surplus self-adhesive paper around the stamps retained.

(Des CommArts Design. Litho Southern Colour Print, Dunedin)

2004 (30 Jan). Hong Kong 2004 International Stamp Exhibition. Sheet 110×80 mm containing Nos. 2627/2628. Phosphorised paper. Perf 14.

MS2672 $1.50 All Blacks jersey; $2 New Zealand v England, 1997............... 2·50 3·50

(Des CommArts Design. Litho Southern Colour Print, Dunedin)

2004 (25 Feb). Rugby Sevens. T **631** and similar horiz designs. Multicoloured. Phosphorised paper. Perf 14×14½.

2673	40c. Type **631**	30	25
2674	90c. Hong Kong team	60	70
2675	$1.50 Hong Kong Stadium	1·00	1·50
2676	$2 Westpac Stadium, Wellington	1·25	2·00
2673/2676	Set of 4	2·75	4·00
MS2677	125×85 mm. Nos. 2673/2676	2·75	4·00

Stamps of the same design were issued by Hong Kong.

632 Parliament Building, Auckland, 1854

(Des D. Gray. Litho Walsall)

2004 (3 Mar–5 Apr). 150th Anniversary of First Official Parliament in New Zealand. T **632** and similar horiz designs. Phosphorised paper. Perf 14

2678	**632**	40c. purple and black	30	35
2679		45c. purple and black (5.4)	55	60
2680	–	90c. deep lilac and black	60	90
2681	–	$1.30 brownish grey and black	90	1·50
2682	–	$1.50 greenish blue and black	1·00	1·50
2683	–	$2 deep grey-green and black	1·25	1·75
2678/2683	Set of 6		4·25	6·00
MS2684	186×65 mm. Nos. 2678 and 2680/2683		3·00	5·00

Designs: 90c. Parliament Buildings, Wellington, 1865; $1.30 Parliament Buildings, Wellington, 1899; $1.50 Parliament House, Wellington, 1918; $2 The Beehive, Wellington, 1977.

Nos. 2685/2694. The three sets previously listed as Nos. 2685/2688, Draw it Yourself, Nos. 2689/2691, Wild Food, and Nos. 2692/2694, Kiwi Characters, have been deleted from this catalogue as it is now clear that they did not conform to listing criteria. *Prices (complete sets):*

Draw it Yourself. £10 *unused*, £25 *used*
Wild Food. £10 *unused*, £15 *used*
Kiwi Characters. £10 *unused*, £15 *used*

636 Kinnard Haines Tractor

637 Dragonfish

(Des R. Jones. Litho Southern Colour Print, Dunedin)

2004 (5 Apr). Historic Farm Equipment. T **636** and similar horiz designs. Multicoloured. Phosphorised paper. Perf 14.

2695	45c. Type **636**	45	25
2696	90c. Fordson F tractor with plough	80	65
2697	$1.35 Burrell traction engine	1·25	2·00
2698	$1.50 Threshing mill	1·25	1·60
2699	$2 Duncan's Seed Drill	1·60	2·00
2695/2699	Set of 5	4·75	6·00

The stamps also exist in six miniature sheets, each 148×109 mm with a line of roulettes at left. The stamps in these miniature sheets are larger than Nos. 2695/2699.

Five of the miniature sheets contain Nos. 2695/2699 as single stamps and the sixth sheet contains all six designs.

These miniature sheets were only available from a booklet, No. SP5, printed by Wyatt and Wilson, containing stamps with a face value of $12.40, but sold at $19.95.

(Des Cato Design. Litho Southern Colour Print, Dunedin)

2004 (5 May). Wearable Art. T **637** and similar vert designs. Multicoloured. Phosphorised paper. Perf 14.

2701	45c. Type **637**	25	15
2702	90c. Persephone's Descent (man in armour costume)	50	50
2703	$1.35 Meridian (woman in silk costume)	70	1·10
2704	$1.50 Taunga Ika (woman in net costume)	75	1·25
2705	$2 Cailleach Na Mara (woman in sea witch costume)	90	1·50
2701/2705	Set of 5	2·75	4·00

638 Magnolia, Vulcan

639

(Des CommArts Design. Litho Southern Colour Print, Dunedin)

2004 (2 June). Garden Flowers. T **638** and similar vert designs. Multicoloured. Phosphorised paper. Perf 13½.

2706	45c. Type **638**	30	15
2707	90c. Helleborus (unnamed hybrid)	55	50
2708	$1.35 Nerine, Anzac	80	1·25
2709	$1.50 Rhododendron, Charisma	80	1·40
2710	$2 Delphinium, Sarita	1·25	1·50
2706/2710	Set of 5	3·25	4·25
MS2711	160×65 mm. Nos. 2706/2710	3·25	4·25

The 45c. stamp in No. **MS**2711 was impregnated with the fragrance of Magnolia.

NEW ZEALAND

(Litho Southern Colour Print, Dunedin)

2004 (26 June). Salon du Timbre International Stamp Exhibition, Paris. Sheet, 125×95 mm, containing designs from Nos. **MS**2664 and 2676. Perf 14 ($1.50) or 14×14½ ($2).
MS2712 $1.50 New Zealand v France, 1986; $1.50 All Blacks jersey; $2 Westpac Stadium............... 2·75 3·50

2004 (29 June). Emergency 5c. Provisional Stamp. Die-cut wavy line.
2713 **639** 5c. steel-blue and scarlet-vermilion ..... 2·00 2·50

640 Skippers Canyon (The Ford of Bruinen)

(Des CommArts Design. Litho Southern Colour Print, Dunedin (Nos. 2714/2722) or SNP Sprint (Nos. 2723/2726))

2004 (7 July). Making of *The Lord of the Rings* Film Trilogy (4th issue). *Home of Middle Earth*. T **640** and similar horiz designs. Multicoloured.

(a) Ordinary gum. Designs 40×30 mm. Phosphorised paper. Perf 14.

2714	45c. Type **640**	35	50
	a. Vert pair. Nos. 2714/2715...............	70	1·00
	b. Block of 8. Nos. 2714/2721	6·50	9·00
2715	45c. Arwen facing Black Riders	35	50
2716	90c. Mount Olympus (South of Rivendell).....	65	1·00
	a. Vert pair. Nos. 2716/2717...............	1·25	2·00
2717	90c. Gimli and Legolas	65	1·00
2718	$1.50 Erewhon (Edoras).............................	1·10	1·75
	a. Vert pair. Nos. 2718/2719...............	2·10	3·50
2719	$1.50 Gandalf the White, Legolas, Gimli and Aragorn riding to Rohan	1·10	1·75
2720	$2 Tongariro (Emyn Muil, Mordor)	1·50	2·00
	a. Vert pair. Nos. 2720/2721...............	3·00	4·00
2721	$2 Frodo and Sam	1·50	2·00
2714/2721 Set of 8...		6·50	9·00
MS2722 100×180 mm. Nos. 2714/2721...................		7·25	9·00

(b) Designs 29×24 mm. Self-adhesive. One side phosphor band. Perf 11½×11.

2723	45c. Skippers Canyon (The Ford of Bruinen)	45	45
	a. Block of 4. Nos. 2723/2726	2·00	2·50
	ba. Booklet pane. Nos. 2723/2724 each×3 and Nos. 2725/2726 each×2...............	5·50	
2724	45c. Arwen facing Black Riders	45	45
2725	90c. Mount Olympus (South of Rivendell).....	65	1·00
2726	90c. Gimli and Legolas	65	1·00
2723/2726 Set of 4...		2·00	2·50

Nos. 2714/2721 were printed together, *se-tenant*, as vertical pairs in blocks of eight or throughout sheets of 50.

Nos. 2714/2721 also exist as horizontal pairs in a miniature sheet (No. **MS**2722).

Nos. 2723/2726, on which the phosphor shows pink under UV light, were printed in sheets of 100 (45c.) sheets of 50 (90c.) or as a coil of 100 (45c.).

Nos. 2723/2726 were also available as blocks of four and in $6.30 booklet, No. SB124, containing pane No. 2723ba with the surplus self-adhesive paper retained in both instances.

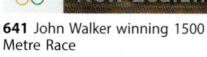

641 John Walker winning 1500 Metre Race

642 Children playing in the Sea

(Des Saatchi and Saatchi, Wellington. Litho and lenticular Xtreme Graphics USA)

2004 (2 Aug). Olympic Games, Athens. Gold Medal Winners. T **641** and similar horiz designs. Multicoloured. Self-adhesive. Perf 10½.

2727	45c. Type **641**	60	40
	a. Horiz strip of 4. Nos. 2727/2730	4·50	4·75
2728	90c. Yvette Williams (long jump).................	95	1·00
2729	$1.50 Ian Ferguson and Paul MacDonald (kayaking)..	1·60	2·00
2730	$2 Peter Snell (800 metre race)..................	1·75	1·75
	a. Lenticular image inverted	£2000	
2727/2730 Set of 4...		4·50	4·75

Nos. 2727/2730 were available as strips of four stamps or in sheets of 16. They were printed by lenticular process, producing 3-D animated images. Examples of No. 2730a were sold from at least three post offices. Other values purporting to have the lenticular image inverted are considered to be forgeries.

(Litho Southern Colour Print)

2004 (28 Aug). World Stamp Exhibition, Singapore. Sheet 125×95 mm containing Nos. 2716/2719. Multicoloured. Phosphorised paper. Perf 14.
MS2731 90c. Gimli and Legolas; 90c. Mount Olympus (South of Rivendell); $1.50 Gandalf the White, Legolas, Gimli and Aragorn riding to Rohan; $1.50 Erewhon (Edoras)................................ 3·00 4·00

(Des CommArts Design. Litho Southern Colour Print, Dunedin)

2004 (1 Sept). Tourism (1st series). Horiz designs as T **622**, Multicoloured. Phosphorised paper. Perf 13½.

2732	$1.50 The Bath House, Rotorua	1·25	1·75
2733	$1.50 Pohutu Geyser, Rotorua	1·25	1·75
2734	$1.50 Hawke's Bay	1·25	1·75
2735	$1.50 Lake Wakatipu, Queenstown...........	1·25	1·75
2736	$1.50 Mitre Peak, Milford Sound..............	1·25	1·75
2737	$1.50 Kaikoura	1·25	1·75
2732/2737 Set of 6...		6·50	9·50

See also Nos. 2868/2873.

(Des Chromotoaster. Litho Southern Colour Print, Dunedin)

2004 (1 Sept). Children's Health. A Day at the Beach. T **642** and similar vert designs. Multicoloured.

(a) Size 30×40 mm. Ordinary gum. Phosphorised paper. Perf 14.

2738	45c.+5c. Type **642**....................................	35	60
2739	90c.+5c. People in dinghy and swimmer............	65	1·00
MS2740 102×90 mm. Nos. 2738/2739 and 45c.+5c. Children fishing (25×30 mm). (Perf 14×14½)............		1·40	2·00

No. 2741 was available as single stamps or in sheets of 100.

Some examples of No. 2741 showed phosphor bands of various sizes at the foot of the stamp.

(b) Size 24×29 mm. Self-adhesive. Phosphor frame. Perf 9½×10.

2741	45c.+5c. Children fishing	35	60

643 Christmas Dinner

644 Christmas Dinner

(Des P. Hooker. Litho Southern Colour Print, Dunedin)

2004 (4 Oct). Christmas. T **643** and similar diamond-shaped designs. Multicoloured.

(a) Ordinary gum. Designs 49×49 mm. Phosphorised paper. Perf 14½.

2742	45c. Type **643**..	40	10
2743	90c. Traditional Maori meal.......................	65	45
2744	$1.35 Barbecued Prawns and Salmon.......	95	1·25
2745	$1.50 Pie and salad...................................	1·00	1·50
2746	$2 Plum pudding and pavlova...................	1·40	1·75
2742/2746 Set of 5...		4·00	4·50

*(b) Vert designs as T **644**. Self-adhesive. Phosphor frame. Perf 10.*

2747	45c. Type **644**..	45	40
	a. Booklet pane. No. 2747×10................	4·00	
2748	90c. Traditional Maori meal.......................	80	1·50
2749	$1 Christmas cake and cards.....................	95	1·25
	a. Booklet pane. No. 2749×8.................	7·00	

Nos. 2742/2746 and No. 2748 were each printed in sheets of 50 stamps. No. 2747 was issued in rolls of 100 and $4.50 stamp booklet, No. SB125. No. 2749 was issued in $8 booklet, No. SB126.

The surplus self-adhesive paper around each stamp in booklets Nos. SB125/SB126 was retained.

(Litho Southern Colour Print, Dunedin)

2004 (29 Oct). Baypex 2004 Hawke's Bay Stamp Show. Sheet 130×70 mm, containing Nos. 1934f and 2734. Multicoloured. Phosphorised paper. Perf 13½.
MS2750 $1.50 Hawke's Bay, $3 Cape Kidnappers............ 3·25 4·50

NEW ZEALAND

645 White-water Rafting   **646** Sheep

(Des CommArts Design. Litho Southern Colour Print, Dunedin)

2004 (1 Dec). Extreme Sports. T **645** and similar horiz designs. Multicoloured. Phosphorised paper. Perf 14.

2751	45c. Type **645**	35	25
2752	90c. Snowsports	60	80
2753	$1.35 Skydiving	1·00	1·50
2754	$1.50 Jet boating	1·00	1·60
2755	$2 Bungy jumping	1·25	1·75
2751/2755 Set of 5		3·75	5·50

The stamps also exist in six miniature sheets, each 148×110 mm with a line of roulettes at left.

Five of the miniature sheets contain Nos. 2751/2755 as single stamps and the sixth miniature sheet contains all six designs.

These miniature sheets were only available from a booklet, No. SP6, containing stamps with a face value of $12.40, but sold at $14.95.

Best of 2004. A further set of miniature sheets as described below No. 2042 were distributed by the Philatelic Bureau to customers purchasing a certain amount of material during 2004. The sheets comprised; 1. Nos. 2669, 2676 and 2683; 2. Nos. 2699, 2705 and 2710; 3. Nos. 2720, 2755 and 2746.

Imperforate sheets and mint and cancelled *se-tenant* strips of Nos. 2701/2705 were also distributed.

(Des S. Sakaria. Litho Southern Colour Print, Dunedin)

2005 (12 Jan). Farmyard Animals and Chinese New Year. Year of the Rooster. T **646** and similar vert designs. Multicoloured.

(a) Ordinary gum. Phosphorised paper. Perf 14.

2757	45c. Type **646**	45	40
	a. Horiz strip of 5. Nos. 2757/2761	4·75	5·50
2758	90c. Sheep Dog and Puppy	80	90
2759	$1.35 Pigs	1·25	1·50
2760	$1.50 Rooster	1·25	1·40
2761	$2 Rooster perched on farm equipment	1·60	1·75
2757/2761 Set of 5		4·75	5·50
MS2762 126×90 mm. Nos. 2760/2761		3·50	4·25

(b) Size 24×30 mm. Self-adhesive. Phosphor frame. Perf 11.

2763	45c. Sheep	45	40
	a. Booklet pane. No. 2763×10	4·00	

Nos. 2757/2761 were available printed *se-tenant* as horizontal strips of five with the backgrounds forming a composite design and also in single stamp sheets.

No. 2763 was issued in rolls of 100 and $4.50 stamp booklet, No. SB127, both of which have the surplus self-adhesive paper retained.

647 Beneficiaries (Centenary of Rotary International)   **648** 1855 Full Face Queen (Chalon head), London Print (No. 1)

(Des R. Jones. Litho Southern Colour Print, Dunedin)

2005 (2 Feb). Anniversaries of Organisations. T **647** and similar horiz designs. Multicoloured. Phosphorised paper. Perf 14.

2764	45c. Type **647**	45	50
2765	45c. Rural development (50th Anniversary of the Lions)	45	50
2766	45c. Canoeists (150th Anniversary of YMCA)	45	50
2767	$1.50 Building development (Centenary of Rotary International)	1·00	1·50
2768	$1.50 Miniature train (50th Anniversary of the Lions)	1·00	1·50
2769	$1.50 Beneficiaries jumping (150th Anniversary of YMCA)	1·00	1·50
2764/2769 Set of 6		4·00	5·25
MS2770 130×100 mm. Nos. 2764/2769 and central gutter		4·50	5·25

(Des Totem Design. Litho Southern Colour Print, Dunedin)

2005 (2 Mar). 150th Anniversary of New Zealand Stamps (1st issue). Stamps of 1855–1905. T **648** and similar vert designs. Multicoloured. Phosphorised paper. Perf 14.

2771	45c. Type **648**	35	25
2772	90c. 1873 Newspaper (Nos. 143/145)	60	90
2773	$1.35 1891 Government Life (No. L5)	90	1·60
2774	$1.50 1989 Pictorial, Mount Cook (No. 259)	1·00	1·75
2775	$2 1901 Universal Postage (No. 277)	1·25	1·75
2771/2775 Set of 5		3·50	5·50
MS2776 160×80 mm. Nos. 2771/2775		3·50	5·50

See also Nos. 2777/2784 and 2791/**MS**2796.

(Des Totem Design. Litho SNP Sprint (Nos. 2783/2784) or Southern Colour Print, Dunedin (others))

2005 (6 Apr). 150th Anniversary of New Zealand Stamps (2nd issue). Stamps of 1905–1955. Vert designs as T **648**. Multicoloured.

(a) Phosphorised paper. Ordinary gum. Perf 14.

2777	45c. 1906 New Zealand Exhibition (No. 371)	35	25
2778	90c. 1931 Health (No. 546)	60	90
2779	$1.35 1935 Airmail (No. 571)	90	1·60
2780	$1.50 1946 Peace (No. 676)	1·00	1·75
2781	$2 1954 Queen Elizabeth II (No. 736)	1·25	1·75
2777/2781 Set of 5		3·50	5·50
MS2782 160×80 mm. Nos. 2777/2781		3·50	5·50

(b) Designs 25×30 mm. Phosphor frame. Self-adhesive. Perf 13.

2783	45c. As No 2777	50	65
	a. Horiz pair. Nos. 2783/2784	1·25	1·60
	b. Perf 11	50	65
	ba. Booklet pane. No. 2783×10	4·50	
2784	90c. As No 2778	75	1·00
	b. Perf 11	75	1·00
	ba. Booklet pane. No. 2784×10	7·00	

Nos. 2783/2784, on which the phosphor shows pink under UV light, were printed together, *se-tenant*, as horizontal pairs and separately in booklets of ten.

No. 2784 was also available as a coil of 100 stamps.

(Litho Southern Colour Print, Dunedin)

2005 (21 Apr). Pacific Explorer World Stamp Exhibition, Sydney. Phosphorised paper. Perf 14.

MS2785 109×90 mm. Nos. 2775 and 2781 .... 2·50 3·50

649 Café, 1910s   **650** All Blacks Jersey

(Litho Wyatt and Wilson)

2005 (4 May). Café Culture. T **649** and similar cup-shaped designs. Multicoloured. Phosphor frame. Self-adhesive. Die-cut.

2786	45c. Type **649**	45	30
	a. Horiz strip of 5. Nos. 2786/2790	4·75	6·00
2787	90c. Café, 1940s	80	90
2788	$1.35 Café, 1970s	1·25	1·50
2789	$1.50 Tables outside café on pavement, 1990s	1·25	2·00
2790	$2 Internet café, 2005	1·60	1·75
2786/2790 Set of 5		4·75	5·75

Nos. 2786/2790 were printed together, *se-tenant*, in horizontal strips of five stamps, and also in separate sheets of 25.

(Des Totem Design. Litho Southern Colour Print, Dunedin)

2005 (7 June). 150th Anniversary of New Zealand Stamps (3rd issue). Stamps of 1955–2005. Vert designs as T **648**. Multicoloured. Phosphorised paper. Perf 14.

2791	45c. 1965 50th Anniversary of the Gallipoli Landing (No. 827)	35	25
2792	90c. 1988 Round Kiwi (No. 1490)	60	90
2793	$1.35 1990 The Achievers Katherine Sheppard (No. 1550)	90	1·60
2794	$1.50 1994 Maori Myths Maui (No. 1807)	1·00	1·75
2795	$2 2003 Centenary of New Zealand Test Rugby (No. 2627)	1·25	1·75
2791/2795 Set of 5		3·50	5·50
MS2796 160×80 mm. Nos. 2791/2795		3·50	5·50

NEW ZEALAND

(Des Saatchi and Saatchi. Litho Southern Colour Print, Dunedin)

2005 (1 June). DHL New Zealand Lions Rugby Series. T **650** and similar jersey-shaped designs. One phosphor band at foot. Self-adhesive. Die-cut.

2797	45c. black and grey	30	50
	a. Pair. Nos. 2797/2798	60	1·00
2798	45c. multicoloured	30	50
2799	$1.50 black and grey	75	1·00
	a. Pair. Nos. 2799/2800	1·50	2·00
2800	$1.50 multicoloured	75	1·00
2797/2800 Set of 4		1·90	2·75

Designs: No. 2797, T **650**; No. 2798, Red Lions jersey; No. 2799, As No. 2797; No. 2800, As No. 2798.

Nos. 2797/2798 and 2799/2800 were each printed together, *se-tenant*, as horizontal pairs in sheets of 24 stamps.

651 Kiwi

652 Kakapo ('Relies heavily on camouflage for defence')

(Litho Southern Colour Print, Dunedin)

2005 (6 July). Personalised Stamps. T **651** and similar square designs. Multicoloured. Phosphorised paper. Perf 14.

2801	45c. Type **651**	45	75
	a. Sheetlet of 10. Nos. 2801/2810	7·00	9·75
2802	45c. Pohutukawa (native Christmas tree)	45	75
2803	45c. Champagne glasses	45	75
2804	45c. Balloons	45	75
2805	45c. Wedding bands	45	75
2806	45c. Gift box	45	75
2807	45c. Baby's hand	45	75
2808	$1.50 Globe	1·25	1·60
2809	$2 As Type **651**	1·60	2·00
2810	$2 Fern	1·60	2·00
2801/2810 Set of 10		7·00	9·75

Nos. 2801/2810 were each printed together, *se-tenant*, in sheetlets of ten stamps.

(Des Cue Design. Litho Southern Colour Print, Dunedin)

2005 (3 Aug). Endangered Species. Kakapo. T **652** and similar horiz designs showing the Kakapo with different facts inscribed. Multicoloured. Phosphorised paper. Perf 14.

2811	45c. Type **652**	80	1·00
	a. Strip of 4. Nos. 2811/2814	3·00	3·50
2812	45c. 'Night Parrot unique to New Zealand'	80	1·00
2813	45c. 'Nocturnal bird living on the forest floor'	80	1·00
2814	45c. 'Endangered – only 86 known surviving'	80	1·00
2811/2814 Set of 4		3·00	3·50

Nos. 2811/2814 were each printed together, *se-tenant*, in horizontal and vertical rows within sheets of 16 stamps.

653 Child and Horse

654 Baby Jesus

(Des Donna Cross. Litho Southern Colour Print, Dunedin)

2005 (3 Aug). Children's Health. Pets. T **653** and similar vert designs. Multicoloured.

(a) Size 30×40 mm. Ordinary gum. Phosphorised paper. Perf 14.

2815	45c.+5c. Type **653**	55	55
2816	90c.+5c. Child holding Rabbit	90	95
MS2817 100×90 mm. Nos. 2815/2816 and 45c.+5c. Children and Dog (25×30 mm) (Perf 14½×14)		2·50	2·50

(b) Size 25×30 mm. Self-adhesive. Phosphor frame. Die-cut perf 9½×10.

| 2818 | 45c.+5c. Children and Dog | 50 | 70 |

No. 2818 was available as single stamps or in sheets of 100.

(Litho Southern Colour Print, Dunedin)

2005 (18 Aug). TAIPEI 2005 International Stamp Exhibition. Sheet, 110×90 mm, containing Nos. 2733 and 2737. Phosphorised paper. Perf 13½.
MS2819 $1.50 Kaikoura; $1 Pohutu Geyser, Rotorua... 2·50 3·25

(Des A. Petrov. Litho Southern Colour Print, Dunedin (Nos. 2820/2824) or SEP Sprint, Australia (Nos. 2825/2826))

2005 (5 Oct–2 Nov). Christmas. T **654** and similar multicoloured designs.

(a) Ordinary gum. Designs 35×35 mm. Phosphorised paper. Perf 14½.

2820	45c. Type **654** (2.11)	30	15
	a. Horiz strip of 5. Nos. 2820/2824	3·50	6·00
2821	90c. Mary and Joseph (2.11)	55	55
2822	$1.35 Shepherd (2.11)	90	1·10
2823	$1.50 Wise Men (2.11)	1·10	1·50
2824	$2 Star (2.11)	1·25	2·00
2820/2824 Set of 5		3·50	4·75

(b) Size 24×29 mm. Self-adhesive. Phosphor frame. Die-cut perf 11.

2825	45c. Type **654** (2.11)	45	35
	a. Booklet pane. No. 2825×10	4·00	
2826	$1 Gifts on straw	85	1·00
	a. Booklet pane. No. 2826×10	7·50	

Nos. 2820/2824 were printed together, *se-tenant*, in horizontal strips of five stamps and separately in sheets of 50.

No. 2825 was issued in rolls of 100 and $4.50 stamp booklet, No. SB130.

No. 2826 was issued in $10 stamp booklet, No. SB131.

The surplus self-adhesive paper around in each stamp in booklets Nos. SB130/SB131 was retained.

655 King Kong

656 Lucy opening the Wardrobe

(Des Saatchi & Saatchi. Litho Southern Colour Print, Dunedin)

2005 (19 Oct). *King Kong* (film). T **655** and similar vert designs. Multicoloured. Phosphorised paper. Perf 14½×15.

2827	45c. Type **655**	40	35
	a. Horiz strip of 5. Nos. 2827/2831	4·75	5·50
2828	90c. Carl Denham	75	70
2829	$1.35 Ann Darrow	1·25	1·50
2830	$1.50 Jack Driscoll	1·40	1·50
2831	$2 Ann Darrow and Jack Driscoll	1·60	1·75
2827/2831 Set of 5		4·75	5·25
MS2832 180×65 mm. Nos. 2827/2831		5·25	6·00

Nos. 2827/2831 were printed together, *se-tenant*, in horizontal strips of five stamps and separately in sheets of 25.

(Des A. Hollows. Litho Southern Colour Print, Dunedin)

2005 (17 Nov). National Stamp Show, Auckland. Sheet, 120×90 mm, containing Nos. 2774, 2780 and 2794. Phosphorised paper. Perf 14.
MS2833 $1.50 1989 Pictorial, Mount Cook (No. 259); $1.50 1946 Peace (No. 676); $1.50 1994 Maori Myths, Maui (No. 1807) ... 4·00 5·00

(Des Commarts Design)

2005 (1 Dec). Making of *The Chronicles of Narnia. The Lion the Witch and the Wardrobe* (film). T **656** and similar multicoloured designs.

(a) Ordinary gum. Litho Southern Colour Print. Phosphorised paper. Perf 14×14½ (vert) or 14½×14 (horiz).

2834	45c. Type **656**	40	25
2835	90c. Lucy, Edmund, Peter and Susan (*horiz*)	75	80
2836	$1.35 The White Witch tempting Edmund (*horiz*)	1·25	2·00
2837	$1.50 Dissenters turned to stone statues	1·40	1·60
2838	$2 Lucy and body of Aslan (*horiz*)	1·60	2·00
2834/2838 Set of 5		4·75	6·00

(b) Self-adhesive. Litho Wyatt & Wilson. Designs as Nos. 2834/2838 but smaller. Phosphor frame. Die-cut perf 13×12½.

MS2839 200×70 mm. 45c. Type **656** (25×35 mm); 90c. As No. 2835 (35×25 mm); $1.35 As No. 2836 (35×25 mm); $1.50 As No. 2837 (25×35 mm); $2 As No. 2838 (35×25 mm) ... 8·00 9·00

Nos. 2834/2838 also exist as a set of five miniature sheets, each containing a single stamp, which was sold at $8.70, a premium of $2.50 over the face value.

BEST OF 2005. A further set of miniature sheets as described below No. 2042 were distributed by the Philatelic Bureau to customers purchasing a certain amount of material during 2005. The sheets comprised: 1. Nos. 2771, 2774 and 2775; 2. Nos. 2777, 2780 and 2781; 3. Nos. 2791, 2794 and 2795.

Imperforate sheets of Nos. 2791/2795 and a perforated *se-tenant* strip comprising the same five stamps were also distributed.

NEW ZEALAND

657 Labrador Retriever Guide Dog

658 Street Scene, *circa* 1930

(Des Stephen Fuller)

2006 (4 Jan). Chinese New Year. Year of the Dog. T **657** and similar vert designs. Multicoloured.

(a) Ordinary gum. Litho Southern Colour Print. Phosphorised paper. Perf 14.

2840	45c. Type **657**	50	25
2841	90c. German Shepherd Dog	90	70
2842	$1.35 Jack Russell Terrier	1·40	1·25
2843	$1.50 Golden Retriever	1·50	1·90
2844	$2 Huntaway (New Zealand Sheepdog)	1·75	2·00
2840/2844	Set of 5	5·50	5·50
MS2845	124×89 mm. Nos. 2843/2844	5·50	6·00

(b) Self-adhesive. Size 25×30 mm
(i) Litho Pemara, Australia. Phosphor frame on three sides. Die-cut perf 13.

2846	45c. Type **657**	50	70

(ii) Litho Sprintpak, Australia. Phosphor frame. Die-cut perf 11½.

2847	45c. Type **657**	50	70
	a. Booklet pane. No. 2847×10	5·00	

No. 2846 was issued in rolls of 100. No. 2847 was issued in $4.50 stamp booklet, No. SB132.

(Des CommArts Design. Litho Southern Colour Print, Dunedin)

2006 (3 Feb). 75th Anniversary of Hawke's Bay Earthquake. T **658** and similar horiz designs. Multicoloured. Phosphorised paper. Perf 14.

2848	45c. Type **658**	70	70
	a. Sheetlet of 20. Nos. 2848/2867	12·00	12·00
2849	45c. Aerial view of devastated city of Napier	70	70
	a. Horiz pair. Nos. 2849/2850	1·40	1·40
2850	45c. Aerial view with roofless church and intact Public Trust Building, Napier	70	70
2851	45c. Fire engine and crew	70	70
2852	45c. HMS *Veronica*	70	70
2853	45c. Sailors from HMS *Veronica* clearing debris	70	70
2854	45c. Red Cross nurses with hospital patient	70	70
2855	45c. Rescue services	70	70
2856	45c. Abandoned vehicles on broken road ('Devastation')	70	70
2857	45c. Outdoor hospital ward, Botanical Gardens, Napier ('Medical services')	70	70
2858	45c. Emergency mail plane	70	70
2859	45c. Refugees on road	70	70
2860	45c. Refugee tents, Nelson Park	70	70
2861	45c. Makeshift cooking facilities, Hastings	70	70
2862	45c. Maori women ('Community spirit')	70	70
2863	45c. Refugees boarding train	70	70
2864	45c. Reconstruction work ('Building industry')	70	70
2865	45c. Hastings Street rebuilt in Art Deco style, 1933	70	70
2866	45c. Carnival procession ('Celebrations')	70	70
2867	45c. Entrance to National Tobacco Company building, Ahuriri, 2005	70	70
2848/2867	Set of 20	12·00	12·00

Nos. 2848/2867 were printed together, *se-tenant*, in sheetlets of 20 stamps.

Nos. 2849/2850 form a composite design showing an aerial view of Napier after the earthquake.

Nos. 2848/2867 do also exist in seven miniature sheets, each 150×110 mm, containing two examples each of Nos. 2848/2850, 2865/2867, 2851/2853, 2854/2855, 2856, 2858 and 2863, 2857 and 2859/2860 and 2861/2862 and 2864.

These only came from a miniature sheet booklet, No. SP7, containing stamps with a face value of $18.80, which was sold for $19.95.

(Des CommArts Design. Litho Southern Colour Print, Dunedin)

2006 (1 Mar). Tourism (2nd series). Horiz designs as T **622**. Multicoloured. Phosphorised paper. Perf 13½×14.

2868	$1.50 Lake Wanaka	1·40	1·75
2869	$1.50 Mount Taranaki	1·40	1·75
2870	$1.50 Halfmoon Bay, Stewart Island	1·40	1·75
2871	$1.50 Franz Josef Glacier, West Coast	1·40	1·75
2872	$1.50 Huka Falls, Taupo	1·40	1·75
2873	$1.50 Cathedral Cove, Coromandel	1·40	1·75
2868/2873	Set of 6	7·50	9·50

659 Queen Elizabeth II

660 Champagne Glasses

(Litho and embossed Cartor)

2006 (21 Apr). 80th Birthday of Queen Elizabeth II. Perf 13½.

2874	**659** $5 multicoloured	4·25	6·00
MS2875	150×100 mm. No. 1272 of Jersey; $5 Type **659** (sold at $17.50)	12·00	12·00

An identical miniature sheet was issued by Jersey on the same date.

(Des Communication Arts. Litho Southern Colour Print, Dunedin)

2006 (3 May). Personalised Stamps. T **660** and similar horiz designs. Multicoloured. Phosphorised paper. Perf 14.

2876	45c. Type **660**	45	65
	a. Sheetlet of 10. Nos. 2876/2885 and 5 stamp-size labels	7·00	9·00
2877	45c. Buzzy Bee (toy)	45	65
2878	45c. Silver Fern	45	65
2879	45c. Pohutukawa flower	45	65
2880	45c. Christmas star decorations	45	65
2881	45c. Engagement and wedding rings	45	65
2882	45c. Red Rose	45	65
2883	$1.50 As No. 2878	1·25	1·60
2884	$2 As No. 2879	1·60	2·00
2885	$2 As No. 2880	1·60	2·00
2876/2885	Set of 10	7·00	9·00

Nos. 2876/2885 were printed together, *se-tenant*, in sheetlets of ten stamps containing two horizontal strips of five stamps separated by five stamp-size labels inscribed 'Personalised Stamps 2006'.

2006 (27 May). Washington 2006 World Philatelic Exhibition. Sheet, 120×80 mm containing designs as Nos. 2809/2810 but without imprint date. Phosphorised paper. Perf 14.

MS2886	$2 Fern; $2 Type **651**	4·50	4·50

Maori Performing Arts. A set of five stamps (45c., 90c., $1.35, $1.50 and $2) with the above title was due to be issued on 7 June 2006. The stamps were conventionally gummed but the 45c. value was also prepared in self-adhesive coils and booklets of ten stamps.

Three days prior to issue date, New Zealand Post announced that the issue would be withdrawn, but some stamps, in each format, including first day covers, had already been sent out to Philatelic Bureau customers.

661 Wind Farm, Tararua, Palmerston North

662 '5' and Tomatoes

(Des Watermark. Litho Southern Colour Print, Dunedin)

2006 (5 July). Renewable Energy. T **661** and similar multicoloured designs. Phosphorised paper. Perf 14.

2887	45c. Type **661**	75	25
2888	90c. Roxburgh Dam, Central Otago (hydro).	1·50	90
2889	$1.35 Biogas production, Waikato	1·75	1·50
2890	$1.50 Wairakei Geothermal Power Station	2·00	2·50
2891	$2 Solar-powered lighthouse, Cape Reinga (vert)	3·50	3·00
2887/2891	Set of 5	8·50	7·25

(Des Cue Design. Litho Southern Colour Print, Dunedin)

2006 (2 Aug). Children's Health. 5+A Day Healthy Eating Campaign. T **662** and similar multicoloured designs.

(a) Ordinary gum. Phosphorised paper. Perf 14.

2892	45c.+5c. Type **662** (30×40 mm)	85	1·00
2893	90c.+10c. +and Oranges (30×40 mm)	1·50	2·00
2894	$1.35 a and Garlic (30×30 mm)	1·75	2·00

NEW ZEALAND

2895	$1.50 DAY and Kiwi Fruit (40×30 mm)	2·25	2·75
2896	$2 Hand silhouette and Red Cabbage (30×40 mm)	2·50	3·00
2892/2896 Set of 5		8·00	9·75
MS2897 120×90 mm. Nos. 2892/2896		9·00	10·00

(b) Self-adhesive. Phosphor frame. Die-cut perf 10.

2898	45c.+5c. Type **662** (25×30 mm)	1·25	1·25

663 Gold Panning, circa 1880s

664 Decorated Silver Fern (Hanna McLachlan)

(Des Cato Partners. Litho Southern Colour Print, Dunedin)

2006 (6 Sept). Gold Rush. T **663** and similar multicoloured designs. Phosphorised paper. Perf 14.

2899	45c. Type **663**	75	25
2900	90c. Settlement at Kurunui Creek, Thames, circa 1868 (horiz)	1·40	1·00
2901	$1.35 Chinese prospectors at Tuapeka, Otago, circa 1900s (horiz)	1·75	2·00
2902	$1.50 Last Otago gold escort at Roxburgh, 1901 (horiz)	1·90	2·50
2903	$2 Waterfront at Dunedin, circa 1900s (horiz)	2·25	3·00
2899/2903 Set of 5		7·25	8·00
MS2904 125×90 mm. As Nos. 2899/2903 but 'NEW ZEALAND' on stamp and fern symbol in gold		11·00	12·00

The bottom of the prospector's pan on Nos. 2899 and **MS**2904 is printed in thermochromic ink which fades temporarily when exposed to heat, making the gold nuggets visible.

The stamps within No. **MS**2904 have the country inscription 'NEW ZEALAND' on stamp and fern symbol die-stamped in gold.

(Litho Southern Colour Print, Dunedin)

2006 (4 Oct). Christmas. T **664** and similar square designs showing winning entries in children's stamp design competition What Christmas Means to Me. Multicoloured.

(a) Ordinary gum. Designs 34×34 mm. Phosphorised paper. Perf 14½.

2905	45c. Type **664**	60	15
	a. Sheetlet of 6. Nos. 2905/2910	3·25	2·75
2906	45c. Angel appearing to shepherds and magi (Isla Hewitt)	60	60
	a. Horiz strip of 5. Nos. 2906/2910	2·75	2·75
2907	45c. Extended family around Christmas tree (Caitlin Davidson)	60	60
2908	45c. Virgin Mary and baby Jesus (Maria Petersen)	60	60
2909	45c. Beach and Pohutakawa tree (Deborah Yoon)	60	60
2910	45c. New Zealand Wood Pigeon and Christmas star (Hannah Webster)	60	60
2911	90c. Santa hat on Kiwi Fruit (Pierce Higginson)	1·00	1·00
2912	$1.35 Kiwiana Christmas trees (Rosa Tucker)	1·50	1·60
2913	$1.50 Pattern of four Pohutakawa flowers (Sylvie Webby)	1·75	1·75
2914	$2 Camping at Christmas (Gemma Baldock)	2·00	2·00
2905/2914 Set of 10		9·00	8·50

(b) Size 24×29 mm. Self-adhesive. Phosphor frame. Die-cut perf 10.

2915	45c. Type **664**	50	40
	a. Booklet pane. No. 2915×10	5·00	
2916	$1.50 As No. 2913	1·40	1·75
	a. Booklet pane. No. 2916×10	14·00	

Nos. 2905/2910 were printed together, *se-tenant*, in sheetlets of six stamps. No. 2905 was also printed in ordinary sheets.

Nos. 2906/2910 were printed together, *se-tenant*, in horizontal strips of five stamps in sheets of 50.

No. 2915 was issued in rolls of 100 and $4.50 stamp booklet, No. SB133.

No. 2916 was issued in stamp booklet, No. SB134, sold at $13.50, providing a discount of $1.50 off the face value of the stamps.

Nos. 2915/2916 could be purchased as *se-tenant* pairs from the Philatelic Bureau.

665 Dragon Boat Festival

(Des The Church. Litho Southern Colour Print, Dunedin)

2006 (1 Nov). Summer Festivals. T **665** and similar horiz designs. Multicoloured. Phosphorised paper. Perf 14½.

2917	45c. Type **665**	75	40
	a. Horiz strip of 5. Nos. 2917/2921	7·25	7·25
2918	90c. Race day	1·40	90
2919	$1.35 Teddy bears' picnic	1·75	1·50
2920	$1.50 Outdoor concert	1·90	2·50
2921	$2 Jazz festival	2·25	2·75
2917/2921 Set of 5		7·25	7·25
MS2922 185×80 mm. Nos. 2917/2921		9·00	10·00

Nos. 2917/2921 were printed together, *se-tenant*, as horizontal strips of five in sheets of 25, and also in separate sheets.

2006 (2 Nov). Kiwipex 2006 International Stamp Exhibition, Christchurch. Sheet 120×90 mm. Phosphorised paper. Perf 14.

MS2923 As Nos. 2809/2810 but without imprint date (sold at $5)	4·50	7·00

No. **MS**2923 was sold at $5, a premium of $1 above the face value. The premium funded the NZ National Philatelic Trust.

(Litho Southern Colour Print, Dunedin)

2006 (16 Nov). Belgica '06 International Stamp Exhibition, Brussels. Sheet 120×90 mm. Phosphorised paper. Perf 14.

MS2924 Nos. 2883×2 and 2884	4·50	7·00

BEST OF 2006. A further set of miniature sheets as described below No. 2042 were distributed by the Philatelic Bureau to customers purchasing a certain amount of material in 2006. The sheets comprised: 1. Nos. 2844, 2852 and 2872; 2. Nos. 2879, 2891 and 2896; 3. Nos. 2903, 2914 and 2921.

Imperforate sheets of Nos. 2899/2903 and a perforated *se-tenant* strip comprising the same five stamps were also distributed.

666 Opening Ceremony, 1957

(Litho Southern Colour Print, Dunedin)

2007 (20 Jan). 50th Anniversary of Scott Base, Antarctica. T **666** and similar horiz designs. Multicoloured. Phosphorised paper. Perf 14.

2925	45c. Type **666**	1·50	40
2926	90c. Scott Base, 1990	2·50	1·10
2927	$1.35 Aerial view of Scott Base, 2000	3·00	2·00
2928	$1.50 'SCOTT BASE' sign	3·50	4·50
2929	$2 Scott Base, 2005	3·50	4·50
2925/2929 Set of 5		12·50	11·00

Nos. 2925/2929 also exist as a set of five miniature sheets, each containing a single stamp, which was sold at $8.70, a premium of $2.50 over the face value.

667 Kunekune Piglet   **668** Tuatara

(Des Cue Design. Litho Sprintpak, Australia)

2007 (7 Feb). Chinese New Year. Year of the Pig. T **667** and similar horiz designs. Multicoloured. Perf 14½×14.

2930	45c. Type **667**	75	40
2931	90c. Kunekune Pig	1·40	1·00
2932	$1.35 Arapawa Pig	1·75	2·00
2933	$1.50 Auckland Island Pig	1·90	3·00
2934	$2 Kunekune Pig, young sow, Ruby	2·25	3·00
2930/2934 Set of 5		7·00	8·50
MS2935 125×90 mm. Nos. 2933/2934		4·25	4·75

NEW ZEALAND

(Des P. Faulkner. Litho Southern Colour Print, Dunedin)

2007 (7 Mar). Native Wildlife. T **668** and similar circular designs. Multicoloured. Phosphorised frame. Self-adhesive. Die-cut perf 11½.

2936	45c. Type **668**		75	40
	a. Horiz strip of 5. Nos. 2936/2940		8·00	10·00
2937	90c. Kiwi		1·40	90
2938	$1.35 Hamilton's Frog		1·75	1·60
2939	$1.50 Yellow-eyed Penguin		2·50	3·00
2940	$2 Hector's Dolphin		2·50	3·00
2936/2940 Set of 5			8·00	8·00

The backing paper of Nos. 2936/2940 is divided into squares by lines of rouletting.

Nos. 2936/2940 were issued in separate sheets.

No. 2936a could only be purchased from the Philatelic Bureau.

(Litho Southern Colour Print, Dunedin)

2007 (30 Mar). Northland 2007 National Stamp Exhibition, Whangarei. Sheet 119×80 mm. Phosphorised paper. Perf 14.

MS2941 Nos. 2884 and 2891		7·00	8·00

669 Scouts of 1908 and Lieutenant Colonel David Cossgrove (NZ Scouts founder)

(Des S. Fuller. Litho Southern Colour Print, Dunedin)

2007 (24 Apr). Centenaries. T **669** and similar horiz designs. Multicoloured. Phosphorised paper. Perf 14.

2942	50c. Type **669**	1·25	1·40
	a. Horiz strip of 4. Nos. 2942/2945	4·25	4·75
	b. Block of 8. Nos. 2942/2949	16·00	18·00
2943	50c. Dr Truby King (founder of Plunket Society) and nurse with baby, 1920s	1·25	1·40
2944	50c. All Golds, first New Zealand rugby league team, 1907	1·25	1·40
2945	50c. Sister Suzanne Aubert (founder) and classroom at Home of Compassion, 1907	1·00	1·00
2946	$1 Parents with baby, 2007 (Plunket Society)	2·00	90
2947	$1.50 Elderly lady and carer, 2007 (Home of Compassion)	2·50	2·75
2948	$2 Kiwi rugby league team, 2007	3·50	4·75
	a. Horiz pair. Nos. 2948/2949	7·00	9·50
2949	$2 Scouts abseiling, 2007	3·50	4·75
2942/2949 Set of 8		16·00	18·00

Nos. 2942/2945 were printed together, *se-tenant*, in horizontal strips of four stamps in sheets of 20.

Nos. 2948/2949 were printed together, *se-tenant*, in horizontal pairs in sheets of 20.

No. 2942b could only be purchased from the Philatelic Bureau.

No. 2945 could also be purchased in sheets of 20 of the same design at $10 a sheet from the Philatelic Bureau.

Centenaries: Nos. 2942, 2949 World Scout Movement; Nos. 2943, 2946 Plunket Society; Nos. 2944, 2948 Rugby League in New Zealand; Nos. 2945, 2947 Home of Compassion.

2007 (9 May). Personalised Stamps. As Nos. 2876/2882 but new values. Multicoloured. Phosphorised paper. Perf 14.

2950	50c. Buzzy Bee (toy)	70	70
	a. Sheetlet of 7. Nos. 2950/2956 and 8 stamp-size labels	3·75	3·75
2951	50c. Pohutukawa flower	70	70
2952	50c. Engagement and wedding rings	70	70
2953	50c. Silver Fern	70	70
2954	50c. Type **660**	70	70
2955	50c. Red Rose	70	70
2956	50c. Christmas star decorations	70	70
2950/2956 Set of 7		3·75	3·75

Nos. 2950/2956 were printed together, *se-tenant*, in sheetlets of seven stamps alternated with eight stamp-size labels inscribed 'Personalised Stamps'.

670 Southern Cross and 0.5 m Zeiss Telescope at Stardome Observatory, Auckland

671 'good as gold'

(Des Capiche Design. Litho SEP Sprint)

2007 (6 June). Southern Skies. T **670** and similar horiz designs. Multicoloured. Phosphorised paper. Perf 13×13½.

2957	50c. Type **670**	1·50	45
2958	$1 Pleiades and 1 m McLellan telescope, Mount John Observatory, Tekapo	2·00	1·00
2959	$1.50 Trifid Nebula and 24 cm telescope, Ward Observatory, Wanganui	2·75	2·25
2960	$2 Southern Pinwheel and 1.8 m MOA telescope, Mount John Observatory	3·25	4·00
2961	$2.50 Large Magellanic Cloud and 11 m Southern African large telescope	4·00	4·50
2957/2961 Set of 5		12·00	11·00

The stamps also exist in six miniature sheets, each 150×110 mm with a line of roulettes at left. Five of the miniature sheets contain Nos. 2957/2961 as single stamps and the sixth sheet contains all five designs. These miniature sheets are only available from a booklet, No. SP8, containing stamps with a face value of $15, but sold for $19.90.

(Des Stamps Business. Litho Southern Colour Print)

2007 (4 July). Classic Kiwi (Kiwi slang). T **671** and similar horiz designs. Multicoloured. Phosphorised paper. Perf 14.

2962	50c. Type **671**	80	80
	a. Sheetlet of 20. Nos. 2962/2981	14·00	15·00
2963	50c. 'sweet as'	80	80
2964	50c. 'she'll be right'	80	80
2965	50c. 'hissy fit'	80	80
2966	50c. 'sparrow fart'	80	80
2967	50c. Kiwi and 'cuz'	80	80
2968	50c. 'away laughing'	80	80
2969	50c. 'tiki tour'	80	80
2970	50c. 'away with the fairies'	80	80
2971	50c. 'wop-wops'	80	80
2972	50c. 'hard yakka'	80	80
2973	50c. 'cods wallop'	80	80
2974	50c. 'boots and all'	80	80
2975	50c. 'shark and taties'	80	80
2976	50c. 'knackered'	80	80
2977	50c. 'laughing gear'	80	80
2978	50c. 'everyman and his dog'	80	80
2979	50c. 'bit of a dag'	80	80
2980	50c. 'dreaded lurgy'	80	80
2981	50c. 'rark up'	80	80
2962/2981 Set of 20		14·00	15·00

The shiny black portions at the right of Nos. 2962/2981 are printed in thermochromic ink which fades temporarily when exposed to heat, revealing translations of the Kiwi slang on the stamps.

Nos. 2962/2981 were printed together, *se-tenant*, in sheetlets of 20 stamps.

672 Electric Fence (Bill Gallagher), 1969

673 Girl releasing Peace Dove

(Des Tim Garman. Litho Southern Colour Print)

2007 (1 Aug). Clever Kiwis. New Zealand Inventions. T **672** and similar horiz designs. Multicoloured. Phosphorised paper. Perf 14.

2982	50c. Type **672**	60	30
2983	$1 Spreadable butter (Norris and Illingworth)	1·25	1·10
2984	$1.50 Mountain buggy, 1992	2·00	2·00
2985	$2 Jet boat (Bill Hamilton)	3·25	3·75
2986	$2.50 Tranquilliser gun (Colin Murdoch), 1950s	3·75	4·00
2982/2986 Set of 5		9·75	10·00

NEW ZEALAND

(Des Stamps Business. Litho Southern Colour Print)

2007 (3 Aug). Bangkok 2007 20th Asian International Stamp Exhibition. Sheet 80×70 mm. Phosphorised paper. Perf 14×14½.

MS2987	Nos. 2735/2736	4·00	4·00

(Des Stamps Business. Litho Southern Colour Print, Dunedin)

2007 (31 Aug). Huttpex 2007 Stampshow (National Exhibition), Lower Hutt. Sheet 120×90 mm. Phosphorised paper. Perf 14.

MS2988	Nos. 2960/2961	5·50	5·50

(Des Donna McKenna. Litho Southern Colour Print, Dunedin)

2007 (5 Sept). Children's Health. Peaceful World. T **673** and similar vert designs. Multicoloured.

(a) Size 30×40 mm. Ordinary gum. Phosphorised paper. Perf 14.

2989	50c.+10c. Type **673**	1·00	1·00
2990	$1+10c. Boy holding Japanese Crane	1·75	1·75
MS2991	100×90 mm. 50c.+10c. Girls with Peace Lily (24×29 mm) (Perf 14½×14) and Nos. 2989/2990	3·00	3·00
	a. Perf 14½×14×13½ (Girls with Peace Lily design), Perf 13½ (others)	3·00	3·00

(b) Size 24×29 mm. Self-adhesive. Irregular phosphor frame. Perf 10.

2992	50c.+10c. Girls with Peace Lily	1·50	1·50

674 Queen Elizabeth II and Prince Philip, circa 2007

675 Christmas Symbols (Sione Vao)

(Des Communication Arts. Litho Southern Colour Print, Dunedin)

2007 (5 Sept). Diamond Wedding of Queen Elizabeth II and Prince Philip. T **674** and similar vert design. Multicoloured. Phosphorised paper. Perf 14.

2993	50c. Type **674**	50	50
2994	$2 On their wedding day, 1947	2·75	2·75
MS2995	110×90 mm. Nos. 2993/2994	3·25	3·25

(Adapted by Communication Arts) Litho Pemara, Australia (Nos. 3000/3001) or Southern Colour Print (others))

2007 (3 Oct). Christmas. T **675** and similar multicoloured designs showing winning entries in children's stamp design competition Christmas Symbols.

(a) Ordinary gum. Litho Southern Colour Print, Dunedin. Designs 34×34 mm. Phosphorised paper. Perf 14½.

2996	50c. Type **675**	60	10
2997	$1 Robin wearing Santa hat (Reece Cateley)	1·10	40
2998	$1.50 Baby Jesus (Emily Wang)	2·25	2·00
2999	$2 Beach cricket (Alexandra Eathorne)	3·00	3·50
3000	$2.50 Fantail (Jake Hooper)	3·75	4·50
2996/3000	Set of 5	9·50	9·50

(b) Self-adhesive. Litho SEP Sprint, Australia. Size 24×29 mm. Partial phosphor frame (at left and foot). Die-cut perf 11½ (Nos. 3001/3002) or 13 (Nos. 3001b/3002b).

3001	50c. As Type **675**	60	70
	a. Booklet pane. No. 3001×10	5·50	
	b. Perf 13	60	70
	ba. Horiz pair. Nos. 3001b/3002b	2·25	3·00
3002	$1.50 As No. 2998	1·75	2·00
	a. Booklet pane. No. 3002×10	15·00	
	b. Perf 13	1·75	2·50

No. 3001 was issued in $4.50 stamp booklets, No. SB138.
No. 3001b was issued in rolls of 100.
No. 3002 was issued in stamp booklet, No. SB139, sold at $13.50, providing a discount of $1.50 off the face value of the stamps.
Nos. 3001b/3002b could be purchased as *se-tenant* pairs from the Philatelic Bureau.

676 'GO YOU GOOD THING'

677 Dusky Sound, Fiordland

(Des Saatchi & Saatchi. Litho Southern Colour Print, Dunedin)

2007 (7 Nov). Personalised Stamps. T **676** and similar horiz designs. Multicoloured. Phosphorised paper. Perf 14.

3003	50c. Type **676**	75	75
	a. Sheetlet of 10. Nos. 3003/3012	11·00	11·00
3004	50c. 'Look Who it is!'	75	75
3005	50c. 'Love Always'	75	75
3006	50c. 'THANKS A MILLION'	75	75
3007	50c. 'WE'VE GOT NEWS'	75	75
3008	50c. 'Wish you were here'	75	75
3009	$1 'Time to Celebrate'	1·40	1·40
3010	$1 'Kia Ora'	1·40	1·40
3011	$1.50 'You gotta love Christmas'	2·25	2·25
3012	$2 Chinese inscription	3·00	3·00
3003/3012	Set of 10	11·00	11·00

Nos. 3003/3012 were printed together, *se-tenant*, in sheetlets of ten stamps and five stamp-size labels.

BEST OF 2007. A further set of miniature sheets as described below No. 2042 were distributed by the Philatelic Bureau to customers purchasing a certain amount of material during 2007. The sheets comprised: 1. Nos. 2934, 2929 and 2960; 2. Nos. 2948/2949 and 2985; 3. Nos. 2998, 2994 and 3012.
Imperforate sheets of Nos. 2957/2961 and a perforated *se-tenant* strip comprising the same five stamps were also distributed.

(Des Tim Garman)

2008 (9 Jan). Underwater Reefs. T **677** and similar horiz designs. Multicoloured.

(a) Ordinary gum. Litho Cartor. Designs 39×29 mm. Phosphorised paper. Perf 13×13½.

3013	50c. Type **677**	75	30
3014	$1 *Callanthias australis* (Splendish Perch) and *Ecklonia radiata* (Common Kelp), Mayor Island, Bay of Plenty	1·50	1·25
3015	$1.50 Hydrocoral *Errina novaezealandiae* (Red Coral), Fiordland	2·25	2·50
3016	$2 *Diadema palmeri* (Diadema Urchin), Volkner Rocks, White Island, Bay of Plenty	3·00	3·50
3013/3016	Set of 4	6·75	6·75
MS3017	120×80 mm. Nos. 3013/3016	11·00	11·00

(b) Self-adhesive. Litho SEP Sprint, Australia. Size 29×24 mm. Phosphor frame. Die-cut perf 11½.

3018	50c. Type **677**	90	75
	a. Booklet pane. No. 3018×10	9·00	
	b. Horiz pair. Nos. 3018/3019	2·10	2·50
3019	$1 As No. 3014	1·40	1·75
	a. Booklet pane. No. 3019×10	14·00	

No. 3018 was issued in rolls of 100 and $5 stamp booklet, No. SB140.
No. 3019 was issued in $10 stamp booklet, No. SB141.
Nos. 3018/3019 could be purchased as *se-tenant* pairs (No. 3018b) from the Philatelic Bureau.

678 Rabbits

679 Drought, 1997–1998

(Des Lindy Fisher. Litho Southern Colour Print, Dunedin)

2008 (7 Feb). Chinese New Year. Year of the Rat. Pocket Pets. T **678** and similar horiz designs. Multicoloured. Phosphorised paper. Perf 14.

3020	50c. Type **678**	1·00	30
3021	$1 Guinea Pigs	1·75	1·25
3022	$1.50 Rats	2·50	3·00
3023	$2 Mice	3·25	3·50
3020/3023	Set of 4	7·75	7·25
MS3024	125×90 mm. Nos. 3022/3023	7·00	7·50

(Des Vertigo Design. Litho Southern Colour Print)

2008 (5 Mar). Weather Extremes. T **679** and similar horiz designs. Multicoloured. Phosphorised paper. Perf 14.

3025	50c. Type **679**	1·00	75
3026	50c. Pedestrians in gale, Auckland, March 2007	1·00	75
	a. Magenta, yellow and orange-brown omitted	£1200	
3027	$1 Storm waves, Evans Bay, Wellington, January 2001	1·60	1·40
3028	$1.50 Flooded farmland, Hikurangi, 2007	2·50	2·25
3029	$2 Snow storm, Ohai, Southland, May 2001	3·00	3·50
3030	$2.50 Heat, Matarangi beach, Coromandel, 2005	4·00	3·75
3025/3030	Set of 6	12·00	11·00

NEW ZEALAND

2008 (7 Mar). Taipei 2008 21st Asian International Stamp Exhibition. Sheet 120×90 mm. Phosphorised paper.
MS3031 No. 3012 (Perf 14) and as No. 3023 (Perf 13½).... 6·50 6·50

680 Sapper John Luamanu and Baby Daughter, ANZAC Day Parade, 2007

(Des Cue Design. Litho Southern Colour Print, Dunedin)

2008 (2 Apr). ANZAC (1st series). T **680** and similar horiz designs. Multicoloured. Phosphorised paper. Perf 14.

3032	50c. Type **680**	1·00	75
3033	50c. Auckland Infantry Battalion landing at Gallipoli, 25 April 1915	1·00	75
3034	$1 New Zealand soldiers on Western Front, April 1918	1·75	1·40
3035	$1.50 Sling Camp and chalk kiwi on Salisbury Plain, England, 1919	2·75	2·50
3036	$2 Maori Battalion performing haka, Helwan, Egypt, June 1941	3·50	3·25
3037	$2.50 161 Battery, Nui Dat, Vietnam, 1965–1971	4·25	4·25
3032/3037	Set of 6	13·00	11·50

The stamps also exist in seven miniature sheets, each 148×110 mm with a line of roulettes at left. Six of the miniature sheets contain Nos. 3032/3037 as single stamps and the seventh sheet contains all six designs. These miniature sheets are only obtainable from a booklet, No. SP9, containing stamps with a face value of $16 but sold for $19.90.

See also Nos. 3131/3136, 3199/3204, 3441/**MS**3447, 3541/**MS**3553 and 4063/**MS**4069.

681 Miro Whero, Miro Ma, Miro Pango **682** The Pevensie Children playing in the Surf

(Des Len Hetet. Litho Southern Colour Print, Dunedin)

2008 (2 May). 150 Years of Kingitanga (Maori King) Movement. T **681** and similar multicoloured designs showing art by Fred Graham. Phosphorised paper. Perf 14.

3038	50c. Type **681**	75	40
3039	$1.50 He Piko He Taniwha	2·00	2·25
3040	$2.50 Kia Mau (horiz)	3·75	4·00
3038/3040	Set of 3	6·00	6·00

(Des CommArts, Wellington. Litho Sprintpak, Australia)

2008 (7 May). Making of *The Chronicles of Narnia. Prince Caspian* (film). T **682** and similar horiz designs. Multicoloured. Phosphorised paper. Perf 14½×14.

3041	50c. Type **682**	1·25	45
3042	$1 Queen Susan	2·00	1·50
3043	$1.50 High King Peter	3·25	4·00
3044	$2 Prince Caspian	4·00	4·50
3041/3044	Set of 4	9·50	9·50

Nos. 3041/3044 also exist as a set of four miniature sheets, each containing a single stamp, which were sold at $7, a premium of $2 over the face value.

683 'Ranginui' (sky)

(Des Len Hetet. Litho Southern Colour Print)

2008 (5 June). Matariki (Maori New Year). T **683** and similar horiz designs. Multicoloured. Perf 14.

3045	50c. Type **683**	75	60
3046	50c. 'Te Moana Nui A Kiwa' (prow of war canoe and Pacific Ocean)	75	60
3047	$1 'Papatuanuku' (land) (silver fern fronds)	1·50	1·10
3048	$1.50 'Whakapapa' (genealogy) (sunset)	2·50	2·25
3049	$2 'Takoha' (passing of tiki neck pendant to next generation)	3·00	3·50
3050	$2.50 'Te Tau Hou' (woodcarving and moon rising over sea)	4·00	4·50
3045/3050	Set of 6	11·00	11·00
MS3051	150×90 mm. Nos. 3045/3050	11·00	11·00

684 Girl riding Bicycle ('INSPIRE')

(Des Martin Bailey. Litho Southern Colour Print)

2008 (2 July). Children's Health. T **684** and similar diamond-shaped designs. Multicoloured.

(a) Ordinary gum. Phosphorised paper. Perf 14½.

3052	50c.+10c. Type **684**	1·25	1·25
3053	$1+10c. Boy kayaking ('PASSION')	1·60	1·75
MS3054	140×90 mm. 50c.+10c. Boy with arms outstretched in triumph (34×32 mm) (Perf 14×14½) and Nos. 3052/3053	3·00	3·00

(b) Self-adhesive. Perf 10.

3055	50c.+10c. Boy with arms outstretched in triumph ('EXCEL') (34×32 mm)	1·00	1·00

685 Rower ('CELEBRATE')

(Des Martin Bailey. Litho Southern Colour Print)

2008 (2 July). Olympic Games, Beijing. T **685** and similar diamond-shaped designs. Multicoloured. Phosphorised paper. Perf 14½.

3056	50c. Type **685**	1·25	1·00
3057	50c. Cyclist ('PASSION')	2·00	1·25
3058	$1 Kayaker ('SUCCEED')	2·00	1·50
3059	$2 Athlete ('MOTIVATE')	3·25	4·00
3056/3059	Set of 4	7·75	7·00

686 a is for Aotearoa **687** Last Spike Ceremony, Manganui-o-te-Ao, 1908

(Des Clemenger BBDO. Litho Southern Colour Print)

2008 (6 Aug). The A to Z of New Zealand. T **686** and similar horiz designs. Multicoloured. Phosphorised paper. Perf 14½.

3060	50c. Type **686**	80	80
	a. Sheetlet of 26. Nos. 3060/3085	18·00	20·00

NEW ZEALAND

3061	50c. B is for Beehive (Parliament House, Wellington)	80	80
3062	50c. C is for Cook (Captain Cook)	80	80
3063	50c. D is for Dog (from *Footrot Flats* cartoon strip)	80	80
3064	50c. E is for Edmonds (Thomas Edmonds)	80	80
3065	50c. F is for Fantail (bird)	80	80
3066	50c. G is for Goodnight Kiwi (TV cartoon)	80	80
3067	50c. H is for Haka	80	80
3068	50c. I is for Interislander (ferry)	80	80
3069	50c. J is for Jelly Tip (ice cream)	80	80
3070	50c. K is for Kia Ora	80	80
3071	50c. L is for log o'wood (Ranfurly Shield rugby trophy)	80	80
3072	50c. M is for Mudpools	80	80
3073	50c. N is for Nuclear Free	80	80
3074	50c. O is for OE (overseas experience)	80	80
3075	50c. P is for Pinetree (All Black player Colin Meads)	80	80
3076	50c. Q is for Quake (earthquakes)	80	80
3077	50c. R is for Rutherford (nuclear physicist Sir Ernest Rutherford)	80	80
3078	50c. S is for Southern Cross	80	80
3079	50c. T is for Tiki (carved by Lewis Gardiner)	80	80
3080	50c. U is for Upham (Captain Charles Upham's Victoria Cross)	80	80
3081	50c. V is for Vote (suffragette Kate Sheppard)	80	80
3082	50c. W is for Weta (model of insect)	80	80
3083	50c. X is for x-treme sports	80	80
3084	50c. Y is for Yarn	80	80
3085	50c. Z is for Zeeland (explorer Abel Tasman)	80	80
3060/3085 Set of 26		18·00	20·00

Nos. 3060/3085 were printed together, *se-tenant*, in sheetlets of 26 stamps.

(Des Communication Arts. Litho Southern Colour Print)

2008 (3 Sept). Centenary of the North Island Main Trunk Railway Line. T **687** and similar horiz designs. Multicoloured. Phosphorised paper. Perf 14.

3086	50c. Type **687**	1·00	40
3087	$1 KA 947 class steam locomotive on display at Taumarunui, 1958	1·75	1·10
3088	$1.50 Steam hauled goods train on Makatote Viaduct, 1963	2·25	2·00
3089	$2 Steam hauled goods train climbing the Raurimu Spiral, 1964	3·00	3·75
3090	$2.50 EF powered Overlander crossing Hapuawhenua Viaduct, 2003	4·00	4·50
3086/3090 Set of 5		11·00	10·50

2008 (18 Sept). WIPA08 International Stamp Exhibition, Vienna. Sheet 121×85 mm. Phosphorised paper. Perf 14.

MS3091 Nos. 3046 and 3048/3049 .... 4·50   4·75

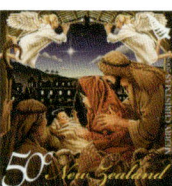 

688 Nativity   **689** Sheep wearing Santa Hat and Jandals (Kirsten Fisher-Marsters)

(Des Martin Bailey. Litho Southern Colour Print (Nos. 3092/3094) or Sprintpak, Australia (Nos. 3095/3096))

2008 (1 Oct). Christmas (1st issue). T **688** and similar square designs. Multicoloured.

(a) Ordinary gum. Phosphorised paper. Perf 14½.

3092	50c. Type **688**	60	10
3093	$1 Holy Family	1·10	40
3094	$1.50 Mary and baby Jesus	1·75	2·25
3092/3094 Set of 3		3·00	2·50

(b) Self-adhesive. Size 24×29 mm. Phosphor frame. Die-cut perf 11½ (Nos. 3095/3096) or 13 (Nos. 3095b/3096b).

3095	50c. As Type **688**	60	50
	a. Booklet pane. No. 3095×10	5·50	
	b. Perf 13	65	50
	ba. Horiz pair. Nos. 3095b/3096b	2·25	2·50
3096	$1.50 As No. 3094	1·60	1·75
	a. Booklet pane. No. 3096×10	14·00	
	b. Perf 13	1·60	2·00

No. 3095 was issued in $5 booklet, No. SB142.
No. 3096 was issued in $15 booklet, No. SB143.
No. 3095b was issued in rolls of 100.
Nos. 3095b/3096b could be purchased in *se-tenant* pairs from the Philatelic Bureau.

(Adapted Communication Arts. Litho Southern Colour Print)

2008 (1 Oct). Christmas (2nd issue). T **689** and similar square designs showing winning entries in children's stamp design competition Kiwi Christmas. Multicoloured. Phosphorised paper. Perf 14½.

3097	50c. Type **689**	60	10
3098	$2 Pohutukawa flowers and koru (Tamara Jenkin)	2·25	2·75
3099	$2.50 Kiwi wearing Santa hat (Molly Bruhns)	2·50	3·25
3097/3099 Set of 3		4·75	5·50

(Litho Southern Colour Print)

2008 (20 Oct). 90th Anniversary of the End of World War I. Sheet 150×90 mm. Multicoloured. Perf 14.

MS3100 Nos. 3033/3035 .... 6·50   6·50

690 Sir Edmund Hillary   **691** Pencarrow Lighthouse

(Des Vertigo Design. Litho Southern Colour Print)

2008 (5 Nov). Sir Edmund Hillary Commemoration. T **690** and similar vert designs. Multicoloured. Phosphorised paper. Perf 15.

3101	50c. Type **690**	1·00	40
3102	$1 Edmund Hillary and Tenzing Norgay during first ascent of Mount Everest, 1953	1·75	1·10
3103	$1.50 On tracked vehicle, Trans-Antarctic Expedition, 1955–1958	2·50	2·25
3104	$2 Sir Edmund Hillary (founder of Himalayan Trust, 1960) with Nepalese children	3·00	3·50
3105	$2.50 Appointed to the Order of the Garter, 1995	3·00	3·50
3101/3105 Set of 5		10·00	9·75

(Litho Southern Colour Print)

2008 (7 Nov). Tarapex 2008 National Stamp Exhibition, New Plymouth. Sheet 138×86 mm. Multicoloured. Perf 13½.

MS3106 $4.50 As Nos. 2609 and 2869 but without imprint dates .... 5·00   5·50

BEST OF 2008. A further set of miniature sheets as described below No. 2042 were distributed by the Philatelic Bureau to customers purchasing a certain amount of material during 2008. The sheets comprised: 1. Nos. 3016, 3023 and 3030; 2. Nos. 3037, 3040 and 3050; 3. Nos. 3090, 3094 and 3105.

Imperforate sheets of Nos. 3025/3030 and a perforated *se-tenant* block comprising the same six stamps were also distributed.

(Des Vertigo Design. Litho Sprintpak)

2009 (7 Jan). Lighthouses of New Zealand. T **691** and similar horiz designs. Multicoloured. Phosphorised paper. Perf 13.

3107	50c. Type **691**	1·25	45
3108	$1 Dog Island Lighthouse	2·00	1·00
3109	$1.50 Cape Brett Lighthouse	2·75	2·50
3110	$2 Cape Egmont Lighthouse	3·75	4·00
3111	$2.50 Cape Reinga Lighthouse	3·75	4·25
3107/3111 Set of 5		12·00	11·00

Nos. 3107/3111 commemorate the 150th anniversary of New Zealand's first lighthouse (Pencarrow Head).

The beams of light shining from the lighthouses on Nos. 3107/3111 are printed in luminous ink.

692 Lunar Ox Symbol   **693** Scott Dixon in Honda Indycar

(Des Bananaworks. Litho Cartor)

2009 (7 Jan). Chinese New Year. Year of the Ox. T **692** and similar vert designs. Multicoloured. Phosphorised paper. Perf 13.

3112	50c. Type **692**	80	65
3113	$1 Ox	1·40	1·40
3114	$2 Chinese lanterns and Auckland Harbour Bridge	2·75	3·50
3112/3114 Set of 3		4·50	5·00
MS3115 Nos. 3112/3114		4·50	5·00

(Des Communication Arts. Litho Southern Colour Print)

2009 (4 Feb). New Zealand Champions of Motorsport. T **693** and similar horiz designs. Multicoloured.

(a) Ordinary gum. Phosphorised paper. Perf 14.

3116	50c. Type **693**	1·25	45
3117	$1 Bruce McLaren in Formula One car	2·00	1·25
3118	$1.50 Ivan Mauger on speedway motorcycle	2·75	2·50
3119	$2 Denny Hulme in Formula One car	3·50	3·50
3120	$2.50 Hugh Anderson on Grand Prix motorcycle	4·00	4·25
3116/3120 Set of 5		12·00	11·00
MS3121 150×90 mm. Nos. 3116/3120		12·00	11·00

(b) Self-adhesive. Size 30×25 mm. Phosphor frame. Die-cut perf 10×9½.

3122	50c. As Type **693**	1·00	1·00
	a. Booklet pane. No. 3122×10	9·00	
3123	$1 As No. 3117	1·50	1·50
	a. Booklet pane. No. 3123×10	13·50	

No. 3122 was issued in $5 booklet, No. SB142, and also in rolls of 100.
No. 3123 was issued in $10 booklet, No. SB143.
Nos. 3122/3123 could be purchased in *se-tenant* pairs from the Philatelic Bureau.

694 Giant Moa

(Des Dave Gunson. Litho Southern Colour Print)

2009 (4 Mar). Giants of New Zealand. T **694** and similar horiz designs. Multicoloured. Phosphorised paper. Perf 14½.

3124	50c. Type **694**	1·50	65
3125	$1 Colossal Squid	2·25	1·25
3126	$1.50 Southern Right Whale	3·50	2·75
3127	$2 Giant Eagle	4·25	4·50
3128	$2.50 Giant Weta	4·50	4·75
3124/3128 Set of 5		14·50	12·50
MS3129 179×90 mm. Nos. 3124/3128		14·50	13·50

2009 (4 Mar). International Polar Year 2007–2009. Sheet 120×80 mm. Multicoloured. Perf 13×13½.

MS3130 As No. 2871×2 but without imprint dates		7·50	7·50

695 Funeral Procession of the Unknown Warrior, Wellington, 2004

(Des Communication Arts. Litho Southern Colour Print)

2009 (1 Apr). ANZAC (2nd series). Comrades in Arms. T **695** and similar horiz designs. Multicoloured. Perf 13½×13.

3131	50c. Type **695**	1·40	1·00
3132	50c. NZ (Maori) Pioneer Battalion on break from trench improvement, World War I	1·40	1·00
3133	$1 No. 75 (NZ) Squadron RAF and Wellington bomber, World War II	2·75	1·75
3134	$1.50 HMS *Achilles* (Leander class cruiser), World War II	3·00	2·50
3135	$2 Kayforce gun crew in action, Korea, 1 April 1952	3·75	4·00
3136	$2.50 Soldiers of ANZAC Battalion boarding RAAF Iroquois helicopter, Vietnam, 23 March 1968	4·00	4·25
3131/3136 Set of 6		14·50	13·00

The stamps also exist in seven miniature sheets, each 151×110 mm with a line of roulettes at left. Six of the miniature sheets contain Nos. 3131/3136 as single stamps and the seventh sheet contains all six designs. Stamps from these miniature sheets are all perforated 14. The miniature sheets are only obtainable from a booklet, No. SP10, containing stamps with a face value of $16 but sold for $19.90.

2009 (1 Apr). China 2009 World Stamp Exhibition, Luoyang, China. Sheet 95×90 mm. Multicoloured. Perf 13×13½.

MS3137 Nos. 3010, 3012 and 3113		5·25	5·50

No. **MS**3137 is cut in a semicircle at left and foot.

696 Pedestrians crossing Bridge before its opening to Traffic, 1959

697 Heitiki from Te Maori Exhibition, 1984

(Des Mata Limited. Litho Southern Colour Print)

2009 (1 May). 50th Anniversary of Auckland Harbour Bridge. T **696** and similar horiz designs. Multicoloured. Phosphorised paper. Perf 13½×13.

3138	50c. Type **696**	1·00	40
3139	$1 Auckland Harbour Bridge (with two extra lanes) in 2009	1·50	1·10
3140	$1.50 Auckland Harbour Bridge in 1961	2·50	3·00
3141	$2 Auckland Harbour Bridge at night, 2009	3·00	3·25
3138/3141 Set of 4		7·25	7·00

A 50c. self-adhesive stamp as T **696** was only available from the Philatelic Bureau as a single stamp or from PostShops as part of the set (*Price £1·50 mint or used*).

(Des Len Hetet. Litho Southern Colour Print)

2009 (24 June). Matariki (Maori New Year). T **697** and similar vert designs. Multicoloured.

(a) Self-adhesive. Die-cut perf 10×9½.

3143	50c. Type **697**	75	45
	a. Pane. Nos. 3143/3148	12·00	12·00
3144	$1 Heitiki by Raponi	1·40	1·10
3145	$1.50 Heitiki made from corian by Rangi Kipa	2·25	2·25
3146	$1.80 Female heitiki made from greenstone	2·50	2·50
3147	$2 Female heitiki, *circa* 1849, from the Museum of New Zealand	3·00	3·25
3148	$2.30 Heitiki made from paraoa by Rangi Hetet, 1991	3·50	3·75
3143/3148 Set of 6		12·00	12·00

(b) Ordinary gum. Phosphorised paper. Perf 13×13½.

MS3149 150×90 mm. As Nos. 3143/3148		12·00	12·00

Nos. 3143/3148 were issued in separate sheets of 25.
The *se-tenant* pane, No. 3143a, was only available from the Philatelic Bureau.
A *se-tenant* strip of six stamps containing Nos. 3143/3148 was only available from presentation packs and the limited edition pack (*Price £30 mint or used*).

(Des Stamps Business, New Zealand Post. Litho Southern Colour Print)

2009 (1 July). New Zealand Landscapes (2nd series). Horiz designs as T **622**. Multicoloured.

(a) Ordinary gum. Perf 13×13½.

3150	30c. Tolaga Bay	75	45
3151	$1.80 Russell	3·00	3·00
3152	$2.30 Lake Wanaka	3·50	3·50
3153	$2.80 Auckland	3·75	3·75
3154	$3.30 Rakaia River	4·25	4·25
3155	$4 Wellington	5·50	7·50
3150/3155 Set of 6		19·00	20·00

(b) Self-adhesive. Phosphor frame. Perf 10×9½.

3156	$1.80 As No. 3151	2·75	3·00
	a. Booklet pane. No. 3156×5 and 2 International Air labels	12·00	

No. 3156 was issued in $9 booklet, No. SB146.

NEW ZEALAND

698 Lighthouse (Cape Reinga) and Angler

699 1996 Child Safety 40c.+5c. Stamp

(Des Assignment Group. Litho Southern Colour Print)

2009 (5 Aug). A Tiki Tour of New Zealand (1st issue). Sheet 190×280 mm containing T **698** and similar square designs. Multicoloured. Phosphorised paper. Perf 14.

MS3157	50c.×24 Type **698**; Hole in the Rock Tour (Cape Brett); *Maui snaring the sun* (Maori legend); Yachting; Sky Tower (Auckland) and surf boat; Marlin fishing; Waikato rugby (Mooloos); Rower, statue of shearer and Maori carving; Pohutukawa tree, east coast style whare (meeting house); surfing and horse riding; Mount Taranaki; Gumboot and wind turbines; Gannet (Cape Kidnappers); Tribute state (Greymouth) and Municipal Building (Westport); Grapes, fly fishing and glassblowing; Richard Seddon statue (Parliament) and windsurfer; Mount Cook Lily and statue of Mackenzie's Dog (Lake Tekapo); Roadside crayfish caravan (Kaikoura) and Neil Dawson's Chalice sculpture (Christchurch); Whale watching; Crayfish, Black Robin and fishing boat (Chatham Islands); Milford Sound and jet boat (Shotover river); Wings over Wanaka (biplane); Kakapo; Curling; Stewart Island Shag and chain sculpture (Rakiura track, Oban)	20·00	28·00

No. **MS**3157 contains 24 stamps and one stamp-size label, the backgrounds forming a composite design of a map of New Zealand.

See also No. **MS**3379.

(Des Hamish Thompson. Litho Southern Colour Print, New Zealand)

2009 (7 Sept). 80th Anniversary of Children's Health Stamps. T **699** and similar vert designs. Multicoloured. Phosphorised paper.

(a) Ordinary gum. Perf 13×13½.

3158	50c.+10c. Type **699**	1·75	1·75
3159	$1+10c. 1932 Hygeia 1d.+1d. Health stamp	2·25	2·25
MS3160	100×90 mm. 50c.+10c. 1943 Princess Elizabeth 2d.+1d. Health stamp (25×30 mm) (Perf 14×14½) and as Nos. 3158/3159 (Perf 14)	3·25	3·25

(b) Self-adhesive. Die-cut perf 9½×10.

3161	50c.+10c. 1943 Princess Elizabeth 2d.+1d. Health stamp (25×30 mm)	1·75	1·75

700 Beach Cricket

701 Three Shepherds

(Des Robertson Communications. Litho Australia Post Sprintpak (Nos. 3162C/3171C) or Southern Colour Print (others))

2009 (7 Sept). KiwiStamps (1st issue). T **700** and similar vert designs. Multicoloured. Self-adhesive. Die-cut.

(a) Folded sheets of 50. Design size 21½×26½ mm. Perf 10×9½.

3162A	(50c.) Type **700**	1·00	1·00
3163A	(50c.) Kiwi Fruit	1·00	1·00
3164A	(50c.) State Highway 1 road sign	1·00	1·00
3165A	(50c.) Windfarm and umbrella blown inside out	1·00	1·00
3166A	(50c.) Lawnmower	1·00	1·00
3167A	(50c.) Caravan	1·00	1·00
3168A	(50c.) Flying duck wall ornaments	1·00	1·00
3169A	(50c.) Fish and chips at the beach	1·00	1·00
3170A	(50c.) Swanndri jacket on barbed wire	1·00	1·00
3171A	(50c.) Sausage on fork and barbecue	1·00	1·00
3162A/3171A	Set of 10	9·00	9·00

(b) Coil stamps. Design size 21x26 mm. Perf 9½×10.

3162B	(50c.) Type **700**	1·00	1·00
	a. Pane of 10. Nos. 3162B/3171B	9·00	9·00
	b. Vert strip of 10. Nos. 3162B/3171B	9·00	9·00
3163B	(50c.) As No. 3163A	1·00	1·00
3164B	(50c.) As No. 3164A	1·00	1·00
3165B	(50c.) As No. 3165A	1·00	1·00
3166B	(50c.) As No. 3166A	1·00	1·00
3167B	(50c.) As No. 3167A	1·00	1·00
3168B	(50c.) As No. 3168A	1·00	1·00
3169B	(50c.) As No. 3169A	1·00	1·00
3170B	(50c.) As No. 3170A	1·00	1·00
3171B	(50c.) As No. 3171A	1·00	1·00
3162B/3171B	Set of 10	9·00	9·00

(c) Booklet stamps. Design size 21×26 mm. Perf 11.

3162C	(50c.) Type **700**	1·00	1·00
	a. Booklet pane of 10. Nos. 3162C/3171C	9·00	
3163C	(50c.) As No. 3163A	1·00	1·00
3164C	(50c.) As No. 3164A	1·00	1·00
3165C	(50c.) As No. 3165A	1·00	1·00
3166C	(50c.) As No. 3166A	1·00	1·00
3167C	(50c.) As No. 3167A	1·00	1·00
3168C	(50c.) As No. 3168A	1·00	1·00
3169C	(50c.) As No. 3169A	1·00	1·00
3170C	(50c.) As No. 3170A	1·00	1·00
3171C	(50c.) As No. 3171A	1·00	1·00
3162C/3171C	Set of 10	9·00	9·00

Nos. 3162A/3171C were all inscribed 'Kiwistamp' and were valid for standard post letters within New Zealand.

Nos. 3162A/3171A were issued in sheets of 50, containing five stamps of each design in different combinations *se-tenant* throughout the sheet.

Nos. 3162B/3171B were issued in rolls of 100, containing all ten designs in sequence, with a join every 20 stamps. They were also available in Jumbo panes of ten (5×2), originally produced for first day covers (No. 3162Ba); these were only available from the philatelic bureau.

Nos. 3162C/3171C were issued in booklets of ten, No SB147, originally sold for $5.

There are design differences between the sheet, coil and booklet stamps due to varied scaling and cropping of the original artwork.

As well as the size and perforation differences, stamps from the different sources may be identified by the fact that the sheet stamps have interlocking perforations with no matrix between the stamps; booklet stamps and stamps from the Jumbo coil pane (No. 3162Ba) are separated by a matrix which is intact; stamps from the coils of 100 have the matrix removed.

Stamps in these designs but with silver foil Kiwistamp and silver fern emblems were issued in numbered sheets of 50 and numbered booklets of ten in limited quantities (11,000 booklets and 3000 sheets).

See also Nos. 3269/3273

(Des Stephen Fuller. Litho Southern Colour Print)

2009 (7 Oct). Christmas (1st issue). T **701** and similar square designs. Multicoloured.

(a) Ordinary gum. Phosphorised paper. Perf 14.

3172	50c. Type **701**	85	10
3173	$1 Mary, Joseph and Infant Jesus	1·60	80
3174	$1.80 Three magi with gifts	2·75	3·50
3172/3174	Set of 3	4·75	4·00

(b) Self-adhesive. Size 30×25 mm. Die-cut perf 10×9½.

3175	50c. As Type **701**	85	75
	a. Booklet pane. No. 3175×10	7·50	
	b. Horiz pair. Nos. 3175/3176	3·25	3·00
3176	$1.80 As No. 3174	2·50	2·25
	a. Booklet pane. No. 3176×10	22·00	

No. 3175 was issued in $5 booklet, No. SB148, and in rolls of 100.

No. 3176 was issued in booklet, No. SB149 sold at $15, providing a $3 discount off the face value of the stamps.

The *se-tenant* pair, No. 3175b, could be purchased from the Philatelic Bureau.

702 Seaside Chair and Pohutukawa Tree (Felix Wang)

703 Sir Peter Blake ('Inspirational Leader')

(Des Communication Arts. Litho Southern Colour Print)

2009 (7 Oct). Christmas (2nd issue). T **702** and similar square designs showing winning entries in children's stamp design competition What do you love about Christmas? Multicoloured. Phosphorised paper. Perf 14.

3177	50c. Type **702**	75	10
3178	$2.30 *New Zealand pigeon wearing Christmas hat* (Dannielle Aldworth)	3·00	3·75
3179	$2.80 *Christmas presents* (Apun Bakshi)	4·25	4·50
3177/3179	Set of 3	7·25	7·50

NEW ZEALAND

2009 (16 Oct). Timpex 2009 National Stamp Exhibition, Timaru. Sheet 170×90 mm. Multicoloured.
MS3180 As Nos. 3101/3102 and 3105 (all Perf 14) and
specimen stamp as Type **501** (Perf 14½×15)............ 8·00 8·00

No. **MS**3180 was sold for $6.50, with a $2.50 surcharge to fund the Philatelic Trust.
The $20 specimen stamp as T **501** differs from No. 1784 by being printed in lithography and having no watermark. It was not valid for postage.

(Des Cue Design. Litho Southern Colour Print)

2009 (25 Nov). Sir Peter Blake (yachtsman) Commemoration. T **703** and similar vert designs. Multicoloured. Phosphorised paper. Perf 13½.
3181	50c. Type **703**............	1·00	45
3182	$1 Sir Peter Blake at wheel and yacht ('Whitbread Round the World Yachtsman')............	1·75	1·25
3183	$1.80 Sir Peter Blake using winch and catamaran ('Jules Verne Trophy Record Breaker')............	3·00	2·75
3184	$2.30 Sir Peter Blake, Americas Cup trophy and yacht *New Zealand* ('Passionate Kiwi')............	4·00	4·50
3185	$2.80 Sir Peter Blake and yacht *Seamaster* on expedition in Antarctica ('Environmentalist')............	4·50	4·75
3181/3185 *Set of 5*............		13·00	12·50
MS3186 160×58 mm. Nos. 3181/3185............		13·00	13·00

BEST OF 2009. A further set of miniature sheets as described below No. 2042 were distributed by the Philatelic Bureau to customers purchasing a certain amount of philatelic material during 2009. The sheets comprised: 1. Nos. 3111, 3114 and 3120; 2. Nos. 3128, 3136 and 3141; 3. Nos. 3148, 3174 and 3185.
Imperforate sheets of Nos. 3150/3155 and a perforated *se-tenant* block comprising the same six stamps were also distributed.

704 Lunar Tiger Symbol

705 Heitiki

(Des Bananaworks. Litho Southern Colour Print)

2010 (6 Jan). Chinese New Year. Year of the Tiger. T **704** and similar vert designs. Multicoloured. Perf 14 (Nos. 3187/3190) or 13½ (No. **MS**3191).
3187	50c. Type **704**............	1·00	75
3188	$1 Tiger............	1·90	1·90
3189	$1.80 Head of Tiger............	2·75	2·75
3190	$2.30 Beehive (Parliament House, Wellington)............	3·75	4·00
3187/3190 *Set of 4*............		8·50	8·50
MS3191 150×90 mm. Nos. 3187/3190............		8·50	8·50

(Des YouXD. Litho Southern Colour Print)

2010 (10 Feb). Personalised Stamps. Sheet 94×82 mm containing T **705** and designs as Nos. 2876, 2879 and 2881 but 35×20 mm and with new values. Multicoloured. Phosphorised paper. Perf 15×14.
MS3192 $1.80 Type **705**; $2.30 As Type **660**;
$2.30 Engagement and wedding rings; $2.30
Pohutukawa flower............ 13·00 14·00

No. **MS**3192 contains four stamps in two horizontal pairs separated by two stamp-size labels inscribed 'Personalised Stamps 2010'.

706 Allosaurus

(Des Eklektus Inc. Litho Southern Colour Print)

2010 (3 Mar). Dinosaurs of New Zealand. T **706** and similar horiz designs. Multicoloured.
(a) Ordinary gum. Phosphorised paper. Perf 14½.
3193	50c. Type **706**............	95	85
3194	$1 Anhanguera............	2·25	2·25
3195	$1.80 Titanosaurus............	3·00	3·00
3196	$2.30 Moanasaurus............	3·75	3·75
3197	$2.80 Mauisaurus............	4·50	4·50
3193/3197 *Set of 5*............		13·00	13·00

(b) Self-adhesive. Sheet 230×200 mm. Partial phosphor frames. Die-cut perf 10×9½.
MS3198 As Nos. 3193/3197............ 13·00 13·00

Stamps from No. **MS**3198 have a phosphor frame at left, right and foot of the stamps.
A gummed miniature sheet containing Nos. 3193/3197 was only sold in a limited edition pack.

707 ANZAC Soldier

708 Peony and Pohutukawa Flowers

(Des Cue Design. Litho Southern Colour Print, New Zealand)

2010 (7 Apr). ANZAC (3rd series). Remembrance. T **707** and similar horiz designs. Multicoloured. Phosphorised paper. Perf 13½.
3199	50c. Type **707**............	1·50	1·25
3200	50c. Gallipoli veterans marching, ANZAC Day, 1958............	1·50	1·25
3201	$1 Posthumous VC Award Ceremony for Second Lieutenant Te Moana-Nui-a-Kiwa Ngarimu, Ruatoria, 1943............	2·50	1·75
3202	$1.80 Nurses laying wreath, Cairo Cemetery, ANZAC Day, 1940............	3·50	3·00
3203	$2.30 ANZAC War Memorial, Port Said, Egypt, 1932............	4·50	5·00
3204	$2.80 Veteran at Sangro War Cemetery, Italy, 2004............	4·50	5·00
3199/3204 *Set of 6*............		16·00	15·00

The stamps also exist in seven miniature sheets, each 151×110 mm, with a line of roulettes at left. Six of the miniature sheets contain Nos. 3199/3204 as single stamps and the seventh sheet contains all six designs. Stamps from these miniature sheets are all perforated 14. The miniature sheets are only obtainable from a booklet, No. SP11, containing stamps with a face value of $17.80 but sold for $19.90.

(Des Assignment Group. Litho Southern Colour Print)

2010 (30 Apr). Expo 2010, Shanghai, China. T **708** and similar vert designs, with the two images on each stamp laid *tête-bêche*. Multicoloured. Phosphorised paper. Perf 14.
3205	50c. Type **708**............	95	95
3206	$1 Maori Kaitiaki (carved by Lyonel Grant for New Zealand pavilion) and Chinese Fu Dog............	1·75	1·75
3207	$1.80 Pan Gu (Chinese creation story) and Tane creating world of light (Maori legend)............	2·25	2·25
3208	$2.30 Shanghai and Auckland skylines............	2·50	2·75
3209	$2.80 Jade cong (Chinese good luck symbol) and jade heitiki............	2·75	3·00
3205/3209 *Set of 5*............		9·00	9·50
MS3210 180×140 mm. As Nos. 3205/3209............		9·00	9·50

Nos. 3205/3209 have text in English and Chinese printed on the back of the stamps.
Stamps from No. **MS**3210 do not have text printed on the reverse.

NEW ZEALAND

(Litho Southern Colour Print)

2010 (30 Apr). London 2010 Festival of Stamps. Sheet 130×90 mm. Multicoloured. Perf 14.
MS3211 Nos. 3199 and 3203/3204...................... 9·00 9·00

709 Manu Aute

710 Centenary Series Jersey

(Des Len Hetet. Litho Southern Colour Print)

2010 (9 June). Matariki. Manu Tukutuku (traditional Maori kites). T **709** and similar multicoloured designs. Phosphorised paper. Perf 14.
3212	50c. Type **709**	1·00	80
3213	$1 Manu patiki (*vert*)	1·75	1·75
3214	$1.80 Manu taratahi (*vert*)	3·00	3·00
3215	$2.30 Upoko tangata	3·75	4·50
3212/3215 Set of 4		8·50	9·00
MS3216 150×90 mm. Nos. 3212/3215		8·75	9·00

(Des Len Hetet. Litho Southern Colour Print)

2010 (9 June). Centenary of Maori Rugby. T **710** and similar vert design. Multicoloured. Phosphorised paper. Perf 14.
3217	50c. Type **710**	1·25	80
3218	$1.80 Centenary logo	3·00	3·00
MS3219 160×90 mm. Nos. 3217/3218		3·50	3·50

711 Monarch Butterfly

(Des YouXD. Litho Southern Colour Print)

2010 (7 July). Children's Health. Butterflies. T **711** and similar multicoloured designs.
(a) Ordinary gum. Phosphorised paper. Perf 14.
3220	50c.+10c. Type **711**	1·50	1·50
3221	$1+10c. Tussock Butterfly	2·00	2·00
MS3222 166×95 mm. 50c.+10c. Boulder Copper Butterfly (26×30 mm) and Nos. 3220/3221		3·25	3·25

(b) Self-adhesive. Size 25×30 mm. Die-cut perf 9½×10.
3223	50c.+10c. Boulder Copper Butterfly	1·75	1·75

No. MS3222 is cut around in the shape of a butterfly.

712 Silver Fern (All Blacks emblem)

2010 (4 Aug). All Blacks (national rugby team). Phosphorised paper. Perf 13½.
3224	**712** 60c. black	1·00	80
3225	$1.90 black	5·00	4·00
MS3226 90×78 mm. As Nos. 3224/3225 but 35×20 mm (Perf 15×14½) and Nos. 3224/3225		4·00	6·00

See also Nos. 3368/**MS**3369 and 3562/**MS**3564.

(Litho Southern Colour Print)

2010 (4 Aug)–**2012**. New Zealand Landscapes (3rd series). Horiz designs as T **622**. Multicoloured.
(a) Ordinary gum. Phosphorised paper. Perf 13½.
3227	$1.20 Mitre Peak, Milford Sound	1·60	1·60
3228	$1.90 Queenstown	2·75	2·75
3229	$2.40 Lake Rotorua	3·75	3·75
3230	$2.90 Kaikoura	4·50	4·50
3231	$3.40 River Avon at Christchurch	5·50	5·50
3227/3231 Set of 5		16·00	16·00

(b) Self-adhesive. Phosphor frame. Die-cut perf 10×9½.
3232	$1.20 As No. 3227	1·75	1·75
	a. Booklet pane. No. 3232×10	16·00	
3233	$1.90 As No. 3228	3·00	3·00
	a. Booklet pane. No. 3233×5 and 2 International Air labels	13·00	
3233*b*	$2.40 As No. 3229 (1.2.12)	3·75	4·00
	ba. Booklet pane. No. 3233*b*×5 and 2 International Air labels	17·00	
3232/3233*b* Set of 3		7·75	8·00

Nos. 3232/3233 were normally only available from separate $9.50 or $12 booklets, Nos. SB150/SB151, but the set of two single stamps with plain backing paper could be purchased from the Philatelic Bureau.

No. 3233*b* was available in $12 booklet, No. SB158, and also as a single stamp with plain backing paper from the Philatelic Bureau.

Nos. 3232/3233*b* all have the surplus self-adhesive paper around each stamp retained.

The original printings of No. 3233*b* showed a '2012' imprint, but with the two kiwi reprint booklet issued on 1 November 2013 this was altered to '2010'.

713 Emblem

(Litho Southern Colour Print)

2010 (9 Sept). Rugby World Cup, New Zealand (2011). Phosphorised paper. Perf 13½.
3234	**713**	60c. multicoloured	1·00	1·00
3235	**713**	$1.90 multicoloured	3·00	3·00
MS3236 91×79 mm. As Nos. 3234/3235 but 35×20 mm (Perf 15×14½) and Nos. 3234/3235			7·75	7·75

Stamps as Nos. 3234/3235 but 35×20 mm as in No. MS3236 were sold in sheets of 20 as personalised stamps.

(Des YouXD. Litho Southern Colour Print)

2010 (9 Sept). Personalised Stamps. As Nos. 2950/2955 with new values and new design and as No. **MS**3192 with new values. Multicoloured. Phosphorised paper. Perf 15×14½.
MS3237 165×82 mm. 60c.×8 As Type **660**; Buzzy Bee (toy); Silver Fern; Pohutukawa flower; Engagement and wedding rings; Red Rose; As Type **705**; Teddy bear.............. 7·50 7·50
MS3238 94×82 mm. $1.90 As Type **705**; $2.40 As Type **660**; $2.40 Engagement and wedding rings; $2.40 Pohutukawa flower.............. 18·00 19·00

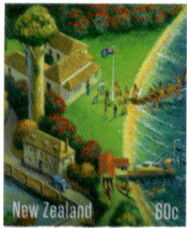
714 Tane Mahuta (oldest tree), Kerikeri Stone Store and Treaty House at Waitangi

715 1960 2d. *The Adoration of the Shepherds* (Rembrandt) Stamp

NEW ZEALAND

(Des Assignment Group. Litho Southern Colour Print)

2010 (6 Oct). New Zealand A Slice of Heaven. Sheet 185×254 mm containing T **714** and similar vert designs. Multicoloured. Phosphorised paper. Perf 14.

MS3239	60c.×25 Type **714**; Fountain and waterfront, Oriental Bay, Wellington; Octagon Plaza with Dunedin Cathedral and St Paul's Church, Dunedin; Auckland Ferry Terminal; The Beehive, Wellington; Sky Tower, Auckland; One Tree Hill, Auckland; Mount Ruapehu and Waikato River; Hot air balloons shaped as Sheep, Cow's head and kiwi; Christchurch Cathedral and River Avon; Horse race; Rural garage, coffee shop and church; Mount Cook, helicopter and aeroplane; War memorial, ploughed field and lake shore; Lake Taupo, Huka Falls and bridge; Champagne Pool, geysers, mud pools and marae; Rugby match; Queenstown, Lake Wakatipu and the Remarkables Range; Skiers, biplane, glider and golf course; Shotover River and Skippers Suspension Bridge; Seaside caravan park; Titahi Bay boatsheds; Hawke's Bay vineyard; Farm with Sheep in pens; Nugget Point.............................	27·00	30·00

The stamps and margins of No. **MS**3239 form a composite design.

An imperforate version of No. **MS**3239 was included in The New Zealand Collection 2010 Yearbook.

(Des Hamish Thompson. Litho Southern Colour Print)

2010 (20 Oct). Christmas. 50th Anniversary of New Zealand Christmas Stamps. T **715** and similar vert designs showing stamps. Multicoloured.

(a) Phosphorised paper. Perf 13½.

3240	60c. Type **715**	1·00	30
3241	$1.20 1970 3c. stamp showing The Holy Family stained glass window from Invercargill Presbyterian Church	2·75	1·50
3242	$1.90 1979 35c. Pohutukawa tree stamp	3·00	3·00
3243	$2.40 1983 45c. The Glory of Christmas stamp showing star and flowers	4·00	4·75
3244	$2.90 2000 40c. Virgin Mary and Baby Jesus stamp	4·75	5·00
3240/3244	*Set of 5*	14·00	13·00

(b) Self-adhesive. Size 25×30 mm. Die-cut perf 11.

3245	60c. As Type **715**	1·00	1·00
	a. Booklet pane. No. 3245×10	9·00	
	b. Perf 12½	1·00	1·00
	ba. Horiz pair. Nos. 3245b/3246b	2·00	2·00
3246	$1.90 As No. 3242	2·75	3·25
	a. Booklet pane. No. 3246×10	25·00	
	b. Perf 12½	2·75	3·25

No. 3245 was issued in booklet, No. SB152, sold at $5.40, a 60c. discount off the face value of the stamps.

No. 3245b was issued in rolls of 100.

The *se-tenant* pair, No. 3245ba, could be purchased from the Philatelic Bureau.

No. 3246 was issued in booklet, No. SB153, sold at $16, a $3 discount off the face value of the stamps.

716 Surf Lifeguard with Rescue Tube

(Des Creature. Litho Cartor)

2010 (3 Nov). Centenary of Surf Lifesaving. T **716** and similar horiz designs. Multicoloured. Phosphorised paper. Perf 13×13½.

3247	60c. Type **716**	1·10	60
3248	$1.20 Lifeguards in inflatable rescue boat (IRB)	2·25	1·40
3249	$1.90 Ski paddlers in Surf Lifesaving Championships	2·75	2·75
3250	$2.40 Surf boat	3·75	4·25
3251	$2.90 March past of lifeguards in 1930s surf carnival	5·00	5·00
3247/3251	*Set of 5*	13·50	12·50

(Litho Southern Colour Print)

2010 (12 Nov). Palmpex 2010 National Stamp Exhibition, Palmerston North. Sheet 150×90 mm. Phosphorised paper. Multicoloured. Perf 14.

MS3252	No. 2090b×3	8·00	8·00

BEST OF 2010. A further set of miniature sheets as described below No. 2042 were distributed by the Philatelic Bureau to customers purchasing a certain amount of philatelic material during 2010. The sheets comprised: 1. Nos. 3190, 3197 and 3204; 2. Nos. 3209, 3215 and 3221; 3. Nos. 3230, 3244 and 3251.

Imperforate sheets of Nos. 3212/3215 and a perforated *se-tenant* block of the same four stamps were also distributed.

717 Rabbit Symbol

(Des AsiaWorks. Litho Cartor)

2011 (12 Jan). Chinese New Year. Year of the Rabbit. T **717** and similar vert designs. Multicoloured. Phosphorised paper. Perf 13½×13.

3253	60c. Type **717**	1·10	60
3254	$1.20 Chinese style Rabbit	1·90	1·50
3255	$1.90 Leaping Rabbit	3·25	3·50
3256	$2.40 Christchurch Cathedral and Chinese kite	3·75	4·25
3253/3256	*Set of 4*	9·00	9·00
MS3257	150×90 mm. Nos. 3253/3256	10·00	10·00

(Litho Southern Colour Print)

2011 (12 Feb). INDIPEX 2011 World Philatelic Exhibition, New Delhi. Sheet 120×90 mm. Multicoloured. Perf 13½.

MS3258 Nos. 3227/3229	9·00	9·00

718 Whakaeke (choreographed entrance)

(Des Tai Kerekere, KE Design. Litho Southern Colour Print)

2011 (17 Feb). Kapa Haka (Maori performing arts). T **718** and similar vert designs. Multicoloured.

(a) Self-adhesive. Die-cut perf 10×9½.

3259	60c. Type **718**	90	1·10
	a. Block of 6. Nos. 3259/3264	11·00	13·00
3260	60c. Poi (dancer swinging taupo ball on flax cord)	90	1·10
3261	$1.20 Waiata-a-ringa (action songs)	1·75	2·25
3262	$1.90 Haka	2·50	3·00
3263	$2.40 Whakawatea (choreographed exit)	3·00	3·25
3264	$2.90 Moteatea (traditional chant)	3·50	4·00
3259/3264	*Set of 6*	11·00	13·00

(b) Ordinary gum. Perf 13½.

MS3265	150×90 mm. As Nos. 3259/3264	11·00	13·50

Nos. 3259/3264 were each issued in separate sheets of 25.

The *se-tenant* block, No. 3259a, is probably from the jumbo roll printing.

719 Prince William and Miss Catherine Middleton

NEW ZEALAND

(Des Datam. Litho Southern Colour Print)

2011 (23 Mar). Royal Wedding. T **719** and similar vert design. Multicoloured. Phosphorised paper. Perf 14½.

3266	$2.40 Type **719**	4·00	4·00
	a. Horiz pair. Nos. 3266/3267	8·00	8·00
3267	$2.40 Prince William and Miss Catherine Middleton embracing	4·00	4·00
MS3268	135×91 mm. Nos. 3266/3267	8·00	8·00

Nos. 3266/3267 were printed together, *se-tenant*, as horizontal pairs in sheets of 20.

720 Hokey Pokey (vanilla and crunchy toffee ice cream)

721 Charles Heaphy, 11 February 1864, Waikato, New Zealand

(Des Datam. Litho Southern Colour Print or Australia Post Sprintpak (Nos. 3269b/3273b, first three printings))

2011 (23 Mar). KiwiStamps (2nd issue). T **720** and similar horiz designs. Multicoloured. Self-adhesive. Phosphor frame. Die-cut perf 10.

3269	(60c.) Type **720**	95	95
	a. Horiz strip of 5. Nos. 3269/3273	4·25	4·25
	b. Perf 11	95	95
	ba. Booklet pane. Nos. 3269b/3273b, each×2	8·50	
	bb. Imperf		
3270	(60c.) Kiwi road sign	95	95
	b. Perf 11	95	95
3271	(60c.) Beach	95	95
	b. Perf 11	95	95
3272	(60c.) Trout fishing	95	95
	b. Perf 11	95	95
3273	(60c.) Mountain biking	95	95
	b. Perf 11	95	95
3269/3273 Set of 5		4·25	4·25

Nos. 3269/3273b were all inscr 'KiwiStamp' and were valid for Standard Post medium letters in New Zealand (originally 60c. each).

Nos. 3269/3273 were issued in sheets and in rolls of 100 containing all five designs in sequence.

Nos. 3269b/3273b were issued in booklets of ten, No. SB154, originally sold for $6.

Prior to May 2014 printing was by Australia Post Sprintpak but after that date Southern Colour Print took over the booklet printing contract.

(Des Cue Design. Litho Southern Colour Print)

2011 (14 Apr). Victoria Cross. The New Zealand Story. T **721** and similar vert designs showing New Zealand recipients of Victoria Cross. Multicoloured. Phosphorised paper. Perf 13½.

3274	60c. Type **721**	1·25	1·25
	a. Sheetlet of 22. Nos. 3274/3295	25·00	25·00
3275	60c. William James Hardham, 28 January 1901, South Africa	1·25	1·25
3276	60c. Cyril Royston Guyton Bassett, 7 August 1915, Gallipoli	1·25	1·25
3277	60c. Donald Forrester Brown, 15 September 1916, High Wood, France	1·25	1·25
3278	60c. Samuel Frickleton, 7 June 1917, Messines, Belgium	1·25	1·25
3279	60c. Leslie Wilton Andrew, 31 July 1917, La Basse Ville, France	1·25	1·25
3280	60c. Henry James Nicholas, 3 December 1917, Polderboek, Belgium	1·25	1·25
3281	60c. Richard Charles Travis, 24 July 1918, Hébuterne, France	1·25	1·25
3282	60c. Samuel Forsyth, 24 August 1918, Grévillers, France	1·25	1·25
3283	60c. Reginald Stanley Judson, 26 August 1918, Bapaume, France	1·25	1·25
3284	60c. Harry John Laurent, 12 September 1918, Gouzeaucourt Wood, France	1·25	1·25
3285	60c. James Crichton, 30 September 1918, Crevecoeur, France	1·25	1·25
3286	60c. John Gildroy Grant, 1 September 1918, Bancourt, France	1·25	1·25
3287	60c. James Edward Allen Ward, 7 July 1941, on operations over Holland	1·25	1·25
3288	60c. Charles Hazlitt Upham, 22–30 May 1941, Crete and 14–15 July 1942, Western Desert	1·25	1·25
3289	60c. Alfred Clive Hulme, 20–28 May 1941, Crete	1·25	1·25
3290	60c. John Daniel Hinton, 28–29 April 1941, Greece	1·25	1·25
3291	60c. Keith Elliott, 15 July 1942, Western Desert	1·25	1·25
3292	60c. Moana-Nui-a-Kiwa Ngarimu, 26–27 March 1943, Tunisia	1·25	1·25
3293	60c. Lloyd Allen Trigg, 11 August 1943, sea patrol, Atlantic Ocean	1·25	1·25
3294	60c. Leonard Henry Trent, 3 May 1943, on operation over Holland	1·25	1·25
3295	60c. Victoria Cross of New Zealand (awarded to Bill Henry Apiata, 2004, Afghanistan)	1·25	1·25
3274/3295 Set of 22		25·00	25·00

Nos. 3274/3295 were printed together, *se-tenant*, in sheetlets of 22 stamps.

An imperforate version of the sheetlet, No. 3274a, was included in The New Zealand Collection 2011 Yearbook.

722 Humpback Whale   **723** Modern Greenstone Hei Matau by Lewis Gardiner

(Des Dave Gunson. Litho Southern Colour Print)

2011 (4 May). Beyond the Coast. Sheet 180×250 mm containing T **722** and similar multicoloured designs. Self-adhesive. Phosphorised paper. Die-cut perf 10×9½ (vert) or 9½×10 (horiz).

MS3296 60c.×10 Type **722**; White-faced Storm Petrel (*horiz*); John Dory (*horiz*); Yellowfin Tuna (*horiz*); Hammerhead Shark (*horiz*); Kingfish (*horiz*); Lord Howe Coralfish; Snapper (*horiz*); Arrow Squid (*horiz*); Orange Roughy (*horiz*) $1.90 Yellow Moray Eel (*horiz*); $1.90 King Crab..... 17·00 18·00

The stamps and margins of No. **MS**3296 form a composite design showing marine life from the surface to the seabed.

(Des Len Hetet. Litho Southern Colour Print)

2011 (1 June). Matariki. Hei Matau. T **723** and similar vert designs. Multicoloured. Phosphorised paper.

(a) Self-adhesive. Die-cut perf 10×9½.

3297	60c. Type **723**	90	1·10
	a. Block of 6. Nos. 3297/3302	11·00	13·50
3298	60c. Functional whalebone fish hook, 1500–1800	90	1·10
3299	$1.20 Inanga greenstone hei matau, *circa* 1800	1·75	2·25
3300	$1.90 Modern hei matau in multiple materials by Lewis Gardiner	2·50	3·00
3301	$2.40 Wooden hei matau with bone barb, *circa* 1800	3·00	3·25
3302	$2.90 Symbolic Maui's hook made from whalebone, 1750–1850	3·50	4·00
3297/3302 Set of 6		11·00	13·50

(b) Ordinary paper. Perf 13½.

MS3303 150×90 mm. As Nos. 3297/3302..... 11·00 13·50

Nos. 3297/3302 were each issued in separate sheets of 25, and also in a *se-tenant* block, No. 3297a.

724 Kiwi

(Litho Southern Colour Print)

2011 (6 July). Children's Health. Flightless Birds. T **724** and similar multicoloured designs.

(a) Ordinary gum. Perf 14.

3304	60c.+10c. Type **724**	1·75	1·75
3305	$1.20+10c. Kakapo	2·75	3·00
MS3306	130×90 mm. 60c.+10c. Takahe (26×30 mm) and Nos. 3304/3305	4·75	4·75

(b) Self-adhesive. Size 26×30 mm. Die-cut perf 9½×10.

3307	60c.+10c. Takahe	1·75	1·75

NEW ZEALAND

The upper and left portions of No. **MS**3306 are cut around in the shape of a takahe.

(Litho Southern Colour Print)

2011 (6 July). Round Kiwi Stamps. Phosphorised paper. Phosphorised paper. Perf 14½.
3308	445	$1.20 black	3·00	3·50
		a. Horiz strip of 3. Nos. 3308/3310	8·50	11·50
3309	445	$1.90 silver	3·25	4·50
3310	445	$2.40 blue	3·50	5·00
3308/3310 Set of 3			8·50	11·50

Nos. 3308/3310 were each perforated in a circle contained within an outer perforated square which had a silver fern leaf in the four corners. The design of the stamp was also altered, to include the NZ Post Silver Fern logo above the Kiwi's neck.

Nos. 3308/3310 were each printed in sheets of ten.

Nos. 3308/3310 were also available in a horizontal strip of three, No. 3308a.

(Litho Southern Colour Print)

2011 (28 July). Philanippon 2011 World Stamp Exhibition, Yokohama, Japan. Sheet 130×90 mm. Phosphorised paper. Multicoloured. Perf 14½ (circular Kiwi stamp as No. 3309) or 13½ (others).
MS3311 No. 3225×2 and No. 3309................... 11·00 11·00

725 1 State Highway

726 Webb Ellis Cup (Motionstamp HDR 3D Technology Outer Aspect, Auckland)

(Des Assignment Group. Litho Southern Colour Print)

2011 (10 Aug). Counting in Kiwi. Sheet 190×226 mm containing T **725** and similar vert designs. Multicoloured. Phosphorised paper. Perf 14.
MS3312 60c.×21 1, Type **725**; 2, jandals; 3, hour ferry ride across Cook Strait (Seagull and ferry); 4, players of Southern Cross; 5, year old starting school; 6, runs in cricket - out of the park; 7, players in netball team (ball landing in net); 8, wire; 9, dressed to the nines; 10, guitar; First 11; 12, Bluff Oysters; 13, lamingtons (cakes); 14, national parks (fish and lake); 15, players in rugby team; 16, driving age (car mirror and dice); 17, Captain Cook's landing, 1769; 18, voting age; 19, protected surf breaks (surfboard and wave); 20, bucks (parrot wearing crown); 21, key to the door.......................... 23·00 25·00

(Motionstamp HDR 3D Technology Outer Aspect, Auckland)

2011 (7 Sept). Webb Ellis Cup (World Cup Rugby, New Zealand). Die-cut perf 10.
3313 **726** $15 gold, black and grey .... 17·00 24·00

No. 3313 was produced using Motionstamp technology, giving a three dimensional effect to the trophy.

No. 3313 is laser perforated.

No. 3313 was only available mounted in a display card or as a first day cover.

727 Hiker

728 Baby Jesus in Manger

(Des Cue Design. Litho Southern Colour Print, New Zealand)

2011 (5 Oct). The New Zealand Experience. T **727** and similar vert designs. Multicoloured. Phosphorised paper. Perf 14.
3314	60c. Type **727**	1·40	1·25
3315	60c. Sailing dinghy, motor boat and windsurfer	1·40	1·25
3316	$1.20 Fishing	2·25	2·00
3317	$1.90 Maori man performing kapa haka and marae	3·50	3·75
3318	$2.40 Skier and helicopter	4·00	4·75
3319	$2.90 Bungy jumping	5·00	5·50
3314/3319 Set of 6		16·00	17·00
MS3320 160×90 mm. Nos. 3314/3319		16·00	17·00

(Des Karen Mounsey-Smith. Litho Australia Post Sprintpak (Nos. 3326b/3326ba) or Southern Colour Print (others))

2011 (2 Nov). Christmas. T **728** and similar multicoloured designs.

(a) Ordinary paper. Phosphorised paper. Perf 14.
3321	60c. Type **728**	1·90	60
3322	$1.20 Angel appearing to shepherds	2·75	1·75
3323	$1.90 Mary, Joseph and baby Jesus	3·25	3·25
3324	$2.40 Shepherds with baby Jesus	3·75	4·25
3325	$2.90 Wise men with baby Jesus	5·00	7·00
3321/3325 Set of 5		15·00	15·00

(b) Self-adhesive. Size 25×30 mm. Die-cut perf 9½×10.
3326	60c. As Type **728**	1·60	1·00
	a. Horiz strip of 3. Nos. 3326/3328	8·50	9·50
	b. With phosphor frame. Perf 11	1·40	1·00
	ba. Booklet pane. No. 3326b×10	12·00	
3327	$1.90 As No. 3323	3·25	3·50
	a. Booklet pane. No. 3327c×10	30·00	
3328	$2.40 As No. 3324	4·25	4·50
	a. Booklet pane. No. 3328c×10	35·00	
3326/3328 Set of 3		8·50	8·50

No. 3326 was issued in rolls of 100.

The *se-tenant* strip, No. 3326a, could be purchased from the Philatelic Bureau.

No. 3326b was issued in $6 booklet, No. SB155.

No. 3327 was issued in booklet, No. SB156, sold at $17.10, a $1.90 discount off the face value of the stamps.

No. 3328 was issued in booklet, No. SB157, sold at $21.60, a $2.40 discount off the face value of the stamps.

(Litho Southern Colour Print)

2011 (11 Nov). China 2011 27th Asian International Stamp Exhibition, Wuxi, China. Sheet 130×90 mm. Multicoloured. Phosphorised paper. Perf 14½.
MS3329 Nos. 3308/3310... 9·25 10·00

BEST OF 2011. A further set of miniature sheets as described below No. 2042 were distributed by the Philatelic Bureau to customers purchasing a certain amount of philatelic material during 2011. The sheets comprised: 1. Nos. 3256, 3267 and 3264; 2. Nos. 3295, 3305 and 3302; 3. Nos. 3319, 3310 and 3325.

Imperforate sheets of Nos. 3321/3325 and a perforated *se-tenant* strip comprising the same five stamps were also distributed.

729 Chinese Character for Dragon

730 Pohutukawa (*Metrosideros exselsa*)

(Des Bananaworks. Litho Cartor)

2012 (5 Jan). Chinese New Year. Year of the Dragon. T **729** and similar vert designs. Multicoloured. Phosphorised paper. Perf 13.
3330	60c. Type **729**	1·25	60
3331	$1.20 Paper-cut Dragon	2·00	1·50
3332	$1.90 Dragon lantern	2·50	2·50
3333	$2.40 Dunedin Railway Station and pair of Swallows	6·00	7·00
3330/3333 Set of 4		10·50	10·50
MS3334 150×90 mm. Nos. 3330/3333		10·75	10·75

See also No. **MS**3423.

(Des 2Di4 Design. Litho Southern Colour Print)

2012 (1 Feb). Native Trees. T **730** and similar vert designs. Multicoloured. Phosphorised paper. Perf 13×13½.
3335	60c. Type **730**	1·50	60
3336	$1.20 Cabbage tree (*Cordyline australis*)	2·50	2·00
3337	$1.90 Kowhai (*Sophora microphylla*)	3·25	2·75

NEW ZEALAND

3338	$2.40 Nikau (*Rhopalostylis sapida*)		4·75	5·00
3339	$2.90 Manuka (*Leptospermum scoparium*)		5·50	6·00
3335/3339 Set of 5			16·00	14·50
MS3340 160×90 mm. Nos. 3335/3339			16·00	16·00

731 Tiger Moth ('The Beginning')

732 Official New Zealand Portrait of Queen Elizabeth II

(Des Strategy Design and Advertising. Litho Southern Colour Print)

2012 (15 Mar). 75th Anniversary of the RNZAF (Royal New Zealand Air Force). T **731** and similar horiz designs. Multicoloured. Phosphorised paper. Perf 14½.

3341	60c. Type **731**	1·75	1·75
	a. Sheetlet of 15. Nos. 3341/3355	24·00	24·00
3342	60c. Air Training Corps cadets	1·75	1·75
3343	60c. Pilot and navigator in cockpit of Wellington bomber ('WWII Europe')	1·75	1·75
3344	60c. Women's Auxiliary Air Force members in front of de Havilland Express aircraft	1·75	1·75
3345	60c. Servicing Unit aircraft maintenance area, Ondonga, New Georgia, 1943 ('WWII Pacific')	1·75	1·75
3346	60c. Loading hopper into modified bomb bay of Avenger NZ2504 for aerial topdressing trials, Masterton Aerodrome, 1949	1·75	1·75
3347	60c. Territorial Air Force No. 3 (Canterbury) Squadron	1·75	1·75
3348	60c. de Havilland Venom WK428 of 14 Squadron over RAF Station, Changi, Singapore ('South East Asia')	1·75	1·75
3349	60c. RNZAF A-4 Skyhawk and HMAS *Adelaide* off Perth, 1996 ('ANZAC')	1·75	1·75
3350	60c. Super Sea Sprite helicopter SH-2G taking off from flight deck of Anzac class ship HMNZS *Te-Mana* ('Naval Support')	1·75	1·75
3351	60c. RNZAF Hercules at McMurdo Base, Antarctica ('Transport')	1·75	1·75
3352	60c. Three 'Huey' Iroquois helicopters, Timor, 2001 ('Peacekeeping')	1·75	1·75
3353	60c. Search and rescue training and RNZAF Iroquois helicopter	1·75	1·75
3354	60c. Aircraft flying in 'missing man' formation ('Remembrance')	1·75	1·75
3355	60c. NH90 advance medium utility helicopter ('The Future')	1·75	1·75
3341/3355 Set of 15		24·00	28·00

Nos. 3341/3355 were printed together, *se-tenant*, in sheetlets of 15 stamps.

The stamps also exist in eight miniature sheets, each 135×150 mm, with a line of roulettes at left. The miniature sheets contain: Nos. 3341/3342, each×2; Nos. 3343/3344, each×2; Nos. 3345/3346, each×2; Nos. 3347/3348, each×2; Nos. 3349/3350, each×2; Nos. 3351/3352, each×2; Nos. 3353 and 3355, each×2; No. 3354×2. These miniature sheets were only available from a booklet, No. SP12, containing stamps with a face value of $18 but sold for $19.90.

(Des Capiche Design. Litho Southern Colour Print)

2012 (9 May). Diamond Jubilee. T **732** and similar vert designs. Multicoloured. Phosphorised paper. Perf 13×13½.

3356	70c. Type **732**	1·40	1·40
3357	70c. Official New Zealand portrait of Queen Elizabeth II and Duke of Edinburgh	1·40	1·40
3358	$1.40 Queen Elizabeth II and Duke of Edinburgh wearing ceremonial cloaks for Maori reception, Hastings, New Zealand, 1986	2·50	2·50
3359	$1.90 Queen Elizabeth II and Duke of Edinburgh waving from car, Wellington, 1981	3·25	3·25
3360	$2.40 Queen Elizabeth II and Duke of Edinburgh on Silver Jubilee tour, Wellington, 1981	3·75	3·75
3361	$2.90 Queen Elizabeth II giving Christmas broadcast from Government House, Auckland, 1953	4·25	4·25
3356/3361 Set of 6		15·00	15·00
MS3362 101×97 mm. Nos. 3356/3361		18·00	18·00

(Litho Southern Colour Print)

2012 (23 May). New Zealand Landscapes (4th series). Horiz designs as T **622**. Multicoloured.

(a) Ordinary gum. Perf 13×13½.

3363	$1.40 Cape Reinga	2·50	3·00
3364	$2.10 Stewart Island	3·75	4·25
3365	$3.50 Lake Matheson	6·25	8·00
3363/3365 Set of 3		11·00	14·00

(b) Self-adhesive. Die-cut perf 10×9½.

3366	$1.40 As No. 3363	2·50	3·00
	a. Booklet pane. No. 3366×10	22·00	
	b. Horiz pair. Nos. 3366/3367	6·25	7·00
3367	$2.10 As No. 3364	3·75	4·25
	a. Booklet pane. No. 3367×5	16·00	

Nos. 3366/3367 were issued in separate booklets, Nos. SB159/SB160. The *se-tenant* pair, No. 3266b, could be purchased from the Philatelic Bureau.

(Litho Southern Colour Print)

2012 (23 May). All Blacks (National Rugby Team). As Nos. 3224 and **MS**3226 with new face value. Perf 13½.

3368	**712** 70c. black	1·75	1·75
MS3369 90×61 mm. As No. 3368 but 35×20 mm (Perf 15×14½) and No. 3368		2·50	2·50

733 Pouakai (birdman), Pareora

(Des Dave Burke. Litho Southern Colour Print)

2012 (6 June). Matariki. Maori Rock Art. T **733** and similar horiz designs. Multicoloured. Phosphorised paper.

(a) Self-adhesive. Die-cut perf 9½×10.

3370	70c. Type **733**	1·25	1·25
	a. Pane. Nos. 3370/3375	16·00	16·00
3371	70c. Seated tiki figure on ceiling of shelter, Maerewhenua	1·25	1·25
3372	$1.40 Two people on mokihi (bulrush water craft), Opihi	2·50	2·50
3373	$1.90 Te Puawaitanga, Waitaki	3·50	3·50
3374	$2.40 Tiki figure, Te Ana a Wai	4·25	4·25
3375	$2.90 Taniwha on ceiling of shelter, Opihi	5·25	5·25
3370/3375 Set of 6		16·00	16·00

(b) Ordinary gum. Perf 13½.

MS3376 150×91 mm. As Nos. 3370/3375	16·00	16·00

(Litho)

2012 (6 June). Personalised Stamps. As No. **MS**3237 with new face values. Multicoloured. Perf 15×14½.

MS3377 70c.×8 as Type **660**; Buzzy Bee (toy); Silver Fern; Pohutukawa flower; Engagement and wedding rings; Red Rose; As Type **705**; Teddy bear.. 9·00 16·00

No. **MS**3377 contains two horizontal strips of four stamps separated by a gutter containing labels inscribed 'Personalised Stamps 2012'.

(Litho Southern Colour Print)

2012 (18 June). Indonesia 2012 World Stamp Championship and Exhibition, Jakarta. Sheet 120×90 mm containing Nos. 3335 and 3337/3338. Phosphorised paper. Multicoloured. Perf 13×13½.

MS3378 Nos. 3335 and 3337/3338 .... 8·00 9·00

734 Cape Reinga and Kaitaia

735 Selu Tuiga depicting Samoan Parliament and Beehive, Wellington

NEW ZEALAND

(Des Evan Purdie and Geoff Francis, Assignment Group. Litho Southern Colour Print)

2012 (4 July). Tiki Tour of New Zealand (2nd issue). Sheet 185×254 mm containing T **734** and similar vert designs. Multicoloured. Phosphorised paper. Perf 14.

MS3379	70c.×20 Type **734**; Whangarei and Bay of Islands; Cape Brett; Lion Rock; Auckland, Hamilton and Tauranga; White Island and East Cape; Mount Taranaki, New Plymouth and Hawera; Rotorua, Taupo and Palmerston North; Napier and Gisborne; Fish and boat; Westport and Greymouth; Nelson and Kaikoura; Wellington; Chatham Islands; Milford Sound and Mitre Peak; Mount Cook, Queenstown and Timaru; Christchurch; Invercargill, Gore and Stewart Island; Dunedin; Taiaroa Head	29·00	35·00

The stamps and background of No. **MS**3379 form a composite design showing a map of New Zealand.

An imperforate version of No. **MS**3379 was included in The New Zealand Collection 2012 yearbook.

(Des Michael Tuffery. Litho Southern Colour Print)

2012 (1 Aug). 50th Anniversary of Treaty of Friendship between New Zealand and Samoa. Selu Tuiga (Samoan head comb in shape of traditional tuiga headdress). T **735** and similar vert designs. Multicoloured. Phosphorised paper. Perf 14.

3380	70c. Type **735**	1·25	1·25
3381	$1.40 Tuiga with niu (Coconut tree) design	2·50	2·50
3382	$1.90 Selu Tuiga depicting Maota Fa'amasino (Courthouse, Apia)	3·50	3·50
3383	$2.40 Selu Tuiga with tatau (tattoo) motifs and patterns	4·25	4·25
3384	$2.90 Selu Tuiga depicting Immaculate Conception of Mary Cathedral, Mulivai	5·25	5·25
3380/3384	Set of 5	15·00	15·00
MS3385	150×90 mm. Nos. 3380/3384	16·00	16·00

736 Sea Lion Pup

737 *Aramoana* (Picton to Wellington ferry, 1962–1984)

(Litho Southern Colour Print)

2012 (1 Aug). Children's Health. New Zealand Sea Lion (*Phocarctos hookeri*). T **736** and similar multicoloured designs.

(a) Ordinary gum. Perf 14.

3386	70c.+10c. Type **736**	1·75	1·75
3387	$1.40+10c. Sub-adult male	3·00	3·25
MS3388	147×91 mm. 70c.+10c. Sea Lion Pup (head) (26×30 mm) and Nos. 3386/3387	7·00	7·50

(b) Self-adhesive. Size 26×30 mm. Die-cut perf 9½×10.

3389	70c.+10c. Sea Lion Pup (head)	1·75	1·75

No. **MS**3388 is cut in the shape of a female Sea Lion and Pup.

(Des Creature, Wellington. Litho Southern Colour Print)

2012 (5 Sept). Great Voyages of New Zealand. T **737** and similar horiz designs. Multicoloured. Phosphorised paper (Nos. 3390/3394) or ordinary paper (No. **MS**3395). Perf 14.

3390	70c. Type **737**	2·00	1·25
3391	$1.40 Waka (Maori canoe) crossing Cook Strait	2·75	2·50
3392	$1.90 *Earnslaw* (Kingston–Queenstown–Glenorchy steamer), Lake Wakatipu	4·25	3·50
3393	$2.40 *Dunedin* (Port Chalmers to London, 1874–1990)	5·00	5·50
3394	$2.90 *Rotomahana* (Wellington to Lyttelton, Australia), 1870s–1925	6·50	6·50
3390/3394	Set of 5	18·00	17·00
MS3395	136×75 mm. Nos. 3390/3394	19·00	18·00

738 Mary, Joseph and Baby Jesus

739 Bilbo Baggins

(Des Donna MacKenna. Litho Southern Colour Print (Nos. 3396/3400, 3401b) or Australia Post Sprintpak (Nos. 3401/3403))

2012 (3 Oct). Christmas. T **738** and similar vert designs. Multicoloured.

(a) Ordinary gum. Perf 14.

3396	70c. Type **738**	1·25	60
3397	$1.40 Shepherds	2·50	1·25
3398	$1.90 Angel	3·50	3·25
3399	$2.40 Three Wise Men offering gifts	4·25	4·75
3400	$2.90 Journey of the Three Wise Men	5·25	5·75
3396/3400	Set of 5	15·00	14·00

(b) Self-adhesive. Size 25×30 mm. Die-cut perf 9½×10 (3401b) or 11 (others).

3401	70c. As Type **738**	1·25	1·25
	a. Booklet pane. No. 3401×10	11·00	
	b. Partial phosphor frame only. Die-cut perf 9½×10	1·25	1·25
	c. Phosphor as No. 3401 but baby has phosphor halo only. Perf 11	1·25	1·25
	ca. Horiz strip of 3. Nos. 3401c/3403	8·00	8·00
3402	$1.90 As No. 3398	3·50	3·50
	a. Booklet pane. No. 3402×10	30·00	
3403	$2.40 As No. 3399	4·25	4·25
	a. Booklet pane. No. 3403×10	35·00	

No. 3401, issued in $7 booklet, No. SB161, has phosphor as No. 3401c but with the addition of phosphor over the baby's clothes.

Nos. 3402/3403 were issued in $17.10 or $21.60 booklets, Nos. SB162/SB163.

No. 3401b, issued in rolls of 100, has a partial phosphor frame at the foot and part way up the sides of the stamp.

No. 3401c has a phosphor band at the foot of the stamp, phosphor haloes for the Holy Family and phosphor around the sides of the filigree frame of the stamp design. It was only issued in horizontal strips of three with Nos. 3402/3403 and could be purchased from the Philatelic Bureau.

(Litho Southern Colour Print)

2012 (12 Oct). Blenpex 2012 National Stamp Exhibition, Marlborough. Sheet 131×91 mm. Phosphorised paper. Phosphorised paper. Perf 13×13½.

MS3404	Nos. 3356, 3359 and 3361	9·00	10·00

(Litho Southern Colour Print (Nos. 3405/3410) or Australia Post Sprintpak (Nos. 3417/3422))

2012 (1 Nov). *The Hobbit* (film trilogy). *An Unexpected Journey* (1st issue). T **739** and similar multicoloured designs.

(a) Ordinary gum. Phosphorised paper. Perf 14½×14 (vert) or 14×14½ (horiz).

3405	70c. Type **739**	1·50	70
3406	$1.40 Gollum (Andy Serkis)	2·75	1·50
3407	$1.90 Gandalf (Ian McKellen)	3·75	4·00
3408	$2.10 Thorin Oakenshield (Richard Armitage) (horiz)	4·00	4·50
3409	$2.40 Radagast (Sylvester McCoy)	4·50	4·75
3410	$2.90 Elrond (Hugo Weaving)	5·50	6·50
3405/3410	Set of 6	20·00	20·00

Nos. 3411/3416 are vacant.

(b) Self-adhesive. Size 26×37 mm or 37×26 mm. Die-cut perf 11½.

3417	70c. As Type **739**	1·25	1·25
	a. Booklet pane. Nos. 3417×4, 3418×2 and 3419/3422 (horiz)	25·00	
	b. Pane. Nos. 3417/3422	18·00	18·00
3418	$1.40 As No. 3406	2·50	2·50
3419	$1.90 As No. 3407	3·50	3·50
3420	$2.10 As No. 3408	3·75	3·75
3421	$2.40 As No. 3409	4·25	4·25
3422	$2.90 As No. 3410	5·25	5·25
3417/3422	Set of 6	18·00	18·00

A set of six miniature sheets containing Nos. 3405/3410 as single stamps were sold at $14.40 per set, a $3 premium over face value.

Nos. 3417/3422 were issued in $14.90 stamp booklet, No. SB164.

No. 3417b could be purchased from the Philatelic Bureau.

See also Nos. 3512/3523 and 3623/3635.

NEW ZEALAND

(Litho Southern Colour Print)

2012 (2 Nov). Beijing 2012 International Stamp and Coin Expo. Sheet 121×90 mm. Phosphorised paper. Multicoloured. Perf 13×13½.
MS3423 As Nos. 3330 and 3332/3333.................... 7·00 7·50

BEST OF 2012. A further set of miniature sheets as described below No. 2042 were distributed by the Philatelic Bureau to customers purchasing a certain amount of philatelic material during 2012. The sheets comprised: 1. Nos. 3333, 3339 and 3355; 2. Nos. 3361, 3375 and 3384; 3. The Taiaroa Head stamp from Nos. **MS**3379, Nos. 3387 and 3394.
Imperforate sheets of Nos. 3390/3394 and a perforated *se-tenant* strip comprising the same four stamps were also distributed.

740 Calligraphic Snake by Zhao Meng-fu (1254–1322)

741 Hen and Chickens Fern (*Asplenium bulbiferum*)

(Des Bananaworks, Auckland. Litho Cartor)

2013 (9 Jan). Chinese New Year. Year of the Snake. T **740** and similar vert designs. Multicoloured. Phosphorised paper. Perf 13½×13.
3424   70c. Type **740** .... 1·25   60
3425 $1.40 Paper-cut greeting Snake patterned with Silver Ferns and Pomegranates ..... 2·50   1·50
3426 $1.90 Lantern with koru-shaped Snake design .... 3·50   4·00
3427 $2.40 Koru-snake lanterns on Skyline Gondola, Queenstown....................... 4·25   4·75
3424/3427 Set of 4 .... 10·50 9·75
MS3428 150×90 mm. Nos. 3424/3427................... 10·50 10·50

(Des 2Di4 Design, Wellington. Litho Cartor)

2013 (7 Feb). Native Ferns. T **741** and similar horiz designs. Multicoloured. Phosphorised paper. Perf 13×13½.
3429   70c. Type **741** .... 1·25   60
3430 $1.40 Kidney Fern (*Cardiomanes reniforme*)..... 2·50   1·50
3431 $1.90 Colenso's Hard Fern (*Blechnum colensoi*).. 3·50   3·50
3432 $2.40 Umbrella Fern (*Sticherus cunninghamii*).. 4·25   4·75
3433 $2.90 Silver Fern (*Cyathea dealbata*)............. 5·25   5·75
3429/3433 Set of 5 .... 15·00 14·50
MS3434 160×90 mm. Nos. 3429/3433................... 16·00 16·00

742 *A Lion in the Meadow*

743 Kiwi Team One on Patrol, North-east Bamyan, Afghanistan, 2011

(Des Tim Garman, Silver-i-Design Associates. Litho Southern Colour Print)

2013 (13 Mar). Margaret Mahy (children's writer) Commemoration. T **742** and similar horiz designs. Multicoloured. Phosphorised paper. Perf 14.
3435   70c. Type **742** .... 1·25   60
3436 $1.40 *A Summery Saturday Morning*.................. 2·50   1·50
3437 $1.90 *The Word Witch* .... 3·50   3·50
3438 $2.40 *The Great White Man-eating Shark* .... 4·25   4·75
3439 $2.90 *The Changeover* .... 5·25   5·75
3435/3439 Set of 5 .... 15·00 14·50
MS3440 140×85 mm. Nos. 3435/3439................... 15·00 15·00

(Des Strategy Design and Advertising, Wellington. Litho Southern Colour Print)

2013 (10 Apr). ANZAC (4th series). New Zealanders serving Abroad. T **743** and similar horiz designs. Multicoloured. Phosphorised paper. Perf 14.
3441   70c. Type **743** .... 1·25   1·25
3442   70c. RNZAF Iroquois helicopter carrying Australian troops, Dili, Timor-Leste, 2008... 1·25   1·25
3443 $1.40 Territorial Army members performing haka, Honiara, Solomon Islands, 2009 .. 2·50   2·50
3444 $1.90 M113A1 tank of Queen Alexandra's Mounted Rifles on checkpoint duty, Bosnia Herzegovina, 2007 .... 3·50   3·50
3445 $2.40 ANZAC class frigate *Te Kaha* on patrol off Antarctica, 1999............................ 4·25   4·25
3446 $2.90 Kiwi symbol on hillside at post Armistice Korean headquarters of 16th Field Regiment, Royal New Zealand Artillery, 1953..................................... 5·25   5·25
3441/3446 Set of 6 .... 16·00 16·00
MS3447 Seven sheets, each 155×110 mm. (a) No. 3441. (b) No. 3442. (c) No. 3443. (d) No. 3444. (e) No. 3445. (f) No. 3446. (g) Nos. 3441/3446.................. 32·00 32·00
Nos. **MS**3447 were only available from $19.90 stamp booklet, No. SB165, with each miniature sheet having a line of roulettes at left.

744 Portrait by Mary Gillick, 1953

745 Piko (Silver Fern) and Tane Mahuta (God of the Forest)

(Recess and litho Southern Colour Print)

2013 (8 May). 60th Anniversary of the Coronation. Portraits of Queen Elizabeth II from New Zealand Coins. T **744** and similar vert designs. Multicoloured. Phosphorised paper. Perf 14.
3448   70c. Type **744** .... 1·75   1·50
3449   70c. Re-engraved portrait by Mary Gillick, 1956... 1·75   1·50
3450 $1.40 Portrait by Arnold Machin, 1967 .... 3·00   2·50
3451 $1.90 Portrait by James Berry, 1979................. 4·00   3·75
3452 $2.40 Portrait by Raphael Maklouf, 1986 .... 4·75   5·50
3453 $2.90 Portrait by Ian Rank-Broadley, 1999...... 5·50   6·00
3448/3453 Set of 6 .... 19·00 19·00
MS3454 150×90 mm. Nos. 3448/3453................... 22·00 22·00

2013 (10 May). Australia 2013 World Stamp Exhibition, Melbourne. Sheet 150×91 mm. Phosphorised paper. Multicoloured. Perf 14.
MS3455 Nos. 3448, 3450 and 3453....................... 9·00   9·00

(Des Dave Burke Design. Litho Southern Colour Print)

2013 (5 June). Matariki. Koru (pattern derived from Silver Fern frond, symbolising renewal). T **745** and similar horiz designs. Multicoloured. Phosphorised paper.

(a) *Self-adhesive. Die-cut perf 9½×10.*
3456   70c. Type **745** .... 1·25   1·25
       a. Pane. Nos. 3456/3461 .... 16·00 16·00
3457   70c. Manu Tukutuku (kite) and koru pattern symbolising wind........................... 1·25   1·25
3458 $1.40 Nguru (flute) and Hine Raukatauri (Goddess of Flute Music)........................ 2·50   2·50
3459 $1.90 Pataka (storehouse) covered in Koru...... 3·50   3·50
3460 $2.40 Kotiate (club) and Mangopare design representing Hammerhead Shark........... 4·25   4·25
3461 $2.90 Patiki (flounder) design symbolising hospitality... 5·25   5·25
3456/3461 Set of 6 .... 16·00 16·00

(b) *Ordinary gum. Perf 13½.*
MS3462 151×91 mm. Nos. 3456/3461................... 16·00 16·00

746 Bee gathering Nectar

747 Napier, 1933

NEW ZEALAND

(Des Strategy Design and Advertising, Wellington. Litho Southern Colour Print)

2013 (3 July). Honey Bees. T **746** and similar horiz designs. Multicoloured. Phosphorised paper. Perf 14.

3463	70c. Type **746**	1·00	1·50
3464	$1.40 Bees returning to hive	1·75	1·50
3465	$1.90 Worker Bees transferring nectar to honey storage area of hive	2·50	2·50
3466	$2.40 Beekeeper removing honeycomb	3·75	4·25
3467	$2.90 Honey	4·50	4·75
3463/3467	Set of 5	12·00	12·00
MS3468	137×81 mm. Nos. 3463/3467	12·00	12·00

(Des Hamish Thompson. Litho Southern Colour Print)

2013 (7 Aug). Classic Travel Posters. T **747** and similar vert designs. Multicoloured. Phosphorised paper. Perf 14×14½.

3469	70c. Type **747**	1·40	1·40
	a. Sheetlet of 20. Nos. 3469/3488	25·00	25·00
3470	70c. New Zealand The Sportsman's Paradise (game fishing, hooked Marlin)	1·40	1·40
3471	70c. Tree Fern	1·40	1·40
3472	70c. Rata Blossom Franz Josef Glacier	1·40	1·40
3473	70c. For the Worlds Best Sport (angler)	1·40	1·40
3474	70c. Cities of New Zealand, Wellington	1·40	1·40
3475	70c. Your New Zealand Holiday Fly Teal (carved Maori figure, Arthur Thompson), 1950s	1·40	1·40
3476	70c. Get in the Queue for Queenstown	1·40	1·40
3477	70c. Timaru by the Sea	1·40	1·40
3478	70c. New Zealand (lake and mountains)	1·40	1·40
3479	70c. Tauranga for Winter Sunshine	1·40	1·40
3480	70c. Kea (Alpine Parrot)	1·40	1·40
3481	70c. Southern Alps Travel the Mount Cook way!	1·40	1·40
3482	70c. Marlborough Sounds	1·40	1·40
3483	70c. Sheep Droving in New Zealand	1·40	1·40
3484	70c. New Zealand for your next holiday (Maori woman)	1·40	1·40
3485	70c. For Winter Thrills Mount Cook Train to Timaru (skier)	1·40	1·40
3486	70c. Mount Egmont 8,260 ft	1·40	1·40
3487	70c. Fly Teal to nearby New Zealand (Maori figures, geyser and Mount Cook)	1·40	1·40
3488	70c. Blue Baths, Rotorua	1·40	1·40
3469/3488	Set of 20	25·00	25·00

Nos. 3469/3488 were printed together, *se-tenant*, in sheetlets of 20. An imperforate version of the sheetlet, No. 3469a, was included in The New Zealand Collection 2013 yearbook.

748 Castlepoint (centenary of lighthouse), Wairarapa Coast

(Des Creature, Wellington. Litho Southern Colour Print)

2013 (4 Sept). Coastlines. T **748** and similar horiz designs. Multicoloured. Phosphorised paper. Perf 13×13½.

3489	70c. Type **748**	1·00	1·00
3490	$1.40 Nugget Point	1·75	2·00
3491	$1.90 East Cape	2·50	3·00
3492	$2.40 Pencarrow Head, near Wellington	3·75	4·50
3493	$2.90 Cape Campbell	4·50	5·50
3489/3493	Set of 5	12·00	14·50
MS3494	160×91 mm. Nos. 3489/3493	12·00	14·50

749 Boy with Pet Lamb

750 Duke and Duchess of Cambridge with Prince George outside St Mary's Hospital, 22 July 2013

(Des Stephen Fuller. Litho Southern Colour Print)

2013 (4 Sept). Children's Health. Country Pets. T **749** and similar vert designs. Multicoloured.

(a) Ordinary gum. Phosphorised paper. Perf 13½ (No. MS3497) or 14 (others).

3495	70c.+10c. Type **749**	1·75	1·75
3496	$1.40+10c. Girl with Piglet	2·25	2·75
MS3497	140×90 mm. Nos. 3495/3496 and 70c.+10c. Boy with Goat on school Pet Day (25×30 mm)	4·25	5·00

(b) Self-adhesive. Size 25×30 mm. Phosphor frame. Die-cut perf 9½×10.

3498	70c.+10c. Boy with Goat on school Pet Day	1·50	1·75

(Litho Southern Colour Print)

2013 (11 Sept). Birth of Prince George of Cambridge. T **750** and similar vert designs. Multicoloured. Perf 14½.

3499	70c. Type **750**	2·00	2·25
	a. Horiz strip of 4. Nos. 3499/3502	13·00	14·00
3500	$1.90 Prince William holding Prince George	3·25	3·75
3501	$2.40 Duke and Duchess of Cambridge, Duchess holding Prince George	4·25	4·75
3502	$2.90 Catherine, Duchess of Cambridge holding Prince George	4·75	5·00
3499/3502	Set of 4	13·00	14·00

No. 3499a could be purchased from the Philatelic Bureau at $7.90 per strip. It was not available in sheets.

(Litho Southern Colour Print)

2013 (13 Sept). Upper Hutt 2013 National Stamp Show. Sheet 141×80 mm. Phosphorised paper. Multicoloured. Perf 13½.

MS3503	As Nos. 3432/3433	9·50	11·00

751 Giving Christmas Present

(Des Martin Bailey. Litho Southern Colour Print)

2013 (2 Oct). Christmas. T **751** and similar square designs. Multicoloured. Phosphorised paper.

(a) Ordinary gum. Perf 14.

3504	70c. Type **751**	1·00	50
3505	$1.40 Christmas lunch	2·00	1·40
3506	$1.90 Decorating the tree	2·50	2·75
3507	$2.40 Cricket on the beach	4·25	4·50
3508	$2.90 Carol singing	4·75	5·50
3504/3508	Set of 5	13·00	13·00

(b) Self-adhesive. Size 25×30 mm. Die-cut perf 9½×10
(i) Domestic mail.

3509	70c. As Type **751**	1·00	1·00
	a. Booklet pane. No. 3509×10	9·00	
	b. With phosphor bar at foot	1·00	1·00
	ba. Horiz strip of 3. Nos. 3509b/3511	6·50	7·50

(ii) International Post. Die-cut perf 9½×10.

3510	$1.90 As No. 3506	2·50	3·25
	a. Booklet pane. No. 3510×10	22·00	
3511	$2.40 As No. 3507	3·75	4·50
	a. Booklet pane. No. 3511×10	30·00	
3509/3511	Set of 3	6·50	8·00

No. 3509 was issued in $7 booklet, No. SB166.
No. 3509b was issued in rolls of 100 and in No. 3509ba.
The *se-tenant* strip of three, No. 3509ba, could be purchased from the Philatelic Bureau.
No. 3510 was issued in booklet, No. SB167, sold at $17.10, providing a $1.90 discount off the face value of the stamps.
No. 3511 was issued in booklet, No. SB168, sold at $21.60, providing a $2.40 discount off the face value of the stamps.

(Litho Southern Colour Print)

2013 (1 Nov). *The Hobbit* (film trilogy). *The Desolation of Smaug* (2nd issue). Multicoloured designs as T **739**.

(a) Ordinary gum. Phosphorised paper. Perf 14½×14 (vert) or 14×14½ (horiz).

3512	70c. Thorin Oakenshield (Richard Armitage)	1·50	70
3513	$1.40 Gandalf (Ian McKellen)	2·25	1·50
3514	$1.90 Tauriel (Evangeline Lilly) (*horiz*)	3·00	2·50
3515	$2.10 Bilbo Baggins (Martin Freeman) (*horiz*)	3·00	3·00
3516	$2.40 Legolas Greenleaf (Orlando Bloom)	4·00	4·25
3517	$2.90 Bard the Bowman (Luke Evans)	4·50	4·75
3512/3517	Set of 6	16·00	15·00

NEW ZEALAND

(b) Self-adhesive. Size 26×37 mm (vert) or 37×26 mm (horiz). Phosphor frame. Die-cut perf 10×9½ (vert) or 9½×10 (horiz).

3518	70c. As No. 3512	1·00	1·00
	a. Booklet pane. Nos. 3518×4, 3519×2 and 3520/3523	20·00	
	b. Pane. Nos. 3518/3523	16·00	18·00
3519	$1.40 As No. 3513	1·75	1·75
3520	$1.90 As No. 3514	3·00	3·50
3521	$2.10 As No. 3515	3·25	3·75
3522	$2.40 As No. 3516	4·50	5·00
3523	$2.90 As No. 3517	4·75	5·50
3518/3523 Set of 6		16·00	18·00

A set of six miniature sheets containing Nos. 3512/3517 as single stamps were sold at $14.40 per set, a $3 premium over face value.

Nos. 3518/3523 were issued in $14.90 stamp booklet, No. SB169.

No. 3518b could be purchased from the Philatelic Bureau.

BEST OF 2013. A further set of miniature sheets as described below No. 2042 were distributed by the Philatelic Bureau to customers purchasing a certain amount of philatelic material during 2013. The sheets comprised: 1. Nos. 3433, 3427 and 3439; 2. Nos. 3446, 3461 and 3467; 3. Nos. 3470, 3493 and 3508.

Imperforate sheets of Nos. 3463/3467 and a perforated *se-tenant* strip of the same five values were also distributed.

752 Horse Pictogram

(Des Asiaworks, Auckland. Litho Cartor)

2014 (8 Jan). Chinese New Year. Year of the Horse. T **752** and similar vert designs. Multicoloured. Perf 13½×13.

3524	70c. Type **752**	1·00	75
3525	$1.40 Paper-cut Horse	1·75	1·50
3526	$1.90 Show jumping	2·50	2·75
3527	$2.40 Rotorua Museum of Art and History	3·75	4·50
3524/3527 Set of 4		8·00	8·50
MS3528 150×90 mm. Nos. 3524/3527		8·00	8·50

753 *Hormosira banksii* (Neptune's Necklace)   **754** Colonial Cottage

(Des 2Di4 Design. Litho Southern Colour Print)

2014 (5 Feb). Native Seaweeds. T **753** and similar vert designs. Multicoloured. Phosphorised paper. Perf 13½ (No. MS3534) or 14 (others).

3529	70c. Type **753**	1·00	75
3530	$1.40 *Landsburgia quercifolia*	1·75	1·50
3531	$1.90 *Caulerpa brownii* (Sea Rimu)	2·50	2·50
3532	$2.40 *Marginariella boryana*	3·75	4·50
3533	$2.90 *Pterocladia lucida* (Agar Weed)	4·50	5·00
3529/3533 Set of 5		12·00	13·00
MS3534 160×90 mm. Nos. 3529/3533		12·00	13·00

(Litho Southern Colour Print)

2014 (5 Mar). Construction of a Nation. T **754** and similar horiz designs. Multicoloured. Phosphorised paper. Perf 14.

3535	70c. Type **754**	1·00	75
3536	$1.40 Villa	1·75	1·50
3537	$1.90 Californian bungalow	2·50	2·50
3538	$2.40 Art Deco house	3·75	4·50
3539	$2.90 State House	4·50	5·00
3535/3539 Set of 5		12·00	13·00
MS3540 130×89 mm. Nos. 3535/3539		12·00	13·00

The top margin of No. MS3540 is cut around in the shape of a house roof.

755 Recruitment Poster for Air Training Corps, 1942   **756** Duke and Duchess of Cambridge with Prince George, August 2013

(Litho Southern Colour Print, New Zealand)

2014 (2 Apr). ANZAC (5th series). World War II Poster Art. T **755** and similar vert designs. Multicoloured. Phosphorised paper. Perf 14½.

3541	70c. Type **755**	1·50	1·50
3542	70c. Woman driving tractor ('HELP FARM FOR VICTORY', Women's Land Service), October 1943	1·50	1·50
3543	$1.40 Pilot ('THE AIR FORCE NEEDS MEN!', Royal New Zealand Air Force), February 1941	2·75	2·75
3544	$1.90 Warship ('NAVY WEEK') on fund raising poster for 3rd Liberty Loan, June 1943	3·75	3·75
3545	$2.40 Soldier throwing grenade ('ARMY WEEK' on fund raising poster for 3rd Liberty Loan, June 1943	4·50	4·50
3546	$2.90 Maori soldier and fund raising poster in Maori language ('TARINGA WHAKARONGO!'), 1941	5·50	5·50
3541/3546 Set of 6		18·00	18·00
MS3547 165×110 mm. No. 3541		2·00	2·00
MS3548 165×110 mm. No. 3542		2·00	2·00
MS3549 165×110 mm. No. 3543		3·25	3·25
MS3550 165×110 mm. No. 3544		3·75	3·75
MS3551 165×110 mm. No. 3545		4·50	4·50
MS3552 165×110 mm. No. 3546		5·50	5·50
MS3553 165×110 mm. No. 3541/3546		19·00	19·00

Nos. MS3547/MS3553 were only available from $19.90 stamp booklet, No. SB170, containing stamps with a face value of $20.

(Litho Southern Colour Print)

2014 (7 Apr). Visit of Duke and Duchess of Cambridge to New Zealand, April 2014. T **756** and similar vert design. Multicoloured. Phosphorised paper. Perf 14½.

3554	70c. Type **756**	1·75	1·50
3555	$2.40 Official Christening photograph, Clarence House, London	4·75	4·75

757 Franz Josef Glacier

(Litho Southern Colour Print)

2014 (7 May). New Zealand Landscapes (5th series). T **757** and similar horiz designs. Multicoloured.

(a) Ordinary gum. Phosphorised paper. Perf 13×13½.

3556	60c. Type **757**	1·10	1·10
3557	$1.60 Moeraki Boulders	3·00	3·00
3558	$2.50 Pancake Rocks	4·50	4·50
3559	$3.60 Waikato River	6·50	6·50
3556/3559 Set of 4		13·50	13·50

(b) Self-adhesive. Phosphor frame. Die-cut perf 10×9½.

3560	$2 Mount Taranaki	3·50	3·50
	a. Booklet pane. No. 3560×5	16·00	
	b. Horiz pair. Nos. 3560/3561	8·00	8·00
3561	$2.50 As No. 3558	4·50	4·50
	a. Booklet pane. No. 3561×5	20·00	

Nos. 3560/3561 were issued in $10 or $12.50 booklets, Nos. SB171/SB172.

No. 3560 on ordinary gummed paper comes from a limited edition miniature sheet.

See also Nos. 3895/3896, 3991/3994, 4076/4080, 4151/4152 and 4159/4162.

NEW ZEALAND

(Litho Southern Colour Print)

2014 (7 May). All Blacks (National Rugby Team). As Nos. 3224/**MS**3226 with new face values. Perf 13½.
3562	712	80c. black	1·40	1·40
3563		$2.50 black	4·50	4·50
MS3564		90×80 mm. As Nos. 3562/3563 but 35×19 mm (Perf 15×14½) and Nos. 3562/3563	11·00	12·00

758 Wedding Rings

(Litho Southern Colour Print)

2014 (7 May). Personalised Stamps. T **758** and similar horiz designs. Multicoloured. Perf 15×14½.
MS3565 164×82 mm. 80c.×8 Type **758**; Silver Fern; 'love'; Two glasses of champagne; Teddy bear; Pohutukawa flowers; Cupcake with birthday candles; Balloons.. 8·75 10·00
MS3566 94×82 mm. $2 As Type **758**; $2 Silver Fern; $2.50 Two glasses of champagne; $2.50 Pohutukawa flowers.. 12·50 14·00

No. **MS**3565 contains two horizontal strips of four stamps separated by a gutter containing labels inscribed '2014 Personalised Stamps'.

759 Te wehenga o Rangi raua ko Papa (Cliff Whiting)

760 Giant Peaches, Cromwell

(Des Rangi Kipa, Te Atiawa, Taranaki Tuturu. Litho Southern Colour Print)

2014 (4 June). Matariki. Papatuanuku and Ranginui. T **759** and similar multicoloured designs.
(a) Self-adhesive. Die-cut perf 10×9½ (vert) or 9½×10 (horiz).
3567	80c. Type **759**	1·10	95
	a. Pane. Nos. 3567/3572	13·00	13·50
3568	80c. Rangi and Papa (Phil Mokaraka Berry)	1·10	95
3569	$1.40 Te whakamamae o te wehenga (Kura Te Waru Rewiri)	2·00	1·60
3570	$2 The Separation of Rangi and Papa (Fred Graham) (*horiz*)	2·75	2·75
3571	$2.50 The Children of Rangi and Papa (Pauline Kahurangi Yearbury) (*horiz*)	3·50	4·00
3572	$3 The Ranginui Doorway (Robert Jahnke) (*horiz*)	4·25	4·75
3567/3572 Set of 6		13·00	13·50

(b) Ordinary gum. Perf 13½.
MS3573 150×90 mm. As Nos. 3567/3572 .... 13·00 13·50

(Des Graeme Mowday and Tim Christie. Litho Southern Colour Print)

2014 (2 July). Legendary Landmarks (town icons). T **760** and similar square designs. Multicoloured. Phosphorised paper. Perf 14½.
3574	80c. Type **760**	1·40	1·40
	a. Sheetlet of 18. Nos. 3574/3591	23·00	23·00
3575	80c. New Zealand flag on giant Kiwi ('Otorohanga Kiwiana Town')	1·40	1·40
3576	80c. Kiwi Fruit ('TEPUKE HEART OF KIWI FRUIT COUNTRY')	1·40	1·40
3577	80c. Lemon and Paeroa bottle ('PAEROA HOME OF A KIWI FAVOURITE')	1·40	1·40
3578	80c. Deer statue ('MOSSBURN Deer capital of NZ')	1·40	1·40
3579	80c. Surfer on wave ('Surf's Up at Colac Bay')	1·40	1·40
3580	80c. Giant Carrot ('OHAKUNE CARROT CAPITAL OF NZ')	1·40	1·40
3581	80c. Giant fish ('Rakaia means great fishing')	1·40	1·40
3582	80c. Giant Sheep's head ('Tirau's Big Sheep')	1·40	1·40
3583	80c. Multicoloured giant gumboot ('TAIHAPE WHERE GUMBOOTS RULE')	1·40	1·40
3584	80c. Chain-link sculpture ('Rakiura the chain holding us together')	1·40	1·40
3585	80c. Bronze statue of child with Opo the dolphin ('Opononi HOME OF THE FRIENDLY DOLPHIN')	1·40	1·40
3586	80c. Dog statue ('HUNTERVILLE THE HUNTAWAY'S HOME')	1·40	1·40
3587	80c. Bicycle with cyclist in front wheel ('TAUPO THE CYCLIST'S DELIGHT')	1·40	1·40
3588	80c. Giant Sandfly ('PUKEKURA'S GIANT SANDFLY')	1·40	1·40
3589	80c. Sculpture of shepherd and Dog ('Feilding celebrating the land')	1·40	1·40
3590	80c. Cart Horses ('Clinton celebrates our rural heritage')	1·40	1·40
3591	80c. Loaf of bread ('Farewell from MANAIA BREAD CAPITAL')	1·40	1·40
3574/3591 Set of 18		23·00	23·00

Nos. 3574/3591 were printed together, *se-tenant*, in sheetlets of 18 stamps, each sheetlet forming a composite background design depicting postcards stuck on a fridge.

761 Lord Kitchener (1850–1916)

(Des Strategy Design and Advertising, Wellington. Litho Southern Colour Print)

2014 (29 July). Centenary of the First World War (1st issue). 1914 For King and Empire. T **761** and similar square designs. Multicoloured. Phosphorised paper. Perf 14½.
3592	80c. Type **761**	1·40	1·40
	a. Block of 6. Nos. 3592/3597	7·50	7·50
3593	80c. Military training poster ('New Zealand called to prepare')	1·40	1·40
3594	80c. Governor of New Zealand (Earl of Liverpool) with New Zealand Parliament reading message from King George V ('War announced')	1·40	1·40
3595	80c. Melville Mirfin ('Serving his country')	1·40	1·40
3596	80c. Mirfin family ('Family portrait')	1·40	1·40
3597	80c. New Zealand Expeditionary Force aboard the troopship *Limerick*, 1914 ('Troopships depart')	1·40	1·40
3598	$2 Training camp, Canterbury	3·00	3·00
	a. Horiz pair. Nos. 3598/3599	6·00	6·00
3599	$2 Karaka Bay, Wellington, 1914 ('The home front')	3·00	3·00
3600	$2.50 Letter from Melville Mirfin to his father ('Letters and stories from Samoa')	4·00	4·50
	a. Horiz pair. Nos. 3600/3601	8·00	9·00
3601	$2.50 New Zealand Expeditionary Force by the Pyramids, Egypt, 1914 ('Serving abroad')	4·00	4·50
3592/3601 Set of 10		20·00	20·00
MS3602 175×90 mm. Nos. 3592/3597		9·00	9·50
MS3603 141×90 mm. Nos. 3598/3601		13·00	14·00

Nos. 3592/3597 were printed together, *se-tenant*, as blocks of six stamps in sheets of 24 (6×4).

Nos. 3598/3599 and 3600/3601 were each printed together, *se-tenant*, as horizontal pairs in sheets of 24 (6×4).

Nos. 3592/3601 were also issued in premium booklet, No. SP13, containing stamps with a face value of $27.60 but sold for $39.90.

See also Nos. 3663/**MS**3674, 3760/**MS**3771, 3879/**MS**3890a and 3964/**MS**3976.

762 Antipodean Albatross

763 Girl holding Carrots

NEW ZEALAND

(Litho Southern Colour Print)

2014 (3 Sept). Endangered Seabirds. T **762** and similar horiz designs. Multicoloured. Perf 14 (Nos. 3604/3608) or 13½ (No. **MS**3609).

3604	80c. Type **762**	1·40	1·25
3605	$1.40 New Zealand Fairy Tern	2·25	2·00
3606	$2 Chatham Island Shag	3·00	3·00
3607	$2.50 Black-billed Gull	3·50	4·00
3608	$3 Chatham Island Taiko	4·25	4·75
3605/3608 Set of 5		13·00	13·50
MS3609 160×74 mm. Nos. 3604/3608		13·50	14·50

(Des Insight, Wellington. Litho Southern Colour Print)

2014 (3 Sept). Children's Health. Growing a Healthy Future. T **763** and similar vert designs.

*(a) Ordinary gum. Phosphorised paper. Perf 13½ (No. **MS**3612) or 14 (others).*

3610	80c.+10c. Type **763**	1·10	1·25
3611	$1.40+10c. Boy holding Apples on shoulders	2·00	2·00
MS3612 140×90 mm. As Nos. 3610/3611 and 80c.+10c. boy holding Pumpkin (25×30 mm)		3·00	3·50

(b) Self-adhesive. Size 25×30 mm. Phosphor frame. Die-cut perf 9½×10.

| 3613 | 80c.+10c. Boy holding Pumpkin | 1·25 | 1·25 |

764 Mary and Jesus

(Des Lindy Fisher. Litho Southern Colour Print)

2014 (1 Oct). Christmas. Children in Nativity Play. T **764** and similar horiz designs. Multicoloured.

(a) Ordinary gum. Perf 14.

3614	80c. Type **764**	1·10	95
3615	$1.40 Joseph	2·00	1·60
3616	$2 Wise man	2·75	2·75
3617	$2.50 Angel	3·50	4·00
3618	$3 Shepherd	4·25	4·75
3614/3618 Set of 5		12·00	12·50

(b) Self-adhesive. Size 30×25 mm.
(i) Domestic mail. Die-cut perf 10×9½.

3619	80c. As Type **764**	1·10	1·25
	a. Booklet pane. No. 3619×10	10·00	
	b. With irregular phosphor bar at left	1·10	1·25
	ba. Horiz strip of 3. Nos. 3619b/3621b	6·50	7·50

(ii) International Post. Die-cut perf 10×9½.

3620	$2 As No. 3616	2·75	3·25
	a. Booklet pane. No. 3620×10	25·00	
	b. With irregular phosphor bar at left	2·75	3·00
3621	$2.50 As No. 3617	3·50	4·00
	a. Booklet pane. No. 3621×10	32·00	
	b. With irregular phosphor bar at left	3·50	4·00
3619/3621 Set of 3		6·50	7·50

No. 3619 was issued in $8 booklet, No. SB173.
Nos. 3619/3621b were issued in No. 3619ba.
The *se-tenant* strip of three, No. 3619ba, could be purchased from the Philatelic Bureau.
No. 3620 was issued in booklet No. SB174, sold at $18, providing a $2 discount off the face value of the stamps.
No. 3621 was issued in booklet No. SB175, sold at $22.50, providing a $2.50 discount off the face value of the stamps.

765 Gandalf and the Companions

(Litho Southern Colour Print)

2014 (15 Oct). Personalised Stamps. *The Hobbit*. Multicoloured. Phosphorised paper. Perf 15×14½.

MS3622 110×66 mm. 80c. Type **765**; $2.50 As Type **765**. 4·50 5·00

(Litho Southern Colour Print)

2014 (12 Nov). *The Hobbit* (film trilogy). *The Battle of the Five Armies* (3rd issue). Multicoloured designs as T **739**.

(a) Ordinary gum. Phosphorised paper. Perf 14½×14 (vert) or 14×14½ (horiz).

3623	80c. Smaug the Dragon	1·10	95
3624	$1.40 Bilbo Baggins	2·00	1·60
3625	$2 Gandalf (*horiz*)	2·75	2·75
3626	$2.10 Thranduil (*horiz*)	3·00	3·50
3627	$2.50 Bard the Bowman	3·50	4·00
3628	$2.50 Door to Bag End	3·50	4·00
3629	$3 Tauriel	4·25	4·75
3623/3629 Set of 7		18·00	19·00

(b) Self-adhesive. Size 26×37 mm or 37×26 mm. Die-cut perf 10×9½ (vert) or 9½×10 (horiz).

3630	80c. As No. 3623	1·10	95
	a. Booklet pane. Nos. 3630×4, 3631×2 and 3632/3635	20·00	
	b. Pane. Nos. 3630/3635	15·00	16·00
3631	$1.40 As No. 3624	2·00	1·60
3632	$2 As No. 3625	2·75	2·75
3633	$2.10 As No. 3626	3·00	3·50
3634	$2.50 As No. 3627	3·50	4·00
3635	$3 As No. 3629	4·25	4·75
3630/3635 Set of 6		15·00	16·00

No. 3628 has ground wood from the Hobbiton film set affixed to the Bag End door.
A set of seven miniature sheets containing Nos. 3623/3629 as single stamps were sold at $17.80 per set, a $3.50 premium over face value (*price £28*).
Nos. 3630/3635 were issued in $15.60 stamp booklet, No. SB176.
No. 3630b could be purchased from the Philatelic Bureau.

(Litho Southern Colour Print)

2014 (14 Nov). BAYPEX 2014 National Stamp Exhibition, Hawke's Bay. Sheet 140×90 mm. Phosphorised paper. Multicoloured. Perf 14½.

MS3636 Nos. 3597/3598 and 3601 11·00 12·00

No. **MS**3636 was sold at $7.80, a $2.80 premium over face value. The surcharge was for the Philatelic Trust.

766 Chinese Character for Sheep

767 ZK-AMA *Aotearoa* Short S.30 Empire Class Flying Boat on First TEAL Flight Auckland to Sydney, 30 April 1940

(Des Asiaworks. Litho Southern Colour Print)

2015 (14 Jan). Chinese New Year. Year of the Sheep. T **766** and similar vert designs. Multicoloured. Phosphorised paper. Perf 14 (Nos. 3637/3640) or 13½ (No. **MS**3641).

3637	80c. Type **766**	1·10	1·00
3638	$1.40 Paper-cut of Sheep decorated with traditional Chinese patterns	2·00	1·75
3639	$2 Sheep pasture in New Zealand	2·75	3·00
3640	$2.50 Church of the Good Shepherd, Lake Tekapo	3·50	4·00
3637/3640 Set of 4		8·50	8·75
MS3641 150×90 mm. Nos. 3637/3640		9·00	9·00

(Des Insight Creative. Litho Southern Colour Print)

2015 (14 Jan). 75th Anniversary of New Zealand National Airlines Connecting New Zealand and the World. T **767** and similar horiz designs. Multicoloured. Phosphorised paper. Perf 14½.

3642	80c. Type **767**	1·40	1·25
3643	$1.40 Mrs Margaret Gould, NAC's first ground stewardess with child and Kawatere NZNAC Lockheed Lodestar on ground, 1948 ('Travelling the Country with NAC')	2·50	2·00
3644	$2 TEAL (Tasman Empire Airways Ltd) coral route luggage label, 1951 to 1960 ('Exploring the Pacific with TEAL')	3·50	3·50
3645	$2.50 Two children on board Douglas DC-10 Series 30, 1977 ('Sharing the Flying Experience') (NAC merged with Air New Zealand, 1978)	4·00	4·25
3646	$3 Air New Zealand Boeing 787-9 taking off, 2014	4·50	5·00
3642/3646 Set of 5		14·00	14·50
MS3647 119×91 mm. Nos. 3642/3646		14·00	14·50

NEW ZEALAND

768 India

(Litho Southern Colour Print)

2015 (4 Feb). ICC Cricket World Cup, New Zealand and Australia. T **768** and similar round designs showing emblem and National Flags of participating countries on cricket balls. Multicoloured. Phosphorised paper. Self-adhesive. Die-cut.

3648	80c. Type **768**	1·25	1·25
	a. Sheetlet of 14. Nos. 3648/3661	16·00	16·00
3649	80c. England (white ball)	1·25	1·25
3650	80c. South Africa (bright blue-green ball)	1·25	1·25
3651	80c. Pakistan (bright yellow-green ball)	1·25	1·25
3652	80c. United Arab Emirates (grey ball)	1·25	1·25
3653	80c. Sri Lanka (Royal blue ball)	1·25	1·25
3654	80c. West Indies (lake ball)	1·25	1·25
3655	80c. Afghanistan (bright blue ball)	1·25	1·25
3656	80c. Ireland (emerald ball)	1·25	1·25
3657	80c. Bangladesh (bright scarlet ball, green dotted lines)	1·25	1·25
3658	80c. Australia (greenish yellow ball)	1·25	1·25
3659	80c. New Zealand (grey ball)	1·25	1·25
3660	80c. Zimbabwe (bright scarlet ball, white dotted lines)	1·25	1·25
3661	80c. Scotland (deep dull blue)	1·25	1·25
3648/3661 Set of 14		16·00	16·00

Nos. 3648/3661 were printed together in sheetlets of 14 stamps.
A second version of No. 3648a was printed for the Indian Philatelic Bureau and sold only from there. The stamps are on non-phosphorised paper and there are differences to the sheet border and central image.

769 Ngapuhi Chief Tamati Waka Nene shaking hands with William Hobson (first Governor of New Zealand)

770 Catafalque Sentry, Bugler, Australian Golden Wattle and Anzac Cove

(Des Rangi Kipa, Te Atiawa, Taranaki Tuturu and Roy McDougall. Litho Southern Colour Print)

2015 (4 Feb). 175th Anniversary of the Treaty of Waitangi. Sheet 149×90 mm. W **502**. Perf 14×14½.
MS3662 **769** $2.50 multicoloured .... 4·00 4·50

(Des Strategy Design and Advertising, Wellington. Litho Southern Colour Print)

2015 (23 Mar). Centenary of the First World War (2nd issue). 1915 The Spirit of ANZAC. Square designs as T **761**. Multicoloured. Phosphorised paper. Perf 14½.

3663	80c. Evelyn Brooke (matron in New Zealand Army Nursing Service)	1·40	1·40
	a. Block of 6. Nos. 3663/3668	7·50	7·50
3664	80c. Postcard from Egypt, 1915	1·40	1·40
3665	80c. Landing at Anzac Cove, 1915	1·40	1·40
3666	80c. The Battle of Chunuk Bair, 8 August 1915 (Ion Brown)	1·40	1·40
3667	80c. 'HELP OUR WOUNDED' in lights, Queen Carnival, Auckland, 1915	1·40	1·40
3668	80c. Stained glass window depicting First and Second World War nurses, Marquette Memorial Chapel, Christchurch	1·40	1·40
3669	$2 Watercolour *The Sapper and his Donkey* (Horace Moore-Jones)	3·25	3·25
	a. Horiz pair. Nos. 3669/3670	6·50	6·50
3670	$2 War Census, 1915	3·25	3·25
3671	$2.50 Hospital ship NZHS *Maheno*	4·00	4·50
	a. Horiz pair. Nos. 3671/3672	8·00	9·00
3672	$2.50 Poster of Australian and New Zealand soldiers bearing Union Jack flags (Otho Hewett)	4·00	4·50
3663/3672 Set of 10		21·00	22·00
MS3673 175×90 mm. Nos. 3663/3668		9·00	9·00
MS3674 140×90 mm. Nos. 3669/3672		13·00	14·00

Nos. 3663/3668 were printed together, *se-tenant*, as blocks of six stamps in sheets of 24 (6×4).
Nos. 3669/3670 and 3671/3672 were each printed together, *se-tenant*, as horizontal pairs in sheets of 24 (6×4).
Nos. 3663/3672 were also issued in premium booklet No. SP14, containing stamps with a face value of $27.60 but sold for $39.90.

(Des Australia Post Design Studio. Litho McKellar Renown)

2015 (7 Apr). ANZAC Centenary. T **770** and similar vert design. Multicoloured. Phosphorised paper. Perf 14½×14.

3675	80c. Type **770**	1·50	1·25
3676	$2 Bugler, catafalque sentry, New Zealand Silver Fern and ANZAC Cove	3·50	3·50
MS3677 105×70 mm. Nos. 3675/3676		5·00	4·75

Similar designs were issued on the same date by Australia.

771 Silver Paua (*Haliotis australis*)

772 Digiwhaiwhai (Johnson Witehira)

(Litho Southern Colour Print)

2015 (6 May). Native Seashells. T **771** and similar vert designs. Multicoloured. Phosphorised paper. Perf 14 (Nos. 3678/3682) or 13½ (No. MS3683).

3678	80c. Type **771**	1·10	1·00
3679	$1.40 Scott's Murex (*Rolandiella scotti*)	2·00	2·00
3680	$2 Golden Volute (*Provocator mirabilis*)	2·75	3·00
3681	$2.50 Fan Shell (*Talochlamys gemmulata*)	3·50	4·00
3682	$3 Opal Top Shell (*Cantharidus opalus*)	4·25	4·75
3679/3682 Set of 5		12·00	13·00
MS3683 140×90 mm. Nos. 3678/3682		13·00	14·00

(Des Rangi Kipa and Roy McDougall. Litho Southern Colour Print)

2015 (3 June). Matariki. Kowhaiwhai. T **772** and similar multicoloured designs.

(a) Self-adhesive. Die-cut perf 10×9½ (vert) or 9½×10 (horiz).

3684	80c. Type **772**	1·10	1·50
	a. Pane. Nos. 3684/3689	13·00	15·00
3685	80c. Tenai au tenai au (This is me, this is me) (Kura Te Waru Rewiri)	1·10	1·50
3686	$1.40 *Haki* from the series *Whakahokia mai te mauri* (Kylie Tiuka)	2·00	2·00
3687	$2 *Banner Moon* from the series *Land Protest 1975–1976*, reworked 1982 (Buck Nin) (horiz)	2·75	3·25
3688	$2.50 Part of the *Te Hatete o te Reo* series (Ngatai Taepa) (horiz)	3·50	4·00
3689	$3 *Taona Marama* (Night Lights of the City) (Sandy Adsett)	4·25	4·75
3684/3689 Set of 6		13·00	15·00

(b) Ordinary gum. Perf 14.

MS3690 150×90 mm. As Nos. 3684/3689 .... 14·00 15·00

773 Asparagus Rolls

774 Emerald Lakes, Tongariro National Park

(Des Jason Kelly. Litho Southern Colour Print)

2015 (1 July). Kiwi Kitchen. T **773** and similar square designs. Multicoloured. Phosphorised paper. Perf 14½.

3691	80c. Type **773**	1·10	1·10
	a. Sheetlet of 18. Nos. 3691/3708	19·00	19·00
3692	80c. Kiwi Onion Dip	1·10	1·10

NEW ZEALAND

3693	80c. Puha Pork	1·10	1·10
3694	80c. Bluff Oysters	1·10	1·10
3695	80c. Meat Loaf	1·10	1·10
3696	80c. Hokey Pokey ice cream	1·10	1·10
3697	80c. Shrimp Cocktail	1·10	1·10
3698	80c. Cheese Rolls	1·10	1·10
3699	80c. Pikelets	1·10	1·10
3700	80c. Lambington	1·10	1·10
3701	80c. Mince on Toast	1·10	1·10
3702	80c. Whitebait Fritters	1·10	1·10
3703	80c. Curried Egg	1·10	1·10
3704	80c. Saveloy and Tomato Sauce	1·10	1·10
3705	80c. Bacon and Egg	1·10	1·10
3706	80c. Pavlova	1·10	1·10
3707	80c. Fairy Bread	1·10	1·10
3708	80c. Mousetrap	1·10	1·10
3691/3708 Set of 18		19·00	19·00

Nos. 3691/3708 were printed together, *se-tenant*, in sheetlets of 18 stamps.

(Litho Southern Colour Print)

2015 (5 Aug). UNESCO World Heritage Sites. Multicoloured. Phosphorised paper. Perf 14.

3709	80c. Type **774**	1·10	95
3710	$1.40 Franz Josef Glacier, Te Wahipounamu (south-west New Zealand)	2·00	1·60
3711	$2 Enderby Island, New Zealand sub Antarctic islands	2·75	2·75
3712	$2.20 Mount Ngauruhoe, Tongariro National Park	3·00	3·50
3713	$2.50 Lake MacKenzie, Te Wahipounamu (south-west New Zealand)	3·50	4·00
3714	$3 Campbell Island, New Zealand sub Antarctic islands	4·25	4·75
3710/3714 Set of 6		15·00	16·00
MS3715 160×90 mm. Nos. 3709/3714		16·00	17·00

775 Parliament House, Wellington, New Zealand

776 Girl under Sun Umbrella

(Litho Southern Colour Print)

2015 (14 Aug). World Stamp Exhibition, Singapore. T **775** and similar horiz designs. Multicoloured. Phosphorised paper. Perf 14.

3716	$2.50 Type **775**	3·50	4·00
MS3717 120×80 mm. 70c. Parliament House, Canberra, Australia; $1.30 Parliament House, Singapore; No. 3716		2·75	3·75

Similar designs were issued by Australia and Singapore.

(Des Donna McKenna. Litho Southern Colour Print)

2015 (2 Sept). Children's Health. Being Sunsmart. Slip, Slop, Slap & Wrap. T **776** and similar vert designs. Multicoloured.

(a) Ordinary gum. Phosphorised paper. Perf 14 (Nos. 3718/3720) or 13½ (No. MS3721).

3718	80c.+10c. Type **776**	1·25	1·00
3719	$1.40+10c. Boy wearing cap with flaps and applying sunscreen	2·00	2·00
3720	$2+10c. Girl with huge wide-brimmed hat	3·00	3·50
3718/3720 Set of 3		5·75	6·00
MS3721 149×90 mm. As Nos. 3718/3720 and 80c.+10c. Boy with huge sunglasses (25×30 mm)		7·00	8·50

(b) Self-adhesive. Size 25×30 mm. Die-cut perf 9½×10.

3722	80c.+10c. Boy with huge sunglasses (25×30 mm)	1·25	1·25

The top of No. **MS**3721 is cut around in the shape of a sun umbrella. This miniature sheet contains photochromic ink and the sun umbrella on the upper sheet margin turns from yellow and white to purple and green when exposed to sunlight.

777 All Blacks Jersey

(Des Dave Burke. Litho Southern Colour Print)

2015 (2 Sept). All Blacks (National Rugby Team) Jersey. Phosphorised paper. Perf 13½.

3723	**777**	$15 multicoloured	20·00	25·00

No. 3723 was issued in a folder sold for $15.
The shirt was of screen-printed fabric affixed to the background frame. A sheet containing six $2.50 All Blacks stamps as No. 3563 was issued on 1 November 2015 to mark New Zealand's victory in the Rugby World Cup and sold by New Zealand Post for $19.90 per sheet.

778 Queen Elizabeth II, 1950s

779 Angel (from St Mark's Church, Carterton)

(Litho Southern Colour Print)

2015 (7 Oct). Queen Elizabeth II. New Zealand's Longest Reigning Monarch. T **778** and similar vert designs. Multicoloured. Phosphorised paper. Perf 14½.

3724	80c. Type **778**	1·10	1·25
3725	80c. Queen Elizabeth II, 1960s	1·10	1·25
3726	$1.40 Queen Elizabeth II, 1970s	2·00	1·75
3727	$2 Queen Elizabeth II, 1980s	2·75	2·75
3728	$2.20 Queen Elizabeth II, 1990s	3·00	3·50
3729	$2.50 Queen Elizabeth II, 2000s	3·50	4·00
3730	$3 Queen Elizabeth II, 2010s	4·25	4·75
3725/3730 Set of 7		16·00	17·00
MS3731 158×85 mm. Nos. 3724/3730		17·00	17·00

(Litho Southern Colour Print)

2015 (23 Oct). The Capital Stamp Show, Wellington. Sheet 130×90 mm containing Nos. 3665, 3669 and 3671. Phosphorised paper. Multicoloured. Perf 14½.

MS3732 Nos. 3665, 3669 and 3671	7·00	7·00

(Des Hannah Stancliffe-White. Litho Southern Colour Print)

2015 (4 Nov). Christmas. Stained Glass Windows. T **779** and similar vert designs. Multicoloured. Phosphorised paper (except No. **MS**3738).

(a) Ordinary gum. Perf 14.

3733	80c. Type **779**	1·10	95
3734	$1.40 Dove (from St Aidan's Anglican Church, Remuera, Auckland)	2·00	1·50
3735	$2 Mary and Jesus (from St Mary's-in-Holy Trinity Cathedral, Parnell, Auckland)	2·75	2·75
3736	$2.50 Pohutukawa (from Christchurch Hospital Nurses Memorial Chapel)	3·50	4·00
3737	$3 Three Wise Men (from St Benedict's Church, Auckland)	4·25	4·75
3733/3737 Set of 5		12·00	12·50
MS3738 177×79 mm. As Nos. 3733/3737		12·00	13·00

(b) Self-adhesive. Size 25×30 mm.
(i) Domestic mail. Die-cut perf 9½×10.

3739	80c. As Type **779**	1·10	95
	a. Booklet pane. No. 3739×10	10·00	
	b. Horiz strip of 3. Nos. 3739/3741	7·25	7·50

(ii) International Post. Die-cut perf 9½×10.

3740	$2 As No. 3735	2·75	2·75
	a. Booklet pane. No. 3740×10	25·00	
3741	$2.50 As No. 3736	3·50	4·00
	a. Booklet pane. No. 3741×10	32·00	
3739/3741 Set of 3		6·50	7·00

No. 3739 was issued in $8 booklet No. SB177.
The *se-tenant* strip of three, No. 3739b, could be purchased from the Philatelic Bureau.

No. 3740 was issued in booklet No. SB178. sold at $18, providing a $2 discount off the face value of the stamps.

No. 3741 was issued in booklet No. SB179, sold at $22.50, providing a $2.50 discount off the face value of the stamps.

BEST OF 2015. A further set of miniature sheets as described below No. 2042 were distributed by the Philatelic Bureau to customers purchasing a certain amount of philatelic material during 2015. The sheets comprised: 1. No. 3640, the $2.50 stamp from No. **MS**3662 and No. 3689; 2. Nos. 3682, 3646 and 3670; 3. Nos. 3714, 3730 and 3737.

Imperforate sheets of Nos. 3678/3682 and a *se-tenant* strip of the same five values was also distributed.

780 Pictogram

(Des Asiaworks, Auckland. Litho Southern Colour Print, New Zealand)

2016 (13 Jan). Chinese New Year. Year of the Monkey. T **780** and similar vert designs. Multicoloured. Phosphorised paper. Perf 14 (Nos. 3742/3745) or 13½ (No. **MS**3746).

3742	80c. Type **780**	1·10	95
3743	$1.40 Paper-cut Monkey holding Peach	2·00	1·50
3744	$2 Monkey	2·75	2·75
3745	$2.50 Monkey Island	3·50	4·00
3742/3745 Set of 4		8·50	8·25
MS3746 150×90 mm. As Nos. 3742/3745		9·00	9·00

781 National Meeting of Returned Soldiers, Wellington, 28 April 1916 ('THE RETURNED')

782 Glowworms, Mangawhitikau Cave

(Des Richard Payne. Litho Southern Colour Print)

2016 (3 Feb). Centenary of RSA (Royal New Zealand Returned and Services' Association). T **781** and similar square designs. Multicoloured. Phosphorised paper. Perf 14½.

3747	80c. Type **781**	1·10	95
3748	$1.40 'THE POPPY'	2·00	2·00
3749	$2 'SUPPORTING THOSE WHO SERVED'	2·75	2·75
3750	$2.20 Inside RSA clubroom ('AT THE RSA')	3·00	3·50
3751	$2.50 RSA badge ('THE BADGE')	3·50	4·00
3752	$3 'WE WILL REMEMBER THEM'	4·25	4·75
3748/3752 Set of 6		15·00	15·50
MS3753 165×90 mm. Nos. 3747/3752		16·00	16·00

(Des Hannah Stancliffe-White. Litho Southern Colour Print)

2016 (2 Mar). New Zealand Native Glowworms (*Arachnocampa luminosa*). T **782** and similar vert designs. Multicoloured.

(a) Ordinary gum. Phosphorised paper. Perf 14½×14.

3754	80c. Type **782**	1·10	1·00
3755	$1.40 Nicau Cave	2·00	2·00
3756	$2 Ruakuri Cave	2·75	2·75
3757	$2.50 Waipu Cave	3·50	4·00
3754/3757 Set of 4		8·50	8·75
MS3758 149×70 mm. Nos. 3754/3757		9·00	9·00

(b) Self-adhesive. Size 25×36 mm. Die-cut perf 9½×10.

3759	$2 As No. 3756	2·75	2·75
	a. Booklet pane. No. 3759×10	25·00	

Nos. 3754/3759 were printed using glow-in-the-dark ink, and will light up if exposed to sunlight and then taken into a dark place.

No. 3759 was issued in $20 stamp booklet No. SB180. It was also available as a self-adhesive stamp on plain white backing paper.

(Des Strategy Design and Advertising. Litho Southern Colour Print)

2016 (6 Apr). Centenary of the First World War (3rd issue). 1916 Courage and Commitment. Square designs as T **761**. Multicoloured. Phosphorised paper. Perf 14½.

3760	80c. Solomon Isaacs in uniform, February 1916	1·25	1·25
	a. Block of 6. Nos. 3760/3765	6·75	6·75
3761	80c. Pioneer Battalion	1·25	1·25
3762	80c. Graffiti 'KIAORA NZ' by the New Zealand Tunnelling Company (NZTC) in the Arras tunnels	1·25	1·25
3763	80c. Newspaper headline of 26 August 1916 'CONSCRIPTION COMES!'	1·25	1·25
3764	80c. New Zealand Mounted Rifles in the Middle East	1·25	1·25
3765	80c. The Somme	1·25	1·25
3766	$2 Service on church steps, Nelson, 25 April 1916 ('The first Anzac Day')	3·00	3·00
	a. Horiz pair. Nos. 3766/3767	6·00	6·00
3767	$2 NZEF Headquarters, Bloomsbury Square, London ('Away from the front')	3·00	3·00
3768	$2.50 Indefatigable-class battlecruiser HMS *New Zealand*, 31 May 1916 ('Battle of Jutland')	3·75	4·50
	a. Horiz pair. Nos. 3768/3769	7·50	9·00
3769	$2.50 Kaikoura Post & Telegraph office ('The home front')	3·75	4·50
3760/3769 Set of 10		19·00	20·00
MS3770 174×89 mm. Nos. 3760/3765		8·00	8·50
MS3771 137×89 mm. Nos. 3766/3769		14·00	15·00

Nos. 3760/3765 were printed together, *se-tenant*, as blocks of six stamps in sheets of 24 (6×4).

Nos. 3766/3767 and 3768/3769 were each printed together, *se-tenant*, as horizontal pairs in sheets of 24 (6×4).

Nos. 3760/3769 were also issued in premium booklet No. SP15, containing stamps with a face value of $27.60 but sold for $39.90.

783 Duke and Duchess of York with Baby Elizabeth, 1926

(Des Jonathan Gray. UV offset printing Enschedé)

2016 (4 May). 90th Birthday of Queen Elizabeth II. Sheet 179×92 mm containing T **783** and similar horiz designs. Multicoloured. Self-adhesive. Die-cut.

MS3772 Type **783**, Princess Elizabeth and Duke of Edinburgh with Prince Charles, 1949, Queen Elizabeth II in New Zealand, 2016; $5 Young Princesses Elizabeth and Margaret, 1936, Queen Elizabeth II and Duke of Edinburgh opening New Zealand's Parliament, 1963, Queen Elizabeth II, New Zealand, 2002; $5 Wedding of Princess Elizabeth, 1947, Queen Elizabeth II, New Zealand, 1977, Queen Elizabeth II, New Zealand, 2016	20·00	25·00

No. **MS**3772 contains three lenticular stamps, each stamp containing three images which change as the miniature sheet is tilted.

(Des Richard Payne. Litho Southern Colour Print)

2016 (18 May). New Zealand Landscapes (6th series). Horiz designs as T **757**. Multicoloured.

(a) Ordinary gum. Phosphorised paper. Perf 13×13½.

3773	40c. Church of the Good Shepherd, Lake Tekapo	55	45
3774	80c. Chatham Islands	1·10	95
3775	$2.20 Awaroa Bay, Abel Tasman Scenic Reserve	3·00	3·50
3776	$2.70 Vineyards, Marlborough	3·75	4·25
3777	$3.30 Dunedin Railway Station	4·50	5·00
3778	$3.80 Te Mata Peak, Hawke's Bay	5·25	5·75
3773/3778 Set of 6		16·00	18·00

(b) Self-adhesive. Phosphor frame. Die-cut perf 10×9½.

3779	$2.20 As No. 3775	3·00	3·50
	a. Booklet pane. No. 3779×5	13·50	
	b. Horiz pair. Nos. 3779/3780	6·75	7·75
3780	$2.70 As No. 3776	3·75	4·25
	a. Booklet pane. No. 3780×5	17·00	

No. 3779 was issued in $11 booklet No. SB181.
No. 3780 was issued in $13.50 booklet No. SB182.

NEW ZEALAND

784 Kete Taniko with Serpent's Teeth and Duck's Feet Pattern (Cori Marsters)

785 Athlete and New Zealand Landscape

(Des Rangi Kipa and Roy McDougall. Litho Southern Colour Print)

2016 (1 June). Matariki. Kete. T **784** and similar multicoloured designs. Phosphorised paper.

(a) Self-adhesive. Die-cut perf 10×9½ (vert) or 9½×10 (horiz).

3781	$1 Type **784**	1·40	1·10
	a. Pane. Nos. 3781/3786	15·00	15·00
3782	$1 Basket with plaited bottom (Pip Devonshire)	1·40	1·10
3783	$1.80 Poutama (male lineage) design (Te Atiwei Ririnui)	2·50	2·00
3784	$2.20 Mount Taranaki and Royal Albatross feather design (Audra Potaka) (*horiz*)	3·00	3·50
3785	$2.70 Aramoana (navigate the ocean) design (Matthew McIntyre Wilson) (*horiz*)	3·75	4·25
3786	$3.30 Tatai whetu ki te rangi (clusters of stars in the heavens) (Sonia Snowden)	4·50	5·00
3781/3786	Set of 6	15·00	15·00

(b) Ordinary gum. Perf 13½.

MS3787	150×90 mm. As Nos. 3781/3786	15·00	15·00

(Litho Southern Colour Print)

2016 (22 June). Personalised Stamps. Horiz designs as T **758**. Multicoloured. Phosphorised paper. Perf 14½.

3788	$1 As Type **758**	1·40	1·75
	a. Sheetlet of 10. Nos. 3788/3797	18·00	21·00
3789	$1 Silver Fern	1·40	1·75
3790	$1 'love'	1·40	1·75
3791	$1 Two glasses of champagne	1·40	1·75
3792	$1 Teddy bear	1·40	1·75
3793	$1 Pohutukawa flowers	1·40	1·75
3794	$1 Balloons	1·40	1·75
3795	$2.20 As No. 3789	3·00	3·50
3796	$2.20 As Type **758**	3·00	3·50
3797	$2.70 As No. 3793	3·75	4·00
3788/3797	Set of 10	18·00	21·00

Nos. 3788/3797 were printed together, *se-tenant*, in sheetlets of ten stamps containing two horizontal strips of five stamps separated by a gutter containing stamp-size labels inscribed '2016 Personalised Stamps'.

(Des Jonathan Gray. Litho Southern Colour Print)

2016 (6 July). Olympic Games, Rio de Janeiro, Brazil. Road to Rio. T **785** and similar parallelogram designs showing silhouettes of athletes in New Zealand landscapes. Multicoloured. Phosphorised paper. Perf 14.

3798	$1 Type **785**	1·40	1·50
	a. Block of 10. Nos. 3798/3807	12·50	13·50
3799	$1 Boxer	1·40	1·50
3800	$1 Canoeist (on mountain river with gravel banks)	1·40	1·50
3801	$1 Swimmer	1·40	1·50
3802	$1 Equestrian	1·40	1·50
3803	$1 Hockey player	1·40	1·50
3804	$1 Triathlete	1·40	1·50
3805	$1 Cyclist	1·40	1·50
3806	$1 Rower (on river with forested banks)	1·40	1·50
3807	$1 Sailor	1·40	1·50
3798/3807	Set of 10	12·50	13·50

Nos. 3798/3807 were printed together, *se-tenant*, as blocks of ten stamps in sheetlets of 20 (5×4).

786 Natalie Rooney (silver, shooting trap, women)

(Des Jonathan Gray. Litho. New Zealand Post)

2016 (8 Aug). New Zealand Olympic Medal Winners, Rio de Janeiro, Brazil. T **786** and similar parallelogram designs. Multicoloured. Phosphorised paper. Perf 14.

3808	$1 Type **786**	1·40	1·40
	a. Sheetlet of 6. No. 3808×6	8·00	
	b. Sheetlet of 18. Nos. 3808/3825	24·00	
3809	$1 New Zealand team (silver, rugby sevens women)	1·40	1·40
	a. Sheetlet of 6. No. 3809×6	8·00	
3810	$1 Eric Murray and Hamish Bond (gold, rowing pair men)	1·40	1·40
	a. Sheetlet of 6. No. 3810×6	8·00	
3811	$1 Luuka Jones (silver, slalom, K-1 women)	1·40	1·40
	a. Sheetlet of 6. No. 3811×6	8·00	
3812	$1 Ethan Mitchell, Sam Webster and Eddie Dawkins (silver, cycling, track, team sprint men)	1·40	1·40
	a. Sheetlet of 6. No. 3812×6	8·00	
3813	$1 Genevieve Behrent and Rebecca Scown (silver, rowing, pair women)	1·40	1·40
	a. Sheetlet of 6. No. 3813×6	8·00	
3814	$1 Valerie Adams (silver, athletics, shot put women)	1·40	1·40
	a. Sheetlet of 6. No. 3814×6	8·00	
3815	$1 Mahe Drysdale (gold, rowing, single scull men)	1·40	1·40
	a. Sheetlet of 6. No. 3815×6	8·00	
3816	$1 Lisa Carrington (gold, sprint, K-1, 200 m women)	1·40	1·40
	a. Sheetlet of 6. No. 3816×6	8·00	
3817	$1 Sam Meech (bronze, sailing, laser men)	1·40	1·40
	a. Sheetlet of 6. No. 3817×6	8·00	
3818	$1 Lisa Carrington (bronze, sprint, K-1, 500 m women)	1·40	1·40
	a. Sheetlet of 6. No. 3818×6	8·00	
3819	$1 Jo Aleh and Polly Powrie (silver, sailing, 470 women)	1·40	1·40
	a. Sheetlet of 6. No. 3819×6	8·00	
3820	$1 Peter Burling and Blair Tuke (gold, sailing, 49er men)	1·40	1·40
	a. Sheetlet of 6. No. 3820×6	8·00	
3821	$1 Molly Meech and Alex Maloney (silver, sailing, 49er women)	1·40	1·40
	a. Sheetlet of 6. No. 3821×6	8·00	
3822	$1 Tomas Walsh (athletics, shot put men)	1·40	1·40
	a. Sheetlet of 6. No. 3822×6	8·00	
3823	$1 Eliza McCartney (bronze, athletics, pole vault women)	1·40	1·40
	a. Sheetlet of 6. No. 3823×6	8·00	
3824	$1 Lydia Ko (silver, golf, individual women)	1·40	1·40
	a. Sheetlet of 6. No. 3824×6	8·00	
3825	$1 Nick Willis (bronze, athletics, 1500 m men)	1·40	1·40
	a. Sheetlet of 6. No. 3825×6	8·00	
3808/3825	Set of 18	24·00	24·00

Nos. 3808/3825 were issued in a *se-tenant* sheetlet containing the 18 designs and two labels.

Nos. 3808/3825 were also each issued in sheetlets of six stamps of the same design.

787 'At that moment Trev had a bit of an idea'

788 Children playing Touch Rugby (Aerobic)

(Des Chris Davidson (illustration), Graeme Mowday and Jack Faulkner. Litho Southern Colour Print)

2016 (7 Sept). It's a Kiwi Thing. T **787** and similar square designs. Multicoloured. Phosphorised paper. Perf 14½.

3826	$1 Type **787**	1·40	1·40
	a. Sheetlet of 14. Nos. 3826/3839	18·00	19·00
3827	$1 'I'll have a trim, decaf latte with a twist and a...'	1·40	1·40
3828	$1 'Breaking the tackle in the big game' (streaker on rugby pitch)	1·40	1·40
3829	$1 'The traditional Kiwi sand-wich'	1·40	1·40
3830	$1 'GONE BUT NOT FORGOTTEN 2011–2016 (jandals)'	1·40	1·40
3831	$1 'A kea ate my car'	1·40	1·40
3832	$1 'Catching a glimpse of our national bird'	1·40	1·40
3833	$1 'A cool splash followed by a hot dash' (hot beach sand)	1·40	1·40
3834	$1 'Water skiing on Lake Taupo' (angler towed by trout)	1·40	1·40

3835	$1 'Another smooth landing in the capital'	1·40	1·40
3836	$1 'At this time of year we'd be lucky to see a whale'	1·40	1·40
3837	$1 'Another successful day's whitebaiting'	1·40	1·40
3838	$1 'Just a friendly game of beach cricket'	1·40	1·40
3839	$1 'Always blow on the pie'	1·40	1·40
3826/3839	Set of 14	18·00	19·00

Nos. 3826/3839 were printed together, *se-tenant*, in sheetlets of 14 stamps.

(Des Stephen and Di Fuller. Litho Southern Colour Print)

2016 (7 Sept). Children's Health. Being Active. T **788** and similar horiz designs. Multicoloured. Phosphorised paper. Perf 14.

3840	$1+10c. Type **788**	1·50	1·75
	a. Horiz strip of 3. Nos. 3840/3842	7·00	8·50
3841	$1.80+10c. Children playing tug of war (Strength)	2·75	3·25
3842	$2.20+10c. Stretching exercises (Flexibility)	3·25	4·50
3840/3842	Set of 3	7·00	8·50
MS3843	150×90 mm. Nos. 3840/3842	7·00	8·50

No. 3840a could be purchased from the Philatelic Bureau.

789 Bruce and William Anderson (Loss of HMS *Neptune*)

(Des Helcia Knap. Litho Southern Colour Print)

2016 (5 Oct). 75th Anniversary of the Royal New Zealand Navy (RNZN). T **789** and similar horiz designs. Multicoloured. Phosphorised paper. Perf 14½×14.

3844	$1 Type **789**	1·75	1·40
3845	$1 Frigate RNZN *Pukaki* (Conflict in Korea)	1·75	1·10
3846	$1.80 Women at sea	2·50	2·75
3847	$2.20 Frigate HMNZS Te Mana, 2004 (Supporting the United Nations)	3·50	3·50
3848	$2.70 Disaster relief in Christchurch, 2011	4·25	4·50
3849	$3.30 The Navy family	5·00	5·50
3844/3849	Set of 6	17·00	17·00
MS3850	160×110 mm. Nos. 3844/3849	17·00	17·00

Nos. 3844/3849 and the stamps within No. **MS**3850 each show an image, coated with spot UV to give the effect of looking through glass, within a brass scuttle recovered from the wreck of the *Moa* In 1943.

A Journey through Middle Earth miniature sheet with a $10 stamp showing the One Ring embossed in gold foil was issued on 19 October 2016 and sold for $10.50, a 50c. premium over face value.

790 Jesus in Manger

(Des Donna McKenna. Litho Southern Colour Print)

2016 (2 Nov). Christmas. T **790** and similar multicoloured designs. Phosphorised paper.

(a) Ordinary gum. Square designs as T **790**. Perf 14.

3851	$1 Type **790**	1·40	1·00
3852	$1.80 Joseph	2·50	2·00
3853	$2.20 Shepherd	2·75	2·75
3854	$2.70 Mary	3·25	3·50
3855	$3.30 Wise Man	4·00	4·50
3851/3855	Set of 5	12·50	13·00
MS3856	160×110 mm. Nos. 3851/3855	12·50	13·00

(b) Self-adhesive. Size 25×30 mm.
(i) Domestic mail. Die-cut perf 10.

3857	$1 As Type **790**	1·40	1·25
	a. Booklet pane. No. 3857×10	11·00	1·10
	b. Horiz strip of 3. Nos. 3857/3859	6·50	7·25

(ii) International Post.

3858	$2.20 As No. 3853	2·75	3·00
	a. Booklet pane. No. 3858×10	22·00	3·50
3859	$2.70 As No. 3854	3·25	3·75
	a. Booklet pane. No. 3859×10	25·00	4·25
3857/3859	Set of 3	6·50	7·25

No. 3857 was issued in $10 booklet No. SB183.
The *se-tenant* strip of three, No. 3857b, could be purchased from the Philatelic Bureau.
No. 3858 was issued in booklet No. SB184, sold at $19.80, providing a $2.20 discount off the face value of the stamps.
No. 3859 was issued in booklet No. SB185, sold at $24.30, providing a $2.70 discount off the face value of the stamps.

(Litho Southern Colour Print)

2016 (18 Nov). CHRISTCHURCH 2016 Stamp and Postcard Exhibition. Sheet 140×85 mm. Multicoloured. Phosphorised paper. Perf 13½.

MS3860	Nos. 3230/3231	10·00	10·00

An imperforate master sheet of 20×No. **MS**3860 was donated by New Zealand post to raise funds for the exhibition.

BEST OF 2016. A further set of miniature sheets as descibed below No. 2042 were distributed by the Philatelic Bureau to customers purchasing a certain amount of philatelic material during 2016. The sheets comprised: 1. Nos. 3745, 3752 and 3757. 2. No. 3768, the $3.30 stamp from No. **MS**3787 and No. 3834. 3. Nos. 3842, 3849 and 3855.
Imperforate sheets of Nos. 3844/3849 and a perforated *se-tenant* block of the same six stamps were also distributed.

791 Calligraphic Character for Rooster

792 Southern Lights

(Des Asiaworks, Auckland. Litho Southern Colour Print)

2017 (11 Jan). Chinese New Year. Year of the Rooster. T **791** and similar vert designs. Multicoloured. Phosphorised paper. Perf 13½×13.

3861	$1 Type **791**	1·40	1·00
3862	$1.80 Paper-cut Rooster	2·50	2·00
3863	$2.20 Rooster	2·75	2·75
3864	$2.70 Chinese lantern with Rooster design and Auckland War Memorial Museum (Lantern Festival)	3·25	3·50
3861/3864	Set of 4	9·00	8·25
MS3865	150×90 mm. Nos. 3861/3864	9·00	9·50

2017 (8 Feb). Southern Lights. T **792** and similar horiz designs. Multicoloured. Perf 14½×14.

3866	$1 Type **792**	1·40	1·00
3867	$1.80 Southern Lights (yellow and red)	2·50	2·25
3868	$2 Mount John Observatory and Southern Lights	2·50	2·75
3869	$2.20 Southern Lights (yellow and magenta)	2·75	3·00
3870	$2.70 Southern Lights over Mount John Observatory and other buildings	3·25	3·50
3871	$3.30 Southern Lights (green and red) over Mount John Observatory and other buildings	4·25	4·75
3866/3871	Set of 6	15·00	16·00
MS3872	180×110 mm. As Nos. 3866/3871 but with silver foil	15·00	16·00

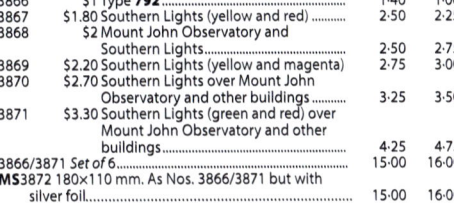

793 Lowland Longjaw Galaxias

(Des Stephen Fuller. Litho Southern Colour Print, New Zealand)

2017 (1 Mar). Native Freshwater Fish. T **793** and similar horiz designs. Multicoloured. Perf 14×14½.

3873	$1 Type **793**	1·40	1·00
3874	$1.80 Redfin Bully	2·50	2·00
3875	$2.20 Longfin Eel	2·75	2·75
3876	$2.70 Lamprey	3·25	3·50
3877	$3.30 Torrentfish	4·25	4·50
3873/3877	Set of 5	12·50	12·50
MS3878	160×90 mm. Nos. 3873/3877	12·50	13·00

NEW ZEALAND

(Des Strategy Creative, Wellington. Litho Southern Colour Print)

2017 (5 Apr). Centenary of the First World War (4th issue). The Darkest Hour. Square designs as T **761**. Multicoloured. Perf 14½.

3879	$1 A mother mourns, Ellen Knight	1·40	1·40
	a. Block of 6. Nos. 3879/3884	7·50	7·50
3880	$1 Major General Edward Walter Clervaux Chaytor and Brigadier General William Meldrum of Australian and New Zealand Mounted Division outside a mosque in Beersheba, Palestine ('From Egypt to Jerusalem')	1·40	1·40
3881	$1 Letter postmarked Sling Camp, Salisbury and NZ Hastings, 1917 ('Sling Camp')	1·40	1·40
3882	$1 Tank, Battle of Messines, 1917 ('Technology of war')	1·40	1·40
3883	$1 Harold Gillies in The Queen's Hospital, Kent, 1917 ('Plastic surgery')	1·40	1·40
3884	$1 Relatives at Tyne Cot Cemetery, Passchendaele	1·40	1·40
3885	$2.20 General Godley salutes surviving soldiers of 2nd Infantry Brigade after Battle of Messines, Belgium	3·00	3·00
	a. Horiz pair. Nos. 3885/3886	6·00	6·00
3886	$2.20 'SIX O'CLOCK CLOSING IS IT JUSTIFIED ON MILITARY GROUNDS? BUSINESS MEN'S RESOLUTION REQUEST TO DEFER ACTION' ('Social change at home')	3·00	3·00
3887	$2.70 Australian supply ship SS *Port Kembla* (sunk by German mine in New Zealand waters)	3·50	4·00
	a. Horiz pair. Nos. 3887/3888	7·00	8·00
3888	$2.70 Women in Census and Statistics Office Military Service Section in Routh's building, Wellington, during military service ballot ('A changing workforce')	3·50	4·00
3879/3888 *Set of 10*		19·00	20·00
MS3889 175×90 mm. Nos. 3879/3884		9·00	9·50
MS3890 138×90 mm. Nos. 3885/3888		13·00	14·00
MS3890*a* 169×91 mm. Nos. 3879/3888		19·00	20·00

Nos. 3879/3884 were printed together, *se-tenant*, as blocks of six stamps in sheets of 24 (6×4).

Nos. 3885/3886 and 3887/3888 were each printed together, *se-tenant*, as horizontal pairs in sheets of 24 (6×4).

Nos. 3879/3888 were also issued in premium booklet No. SP16, containing stamps with a face value of $31.60 but sold for $39.90.

794 Lion and Team Colours on Map of Whangarei Area

795 Modern Man and Rangatira (Maori leader) of 1835

(Des Dave Burke. Litho Southern Colour Print)

2017 (3 May). The British and Irish Lions 2017 Rugby Tour to New Zealand. T **794** and similar horiz designs. Multicoloured. Perf 14×14½.

MS3891 180×235 mm. $2.70 Type **794**; $2.70 Lion over map of Auckland area with flowers; $2.70 Lion over map of Hamilton area with yellow and black design; $2.70 Lion over map of Rotorua area with black and grey design; $2.70 Lion over map of Wellington area (southern tip of North Island) with yellow filigree pattern; $2.70 Lion over map of Christchurch area with red and black stripes; $2.70 Lion over map of Dunedin area with tartan pattern ... 19·00 22·00

The stamps and background of No. **MS**3891 form a composite design showing an outline map of New Zealand.

(Des Spencer Levine, Story Inc. Litho Southern Colour Print)

2017 (17 May). He Tohu Exhibition, Wellington. T **795** and similar horiz designs. Multicoloured. Perf 14.

3892	$1 Type **795** (Declaration of Independence of the United Tribes of New Zealand)	1·25	1·25
3893	$2 Maori boy and white girl (Treaty of Waitangi)	2·00	2·50
3894	$2.20 Modern woman and suffragist of 1890s (Women's Suffrage Petition)	2·25	2·50
3892/3894 *Set of 3*		5·00	5·50

(Litho Southern Colour Print)

2017 (7 June). New Zealand Landscapes (7th series). Horiz designs as T **757**. Multicoloured. Perf 13×13½.

3895	$2.30 Mangamaunu, Kaikoura	2·50	2·75
3896	$4.30 Manu Bay, Raglan	4·75	5·50

796 Piha Bar, Piha

(Des Hannah Stancliffe-White. Litho Southern Colour Print)

2017 (7 June). Surf Breaks. T **796** and similar horiz designs. Multicoloured. Perf 14×14½.

3897	$1 Type **796**	1·40	1·10
3898	$2.20 Manu Bay, Raglan	2·50	2·75
3899	$2.30 Surf Highway 45, Taranaki	2·50	2·75
3900	$2.70 Mangamaunu, Kaikoura	3·00	3·25
3901	$3.30 Aramoana Spit, Dunedin	3·50	4·25
3897/3901 *Set of 5*		11·50	12·50
MS3902 187×78 mm. Nos. 3897/3901		11·50	14·00

BERMUDA 2017 WINNERS. On 3 July 2017 a sheetlet comprising six $2.70 stamps was issued in celebration of New Zealand's victory in the Americas Cup. The sale price was in excess of the face value of the stamps.

797 Couple, Lighthouse and Pohutukawa Tree (Cape Reinga)

(Des Graeme Mowday, Chris Boniface (artwork) and Chris Davidson (illustration). Litho Southern Colour Print)

2017 (12 July). The Great Kiwi Road Trip. T **797** and similar horiz designs depicting couple with campervan. Multicoloured. Perf 14½×14.

MS3903 180×235 mm. $1 Type **797**; $1 Couple at Ninety Mile Beach and Pohutukawa tree; $1 Campervan stuck among Sheep, Mount Taranaki in background; $1 Couple, geyser and ROTOVEGAS sign (Rotorua); $1 Campervan gridlocked in Auckland traffic; $1 Couple, campervan, Kiwi sign and longest Maori place name; $1 Couple, campervan and DESSERT ROAD sign (Central Plateau); $1 Couple crossing Cook Strait on ferry, WELLINGTON and PICTON signs; $1 Surfer and beach (Canterbury); $1 Couple in rain in mountain forest and WELCOME TO THE WEST COAST; $1 Campervan at seaside with Whale and Dolphins offshore (KAIKOURA and OPEN for BUSINESS signs); $1 BALDWIN STREET and THE WORLD'S STEEPEST STREET (Dunedin); $1 Couple hiking in Fiordland forest (LOST REALLY LOST NOT THIS WAY); $1 Campervan on coast road and BLUFF sign with Oysters ... 20·00 22·00

798 Campbell Island Teal

799 Waea Pūkoro (mobile phone)

NEW ZEALAND

(Des Jonathan Gray. Litho Southern Colour Print)

2017 (2 Aug). Recovering Native Birds. T **798** and similar horiz designs. Multicoloured. Phosphorised paper. Perf 14½×14 (Nos. 3904/3908) or 14 (No. **MS**3909).

3904	$1 Type **798**	1·75	1·25
3905	$2.20 Black Stilt	3·00	2·75
3906	$2.30 North Island Kaka	3·00	2·75
3907	$2.70 South Island Saddleback	3·25	3·25
3908	$3.30 Northern New Zealand Dotterel	4·00	4·50
3904/3908 Set of 5		13·50	13·00
MS3909 106×100 mm. Nos. 3904/3908		13·50	14·00

(Des Elisabeth Vüllings (illustrator) and David Hakaraia. Litho Southern Colour Print)

2017 (6 Sept). Te Reo Māori. Māori Language. New Words. T **799** and similar vert designs. Multicoloured. Perf 13×13½.

3910	$1 Type **799**	1·10	1·10
	a. Block of 8. Nos. 3910/3917	8·00	8·00
3911	$1 Pātuhi (text)	1·10	1·10
3912	$1 Rorohiko (computer)	1·10	1·10
3913	$1 Pūmahara (flash drive)	1·10	1·10
3914	$1 Uruwhenua (passport)	1·10	1·10
3915	$1 Taunga rererangi (airport)	1·10	1·10
3916	$1 Pūnaha kimi ahunga (global positioning system)	1·10	1·10
3917	$1 Whare Tikoke (skyscraper)	1·10	1·10
3918	$2.20 Ahokore (wifi)	2·50	2·75
3919	$2.70 Waka Hiko (electric car)	2·75	3·25
3910/3919 Set of 10		12·50	13·00
MS3920 185×266 mm. Nos. 3910/3919		12·50	14·00

Nos. 3910/3917 were printed together, *se-tenant*, as blocks of eight in sheetlets of 20 (4×5), giving two blocks of eight and one horizontal strip of four (Nos. 3910/3913).

800 Basil

801 Angel

(Des Hannah Stancliffe-White. Litho Southern Colour Print)

2017 (4 Oct). Grow Your Own. T **800** and similar vert designs. Multicoloured. Phosphorised paper. Perf 14×14½.

3921	$1 Type **800**	1·25	1·25
3922	$1 Carrots	1·25	1·25
3923	$2.20 Parsley	2·50	2·50
3924	$2.30 Chives	2·50	2·50
3925	$2.70 Broccoli	2·75	3·00
3926	$3.30 Lettuce	3·25	4·00
3921/3926 Set of 6		12·00	13·00
MS3927 185×90 mm. Nos. 3921/3926		12·00	14·00

Nos. 3921/3926 and stamps from No. **MS**3927 have V-shaped roulettes at the foot of the stamp.

Nos. 3921/3926 have white margins under the roulettes and above the perforations at the top of the stamp.

Stamps from No. **MS**3927 have the V-shaped roulettes at the foot of the stamp, and sheet margins showing soil, with no white margins. They also have 'PLANT ME' over the top. To comply with export regulations, miniature sheets sold overseas did not include the seeds but showed an image of the seed panel with 'PLANT ME' above (*Price, the same in either form*).

(Des Yulia Brodskaya (artwork) and Nicky Dyer. Litho Southern Colour Print)

2017 (1 Nov). Christmas. Quilled Christmas Decorations. T **801** and similar vert designs. Multicoloured. Phosphorised paper. Perf 14.

(a) Ordinary gum. Perf 14.

3928	$1 Type **801**	1·25	1·00
3929	$2.20 Bauble	2·50	2·50
3930	$2.30 Star	2·50	2·50
3931	$2.70 Bell	2·75	3·00
3932	$3.30 Wreath	3·25	3·00
3928/3932 Set of 5		11·00	11·00
MS3933 115×101 mm. Nos. 3928/3932		11·00	13·00

(b) Self-adhesive. Size 22×27 mm. Die-cut perf 9½×10.
(i) Domestic mail.

3934	$1 As Type **801**	1·25	1·25
	a. Booklet pane. No. 3934×10	10·00	
	b. With phosphor frame	1·25	1·25
	ba. Horiz strip of 3. Nos. 3934b/3936b	6·50	

(ii) International Post.

3935	$2.20 As No. 3929	2·75	3·00
	a. Booklet pane. No. 3935×10	22·00	
	b. With phosphor frame	2·75	3·00
3936	$2.70 As No. 3931	3·25	3·50
	a. Booklet pane. No. 3936×10	25·00	
	b. With phosphor frame	3·25	3·50
3934/3936 Set of 3		6·50	7·00

No. 3934 was issued in $10 booklet No. SB186.

Nos. 3934b/3936b were issued in No. 3634ba, which could be purchased from the Philatelic Bureau.

No. 3935 was issued in booklet No. SB187, sold at $19.80, providing a $2.20 discount off the face value of the stamps.

No. 3936 was issued in booklet No. SB188, sold at $24.30, providing a $2.70 discount off the face value of the stamps.

802 Engagement of Princess Elizabeth and Lieutenant Philip Mountbatten

(Des Jonathan Gray. Litho Southern Colour Print)

2017 (20 Nov). Platinum Wedding Anniversary of Queen Elizabeth II and Prince Philip Duke of Edinburgh. T **802** and similar vert designs. Multicoloured. Phosphorised paper. Perf 14.

3937	$1 Type **802**	1·75	1·25
3938	$2 Wedding of Princess Elizabeth and Duke of Edinburgh	2·75	2·50
3939	$2.20 Queen Elizabeth II, Prince Philip, Princes Charles, Andrew and Edward and Princess Anne, 1972	2·75	2·50
3940	$2.30 Queen Elizabeth II and Prince Philip in New Zealand, 30 January–8 February 1974	2·75	2·50
3941	$2.70 Queen Elizabeth II, Prince Philip, Princes Charles, William, Harry and George, and Catherine, Duchess of Cambridge holding Princess Charlotte, Buckingham Palace balcony, 2016	3·00	3·00
3942	$3.30 Queen Elizabeth II and Prince Philip watching Trooping the Colour from Buckingham Palace balcony, 2017	3·50	4·00
3937/3942 Set of 6		15·00	14·00
MS3943 115×101 mm. Nos. 3937/3942		15·00	15·00

(Litho Southern Colour Print)

2017 (24 Nov). Royalpex 2017 National Stamp Exhibition, Hamilton. Sheet 115×100 mm containing Nos. 3904/3906. Phosphorised paper. Perf 14.

MS3944 Nos. 3904/3906		8·00	9·00

BEST OF 2017. A further set of miniature sheets as described below No. 2042 were distributed by the Philatelic Bureau to customers purchasing a certain amount of philatelic material during 2017. The sheets comprised: 1. Nos. 3871, 3864 and 3877. 2. Nos. 3906, 3887 and 3894. 3. Nos. 3919, 3901 and 3932.

Imperforate sheets of Nos. 3897/3901 and a *se-tenant* block of the same five stamps, plus a label were also distributed.

NEW ZEALAND

803 Calligraphy **804** Alps 2 Ocean Cycle Trail

(Des Asiaworks, Auckland. Litho Cartor)

2018 (10 Jan). Chinese New Year. Year of the Dog. T **803** and similar vert designs. Multicoloured. Phosphorised paper. Perf 13½×13.
3945	$1 Type **803**	1·40	1·00
3946	$2.20 Paper-cut Dog	2·75	2·50
3947	$2.70 Huntaway (New Zealand Sheepdog)	3·00	3·25
3948	$3.30 Bronze statue of Sheepdog, Lake Tekapo	3·50	4·00
3945/3948 Set of 4		9·50	9·75
MS3949 150×90 mm. Nos. 3945/3948		9·50	10·00

(Des Strategy Creative. Litho Southern Colour Print)

2018 (7 Feb). Cycle Trails. T **804** and similar horiz designs. Multicoloured. Phosphorised paper. Perf 14×14½.
3950	$1 Type **804**	1·50	1·40
3951	$1 Mountains to Sea	1·50	1·40
3952	$2 Otago Central Rail Trail	2·50	2·50
3953	$2.20 Old Ghost Road	2·50	2·50
3954	$2.70 Queen Charlotte Track	2·75	3·00
3955	$3.30 Timber Trail	3·50	4·00
3950/3955 Set of 6		13·00	13·50
MS3956 175×100 mm. Nos. 3950/3955		14·00	19·00

805 *Wahine* ('World's Finest Drive-on Vessel') in Wellington Harbour

(Des Jonathan Gray. Litho Southern Colour Print)

2018 (7 Mar). 50th Anniversary of the Sinking of the *Wahine*. T **805** and similar horiz designs. Multicoloured. Phosphorised paper. Perf 14½×14.
3957	$1 Type **805**	1·50	1·40
3958	$1 *Wahine* forced onto Barrett Reef, near Wellington, 10 April 1968 ('*Wahine* in Trouble')	1·50	1·40
3959	$2 Passengers in lounge ('Waiting to Abandon Ship')	2·50	2·50
3960	$2.20 'Lifeboats make Land'	2·50	2·50
3961	$2.70 'Hundreds rescued from Wellington Harbour'	2·75	3·00
3962	$3.30 *Aranui* passes wreck of *Wahine*	3·50	4·00
3957/3962 Set of 6		13·00	13·50
MS3963 190×100 mm. Nos. 3957/3962		13·00	14·00

(Des Strategy Creative, Wellington. Litho Southern Colour Print)

2018 (4 Apr). Centenary of the First World War (5th issue). 1918 Back from the Brink. Square designs as T **761**. Perf 14½.
3964	$1 Arthur Gordon (1895–1978)	1·40	1·40
	a. Block of 6. Nos. 3964/3969	7·50	7·50
3965	$1 Hundred days offensive	1·40	1·40
3966	$1 Influenza depot in Christchurch ('The flu pandemic')	1·40	1·40
3967	$1 Returned soldier and family ('Demobilisation')	1·40	1·40
3968	$1 Resettlement	1·40	1·40
3969	$1 Sopwith Camel biplane ('Great air war')	1·40	1·40
3970	$2.20 Auckland Town Hall lit for Peace Festival celebrations, 28 June 1919 ('Armistice')	3·00	3·00
	a. Horiz pair. Nos. 3970/3971	6·00	6·00
3971	$2.20 Maori Battalion marching up Queen Street, Auckland, 6 April 1919 ('Maori battalion return')	3·00	3·00
3972	$2.70 New Zealand soldiers scaling the walls of fortress town of Le Quesnoy, 4 November 1918 (stained glass window, St Andrew's Anglican Church, Cambridge)	3·50	4·00
	a. Horiz pair. Nos. 3972/3973	7·00	8·00
3973	$2.70 Badge of the New Zealand War Amputees' Association ('Rehabilitation')	3·50	4·00
3964/39736 Set of 10		19·00	20·00
MS3974 175×90 mm. Nos. 3964/3969		9·00	9·50
MS3975 138×90 mm. Nos. 3970/3973		13·00	14·00
MS3976 205×107 mm. Nos. 3964/3973		19·00	20·00

Nos. 3964/3969 were printed together, *se-tenant*, as blocks of six stamps in sheets of 24 (6×4).

Nos. 3970/3971 and 3972/3973 were each printed together, *se-tenant*, in horizontal pairs throughout the sheets.

Nos. 3964/3973 were also issued in premium booklet No. SP17, containing stamps with a face value of $31.60 but sold for $39.90.

806 State Highway 1 moved Seawards away from Landslide, Irongate Stream, north of Kaikoura (Shape of the Future)

807 Māui stows away on board his Brothers' Waka (An Impending Storm)

(Des Saint Andrew Matautia. Litho Southern Colour Print)

2018 (2 May). Reconnecting New Zealand (after earthquake of 14 November 2016). T **806** and similar horiz designs. Multicoloured. Phosphorised paper. Perf 14½×14.
3977	$1 Type **806**	1·50	1·40
3978	$1 Abseiler installing geomesh on cliff to prevent rockfalls (Taming the Cliffs)	1·50	1·40
3979	$2 Earth moving machinery clearing landslide, south of Peketa (Moving Mountains)	2·50	2·50
3980	$2.20 Construction of seawall (A Hard Road)	2·50	2·50
3981	$2.70 Temporary Bridge 131 at Wharenui, built to allow KiwiRail's specialised work trains into coastal corridor (Engines That Could)	2·75	3·00
3982	$3.30 First freight train to travel the main North Line after the earthquake, en route from Picton to Christchurch, 15 September 2017 (A Special Delivery)	3·50	4·00
3977/3982 Set of 6		13·00	13·50
MS3983 190×100 mm. Nos. 3977/3982		13·00	14·00

A sheetlet of six $2.70 Royal Wedding stamps perforated 14½ depicting Prince Harry and Ms. Meghan Markle was issued on 21 May 2018, and sold for $19.90, $3.70 premium over face value.

(Des David Hakaria. Litho Southern Colour Print)

2018 (6 June). Māui and the Fish. T **807** and similar vert designs. Multicoloured. Phosphorised paper.

(a) Self-adhesive. Die-cut perf 10×9½.
3984	$1.20 Type **807**	1·25	1·40
	a. Pane. Nos. 3984/3989	11·00	13·00
3985	$1.20 Launch the waka	1·25	1·40
3986	$1.20 Māui holding his late grandmother's heirloom jawbone (A legendary heirloom)	1·25	1·40
3987	$2.40 Māui hauling in the huge fish (The fierce battle)	2·25	2·50
3988	$3 Fish breaks the surface and hardens into huge land mass, which Māui's brothers carved up with the jawbone (The carving of the land)	3·00	3·50
3989	$3.60 North and South Islands of New Zealand (The fish of Māui and the waka)	3·50	4·00
3984/3989 Set of 6		11·00	13·00

(b) Ordinary gum. Perf 14×13½.
MS3990 150×90 mm. As Nos. 3984/3989		11·00	14·00

(Litho Southern Colour Print)

2018 (6 June). New Zealand Landscapes (8th series). Horiz designs as T **757**. Multicoloured. Phosphorised paper.

(a) Ordinary gum. Perf 13×13½.
3991	$2.40 Mount Maunganui, Tauranga	2·50	2·75
3992	$4.40 Lake Te Anau, Fiordland	4·75	5·50

(b) Self-adhesive. Die-cut perf 10×9½.
3993	$2.40 As No. 3991	2·50	2·75
	a. Booklet pane. No. 3993×5	10·00	

NEW ZEALAND

	b. Horiz pair. Nos. 3993/3994	5·75	6·25
3994	$3 Tongaporutu, Taranaki	3·25	3·50
	a. Booklet pane. No. 3994×5	13·00	

The design of No. 3994 is as No. 2609 but with redrawn country inscription and face value.
No. 3993 was issued in $12 booklet No. SB189.
No. 3994 was issued in $15 booklet No. SB190.

(Litho Southern Colour Print)

2018 (6 June). Personalised Stamps. As Nos. 3788/3797 but new face values. Phosphorised paper. Perf 15×14½.
MS3995 185×70 mm. $1.20 As Type **758**; $1.20 Silver fern; $1.20 'love'; $1.20 Two glasses of champagne; $1.20 Teddy bear; $1.20 Pohutukawa flowers; $1.20 Balloons; $2.40 Silver fern; $2.40 As Type **758**; $3 Pohutukawa flowers................ 13·00 14·00

No. MS3995 contains two horizontal strips of five stamps separated by a gutter containing labels inscribed '2018 Personalised Stamps'.

808 Brown Kiwi

809 Tui, Stitchbird and Saddleback (Tuneful Backyards)

(Des Dave Burke Design. Litho Southern Colour Print)

2018 (4 July). Round Kiwi Stamps. T **808** and similar circular designs. Multicoloured. Phosphorised paper. Perf 14½.

3996	$1.20 Type **808**	1·40	1·40
	a. Booklet pane. No. 3996×6	7·00	
3997	$1.20 Great Spotted Kiwi	1·40	1·40
3998	$2.40 Little Spotted Kiwi	2·50	2·75
3999	$3 Tokoeka	3·00	3·50
4000	$3.60 Rowi	3·50	4·00
3996/4000 Set of 5		10·50	11·00
MS4001 170×90 mm. Nos. 3996/4000		10·50	12·50

(Des Stephen Fuller, Wellington. Litho Southern Colour Print)

2018 (1 Aug). Predator Free 2050. T **809** and similar horiz designs. Multicoloured. Phosphorised paper. Perf 14½×14.

4002	$1.20 Type **809**	1·75	1·50
4003	$1.20 White Heron, Blue Ducks, kingfisher and frog (Thriving wetland cycleways)	1·75	1·50
4004	$2.40 Wood Pigeon, Tuatara, Jewelled Gecko, Weka and Red Admiral Butterfly (Picnic in the park)	3·00	2·75
4005	$3 Whitehead, Tomtit, North Island Robin and Forbes' Parakeet (Urban oasis)	3·75	3·75
4006	$3.60 Owl, giant snail, Great Spotted Kiwi and Giant Weta (Nocturnal wonderland)	4·50	4·75
4002/4006 Set of 5		13·50	13·00
MS4007 170×95 mm. Nos. 4002/4006		13·50	14·00

810 Log Splitters

811 Kate Sheppard (1847–1934, suffragist)

(Des EightyOne, Wellington. Litho Southern Colour Print)

2018 (5 Sept). Thinking Outside the Square. Celebrating Kiwi Innovation and Ingenuity. T **810** and similar square designs. Multicoloured. Phosphorised paper. Perf 14½.

4008	$1.20 Type **810**	1·50	1·50
	a. Sheetlet of 12. Nos. 4008/4019	16·00	16·00
4009	$1.20 Lifepod incubators	1·50	1·50
4010	$1.20 Instant coffee	1·50	1·50
4011	$1.20 The Jogging Movement	1·50	1·50
4012	$1.20 Self-resetting traps	1·50	1·50
4013	$1.20 Retractable boat wheels	1·50	1·50
4014	$1.20 Automatic chook (chicken) feeder	1·50	1·50
4015	$1.20 Ref's whistle	1·50	1·50
4016	$1.20 Land yachting	1·50	1·50
4017	$1.20 Robust brollies	1·50	1·50
4018	$1.20 Kid-proof caps	1·50	1·50
4019	$1.20 3-stage bikes	1·50	1·50
4008/4019 Set of 12		16·00	16·00

Nos. 4008/4019 were printed together, *se-tenant*, as sheetlets of 12 stamps (4×4) surrounding a central 74×74 mm label.

(Des Helcia Berryman, Grange Park Creative, Raumati South. Litho Southern Colour Print)

2018 (5 Sept). 125th Anniversary of Women's Suffrage in New Zealand. T **811** and similar vert designs. Multicoloured. Phosphorised paper. Perf 14.

4020	$3 Type **811**	3·00	3·50
	a. Horiz pair. Nos. 4020/4021	6·00	7·00
4021	$3 White Camellia (symbol of suffrage movement) named Kate Sheppard	3·00	3·50
MS4022 115×85 mm. Nos. 4020/4021		6·00	7·00

Nos. 4020/4021 were printed together, *se-tenant*, as horizontal pairs in sheets of 24 (6×4).

(Litho Southern Colour Print)

2018 (21 Sept). Macau 2018 35th Asian International Stamp Exhibition. Two sheets, containing Nos. 3996/3998 (No. MS4023) or as Nos. 4002/4004 but smaller (42×28 mm) (No. MS4024). Phosphorised paper. Perf 14½.
MS4023 130×90 mm. $1.20 Type **808**; $1.20 Great Spotted Kiwi; $2.40 Little Spotted Kiwi (sold for $5.80).................. 5·00 6·50
MS4024 160×90 mm. $1.20 As Type **809**; $1.20 White Heron, Blue Ducks, kingfisher and frog (Thriving wetland cycleways); $2.40 Wood Pigeon, Tuatara, Jewelled Gecko, Weka and Red Admiral Butterfly (Picnic in the park).................. 5·00 6·50

Nos. MS4023/MS4024 were each sold at $5.80, a $1 surcharge over face value for the New Zealand Philatelic Trust.

812 Pilots of 1918 and 2018 (Air Force)

813 Viirgin Mary

(Des Dave Burke. Litho Southern Colour Print)

2018 (1 Oct). Centenary of the Armistice. T **812** and similar horiz designs. Multicoloured. Phosphorised paper. Perf 14.

4025	$1.20 Type **812**	1·50	1·40
4026	$1.20 Nurse of 1918 and doctor (serving medical personnel)	1·50	1·40
4027	$2.40 Soldiers of 1918 and 2018	3·00	2·50
4028	$3 Navy of 1918 and 2018	3·75	3·75
4029	$3.60 RNZRSA Poppy	4·50	4·50
4025/4029 Set of 5		13·00	12·50
MS4030 184×95 mm. Nos. 4025/4029		13·00	13·00

(Des Saint Andrew Matautia. Litho Southern Colour Print)

2018 (7 Nov). Christmas. T **813** and similar vert designs. Multicoloured. Phosphorised paper.

(a) Ordinary gum. Perf 14.

4031	$1.20 Type **813**	1·25	1·25
	a. Pair. Nos. 4031/4032	2·50	2·50
4032	$1.20 Joseph and Mary holding baby Jesus	1·25	1·25
4033	$2.40 Angel	2·50	2·25
4034	$3 The Three Wise Men holding baby Jesus	3·00	3·25
4035	$3.60 Shepherd	3·50	3·75
4031/4036 Set of 5		10·50	10·50
MS4036 115×102 mm. As Nos. 4031/4035 but with gold foil		10·50	12·00

(b) Self-adhesive. Phosphor frame (No. 4037ba) or phosphorised paper (others). Die-cut perf 9½×10
(i) Domestic mail.

4037	$1.20 As Type **813**	1·25	1·25
	a. Booklet pane. Nos. 4037/4038, each×5	10·00	
	b. With phosphor frame	1·25	1·25
	ba. Horiz strip of 4. Nos. 4037b/4040b	7·00	7·25
4038	$1.20 As No. 4032	1·25	1·25
	b. With phosphor frame	1·25	1·25

NEW ZEALAND

(ii) International Post.

4039	$2.40 As No. 4033		2·50	2·50
	a. Booklet. No. 4039×10		21·00	
	b. With phosphor frame		2·50	2·50
4040	$3 As No. 4034		3·00	3·25
	a. Booklet pane. No. 4040×10		26·00	
	b. With phosphor frame		3·00	3·25
4037/4040 Set of 4			7·00	7·25

Nos. 4031/4032 were printed together, *se-tenant*, as horizontal and vertical pairs in sheets of 25.

No. 4037 was issued in $12 booklet No. SB192.

Nos. 4037b/4040b were issued in No. 4037ba, which could be purchased from the Philatelic Bureau.

No. 4039 was issued in booklet No. SB193, sold at $21.60, providing a $2.40 discount off the face value of the stamps.

No. 4040 was issued in booklet No. SB194, sold at $27, providing a $3 discount off the face value of the stamps.

(Litho Southern Colour Print)

2018 (9 Nov). The Armistice Stamp Show, Dunedin. Multicoloured. Phosphorised paper. Perf 14.

MS4041 146×82 mm. Nos. 4025 and 4027/4028 (*sold at $9.10*)... 9·00 9·50

No. **MS**4041 was sold at $9.10, a $2.50 premium over face value. The surcharge was for the New Zealand Philatelic Trust.

(Litho Southern Colour Print)

2018 (28 Nov). Thailand 2018 World Stamp Exhibition, Bangkok. Phosphorised paper. Perf 14½ (No. **MS**4042) or 14½×14 (No. **MS**4043).

MS4042 130×90 mm. Nos. 3996/3998 (*sold at $5.80*)...... 5·00 5·50
MS4043 120×100 mm. Nos. 4002/4003 and 4005 (*sold at $6.40*)... 6·00 6·50

No. **MS**4042 was sold at $5.80 and No. **MS**4043 at $6.40. The $1 surcharges over face value were for the New Zealand Philatelic Trust.

BEST OF 2018. A further set of miniature sheets as described below No. 2042 were distributed by the Philatelic Bureau to customers purchasing certain amount of material during 2018. The sheets comprised: 1. Nos. 3962, 3948 and 3955. 2. Nos. 3972, 3982 and 3989. 3. Nos. 4006, 4000 and 4035.

Imperforate sheets of Nos. 3996/4000 and a *se-tenant* block of the same five stamps, plus a label, were also distributed.

814 Calligraphy   **815** Mountain Buttercup (*Ranunculus insignis*)

(Des Asiaworks, Auckland. Litho Cartor)

2019 (16 Jan). Chinese New Year. Year of the Pig. T **814** and similar vert designs. Multicoloured. Phosphorised paper. Perf 13½×13.

4044	$1.20 Type **814**	1·25	1·00
4045	$2.40 Paper-cut pig	2·25	2·00
4046	$3 Arapawa pig	3·00	3·25
4047	$3.60 State Highway 85 (Pig Route)	3·50	4·50
4044/4047 Set of 4		9·00	9·75
MS4048 150×90 mm. Nos. 4044/4047		9·00	11·00

(Des Stephen Fuller. Litho Southern Colour Print)

2019 (13 Feb). Native Alpine Flora. T **815** and similar vert designs. Multicoloured. Perf 14.

4049	$1.20 Type **815**	1·25	1·25
4050	$1.20 Penwiper Plant (*Notothlaspi rosulatum*)	1·25	1·25
4051	$1.20 Black Scree Button Daisy (*Leptinella atrata* subsp. *atrata*)	1·25	1·25
4052	$2.40 Woollyhead (*Craspedia incana*)	2·25	2·25
4053	$3 Mount Cook Lily (*Ranunculus lyallii*)	3·00	3·50
4054	$3.60 Moss-dwelling Forget-me-not (*Myosotis bryonoma*)	3·50	4·50
4049/4054 Set of 6		11·00	13·00
MS4055 140×90 mm. Nos. 4049/4054		11·00	14·00

For the miniature sheet containing Nos. 4049 and 4051/4052, see No. **MS**4090.

816 Pouto Lighthouse, Northland

(Des Hannah Fortune. Litho Southern Colour Print)

2019 (6 Mar). Lighthouse Perspectives. T **816** and similar horiz designs. Multicoloured. Phosphorised paper. Perf 14½×14.

4056	$1.20 Type **816**	1·75	1·75
4057	$1.20 Manukau Heads Lighthouse, Auckland	1·75	1·75
4058	$1.20 Baring Head Lighthouse, Greater Wellington	1·75	1·75
4059	$2.40 French Pass Lighthouse, Marlborough	2·75	2·75
4060	$3 Nugget Point Lighthouse, Catlins	3·75	3·75
4061	$3.60 Puysegur Point Lighthouse, Fiordland	4·50	4·50
4056/4061 Set of 6		14·50	14·50
MS4062 170×95 mm. Nos. 4056/4061		14·50	14·50

817 Anzac Day Dawn Service at Auckland War Memorial and Cenotaph

(Des Helcia Berryman, Grange Park Creative. Litho Southern Colour Print)

2019 (3 Apr). ANZAC (6th series). Dawn Service. T **817** and similar horiz designs. Multicoloured. Phosphorised paper. Perf 14×14½.

4063	$1.20 Type **817**	1·75	1·75
4064	$1.20 Ride to remember Canterbury Mounted Rifles in First World War, Kaikoura	1·75	1·75
4065	$1.20 Anzac Dawn Service, Oban, Halfmoon Bay, Stewart Island	1·75	1·75
4066	$2.40 Anzac Day at Scott Base, Antarctica	3·75	3·75
4067	$3 Dawn service at Whangarei District War Memorial	4·50	4·50
4068	$3.60 Anzac Dawn Service at Dannevirke	4·50	4·50
4063/4068 Set of 6		14·50	14·50
MS4069 160×90 mm. Nos. 4063/4068		14·50	14·50

818 Beatrice Hill Tinsley (cosmologist)

*(Des Hannah Fortune (Nos. 4070/4074) or Sam Taylor (No. **MS**4075). Litho Southern Colour Print (Nos. 4070/4074) or Cartor (No. **MS**4075))*

2019 (1 May). New Zealand Space Pioneers. T **818** and similar square designs. Multicoloured. Phosphorised paper (Nos. 4070/4074). Perf 14½ (Nos. 4070/4074) or 14 (No. **MS**4075).

4070	$1.20 Type **818**	1·75	1·75
	a. Vert strip of 5. Nos. 4070/4074	12·50	12·50
4071	$1.20 Alan Gilmore and Pamela Kilmartin (comet and nova hunters, discoverers of minor planets)	1·75	1·75
4072	$2.40 Charles Gifford (astronomer)	2·75	2·75
4073	$3 Albert Jones (visual astronomer)	3·50	3·50
4074	$3.60 Sir William Pickering (rocket scientist)	4·00	4·00
4070/4074 Set of 5		12·50	12·50
MS4075 200×100 mm. $4 Voyager 1 spacecraft; $4 Space Shuttle; $4 First moonwalk, 20 July 1969; $4 Apollo Lunar Module (all 30×40 mm)		18·00	20·00

Nos. 4070/4074 each have a circle of ground meteor dust applied to overgloss surrounding the portraits.

No. 4070a could be purchased from the Philatelic Bureau. The centre of the strip of five forms a composite background design of a rocket.

No. **MS**4075 is a lenticular miniature sheet with a 3D effect.

NEW ZEALAND

(Litho Southern Colour Print)

2019 (5 June). New Zealand Landscapes (9th series). Horiz designs as T **757**. Multicoloured.

(a) Ordinary gum. Phosphorised paper. Perf 13½.

4076	$2.60 Escarpment Walkway, Paekākāriki..........	2·75	2·75
4077	$3.90 Akaroa Harbour, Canterbury	4·00	4·25
4078	$4.50 Shotover River Valley, Otago	4·75	5·00
4076/4078	Set of 3	10·50	11·00

No. 4077 is incorrectly inscribed 'Banks Peninsula, Canterbury'.

(b) Self-adhesive. Phosphor frame. Die-cut perf 10×9½.

4079	$2.60 As No. 4076	2·75	2·75
	a. Booklet pane. No. 4079×5	11·00	
	b. Horiz pair. Nos. 4079/4080	6·25	6·25
4080	$3.30 Dunedin Railway Station	3·50	3·50
	a. Booklet pane. No. 4080×5	14·00	

The design of No. 4080 is as No. 3777.
No. 4079 was issued in $13 booklet No. SB195.
No. 4080 was issued in $16.50 booklet No. SB196.

819 The Journey Begins

(Des Dave Burke. Litho Southern Colour Print)

2019 (5 June). Kupe the Great Navigator. T **819** and similar horiz designs. Multicoloured. Phosphorised paper. Perf 14.

4081	$1.30 Type **819**...	1·75	1·75
	a. Block of 8. Nos. 4081/4088	12·00	12·00
4082	$1.30 Kupe the Great Navigator (standing waist deep in sea, arm outstretched towards New Zealand).................................	1·75	1·75
4083	$1.30 Star Compass (Navigating canoe at night by moon and stars)	1·75	1·75
4084	$1.30 First Sight of New Zealand (Kupe's wife Hine-te-Aparangi sees colour distortion on the horizon)	1·75	1·75
4085	$1.30 The Arrival at New Zealand......................	1·75	1·75
4086	$1.30 The Battle with the Giant Octopus........	1·75	1·75
4087	$1.30 Kupe's daughters and Pariwhero (Red Rocks)..	1·75	1·75
4088	$1.30 Kupe's adze and the Return Home.........	1·75	1·75
4081/4088	Set of 8..	12·00	12·00
MS4089	205×115 mm. Nos. 4081/4088..........................	12·00	12·00

Nos. 4081/4088 were printed together, *se-tenant*, as blocks of eight stamps in sheets of 24 (4×6).

(Litho Southern Colour Print)

2019 (11 June). China 2019 World Stamp Exhibition, Wuhan. Phosphorised paper. Perf 13½.

MS4090	120×90 mm. As Nos. 4049 and 4051/4052.........	5·00	6·00

Sheets sold at the exhibition were numbered in the bottom right corner. Only 300 such sheets were sold on each day of the show.

820 *IAM* (oil on jute canvas), 1954

(Des Alan Hollows. Litho Southern Colour Print)

2019 (3 July). Birth Centenary of Colin McCahon (1919–1987, artist). T **820** and similar multicoloured designs. Phosphorised paper. Perf 14.

4091	$1.30 Type **820**...	1·50	1·50
4092	$1.30 *Titirangi Landscape* (oil on canvas, 1954)	1·50	1·50
4093	$2.60 *The Angel of the Annunciation* (oil on cardboard, 1947) (vert)	2·75	3·00
4094	$3.30 *Red on Black Landscape* (enamel on sand on hardboard, 1959) (vert).............	3·50	3·75
4095	$4 *The First Waterfall* (oil on jute on board, 1964) (vert)	4·25	4·25
4091/4095	Set of 5	12·00	13·00
MS4096	145×95 mm. Nos. 4091/4095..............................	12·00	14·00

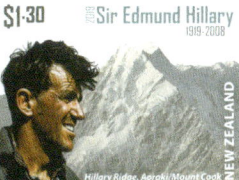

821 Edmund Hillary and Hillary Ridge on Aoraki/Mount Cook

822 Kaiaraara, Northland

(Des Helcia Berryman. Litho Southern Colour Print)

2019 (23 July). Birth Centenary of Sir Edmund Hillary (1919–2008, mountaineer and explorer). T **821** and similar horiz designs. Multicoloured. Phosphorised paper. Perf 14.

4097	$1.30 Type **821**...	1·75	1·75
	a. Horiz strip of 5. Nos. 4097/4101	8·00	8·00
4098	$1.30 Sir Edmund Hillary and Mount Everest....	1·75	1·75
4099	$1.30 Sir Edmund Hillary and Hillary, Derek Wright and Murray Ellis arriving at the South Pole in tractors, 20 January 1958 (South Pole Expedition).................................	1·75	1·75
4100	$1.30 Sir Edmund Hillary and children outside Khumjung School, 1961 (Himalayan Trust)	1·75	1·75
4101	$1.30 Sir Edmund Hillary and Ocean to Sky jet boat expedition from mouth to source of Ganges, India, 1977.................................	1·75	1·75
4097/4101	Set of 5	8·00	8·00

Nos. 4097/4101 were printed together, *se-tenant*, as horizontal strips of five in sheets of 25 (5×5).

A special printing of 2019 numbered sheets of 25 were also produced, each stamp having a silver fern additionally printed in the lower right corner. On normal sheets the fern is printed in varnish ink.

(Des Eighty One Group. Litho Southern Colour Print)

2019 (7 Aug). Rock Legends New Zealand Tour. T **822** and similar square designs. Multicoloured. Phosphorised paper. Perf 14.

MS4102	180×235 mm. $1.30×9 Type **822**; Lion Rock, Auckland; Elephant Rock, Taranaki; Te Hoho Rock, Coromandel; Castlepoint Reef, Wairarapa; Motukiekie, west coast; Tunnel Beach, Otago; Punakaiki, west coast; Anapai Bay, Tasman...............	13·00	14·00

823 Ninety Mile Beach, Northland

(Des Hannah Fortune. Litho Southern Colour Print)

2019 (4 Sept). Te Araroa Trail. T **823** and similar horiz designs. Multicoloured. Phosphorised paper. Perf 14½×14.

4103	$1.30 Type **823**...	1·50	1·50
4104	$1.30 Karamu Walkway, Waikato.......................	1·50	1·50
4105	$1.30 Tongariro Alpine Crossing.........................	1·50	1·50
4106	$2.60 Nelson Lakes, Tasman	2·50	2·50
4107	$3.30 Stag Saddle, Canterbury	3·25	3·25
4108	$4 Lake Hāwea, Otago	4·00	4·50
4103/4108	Set of 6	13·00	13·50
MS4109	161×90 mm. Nos. 4103/4108..............................	13·00	15·00

824 Silver Fern (All Blacks emblem), 1905

NEW ZEALAND

(Des Dave Burke. Litho Southern Colour Print)

2019 (20 Sept). All Blacks (National Rugby Team). T **824** and similar horiz designs. Multicoloured. Perf 13½.
MS4110 160×85 mm. $2.60×6 Type **824**; Silver fern, 1921; Silver fern, 1924; Silver fern, 1967; Silver fern, 1986; Silver fern, 2003 .... 22·00 24·00

(Des Michel Tuffery (illustrations) and Saint Andrew Matautia. Litho Southern Colour Print)

2019 (2 Oct). Tuia 250. Michel Tuffery's Artistic Journey of Discovery. T **825** and similar vert designs. Multicoloured. Phosphorised paper. Perf 14.
4111	$1.30 Type **825**..	1·75	1·40
4112	$1.30 Nicholas Young and Taiato arrive in New Zealand, October 1769	1·75	1·40
4113	$2.60 Daniel Solander and Te Maro, Turanganui River, 1769	3·75	4·25
4114	$3.30 Natural history artist Sydney Parkinson at Opoutama, 1769	4·50	5·00
4115	$4 Captain Cook	5·50	6·00
4111/4115 Set of 5...		16·00	16·00
MS4116 115×106 mm. Nos. 4111/4115............................		17·00	19·00

826 Madonna and Child

(Des Donna McKenna Studio. Litho Southern Colour Print, New Zealand)

2019 (6 Nov). Christmas. T **826** and similar multicoloured designs.
(a) Ordinary gum. Perf 14.
4117	$1.30 Type **826**..	1·75	1·40
	a. Horiz pair. Nos. 4117/4118	3·50	2·75
4118	$1.30 Joseph..	1·75	1·40
4119	$2.60 Shepherd playing flute	3·75	4·25
4120	$3.30 Three Wise Men carrying gifts of gold, frankincense and myrrh	4·50	5·00
4121	$4 Angel	5·50	6·00
4117/4121 Set of 5...		16·00	16·00
MS4122 140×90 mm. Nos. 4117/4121............................		17·00	19·00

(b) Self-adhesive. Size 22×28 mm. Phosphor frame. Die-cut perf 9½×10.
(i) Domestic mail.
4123	$1.30 As Type **826**................................	1·75	1·40
	a. Booklet pane. No. 4123/4124, each×5..	13·50	
	b. Horiz strip of 4. Nos. 4123/4126	10·50	
4124	$1.30 As No. 4118	1·75	1·40

(ii) International Post.
4125	$2.60 As No. 4119	3·75	4·25
	a. Booklet pane. No. 4125×10.................	30·00	
4126	$3.30 As No. 4120	4·50	5·00
	a. Booklet pane. No. 4126×10.................	35·00	

Nos. 4117/4118 were printed together, *se-tenant*, as horizontal and vertical pairs in sheets of 25.

No. 4123/4124 were issued in $13 booklet No. SB197, and also in coils of 100 with the two designs alternating through the roll.

Pairs of Nos. 4123/4124 from the roll of 100 were vertical.

No. 4123b was a horizontal strip of four containing Nos. 4123/4126 available from the Philatelic Bureau.

No. 4125 was issued in booklet No. SB198, sold at $23.40, providing a $2.60 discount off the face value of the stamps.

No. 4126 was issued in booklet No. SB199, sold at $29.70, providing a $3.30 discount off the face value of the stamps.

A sheetlet of six Royal Visit stamps ($1.30, $2.60 and $3.30, each×2) perforated 14½ depicting Prince Charles and Camilla, Duchess of Cornwall was issued on 22 November 2019, and sold for $19.90, a $5.50 premium over face value.

827 Calligraphy   828 *Notoreas blax*

(Des Asiaworks, Auckland. Litho Australia Post)

2019 (4 Dec). Chinese New Year. Year of the Rat. T **827** and similar vert designs. Multicoloured. Phosphorised paper. Perf 13.
4127	$1.30 Type **827**..	1·75	1·40
4128	$2.60 Paper-cut rat...................................	3·75	4·25
4129	$3.30 Rat on New Zealand coast and sailing ship	4·50	5·00
4130	$4 Sky Tower, Auckland	5·50	6·00
4127/4130 Set of 4...		14·00	15·00
MS4131 150×90 mm. Nos. 4127/4130............................		16·00	18·00

A circular sheet containing 12 circular $1.30 stamps, one for each animal on the Chinese Lunar Calendar was also produced, but had limited distribution.

BEST OF 2019. A further set of miniature sheets as described below No. 2042 were distributed by the Philatelic Bureau to customers purchasing a certain amount of philatelic material during 2019. The sheets comprised:
1. Nos. 4047, 4054 and 4061. 2. Nos. 4068, 4095 and 4098. 3. Nos. 4108, 4115 and 4121.

Se-tenant sheetlets of Nos. 4091/4095 were also distributed.

(Des Stephen Fuller. Litho Southern Colour Print, New Zealand)

2020 (5 Feb). Native Daphne Moths. T **828** and similar vert designs. Multicoloured. Perf 14.
4132	$1.30 Type **828**..	1·75	1·40
4133	$1.30 *Notoreas casanova*	1·75	1·40
4134	$1.30 *Notoreas edwardsi*	1·75	1·40
4135	$2.60 *Notoreas mechanitis*	3·75	4·25
4136	$3.30 *Notoreas*, Wellington Coast (new species)..	4·50	5·00
4137	$4 *Notoreas*, Kaitorete Spit (new species)..	5·50	6·00
4132/4137 Set of 6...		17·00	18·00
MS4138 140×90 mm. Nos. 4132/4137............................		18·00	20·00

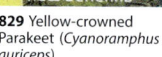

829 Yellow-crowned Parakeet (*Cyanoramphus auriceps*)   830 Exhibition Emblem and Auckland Harbour Bridge within Lifebelt

(Des Tim Garman. Litho Southern Colour Print)

2020 (4 Mar). Kakariki (New Zealand Parakeets). T **829** and similar square designs. Multicoloured. Perf 14.
4139	$1.30 Type **829**..	1·75	1·40
4140	$1.30 Orange-fronted Parakeet (*Cyanoramphus malherbi*)	1·75	1·40
4141	$2.60 Red-crowned Parakeet (*Cyanoramphus novaezelandiae*)	3·75	4·25
4142	$3.30 Forbes' Parakeet (*Cyanoramphus forbesi*)	4·50	5·00
4143	$4 Antipodes Island Parakeet (*Cyanoramphus unicolor*)	5·50	6·00
4139/4143 Set of 5...		16·00	16·00
MS4144 150×85 mm. Nos. 4139/4143............................		18·00	20·00

(Des Alan Hollows. Litho Southern Colour Print)

2020 (19 Mar). NZ 2020 FIAP International Stamp Exhibition, Auckland. Phosphorised paper. Perf 14 (Nos. **MS**4145, **MS**4147), 14½×14 (No. **MS**4146) or 13×13½ (No. **MS**4148).

MS4145 160×90 mm. $1.30 Type **830**; $1.30 Emblem and image of yachts passing under Auckland Harbour Bridge within lifebelt; $2.60 Emblem and image of city of Auckland and Sky Tower within lifebelt... 7·25 7·75
MS4146 160×90 mm. Nos. 4056/4058 (Lighthouse Perspectives).. 3·25 3·75
MS4147 130×80 mm. Nos. 4081/4083 and 4085 (Kupe the Navigator)... 5·50 6·00
MS4148 130×90 mm. Nos. 4127/4129 (Year of the Rat)... 16·00 18·00

The NZ 2020 FIAP International Stamp Exhibition became a National Exhibition and closed early on Saturday 21 March at 1pm due to Coronavirus, but the exhibition miniature sheets were available at the show and from New Zealand Post.

NEW ZEALAND

831 Returning Soldier and Children, Wellington ('Mobilising the nation')

(Des Nicky Dyer. Litho Southern Colour Print)

2020 (1 Apr). 75th Anniversary of the End of World War II. T **831** and similar horiz designs. Multicoloured. Phosphorised paper. Perf 14½×14.

MS4149 180×250 mm. $1.30×15 Type **831**; Crowd watching HMS *Achilles* return to Auckland, 1940; New Zealand fighter pilots and Supermarine Spitfire, England, 15 July 1942; Assisting injured soldier off ship, Alexandria, Egypt, 1941 ('Retreat from Crete'); Kiwi Cribb, David McClutchie, Whiwhi Winiata, Repoma Thompson and Dick Huata of 28th (Maori) Battalion driving through Sora, Italy, 3 June 1944; Women's War Service auxiliaries; Men of the New Zealand Railway Construction Company laying track, North African desert, *circa* October 1941; Members of the 3rd Division at Vella Lavella, Solomon Islands, *circa* 1944 ('At rest in the Pacific'); American servicemen with New Zealand women, Oriental Bay, Wellington, *circa* 1942; Merchant seamen on Union Steam Ship Company's *Kaiwarra*, Auckland, December 1940; Members of 75 (NZ) Squadron passing a Wellington Mk I bomber, RAF Feltwell, England, ('Bomber Command'); Pupils and teachers of Devonport School entering air raid shelters during drill, Auckland, April 1942; Home Guard members training in Waikato; Gordon Reid of 4th Armoured Brigade operating communications equipment in the ruins of Monte Cassino, 18 May 1944; Peace celebrations, Wellington, 15 August 1945.................. 27·00 29·00

Stamps as within No. **MS**4149 were also issued in $39.90 premium booklet No. SP18.

An imperforate version of No. **MS**4149 was included in the 2020 New Zealand Collection yearbook.

832 Theodore Bear

(Des Cam Price. Litho New Zealand Post)

2020 (20 May). New Zealand Bear Hunt. T **832** and similar square designs. Multicoloured. Phosphorised paper. Perf 14½.

MS4150 260×170 mm. $1.30 Type **832**; $1.30 Hay Hay Teddy (made from hay bales); $1.30 Lubert (wearing jersey); $2.60 Little Ted (looking out of letter box); $2.60 Childhood Bear (wearing scarf and Poppy); $2.60 Frontliner Bear (with face mask).. 16·00 18·00

No. **MS**4150 was sold for $14.70 which included a $3 donation to the New Zealand Red Cross.

(Litho Southern Colour Print)

2020 (3 June). New Zealand Landscapes (10th series). Horiz designs as T **757**. Multicoloured. Phosphorised paper. Perf 13×13½.
4151	$4 Island Bay, Wellington...................	5·50	6·00
4152	$10 Aoraki Mount Cook.......................	13·50	14·00

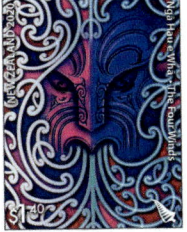 

833 Te Hau Raki (northerly)   **834** Anzac Biscuits

(Des Dave Burke. Litho Southern Colour Print)

2020 (3 June). Matariki. Ngā Hau e Whā (The Four Winds). Tāwhirimātea (Father of the Four Winds). T **833** and similar vert designs. Multicoloured. Perf 14.
4153	$1.40 Type **833**.................................	2·00	1·50
4154	$2.70 Te Hau Rāwhiti (easterly).............	3·75	4·25
4155	$3.30 Te Hau-ā-uru (westerly)..............	4·50	5·00
4156	$4 Te Hau Tonga (southerly)................	5·50	6·00
4153/4156 Set of 4..		14·00	15·00
MS4157 180×90 mm. Nos. 4153/4156................		16·00	17·00

(Des Graeme Mowday. Litho Southern Colour Print)

2020 (1 July). Cakes and Bakes. T **834** and similar square designs. Multicoloured. Phosphorised paper. Perf 14.

MS4158 235×180 mm. $1.40×15 Type **834**; Pavlova; Churchill Slice; Cheese Rolls; Lolly Cake; Neenish Tarts; Lamingtons; Cheese Scones; Custard Square; Chocolate Crackles; Ginger Biscuits; Melting Moments; Louise Cake; Afghans; Banana Cake......... 28·00 29·00

(Des Nicky Dyer. Litho Southern Colour Print)

2020 (5 Aug). New Zealand Landscapes (11th series). Horiz designs as T **757**. Multicoloured.

(a) Ordinary gum. Perf 13×13½.
4159	$3.50 Fitzroy Bay, Marlborough Sounds...........	4·75	5·25
4160	$4.20 Whanganui River................................	5·75	6·25
4161	$4.70 Mount Ngauruhoe...............................	6·50	7·00
4159/4161 Set of 3..		15·00	17·00

(b) Self-adhesive. Die-cut perf 10×9½.
4162	$3.50 As No. 4159.....................................	4·75	5·25
	a. Booklet pane. No. 4162×5	19·00	

No. 4162 was issued in $17.50 booklet No. SB200.

835 General Hospital, Crete, 20 May 1941   **836** 'AROHA' (love, affection, respect, compassion, empathy)

(Des Nicky Dyer. Litho Southern Colour Print)

2020 (5 Aug). Peter McIntyre's World War II. T **835** and similar square designs. Multicoloured. Phosphorised paper. Perf 14½.
4163	$1.40 Type **835**.................................	2·00	1·50
4164	$2.70 Building the railway to Tobruk, 1941	3·75	4·25
4165	$3.50 The Grants (tanks) go into action, El Alamein, *circa* November 1942................	4·75	5·25
4166	$4 Medical Officer attending wounded Germans after final surrender in Tunisia, 1 May 1943.....................................	5·50	6·00
4163/4166 Set of 4..		14·50	15·00
MS4167 120×95 mm. Nos. 4163/4166................		16·00	17·00

(Des Dave Burke. Litho Southern Colour Print, New Zealand)

2020 (2 Sept). Te Wiki o Te Reo (Maori Language Week). T **836** and similar horiz designs. Multicoloured. Phosphorised paper. Perf 14.
4168	$1.40 Type **836**.................................	2·00	1·50
4169	$2.70 'WHĀNAU' (family).........................	3·75	4·25
4170	$3.50 'TĀNE' (man)................................	4·75	5·25
4171	$4 'WAHINE' (woman)............................	5·50	6·00
4168/4171 Set of 4..		14·50	15·00
MS4172 180×90 mm. Nos. 4168/4171................		16·00	17·00

NEW ZEALAND

837 Track

838 Angel Gabriel (The Annunciation)

(Des Hannah Fortune. Litho Southern Colour Print)

2020 (7 Oct). Olympic Games, Tokyo. Centenary of the New Zealand Olympic Team. T **837** and similar multicoloured designs. Phosphorised paper. Perf 14½×14 (Nos. 4173/4174, 4177/4178, **MS**4179) or 14×14½ (Nos. 4175/4176).

4173	$1.40 Type **837**	2·00	1·50
4174	$1.40 Surfing	2·00	1·50
4175	$1.40 Pole vault (*horiz*)	2·00	1·50
4176	$2.70 Hockey (*horiz*)	3·75	4·25
4177	$3.50 Rugby sevens	4·75	5·25
4178	$4 Shot put	5·50	6·00
4173/4178 Set of 6		18·00	18·00
MS4179 182×57 mm. As Nos. 4173/4178		20·00	21·00

(Des Jon Ward. Litho Southern Colour Print)

2020 (4 Nov). Christmas. T **838** and similar square designs. Multicoloured.
(*a*) *Ordinary gum. Perf 14.*

4180	$1.40 Type **838**	2·00	1·50
4181	$2.70 Mary and Jesus (The Birth of Jesus Christ)	3·75	4·25
4182	$3.50 The Star of Bethlehem	4·75	5·25
4183	$4 The Wise Men's Gifts	5·50	6·00
4180/4183 Set of 4		14·50	15·00
MS4184 161×90 mm. Nos. 4180/4183		16·00	17·00

(*b*) *Self-adhesive. size 25×30 mm.*
(i) *Domestic mail. Die-cut perf 9½×10.*

4185	$1.40 As Type **838**	2·00	1·50
	a. Booklet pane. No. 4185×10	16·00	
	b. Horiz strip of 3. Nos. 4185/4187	9·50	10·00

(ii) *International Post.*

4186	$2.70 As No. 4181	3·75	4·25
	a. As No. 4181	30·00	
4187	$3.50 As No. 4182	4·75	5·25
	a. Booklet pane. No. 4187×10	38·00	

Nos. 4180/4187 have an Augmented Reality Christmas experience, accessed by downloading the Magenta app to a phone or tablet, and holding the device over the stamp or booklet, each stamp telling a part of the Nativity story.

The bottom right corner of No. **MS**4184 was cut in a semi circular shape.

No. 4185 was issued in $14 booklet No. SB201.
No. 4186 was issued in $27 booklet No. SB202.
No. 4187 was issued in $35 booklet No. SB203.

839 Ox, Smiling Infant and Flowers (Happiness)

840 Daniel Quasar's Progress Pride Flag

(Des Ying-Min Chu, YMC Design. Litho Southern Colour Print)

2020 (2 Dec). Chinese New Year. Year of the Ox. T **839** and similar vert designs. Multicoloured. Phosphorised paper. Perf 13×13½.

4188	$1.40 Type **839**	2·00	1·50
4189	$2.70 Ox and two infants in New Year procession (Fortune)	3·75	4·25
4190	$3.50 Toddler raising ox kite	4·75	5·25
4191	$4 Ox and infant sharing apples (Peace)	5·50	6·00
4188/4191 Set of 4		14·50	15·00
MS4192 135×90 mm. Nos. 4188/4191		16·00	17·00

BEST OF 2020. A further set of miniature sheets as described below No. 2042 were distributed by the Philatelic Bureau to customers purchasing a certain amount of philatelic material during 2020. The sheets comprised: 1. Nos. 4130, 4137 and 4143. 2. the 'Peace Celebration' stamp from No. **MS**4149 and Nos. 4156 and 4166. 3. Nos. 4171, 4178 and 4183.

(Des Cam Price. Litho Southern Colour Print Ltd)

2021 (3 Feb). Pride. Phosphorised paper. Perf 14.

4193	840	$1.40 multicoloured	2·00	1·50

841 M for Mount Taranaki

842 Te Rehutai, 2020

(Des YMC Design. Litho Southern Colour Print Ltd)

2021 (3 Feb). Holiday at Home. I spy with my little eye something beginning with. T **841** and similar vert designs. Multicoloured. Phosphorised paper. Perf 14.

MS4194 155×200 mm. $1.40×9 Type **841**; K for Kiwi, Stewart Island; S for Stargazing, Tekapo; D for Dolphins, Akaroa; T for Treaty Grounds, Waitangi; L for Lighthouse, Wairarapa; G for Gardens, Hamilton; C for Canoeing, Whanganui; B for Boats, Marlborough Sounds........ 17·00 18·00

(Des John Morris. Litho Southern Colour Print Ltd)

2021 (2 Mar). 150th Anniversary of Royal New Zealand Yacht Squadron (RNZYS). T **842** and similar vert designs. Multicoloured. Phosphorised paper. Perf 14×14½.

4195	$1.40 Type **842**	2·00	1·50
4196	$2.70 *Steinlager II*, 1989	3·75	4·25
4197	$3.50 *Rainbow II*, 1969	4·75	5·25
4198	$4 *Rainbow I*, 1898	5·50	6·00
4195/4198 Set of 4		14·50	15·00
MS4199 150×90 mm. Nos. 4195/4198		16·00	17·00

843 Princess Elizabeth

844 *Clematis paniculata* (Puawananga)

(Des Nicky Dyer. Litho Southern Colour Print)

2021 (7 Apr). 95th Birthday of Queen Elizabeth II. T **843** and similar vert designs. Multicoloured. Phosphorised paper. Perf 14.

4200	$1.40 Type **843**	2·00	1·50
4201	$2.70 Queen Elizabeth II during Coronation Tour of New Zealand, 1953–1954	3·75	4·25
4202	$3.50 Queen Elizabeth II, 1970s	4·75	5·25
4203	$4 Queen Elizabeth II in recent years	5·50	6·00
4200/4203 Set of 4		14·50	15·00
MS4204 120×95 mm. Nos. 4200/4203		16·00	17·00

(Des Hannah Fortune. Litho Southern Colour Print, New Zealand)

2021 (5 May). Sarah Featon. Botanical Artist. T **844** and similar vert designs. Multicoloured. Phosphorised paper. Perf 13×13½.

4205	$1.40 Type **844**	2·00	1·50
4206	$2.70 *Corynocarpus laevigatus* (Karaka)	3·75	4·25
4207	$3.50 *Clianthus puniceus* (Kōwhai-ngutu-kaka)	4·75	5·25
4208	$4 *Pleurophyllum speciosum* (Campbell Island Daisy)	5·50	6·00
4205/4208 Set of 4		14·50	15·00
MS4209 80×95 mm. Nos. 4205/4208		16·00	17·00

NEW ZEALAND

(Litho Southern Colour Print)

2021 (2 June). New Zealand Landscapes. Horiz designs as T **757**. Multicoloured.

(a) Self-adhesive. Phosphor frames. Die-cut perf 10×9½.

4210	$2.80 Auckland	3·75	3·75
	a. Booklet pane. No. 4210×5	15·00	
	b. Horiz pair. Nos. 4210/4211	8·00	
4211	$3.60 Waikato River	5·00	5·00
	a. Booklet pane. No. 4211×5	20·00	

(b) Ordinary gum. Phosphorised paper. Perf 13×13½.

4212	$4.10 Castle Hill, Canterbury	5·50	5·50

No. 4210 was issued in $14 booklet No. SB204.
No. 4211 was issued in $18 booklet No. SB205.

848 Prince Philip, Duke of Edinburgh

(Des Helcia Berryman, Mopsy Creative. Litho Southern Colour Print)

2021 (4 Aug). Prince Philip, Duke of Edinburgh (1921–2021) Commemoration. Phosphorised paper. Perf 14.

MS4228	150×75 mm. **848** $3.60 multicoloured	4·75	5·00

845 Marama (the Moon) drawing Rona to Her

846 Kayaking, Milford Sound

(Des Dave Burke. Litho Southern Colour Print)

2021 (2 June). Matariki. Whānau Mārama the Family of Light (the sun, moon and Pleiades star cluster). T **845** and similar horiz designs. Multicoloured. Phosphorised paper. Perf 14.

4213	$1.50 Type **845**	2·00	1·50
4214	$2.80 Marama (the moon) the Eye of the Night	3·75	4·25
4215	$3.60 Tamanuiterā fast to rise, fast to set	4·75	5·25
4216	$4.10 Tamanuiterā: Summer path, winter path	5·50	6·00
4213/4216	Set of 4	14·50	15·00
MS4217	180×90 mm. Nos. 4213/4216	16·00	17·00

Nos. 4213/4216 were perforated 14.0×14.2 and No. **MS**4217 13.8×14.2.

(Des Alan Hollows. Litho Southern Colour Print)

2021 (7 July). Kiwi Stamps. T **846** and similar horiz designs. Multicoloured. Self-adhesive. Phosphorised paper. Die-cut perf 10×9½.

4218	($1.50) Type **846**	2·00	1·50
	a. Horiz strip of 5. Nos. 4218/4222	9·00	10·00
4219	($1.50) Cycling, Tasman region	2·00	1·50
4220	($1.50) Skiing	2·00	1·50
4221	($1.50) Bushwalking, Te Urewera National Park	2·00	1·50
4222	($1.50) Motorhome (Road Trip)	2·00	1·50
4218/4222	Set of 5	9·00	10·00

Nos. 4218/4222 were originally valid for $1.50 each. They were issued in coils of 100 containing the five designs in sequence, and also in booklets of ten sold for $15, not yet received by us.

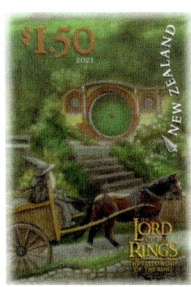

849 Gandalf arrives at Bag End, Hobbiton (The Journey Begins)

(Des Sacha Lees. Litho Southern Colour Print)

2021 (1 Sept). 20th Anniversary of *The Lord of the Rings. The Fellowship of the Ring* (film). T **849** and similar vert designs. Multicoloured. Phosphorised paper. Perf 14×14½.

4229	$1.50 Type **849**	2·00	1·50
4230	$1.50 Frodo and his friends hiding from the Black Rider	2·00	1·50
4231	$1.50 Frodo and his friends in the Prancing Pony inn at Bree, Aragorn in background	2·00	1·50
4232	$2.80 Arwen fleeing from Black Riders with wounded Frodo (Flight to the Ford)	3·75	4·25
4233	$3.60 The fire-breathing Balrog in the Mines of Moria (The Bridge of Khazad-dum)	4·75	5·25
4234	$4.10 The Fellowship in three boats on the river Anduin reach giant stone statues at the Gates of Argonath	5·50	6·00
4229/4234	Set of 6	18·00	18·00
MS4235	112×66 mm. As No. 4229	2·25	2·50
MS4236	112×66 mm. As No. 4230	2·25	2·50
MS4237	112×66 mm. As No. 4231	2·25	2·50
MS4238	112×66 mm. As No. 4232	4·00	4·50
MS4239	112×66 mm. As No. 4233	5·00	5·50
MS4240	112×66 mm. As No. 4234	5·75	6·25

(Des Sacha Lees. Litho Southern Colour Print)

2021 (10 Sept). Royalpex 2021 National Stamp Exhibition, Palmerston North. Sheet containing Nos. 4233/4234. Multicoloured. Phosphorised paper. Perf 14×14½.

MS4241	150×90 mm. $3.60 The fire-breathing Balrog in the Mines of Moria (The Bridge of Khazad-dum); $4.10 The Fellowship in three boats on the river Anduin reach giant stone statues at the Gates of Argonath	5·00	5·00

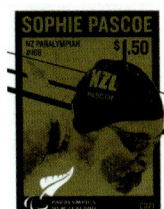

847 Sophie Pascoe (swimmer)

(Des John Morris. Litho Southern Colour Print)

2021 (4 Aug). Paralympic Games, Tokyo. T **847** and similar vert designs. Multicoloured. Phosphorised paper. Perf 14.

4223	$1.50 Type **847**	2·00	1·50
4224	$2.80 Cameron Leslie (wheelchair rugby and swimmer)	3·75	4·25
4225	$3.60 Emma Foy and Hannah van Kampen (cycling)	4·75	5·25
4226	$4.10 'SPIRIT OF GOLD'	5·50	6·00
4223/4226	Set of 4	14·50	15·00
MS4227	150×90 mm. Nos. 4223/4226	15·00	16·00

850 Diwali Lamp   851 Angel

NEW ZEALAND

(Des John Morris. Litho Southern Colour Print)

2021 (7 Oct). Shubh Diwali. T **850** and similar diamond-shaped designs. Multicoloured. Phosphorised paper. Perf 14.

4242	$1.50 Type **850**	2·00	1·50
4243	$2.80 Sparkler	3·75	4·25
4244	$3.60 Diwali sweets	4·75	5·25
4245	$4.10 Diwali lamps in lotus pattern	5·50	6·00
4242/4245 Set of 4		14·50	15·00
MS4246 175×107 mm. Nos. 4242/4245		16·00	17·00

Nos. 4242/4245 were printed in individual value sheets. However Philatelic Bureau customers were provided with *se-tenant* blocks of four taken from the first printing of No. **MS**4246 which was replaced due to a fault in the margin design (*Price £15 mint or used*).

854 Poppy of 1922, made in France

855 '7' in Form of Harp

(Des Cam Price. Litho)

2021 (3 Nov). Christmas. T **851** and similar vert designs. Multicoloured.

(a) Ordinary gum. Phosphorised paper. Perf 14.

4247	$1.50 Type **851**	2·00	1·50
4248	$2.80 Baby Jesus in manger	3·75	4·25
4249	$3.60 Shepherd	4·75	5·25
4250	$4.10 Wise Man	5·50	6·00
4247/4250 Set of 4		14·50	15·00
MS4251 150×90 mm. Nos. 4247/4250		16·00	17·00

(b) Self-adhesive. Size 25×30 mm. Phosphor frames. Die-cut perf 9½×10.
(i) Domestic mail.

4252	$1.50 As Type **851**	2·00	1·50
	a. Booklet pane. No. 4252×10	16·00	
	b. Horiz strip of 3. Nos. 4252/4254	10·00	10·50

(ii) International Post.

4253	$2.80 As No. 4248	3·75	4·25
	a. Booklet pane. No. 4253×10	30·00	
4254	$3.60 As No. 4249	4·75	5·25
	a. Booklet pane. No. 4254×10	38·00	

(Des Nicky Dyer. Litho Southern Colour Print)

2022 (2 Mar). Centenary of the Poppy Appeal. T **854** and similar vert designs. Multicoloured. Perf 13½.

4265	$1.50 Type **854**	2·00	1·50
	a. Horiz strip of 5. Nos. 4265/4269	20·00	
4266	$2.80 RSA poppy of 1960s or 1970s	3·75	4·25
4267	$3.60 Modern poppy, 1978 onwards	4·75	5·25
4268	$4.10 Australian poppy from emergency shipment of 2015	5·50	6·00
4269	$4.90 Home-made poppy from COVID-19 lockdown of April 2020	6·50	7·00
4265/4259 Set of 5		20·00	21·00
MS4270 170×90 mm. Nos. 4265/4269		22·00	24·00

Nos. 4265/4269 were printed in separate sheets of 25 (5×5).
No. 4265a could be purchased from the Philatelic Bureau.

(Des Hannah Fortune. Litho Southern Colour Print)

2022 (2 Mar). 75th Anniversary of NZSO (New Zealand Symphony Orchestra). T **855** and similar vert design. Multicoloured. Perf 13½.

MS4271 131×82 mm. $1.50 Type **855**; $4.10 '75' containing horn		7·50	8·00

852 Infant and Tiger (Balance)

853 Early Trading between Maori and Pakeha at Tata Beach, 1843

856 Arabic Calligraphy over Mosque Silhouette

857 Tawhirinuku, Tawhirirangi, Tawhirimatea e (Tawhirimatea gave his eyes to his father Ranginui)

(Des YMC Design. Litho Southern Colour Print)

2021 (1 Dec). Chinese New Year. Year of the Tiger. T **852** and similar vert designs. Multicoloured. Phosphorised paper. Perf 14.

4255	$1.50 Type **852**	2·00	1·50
4256	$2.80 Infant carrying lantern, tiger and lanterns (The Lantern)	3·75	4·25
4257	$3.60 Infant on tiger's back, gold ingots and bamboo (Fortune)	4·75	5·25
4258	$4.10 Infant carrying tiger mask and firecrackers (Protection)	5·50	6·00
4255/4258 Set of 4		14·50	15·00
MS4259 135×90 mm. Nos. 4255/4258		16·00	17·00

(Des Muhammad and Sameera Waqas (calligraphy) and Chris Jones, Graphetti. Litho Southern Colour Print, New Zealand)

2022 (6 Apr). Eid Mubarak. Multicoloured. Perf 14.

4272	**856**	$1.50 multicoloured	2·00	1·50
4273	**856**	$2.80 multicoloured	3·75	4·25
4274	**856**	$3.60 multicoloured	4·75	5·25
4275	**856**	$6.50 multicoloured	8·75	9·25
4272/4275 Set of 4			14·50	15·00
MS4276 150×90 mm. Nos. 4272/4275			19·00	20·00

(Des Chris Jones, Graphetti. Paintings by Sean Garwood. Litho Southern Colour Print)

2022 (3 Feb). Historic Ships of the 19th Century. T **853** and similar horiz designs. Multicoloured. Phosphorised paper. Perf 14.

4260	$1.50 Type **853**	2·00	1·50
4261	$2.80 Whaling from the *Charles W. Morgan*, Cloudy Bay, 1852	3·75	4·25
4262	$3.60 The *Mataura* on passage from England to New Zealand, 1879	4·75	5·25
4263	$4.10 The *Felicity* and the Blind Bay hookers, Nelson, 1889	5·50	6·00
4260/4263 Set of 4		14·50	15·00
MS4264 108×90 mm. Nos. 4260/4263		16·00	17·00

(Des KE Design. Litho Southern Colour Print)

2022 (4 May). Matariki. Nga Mata o te Ariki Tawhirimatea (the eyes of the god Tawhirimatea). T **857** and similar multicoloured designs. Phosphorised paper. Perf 14.

4277	$1.50 Type **857**	2·00	1·50
4278	$2.80 Nga mata o Tawhirimatea (Tawhirimatea's eyes, now on Ranginui, guide Tamarereti as he guides souls to join their ancestors)	3·75	4·25
4279	$3.60 Te Iwa o Matariki (the nine stars of Matariki shine at dawn) (horiz)	4·75	5·25
4280	$4.10 Hei kahu mo Ranginui (Ranginui's cloak of stars) (horiz)	5·50	6·00
4277/4280 Set of 4		14·50	15·00
MS4281 150×90 mm. Nos. 4277/4280		16·00	17·00

NEW ZEALAND

MACHINE LABELS

An automatic machine dispensing labels, ranging in value from 1c. to $99.99, was installed at the Queen Street Post Office, Auckland, on 3 September 1984 for a trial period. The oblong designs, framed by simulated perforations at top and bottom and vertical rules at the sides, showed the 'Southern Cross', face value and vertical column of six horizontal lines between the 'NEW ZEALAND' and 'POSTAGE' inscriptions. The trial period ended abruptly on 16 October 1984.

Similar labels, with the face value and inscriptions within a plain oblong, were introduced on 12 February 1986 and from 22 August 1988 they were printed on paper showing New Zealand flags. On 12 September 1990 the design printed on the paper was changed to show seaplanes and on 12 August 1992 to a Maori pattern. A further Maori pattern, taken from rafters, in green and grey appeared on 21 February 1996.

A commemorative label was available at 'NEW ZEALAND '90' held at Auckland between 24 August and 2 September 1990.

CUSTOMISED ADVERTISING LABELS (CALs)

The first such label was issued for the Wellington Arts Festival in February 2004, a 40c. value depicting a bright red Kiwi. Subsequent issues were usually at the standard inland postage rate, although higher values were produced. The majority were self-adhesive but several designs had ordinary gum and, although the design size was consistent at 29×21 mm, the format could be vertical or horizontal.

Early labels were printed by Kinetic Vision or Southern Colour Print, but from 2006 to 2019, when the last ones were issued, printing was by NZ Post in Wanganui.

In 2009 the first booklets were released (for Maui Gas), containing ten different 50c. values.

From early 2007 to mid-2019 NZ Post produced an annual pack containing all the labels released during the previous calendar year.

REGIONAL POSTAGE LABELS

In April 2014 New Zealand Post introduced a series of booklets aimed primarily at tourists, available from Visitor Information Centres or 'i-Sites'. The initial issue comprised $7 and $19 booklets, containing 70c. or $1.90 stamps in a selection of locally relevant designs. Subsequent issues comprised $8 and $20, $10 and $22 and $12 and $24 booklets, as postage rates increased, all containing stamps in one design only. In July 2016 the New Zealand Iconic Images labels were also made available in rolls of $2.20 stamps showing ten different designs.

SINCE
1856

Decades of philatelic experience & we're always happy to help

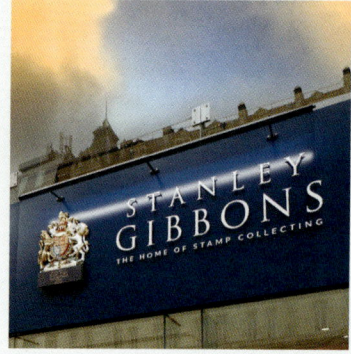

A full range of philatelic equipment, albums, pages & mounts

Over 40 specialised and country stamp catalogues available

The Home of Stamp Collecting

399 Strand
WC2R 0LX
+44 (0) 20 7557 4436
shop@stanleygibbons.com

DESIGN INDEX

The following index is intended to facilitate the identification of all New Zealand stamps from 1946 onwards. Portrait stamps are usually listed under surnames, views under the name of the town or city and other issues under the main subject or a prominent word and date chosen from the inscription. Simple abbreviations have occasionally been resorted to and when the same design or subject appears in more than one stamp, only the first of each series is indicated.

A

A dozen Bluff oysters **MS**3312
A Lion in the Meadow 2272
Abel Tasman National Park 932, 2608
Abel Tasman Scenic Reserve 3775
Achilles (ship) 1380, 3134
Adams, Valerie 3814
Adsett, Sandy 3689
Adzebill 2028
Aerial Top Dressing 794
Afghans **MS**4158
Agate 1278
Agricultural Field Days 1167
Agricultural Technology 934
Ahuriri River Cliffs 1619
Ailsa Mountains 2598, 2601
Air New Zealand 1539
Aircraft 671, 741, 1050, 1423, 1539, 2408, 3341
Airmen 885
Akaroa 1194, 1554
Akaroa Harbour 4077
Alberton 1262
Aleh, Jo 3819
Alexandra Bridge 1367
All Blacks 2623, **MS**2664, **MS**2672, **MS**2712, 3224, **MS**3311, 3368, 3562, 3723
Allosaurus 3196
Alpine Plants 983
America's Cup (yachting) 1655, 1883, 2538, 2562, **MS**2542
Amethyst 1280
Amphibians 1340
Amphilex 2002 .... **MS**2523
Amuri Mounted Rifles 2579
Anakiwa 1488
Anapai Bay **MS**4102
Anderson, Hugh 3120
Andrew, Leslie Wilton 3279
Andrew, Prince 815
Angel 1569
Angus 1312
Angus (cattle) 2047, **MS**2050
Anhanguera 3197
Animals 1820, **MS**1831
Anne, Princess 710
Antarctic Birds 1573
Antarctic Research 1327
Antarctic Treaty 955
Antipodean Albatross 3604
ANZAC 826, 3032, **MS**3100, 3131, 3202, **MS**3214, 3349, 3441, 3541, 3663, 3675, 4063, **MS**4069
Anzac Biscuits **MS**4158
ANZAC Centenary 3675
Aotearoa 1807, 1875, 1952, 2311, 3045, 3060, **MS**3091, 3143, 3215, 3220,
APEC 2278
Apiata, Bill Henry 3295
Apples 1286
Apples and Orchard 872
Aramoana (ship) 3390
Aramoana Spit 3901
Arapawa pig 2932
Arawa (ship) 1546
Architectural Heritage 2484
Armistice 4025, **MS**4030, **MS**4041
Arms of New Zealand 925, 1017
Army 1352
Arrow Squid **MS**3296
Arrowtown 2606
Art Deco 2228, 3538
Art from Nature 2402
Arts Centre, Christchurch 2486
Asaroe rubra 2479
Ashburton 1160
Asian Development Bank 1881
Asian-Oceanic Postal Union 979
Asparagus Rolls 3691
Aubert, Suzanne 2945
Auckland 953, 1221, 1363, 1486, 1520, 1557, 1792, 1855, 2040, 2062, 2217, 2228, 3153, 3211, **MS**3379, 4210
Auckland Harbour Bridge 3138
Auckland Island Pig 2933
Auckland University 1304
Auckland War Memorial Museum 2484
Aunt Daisy 1789
Aupex '97 .... **MS**2122
Australia '99 .... **MS**2245
Australia 2013 .... **MS**3455
Australian Settlement Bicentenary 1474
Authors 1501
Automobile Association 1135
Autumn 1267, 1796
Aviators 1712
Awaroa Bay, Abel Tasman Scenic Reserve 3775
'away laughing' 2968
'away with the fairies' 2970
Ayrshire (cattle) 2046

B

B is for Beehive 3061
Baby's hand 2807
Bacon and egg 3705
Badge 671
Ball Player 1042
Balloons 2417, 2804, **MS**3565, 3794
Banana Cake **MS**4158
Banded Dotterel 1460
Bangkok '93 .... **MS**1769
Bangkok 2003 .... **MS**2651
Bangkok 2007 .... **MS**2987
Barratt-Boyes, Sir Brian 1939
Baskerville, Albert 1891
Bassett, Cyril Royston Guyton 3276
Batten, Jean 1549
Baxter, James K. 1502
Bay of Islands 904, 981, 1163, 1985, **MS**3379
Baypex 2004 .... **MS**2750
BAYPEX 2014 .... **MS**3636
Beach Scene 1184
Bear **MS**4150
Beatrice, Princess 1516
Becks Bay 1396
Behrent, Genevieve 3813
Beijing 2012 .... **MS**3423
Being Active 3840
Being Sunsmart 3718
Belgica 2001 .... **MS**2424
BELGICA '06 .... **MS**2924
Bellbird 839
Benz Velo 639
Bern 1048
Berry, James 3451
Berry, Phil Mokaraka 3568
Beyond the Coast **MS**3296
Bio Gas 2889
Birds 776, 803, 806, 812, 822, 831, 839, 947, 1288, 1459*a*, 1490,1573, 1736, **MS**1745, **MS**1786, **MS**1830, **MS**1854, 2028, 2090, 2369, **MS**2393, 3178, **MS**3296, 3304, 3308, **MS**3312, **MS**3379, 3904, **MS**3909, 4002, **MS**4007
'bit of a dag' 2979
Black-billed Gull 3607
Black Robin 1293
Black Scree Button-Daisy 4051
Black Stilt 3905
Blake, Sir Peter 3181
Blenheim 2038
Blenpex 2012 .... **MS**3404
Blossom Lady (horse) 1947
Blue Duck 1289
Bluff Oysters 3694
Boeing Seaplane 1050
Bomber Pilot Europe 1943 2587
Bond, Hamish 3810
Bonecrusher (horse) 1950
'boots and all' 2974
Bottlenose Dolphin 1997, **MS**2037
Boulder Copper butterfly **MS**3222
Bowls 1045
Boy and Frog 1150
Boy and Pony 1125
Boy Scouts 720, 771
Boys' Brigade 765
Brewster Glacier 1678
Bridal Veil Falls 1123
Bridges 1366
Bristol Freighter (aircraft) 1052
Britannia (ferry) 1334
Broadcasting 1708
Broadgreen 1218
Broccoli 3925
Broken Barrier (film) 2015
Brooke, Evelyn 3663
Brown, Donald Forrester 3277
Brown Kiwi 1463, 1490, 1589, **MS**1745, **MS**1786, 2090, 2163, **MS**2342, 2375
Brown Teal 1291
Brown Trout 871, 2083, **MS**2172
Buck, Peter 1553
Budgerigar 2237
Bungy jumping 1777, 2755, 3319
Burling, Peter 3820
Burnett Range 1040
Burrell Traction Engine 2697
Butler Valley 2280
Butter making 797, 858
Butterflies 914, 957, 1008, 1143, 1635, 3220

C

C is for Cook 3062
Cabbage Tree 3336
Cable 820
Café Culture 2786
Cakes 4159
Californian Bungalow 3537
Cambridge 2182, **MS**2245
Camellias 1681
Campbell Island 3714
Camping 1413
Canberra Pilot 1960 2593
Candle and flowers 2423
Candles on cake 2421
Canpex 2000 .... **MS**2368
Canterbury 703, 999, 2060, 2093, **MS**2173, 4212
Canterbury (ship) 1382
Cape Brett **MS**3379
Cape Brett (lighthouse) 3109
Cape Campbell 3493
Cape Egmont (lighthouse) 3110
Cape Kidnappers 1934*f*, **MS**2328, **MS**2750
Cape Reinga 1927, **MS**1998, 3363, **MS**3379
Cape Reinga (lighthouse) 3111
CAPEX '96 .... **MS**2004
Cardigan Bay (horse) 913
Carmina Burana (ballet) 2572, **MS**2651
Carnelian 1281
Carols 1437, 1480
Carrington, Lisa 3816, 3818
Carrots 3922
Cars 2329, 2639, 3116
Cartoons 2118
Castle Hill 1617
Castlepoint 2610, 3489
Castlepoint Reef **MS**4102
Cats 1320, 1604, 2133, **MS**2139, 2234
Cattle 2043
Cattle and Ship loading 876
Caulerpe brownii (seaweed) 3531
Central Otago 2057, 2598, 2632
Champagne glasses 2803, 2876, 2954, **MS**3192, **MS**3237/**MS**3238, **MS**3377, **MS**3565, 3791, **MS**3995
Champagne Pool 1926, 1983*a*, **MS**1998
Champions of World Motorsport 3116
Charles, Prince 711, 1374
Chatham Island Shag 3606
Chatham Island Taiko 3608
Chatham Islands ... 946, 1505, 1585, 2631, **MS**3379, 3774
Cheese Rolls 3698
Child and Olympic Rings 887
Child Safety 2000, **MS**2004
Child sunbathing 696
Children and Pets 1054, 1079, 1125, 1149, 1741, **MS**1744, 2815
Children at Seaside 762, 1249, 2738
Children picking Apples 755
Children's Health 742, 901, 1516, 1559, 1620, 1687, 1741, **MS**1744, 1813, 1884, 2000, 2086, 2178, 2272, 2360, 2435, 2519, 2635, 2738, 2815, 3052, 3158, 3220, 3304, 3386, 3495, 3610, 3718, 3840
Children's Health 5+a Day 2892, 2989
Children's Health Camps .. 742, 901, 1741, **MS**1744, 1813, 1884
Children's Paintings 1400, 1433, 2086, 2498
Children's Sports 1884, 3052
China 2114, **MS**2123
CHINA '96 .... **MS**1998
China 99 .... **MS**2286
China 2009, Luoyang **MS**3137
China 2011 .... **MS**3329
Chinese inscription 3012, **MS**3031, **MS**3137
Chinese New Year **MS**2139, **MS**2238, 2311, 2386, 2470, 2566, **MS**2670, 2757, 2840, 2930, 3020, 3112, 3187, 3253, 3330, **MS**3423, 3424, 3524, 3637, 3742, 3861, **MS**3868, 3945, **MS**3949, 4044, **MS**4048, 4127, **MS**4131, 4185, **MS**4192
Chives 3924
C.H.O.G.M. 1943
Christchurch ... 1365, 1857, 2041, 2218, 3231, 3256, **MS**3379
Christian Cullen (horse) 2470

NEW ZEALAND Design Index

Christmas 805, 809, 814, 817, 824, 834, 842, 880, 892, 905, 943, 964,990, 1034, 1058, 1083, 1129, 1153, 1182, 1204, 1229, 1253, 1274, 1324, 1349, 1376, 1404, 1437, 1480, 1520, 1569, 1628, 1700, 1746, 1832, 1916, 2020, 2097, 2189, 2288, 2353, 2439, 2524, 2644, 2742, 2820, 2905, 2996, 3092, 3097, 3172, 3240, 3321, 3396, 3504, 3614, 3733, 3851, 3857, 3928, 3934, 4031, 4039, 4117, 4123, 4180, 4185, 4247, 4253
Christmas Lily 1060
Christmas Stamps, 50 Years of 3240
Christmas star decorations 2880, 2956
Church of the Good Shepherd, Lake Tekapo .. 2605, 3773
Church Tower and Cross 945
Churchill, Sir Winston 829
Churchill Slice **MS**4158
Cinderella (ballet) 2574
Cinema 2014
Circular Saw (shell) 1104
Citrus Fruit 1284
Classic Travel Posters 3469
Clay 2493
Cleddau River 1246
Clever Kiwis 2982
Clinton celebrates our rural heritage 3590
Clover 1497
Coarse Dosinia 1101
Coastal Scenery 1395, 1528, 2510
Coastlines 3489
Coat Hanger 1792
Coat of Arms 674, 700, 767, 825, 925, 952, 978, 1017
'cods wallop' 2973
Colac Bay 3579
Colenso's Hard Fern 3431
College of Surgeons 1136
Colonial Cottage 3535
Colossal squid 3125
Columbus 1661
Commonwealth Day 1308
Commonwealth Games 1041, 1530
Commonwealth Heads of Government Meeting 1943
Commonwealth Parliamentary Conference 835, 1207
Computer 3912
Connecting New Zealand and the World 3642
Construction of a Nation 3535
Cook, Captain 906, 2051, 3062, **MS**3312
Cooks Bay 1317
Cooper, Dame Whina 1940
Copland Track 1471
Coromandel 1078, 2599, 2603, 2630, 2873
Coronation 714
Coronation 50th anniversary 2618
Coronation 60th anniversary 3448, **MS**3455
Coronet Peak 1337
Correggio 943, 1153
C.O.R.S.O. 911
Cosimo, Piero di 1274
Cossgrove, Lieut-Col David 2942
Counting in Kiwi **MS**3312
Country Women 948
Courage and Commitment 3760
Crafts 2491
Crichton, James 3285
Cricket 899, 1840
Cromwell 3574
Crump, Barry 1938
Crusader (ship) 1544
Cupcake with candles **MS**3565
Curio Bay, Catlins 2512
Curried Egg 3703
Custard Square **MS**4158
'cuz' 2967
Cycle trails 3950
Cycling 1043, 2435, 3052

D

D is for Dog 3063
d'Oggiono 1253
d'Urville, Dumont 2055
Dairy Farming 877, 1169
Dawkins, Eddie 3812
Dawn Service 4063
de Surville, Jean 2054
Della Robbia, Andrea 1229
Delphinium, Sarita 2710
Demolition 3967
Dempster, C. S. (Stewie) 1688
Devonshire, Pip 3782
DHL New Zealand Lions (rugby) 2797
di Credi, Lorenzo 1349
Diamond Jubilee 3356, **MS**3404
Diamond Wedding 2993
Diana, Princess 1372
Disabled Children 1065
Dinosaurs 1762, **MS**1769, 3196
Discoverers 2051
Diwali 4242
Dixon, Scott 3116
Dog Island (lighthouse) 3108
Dogs 1270, 2232, 2758, **MS**2817, 2840, 3063
Dolls 2360
Dolphin 1791, 2940
Doubtful Sound 1933, 1990, **MS**2005
Doubtless Bay 1397
Draw-it-yourself stamps 2685
'dreaded lurgy' 2980
dressed to the nines **MS**3312
Drysdale, Mahe 3815
du Fresne, Marion 981
Duke and Duchess of Cambridge 3554
Duncan's Seed Drill 2699
Dunedin 1264, 1362, 1858, 2221, 3333, **MS**3379, **MS**3423
Dunedin Railway Station 3777, 4080
Dunedin (sailing ship) 3393
Dürer 809
Dusky Sound, Fiordland 3013

E

E is for Edmonds 3064
Earnslaw (ship) 3392
Earthquake 3977
East Cape **MS**3379, 3491
East Matakitaki 2282
E.C.A.F.E. 1002
Economic Agreement with Australia 1305
Economy Zone 1176
Education 1138
Edward VII **MS**1568
Edward, Prince 1031
Edwin Fox (ship) 1545
Egmont National Park 929
El Greco 1182
Electric car 3919
Electricity 1444
Elephant Rock **MS**4102
Elizabeth II 721, 723, 740, 745, 763, 808, **MS**1046, 1094*a*, **MS**1137, 1170, 1202, 1370, **MS**1568, 2446, 2618, 2874, 3356, **MS**3404, 3448, **MS**3455, 3724, **MS**3772, 4200
Elizabeth II and Duke of Edinburgh 722, 2117, 2993, 3357
Elizabeth II and Prince Charles 701
Elliott, Keith 3291
Emerald Lakes, Tongariro National Park 3709
Empire S.30 (aircraft) 1053, 1539
End of World War One **MS**3100
Endangered Seabirds 3604
Endangered Species 1736
Endeavour (ship) 1542
Enderby Island 3711
Engineer 1939–1945 2584
Entoloma hochstetteri 2478
Environment Protection 1865
Erewhon 2718, **MS**2731
Eros (statue) 690
Escarpment Walkway, Paekakariki 4076
Ethereal (horse) 2474
'everyman and his dog' 2978
Ewelme 1217
'EXCEL' 3055
Expo 70 935
EXPO 2000 ..... **MS**2342
EXPO 2010 3208
Extreme Sports 2751

F

F is for Fantail 3065
Fairy Bread 3707
Falcon 1290
Family 1239
Family entering Church 1036
Fan Shell 3681
Farewell from Manaia Bread Capita 3591
Farm Animals 1894, 2757
Farm Machinery 2695
Farm Transport 1115
Fashion 1707, 1720
Featon Art 4205
Feilding celebrating the land 3589
Feilding, Lieutenat Colonel the Honorable W. H. A. 1237
Ferguson, Ian 2729
Fern 2407, 2810, 2878, **MS**2886, **MS**2923, **MS**2924, 2953, 3224, **MS**3237, **MS**3311, 3368, **MS**3377, 3429, **MS**3503
Fertiliser groundspreading 1166
F.I.A.P. Exhibition **MS**4145
Fighter Pilot Pacific 1943 2588
Fiordland 3015
Fiordland Crested Penguin 1467
Fiordland National Park 1430
Fiori, Federico 905
Fire Engines 1156
First 11 ..... **MS**3312
First Christian Service 824
First Tasman Flight 766
First World War, Centenary 3592, 3663, **MS**3732, 3760
Fish 792, 871, 920, 1012, 1178, 1197, 1525, 2082, **MS**2172, 2206, **MS**2246, **MS**2277, **MS**3296, 3873
Fishing 1225, 1526, 1779, 2082, **MS**2172, 3316, **MS**3379, 3473
Five years old, off to school **MS**3312
Flag 790, 854
Flax 2406, 2492
Flowers 781, 845, 946, 967, 983, 992, 1060, 1086, 1255, 1497, 1681, 2222, 2394, 2418, 2706, 2802, 2879, 2882, **MS**2924, **MS**2941, 2951, 4049
Football 941, 1587
For King and Empire 3592
Ford Model A (car) 1711
Fordson F Tractor with Plough 2696
Forest Ranger 1860s 2577
Forsyth, Samuel 3282
Fountain pen and letter 2420
Four stars of the Southern Cross **MS**3312
Fox Glacier 878, 1679, 1989
Franz Josef Glacier 1675, 2871, 3472, 3556, 3710
Free Milk 1724
FrENZY (ballet) 2575
Freyberg, Bernard 1552
Frickleton, Samuel 3278
Frozen Meat Export 1259
Fungi 2477
Fur Seal 1996, **MS**1999

G

G is for Goodnight Kiwi 3066
Gardens 2038
Garfish 923
Gentle Spirit (boat) 2533
George V **MS**1568
George VI 680, **MS**1568
Geothermal Power 933, 2890
German Shepherd Dog 2841
Giant Eagle 2032, 3127
Giant Kauri tree 1932, **MS**2005
Giant Moa 2033, **MS**2036, 3124
Giant Snail 1738
Giant Weta 3128
Giants of New Zealand 3124
Ginger biscuits **MS**4158
Gillick, Mary 3448, **MS**3455
Girl and Butterfly 1151
Girl and Calf 1126
Girl and Pigeon 1149
Girl Guides 719
Girls and Bird 1127
Girls' Life Brigade 764
Gisborne 1133, 2061, **MS**3379
Glaciers 1675
Glade Copper Butterfly 914
Glass 2495
Global positioning system 3916
Globe 2808
Glowworms 3754
'GO YOU GOOD THING' 3003
Gold Prospector 1506
Gold Rush 2899
Gold-striped Gecko 1344
Golden Retriever 2843
Golden Tainui 1255
Golden Volute 3680
Golden Wedding 2117
Golf 1861
'good as gold' 2962
Goodbye Pork Pie (film) 2016
Gore 2198, **MS**3379
Government Buildings 1220, 2487
Graham, Fred 3570
Graham's Town 1361
Grant, John Gildroy 3286
Grapes 1283
Great Barrier Island 1061, 1934*e*, 2078, **MS**2080, **MS**2122, 2283, **MS**2328
Great Barrier Skink 1341
Great Depression 1721
Great Voyages 3390
'Greedy Cat' 2273
Greenstone 2402
Greetings Stamps 1455, 1594, 1604, 2148, 2414
Grey, Sir George 1186
Greymouth 1325, **MS**3379
Growing a healthy future 3610
Grow Your Own 3921

Design Index NEW ZEALAND

Gunn, Dr Elizabeth ... 901
Gunner Korea 1950-1953 ... 2590

H

H is for Haka ... 3067
Hadlee, Sir Richard ... 1941
Hairy Maclary's Bone ... 2275
Hamadryas Baboon ... 2665
Hamilton ... **MS**3379
Hamilton (Arms) ... 1132
Hamilton's Frog ... 1340, 1738, 2938
Hammerhead Shark ... **MS**3296
'Happy Birthday' ... 1594
'hard yakka' ... 2972
Hardham, William James ... 3275
Hark the Herald Angels Sing ... 1131
Harlequin Gecko ... 1342
Harvest of Grain ... 1168
Harvest of the Sea ... 1175
Hastings ... 2230
Hauraki Gulf ... 930
Hawera ... 1257, 2205, **MS**3379
Hawke's Bay ... 768, 2058, 2095, **MS**2173, 2734, **MS**2750, 3778
Hawke's Bay Earthquake ... 2848
He Tohu Exhibition ... 3892
Health ... 678, 690, 696, 698, 708, 710, 719, 737, 742, 755, 761, 764, 776, 803, 806, 812, 815, 822, 831, 839, 867, 887, 899, 901, 940, 960, 987, 1031, 1054, 1079, 1125, 1149, 1197, 1225, 1249, 1270, 1320, 1345, 1372, 1400, 1433, 1475, 1516, 1559, 1620, 1687, 1741, **MS**1744, 1813, 1884, 2000, 2086, 2178, 2272, 2360, 2435, 2519, 2635, 2738, 2815, 3158
Health Stamps, 50th Anniversary ... 3158
Heaphy, Charles ... 3274
Heaphy Track ... 1470
Heart and ribbon ... 2416
Hector's Dolphin ... 1620, 1736, 2940
Hei Matau ... 3297
Heli-skiing ... 1782, **MS**1785, 3318
Heitiki ... 3143, 3212, **MS**3192, **MS**3237/8, **MS**3377
Helleborus Unnamed Hybrid ... 2707
Hen and Chickens Fern ... 3429
Henry, Prince ... 1373
Herald (ship) ... 1070
Hereford (cattle) ... 2048
Herehere ... 1441
Hericium coralloides ... 2480
High 5 (yacht) ... 2532
Hillary, Sir Edmund ... 3101, **MS**3180, 4097
Hinemoa (film) ... 2014
Hinton, John Daniel ... 3290
'hissy fit' ... 2965
Hobson, Lieutenant-Governor ... **MS**1540
Hockey ... 960
Hodgkins, Frances ... 1027
Hokey Pokey ice cream ... 3696
Holiday hideaways ... 2543
Holidays ... **MS**4194
Holstein-Friesian (cattle) ... 2043
Home of Compassion ... 2945
Hone Heke ... **MS**1540
Honey Bees ... 3463
Hong Kong '94 ... **MS**1785
HONG KONG 2001 ... **MS**2393
Hong Kong 2004 ... **MS**2672
Hong Kong China joint issue ... 2673
Hooker River, Canterbury ... 2634
Horlicks (horse) ... 1949
Hormosira banksii (seaweed) ... 3529
Horses ... 1345, 2236, 2815
Howick ... 1183
Huhu grubs ... 2690
Huia ... 2031, 2161
Huka Falls, Taupo ... 2872
Hulme, Alfred Clive ... 3289
Hulme, Denny ... 3119
Human Rights ... 891
Humpback Whale ... **MS**3296
Huntaway (Dog) ... 2844
Hunterville ... 3586
Hurdling ... 1041
Huttpex 2007 Stampshow ... **MS**2988
Hydro Roxburgh Dam ... 2888
Hygrocybe rubrocarnosa ... 2477

I

I is for Interislander ... 3068
I saw Three Ships ... 1085
ICC Cricket World Cup (2015) ... 3648
'Il Vicolo' (horse) ... 1948
Immigrants ... 2140
INDIPEX 2011 ... **MS**3258
Indonesia 2012 ... **MS**3378
Infantry ... 2583
Insects ... 2104
'INSPIRE' ... 3052
Instant Coffee ... 4010
International Co-operation Year ... 883
International Labour Organisation ... 893
International Orchid Conference ... 1214
International Peace Year ... 1393
International Polar Year 2007–2009 ... **MS**3130
International Telecommunications Network ... 1114
International Women's Year ... 1067
International Year of Child ... 1196
International Year of Disabled ... 1238
International Year of Science ... 1260
International Year of the Ocean ... 2206, **MS**2246
Invercargill ... 954, **MS**3379
Invercargill 2001 ... **MS**2401
Iron Pyrites ... 1279
Isaacs, Solomon ... 3760
Island Bay ... 4151
Israel '98 ... **MS**2172
Italia '98 ... **MS**2214
It's a Kiwi Thing ... 3826
ITU ... 828

J

J is for Jelly Tip ... 3069
Jack, Dr Robert ... 1708
Jack Russell Terrier ... 2842
Jahnke, Robert ... 3572
Jamboree ... 771, 838
Jersey (cattle) ... 2044, **MS**2050
Jessie Kelly (ship) ... 1072
Jet boating ... 1411, 1780, 2307
John Dory (fish) ... 924, 1015, **MS**3296
Joint issue with Vatican City ... 2549
Jones, Luuka ... 3811
Judson, Reginald Stanley ... 3283

K

Kaiauai River ... 1243
Kaikoura ... 1148, 1934*c*, 2094, 2185, 2199, **MS**2401, 2513, 2597, 2600, 2737, **MS**2819, 3230, **MS**3379, 3900
Kaitaia ... **MS**3379
Kaka ... 831, 1739, 2165
Kakapo ... 1288, 2811, 3305
Kakariki ... 812
Kangaroo and Kiwi ... 1305
Kapa Haka ... 3259, 3317
Karaka ... 782, 846
Karamu Walkway ... 4104
Karearea ... 807
Karitane Beach ... 1145
Kauri ... 2405
Kawau ... 1193
Kaweka ... 1077
Kawiti ... **MS**1540
Kea ... 3480
Keep our Roads Safe ... 821
Kereru ... 804
Kerikeri ... 903
Kete ... 3781
Kia Ora ... 3010, 3070, **MS**3137
Kid-proof caps ... 4018
Kidney Fern ... 3430
King ... 760, 2943
King Crab ... **MS**3296
King Kong (film) ... 2827
Kingfish ... **MS**3296
Kingfisher ... 1464
Kingitanga ... 3038
Kinnard Haines Tractor ... 2695
Kitchener, Lord ... 3592
Kiwi ... 1297, 1463, 1490, **MS**1745, **MS**1786, 2090, **MS**2342, 2801, **MS**2886, **MS**2923, 2937, 2967, **MS**3252, 3304, 3308, **MS**3311, **MS**3329, 3575, 3996, 4218
Kiwi (horse) ... 1945
Kiwi (round) ... 3996
Kiwi Characters ... 2692
Kiwi fruit ... 1287, 1806, 3576
Kiwi Inovation ... 4008
Kiwi Kitchen ... 3691
Kiwi Onion Dip ... 3692
Kiwi road trip ... **MS**3903
Kiwiana ... 1797, 2318
Kiwipex 2006 ... **MS**2923
Kiwis Taking on the World ... 2118
KiwiStamp ... 3162, 3269
'knackered' ... 2976
Knights Point ... 1395
Ko, Lydia ... 3824
Koiri ... 1454
Kokako ... 1292
Koromiko ... 788*e*, 852
Korora ... 823
Koru ... 1452, 3456
Kotare ... 803
Kotiate ... 1098
Kotuku ... 806
Kowhai ... 783, 785, 1794, 2224, 3337, **MS**3378
Kowhaiwhai ... 3684
Kunekune Pig ... 2930
Kupe ... 2052, 4081
KZ 1 (yacht) ... 2531

L

L is for log o'wood ... 3071
Labrador Retriever ... 2840
Lake Alexandrina ... 1319, 2341, **MS**2368
Lake Arthur ... 1485
Lake Camp ... 1934*d*, **MS**2401
Lake Coleridge ... 2602
Lake Erie (ship) ... 1069
Lake Hawea ... 1794
Lake Lyndon ... 2336, **MS**2368
Lake MacKenzie ... 3713
Lake Matheson ... 1318, 1988, 3365
Lake Pukaki ... 1484, 1796
Lake Rotorua ... 3229, **MS**3258
Lake Sumner ... 1075
Lake Taupo ... 2159
Lake Te Anan ... 3992
Lake Wakatipu ... 1987, 2166, **MS**2188, **MS**2214, 2337, 2735, **MS**2987, 3392
Lake Wanaka ... 1931, **MS**2005, 2183, 2868, 3152
Lakes ... 993
Lamb Export Trade ... 758
Lambington ... 3700
Land yachting ... 4016
Landsburgia quercifolia (seaweed) ... 3530
Landscapes ... 1690, 2597
'laughing gear' ... 2977
Laughing Owl ... 2029
Laurent, Henry John ... 3284
Law Society ... 894
Le Quesnoy ... 3972
League of Mothers ... 1110
Leather Jacket (fish) ... 922, 1014
Legendary Landmarks ... 3574
Lettuce ... 3926
Longfin Eel ... 3875
Lest we forget ... 3032, **MS**3100, 3131
Letter boxes ... 2064
Lichen Moth ... 918, 1010
Life Savers ... 761
Life Saving ... 1276
Lighthouses ... 3107, 4656
Lincoln College ... 1164
Lindis Pass ... 2187, **MS**2245
Lion Rock ... **MS**3379, **MS**4102
Lions (organisation) ... 2765
Little Spotted Kiwi ... 1297
Lockheed Electra (aircraft) ... 1051
Locomotives ... 1003
LONDON 2010 ... **MS**3214
Look Who it is! ... 3004
Lord Howe Coralfish ... **MS**3296
Lord of the Rings (films) ... 2458, **MS**2490, **MS**2523, 2550, 2652, 2714, **MS**2731, 4229
Lottin Point, East Cape ... 2511
Lotus ... 1498
love ... **MS**3565, 3790, **MS**3995
Love Always ... 3005
Lovelock, J. E. (Jack) ... 1559
Lowland Longjaw ... 3873
Lusk, Doris ... 2268, **MS**2276
Lyell Creek (horse) ... 2471
Lyttelton ... 1223

M

M is for Mudpools ... 3072
Macau 2018 Stamp Exhibition ... **MS**4023
MacDonald, Paul ... 2729
Mace and Black Rod ... 1208
Machiavelli ... 1083
Machin, Arnold ... 3450, **MS**3455
Mackenzie Country ... 1928, **MS**1998
Magnolia, Vulcan ... 2706
Magpie Moth ... 917
Maheno, NZHS ... 3671, **MS**3732
Mahy, Margaret ... 3435
Maklouf, Raphael ... 3452
Malayan Sun Bear ... 2666
Maloney, Alex ... 3821
Manaia ... 3591
Mangahao ... 1224
Mangamauna ... 3895
Mangawhitikau Cave ... 3754
Mangopare ... 1451
Mansfield, Katherine ... 1501
Manu Bay ... 3896, 3898
Manu tukutuku ... 3215
Manuka (tea tree) ... 781, 845, 3339
Maori Bible ... 883

NEW ZEALAND Design Index

Maori Canoe 1541, 2140, 2164
Maori Club 927, 1019
Maori Crafts 1952, **MS**2049
Maori Culture 1562
Maori Fibre-work 1440
Maori Fish Hook 926, 1018
Maori Language 3910
Maori Language Week 4168
Maori Language Year 1875
Maori Mail Carrier 739
Maori Myths 1807, 2311
Maori Rafter Paintings 1451
Maori Rock Art 3370
Maori Rock Drawing 796, 857
Maori Rugby 3220
Maori Tattoo Pattern 928, 1020, 1565
Maori Three Kings 966
Maori Village 1510
Map 1176, 1261, **MS**3157, **MS**3379
Marakopa Falls 1122
Maratta 842, 964
Marginariella boryana (seaweed) 3532
Marine Life 1752, 1958
Marine Mammals 1177, 1992
Marion Plateau 1677
Maripi 1095
Marlborough 772, 2059, 3776
Marsden, Samuel 2097
Marsh, Ngaio 1504
Marsters, Carl 3781
Mason, Bruce 1503
Masterton (Arms) 1134
Matariki 3045, **MS**3091, 3143, 3215, 3297, 3370, 3456, 3567, 3684, 3781, 4153, 4213
Matron RNZN Hospital, 1940s 2585
Matua Tikumu (Mountain Daisy) 787, 850
Mauger, Ivan 3118
Maui 2053, 3984
Maui Gas 1174
Mauisaurus 3200
Mayor Island, Bay of Plenty 3014
McCahon, Colin 2074, 4091
McCartney, Eliza 3823
McIntyre, Peter 2174, **MS**2215, 4163
McLaren, Bruce 3117
Meat Loaf 3695
Meech, Molly 3821
Melting moments **MS**4158
Methodist Church 982
Metric 1111
Meybille Bay, West Coast 2514
Milford Sound 2170, **MS**2214, 3227, **MS**3258, **MS**3379
Milford Track 1469
Military History 1352
Military Uniforms 2577
Millennium Series 2051, 2140, 2216
Mince on Toast 3701
Minerals 1277
Mirfin, Melville 3595
Mission House 1189
Missionaries 1509
Mitchell, Ethan 3812
Mitre Peak 1037, 1929, **MS**1978, 2736, **MS**2987, 3227, **MS**3258, **MS**3379
M.M.P. 2019
Moanasaurus 3199
Model T Ford 2643
Moeraki Boulders 1615, 3557
Monarch butterfly 3220
Montbretia 1499
Moon Landing 1818
Moriori 1505, 1585
Mossburn 3578
Moths 4132
Motorcycles 1389, 3118
Motorsport 3116
Mount Cook 1784, 1793, 1925, 2158, **MS**3180, **MS**3379, 3481, 4152
Mount Cook Lily 1737, 1793
Mount Cook National Park 931, 1429
Mount Egmont 877, 929, 1316, 1487, 1984, 2284, **MS**2295, 3486
Mount Everest 1788, 2308, 2616
Mount Hutt 1336
Mount Maunganui 2184, 4161
Mount Ngauruhoe 1038, 1930, **MS**1998, 3712
Mount Olympus 2716, **MS**2731
Mount Ruapehu 1935, 2168, 2338
Mount Sefton 1039
Mount Taranaki 2869, **MS**3379, 3560
Mountain Climber 737
Mountain oysters 2689
Mountaineer (ferry) 1332
Mountaineering 1415
Mounted Rifles, South Africa 2580
Mousetrap 3708
Moving the Mail 2376, **MS**2424
Mugs 2786
Murillo 834, 990
Murray, Eric 3810
Museum of New Zealand 2131
Music 1407

N

N is for Nuclear Free 3073
Napier 1047, 2042, 2201, 2229, **MS**3379, 3469
Napier Naval Artillery 2578
Narnia *Prince Caspian* 3041
National Airways 980
National Heart Foundation 1180
National Parks 1428, **MS**3312
Native Birds 1459*a*
Native Ferns 3429, **MS**3503
Native Seashells 3678
Native Seaweeds 3529
Native Sulphur 1282
Native Trees 3335, **MS**3378
Nativity Carving 1129
Nativity Play 3614
Nectarines 1285
Neill, Grace 1548
Nelson 767, 1360, **MS**3379
Nelson Lakes 4106
Nephrite 1277
Nepia, George 1560
Nerine, Anzac 2708
Netball 940
New Plymouth 1112, 1230, 2039, **MS**3379
New Plymouth Golf Course 1862
New Zealand 1990 **MS**1547
New Zealand 2005 National Stamp Show **MS**2833
New Zealand A Slice of Heaven **MS**3239
New Zealand and Samoa, 50 Years of Friendship 3380
New Zealand Bear Hunt **MS**4150
New Zealand Day **MS**1046
New Zealand Endeavour (Yacht) 1783
New Zealand Fairy Tern 3605
New Zealand Falcon 1467*a*
New Zealand Football Association 1587
New Zealand Heritage 1484, 1505, 1524, 1541, 1548, 1562
New Zealand Landscapes 2597, 3150, 3227, 3363, 3556, 3773, 3895, 3991, 4076, 4151, 4159
New Zealand National Airlines, 75th Anniversary 3642
New Zealand Native Glowworms 3754
New Zealand Post Vesting Day 1421
New Zealand Sea Lion 3386
New Zealand Symphony Orchestra 2006
New Zealander (ship) 1071
New Zealand's Longest Reigning Monarch 3724
New Zealanders serving Abroad 3441
Ngarimu, Moana-Nui-a-Kiwa 3292
Ngata 1235
Nicholas, Henry James 3280
Night Views 1855
Nikau (tree) 3338, **MS**3378
Nikau Cave 3755
Nin, Buck 3687
Ninety Mile Beach 4103
North Island Kaka 3906
North Island Main Trunk Line Centenary 3086
North Star (boat) 2534
North West Nelson 1076
Northland 2007 **MS**2941
Northpex 2002 **MS**2490
Nostalgia 2239
Nuclear Disarmament 1924, 2309, 3073
Nugget Point 3490, 4060
Number 8 wire **MS**3312
Nurse and Child 698

O

O is for O.E. 3074
Oamaru 1219
Oamaru Stone 2403
Ocean Beach 1146
Ocean Runner (boat) 2535
Ohakune 2197, 3580
Old Ghost Rad 3953
Oldsmobile 2640
Olympic Games 1475, 1663, 1670, 2008, 2018, 2347, 2727, 3056, 3798, 4173
Olympic Medal Winners, Rio de Janeiro 3808
On the Road 2329
Once were Warriors (film) 2017
One Ton Cup 950
Onward 672
Opal Top Shell 3682
Ophir 1265
Opononi Beach 1795
Opononi home of the friendly Dolphin 3585
Orange Roughy (fish) **MS**3296
Orchid **MS**1547
Orchid Conference 1214
Organ Pipes (landmark) 1616
Otago 692, 897, 1068
Otago Skink 1343
Otorohanga Kiwiana Town 3575

P

P is for Pinetree 3075
PACIFIC '97 **MS**2080
Pacific Basin Economic Council 1882
PACIFIC EXPLORER 2005 **MS**2785
Paekakariki 4076
Paeroa 2196, 3577
Palmerston North 952, 1263, **MS**3379
Palmpex 99 **MS**2295
Palmpex 2010 **MS**3252
Pan-Pacific Jamboree 771
Pancake Rocks 3558, 3561
Papakorito Falls 1124
Papanui Point, Raglan 2515
Papatuanuku and Ranginui 3567
Papillon (ballet) 2573, **MS**2651
Paradise Shelduck 1466
Parakeets 4139
Paralympics 4223
Parcel 2414, 2806
Parliament Buildings, New Zealand 668, 1105, 2678, 3716
Parliament House, Australia **MS**3717
Parliament House, Singapore **MS**3717
Parsley 3923
Partridge in a Peartree 1155
PASSION 3053, 3057
Passport 3914
Paua (abalone) 1099, 2404
Pavlova 3706
Peace 677
Peace Monitor 2596
Pearse, Richard 1551
Pembroke Peak 2160
Pencarrow (lighthouse) 3107
Pencarrow Head 3492
Penguins 2452, 2939
people reaching people 1819
Performing Arts 2124
Personalised Stamps 2801, 2876, 2950, 3003, **MS**3137, **MS**3192, **MS**3237/**MS**3238, **MS**3377, **MS**3565, **MS**3622, 3788, **MS**3995
Pets 2332, **MS**2287, 2815, 3495
Petty Officer 2582
Phar Lap (horse) 1722
PHILAKOREA 1994 **MS**1830
Philanippon '01 **MS**2434
Philanippon '11 **MS**3311
PhilexFrance 99 **MS**2276
Photo frame 2419
Picnic Scene 1231
Picton 1195
Piercy Island 1985
Pigeon Post 2078, **MS**2080, **MS**2122
Pigs 2759, 2930
Piha Beach 1147, 3897
Pikelets 3699
Pikiarero (Clematis) 788, 851
Piopio 2030
Piwakawaka 832
Plastic surgery 3883
Platinum Wedding 3937
Playgrounds 2635
Ploughing Championships 1215
Plunket Society 760, 2943
Poaka 777
Pocket Pets 3020, **MS**3031
Pohutu Geyser 802, 862, 879, 1735, **MS**1770, 2733, **MS**2819
Pohutukawa 992, 1206, 1795, 1991, 2802, 2879, **MS**2924, **MS**2941, 2951, 3208, **MS**3192, **MS**3237/**MS**3238, 3242, 3335, **MS**3377, **MS**3378, **MS**3565, 3793, 3797, **MS**3995
Police 1384
Pona 1440
Port Chalmers 1224
Possum pate 2691
POST X '95 **MS**1854
Postage Stamps, 150th Anniversary **MS**1568
Pōtaka, Audra 3784
Poussin, Nicolas 880
Powered Flight 2305
Powrie, Polly 3819
Prehistoric Animals 1762, **MS**1769
Preserve the Polar Regions and Glaciers **MS**3130
Pride 4193
Prince George, Birth of 3499

Design Index NEW ZEALAND

Prince Philip	**MS**4228
'Progress through Co-operation'	1002
Protect the Environment	1865
Provincial Council Buildings	1191
Pterocladia lucida (Seaweed)	3533
Puarangi (Hibiscus)	786, 849
Puha Pork	3693
Pukekura's Giant Sandfly	3588
Punakaiki Rocks	1614
Purakaunui Falls	1121
Puriri	1796
Puriri Moth	919, 1011
Putorino	1096
Puysegur Point Lighthouse	4061

Q

Q is for Quake	3076
Queen Charlotte Track	3954
Queen Elizabeth II, 90th Birthday	**MS**3772
Queen Elizabeth II, 95th Birthday	4200
Queen Elizabeth II New Zealand's Longest Reigning Monarch	3724
Queen Elizabeth the Queen Mother	2343, 2509
Queenstown	1860, 3228, **MS**3258, **MS**3379, 3427, 3476
Queenstown Golf Course	1864

R

R is for Rutherford	3077
Rabbit	2232, 2816, 3020, **MS**3031
Racehorses	913, 1945, 2470
Railway Station, Dunedin	2488
Railways	818, 1003, 2091, **MS**2173
Rainbow I (yacht)	4195
Rainbow II (yacht)	4196
Rainbow Falls	2599
Rainbow Mountain	2339
Rainbow Trout	1306, 2082, **MS**2172
Rakaia means great fishing	3581
Rakaia River	3154
Rakiura	3584
Ramaria aureorhiza	2482
Rangitiki (ship)	1074
Rangitoto Island	1934a, 1990b, **MS**2401, 2604
Ranguatea Maori Church	1275
Rank-Broadley, Ian	3453, **MS**3455
Raphael	1034, 1324
'rark up'	2981
Rata	789, 853
Rau Tau	3221
Raupunga	1453
Red Admiral Butterfly	915, 1008
Red Cross	775
Red Panda	2667
Red Rose	2882, 2955, **MS**3237, **MS**3377
Rembrandt	805
Reptiles	1340
Rescue Services	1979
Rewiri, Kura Te Wharu	3569, 3685
Rhododendron, Charisma	2709
Rifle Shooting	1044
Ring-tailed Lemur	2668
Ririnui, Te Atiwei	3783
River rafting	1416
Riverlands Cottage	1188
Riverton	2202
RNZAF, 75th Anniversary of	3341
RNZB (Royal New Zealand Ballet)	2572, **MS**2651
RNZYS	4195
Road to Rio	3798
Robin	1468
Rock and Roll	1787
Rock legends	**MS**4102
Rock Wren	1463b, 1589a
Rooney, Natalie	3808
Rooster	2760
Roses	967, 1086, 1201, 2114, **MS**2123, 2882
Rotary International	949, 2764
Rotoiti (ship)	1381
Rotomahana	1489, 2162
Rotomahana (ship)	3394
Rotorua	1213, 1730, 1859, 2732, **MS**3379, 3488, 3527
Rotorua Golf Course	1863
Rough Habit (horse)	1946
Round the World Yacht Race	1783
Routeburn Track	1472
Royal Albatross	1933, **MS**2037
Royal Doulton Ceramics Exhibition	1713
Royal Exhibition	**MS**3944
Royal Family	670
Royal Forest Society	1000
Royal New Zealand Air Force	1423
Royal Philatelic Society of New Zealand	1448
Royal Society	881
Royal Visit	721, 1790, 3554
Royal Wedding	1247, 3266
RoyalPex Exhibition	**MS**3944, **MS**4241
RSA Centenary	3747
Ruakuri Cave	3756
Rugby All Blacks	**MS**4110
Rugby Football	867, 1623, 1709, 2248, 2623, **MS**2664, **MS**2672, 2673, **MS**2712, 2797, 3220
Rugby League Centenary	1888, 2944
Rugby Lions Tour	**MS**3891
Rugby Sevens Women	3809
Rugby World Cup 2011	3234, 3313
Russell	1205, 3151
Rutherford, Lord	970, 3077

S

S is for Southern Cross	3078
Saddleback	1295
Sailors	886
Salon du Timbre 2004	**MS**2712
Salperton (yacht)	2536
Salvation Army	1303
SAS Malaya 1955–1957	2592
Sassoferrato	814
Satellite Earth Station	958
Saveloy and tomato sauce	3704
Savings Bank	843
Scallop	1103
Scarlet Parrotfish	920, 1012
Scenic Skies	2182, **MS**2245
Scenic Walks	2279
School Dental Service	962
Scott Base	2925
Scott's Murex	3679
Scown, Rebecca	3813
Sea and Resources	1178, 1524
Seahorses	921, 1013
Seals	1664, 1736
Seashore	1958
Seddon, Richard John	1187
Settlers	1507
Seven netballers make a team	**MS**3312
SHANGHAI '97	**MS**2123
'shark and taties'	2975
Sheep and Wool	875, 1579, 2235, 2566, 2758
Sheep dog	2758
Sheep Grazing	1165
'she'll be right'	2964
Shells	1099
Sheppard, Katherine	1550, 3081
Ships	673, 1069, 1085, 1175, 1259, 1332, 1379, 1529, 1541, 3349
Shotover	1245, 1366, 4078
Shrimp Cocktail	3697
Sightseeing Flights	1412
Silver	2494
Silver Fern	3433, **MS**3503, **MS**3565, 3789, 3795
Silver Jubilee	**MS**1137
Silver Paua	3678
Silvereye	1462
Simmental (cattle)	2045, **MS**2050
Singapore '95 Exhibition	**MS**1914
Singapore 2015 World Stamp Exhibition	**MS**3717
Six runs in cricket out of the park	**MS**3312
Skiing	1336, 3318
Skippers Canyon	2714
Sky Tower, Auckland	2489
Skydiving	2753
Skyscraper	3917
Smith, George	1891
Snapper	**MS**3296
Snell, Peter	2730
Snowden, Sonia	3786
Snowsports	2752
Society for the Prevention of Cruelty to Animals	1258
Solar Lighthouse	2891, **MS**2941
Soldier and Child	678
Soldiers	884
South Rangitikei Bridge	1368
Southern Alps	2092, **MS**2173, 3481
Southern Lights	3866
Southern Right Whale	3126
Southern Skies	2957, **MS**2988
Southland	752
SOUTHPEX '96	**MS**1978
Space pioneers	4070
'sparrow fart'	2966
Sperm Whale	1995
Spider Monkey	2669
Spiny Murex	1102
Splitting the Atom	2306
Sports	2347
Spotless Crake	1459a
Spotted Shag	1465
Spring	1269, 1794
St John Ambulance	1357
St Paul's Cathedral	669
Staff Officer, France 1918	2581
Stag Saddle	4107
Stained Glass Windows	944, 965, 991, 1035, 1059, 1084, 1130, 1154, 1916
Stamp Month (1994)	1820, **MS**1831
Stamp on Stamp	1179, 1219, 1448, 1813, 2771, 2777, **MS**2785, 2791, **MS**2833
Stampex '95 Exhibition	**MS**1887
Stampshow Melbourne 02	**MS**2542
Star biscuits	2422
Star of Bethlehem	1520
State Highway 1	**MS**3312
State Housing	1723, 3539
Statues	2146
Stay in Touch	2148
Steinlager II (yacht)	4197
Stewart Island	1062, 2279, 2870, 3364, **MS**3379
Stitchbird	1294
Stone Store, Kerikeri	2485
Stout-legged Wren	2035
Stratford	1161
Summer	1266, 1795
Summer Festivals	2917
Sunline (horse)	2473
Sunrise	2310
Surf breaks	3897
Surf Life Saving	3247
Surf's Up at Colac Bay	3579
Sutherland Falls	800, 860
Swaggie	1710
Swan Lake (ballet)	2576, **MS**2651
'sweet as'	2963

T

Taepa, Ngatai	3688
Taiaroa Head	1934b, **MS**2328, **MS**2401, **MS**3379
Taihape	3583
Taipei '93	**MS**1744
TAIPEI 2005	**MS**2819
TAIPEI 2008	**MS**3031
Tairua Harbour	2340
Takahe	1296, **MS**3306/**MS**3307
Talbot (car)	2642
Talkies	1725
Taranaki	3899, 3994
TARAPEX '98	**MS**2188
TARAPEX 2008	**MS**3106
Tarapunga	822
Tasman	1659, 2056, 3085
Tasman Glacier	801, 861, 1676
Taupo	**MS**3379
Taupo the Cyclist's Delight	3587
Tauranga	1256, 2096, 2220, **MS**3379, 3479, 3991
Te Ata-O-Tu	1236
Te Hau	1233
Te Heu Heu	1232
Te Hoho Rock	**MS**4102
Te Kanawa	1936
Te Kaukau Point	1618
Te Kuiti	2200
Te Mata Peak, Hawke's Bay	3778
Te Puea	1234
Te Puke	2203, 3576
Te Reo	3910
Te Wiki	4168
Teddy Bears	2360, **MS**3237, **MS**3377, **MS**3565, 3792
Tekapo	2204
Telegraph	810
Telephone	1162
Ten guitars	**MS**3312
Tennis	987
Tete	776
Thailand 2018 Stamp Exhibiton	**MS**4042
Thames Borough	997
THANKS A MILLION	3006
Thaxterogaster porphyreus	2481
The 1920s	1707
The 1930s	1720
The 1940s	1771
The 1950s	1787
The Brothers (islands)	1064
The Capital Stamp Show, Wellington	**MS**3732
The Elms	1190
The Flu Pandemic	3966
The Hobbit An Unexpected Journey (film)	3405
The Hobbit Personalised Stamps	**MS**3622
The Hobbit The Battle of the Five Armies	**MS**3622, 3623
The Hobbit The Desolation of Smaug (film)	3512
The Lion the Witch and the Wardrobe (film)	2834
The New Zealand Experience	3314
The Spirit of Anzac	3663, **MS**3732
The Stamp Show 2000	**MS**2328
Thermal Wonders	1730
Thinking of You	1604
Three-hour ferry ride	**MS**3312

123

NEW ZEALAND Design Index

Threshing Mill ... 2698
Tieke ... 813
Tiki ... 793, 856, 874, 3079
'tiki tour' ... 2969, **MS**3157, **MS**3379
Timaru ... **MS**3379, 3477
Timber ... 791, 855, 873
Time to Celebrate ... 3009
TIMPEX 2009 ... **MS**3180
Tirau's big sheep ... 3582
Titanosaurus ... 3198
Titian ... 817
Titoki ... 784
Tiuka, Kylie ... 3686
Toheroa (clam) ... 1100
Tolaga Bay ... 3150
Tonga Bay ... 2281
Tongaporutu Cliffs, Taranaki ... 2510, 2609
Tongariro ... 798, 859, 878*b*, 1431, 2607, 2720, 4105
Tory (ship) ... 1073, 1543
Tory Channel ... 1986
Tourism 1411, 1777, 2732, **MS**2750, **MS**2819, 2868
Tourism Centenary ... 2425, **MS**2434
Town Icons ... 2196
Toy Buzzy Bee ... 2877, 2950, **MS**3237, **MS**3377
Tramping ... 1781
Trams ... 1360
Travis, Richard Charles ... 3281
Trawler and Fish ... 870
Treaty of Waitangi ... **MS**1540
Treaty of Waitangi, 175th anniv ... **MS**3662, 3893
Trees ... 1511, 2222, **MS**2286, 3335, **MS**3378
Trent, Leonard Henry ... 3294
Trigg, Lloyd Allen ... 3293
Trout ... 792
Trumpet ... 2415
Tuatara ... 1590, 2936
Tuffery, M. ... 4111
Tuke, Blair ... 3820
Tunnel Beach ... **MS**4102
Turkey ... 2146
Turoa ... 1338
Tussock Butterfly ... 916, 1009, 3221
Twelve Days of Christmas ... 1404
Twin Bridges ... 1369
Two jandals ... **MS**3312

U

U is for Upham ... 3080
U-Bix Rugby Super 12 ... 2248
Umbrella Fern ... 3432, **MS**3503
UN Peacekeeper ... 2595
UNESCO World Heritage Sites ... 3709
UNICEF ... 956
United Nations ... 938, 1942
Universal Suffrage ... 890
Upham, Charles ... 1937, 3080, 3288
Upper Hutt 2013 ... **MS**3503
UPU ... 1049
Urban Transformation ... 2216
Urewera National Park ... 1428

V

V is for Vote ... 3081
van Honthorst ... 892
Veteran Vehicles ... 2639
Victoria ... **MS**1568
Victoria Cross ... 3274
Victoria University ... 2247
Villa ... 3536
Vineyards ... 2057, **MS**2081
Vintage Car Rally ... 972
Vogel, Sir Julius ... 1185
Volkner Rocks, White Island ... 3016
Volunteers, 100 Years of ... 3247

W

WAAC Egypt 1942 ... 2586
WAAF Driver 1943 ... 2589
Wahaika ... 1097
Waikana (ferry) ... 1333
Waikato River ... 2633, 3559, 4211
Wahine (ship) ... 3957
Wainui Bay ... 1398
Waipu Cave ... 3757
Waitangi Golf Course ... 1861
Waitomo Limestone Cave ... 1934, **MS**2005
Waka (Maori canoe) ... 3391
Wakatere (ferry) ... 1335
Wakefield ... 1254
Walker, John ... 2727
Walking Trails ... 1469
Wall Hangings from the Beehive ... 1209
Walsh, Tomas ... 3822
Wanganui ... 978, 1555
Ward, James Edward Allen ... 3287
Washington 2006 ... **MS**2886
Water Safety ... 2178
Waterways ... 2630
Wearable Art ... 2701
Weather Extremes ... 3025
Webb Ellis Cup ... 3313
Webster, Sam ... 3812
Wedding Rings ... 2805, 2881, 2952, **MS**3192, **MS**3237/**MS**3238, **MS**3377, **MS**3565, 3788, 3796, **MS**3995
Weka ... 840
Wellington ... 830, 1222, 1350, 1364, 1556, 1856, 2091, 2216, 3155, **MS**3379, 3474
Welpex 2003 ... **MS**2664
Westland ... 778
Westport ... 998, 2219, 2231, **MS**3379
Weta ... 1739, 3082, 3128
WE'VE GOT NEWS ... 3007
Whakapapa ... 1339
Whakarewarewa ... 2597
Whakatane ... 2186
Whales and Whaling ... 752, 1491, 1508, 3126, **MS**3296
Whangarei ... **MS**3379
Whangaroa ... 1192
Whiri ... 1442
Whitau ... 1443
White Heron ... 1994, **MS**1999
White Island ... 1063, **MS**3379
White-faced Storm Petrel ... **MS**3296
White-water Rafting ... 1778, 2751
Whitebait Fritters ... 3702
Whiting, Cliff ... 3567
Wifi ... 3918
Wild Animals ... 1820, **MS**1831
Wild Ginger ... 1500
Wildfood ... 2689
Wilding, Anthony F. ... 1687
William, Prince ... 1372
Williams, Yvette ... 2728
Willis, Nick ... 3825
Wilson, Matthew McIntyre ... 3785
Wind Farm ... 2887
Windsurfing ... 1414, 1524, 3315
Winter ... 1268, 1793
WIPA08 ... **MS**3091
Wish you were here ... 3008
Witehira, Johnson ... 3684
Witz ... 1058
Wolseley (car) ... 2641
Women's Division, Federated Farmers ... 1066
Women's Suffrage ... 2304, 4020
Women's Vote ... 1726
Wood ... 2491
Woollhead (plant) ... 4052
'wop-wops' ... 2971
World Communications Year ... 1307
World Cup (rugby) ... 1623
World Ploughing Championships ... 1215
World Scouting ... 2942
World Stamp Championship 2004 Exhibition ... **MS**2731
World War I ... 3879, 3964
World War II ... **MS**4149
World War II Poster Art ... 3541
Wright, Hercules 'Bumper' ... 2944
Wuhan Exhibition ... **MS**4090
WWF ... 1736

X

X is for x-treme sports ... 3083

Y

Y is for Yarn ... 3084
Yachts ... 708, 950, 1417, 1527, 1655, 1883, 2296, 2531, 2538, 2562, **MS**2542, 4195
Year of the Dog ... 3945
Year of the Dragon ... 2311, 3330
Year of the Horse ... 3524
Year of the Monkey ... 3742
Year of the Ox ... 3112, **MS**3137
Year of the Pig ... 4044
Year of the Rabbit ... **MS**2238, 3253
Year of the Rat ... 4127
Year of the Rooster ... 3861
Year of the Sheep ... 3637
Year of the Snake ... 2386, 3424
Year of the Tiger 1998 ... **MS**2139
Year of the Tiger 2010 ... 3187
Yearbury, Pauline Kahurangi ... 3571
Yellow Moray Eel ... **MS**3296
Yellow-crowned Parakeet ... 4139
Yellow-eyed Penguin ... 1736, 1992, 2939
Yellowfin Tuna ... **MS**3296
Yellowhead ... 1461
YMCA ... 2766
York, Duke and Duchess of ... 1516
You gotta love Christmas ... 3011
Yulestar (horse) ... 2472
YWCA ... 1113

Z

Z is for Zeeland ... 3085
Zabeel (horse) ... 2475
Zoo Animals ... 2665

3-stage bikes ... 4019
13 lamingtons ... **MS**3312
14 national parks ... **MS**3312
15 players make a rugby team ... **MS**3312
16 years old and you can drive ... **MS**3312
17 Captain James Cook lands here ... **MS**3312
18 years, the voting age ... **MS**3312
19 protected surf breaks ... **MS**3312
20 bucks ... **MS**3312
21 years old, the key to the door ... **MS**3312

STAMP BOOKLETS

Nos. SB1 to SB24 are stapled

Nos. SB1/SB5 were sold at ½d. above the face value of the stamps to cover the cost of manufacture.

1901 (1 Apr). White card covers with postage rates.
SB1	1s.½d. booklet containing 12×1d. (No. 278) in blocks of 6	£2500
SB2	2s.6½d. booklet containing 30×1d. (No. 278) in blocks of 6	£3500

Original printings of Nos. SB1/SB2 showed the face value on the cover in small figures. Subsequent printings show large figures of value on the covers and the prices quoted are for this type.

1902 (21 Aug)–**05**. White card covers with postage rates.
SB3	1s.½d. booklet containing 12×1d. in panes of 6 (Nos. 303b or 303cb)	£1800
SB4	2s.½d. booklet containing 24×1d. in panes of 6 (Nos. 303b or 303cb) (21.3.05)	£2250
SB5	2s.6½d. booklet containing 30×1d. in panes of 6 (Nos. 303b or 303cb)	£2750

1910 (Apr). White card cover with postage rates.
SB6	2s. booklet containing 11×½d. in pane of 5 with 1 label (Nos. 387b or 387c) and pane of 6 (No. 387d), and 18×1d. in three panes of 6 (No. 405b)	£5000

1912 (May). White card cover.
SB7	2s. booklet containing 12×½d. and 18×1d. in panes of 6 with bars on the selvedge (Nos. 387e, 405c)	£3000

1915 (Feb). Red card cover.
SB8	2s. booklet containing 12×½d. and 18×1d. in panes of 6 with bars on the selvedge (Nos. 435a or 435ba, 405c)	£1800
	a. Grey cover	
	b. Blue cover	
	c. Yellow-buff cover	
	d. Purple-buff cover	

1924 (1 Dec)–**25**. Cover inscription within frame.
SB9	2s. booklet containing 12×½d. and 18×1d. in panes of 6 with bars on the selvedge (Nos. 441a, 406b) (lilac cover)	£2000
	a. Grey cover	
	b. Pale blue cover	£2250
SB10	2s. booklet containing 12×½d. and 18×1d. in panes of 6 with bars and advertisements on the selvedge (Nos. 446a, 410b) (yellow-buff cover) (1925)	£2500
	a. Grey-green cover	£2500
	b. Grey-buff cover	£2500
	c. Grey-pink cover	£2500

1928–34.
SB11	2s. booklet containing 12×½d. (Perf 14×15) and 18×1d. in panes of 6 with bars on the selvedge (Nos. 446ab, 468b)	£3000
	a. As No. SB11, but ½d. (Perf 14) (Nos. 446ca, 468b)	£1800
	b. As No. SB11 but panes with bars and advertisements on the selvedge (Nos. 446cb, 468c)	£2000
SB12	2s. booklet containing 24×1d. (Perf 14) in panes of 6 with bars and advertisements on the selvedge (No. 468c) (1930)	£1800
	a. As No. SB12, but 1d. (Perf 14×15) (No. 468ea) (1934)	£1700

1935 (18 Nov).
SB15	2s. booklet containing 24×1d., in panes of 6 with advertisements on the selvedge (No. 557ca)	£375

1936 (Nov).
SB16	2s. booklet containing 24×1d. (No. 578) in blocks of 6	£300

B1

1938 (1 July). Cream cover as T **B1**.
SB17	2s. booklet containing 24×1d. (No. 605) in blocks of 6	£375

1938 (Nov). Cream (No. SB18) or blue (No. SB19) covers as T **B1**.
SB18	2s. booklet containing 12×½d. and 18×1d. (Nos. 603, 605) in blocks of 6	£500
SB19	2s.3d. booklet containing 18×1½d. (No. 607) in blocks of 6	£400

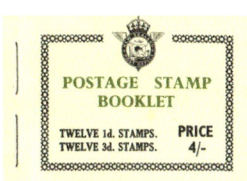

B2

1954 (1 Apr)–**55**. Black and green on cream cover as T **B2**.
SB20	4s. booklet containing 12×1d. and 12×3d. (Nos. 724, 727), each in blocks of 6	4·00
	a. Contents as SB20 but with one pane of airmail labels (9.55)	21·00

1956 (1 May). Black and green on cream cover as T **B2**.
SB21	4s. booklet containing 12×1d. and 12×3d. (Nos. 724, 748), each in blocks of 6, and one pane of airmail labels	10·00

1957 (5 Sept). Black and green on cream cover as T **B2**.
SB22	4s. booklet containing 12×1d. and 12×3d. (Nos. 745, 748), each in blocks of 6, and one pane of airmail labels	11·00
	a. As No. SB22 but 1d. No. 745b and 3d. No. 748b	18·00

B3

1960 (1 Sept). Black and red on cream cover as T **B3**.
SB23	4s. booklet containing 12×1d. and 12×3d. (Nos. 782, 785), each in blocks of 6, and one pane of airmail labels	16·00

1962 (21 May). Black and red on cream cover as T **B3**.
SB24	4s.6d. booklet containing 12×½d., 12×1d. and 12×3d. (Nos. 781, 782, 785), each in blocks of 6, and one pane of airmail labels	50·00

1964. Black and carmine on cream cover as T **B3**. Stitched.
SB25	4s.3d. booklet containing 6×½d. and 12×1d. and 12×3d. (Nos. 781/782, 785), each in blocks of 6, and one pane of airmail labels	18·00

NEW ZEALAND Stamp Booklets

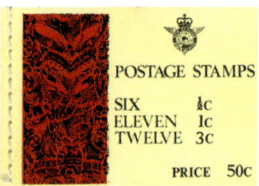

B4 Maori Art

1967 (10 July). Black and carmine on pale lemon cover as T **B4**. Stitched.
SB26   50c. booklet containing ½c. (No. 845) in block of 6, 11×1c. in block of 6 (No. 846) and pane of 5 stamps and 1 label (No. 846a), and 12×3c. (No. 849) in blocks of 6 .... 10·00

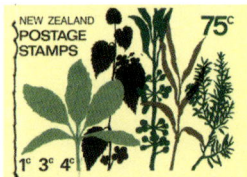

B5 Native Trees

1971 (6 July). Multicoloured cover 70×49 mm, as T **B5**. Stitched.
SB27   75c. booklet containing 9×1c. (No. 915b) in block of 6 and in pane of 3 stamps and three labels (No. 915ba), 6×3c. (No. 918b) and 12×4c. (No. 919b), each in blocks of 6 with sideways inverted or sideways watermarks .... 5·50

1974 (1 Aug). Multicoloured cover 70×49 mm, as T **B5**. Stitched.
SB28   75c. booklet. As No. SB27 but containing stamps without watermark (Nos. 1008/1008a, 1010/1011) .... 5·50
    a. Revised cover design ....

The front cover of No. SB28a was printed in four colours instead of three, with the foliage to the left of the design being in grey-green instead of myrtle-green. The stamps were printed on paper with bluish gum and there were changes to the advertisements.

All booklets from No. SB29 onwards have their panes attached by the selvedge, *unless otherwise stated*. Nos. SB29/SB34 have blank inside covers.

B6 Garden Rose, Josephine Bruce

1977 (1 May). Multicoloured cover 80×58 mm, as T **B6**.
SB29   80c. booklet containing 8c. (No. 1093a) in block of 10 .... 2·25

B7

1977 (1 May). Blue and black printed cover 89×49 mm, as T **B7**.
SB30 $1 booklet containing 10c. (No. 1017) in block of 10 .... 6·00

B8

Two settings of Booklet Cover for No. SB31:
Setting I. Inscription at foot. 'c' aligned at top of '10' (similar to T B8).
Setting II. Inscription at top. 'c' aligned at bottom of '10'.

1978 (Aug)–79. Black and ultramarine printed cover 80×58 mm, as T **B8**.
SB31 $1 booklet containing 10c. (No. 1094a) in block of 10 (Cover Setting I) .... 7·00
    a. Cover Setting II .... 27·00
    b. Containing 10c. (No. 1094ab) (Cover Setting I) (1979) .... 21·00

1978 (1 Aug). Black and orange cover 80×58 mm, as T **B8**.
SB32 $1.20 booklet containing 12c. (No. 1096) in block of 10 .... 2·25

1980 (1 Mar). Black and red cover 80×58 mm, as T **B8**.
SB33 $1.40 booklet containing 14c. (No. 1098) in block of 10 .... 2·25

B9

1980 (12 May). Black and green cover 80×59 mm, as T **B9**.
SB34 $1.40 booklet containing 14c. (No. 1098) in block of 10 .... 2·25

The cover of No. SB34 is inscribed '$1.54' which included a premium payable when purchased from commercial outlets authorised to sell booklets. It was available at $1.40 (value of contents) from the Post Office Philatelic Bureau.

B10

1981. Black and blue cover 95×50 mm, as T **B10**.
SB35 $2 booklet containing 20c. (No. 1099) in block of 10 .... 1·75

B11

1981. Black and green cover 95×50 mm, as T **B11**.
SB36 $2 booklet containing 20c. (No. 1099) in block of 10 .... 1·75

The cover of No. SB36 is inscribed '$2.20'. See note below No. SB34.

Stamp Booklets NEW ZEALAND

1982 (1Apr)–**83**. Black and green cover 83×60 mm, as T **B8**.
SB37 $2.40 booklet containing 24c. (Perf 12½) (No. 1261) in block of 10......... 4·75
    a. Containing 24c. (Perf 14½×14) (No. 1261a) (3.83)................. 14·00

1982 (1 Apr)–**85**. Black and blue cover 83×60 mm, as T **B9**.
SB38 $2.40 booklet containing 24c. (Perf 12½) (No. 1261) in block of 10......... 3·50
    a. Containing 24c. (Perf 14½×14) (No. 1261a) (3.85)................. 20·00

The covers of Nos. SB38/SB38a are inscribed '$2.64'. See note below No. SB34.

B13

1988 (18 May). Personal Message Stamps. Multicoloured cover, 101×60 mm, as T **B13**.
SB47 $2 booklet containing pane of five different 40c. (No. 1455a).......... 2·50

No. SB47 exists overprinted on the front cover with the WORLD STAMP EXPO '89 logo for sale at the International Stamp Exhibition in Washington, USA.

B12 Lake Tekapo, South Island

1985 (1 July). Multicoloured cover as T **B12** with design continuing on back cover.
SB39 $2.50 booklet (Type **B12**) containing 25c. (No. 1370) in block of 10 .... 4·00
SB40 $2.50 booklet (Tongariro Park, North Island) containing 25c. (No. 1370) in block of 10................... 4·00

The cover of No. SB40 is inscribed '$2.75'. See note below No. SB34.

1986 (1 May). Multicoloured covers as T **B12**, but 115×60 mm, with the design continuing on back cover.
SB41 $3 booklet (Matukituki Valley, Otago) containing 30c. (No. 1288) in block of 10....................... 4·00
SB42 $3 booklet (Stream and native bush, Canterbury) containing 30c. (No. 1288) in block of 10.......... 4·00

The cover of No. SB42 is inscribed '$3.30'. See note below No. SB34.

Nos. SB41/SB42 exist overprinted on the front cover with the Stockholmia logo for sale at the International Philatelic Exhibition in Sweden.

1987 (2 Feb–June). Multicoloured covers as T **B12**, but 115×60 mm with the design continuing on back cover.
SB43 $4 booklet (Ahuriri Valley, Otago) containing 40c. (No. 1289) in block of 10................................. 18·00
    a. Revised NZ POST logo without crown (6.87)........................... 18·00
SB44 $4 booklet (Totaranui Beach, Abel Tasman National Park, Nelson) containing 40c. (No. 1289) in block of 10 .... 18·00
    a. Revised NZ POST logo without crown (6.87)........................... 30·00

The covers of booklets Nos. SB44/SB44a are inscribed '$4.40'. See note below No. SB34.

Nos. SB43a and SB44a exist overprinted on the front cover with the CAPEX logo for sale at the International Philatelic Exhibition in Toronto.

1987 (1 Nov). Multicoloured covers as T **B12**, but 115×60 mm, with the design continuing on back cover. New NZ POST logo as shown on T **B14**.
SB45 $4 booklet (Wellington by night) containing 40c. (No. 1289) in block of 10..................................... 5·00
SB46 $4 booklet (Katiki Point) containing 40c. (No. 1289) in block of 10 .... 26·00

The cover of No. SB46 is inscribed '$4.40'. See note below No. SB34.

B14

1988 (7 June). Fast Post Service. Black, bright scarlet and new blue cover, 88×60 mm, as T **B14**.
SB48 $7 booklet containing 70c. (No. 1466) in block of 10....................... 6·50

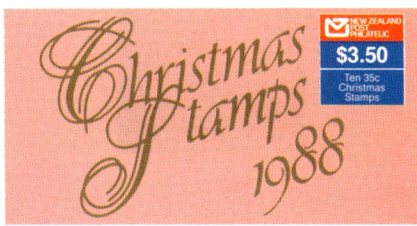

B15

1988 (14 Sept). Christmas. Multicoloured cover, 116×59 mm, as T **B15**.
SB49 $3.50 booklet containing 35c. (No. 1480) in block of 10....................... 3·00

B16

1988 (19 Oct). Multicoloured cover, 86×55 mm, as T **B16**.
SB50 $6 booklet containing pane of 6×$1 (No. 1490a)................................. 9·00

NEW ZEALAND Stamp Booklets

B17 Mount Cook from the Hooker Valley, South Canterbury

B20

1988 (2 Nov). Multicoloured cover, 88×60 mm, as T **B17** with design continuing on back cover.
SB51 $4 booklet containing 40c. (No. 1463) in block of 10.. 4·50

No. SB51 exist overprinted on the front cover with the Stamp World London '90 logo for sale at the International Stamp Exhibition in Great Britain.

1989 (13 Sept). Christmas. Multicoloured cover, 116×59 mm, as T **B15**.
SB52 $3.50 booklet containing 35c. (No. 1520) in block of 10.. 3·00

1991 (15 May). Thinking of You. Multicoloured cover, 101×60 mm, as T **B20**.
SB55 $2 booklet containing pane of five different 40c. (No. 1604a)........................... 3·25

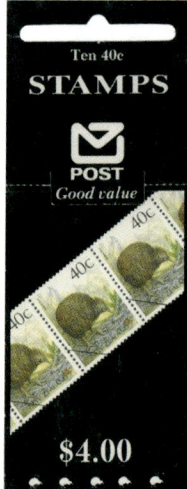

B18

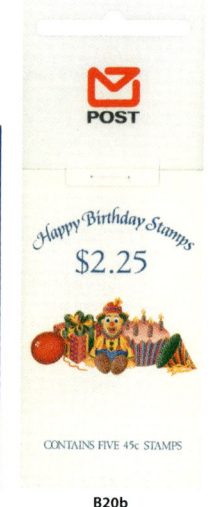

B20a **B20b**

1990 (1 Aug). Black and white cover, 61×96 mm, as T **B18** showing multicoloured stamp No. 1463.
SB53 $4 booklet containing 40c. (No. 1463) in block of 10 with three fastPOST labels . 8·00

No. SB53 has a slot in the cover for hanging display. Booklets in this format were produced for self-service sales.

1991 (1 July). Blue and white cover, 61×96 mm, as T **B18** showing multicoloured stamp No. 1463b. **B20a** in hanging display format with slotted tab as T **B18**.
SB56 $4.50 booklet containing 45c. (No. 1463b) in block of 10.. 4·00

1991 (1 July). Happy Birthday. Multicoloured vert cover, 61×100 mm, as T **B20b**.
SB57 $2.25 booklet containing pane of five different 45c. (No. 1599a)........................... 3·25

B19

B20c

1991 (15 May). Happy Birthday. Multicoloured cover, 101×60 mm, as T **B19**.
SB54 $2 booklet containing pane of five different 40c. (No. 1594a)........................... 3·25

Stamp Booklets NEW ZEALAND

1991 (1 July). Thinking of You. Multicoloured cover, 60×100 mm, as T **B20c** with slotted tab in hanging display format as T **B20b**.
SB58 $2.25 booklet containing pane of five
        different 45c. (No. 1609a)............................ 3·25

BARCODES. All booklets from No. SB59 show a barcode on the reverse, *unless indicated otherwise.*

B21

1991 (1 Oct)–**92**. Bright red and black cover, 86×50 mm, as T **B21** showing multicoloured stamp No. 1463b. Roman 'I' on back.
SB59 $4.50 booklet containing 45c. (No. 1463b) in
        block of 10.. 4·00
        a. Roman 'II' on back (5.92) .... 9·50
        b. With additional slotted tab at right.
            Containing 45c. in pane of ten (No.
            1463bba) ('I' on back) .... 5·50
        ba. Containing 45c. (No. 1463b) in block of
            10 ('II' on back)...................................... 11·00

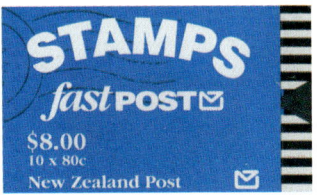

B21a

1992 (Mar–27 May). Bright blue and black cover, 86×50 mm, as T **B21a**. No barcode on reverse.
SB60 $4 booklet containing 80c. (No. 1467) in
        strip of five and pane of six fastPOST
        labels.. 4·00
SB61 $8 booklet containing 80c. (No. 1467) in
        block of 10 and pane of ten fastPOST
        labels.. 30·00
        a. Barcode on back (27.5) .... 8·00

B21b

1992 (1 Sept)–**93**. Landscapes. Bright red and black cover 86×51 mm, as T **B21b** showing multicoloured stamp No. 1693. Roman 'I' on back.
SB62 $4.50 booklet containing pane of ten
        different 45c. (No. 1690a)........................... 4·00
        a. Roman 'II' on back (1993)........................ 13·00
        b. Roman 'III' on back (1993)....................... 35·00
        c. With additional slotted tab at right ('I'
            on back).. 4·50
        ca. Roman 'II' on back (1993)...................... 16·00
        cb. Roman 'III' on back (1993)..................... 35·00

1993 (31 Mar)–**95**. Bright blue and black cover, 86×50 mm, as T **B21a**.
SB63 $8 booklet containing 80c. (No. 1467a) in
        block of 10 and block of 10 fastPOST
        labels.. 8·00
        a. Containing pane No. 1467aab (Perf 12)
            (7.94)... 16·00
        ab. With additional slotted tab right
            (7.95)...

B21c

1993 (9 June). Endangered Species Conservation. Bright red and black cover, 85×50 mm, as T **B21c** showing multicoloured illustration of Tusked Weta.
SB64 $4.50 booklet containing 45c. (No. 1740) in
        block of 10.. 5·50
        a. With additional slotted tab at right .... 9·00

B21d

1993 (1 Sept). Marine Life. Bright red and black cover, 86×50 mm, as T **B21d** showing multicoloured illustration of Grouper (fish).
SB65 $4.50 booklet containing pane of ten
        different 45c. (No. 1752a)........................... 8·00
        a. With additional slotted tab at right .... 11·00

B21e

1993 (1 Oct). Prehistoric Animals. Bright red and black cover, 86×51 mm, as T **B21e** showing multicoloured illustration of Carnosaur.
SB66 $4.50 booklet containing pane of 10×45c.
        plus two labels (No. 1767a)........................ 4·50
        a. With additional slotted tab at right .... 6·50

B21f

1993 (3 Nov). Christmas. Bright red and black cover 86×50 mm as T **B21f** showing multicoloured illustration of Christmas Pudding.
SB67 $4.50 booklet containing pane of 10×45c.
        (No. 1746ba) .... 8·00
        a. With additional slotted tab at right .... 8·00

NEW ZEALAND Stamp Booklets

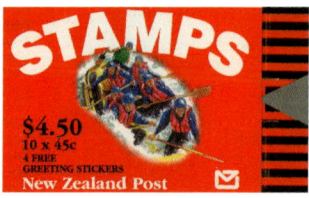

B21g

1994 (19 Jan–Aug). Tourism. Bright red and black cover, 86×50 mm, as T **B21g** showing multicoloured illustration of White-water Rafting.

SB68 $4.50 booklet containing pane of 10×45c.
(No. 1782a) and four half stamp-size
labels (horiz format)...................................... 2·75
    a. Roman 'II' on back (8.94) .... 10·00
    b. Vert format with additional slotted tab
       at top.. 8·00
    ba. Roman 'II' on back (8.94) .... 12·00

1994 (27 Apr). New Zealand Life. Bright red and black cover as T **B21** showing multicoloured illustration of Buzzy Bee.

SB69 $4.50 booklet containing pane of ten
different 45c. (No. 1797a) (horiz
format)... 2·75
    a. Vert format with additional slotted tab
       at right... 3·50

1994 (21 Sept). Christmas. Multicoloured covers as T **B21** showing illustration of Father Christmas and children.

SB70 $4.50 booklet containing 45c. (No. 1832) in
block of 10 (horiz format) .... 3·00
    a. Vert format with additional slotted tab
       at top.. 3·75

1994 (2 Nov). Centenary of New Zealand Cricket Council. Multicoloured covers as T **B21** showing illustration of father and son playing cricket.

SB71 $4.50 booklet containing pane of 10×45c.
(No. 1840a) (horiz format).......................... 6·50
    a. Vert format with additional slotted tab
       at top.. 9·00

 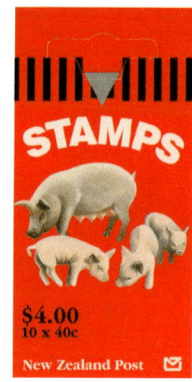

B23   B23a

1995 (1 Sept). Black and bright royal blue cover, 50×99 mm, as T **B23** inscribed 'airPOST INTERNATIONAL'.

SB74 $5 booklet containing pane of 5×$1
and five labels (No. 1645a) inserted
sideways in the cover.................................. 17·00

1995 (1 Sept–2 Oct). Farmyard Animals. Multicoloured covers, 51×99 mm, as T **B23a** showing illustration of Sow and Piglets.

SB75 $4 booklet containing pane of 10×40c.
(No. 1894a) inserted sideways in the
cover (2.10)... 5·50
SB76 $4.50 booklet containing pane of 10×45c.
(No. 1904a) inserted sideways in the
cover... 5·50

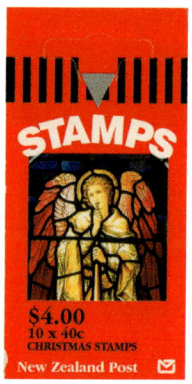

B23b

1995 (9 Nov). Christmas. Multicoloured cover, 51×100 mm, as T **B23b** showing illustration of Angel holding trumpet.

SB77 $4 booklet containing pane of 10×40c.
(No. 1923a)... 4·00

B22   B22a

1995 (22 Mar). Environment. Bright red and black cover, 51×101 mm, as T **B22** showing multicoloured illustration of backpackers.

SB72 $4.50 booklet containing pane of 10×45c.
(No. 1865a) inserted sideways in the
vertical cover.. 6·00

1995 (26 July). Centenary of Rugby League. Multicoloured cover, 51×99 mm, as T **B22a** showing New Zealand and Australian Players.

SB73 $4.50 booklet containing pane of 10×45c.
(No. 1892a)... 3·00

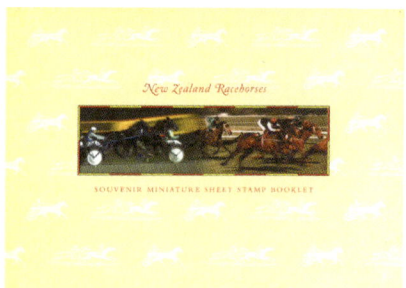

B24 (*Illustration reduced. Actual size 166×110 mm*)

1996 (24 Jan). Famous Racehorses. Multicoloured cover as T **B24** showing illustrations of harness and horse races.

SB78 $13.40 booklet containing seven miniature
sheets (Nos. **MS**1951(a)/**MS**1951(g))..... 14·00

Stamp Booklets NEW ZEALAND

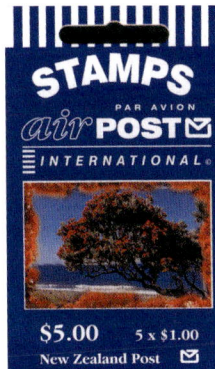

B24a   B25

1996 (21 Feb). Seaside Environment. Multicoloured cover, 50×100 mm, as T **B24a** but vert, showing illustration of seashore.
SB79 $4 booklet containing pane of 10×40c.
         (No. 1958a)... 5·00

1996 (7 Aug). Seaside Environment. Multicoloured cover as No. SB79, but 58×78 mm. Self-adhesive.
SB80 $4 booklet containing pane of 10×40c.
         (No. 1968a)... 4·50

1996 (7 Aug)–**99**. Multicoloured cover, 60×99 mm, as T **B25** showing illustration of Pohutukawa tree. New Zealand Post and logo in white on ultramarine background. Self-adhesive.
SB81 $5 booklet containing pane of 5×$1 (No.
         1991a)... 5·00
     a. New Zealand Post and logo redrawn
        larger in black and red on white panel
        (2.99).. 4·50

1996 (13 Nov)–**2000**. Multicoloured cover, 59×78 mm, as T **B26b** inscr 'fastPOST' with illustration of Doubtful Sound. Self-adhesive.
SB84 $8 booklet containing pane of 10×80c.
         (No. 1990a) incorporating ten half-
         width fastPOST labels on the inner
         cover... 8·00
     a. Incorporating ten full width fastPOST
        labels with barcode on inner cover
        (1.99).. 8·50
     ab. No stamps on first panel, two stamps
        on last panel. Correction to extra large
        envelope size on first panel (12.99)......... 10·00
     ac. Layout as above, extra large envelope
        size information shown correctly
        (8.2000).. 10·00

No. SB84a also shows New Zealand Post and logo redrawn larger.
On Nos. SB84/SB84a there are two stamps on the first panel and none on the last.
No. SB84ab (1 kiwi printing) shows the incorrect extra large envelope size obliterated by a black bar with a correction beneath.
No. SB84ac (2 or 3 kiwi printings) shows the extra large envelope size printed correctly.
The 3 kiwi printing includes increases for some rates in the first panel.

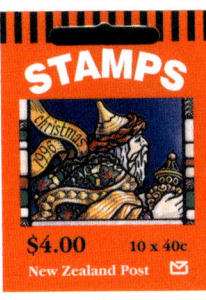
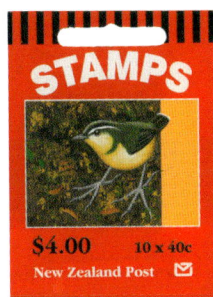

B26   B26a

1996 (4 Sept). Christmas. Multicoloured cover, 58×78 mm as T **B26** showing illustration of King. Self-adhesive.
SB82 $4 booklet containing pane of 10×40c.
         (No. 2027a)... 4·25

1996 (2 Oct). Extinct Birds. Multicoloured cover, 58×79 mm, as T **B26a** showing illustration of Stout-legged Wren. Self-adhesive.
SB83 $4 booklet containing pane of 10×40c.
         (No. 2035a)... 4·75

B27 (Illustration reduced. Actual size 166×110 mm)

1997 (19 Mar). New Zealand Vineyards. Multicoloured cover as T **B27**.
SB85 $13.40 booklet containing seven miniature
         sheets (Nos. **MS**2063(a)/**MS**2063(g))..... 11·00

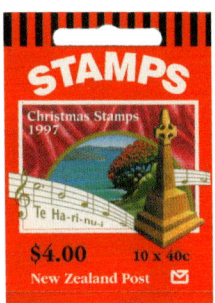

B27a   B27b

1997 (19 Mar). Curious Letter Boxes. Multicoloured cover, 58×79 mm, as T **B27a**, showing letter box. Self-adhesive.
SB86 $4 booklet containing pane of 10×40c.
         (No. 2064a)... 4·50

1997 (3 Sept). Christmas. Multicoloured cover, 59×78 mm, as T **B27b**, showing illustration of Memorial Cross, Pohutukawa, and Bay of Islands. Self-adhesive.
SB87 $4 booklet containing pane of 10×40c.
         (No. 2103a)... 2·75

NEW ZEALAND Stamp Booklets

 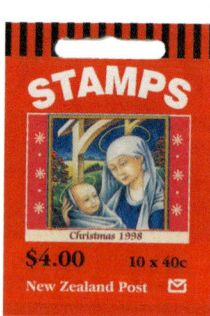

B27c   **B27d**

1997 (1 Oct). Insects. Multicoloured cover, 59×79 mm, as T **B27c** showing illustration of Grasshopper's head. Self-adhesive.
SB88 $4 booklet containing pane of 10×40c.
(No. 2104a) .... 3·50

1998 (14 Jan)–**2001**. Multicoloured (background vermilion) cover, 58×79 mm, as T **B27d** showing New Zealand scenery. Self-adhesive.
SB89 $4 booklet containing pane of 10×40c.
(No. 1984ba) (Motoring Guide advertisement on inner cover) .... 3·25
   a. Background of cover deep rose-red (Scenic Skies presentation pack advertisement on inner cover) (8.98) .... 3·25
   ab. Town Icons presentation pack advertisement on inner cover (5.99) ..... 3·25
   ac. U-BIX Rugby Super 12 Championship stamp packs advertisement on inner cover (10.6.99) .... 3·25
   aca. Stamps printed on backing paper .... 60·00
   ad. Stamp Focus advertisement on inner cover (5.2000) .... 3·75
   ae. Stamp Hunters advertisement on inner cover (6.2000) .... 3·75
   af. New Zealand Stamp Collection 2000 advertisement on inner cover (20.2.2001) .... 4·25
   ag. Threatened Birds presentation pack advertisement on inner cover (20.2.2001) .... 4·25

Nos. SB89a/SB89ac also show New Zealand and logo redrawn larger.
Nos. SB89ad/SB89ae, but not Nos. SB89af/SB89ag, omit the black border to the central star-shaped cut out on the front cover.
For explanation of No. SB89aca see after Nos. 1984/1991.

B28a   **B28b**

1998 (15 Apr). Stay in Touch Greetings Stamps. Multicoloured cover, 60×96 mm, as T **B28a** showing couple on beach. Self-adhesive.
SB91 $4 booklet containing pane of 10×40c.
(No. 2148a) .... 2·75

1998 (2 Sept). Christmas. Multicoloured cover, 58×79 mm, as T **B28b** showing illustration of Virgin Mary and Christ Child. Self-adhesive.
SB92 $4 booklet containing pane of 10×40c.
(No. 2195a) .... 2·75

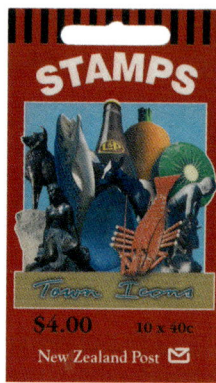 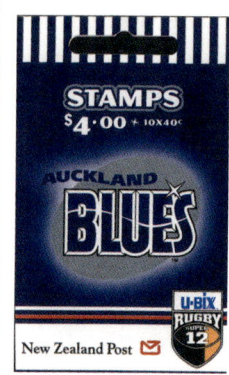

B28c   **B29**

1998 (7 Oct). Town Icons. Multicoloured cover, 60×100 mm, as T **B28c**, showing illustration of town symbols. Self-adhesive.
SB93 $4 booklet containing *se-tenant* pane of 10×40c. (No. 2196a) .... 2·75

1999 (7 Apr). New Zealand U-Bix Rugby Super 12 Championship. Multicoloured covers, 60×96 mm, as T **B29** showing team logos. Self-adhesive.
SB94 $4 booklet containing pane of 10×40c.
(No. 2258a) (Type **B29**) .... 2·25
SB95 $4 booklet containing pane of 10×40c.
(No. 2260a) (Chiefs) .... 2·25
SB96 $4 booklet containing pane of 10×40c.
(No. 2262a) (Wellington Hurricanes) ..... 2·25
SB97 $4 booklet containing pane of 10×40c.
(No. 2264a) (Canterbury Crusaders) ...... 2·25
SB98 $4 booklet containing pane of 10×40c.
(No. 2266a) (Otago Highlanders) .... 2·25

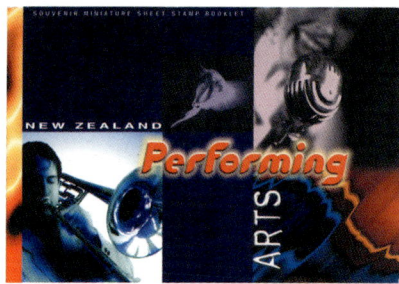

B28 (*Illustration reduced. Actual size 164×110 mm*)

1998 (14 Jan). Performing Arts. Multicoloured cover as T **B28** showing illustration of performers.
SB90 $13.40 booklet containing seven miniature sheets (Nos. **MS**2130(a)/**MS**2130(g)) ..... 10·00

B30 (*Illustration reduced. Actual size 168×110 mm*)

Stamp Booklets NEW ZEALAND

1999 (28 July). Scenic Walks. Multicoloured cover as T **B30** showing illustration of man reading map.
SB99 $13.40 booklet containing seven miniature sheets (Nos. **MS**2285(a)/**MS**2285(g)) ..... 10·00

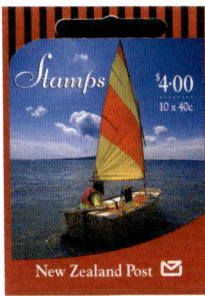 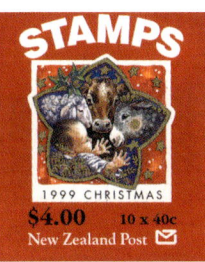

B31 Optimist Sailing Dinghy   **B32** Baby Jesus with Animals

1999 (20 Oct). Yachting. Multicoloured cover, 58×78 mm, as T **B31**. Self-adhesive.
SB100 $4 booklet containing pane of 10×40c. (No. 2303a) .... 2·25

1999 (1 Nov). Christmas. Multicoloured cover, 59×79 mm, as T **B32**. Self-adhesive.
SB101 $4 booklet containing pane of 10×40c. (No. 2294a) .... 2·25

B32a   **B32b**

2000 (3 Apr). Multicoloured (background ultramarine) cover, 59×88 mm, as T **B32a** showing Kaikoura Coast. Self-adhesive.
SB102 $5.50 booklet containing pane of 5×$1.10 (No. 1991bba) .... 4·50

2000 (3 Apr). New Zealand Life (2nd series). Bright red and black cover, 59×79 mm, as T **B32b**, showing Kiwi with envelope. Self-adhesive.
SB103 $4 booklet containing se-tenant pane of 10×40c. (No. 2318a) .... 2·75

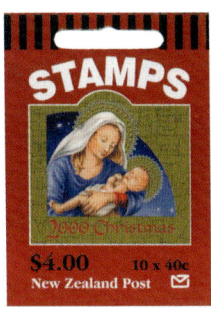 

B32c   **B34** Bungy Jumping

2000 (1 Nov). Christmas. Multicoloured cover, 58×78 mm, as T **B32c** showing Madonna and Child. Self-adhesive.
SB105 $4 booklet containing pane of 10×40c. (No. 2359a) .... 2·25

2001 (4 July). Tourism Centenary. Multicoloured covers as T **B34**. Self-adhesive.
SB106 $4 booklet containing pane of 10×40c. stamps (5×2) (No. 2431b) (cover Type **B34**, 58×79 mm) .... 3·00
SB107 $7.50 booklet containing pane of 5×$1.50 stamps (No. 2433a) and five air post international labels (cover 58×88 mm showing Sea kayaking in Abel Tasman National Park).. 4·00
SB108 $9 booklet containing pane of 10×90c. stamps (5×2) (No. 2432a) (cover 58×79 mm showing sightseeing from Mount Alfred) .... 5·00

No. SB106 and SB108 each include ten fastpost self-adhesive labels on the inner cover.

B34a   **B35** Gandalf (Sir Ian McKellen)

2001 (7 Nov). Christmas. Multicoloured cover, 58×78 mm, as T **B34a** showing Madonna, Child and Angels. Self-adhesive.
SB109 $4 booklet containing pane of 10×40c. (No. 2445b).. 3·00

2001 (4 Dec). Making of *The Lord of the Rings* Film Trilogy (1st issue). *The Fellowship of the Ring*. Multicoloured cover, 61×96 mm, as T **B35**. Self-adhesive.
SB110 $9 booklet containing se-tenant pane of ten (No. 2464b)............................... 7·00

 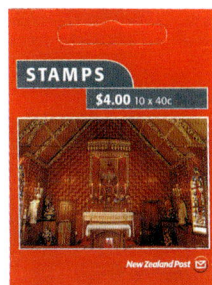

B36 Tongaporutu Cliffs, Taranaki   **B37** Altar, St Werenfrieds Church, Tokaanu

2002 (3 July)–**2003**. Coastlines. Multicoloured covers as T **B36**, each repeating the design of the contents.
SB111 $4 booklet containing pane of 10×40c. (No. 2516b) (cover 58×78 mm) .... 2·25
         a. Containing pane No. 2516ca (Perf 11) (27.5.2003) .... 3·25
SB112 $9 booklet containing pane of 10×90c. (No. 2517b) (cover 58×88 mm) .... 5·50
SB113 $7.50 booklet containing pane of 5×$1.50, (No. 2518b) (cover 58×78 mm) .... 7·00

2002 (4 Sept). Christmas. Church Interiors. Multicoloured cover, 58×78 mm, as T **B37**. Self-adhesive.
SB114 $4 booklet containing pane of 10×40c. (No. 2530ab) .... 3·00

NEW ZEALAND Stamp Booklets

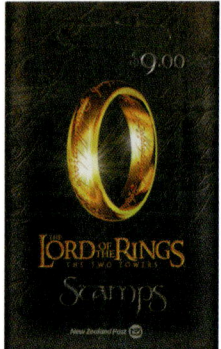 

B37a   **B38** Arrowtown

2002 (4 Dec). Making of *The Lord of the Rings* Film Trilogy (2nd issue). *The Two Towers*. Multicoloured cover, 60×96 mm, as T **B37a** showing the Ring. Self-adhesive.
SB115 $9 booklet containing pane of ten (No. 2556b)... 7·00

2003 (7 May). New Zealand Landscapes. Multicoloured cover, 59×90 mm, as T **B38**. Self-adhesive.
SB116 $7.50 booklet containing pane of 5×$1.50, (No. 2614a)... 7·50

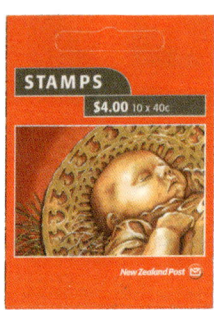

B39 Christ Child in Crib

2003 (1 Oct). Christmas. Decorations. Multicoloured covers, 59×78 mm, as T **B39**, each repeating the design of the contents. Self-adhesive.
SB117 $4 booklet containing pane of 10×40c. (No. 2649b).. 4·00
SB118 $8 booklet containing pane of 8×$1 (No. 2650a) and pane of eight International Economy labels............................. 7·00

B39a   **B40** Hamadryas Baboon

2003 (5 Nov). Making of *The Lord of the Rings* Film Trilogy (3rd issue). *The Return of the King*. Multicoloured cover as 61×95 mm, as T **B39a** showing Gandalf and other horsemen on journey. Self-adhesive.
SB119 $9 booklet containing pane of ten (No. 2658b)... 10·50

2004 (28 Jan). Zoo Animals. Multicoloured cover, 59×79 mm, as T **B40**. Self-adhesive.
SB120 $4 booklet containing pane of 10×40c. (No. 2671ab).. 5·00

B41 Stamps and Tory Channel, Marlborough Sounds   **B41a** Kaikoura

2004 (28 Jan). Multicoloured cover, 58×83 mm, as T **B41**. Self-adhesive.
SB121 $4.40 booklet containing pane of 4×10c. and 10×40c. (No. 1983aab)................. 6·00

2004 (22 Mar). New Zealand Landscapes. Multicoloured cover, 58×79 mm, as T **B41a**. Self-adhesive.
SB122 $4.50 booklet containing pane of 10×45c. (No. 2611a)... 5·50

No. SB122 was re-issued as a one kiwi reprint on 3rd September 2004, two kiwi reprint in March 2005, three and four kiwi reprints both on 20 October 2005, five kiwi reprint in April 2006, six kiwi reprint on 26 September 2006 and seven kiwi reprint on 11 January 2007.

The six and seven kiwi reprints show minor variations in the text on the back covers.

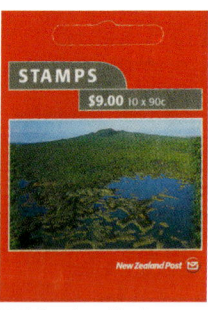 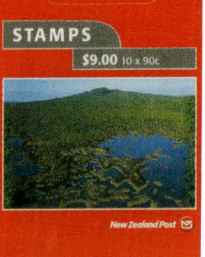

B41b Rangitoto Island   **B42** Aragorn, Legolas, Gimli and Gandalf the White

2004 (5 Apr). New Zealand Scenery. Multicoloured cover, 58×79 mm, as T **B41b**. Self-adhesive.
SB123 $9 booklet containing pane of 10×90c. (1990ba)... 8·00

No. SB123 was re-issued as a one kiwi reprint on 3rd May 2005 and as a two kiwi reprint on 19 May 2006.

The two kiwi reprint shows minor variations in the text on the back cover.

2004 (7 July). Making of *The Lord of the Rings* Film Trilogy (4th issue). *Home of Middle Earth*. Multicoloured cover, 58×79 mm, as T **B42**. Self-adhesive.
SB124 $6.30 booklet containing pane of ten stamps (No. 2723ba)................................ 6·00

Stamp Booklets NEW ZEALAND

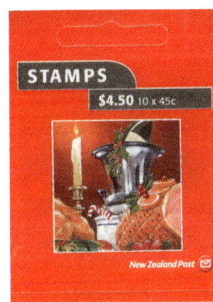

B43 Christmas Dinner   **B43a**

2004 (4 Oct). Christmas. Multicoloured covers, 59×78 mm, as T **B43**. Self-adhesive.
SB125	$4.50 booklet containing pane of 10×45c. (No. 2747a) (cover Type **B43**)	4·00
SB126	$8 booklet containing pane of 8×$1 (No. 2749a) and pane of eight International Economy labels (cover showing Christmas cake and cards)	7·00

2005 (12 Jan). Farmyard Animals and Chinese New Year. Year of the Rooster. Multicoloured cover, 59×79 mm, as T **B43a**. Self-adhesive.
SB127	$4.50 booklet containing pane of 10×45c. (No. 2763a)	5·00

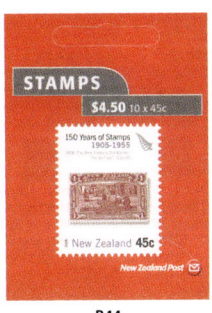

B44   **B45** Baby Jesus

2005 (6 Apr). 150th Anniversary of New Zealand Stamps (2nd issue). Stamps of 1905–1955. Multicoloured covers, 58×78 mm, as T **B44**. Self-adhesive.
SB128	$4.50 booklet containing pane of 10×45c. (No. 2783ba)	5·00
SB129	$9 booklet containing pane of 10×90c. (No. 2784ba)	8·00

2005 (5 Oct–2 Nov). Christmas. Multicoloured covers, 58×78 mm, as T **B45**. Self-adhesive.
SB130	$4.50 booklet containing pane of 10×45c. (No. 2825a) (2.11) (cover Type **B45**)	4·50
SB131	$10 booklet containing pane of 10×$1 (No. 2826a) and pane of ten International Economy labels (cover showing gifts on straw)	8·50

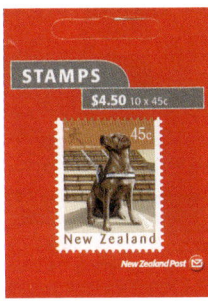
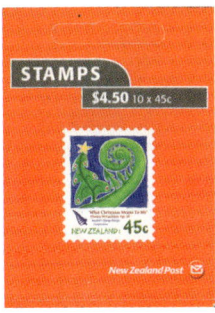

B46 Labrador Retriever Guide Dog   **B47** Decorated Silver Fern (Hanna McLachlan)

2006 (4 Jan). Chinese New Year. Year of the Dog. Multicoloured covers, 57×78 mm, as T **B46**. Self-adhesive.
SB132	$4.50 booklet containing pane of 10×45c. (No. 2847a)	5·00

2006 (4 Oct). Christmas. Multicoloured covers, as T **B47**. Self-adhesive.
SB133	$4.50 booklet containing pane of 10×45c. (No. 2915a) (cover Type **B47**, 58×79 mm)	5·00
SB134	$13.50 booklet containing pane of 10×$1.50, (No. 2916a), ten International Air and ten International Economy labels (cover 58×83 mm showing stamp No. 2916)	14·00

No. SB134 was sold at $13.50, providing a discount of $1.50 off the face value of the stamps.

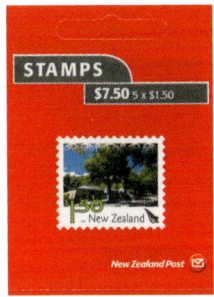
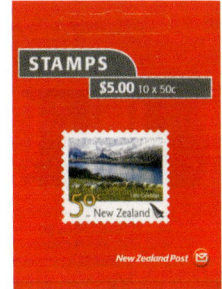

B48   **B49**

2007 (27 Mar)–**2009**. New Zealand Landscapes. Multicoloured cover, 59×78 mm, as T **B48** showing stamp No. 2614. Self-adhesive.
SB135	$7.50 booklet containing pane of 5×$1.50, (No. 2614ba), five International Economy and five International Air labels	10·00
	a. Containing pane No. 2614ca (ordinary paper) (2.3.2009)	10·00
	b. Containing pane No. 2614d (18.5.2009)	10·00
	c. Containing pane No. 2614e (30.10.2009)	7·50

No. SB135 was issued as a one kiwi reprint of No. SB116, but the cover and contents are different.
No. SB135 was re-issued as a two kiwi reprint on 19 November 2007, a three kiwi reprint on 8 July 2008, and a four kiwi reprint on 19 November. The two and three kiwi printings have minor variations to the text on the back cover. The three and four kiwi printings have RRP and (Recommended Retail Price) added to the inscriptions on the front cover.
Nos. SB135a/SB135c all have RRP and (Recommended Retail Price) added to the inscriptions on the front cover.
No. SB135c was issued as one and two kiwi reprints, both on 30 October 2009, a three kiwi reprint in March 2010 and four kiwi reprint on 2 July 2010.

2007 (9 May). New Zealand Landscapes. Multicoloured covers, 59×78 mm, as T **B49** each showing the stamp contained in the booklet. Self-adhesive.
SB136	$5 booklet containing pane of 10×50c. (No. 2612a)	6·25
SB137	$10 booklet containing pane of 10×$1 (No. 2613a)	12·50

No. SB136 was re-issued as a one kiwi reprint on 3 March 2008, a two kiwi reprint on 19 June 2008 and a three kiwi reprint on 25 November 2008. Both the one and two kiwi reprints show variations to the table inside the front cover and the text on the back cover. The two and three kiwi printings have RRP and (Recommended Retail Price) added to the inscriptions on the front cover.
No. SB137 was issued as a one kiwi reprint on 12 December 2007, a two kiwi reprint on 3 March 2008, a three kiwi reprint on 2 July 2008, a four kiwi reprint on 19 November 2008 and a five kiwi reprint on 2 July 2010. The one, two, three and five kiwi printings show variations to the text on the back cover, and the two, three and five kiwi printings also to the table inside the front cover. The three, four and five kiwi printings have RRP and (Recommended Retail Price) added to the inscriptions on the front cover.

2007 (3 Oct). Christmas. Multicoloured covers as T **B47**. Self-adhesive.
SB138	$5 booklet containing pane of 10×50c. (No. 3001a) (cover 58×79 mm, showing stamp Type **675**)	5·50
SB139	$13.50 booklet containing pane of 10×$1.50, (No. 3002a), ten International Air and ten International Economy labels (cover, 58×83 mm, showing stamp No. 3002)	15·00

No. SB139 was sold at $13.50, providing a discount of $1.50 off the face value of the stamps.

NEW ZEALAND Stamp Booklets

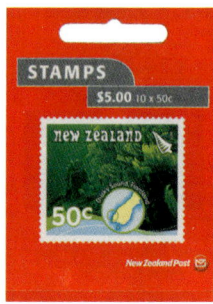
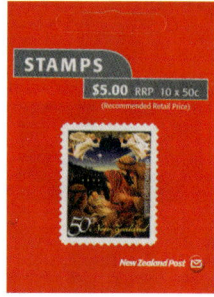

B51   **B52**

2008 (9 Jan). Underwater Reefs. Multicoloured covers, 59×78 mm, as T **B51**, each showing the stamp contained in the booklet. Self-adhesive.
SB140 $5 booklet containing pane of 10×50c.
         (No. 3018a) .... 9·00
SB141 $10 booklet containing pane of 10×$1 (No. 3019a) .... 15·00

2008 (1 Oct). Christmas. Multicoloured covers as T **B52**. Self-adhesive.
SB142 $5 booklet containing pane of 10×50c.
         (No. 3095a) (cover 58×78 mm, Type **B52**) .... 5·50
SB143 $15 booklet containing pane of 10×$1.50, (No. 3096a), ten International Air and ten International Economy labels (cover 58×83 mm, showing stamp No. 3096) .... 15·00

B53   **B54** Russell

2009 (4 Feb). New Zealand Champions of World Motorsport. Multicoloured covers, 58×78 mm, as T **B53**, each showing the stamp contained in the booklet. Self-adhesive.
SB144 $5 booklet containing pane of 10×50c.
         (No. 3122a) .... 9·00
SB145 $10 booklet containing pane of 10×$1 (No. 3123a) .... 15·00

2009 (1 July). New Zealand Landscapes. Multicoloured cover, 59×79 mm, as T **B54**. Self-adhesive.
SB146 $9 booklet containing pane of 5×$1.80
         (No. 3156a) .... 12·00
  No. SB146 was re-issued as a one kiwi reprint in February 2010 and as a two kiwi reprint in January 2011.

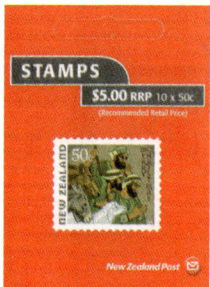

B55 State Highway 1 Road Sign   **B56** Three Shepherds

2009 (7 Sept). KiwiStamps. Multicoloured cover, 61×79 mm, as T **B55**. Self-adhesive.
SB147   ($5) booklet containing pane of ten
         KiwiStamps (No. 3162Ca) .... 9·00

2009 (7 Oct). Christmas. Multicoloured covers, 58×78 mm, as T **B56**. Self-adhesive.
SB148 $5 booklet containing pane of 10×50c.
         (No. 3175a) (cover Type **B56**) .... 7·50
SB149 $15 booklet containing pane of 10×$1.80 (No. 3176a) (green cover showing stamp No. 3174) .... 22·00
  No. SB149 was sold at $15, providing a discount of $3 off the face value of the stamps. The cover was inscr 'International Buy 10 pay $15 save $3'.

B57 Queenstown   **B58** New Zealand 1960 2d. Christmas Stamps

2010 (4 Aug). New Zealand Landscapes. Multicoloured covers, 59×79 mm, as T **B57**. Self-adhesive.
SB150 $9.50 booklet containing pane of 5×$1.90
         (No. 3233a) .... 13·00
SB151 $12 booklet containing pane of 10×$1.20
         (No. 3232a) .... 16·00
  No. SB150 was re-issued as one, two, three, four and five kiwi reprints. The one and two kiwi reprints were issued in 2011, the three kiwi in 2012 and the four and five kiwi reprints in 2013. The two, three, four and five kiwi reprints differ in the wording on the booklet pane about air service indicator stickers.

2010 (20 Oct). Christmas. Multicoloured covers, 58×79 mm, as T **B58**. Self-adhesive.
SB152 $5.40 booklet containing pane of 10×60c.
         (No. 3245a) (cover T **B58**) .... 9·00
SB153 $16 booklet containing pane of ten (No. 3246a) (green cover showing stamp No. 3242) .... 25·00

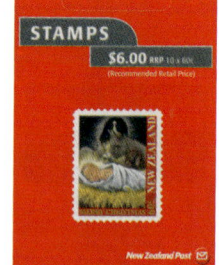

B59 Kiwi Road Sign   **B60** Baby Jesus in Manger

2011 (23 Mar). KiwiStamps. Multicoloured cover, 60×79 mm, as T **B59**. Self-adhesive.
SB154   ($6) booklet containing pane of ten
         KiwiStamps (No. 3269ba) .... 10·00
  No. SB154 was re-issued as one kiwi and two kiwi reprints. The table of required postage is upside down on the original and one kiwi printings only. A new printing by Southern Colour Print, issued in May 2014, had no kiwis. Subsequent Southern Colour Print booklets have one, two, three, four or five kiwis.

Stamp Booklets NEW ZEALAND

2011 (2 Nov). Christmas. Multicoloured covers, 58×79 mm, as T **B60**. Self-adhesive.
SB155 $6 booklet containing pane of 10×60c.
           (No. 3326ba) (cover Type **B60**)................ 12·00
SB156 $17.10 Booklet containing pane of 10×$1.90
           (No. 3327a) (blue cover showing
           stamp No. 3327)........................... 30·00
SB157 $21.60 booklet containing pane of 10×$2.40
           (No. 3328a) (blue cover showing
           stamp No. 3328)........................... 35·00

B61 Lake Rotorua   **B62** Stewart Island

2012 (1 Mar). New Zealand Landscapes. Multicoloured cover, 58×78 mm, as T **B61**. Self-adhesive.
SB158 $12 booklet containing pane of 5×$2.40
           (No. 3233*b*ba).................................. 17·00

No. SB158 was re-issued as a one kiwi reprint on 29 November 2012, a two kiwi reprint on 1 November 2013 and three and four kiwi reprints in 2015.

From 1 November 2013 reprint the stamps showed an imprint date of '2010' as opposed to the '2012' imprint of the original printings. The booklet cover was also amended to show the new imprint.

2012 (23 May). New Zealand Landscapes. Multicoloured covers, 59×79 mm, as T **B62**. Self-adhesive.
SB159 $10.50 booklet containing pane of 5×$2.10
           (No. 3367a) (Type **B62**)................. 16·00
SB160 $14 booklet containing pane of 10×$1.40
           (No. 3366a) (cover showing stamp No.
           3366).. 22·00

No. SB159 was re-issued as a one kiwi reprint on 10 May 2013 and a two kiwi reprint on 1 November 2013.

No. SB160 was re-issued as a one kiwi reprint on 10 April 2013 and a two kiwi reprint in 2015.

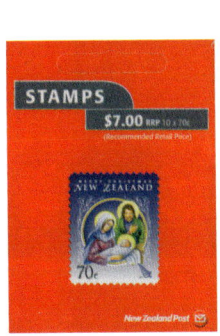 

B63 Mary, Joseph and Baby Jesus   **B64** Bilbo Baggins

2012 (3 Oct). Christmas. Multicoloured covers as T **B63**. Self-adhesive.
SB161 $7 booklet containing pane of 10×70c.
           (No. 3401a) (cover Type **B63**, 58×78
           mm) .... 11·00
SB162 $17.10 booklet containing pane of 10×$1.90,
           (No. 3402a), and ten International Air
           labels (blue cover showing stamp No.
           3402, 58×82 mm)........................... 30·00
SB163 $21.60 booklet containing pane of 10×$2.40,
           (No. 3403a), and ten International Air
           labels (blue cover showing stamp No.
           3403, 58×82 mm)........................... 35·00

No. SB162 was sold at $17.10, providing a discount of $1.90 off the face value of the stamps. The cover was inscr 'International $1.90 Buy 10 pay for 9'.

No. SB163 was sold at $21.60, providing a discount of $2.40 off the face value of the stamps. The cover was inscr 'International $2.40 Buy 10 pay for 9'.

2012 (1 Nov). *The Hobbit* (film trilogy). *An Unexpected Journey* (1st issue). Multicoloured cover, 60×95 mm, as T **B64**. Self-adhesive.
SB164 $14.90 booklet containing pane of ten stamps
           (No. 3417a)...................................... 25·00

B65 Poppy and Bugle

2013 (10 Apr). ANZAC (4th series). New Zealanders serving Abroad. Multicoloured cover, 165×110 mm, as T **B65**.
SB165 $19.90 booklet containing seven miniature
           sheets (Nos. **MS**3447(a)/**MS**3447(g))..... 35·00

B66 Giving Christmas Present

2013 (2 Oct). Christmas. Multicoloured covers as T **B66**. Self-adhesive.
SB166 $7 booklet containing pane of 10×70c.
           (No. 3509a) (cover 59×79 mm) .... 9·00
SB167 $17.10 booklet containing pane of 10×$1.90,
           (No. 3510a), and ten International Air
           labels (cover 59×82 mm, showing
           stamp No. 3510) .... 22·00
SB168 $21.60 booklet containing pane of 10×$2.40,
           (No. 3511a), and ten International Air
           labels (cover 59×82 mm, showing
           stamp No. 3511) .... 30·00

No. SB167 was sold at $17.10, providing a discount of $1.90 off the face value of the stamps. The cover was inscr 'International $1.90 Buy 10 pay for 9 For International sending (Australia and South Pacific only)'.

No. SB168 was sold at $21.60, providing a discount of $2.40 off the face value of the stamps. The cover was inscr 'International $2.40 Buy 10 pay for 9 For International sending'.

2013 (1 Nov). *The Hobbit* (film trilogy). *The Desolation of Smaug* (2nd issue). Multicoloured cover, 60×95 mm, as T **B64**. Self-adhesive.
SB169 $14.90 booklet containing pane of ten stamps
           (No. 3518a)...................................... 22·00

NEW ZEALAND Stamp Booklets

B67 Air Training Corps Recruit playing Bugle

 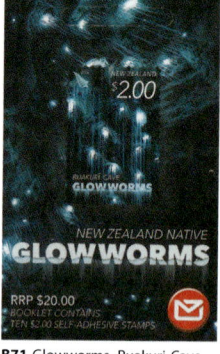

B70 Angel   **B71** Glowworms, Ruakuri Cave

2014 (2 Apr). ANZAC (5th series). World War II Poster Art. Multicoloured cover, 165×110 mm, as T **B67**.
SB170 $19.90 booklet containing seven miniature sheets (Nos. **MS**3547/**MS**3553) .... 35·00

2015 (4 Nov). Christmas. Multicoloured covers as T **B70**. Self-adhesive.
SB177 $8 booklet containing pane of 10×80c. (No. 3739a) (cover Type **B70**, 58×78 mm) .... 10·00
SB178 $18 booklet containing pane of 10×$2, (No. 3740a), and ten International Air labels (cover 58×82 mm, showing stamp No. 3740) .... 25·00
SB179 $22.50 booklet containing pane of 10×$2.50, (No. 3741a), and ten International Air labels (cover 58×82 mm, showing stamp No. 3741) .... 32·00

No. SB178 was sold at $18, providing a discount of $2 off the face value of the stamps. The cover was inscr 'International $2.00 Buy 10 pay for 9 For International sending (Australia & South Pacific only)'.

No. SB1795 was sold at $22.50, providing a discount of $2.50 off the face value of the stamps. The cover was inscr 'International $2.50 Buy 10 pay for 9 For International sending'.

2016 (2 Mar). New Zealand Native Glowworms (*Arachnocampa luminosa*). Multicoloured cover, 60×95 mm, as T **B71**. Self-adhesive.
SB180 $20 booklet containing pane of 10×$2 stamps (No. 3759a) .... 28·00

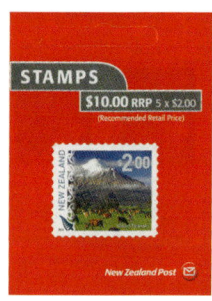 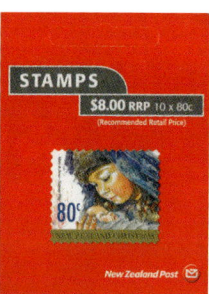

B68 Mount Taranaki   **B69** Mary and Jesus

2014 (7 May). New Zealand Landscapes. Multicoloured covers, 59×78 mm, as T **B68**. Self-adhesive.
SB171 $10 booklet containing pane of 5×$2, (No. 3560a), and two International Air labels (Type **B68**) .... 16·00
SB172 $12.50 booklet containing pane of 5×$2.50, (No. 3561a), and two International Air labels (cover showing stamp No. 3561)   20·00

No. SB172 was re-issued as one and two kiwi reprints in 2015.

No. SB173 was re-issued as one, two and three kiwi reprints in 2015, four kiwi reprint on 11 December 2015 and five kiwi reprint on 12 February 2016.

2014 (1 Oct). Christmas. Children in Nativity Play. Multicoloured covers as T **B69**. Self-adhesive.
SB173 $8 booklet containing pane of 10×80c. (No. 3619a) (cover 58×79 mm) .... 10·00
SB174 $18 booklet containing pane of 10×$2, (No. 3620a), and ten International Air labels (cover 58×82 mm, showing stamp No. 3620) .... 25·00
SB175 $22.50 booklet containing pane of 10×$2.50, (No. 3621a), and ten International Air labels (cover 58×82 mm, showing stamp No. 3621) .... 32·00

No. SB174 was sold at $18, providing a discount of $2 off the face value of the stamps. The cover was inscr 'International $2.00 Buy 10 pay for 9 For International sending (Australia & South Pacific only)'.

No. SB175 was sold at $22.50, providing a discount of $2.50 off the face value of the stamps. The cover was inscr 'International $2.50 Buy 10 pay for 9 For International sending'.

2014 (12 Nov). *The Hobbit* (film trilogy). *The Battle of the Five Armies* (3rd issue). Multicoloured cover, 60×95 mm, as T **B64**. Self-adhesive.
SB176 $15.60 booklet containing pane of ten stamps (No. 3630a) .... 22·00

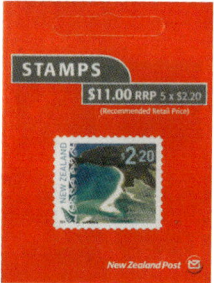 

B72 Awaroa Bay, Abel Tasman Scenic Reserve   **B73** Jesus in Manger

2016 (18 May). New Zealand Landscapes. Multicoloured covers, 58×78 mm, as T **B72**. Self-adhesive.
SB181 $11 booklet containing pane of 5×$2.20 (No. 3779a) (Type **B72**) .... 13·50
SB182 $13.50 booklet containing pane of 5×$2.70 (No. 3780a) (Vineyards, Marlborough). 17·00

2016 (2 Nov). Christmas. Self-adhesive. Multicoloured covers as T **B73**.
SB183 $10 booklet containing pane of 10×$1 (No. 3857a) (cover Type **B73**, 59×79 mm)...... 11·00
SB184 $19.80 booklet containing pane of 10×$2.20, (No. 3858a), and ten International Air labels (cover 59×82 mm, showing stamp No. 3858) .... 22·00
SB185 $24.30 booklet containing pane of 10×$2.70, (No. 3859a), and ten International Air labels (cover 57×82 mm, showing stamp No. 3859) .... 25·00

No. SB184 was sold at $19.80, providing a discount of $2.20 off the face value of the stamps. The cover was inscr 'International $2.20 Buy 10 pay for 9 For International sending (Australia & South Pacific only)'.

No. SB185 was sold at $24.30, providing a discount of $2.70 off the face value of the stamps. The cover was inscr 'International $2.70 Buy 10 pay for 9 For International sending'.

Stamp Booklets NEW ZEALAND

 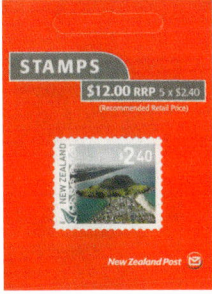

B74 Angel **B75** Mount Maunganui, Tauranga

2017 (1 Nov). Christmas. Quilled Christmas Decorations. Multicoloured covers as T **B74**. Self-adhesive.

SB186	$10 booklet containing pane of 10×$1 (No. 3934a) (cover Type **B74**, 58×78 mm)......	10·00
SB187	$19.80 booklet containing pane of 10×$2.20, (No. 3935a), and ten International Air labels (blue cover 57×82 mm, showing stamp No. 3935)..........................	22·00
SB188	$24.30 booklet containing pane of 10×$2.70, (No. 3936a), and ten International Air labels (blue cover 58×82 mm, showing stamp No. 3936)..........................	25·00

No. SB187 was sold at $19.80, providing a discount of $2.20 off the face value of the stamps. The cover was inscr 'International $2.20 Buy 10 pay for 9 For International sending (Australia & South Pacific only)'.
No. SB188 was sold at $24.30, providing a discount of $2.70 off the face value of the stamps. The cover was inscr 'International $2.70 Buy 10 pay for 9 For International sending'.

2018 (6 June). New Zealand Landscapes. Multicoloured cover, 58×78 mm, as T **B75**. Self-adhesive.

SB189	$12 booklet containing pane of 5×$2.40 (No. 3993a) (Type **B75**)................	10·00
SB190	$15 booklet containing pane of 5×$3 (No. 3994a) (Tongaporutu, Taranaki)	13·00

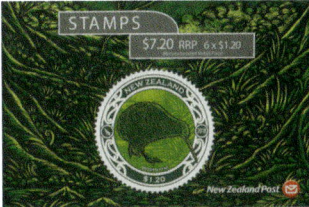

B76 Brown Kiwi Stamp and Woodland Floor

2018 (4 July). Round Kiwi Stamps. Multicoloured cover, 86×55 mm, as T **B76**. Self-adhesive.

SB191	$7.20 Booklet containing pane of six stamps (No. 3996a)...	7·00

 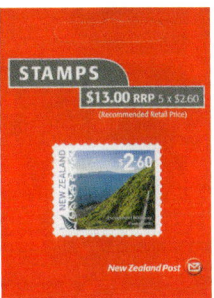

B77 Virgin Mary and Joseph and Mary holding Baby Jesus Stamps   **B78** Escarpment Walkway, Paekakariki

2018 (7 Nov). Christmas. Multicoloured covers as T **B77**. Self-adhesive.

SB192	$12 booklet containing pane of 10×$1.20 (No. 4037a) (cover Type **B77**, 58×78 mm)...	10·00
SB193	$21.60 booklet containing pane of 10×$2.40, (No. 4039a), and ten International Air labels (blue cover 57×82 mm, showing stamp No. 4039)............................	21·00
SB194	$27 booklet containing pane of 10×$3, (No. 4040a), and ten International Air labels (blue cover 58×82 mm, showing stamp No. 4040)............................	26·00

No. SB193 was sold at $21.60, providing a discount of $2.40 off the face value of the stamps. The cover was inscr 'International $2.40 Buy 10 pay for 9 For International sending (Australia & South Pacific only)'.
No. SB194 was sold at $27, providing a discount of $3 off the face value of the stamps. The cover was inscr 'International $3.00 Buy 10 pay for 9 For International sending'.

2019 (5 June). New Zealand Landscapes. Multicoloured cover, 58×78 mm, as T **B78**. Self-adhesive.

SB195	$13 booklet containing pane of 5×$2.60 (No. 4079a) (Type **B78**)................	11·00
SB196	$16.50 booklet containing pane of 5×$3.30 (No. 4080a) (Dunedin Railway Station).	14·00

B79 Madonna and Child and Joseph

2019 (6 Nov). Christmas. Multicoloured covers as T **B79**. Self-adhesive.

SB197	$13 booklet containing pane of 10×$1.30 (No. 4123a) (cover Type **B79**, 58×78 mm)...	13·50
SB198	$23.40 booklet containing pane of 10×$2.60, (No. 4125a), and ten International Air labels (blue cover 58×82 mm, showing stamp No. 4125)............................	30·00
SB199	$29.70 booklet containing pane of 10×$3.30, (No. 4126a), and ten International Air labels (blue cover 58×82 mm, showing stamp No. 4126)............................	35·00

No. SB198 was sold at $23.40, providing a discount of $2.60 off the face value of the stamps. The cover was inscr 'International $2.60 Buy 10 pay for 9 For International sending (Australia & South Pacific only)'.
No. SB199 was sold at $29.70, providing a discount of $3.30 off the face value of the stamps. The cover was inscr 'International $3.30 Buy 10 pay for 9 For International sending'.

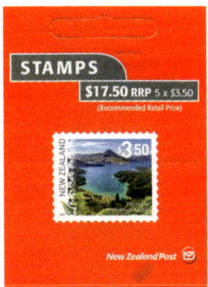

B80 Fitzroy Bay, Marlborough Sound

2020 (5 Aug). New Zealand Landscapes. Multicoloured covers, 58×78 mm, as T **B80**. Self-adhesive.

SB200	$17.50 booklet containing pane of 5×$3.50, (No. 4162a), and two International Air labels	19·00

The postcode of the Collectables and Solutions Centre, Whanganui, is incorrectly shown as 4540 instead of 4541 on the back cover.

NEW ZEALAND Stamp Booklets, Premium Booklets

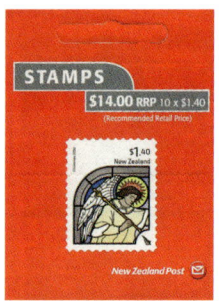 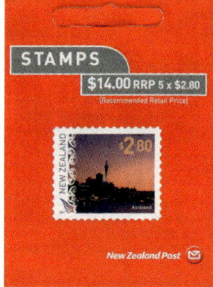

B81 Angel Gabriel (The Annunciation) **B82** Auckland

2020 (4 Nov). Christmas. Multicoloured covers as T **B81**. Self-adhesive.
SB201	$14 booklet containing pane of 10×$1.40 (No. 4185a) (cover Type **B81**, 58×78 mm)	16·00
SB202	$27 booklet containing pane of 10×$2.70, (No. 4186a), and ten International Air labels (blue cover 58×82 mm showing stamp No. 4186)	30·00
SB203	$35 booklet containing pane of 10×$3.50, (No. 4187a), and ten International Air labels (blue cover 58×82 mm showing stamp No. 4187)	38·00

2021 (2 June). New Zealand Landscapes. Multicoloured covers, 58×78 mm, as T **B82**. Self-adhesive.
SB204	$14 booklet containing pane of 5×$2.80 (No. 4210a) (Type **B82**)	15·00
SB205	$18 booklet containing pane of 5×$3.60 (No. 4211a) (Waikato River)	20·00

B83 Angel

2021 (3 Nov). Christmas. Multicoloured covers as T **B83**. Self-adhesive.
SB206	$15 booklet containing pane of 10×$1.50 (No. 4252a) (cover Type **B83**, 58×78 mm)	16·00
SB207	$28 booklet containing pane of 10×$2.80, (No. 4253a), and ten Air labels (cover 58×82 mm showing stamp No. 4253)	30·00
SB208	$36 booklet containing pane of 10×$3.60, (No. 4254a), and ten Air labels (cover 58×82 mm showing stamp No. 4254)	38·00

PREMIUM BOOKLETS

The following booklets were sold at a premium over the face value of the stamps. All are stitched and have text and illustrations on panes and interleaving pages. All (except No. SP12) measure 165×110 mm and are illustrated at one-third actual size.

P1 Ford Zephyr

2000 (1 June). On The Road. Motor Cars. Multicoloured cover as T **P1**. Stitched.
SP1	$14.95 booklet containing seven miniature sheet panes, six containing Nos. 2329/2334 as single stamps and the seventh containing all six designs	11·00

Face value: $13.60.

P2 de Havilland Tiger Moth

2001 (2 May). Aircraft. Multicoloured cover as T **P2**. Stitched.
SP2	$19.95 booklet containing seven miniature sheet panes, six containing Nos. 2408/2413 as single stamps and the seventh containing all six designs	17·00

Face value: $13.80.

P3

2002 (3 Apr). Architectural Heritage. Multicoloured cover as T **P3**. Stitched.
SP3	$16.95 booklet containing seven miniature sheet panes, six containing Nos. 2484/2489 as single stamps and the seventh containing all six designs	12·00

Face value: $13.80.

P4

2003 (2 Apr). New Zealand Military Uniforms. Multicoloured cover as T **P4**. Stitched.
SP4	$19.95 booklet containing five miniature sheet panes containing two examples each of Nos. 2577/2580, 2581/2584, 2585/2588, 2589/2592 and 2593/2596	22·00

Face value: $16.

P5 Heavy Horses Pulling Farm Equipment

2004 (5 Apr). Historic Farm Equipment. Multicoloured cover as T **P5**. Stitched.
SP5 $19.95 booklet containing six miniature sheet panes, five containing Nos. 2695/2699 as single stamps and the sixth containing all five designs............ 22·00
Face value: $12.40.

P8 Trifid Nebula

2007 (6 June). Southern Skies. Multicoloured cover as T **P8**. Stitched.
SP8 $19.90 booklet containing six miniature sheet panes, five containing Nos. 2957/2961 as single stamps and the sixth containing all five designs............ 20·00
Face value: $15.

P6 White-water Rafting

2004 (1 Dec). Extreme Sports. Multicoloured cover as T **P6**. Stitched.
SP6 $14.95 booklet containing six miniature sheet panes, five containing Nos. 2751/2755 as single stamps and the sixth containing all five designs............ 16·00
Face value: $12.40.

P9 Sapper John Luamanu and Baby Daughter, ANZAC Day Parade, 2007

2008 (2 Apr). ANZAC (1st series). Multicoloured cover as T **P9**. Stitched.
SP9 $19.90 booklet containing seven miniature sheet panes, six containing Nos. 3032/3037 as single stamps and the seventh containing all six designs.......... 27·00
Face value: $16.

P7 Street with Wrecked Car and Fallen Masonry

2006 (3 Feb). 75th Anniversary of the Hawke's Bay Earthquake. Grey, brownish grey and red cover as T **P7**. Stitched.
SP7 $19.95 booklet containing seven miniature sheet panes containing two examples each of Nos. 2848/2850, 2865/2867, 2851/2853, 2854/2855 (with two half stamp-size central labels), 2856, 2858 and 2863, 2857 and 2859/2860 and 2861/2862 and 2864.................... 24·00
Face value: $18.80.

P10 Guns and Transport under Simulated Attack by RNZAF Mosquito Aircraft, Final Manoeuvres, Waiouru, 1950

2009 (1 Apr). ANZAC (2nd series). Comrades in Arms. Multicoloured cover as T **P10**. Booklet contains text and illustrations on interleaving pages. Stitched.
SP10 $19.90 booklet containing seven miniature sheet panes, six containing Nos. 3131/3136 as single stamps and the seventh containing all six designs.......... 28·00
Face value: $16
Stamps from booklet No. SP10 are all perforated 14.

NEW ZEALAND Premium Booklets

P11 Carillon Dedication, 25 April 1932

2010 (7 Apr). ANZAC (3rd series). Remembrance. Black, grey and red cover as T **P11**. Booklet contains text and illustrations on interleaving pages. Stitched.

SP11 $19.90 booklet containing seven miniature sheet panes, six containing Nos. 3199/3204 as single stamps and the seventh containing all six designs.......... 32·00

Face value: $17.80

Stamps from booklet No. SP11 are all perforated 14.

P13 Melville Mirfin

2014 (29 July). Centenary of the First World War (1st issue). Grey-black and gold cover, 105×180 mm, as T **P13**. Booklet contains text and illustrations on interleaving pages.

SP13 $39.90 booklet containing Nos. 3592/3601 in panes of single stamps and Nos. 3592/3597 and 3600/3601 in se-tenant panes... 60·00

Face value: $27.60

2015 (23 Mar). Centenary of the First World War (2nd issue). 1915 The Spirit of ANZAC. Grey-black and gold cover, 105×180 mm, as T **P13**. but inscr '1915 THE SPIRIT OF ANZAC NEW ZEALAND'S STORY'. Booklet contains text and illustrations on panes and interleaving pages.

SP14 $39.90 booklet containing Nos. 3663/3672 in panes of single stamps and in se-tenant panes.................................... 60·00

Face value: $27.60

2016 (6 Apr). Centenary of the First World War (3rd issue). 1916 Courage and Commitment. Grey-black, grey and gold cover, 104×179 mm, as T **P13**. but inscr '1916 COURAGE & COMMITMENT NEW ZEALAND'S STORY'. Booklet contains text and illustrations on panes and interleaving pages.

SP15 $39.90 booklet containing Nos. 3760/3769 in panes of single stamps and in se-tenant panes.................................... 60·00

Face value: $27.60

P12

2012 (15 Mar). 75th Anniversary of the RNZAF (Royal New Zealand Air Force). Deep blue cover with silver inscription, 150×150 mm, as T **P12**. Booklet contains text and illustrations on interleaving pages.

SP12 $19.90 booklet containing eight miniature sheet panes as follows: Nos. 3341/3342, each×2; Nos. 3343/3344, each×2; Nos. 3345/3346, each×2; Nos. 3347/3348, each×2; Nos. 3349/3350, each×2; Nos. 3351/3352, each×2; Nos. 3353 and 3355, each×2; No. 3354×2 ..... 32·00

Face value: $18

1917 (5 Apr). Centenary of the First World War (4th issue). 1917 The Darkest Hour. Grey-black, grey and gold cover, 105×180 mm, as T **P13**. but inscr '1917 THE DARKEST HOUR NEW ZEALAND'S STORY'. Booklet contains text and illustrations on panes and interleaving pages.

SP16 $39.90 booklet containing Nos. 3879/3888 in panes of single stamps and in se-tenant panes.................................... 60·00

Face value: $31.60

2018 (4 Apr). Centenary of the First World War (5th issue). 1918 Back from the Brink. Deep brown and gold cover, 105×180 mm, as T **P13**. but inscr '1918 BACK FROM THE BRINK NEW ZEALAND'S STORY'. Booklet contains text and illustrations on panes and interleaving pages.

SP17 $39.90 booklet containing Nos. 3964/3973 in panes of single stamps and in se-tenant panes.................................... 60·00

Face value: $31.60

Premium Booklets, Express Delivery Stamps, Official Stamps — NEW ZEALAND

P14 Kiwi Cribb, David McClutchie, Whiwhi Winiata, Repoma Thompson and Dick Huata of 28th (Maori) Battalion driving through Sora, Italy, 3 June 1944

2020 (1 Apr). 75th Anniversary of the End of World War II. Grey, black and yellow cover, 150×150 mm, as T **P14**. Booklet contains text and illustrations on interleaving pages.
SP18 $39.90 booklet containing the stamp designs from No. **MS**4149 in 15 miniature sheet panes of two stamps .... 60·00

Face value: $39

EXPRESS DELIVERY STAMPS

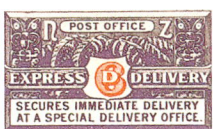

E1

(Typo Govt Printing Office, Wellington)

1903 (9 Feb). Value in first colour. W **43** (sideways). Perf 11.
E1   E1   6d. red and violet .... 42·00   25·00

1926–36. Thick, white, opaque chalk-surfaced Cowan paper. W **43**.
(a) Perf 14×14½.
E2   E1   6d. vermilion and bright violet .... 55·00   28·00
        w. Wmk inverted £300
(b) Perf 14×15 (1936).
E3   E1   6d. carmine and bright violet .... 75·00   65·00

1937–39. Thin, hard, chalk-surfaced Wiggins Teape paper.
(a) Perf 14×14½.
E4   E1   6d. carmine and bright violet .... £110   55·00
(b) Perf 14×15 (4.39).
E5   E1   6d. vermilion and bright violet £180   £400

E2 Express Mail Delivery Van

(Des J. Berry. Eng Stamp Ptg Office, Melbourne. Recess Govt Ptg Office, Wellington)

1939 (16 Aug). W **43**. Perf 14.
E6   E2   6d. violet .... 1·75   2·75
        w. Wmk inverted .... 90·00

No. E6 was withdrawn on 30 June 1948, when the Express Delivery Service ceased.

OFFICIAL STAMPS

1891 (Dec)–**1906**. Contemporary issues handstamped 'O.P.S.O.' in 3½ mm capital letters.
(a) Stamps of 1873 type optd in violet. Perf 12½.
O1   3   ½d. pale dull rose (W **4**) (No. 149) .... —   £1600
O2   ½d. bright rose (W **12b**) (No. 151) .... —   £1200
*(b) Stamps of 1882–1897 optd in rose/magenta. W **12b**.*
O3   13   ½d. black (Perf 10) (No. 217) .... —   £1000
        a. Violet opt .... —   £1300
O4   ½d. black (Perf 10×11) (No. 227) .... —   £1000

O5   1d. rose (Perf 12×11½) (No. 195b) .... —   £1000
        a. Violet opt .... —   £1000
O6   1d. rose (Perf 10) (violet opt) (No. 218)   —   —
O7   1d. rose (Perf 11) (No. 237) .... —   £1000
        a. Violet opt .... —   —
O8   2d. purple (Perf 11) (No. 238) .... —   £1300
        a. Violet opt .... —   —
O9   2d. mauve-lilac (Perf 10) (No. 219) ..... —   £1300
        a. Advert on back (3rd setting) .... —   —
        b. Violet opt .... —   £1500
        ba. Advert on back
O10   2½d. blue (Perf 12×11½) (violet opt) (No. 197) .... —   —
O11   2½d. blue (Perf 11) (violet opt) (No. 239)   —   £1300
O12   2½d. ultramarine (Perf 10) (No. 220) ..... —   £1300
        a. Advert on back .... —   —
        b. Violet opt .... —   —
        ba. Green advert (2nd setting) .... —   —
        bb. Mauve advert (3rd setting) .... —   —
O13   2½d. ultramarine (Perf 10×11) (No. 230)   —   £1300
        a. Violet opt .... —   —
O14   5d. olive-black (Perf 12×11½) (No. 200) .... —   £1500
        a. violet opt .... —   —
O15   6d. brown (Perf 12½×11½) (No. 201) ..... —   £1800
(c) Stamps of 1898–1903 optd in violet. Perf 11
(i) No wmk.
O16   ½d. green (Perf 14) (No. 294) .... —   £1000
        a. Rose or magenta opt .... —   —
O17   2½d. blue (Perf 12–16) (No. 249) .... —   £1200
O18   2½d. blue (No. 260) .... —   £1000
        a. Rose or magenta opt .... —   —
O19   4d. indigo and brown (No. 262) .... —   £1200
O20   5d. purple-brown (No. 263) .... —   £1200
        a. Rose or magenta opt .... —   —
        b. Greenish blue opt .... —   —
O21   8d. Indigo (No. 266) .... —   £1500
O22   1s. red (No. 268) .... —   £2500
*(ii) W **38**.*
O23   ½d. green (No. 273b) .... —   —
O24   1d. carmine (No. 278) .... —   £1000
        a. Blue opt .... —   —
*(iii) W **43** (sideways on 3d. 5d., 1s.).*
O25   ½d. green (Perf 14) (No. 302) .... —   —
        a. Rose or magenta opt .... —   —
O26   1d. carmine (Perf 14) (No. 303) .... —   £1000
        a. Green opt .... —   £1000
O27   1d. carmine (Perf 14) (No. 349) .... —   —
O28   1d. carmine (Perf 14) (No. 356) .... —   £1000
O29   1d. carmine (No. 357) (black opt) .... —   —
O30   2½d. blue (No. 308) .... —   £1000
O31   3d. yellow-brown (No. 309) .... —   £1200
O32   5d. red-brown (No. 311) .... —   —
O33   1s. orange-red (No. 315b) .... —   £2500
O34   2s. green (No. 316) .... —   £4500

The letters signify 'On Public Service Only' and stamps so overprinted were used exclusively at the General Post Office, Wellington, on official correspondence to foreign countries between December 1891 and 31 December 1906.

Four different handstamps were used, differing slightly in the length of the overprint. The handstamp was normally applied diagonally reading upwards but other positions are known.

The stamps were not available unused and such examples with the 'O.P.S.O.' handstamp are generally considered to be reprints.

OFFICIAL.

(O3)

1907–11. Stamps of 1902–1906 optd with T **O3** (vertically, upwards). W **43** (sideways on 3d., 6d., 1s. and 5s.). Perf 14.
O59   23   ½d. yellow-green .... 15·00   2·00
        a. Perf 11×14 .... £350   —
        b. Mixed perfs £350   £350
O60   42   1d. carmine (No. 303) (1.7.07*) .... 12·00   22·00
        a. Booklet pane of 6 .... 55·00
        ab. Imperf horiz (booklet pane of 6) ... £3750
O60b   1d. rose-carmine (Waterlow) (No. 352) ... 35·00   1·50
        ba. Perf 11×14 .... £750   £750
        bb. Mixed perfs £650   £650
        bc. Perf 14×11 .... £1500   £1500
O60c   1d. carmine (Royle) .... 80·00   1·50
        ca. Perf 11×14 .... £500   £750
        cb. Mixed perfs £375   £550
O61   41   2d. purple .... 20·00   2·50
        a. Bright reddish purple .... 15·00   2·25
        ab. Mixed perfs £550   £500
O63   28   3d. bistre-brown .... 50·00   2·75
        a. Mixed perfs .... —   £1800
O64   31   6d. bright carmine-pink .... £450   30·00

NEW ZEALAND Official Stamps

		a. Imperf vert (horiz pair)	£2250	
		b. Mixed perfs	£1200	£1000
		c. Opt inverted (reading downwards)	†	£5000
O65	**34**	1s. orange-red	£180	25·00
O66	**35**	2s. blue-green	£200	£140
		a. Imperf between (pair)	£4000	
		b. Imperf vert (horiz pair)	£2750	
		w. Wmk inverted	£1000	£600
O67	**36**	5s. deep red	£300	£275
		a. Wmk upright (1911)	£1500	£1600

* Though issued in 1907 a large quantity of booklets was mislaid and not utilised until they were found in 1930.

1908–09. Optd as T **O3**. W **43**.

O69	**23**	½d. green (Perf 14×15)	18·00	6·00
O70	**50**	1d. carmine (Perf 14×15)	70·00	4·50
O71	**48**	6d. pink (Perf 14×13, 13½)	£500	75·00
O72		6d. pink (Perf 14×15) (1909)	£600	60·00
O72*a*	**F4**	£1 rose-pink (Perf 14) (No. F89)	£1000	£850

1910. No. 387 optd with T **O3**.

O73	**51**	½d. yellow-green	15·00	1·00
		a. Opt inverted (reading downwards)	†	£4000

1910–16. Nos. 389 and 392/394 optd with T **O3**. Perf 14×14½.

O74	**52**	3d. chestnut	20·00	2·25
		a. Perf 14×13½ (1915)	£225	£180
		ab. Vert pair. Nos. O74/O74a	£500	£950
O75	–	6d. carmine	30·00	12·00
		a. Perf 14 (line) (No. 398)	†	£7500
		b. Deep carmine	35·00	12·00
		w. Wmk inverted		
O76	–	8d. indigo-blue (R.) (5.16)	18·00	30·00
		aw. Wmk inverted	£150	£100
		b. Perf 14×13½	20·00	30·00
		bw. Wmk inverted	£130	£100
		c. Vert pair, Nos. O76 and O76b	£100	£225
		cw. Wmk inverted	£300	£325
O77		1s. vermilion	75·00	35·00
O74/O77 *Set of 4*			£125	70·00

1910–26. Optd with T **O3**.

*(a) W **43**. De La Rue chalk-surfaced paper with toned gum.*

O78	**53**	1d. carmine (No. 405)	5·50	30
		a. 'Feather' flaw	75·00	18·00
		b. 'Globe' flaw	75·00	18·00
		c. 'Q' flaw	80·00	50·00
		y. Wmk inverted and reversed		

*(b) W **43**. Jones chalk-surfaced paper with white gum.*

O79	**53**	1d. deep carmine (No. 406) (1925)	18·00	12·00
		a. 'Feather' flaw	£180	95·00
		b. 'Globe' flaw	£180	95·00

(c) No wmk, but bluish 'NZ' and Star lithographed on back. Art paper.

O80	**53**	1d. rose-carmine (No. 409) (1925)	7·00	25·00
		a. 'Feather' flaw	75·00	
		b. 'Globe' flaw	75·00	

*(d) W **43**. Cowan thick, opaque, chalk-surfaced paper with white gum.*

O81	**53**	1d. deep carmine (No. 410) (1925)	10·00	1·50
		a. 'Feather' flaw	£100	40·00
		b. 'Globe' flaw	£100	40·00
		c. 'N' flaw	£200	£110
		x. Wmk reversed (1926)	75·00	45·00
		xa. 'Feather' flaw	£350	£350
		xb. 'Globe' flaw	£350	£350
		xc. 'N' flaw	£350	£350

1913–25. Postal Fiscal stamps optd with T **O3**.

(i) Chalk-surfaced De La Rue paper
(a) Perf 14 (1913–1914).

O82	**F4**	2s. blue (30.9.14)	75·00	50·00
O83		5s. yellow-green (13.6.13)	£110	£140
O84		£1 rose-carmine (1913)	£1100	£750
O82/O84 *Set of 3*			£1100	£850

(b) Perf 14½×14, comb (1915).

O85	**F4**	2s. deep blue (8.15)	80·00	50·00
		a. No stop after 'OFFICIAL' (R. 2/5)	£200	£160
O86		5s. yellow-green (1.15)	£120	£150
		a. No stop after 'OFFICIAL' (R. 2/5)	£325	£375

(ii) Thick, white, opaque chalk-surfaced Cowan paper. Perf 14½×14 (1925).

O87	**F4**	2s. blue	85·00	£100
		a. No stop after 'OFFICIAL' (R. 2/5)	£250	£300

The overprint on these last, and on Nos. O69 and O72*a* is from a new set of type, giving a rather sharper impression than T **O3**, but otherwise resembling it closely.

1915 (12 Oct)–**34**. Optd with T **O3**. Perf 14×15.

(a) On Nos. 435/440 (De La Rue chalk-surfaced paper with toned gum).

O88	**61**	½d. green	2·25	20
O89	**62**	1½d. grey-black (6.16)	9·00	3·50
O90	**61**	1½d. slate (12.16)	7·50	1·50
O91		1½d. orange-brown (4.19)	5·50	1·00
O92		2d. yellow (4.17)	10·00	50
O93		3d. chocolate (11.19)	18·00	1·75
O88/O93 *Set of 6*			45·00	7·50

(b) On Nos. 441 and 443 (Jones chalk-surfaced paper with white gum).

O94	**61**	½d. green (1924)	5·00	4·50
O95		3d. deep chocolate (1924)	55·00	9·50

(c) On Nos. 446/447 and 448a/449 (Cowan thick, opaque, chalk-surfaced paper with white gum).

O96	**61**	½d. green (1925)	2·50	20
		ax. Wmk reversed (1927)	£100	35·00
		ay. Wmk inverted and reversed (1927)	£400	£130
		b. Perf 14 (1929)	4·00	1·00
		ba. No stop after 'OFFICIAL'	45·00	40·00
O97		1½d. orange-brown (Perf 14) (1929)	25·00	35·00
		a. No stop after 'OFFICIAL'	£130	£130
		b. Perf 14×15 (1934)	60·00	40·00
O98		2d. yellow (Perf 14) (1931)	15·00	1·00
		a. No stop after 'OFFICIAL'	£100	95·00
O99		3d. chocolate (1925)	20·00	1·50
		a. No stop after 'OFFICIAL'	£125	95·00
		b. Perf 14 (1930)	£100	20·00
		ba. No stop after 'OFFICIAL'	£275	£200
O96/O99 *Set of 4*			55·00	29·00

1915 (Dec)–**27**. Optd with T **O3**. Perf 14×13½.

(a) Nos. 420, 422, 425, 428 and 429/430 (Cowan unsurfaced paper).

O100	**60**	3d. chocolate	8·00	2·25
		aw. Wmk inverted	45·00	10·00
		b. Perf 14×14½	11·00	4·50
		bw. Wmk inverted	80·00	15·00
		c. Vert pair, Nos. O100 and O100b	55·00	£225
		cw. Wmk inverted	£200	£275
		d. Opt double	†	£1400
O101		4d. bright violet (4.25)	22·00	7·50
		a. Re-entry (Pl 20 R. 1/6)	£100	60·00
		b. Re-entry (Pl 20 R. 4/10)	£130	70·00
		c. Perf 14×14½ *Deep purple* (4.27)	30·00	5·00
O102		6d. carmine (6.16)	10·00	2·00
		aw. Wmk inverted	£225	
		b. Perf 14×14½	10·00	2·50
		c. Vert pair, Nos. O102 and O102b	75·00	£140
O103		8d. red-brown (8.22)	£120	£200
O104		9d. sage-green (4.25)	50·00	38·00
O105		1s. vermilion (9.16)	30·00	25·00
		aw. Wmk inverted	£275	£180
		ax. Wmk reversed	†	£500
		b. Perf 14×14½	20·00	5·00
		ba. Pale orange-red	35·00	50·00
		bw. Wmk inverted	£250	£275
		c. Vert pair. Nos. O105 and O105b	£100	£350
		cw. Wmk inverted	£650	
O100/O105b *Set of 6*			£200	£225

(b) No. 433 (Thin paper with widely spaced sideways wmk).

O106	**60**	3d. chocolate (Perf 14) (7.16)	10·00	£100
		a. No wmk	75·00	£125

1927–33. Optd with T **O3**. W **43**. Perf 14.

O111	**71**	1d. rose-carmine (No. 468)	3·00	20
		a. No stop after 'OFFICIAL' (R. 1/2, 5/24)	65·00	£150
		bw. Wmk inverted	†	75·00
		c. Perf 14×15	15·00	25
O112	**72**	2s. light blue (No. 469) (2.28)	£130	£150
O113	**F6**	5s. green (1933)	£350	£375
O111/O113 *Set of 3*			£425	£475

Unused examples of No. O111 are known printed on Cowan unsurfaced paper.

No. O111a from R. 1/2 shows a normal 'L' in 'OFFICIAL', that from R. 5/24 shows a shortened base to the 'L'.

Official	*Official*
(O4)	**(O5)**

1936–61. Pictorial issue optd horiz or vert (2s.) with T **O4**.

*(a) W **43** (Single 'N Z' and Star).*

O115	**82**	1d. scarlet (Die I) (Perf 14×13½) (21.3.36)	10·00	1·25
		a. Perf 13½×14	£225	75·00
O116	**83**	1½d. red-brown (Perf 13½×14) (3.36)	30·00	25·00
		a. Perf 14×13½	£23000	
O118	**92**	1s. deep green (Perf 14×13½) (3.36)	75·00	55·00
		w. Wmk inverted	†	£750
O119	**F6**	5s. green (Perf 14) (12.38)	£180	70·00
O115/O119 *Set of 4*			£250	£130

The watermark of No. O119 is almost invisible.

Only four examples of No. O116a exist. The error occurred when a sheet of No. 558a was found to have a block of four missing. This was replaced by a block of No. 558 and the sheet was then sent for overprinting.

*(b) W **98** (Mult 'N Z' and Star).*

O120	**81**	½d. bright green, Perf 14×13½ (7.37)	3·00	3·50
O121	**82**	1d. scarlet (Die II), Perf 14×13½ (11.36)	7·50	50
		w. Wmk inverted (2.37)	55·00	60·00
O122	**83**	1½d. red-brown, Perf 14×13½ (7.36)	25·00	4·50
O123	**84**	2d. orange, Perf 14×13½ (1.38)	10·00	20

Official Stamps, Life Insurance Department   NEW ZEALAND

		aw. Wmk inverted	—	£500
		b. Perf 12½ (1941)	£150	60·00
		c. Perf 14 (1941)	50·00	20·00
O124	85	2½d. chocolate and slate, Perf 13–14×13½ (26.7.38)	50·00	80·00
		a. Perf 14 (1938)	15·00	21·00
O125	86	3d. brown, Perf 14×13½ (1.3.38)	60·00	2·50
		w. Wmk inverted	—	£500
O126	87	4d. black and sepia, Perf 14×13½ (8.36)	15·00	1·10
		a. Perf 14 (8.41)	16·00	4·50
		b. Perf 12½ (12.41)	15·00	7·50
		c. Perf 14×14½ (10.42)	12·00	1·00
		cw. Wmk inverted	—	£1000
O127	89	6d. scarlet, Perf 13½×14 (12.37)	25·00	1·25
		aw. Wmk inverted	†	£1000
		b. Perf 12½ (1941)	18·00	8·00
		c. Perf 14½×14 (7.42)	17·00	1·00
O128	90	8d. chocolate, Perf 12½ (wmk sideways) (17.8.42)	25·00	12·00
		a. Perf 14×14½ (wmk sideways) (8.45)	18·00	10·00
		aw. Wmk sideways inverted	†	†
		b. Perf 14×13½ (1942)	†	£4500
O129	91	9d. red and grey-black (G). (No. 587b), Perf 13½×14 (1.3.38)	£150	35·00
O130		9d. scarlet and black (*chalk-surfaced paper*) (Black.) (No. 631), Perf 14×15 (10.43)	60·00	25·00
O131	92	1s. deep green, Perf 14×13½ (2.37)	50·00	1·50
		aw. Wmk inverted	—	£1000
		b. Perf 12½ (4.42)	30·00	1·50
O132	93	2s. olive-green, Perf 13–14×13½ (5.37)	95·00	35·00
		a. 'CAPTAIN COQK'	£250	£130
		b. Perf 13½×14 (5.39)	£400	7·50
		ba. 'CAPTAIN COQK'	£450	85·00
		c. Perf 12½ (3.42)	80·00	18·00
		ca. 'CAPTAIN COQK'	£225	85·00
		d. Perf 14×13½ (1944)	65·00	8·00
		da. 'CAPTAIN COQK'	£550	£225
O133	F6	5s. green (*chalk-surfaced paper*), Perf 14 (3.43)	60·00	7·50
		aw. Wmk inverted	45·00	6·00
		b. Perf 14×13½. *Yellow-green (ordinary paper)* (10.61)	20·00	35·00
O120/O133 Set of 14			£425	£100

The opt on No. O127b was sometimes applied at the top of the stamp, instead of always at the bottom as on No. O127.

All examples of No. O128b were used by a government office in Whangarei.

The 5s. value on ordinary paper perforated 14×13½ does not exist without the 'Official' overprint.

See notes on perforations after No. 590c.

1938–51. Nos. 603 etc., optd with T **O4**.

O134	108	½d. green (1.3.38)	20·00	2·25
O135		½d. brown-orange (1946)	3·00	1·50
O136		1d. scarlet (1.7.38)	25·00	20
O137		1d. green (10.7.41)	9·00	20
O138	108a	1½d. purple-brown (26.7.38)	80·00	20·00
O139		1½d. scarlet (2.4.51)	14·00	5·00
O140		3d. blue (16.10.41)	7·50	20
O134/O140 Set of 7			£140	27·00

1940 (2 Jan–8 Mar). Centennial. Nos. 613, etc., optd with T **O5**.

O141		½d. blue-green (R.)	3·00	1·00
		a. 'ff' joined, as Type **O4**	55·00	65·00
O142		1d. chocolate and scarlet	5·00	20
		a. 'ff' joined, as Type **O4**	50·00	60·00
O143		1½d. light blue and mauve	5·00	2·50
O144		2d. blue-green and chocolate	7·50	10
		a. 'ff' joined, as Type **O4**	65·00	65·00
O145		2½d. blue-green and ultramarine	5·00	4·00
		a. 'ff' joined, as Type **O4**	50·00	75·00
O146		3d. purple and carmine (R.)	10·00	1·00
		a. 'ff' joined, as Type **O4**	45·00	55·00
O147		4d. chocolate and lake	42·00	2·00
		a. 'ff' joined, as Type **O4**	£120	£100
O148		6d. emerald-green and violet	40·00	2·00
		a. 'ff' joined, as Type **O4**	80·00	75·00
O149		8d. black and red (8.3)	35·00	14·00
		a. 'ff' joined, as Type **O4**	80·00	£120
O150		9d. olive-green and vermilion	15·00	6·00
O151		1s. sage-green and deep green	£100	7·50
O141/O151 Set of 11			£225	35·00

For this issue the T **O4** overprint occurs on R. 4/3 of the 2½d. and on R. 1/10 of the other values.

1947 (1 May)–**51.** Nos. 680, etc., optd with T **O4**.

O152	108a	2d. orange	2·00	10
O153		4d. bright purple	6·50	4·75
O154		6d. carmine	10·00	1·25
O155		8d. violet	13·00	7·50
O156		9d. purple-brown	15·00	7·50
O157	144	1s. red-brown and carmine (wmk upright) (Plate 1)	20·00	3·50
		a. Wmk sideways (Plate 1) (6.49)	13·00	12·00
		aw. Wmk sideways inverted	60·00	50·00
		b. Wmk upright (Plate 2) (4.51)	30·00	8·00
		bw. Wmk inverted	£225	75·00
O158		2s. brown-orange and green (wmk sideways) (Plate 1)	30·00	18·00
		a. Wmk upright (Plate 1)	35·00	48·00
O152/O158 Set of 7			80·00	38·00

O6 Queen Elizabeth II   (**O7**)

(Des J. Berry. Recess B.W.)

1954 (1 Mar)–**63.** W **98.** Perf 14×13½.

O159	O6	1d. orange	75	1·00
		a. White opaque paper (8.7.59)	80	1·00
O160		1½d. brown-lake	2·75	3·50
O161		2d. bluish green	1·00	50
		a. White opaque paper (11.12.58)	50	60
O162		2½d. olive (*white opaque paper*) (1.3.63)	3·00	1·50
O163		3d. vermilion	75	10
		a. White opaque paper (1960)	50	10
		aw. Wmk inverted	40·00	30·00
O164		4d. blue	1·50	75
		a. Printed on the gummed side	£225	
		b. White opaque paper (1.9.61)	1·50	50
O165		9d. carmine	7·50	3·25
O166		1s. purple	3·00	30
		a. White opaque paper (2.10.61)	3·50	1·00
O167		3s. slate (*white opaque paper*) (1.3.63)	32·00	45·00
O159/O167 Set of 9			45·00	50·00

See note re white opaque paper after No. 736.
No. O164a shows the watermark inverted and reversed.

1959 (1 Oct). No. O160 surch with T **O7**.

O168	O6	6d. on 1½d. brown-lake	1·00	1·50

1961 (1 Sept). No. O161 surch as T **O7**.

O169	O6	2½d. on 2d. bluish green	1·25	3·50

Owing to the greater use of franking machines by Government Departments, the use of official stamps was discontinued on 31 March 1965, but they remained on sale at the GPO until 31 December 1965.

STAMP BOOKLET

1907 (1 July). White card cover.

OB1		10s. booklet containing 120×1d. in panes of 6 (No. O60a)	£1500

PROVISIONALS ISSUED AT REEFTON AND USED BY THE POLICE DEPARTMENT

1907 (Jan). Current stamps of 1906, optd 'Official', in red manuscript and handstamped with a circular 'Greymouth—PAID—3'. Perf 14.

P1	23	½d. green	£1300	£1600
P2	40	1d. carmine	£1300	£1500
P3	38	2d. purple	£1500	£2000
P4	28	3d. bistre		£2250
P5	31	6d. pink		£2250
P6	34	1s. orange-red		£3000
P7	35	2s. green		£8500

Only the ½d., 1d. and 2d. are known postally used, cancelled with the Reefton squared circle postmark. The 3d. and 6d. were later cancelled by favour at Wanganui.

LIFE INSURANCE DEPARTMENT

L1 Lighthouse   **L2** Lighthouse   2d. 'Z' flaw (R. 1/5, upper right panel)

(Des W. B. Hudson and J. F. Rogers; Eng. A. E. Cousins. Typo Govt Printing Office, Wellington)

1891 (2 Jan)–**98.**

A. W **12c.** Perf 12×11½.

L1	L1	½d. bright purple	£120	6·50
		a. Mixed perf 12×11 and 12½	†	—
		x. Wmk reversed	†	£190
L2		1d. blue	£100	4·00
		ax. Wmk reversed	†	£190
		ay. Wmk inverted and reversed	†	£110
		b. Wmk **12b**	£180	29·00

NEW ZEALAND Life Insurance Department

L3		bx. Wmk reversed	†	£500
		2d. brown-red	£170	15·00
		ax. Wmk reversed	†	£160
		b. Wmk **12b**	£190	23·00
L4		3d. deep brown	£375	45·00
L5		6d. green	£450	95·00
L6		1s. rose	£800	£200
L1/L6 Set of 6			£1800	£325

B. W **12b** (1893–1898)
(a) Perf 10 (1893).

L7	L1	½d. bright purple	£110	24·00
L8		1d. blue	90·00	2·50
L9		2d. brown-red	£150	5·00
		a. 'Z' flaw	—	£120
L7/L9 Set of 3			£300	27·00

(b) Perf 11×10.

L10	L1	½d. bright purple (1896)	£120	28·00
		a. Perf 10×11	£300	£110
L11		1d. blue (1897)	†	90·00
		a. Perf 10×11	£110	14·00

(c) Mixed perfs 10 and 11 (1897).

L12	L1	2d. brown-red	£1400	£1000

(d) Perf 11 (1897–1898).

L13	L1	½d. bright purple	95·00	4·00
		a. Thin coarse toned paper (1898)	£180	16·00
L14		1d. blue	90·00	75
		a. Thin coarse toned paper (1898)	£190	6·00
		x. Wmk reversed	£275	50·00
		y. Wmk inverted and reversed	£325	55·00
L15		2d. brown-red	£140	3·50
		a. Chocolate	£190	25·00
		b. Thin coarse toned paper (1898)	£300	6·00
		c. 'Z' flaw	—	£110
L13/L15 Set of 3			£300	7·50

1902–04. W **43** (sideways).
(a) Perf 11.

L16	L1	½d. bright purple (1903)	£110	16·00
L17		1d. blue (1902)	95·00	3·25
L18		2d. brown-red (1904)	£225	24·00
L16/L18 Set of 3			£375	38·00

(b) Perf 14×11.

L19	L1	½d. bright purple (1903)	£2500	£1500
L20		1d. blue (1904)	£180	18·00

Nos. L16/L17 and L20 are known without watermark from the margins of the sheet. Note that the W **43** watermark may be found both sideways and sideways inverted.

1905–06. Redrawn, with 'V.R.' omitted. W **43** (sideways).
(a) Perf 11.

L21	L2	2d. brown-red (12.05)	£1500	£160

(b) Perf 14.

L22	L2	1d. blue (7.06)	£350	35·00

(c) Perf 14×11.

L23	L2	1d. blue (7.06)	£850	£225
		a. Mixed perfs	†	£750

Between January 1907 and the end of 1912 the Life Insurance Department used ordinary Official stamps.

1913 (2 Jan)–**37.** New values and colours. W **43**.
(a) De La Rue paper. Perf 14×15.

L24	L2	½d. green	22·00	2·50
		a. Yellow-green	22·00	2·50
L25		1d. carmine	22·00	1·25
		a. Carmine-pink	24·00	1·75
L26		1½d. black (1917)	50·00	9·00
L27		1½d. chestnut-brown (1919)	2·50	3·00
L28		2d. bright purple	50·00	30·00
		w. Wmk inverted	†	£350
L29		2d. yellow (1920)	12·00	4·00
L30		3d. olive-brown	55·00	38·00
L31		6d. carmine-pink	50·00	35·00
L24/L31 Set of 8			£225	£110

(b) Cowan paper
(i) Perf 14×15.

L31a	L2	½d. yellow-green (1925)	45·00	4·50
		aw. Wmk inverted	†	—
L31b		1d. carmine-pink (1925)	42·00	3·50
		bw. Wmk inverted	£200	75·00

(ii) Perf 14.

L32	L2	½d. yellow-green (1926)	24·00	4·00
		w. Wmk inverted	†	90·00
L33		1d. scarlet (1931)	8·50	2·00
		w. Wmk inverted	£100	50·00
L34		2d. yellow (1937)	7·00	13·00
		w. Wmk inverted	£100	£130
L35		3d. brown-lake (1931)	16·00	24·00
		a. 'HREE' for 'THREE' (R. 7/11)	£375	
L36		6d. pink (1925)	55·00	60·00
L32/L36 Set of 5			95·00	90·00

(c) Wiggins Teape paper. Perf 14×15.

L36a	L2	½d. yellow-green (3.37)	8·00	12·00
L36b		1d. scarlet (3.37)	22·00	3·25
L36c		6d. pink (7.37)	35·00	40·00
L36a/L36c Set of 3			60·00	50·00

For descriptions of the various types of paper, see after No. 385. In the 1½d. the word 'POSTAGE' is in both the side-labels instead of at left only.

1944–47. W **98**. Perf 14×15.

L37	L2	½d. yellow-green (7.47)	8·50	7·00
L38		1d. scarlet (6.44)	3·25	2·00
L39		2d. yellow (1946)	17·00	42·00
L40		3d. brown-lake (10.46)	32·00	45·00
		a. 'HREE' for 'THREE' (R. 7/11)	£400	£325
L41		6d. pink (7.47)	20·00	60·00
L37/L41 Set of 5			70·00	£140

L3 Castlepoint Lighthouse    **L4** Taiaroa Lighthouse

L5 Cape Palliser Lighthouse    **L6** Cape Campbell Lighthouse    **L7** Eddystone Lighthouse

L8 Stephens Island Lighthouse    **L9** The Brothers Lighthouse    **L10** Cape Brett Lighthouse

(Des J. Berry. Recess B.W.).

1947 (1 Aug)–**65**. Types **L3/L10**. W **98** (sideways inverted on 1d., 2d., sideways on 2½d.). Perf 13½.

L42	L3	½d. grey-green and orange-red	2·00	1·00
L43	L4	1d. olive-green and pale blue	75	1·25
L44	L5	2d. deep blue and grey-black	2·25	1·00
L45	L6	2½d. black and bright blue (white opaque paper) (4.11.63)	7·00	13·00
L46	L7	3d. mauve and pale blue	3·50	1·25
L47	L8	4d. brown and yellow-orange	3·75	1·75
		a. Wmk sideways (white opaque paper) (13.10.65)	4·00	14·00
L48	L9	6d. chocolate and blue	7·50	3·00
L49	L10	1s. red-brown and blue	6·50	4·25
L42/L49 Set of 8			30·00	23·00

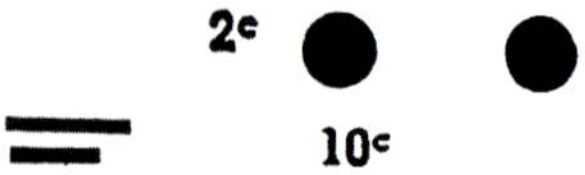

(L11) 2c   (L12) 10c

1967 (10 July)–**68**. Decimal currency. Stamps of 1947–1965, surch as T **L12** or T **L11** (2c.).

L50		1c. on 1d. (No. L43)	2·50	4·25
		a. Wmk upright (white opaque paper) (10.5.68)	1·50	7·00
L51		2c. on 2½d. (No. L45)	5·50	14·00
L52		2½c. on 3d. (No. L46)	2·00	4·00
		a. Horiz pair, one without surcharge	£4250	—
		b. Wmk sideways (white opaque paper) (4.68?)	2·00	4·75
L53		3c. on 4d. (No. L47a)	3·25	5·00
		w. Wmk sideways inverted	£1600	£750
L54		5c. on 6d. (No. L48)	4·00	6·50
		a. White opaque paper	5·00	6·50

Life Insurance Department, Postage Due Stamps NEW ZEALAND

L55		10c. on 1s. (No. L49)	4·00	10·00
		a. Wmk sideways (*white opaque paper*)	3·00	4·00
		aw. Wmk sideways inverted	†	£475
L50/L55a		Set of 6	17·00	32·00

See note re white paper below No. 736.

L13 Moeraki Point Lighthouse

L14 Puysegur Point Lighthouse

L14a Baring Head Lighthouse

L14b Cape Egmont Lighthouse

L14c East Cape

L14d Farewell Spit

L15 Dog Island Lighthouse

(Des J. Berry. Litho B.W.)

1969 (27 Mar)–**76**. Types **L13**/**L15**. No wmk. Chalk-surfaced paper (8c., 10c.), ordinary paper (others). Perf 14 (8c., 10c.) or 13½ (others).

L56	L13	½c. greenish yellow, red and deep blue	75	1·50
L57	L14	2½c. ultramarine, green and pale buff	50	1·00
L58	L14a	3c. reddish brown and yellow	40	60
		a. Chalk-surfaced paper (1974)	40	2·75
		ab. Yellow omitted	£3500	
L59	L14b	4c. light new blue, yellowish green and apple-green	40	75
		a. Chalk-surfaced paper (1975)	40	2·25
L60	L14c	8c. multicoloured (17.11.76)	40	2·00
L61	L14d	10c. multicoloured (17.11.76)	50	2·00
L62	L15	15c. black, light yellow and ultramarine	40	1·25
		a. Chalk-surfaced paper (3.75)	18·00	22·00
		ab. Perf 14 (24.12.76)	90	3·50
L56/L62		Set of 7	3·00	8·00

The ordinary paper stamps have shiny gum and fluoresce brightly under UV light.
The chalk-surfaced paper stamps have matt, PVA gum and the front of the stamps give a dull reaction under UV light.

L16

L17

1978 (8 Mar). As No. L57 but with the addition of new value as T **L16**. Chalk-surfaced paper paper.

L63	L16	25c. on 2½c. ultramarine, green and buff	50	1·50

(Des A. G. Mitchell. Litho Harrison)

1981 (3 June). Perf 14½.

L64	L17	5c. multicoloured	10	10
L65		10c. multicoloured	10	10
L66		20c. multicoloured	15	15
L67		30c. multicoloured	25	25
L68		40c. multicoloured	30	30
L69		50c. multicoloured	30	45
L64/L69		Set of 6	1·00	1·25

Issues for the Government Life Insurance Department were withdrawn on 1 December 1989 when it became the privatised Tower Corporation.

POSTAGE DUE STAMPS

D1

(I)   (II)

(a) Large 'D'   (b) Small 'D'

(Typo Govt Printing Office, Wellington)

1899 (1 Dec)–**1900**. Coarse paper. W **12b**. Perf 11.
I. Type I. Circle of 14 ornaments 17 dots over 'N.Z.', 'N.Z.' large
(a) Large 'D'.

D1	D1	½d. carmine and green	45·00	45·00
		a. No stop after 'D' (Right pane R. 2/3)	£250	£250
D2		8d. carmine and green	95·00	£140
		a. Carmine '8D.' printed double		
D3		1s. carmine and green	£120	£150
D4		2s. carmine and green	£200	£225
D1/D4		Set of 4	£400	£500

To avoid further subdivision the 1s. and 2s. are placed with the pence values, although the two types of 'D' do not apply to the higher values.

(b) Small 'D'.

D6	D1	5d. carmine and green	45·00	50·00
D7		6d. carmine and green	48·00	60·00
D8		10d. carmine and green	£120	£180
D6/D8		Set of 3	£190	£250

II. Type II. Circle of 13 ornaments, 15 dots over 'N.Z.', 'N.Z.' small
(a) Large 'D'.

D9	D1	½d. vermilion and green (5.1900)	5·00	17·00
		a. No stop after 'D' (Right pane R. 2/3)	70·00	£120
D10		1d. vermilion and green	28·00	3·75
D11		2d. vermilion and green	55·00	10·00
D12		3d. vermilion and green	22·00	7·00
D9/D12		Set of 4	95·00	32·00

(b) Small 'D'.

D14	D1	1d. vermilion and green	28·00	3·75
D15		2d. vermilion and green	55·00	7·50
D16		4d. vermilion and green	40·00	25·00
D14/D16		Set of 3	£110	32·00

Nos. D9/D16 were printed from a common frame plate of 240 (4 panes of 60) used in conjunction with centre plates of 120 (2 panes of 60) for the ½d. and 4d. or 240 for the other values. Sheets of the 1d. and 2d. each contained two panes with large 'D' and two panes with small 'D'.

D2

D3

(Des W. R. Bock. Typo Govt Printing Office)

1902 (28 Feb). No wmk. Perf 11.

D17	D2	½d. red and deep green	4·00	9·00

1904–08. Cowan unsurfaced paper. W **43** (sideways).
(a) Perf 11.

D18	D2	½d. red and green (4.04)	4·00	3·00
		a. Imperf between (horiz pair)	£1800	

NEW ZEALAND Postage Due Stamps, Postal Fiscal Stamps

D19		1d. red and green (5.12.05)	25·00	3·75
D20		2d. red and green (5.4.06)	£150	£130
D18/D20 Set of 3			£160	£130

(b) Perf 14.

D21	**D2**	1d. carmine and green (12.06)	27·00	1·50
		a. Rose-pink and green (9.07)	15·00	1·50
D22		2d. carmine and green (10.06)	15·00	11·00
		a. Rose-pink and green (6.08)	11·00	3·00

The note regarding sideways watermark varieties below No. 299 applies here also.

1919 (Jan)–**20**. De La Rue chalk-surfaced paper. Toned gum. W **43**. Perf 14×15.

D23	**D2**	½d. carmine and green (6.19)	3·75	6·50
D24		1d. carmine and green	15·00	15·00
		w. Wmk inverted	†	£500
D25		2d. carmine and green (8.20)	35·00	4·50
D23/D25 Set of 3			45·00	10·50

1925 (May). Jones chalk-surfaced paper. White gum. W **43**. Perf 14×15.

D26	**D2**	½d. carmine and green	48·00	75·00

1925 (July). No wmk, but bluish 'N Z' and Star lithographed on back. Perf 14×15.

D27	**D2**	1d. carmine and green	3·50	26·00
D28		2d. carmine and green	10·00	40·00

1925 (Nov)–**35**. Cowan thick, opaque chalk-surfaced paper. W **43**.

(a) Perf 14×15.

D29	**D2**	½d. carmine and green (12.26)	3·00	14·00
D30		1d. carmine and green	7·50	1·00
D31		2d. carmine and green (6.26)	32·00	4·25
		x. Wmk reversed	75·00	35·00
D32		3d. carmine and green (6.35)	60·00	55·00
D29/D32 Set of 4			90·00	65·00

(b) Perf 14.

D33	**D2**	½d. carmine and green (10.28)	75·00	65·00
D34		1d. rose and pale yellow-green (6.28)	7·50	1·25
D35		2d. carmine and green (10.29)	12·50	3·00
D36		3d. carmine and green (5.28)	45·00	50·00
D33/D36 Set of 4			£120	£100

1937–**38**. Wiggins Teape thin, hard chalk-surfaced paper. W **43**. Perf 14×15.

D37	**D2**	½d. carmine and yellow-green (2.38)	25·00	45·00
D38		1d. carmine and yellow-green (1.37)	18·00	4·25
D39		2d. carmine and yellow-green (6.37)	30·00	15·00
D40		3d. carmine and yellow-green (11.37)	£100	75·00
D37/D40 Set of 4			£160	£120

(Des J. Berry. Typo Govt Printing Office, Wellington)

1939–**49**. Perf 15×14.

*(a) W **43** (sideways inverted) (16.8.39).*

D41	**D3**	½d. turquoise-green	6·00	5·00
D42		1d. carmine	3·50	2·50
		w. Wmk sideways	£250	15·00
D43		2d. bright blue	6·00	2·75
		w. Wmk sideways	£275	
D44		3d. orange-brown	40·00	25·00
		w. Wmk sideways	£225	
D41/D44 Set of 4			50·00	30·00

*(b) W **98** (sideways (1d.), sideways inverted (2d.) or upright (3d.).*

D45	**D3**	1d. carmine (4.49)	20·00	7·50
D46		2d. bright blue (12.46)	11·00	6·00
		w. Wmk sideways (4.49)	5·00	13·00
D47		3d. orange-brown (1943)	60·00	50·00
		a. Wmk sideways inverted (6.45)	40·00	28·00
		aw. Wmk sideways (28.11.49)	12·00	25·00
D45/D47aw Set of 3			35·00	30·00

* The use of Postage Due stamps ceased on 30 September 1951, our used price for No. D45 being for stamps postmarked after this date (*price for examples clearly cancelled 1949–1951, £35*).

POSTAL FISCAL STAMPS

As from 1 April 1882 fiscal stamps were authorised for postal use and conversely postage stamps became valid for fiscal use. Stamps in the designs of 1867 with 'STAMP DUTY' above the Queen's head were withdrawn and although some passed through the mail quite legitimately they were mainly 'philatelic' and we no longer list them. The issue which was specifically authorised in 1882 was the one which had originally been put on sale for fiscal use in 1880.

There is strong evidence that the authorities used up existing low value revenue stamps for postage, delaying the general release of the new 'Postage and Revenue' low values (Types **14**, **15** and **18**–**22**) to achieve this. Used prices for such stamps are for examples with 1882–1883 postal cancellations.

Although all fiscal stamps were legally valid for postage, only values between 2s. and £1 were stocked at ordinary post offices. Other values could only be obtained by request from the GPO, Wellington or from offices of the Stamp Duties Department. From 1884 these stamps were also supplied to major telegraph offices in values between £1 and £10, where they were cancelled with postal datestamps until specific 'Telegraph office' cancellers were provided in the late 1890s. Later the Arms types above £1 could also be obtained from the head post offices in Auckland, Christchurch, Dunedin and also a branch post office at Christchurch North where there was a local demand for them.

It seems sensible to list under Postal Fiscals the Queen Victoria stamps up to the £1 value and the Arms types up to the £5 because by 1931 the higher values were genuinely needed for postal purposes. The £10 was occasionally used on insured airmail parcels and is therefore also listed. Although 2s. and 5s. values were included in the 1898 pictorial issue, it was the general practice for the Postal Department to limit the postage issues to 1s. until 1926 when the 2s. and 3s. appeared. These were then dropped from the fiscal issues and when in turn the 5s. and 10s. were introduced in 1953 and the £1 in 1960 no further printings of these values occurred in the fiscal series.

> **FORGED POSTMARKS.** Our prices are for stamps with genuine postal cancellations. Beware of forged postmarks on stamps from which fiscal cancellations have been cleaned off. Many small post offices acted as agents for government departments and it was the practice to use ordinary postal datestamps on stamps used fiscally, so that when they are removed from documents they are indistinguishable from postally used specimens unless impressed with the embossed seal of the Stamp Duties Department. Datestamps very similar to postal datestamps were sometimes supplied to offices of the Stamp Duties Department and it is not clear when this practice ceased. Prior to the Arms types the only sure proof of the postal use of *off-cover* fiscal stamps is when they bear a distinctive duplex, registered or parcel post cancellation, but beware of forgeries of the first two.

F1　　　　F2　　　　F3

(Die eng W. R. Bock. Typo Govt Ptg Office)

1882 (Feb). W **12a**. Perf 12×11½.

F1	**F1**	1d. lilac	£1500	£750
F2		1d. blue	£300	50·00
		w. Wmk inverted	—	£250

The 1d. fiscal was specifically authorised for postal use in February 1882 owing to a shortage of the 1d. T **5** and pending the introduction of the 1d. T **14** on 1 April.

The 1d. lilac fiscal had been replaced by the 1d. blue in 1878 but postally used copies with 1882 duplex postmarks are known although most postally used examples are dated from 1890 and these must have been philatelic.

1882 (early). W **12a**. Perf 12×11½.

F3	**F2**	1s. grey-green	
F4		1s. grey-green and red	
F4*a*		2s. rose and blue	

Examples of these are known postally used in 1882 and although not specifically authorised for postal use it is believed that their use was permitted where there was a shortage of the appropriate postage value.

> **WATERMARK T F5.** The balance of the paper employed for the 1867 issue was used for early printings of T **F4** introduced in 1880 before changing over to the 'N Z' and Star watermark. The values we list with this watermark are known with 1882–1883 postal datestamps. Others have later dates and are considered to be philatelic but should they be found with 1882–1883 postal dates we would be prepared to add them to the list.

F4　　　　F5

The 12s.6d. value has the head in an oval (as T **10**), and the 15s. and £1 values have it in a broken circle (as T **7**).

Postal Fiscal Stamps NEW ZEALAND

(Dies eng W. R. Bock. Typo Govt Ptg Office)

1882 (1 Apr)–**1930**. T **F4** and similar types. De La Rue paper.

A. W **F5**. Perf 12 (1882).

F5	4d. orange-red	—	£500
F5*a*	6d. lake-brown	—	£1000
F5*b*	8d. green	—	£1000
F5*c*	1s. pink	—	£750
F5*d*	2s.6d. grey-brown	—	£500
F5*e*	4s. brown-rose	—	£400
F5*f*	5s. green	—	£750
F5*g*	6s. rose	—	£750
F5*h*	7s. ultramarine	—	£750
F5*i*	8s. deep blue	—	£750
F5*j*	9s. orange	—	£1000
F5*k*	10s. brown-red	—	£750

B. W **12a** (6 mm). Perf 12 (1882).

F6	6d. lake-brown	—	£375
F8	1s. pink	—	£500
F9	2s. blue	£150	12·00
F10	2s.6d. grey-brown	£200	12·00
F11	3s. mauve	£275	19·00
F12	4s. brown-rose	£325	32·00
F13	5s. green	£375	30·00
	a. Yellow-green	£375	30·00
F14	6s. rose	£400	75·00
F15	7s. ultramarine	£425	£110
F16	7s.6d. bronze-grey	£1600	£325
F17	8s. deep blue	£500	£130
F18	9s. orange	£600	£160
F19	10s. brown-red	£375	35·00
F20	15s. green	£1200	£350
F21	£1 rose-pink	£600	£140

(b) Perf 12½ (1886).

F22	2s. blue	£150	12·00
F23	2s.6d. grey-brown	£200	12·00
F24	3s. mauve	£300	19·00
F25	4s. purple-claret	£325	32·00
	a. Brown-rose	£325	32·00
F26	5s. green	£375	30·00
	a. Yellow-green	£375	30·00
F27	6s. rose	£450	75·00
F28	7s. ultramarine	£450	£110
F29	8s. deep blue	£500	£130
F30	9s. orange	£600	£160
F31	10s. brown-red	£375	35·00
F32	15s. green	£1200	£350
F33	£1 rose-pink	£600	£140

B. W **12b** (7 mm). Perf 12½ (1888).

F34	2s. blue	£150	12·00
F35	2s.6d. grey-brown	£200	12·00
F36	3s. mauve	£275	19·00
F37	4s. brown-rose	£300	32·00
	a. Brown-red	£300	32·00
F38	5s. green	£350	30·00
	a. Yellow-green	£350	30·00
F39	6s. rose	£450	75·00
F40	7s. ultramarine	£475	£110
F41	7s.6d. bronze-grey	£1600	£325
F42	8s. deep blue	£500	£130
F43	9s. orange	£600	£160
F44	10s. brown-red	£375	35·00
	a. Maroon	£375	35·00
F45	£1 pink	£600	£140

C. W **12c** (4 mm). Perf 12½ (1890).

F46	2s. blue	£225	28·00
F46*a*	2s.6d. grey-brown	£325	30·00
F47	3s. mauve	£425	70·00
F48	4s. brown-red	£375	60·00
F49	5s. green	£400	40·00
F50	6s. rose	£500	90·00
F51	7s. ultramarine	£600	£140
F52	8s. deep blue	£600	£150
F53	9s. orange	£650	£200
F54	10s. brown-red	£475	45·00
F55	15s. green	£1500	£350

D. Continuation of W **12b**. Perf 11 (1895–1901).

F56	2s. blue	95·00	12·00
F57	2s.6d. grey-brown	£190	11·00
	a. Inscr 'COUNTERPART' (1901)*	£250	£300
F58	3s. mauve	£250	17·00
F59	4s. brown-red	£300	30·00
F60	5s. yellow-green	£350	30·00
F61	6s. rose	£400	75·00
F62	7s. pale blue	£450	£110
F63	7s.6d. bronze-grey	£1600	£325
F64	8s. deep blue	£500	£120
F65	9s. orange	£600	£190
	a. Imperf between (horiz pair)	£3500	
F66	10s. brown-red	£375	35·00
	a. Maroon	£375	35·00
F67	15s. green	£1200	£350
F68	£1 rose-pink	£600	£140

* The plate normally printed in yellow and inscribed 'COUNTERPART' just above the bottom value panel, was for use on the counterparts of documents but was issued in error in the colour of the normal fiscal stamp and accepted for use.

WATERMARKS. The note regarding sideways watermarks on locally printed stamps (see above No. 300) also applies to Nos. F69/F144.

E. W **43** (sideways)
(i) Unsurfaced Cowan paper
(a) Perf 11 (1903).

F69	2s.6d. grey-brown	£250	11·00
F70	3s. mauve	£300	18·00
F71	4s. orange-red	£300	30·00
F72	6s. rose	£375	75·00
F73	7s. pale blue	£475	£110
F74	8s. deep blue	£500	£120
F75	10s. brown-red	£375	35·00
	a. Maroon	£375	35·00
F76	15s. green	£1300	£350
F77	£1 rose-pink	£550	£140

(b) Perf 14 (1906).

F78	2s.6d. grey-brown	£160	11·00
F79	3s. mauve	£225	17·00
F80	4s. orange-red	£225	27·00
F81	5s. yellow-green	£250	27·00
F82	6s. rose	£350	75·00
F83	7s. pale blue	£400	£110
F84	7s.6d. bronze-grey	£1500	£300
F85	8s. deep blue	£475	£120
F86	9s. orange	£500	£150
F87	10s. maroon	£350	35·00
F88	15s. green	£1300	£350
F89	£1 rose-pink	£500	£140

(c) Perf 14½×14, comb (clean-cut) (1907).

F90	2s. blue	95·00	11·00
F91	2s.6d. grey-brown	£190	11·00
F92	3s. mauve	£250	18·00
F93	4s. orange-red	£250	28·00
F94	6s. rose	£375	75·00
F95	10s. maroon	£350	35·00
F96	15s. green	£1300	£350
F97	£1 rose-pink	£500	£140

(ii) Chalk-surfaced De la Rue paper.
(a) Perf 14 (1913).

F98	2s. blue	75·00	10·00
	a. Imperf horiz (vert pair)	£2000	
F99	2s.6d. grey-brown	90·00	11·00
F100	3s. purple	£180	16·00
F101	4s. orange-red	£180	22·00
F102	5s. yellow-green	£190	24·00
F103	6s. rose	£325	50·00
F104	7s. pale blue	£350	70·00
F105	7s.6d. bronze-grey	£1600	£325
F106	8s. deep blue	£450	80·00
F107	9s. orange	£550	£150
F108	10s. maroon	£350	32·00
F109	15s. green	£1300	£350
F110	£1 rose-carmine	£475	£130

(b) Perf 14½×14, comb (1913–1921).

F111	2s. deep blue	75·00	10·00
F112	2s.6d. grey-brown	90·00	11·00
F113	3s. purple	£180	15·00
F114	4s. orange-red	£180	22·00
F115	5s. yellow-green	£190	24·00
F116	6s. rose	£325	50·00
F117	7s. pale blue	£350	70·00
F118	8s. deep blue	£450	80·00
F119	9s. orange	£500	£150
F120	10s. maroon	£350	32·00
F121	12s.6d. deep plum (1921)	£20000	£7500
F122	15s. green	£1300	£350
F123	£1 rose-carmine	£450	£130

The De La Rue paper has a smooth finish and has toned gum which is strongly resistant to soaking.

(iii) Chalk-surfaced Jones paper. Perf 14½×14, comb (1924).

F124	2s. deep blue	£110	15·00
F125	2s.6d. deep grey-brown	£120	15·00
F126	3s. purple	£250	21·00
F127	5s. yellow-green	£250	30·00
F128	10s. brown-red	£400	35·00
F129	12s.6d. deep purple	£20000	£7500
F130	15s. green	£1200	£350

The Jones paper has a coarser texture, is poorly surfaced and the ink tends to peel. The outline of the watermark commonly shows on the surface of the stamp. The gum is colourless or only slightly toned and washes off readily.

(iv) Thick, opaque, chalk-surfaced Cowan paper. Perf 14½×14, comb (1925–1930).

F131	2s. blue	80·00	12·00
F132	2s.6d. deep grey-brown	95·00	13·00
F133	3s. mauve	£250	26·00
F134	4s. orange-red	£190	32·00
F135	5s. yellow-green	£200	32·00

NEW ZEALAND Postal Fiscal Stamps

	x. Wmk reversed (1927)		£325	65·00
F136	6s. rose		£350	55·00
F137	7s. pale blue		£400	75·00
F138	8s. deep blue		£550	25·00
	a. Blue (1930)		£550	
F139	10s. brown-red		£350	38·00
	x. Wmk reversed (1927)		£450	£300
F140	12s.6d. blackish purple		£20000	£7500
F141	15s. green		£1200	£350
F142	£1 rose-pink		£500	£140

The Cowan paper is white and opaque and the watermark, which is usually smaller than in the Jones paper, is often barely visible.

(v) Thin, hard, chalk-surfaced Wiggins Teape paper. Perf 14½×14, comb (1926).

F143	4s. orange-red		£200	42·00
F144	£1 rose-pink		£500	£225

The Wiggins Teape paper has a horizontal mesh, in relation to the design, with narrow watermark, whereas other chalk-surfaced papers with this perforation have a vertical mesh and wider watermark.

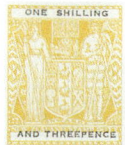

F6   (F7)

PRICES. Collectors should note that in the T **F6** Arms design, prices quoted for unused examples refer to hinged mint for Nos. F145/F168a. Unused prices for Nos. F169/F185 and all subsequent issues are for unmounted examples.

(Des H. L. Richardson. Typo Govt Ptg Office)

1931–40. As T **F6** (various frames). W **43**. Perf 14.
(i) Thick, opaque, chalk-surfaced Cowan paper, with horizontal mesh (1931–1935).

F145	1s.3d. lemon (3.31)		15·00	65·00
F146	1s.3d. orange-yellow (1932)		18·00	22·00
F147	2s.6d. deep brown		17·00	4·50
F148	4s. red		16·00	13·00
F149	5s. green		45·00	16·00
F150	6s. carmine-rose		35·00	21·00
F151	7s. blue		35·00	38·00
F152	7s.6d. olive-grey		85·00	£120
F153	8s. slate-violet		60·00	42·00
F154	9s. brown-orange		60·00	40·00
F155	10s. carmine-lake		28·00	12·00
F156	12s.6d. deep plum (9.35)		£225	£225
F157	15s. sage-green		95·00	50·00
F158	£1 pink		85·00	25·00
F159	25s. greenish blue		£700	£1100
F160	30s. brown (1935)		£425	£250
F161	35s. orange-yellow		£6500	£7500
F162	£2 bright purple		£425	90·00
F163	£2.10s. red		£500	£650
F164	£3 green		£700	£350
F165	£3.10s. rose (1935)		£2250	£3000
F166	£4 light blue (1935)		£950	£250
F167	£4.10s. deep olive-grey (1935)		£2000	£2500
F168	£5 indigo-blue		£500	£160
F168a	£10 deep blue		£1700	£550

(ii) Thin, hard Wiggins Teape paper with vertical mesh (1936–1940).
(a) Chalk-surfaced (1936–1939).

F169	1s.3d. pale orange-yellow		50·00	6·00
F170	2s.6d. dull brown		£130	5·00
F171	4s. pale red-brown		£170	25·00
F172	5s. green		£170	7·50
	w. Wmk inverted		—	£800
F173	6s. carmine-rose		£180	75·00
F174	7s. pale blue		£300	85·00
F175	8s. slate-violet		£325	85·00
F176	9s. brown-orange		£375	£120
F177	10s. pale carmine-lake		£300	9·50
F178	15s. sage-green		£475	£100
F179	£1 pink		£300	55·00
F180	30s. brown (1.39)		£850	£275
F181	35s. orange-yellow		£8000	£7500
F182	£2 bright purple (1937)		£1300	£180
	w. Wmk inverted		£3750	
F183	£3 green (1937)		£1700	£500
F184	£5 indigo-blue (1937)		£2500	£450

(b) Unsurfaced (1940).

F185	7s.6d. olive-grey		£250	£100

Not all values listed above were stocked at ordinary post offices as some of them were primarily required for fiscal purposes but all were valid for postage.

1939. No. F161 and F168a surch as T **F7**.

F186	35/- on 35s. orange-yellow		£950	£475
F186a	£10 on £10 deep blue		£2500	£600
	aw. Wmk inverted			

Because the 35s. orange-yellow could so easily be confused with the 1s.3d. and the £10 with the £5 in similar colours, they were surcharged.

1940 (June). New values surch as T **F7**. Wiggins Teape chalk-surfaced paper. W **43**. Perf 14.

F187	3/6 on 3s.6d. grey-green		80·00	45·00
F188	5/6 on 5s.6d. lilac		£140	75·00
F189	11/- on 11s. yellow		£275	£225
F190	22/- on 22s. scarlet		£700	£500
F187/F190 Set of 4			£1100	£750

These values were primarily needed for fiscal use.

1940–58. As T **F6** (various frames). W **98**. Perf 14.
(i) Wiggins Teape chalk-surfaced paper with vertical mesh (1940–1956).

F191	1s.3d. orange-yellow		21·00	4·25
	w. Wmk inverted		—	£375
F192	1s.3d. yellow and black (wmk inverted) (14.6.55)		9·00	4·50
	aw. Wmk upright (9.9.55)		50·00	45·00
	b. Error. Yellow and blue (wmk inverted) (7.56)		15·00	10·00
F193	2s.6d. deep brown		18·00	1·50
	w. Wmk inverted (3.49)		21·00	1·50
F194	4s. red-brown		40·00	2·00
	w. Wmk inverted (3.49)		50·00	2·75
F195	5s. green		25·00	1·25
	w. Wmk inverted (1.5.50)		35·00	1·25
F196	6s. carmine-rose		55·00	5·00
	w. Wmk inverted (1948)		65·00	5·00
F197	7s. pale blue		60·00	8·50
F198	7s.6d. olive-grey (wmk inverted) (21.12.50)		£120	£100
F199	8s. slate-violet		£100	30·00
	w. Wmk inverted (6.12.50)		£110	30·00
F200	9s. brown-orange (1.46)		£100	60·00
	w. Wmk inverted (9.1.51)		£100	50·00
F201	10s. carmine-lake		60·00	4·50
	w. Wmk inverted (4.50)		70·00	4·50
F202	15s. sage-green		£120	35·00
	w. Wmk inverted (8.12.50)		£120	35·00
F203	£1 pink		50·00	6·00
	w. Wmk inverted (1.2.50)		75·00	7·50
F204	25s. greenish blue (1946)		£850	£1000
	w. Wmk inverted (7.53)		£1000	£1000
F205	30s. brown (1946)		£500	£190
	w. Wmk inverted (9.49)		£500	£170
F206	£2 bright purple (1946)		£225	55·00
	w. Wmk inverted (17.6.52)		£225	45·00
F207	£2.10s. red (wmk inverted) (9.8.51)		£600	£550
F208	£3 green (1946)		£300	£100
	w. Wmk inverted (17.6.52)		£250	£100
F209	£3.10s. rose (11.48)		£4000	£2250
	w. Wmk inverted (5.52)		£4000	£2250
F210	£4 light blue (wmk inverted) (12.2.52)		£350	£225
	w. Wmk upright		†	£1800
F211	£5 indigo-blue		£700	£120
	w. Wmk inverted (11.9.50)		£425	95·00
F191/F211 Set of 21			£7000	£4250

3s.6d. (Type I)

3s.6d. (Type II)

Type I.	Broad serifed, capitals
Type II.	Taller capitals, without serif

*Surcharged as T **F7**.*

F212	3/6 on 3s.6d. grey-green (Type I) (1942)		22·00	10·00
	w. Wmk inverted (12.10.50)		55·00	25·00
F213	3/6 on 3s.6d. grey-green (Type II) (6.53)		45·00	50·00
	w. Wmk inverted (6.53)		55·00	55·00
F214	5/6 on 5s.6d. lilac (1944)		75·00	30·00
	w. Wmk inverted (13.9.50)		90·00	21·00
F215	11/- on 11s. yellow (1942)		£150	75·00
F216	22/- on 22s. scarlet (1945)		£450	£200
	aw. Wmk inverted (1.3.50)		£475	£225
F216b	£10 on £10 deep blue		£1700	£450
	bw. Wmk inverted		£1700	£450
F212/F216 Set of 5			£600	£275

(ii) on £10 14×13½. Wiggins Teape unsurfaced paper with horizontal mesh (1956–1958).

F217	1s.3d. yellow and black (11.56)		7·50	4·50
	w. Wmk inverted		50·00	50·00
F218	£1 pink (20.10.58)		60·00	15·00

No. F192b had the inscription printed in blue in error but as many as 378,000 were printed.

From 1949–1953 inferior paper had to be used and for technical reasons it was necessary to feed the paper into the machine in a certain way which resulted in whole printings with the watermark inverted for most values.

F8

1967 (10 July)–**84**. Decimal currency. W **98** (sideways inverted). Unsurfaced paper. Perf 14 (line).

F219	**F8**	$4 deep reddish violet..............................	4·00	7·00
		a. Perf 14 (comb) (wmk sideways) (17.9.68)...................................	2·00	1·50
		aw. Wmk sideways inverted (6.7.84)....	2·50	9·00
F220		$6 emerald..	7·00	21·00
		a. Perf 14 (comb) (wmk sideways) (17.9.68)...................................	2·50	3·50
		aw. Wmk sideways inverted (6.7.84)....	3·25	11·00
F221		$8 light greenish blue...........................	22·00	38·00
		a. Perf 14 (comb) (wmk sideways) (20.6.68)...................................	4·50	4·50
		aw. Wmk sideways inverted (6.7.84)....		
F222		$10 deep ultramarine...........................	18·00	20·00
		a. Perf 14 (comb) (wmk sideways) (20.6.68)...................................	5·50	3·50
		aw. Wmk sideways inverted (6.7.84)....	25·00	30·00
F219/F222 *Set of 4*			45·00	75·00
F219a/F222a *Set of 4*			14·00	11·50

The original printings were line perforated on paper with the watermark sideways inverted (top of star pointing to left, *when viewed from the back*). In 1968 the stamps appeared comb perforated with the watermark sideways inverted (top of star to right). A further comb perforated printing in July 1984 showed the sideways inverted watermark.

The $6, $8 and $10 values were re-issued on unwatermarked paper in 1986.

1986 (30 Apr–2 May). As Nos. F220/222 but without wmk. Chalk-surfaced paper. Perf 14 (comb).

F223	**F8**	$6 bright green..	5·00	3·50
F224		$8 light greenish blue (2.5.86)..............	6·00	14·00
F225		$10 deep ultramarine (2.5.86)	7·00	6·00
F223/F225 *Set of 3*			16·00	21·00

Subscribe & Save Money
on the cover price*

12-Month Print Subscription

UK £53
Europe (airmail) £90

ROW (airmail) £95

*UK print subscriptions only

Visit stanleygibbons.com/gsm or call
+44 (0)1425 472 363

NEW ZEALAND Antarctic Expeditions, Ross Dependency

ANTARCTIC EXPEDITIONS

VICTORIA LAND

These issues were made under authority of the New Zealand Postal Department and, while not strictly necessary, they actually franked correspondence to New Zealand. They were sold to the public at a premium.

(A1)

1908 (15 Jan). Shackleton Expedition. T **42** of New Zealand (Perf 14), optd with T **A1**, by Coulls, Culling and Co., Wellington.

A1	1d. rose-carmine (No. 356 Royle) (G.)	£475	50·00
	a. Opt double	†	£1600
A1b	1d. rose-carmine (No. 352c Waterlow) (G.)	£1600	£850

Nos. A1/A1b were used on board the expedition ship, *Nimrod*, and at the Cape Royds base in McMurdo Sound. Due to adverse conditions Shackleton landed in Victoria Land rather than King Edward VII Land, the intended destination. The post office was closed on 4 March 1909.

VICTORIA LAND. (A2)   VICTORIA LAND. (A3)

1911 (9 Feb)–**13**. Scott Expedition. Stamps of New Zealand optd with T **A2** (½d.) or T **A3** (1d.) by Govt Printer, Wellington.

A2	51	½d. deep green (No. 387aa) (18.1.13)	£850	£950
A3	53	1d. carmine (No. 405)	60·00	£140
		a. No stop after 'LAND' (R. 7/5)	£425	£850
		b. 'Q' flaw		£650

Nos. A2/A3 were used at the Cape Evans base on McMurdo Sound or on the *Terra Nova*. The post office was closed on 12 February 1913.

ROSS DEPENDENCY

This comprises a sector of the Antarctic continent and a number of islands. It was claimed by Great Britain on 30 July 1923 and soon afterward put under the jurisdiction of New Zealand.

The stamps of New Zealand are also valid in the Dependency.

1 HMS *Erebus*   2 Shackleton and Scott

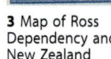

3 Map of Ross Dependency and New Zealand   4 Queen Elizabeth II

(Des E. M. Taylor (3d.), L. C. Mitchell (4d.), R. Smith (8d.), J. Berry (1s.6d.). Recess D.L.R.)

1957 (11 Jan). W **98** of New Zealand (Mult N Z and Star). Perf 13 (1s.6d.) or 14 (others).

1	1	3d. indigo	1·25	60
2	2	4d. carmine-red	1·25	75
3	3	8d. bright carmine-red and ultramarine	1·75	90
		a. Bright carmine-red and blue	4·25	3·75
4	4	1s.6d. slate-purple	2·50	1·00
1/4 Set of 4			6·00	3·00

(New Currency. 100 cents = 1 New Zealand dollar)

5 HMS *Erebus*

1967 (10 July). Decimal currency. As Nos. 1/4 but with values inscr in decimal currency as T **5**. Chalk-surfaced paper (except 15c.). W **98** of New Zealand (sideways on 7c.). Perf 13 (15c.) or 14 (others).

5	5	2c. indigo	12·00	11·00
		a. Deep blue	20·00	15·00
6	2	3c. carmine-red	8·00	7·50
		w. Wmk inverted	95·00	
7	3	7c. bright carmine-red and ultramarine	11·00	11·00
8	4	15c. slate-purple	14·00	12·00
		w. Wmk inverted	£100	
5/8 Set of 4			40·00	38·00

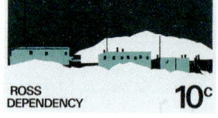

6 McCormick's Skua   7 Scott Base

(Des M. Cleverley. Litho B.W.)

1972 (18 Jan)–**79**. Horiz designs as T **6** (3c. to 8c.) or T **7** (10c., 18c.). Ordinary paper. Perf 14½×14 (10c., 18c.) or 13 (others)

9		3c. black, brownish grey and pale blue	1·25	1·10
		a. Chalk-surfaced paper (2.79)	70	1·40
10		4c. black, royal blue and violet	50	1·10
		a. Chalk-surfaced paper (2.79)	15	1·40
11		5c. black, brownish grey and rose-lilac	35	1·10
		a. Chalk-surfaced paper (2.79)	15	1·40
12		8c. black, yellow-brown and brownish grey	35	1·10
		a. Chalk-surfaced paper (2.79)	15	1·40
13		10c. black, turquoise-green and slate-green	35	1·10
		a. Perf 13½×13. Chalk-surfaced paper (2.79)	15	1·40
14		18c. black, violet and bright violet	50	2·00
		a. Perf 13½×13. Chalk-surfaced paper (2.79)	15	1·50
9/14 Set of 6			3·00	6·75
9a/14a Set of 6			1·25	7·75

Designs: 3c. T **6**; 4c. Lockheed C-130 Hercules aircraft at Williams Field; 5c. Shackleton's Hut; 8c. Supply ship HMNZS *Endeavour*; 10c. T **7**; 18c. Tabular ice floe.

Nos. 9/14 were issued on the 60th anniversary of the arrival at the South Pole of Captain Scott and his party.

8 Adélie Penguins   9 McCormick's Skua

(Des R. Conly. Litho Asher and Co, Melbourne)

1982 (20 Jan). Horiz designs as T **8**. Multicoloured. Perf 15½.

15	5c. Type **8**	1·25	1·60
16	10c. Tracked vehicles	20	1·50
17	20c. Scott Base	20	75
18	30c. Field party	20	40
19	40c. Vanda Station	20	40
20	50c. Scott's hut, Cape Evans	20	40
15/20 Set of 6		2·00	4·50

The post office at Scott Base closed on 30 September 1987 and Nos. 15/20 were withdrawn from sale at philatelic counters in New Zealand on 31 December 1987. Local stamps were subsequently issued by the Armed Forces Canteen Council to cover the cost of mail carriage from Scott Base to New Zealand. These are not listed as they had no national or international validity.

Sets of stamps, showing Whales, Antarctic birds and Seals, inscribed 'NEW ZEALAND ROSS DEPENDENCY', were issued in 1988, 1990 and 1992. These were available from post offices throughout New Zealand, but not in the Ross Dependency.

Ross Dependency NEW ZEALAND

Separate issues for Ross Dependency were resumed in November 1994. Such stamps were only valid on mail from Scott Base, but were not postmarked until arrival at the New Zealand Post Ross Dependency Agency situated at Christchurch.

(Des G. Millen. Litho Southern Colour Print, Dunedin)

1994 (2 Nov)–**95**. Wildlife. T **9** and similar horiz designs. Multicoloured. Perf 13½

21	5c. Type **9**	55	75
22	10c. Snow Petrel chick	65	80
23	20c. Black-browed Albatross	1·00	1·00
24	40c. Emperor Penguins (2.10.95)	3·50	2·50
25	45c. As 40c.	1·60	1·00
26	50c. Chinstrap Penguins	1·60	1·25
27	70c. Adélie Penguin	2·00	1·75
28	80c. Elephant Seals	1·75	1·50
29	$1 Leopard Seal	1·75	1·50
30	$2 Weddell Seal	2·25	2·75
31	$3 Crabeater Seal pup	3·00	3·75
21/31 Set of 11		17·00	17·00

10 Captain James Cook with HMS *Resolution* and HMS *Adventure*

11 Inside Ice Cave

(Des G. Fuller. Litho Questa)

1995 (9 Nov). Antarctic Explorers. T **10** and similar horiz designs. Multicoloured. Perf 14½.

32	40c. Type **10**	1·50	1·50
33	80c. James Clark Ross with HMS *Erebus* and HMS *Terror*	1·75	1·75
34	$1 Roald Amundsen and *Fram*	2·00	2·00
35	$1.20 Robert Scott with *Terra Nova*	2·50	2·50
36	$1.50 Ernest Shackleton with *Endurance*	2·75	2·75
37	$1.80 Richard Byrd with Ford 4-AT-B Trimotor *Floyd Bennett* (aircraft)	2·75	2·75
32/37 Set of 6		12·00	12·00

(Des Diane Prosser. Litho Enschedé)

1996 (13 Nov). Antarctic Landscapes. T **11** and similar multicoloured designs. Perf 14½×14 (vert) or 14×14½ (horiz).

38	40c. Type **11**	75	55
39	80c. Base of glacier	1·25	1·00
40	$1 Glacier ice fall	1·50	1·40
41	$1.20 Climbers on crater rim (*horiz*)	1·75	1·75
42	$1.50 Pressure ridges (*horiz*)	2·00	2·50
43	$1.80 Fumarole ice tower (*horiz*)	2·25	2·75
38/43 Set of 6		8·50	9·00

12 Snow Petrel

13 Sculptured Sea Ice

(Des P. Martinson. Litho Southern Colour Print, Dunedin)

1997 (12 Nov). Antarctic Seabirds. T **12** and similar vert designs. Multicoloured. Perf 14.

(a) With WWF Panda emblem.

44	40c. Type **12**	80	60
45	80c. Cape Petrel	1·25	1·00
46	$1.20 Antarctic Fulmar	1·60	1·50
47	$1.50 Antarctic Petrel	1·60	1·50

(b) Without WWF Panda emblem.

48	40c. Type **12**	2·75	2·75
	a. Block of 6. Nos. 48/53	17·00	16·00
49	80c. Cape Petrel	3·00	2·75
50	$1 Antarctic Prion	3·00	2·50
51	$1.20 Antarctic Fulmar	3·25	3·25
52	$1.50 Antarctic Petrel	3·25	3·50
53	$1.80 Antarctic Tern	3·25	3·25
44/53 Set of 10		21·00	20·00

Nos. 44/47 were printed in sheets containing stamps of one value.

Nos. 48/53 were printed in sheets containing the six values together, *se-tenant*, with the backgrounds forming a composite design.

In addition the $1 and $1.80 were also produced in separate sheets.

(Des S. Fuller. Litho Southern Colour Print, Dunedin)

1998 (11 Nov). Ice Formations. T **13** and similar horiz designs. Multicoloured. Perf 14.

54	40c. Type **13**	60	40
	a. Block of 6. Nos. 54/59	6·50	5·25
55	80c. Glacial tongue	80	70
56	$1 Stranded tabular iceberg	1·00	90
57	$1.20 Autumn at Cape Evans	1·10	1·00
58	$1.50 Sea ice in summer thaw	1·40	1·25
59	$1.80 Sunset at tabular icebergs	1·50	1·50
54/59 Set of 6		6·50	5·25

Nos. 54/59 were printed in sheets of one value or together *se-tenant*, in blocks of six.

14 Sea Smoke, McMurdo Sound

15 RNZAF C-130 Hercules

(Des G. Millen. Litho Southern Colour Print, Dunedin)

1999 (17 Nov). Night Skies. T **14** and similar horiz designs. Multicoloured. Perf 14.

60	40c. Type **14**	1·25	80
61	80c. Alpenglow, Mount Erebus	1·75	1·25
62	$1.10 Sunset, Black Island	1·90	1·60
63	$1.20 Pressure ridges, Ross Sea	2·25	2·00
64	$1.50 Evening light, Ross Island	2·50	2·25
65	$1.80 Mother of pearl clouds, Ross Island	3·00	2·50
60/65 Set of 6		11·50	9·50

(Des Sea Sky Design. Litho Southern Colour Print, Dunedin)

2000 (4 Nov). Antarctic Transport. T **15** and similar horiz designs. Multicoloured. Phosphorised paper. Perf 14.

66	40c. Type **15**	2·00	80
67	80c. Hagglunds BV206 All Terrain carrier	2·25	1·25
68	$1.10 Tracked 4×4 motorbike	2·50	1·50
69	$1.20 ASV track truck	2·50	1·75
70	$1.50 Squirrel helicopter	3·00	2·75
71	$1.80 Elan skidoo	3·00	3·00
66/71 Set of 6		14·00	10·00

(Des Communication Arts Ltd. Litho Southern Colour Print, Dunedin)

2001 (7 Nov). Penguins. Horiz designs as T **604** of New Zealand. Multicoloured. Perf 14½.

72	40c. Two Emperor Penguins	1·40	80
73	80c. Two Adélie Penguins	2·00	1·25
74	90c. Emperor Penguin leaving water	2·00	1·40
75	$1.30 Adélie Penguin in water	2·25	1·75
76	$1.50 Group of Emperor Penguins	2·50	2·25
77	$2 Group of Adélie Penguins	3·00	2·75
72/77 Set of 6		11·50	9·00

16 British Explorers by Sledge

(Des Emdesign. Litho Southern Colour Print, Dunedin)

2002 (6 Nov). Centenary of Discovery Expedition. T **16** and similar horiz designs. Each grey-black, greenish slate and stone. Perf 14.

78	40c. Type **16**	1·50	75
79	80c. HMS *Discovery* at anchor	2·50	1·25
80	90c. HMS *Discovery* trapped in ice	2·50	1·25
81	$1.30 Sledges and tents on ice	2·75	1·90
82	$1.50 Expedition members	3·25	2·25
83	$2 Scott's hut	3·75	2·75
78/83 Set of 6		14·50	9·25

NEW ZEALAND Ross Dependency

17 *Odontaster validus* (Red Seastar)   **18** Penguin and Chick

(Des Chrometoaster. Litho Cartor)

2003 (1 Oct). Marine Life. T **17** and similar horiz designs. Multicoloured. Phosphorised paper. Perf 13×13½.

84	40c. Type **17**	1·50	75
85	90c. *Beroe cucumis* (Comb Jelly)	2·50	1·25
86	$1.30 *Macroptychaster accrescens* (Giant Seastar)	3·00	1·75
87	$1.50 *Sterechinus neumayeri* (Sea Urchin)	3·25	2·25
88	$2 *Perkinsiana littoralis* (Fan Worm)	3·75	2·50
84/88 *Set of 5*		12·50	7·75

(Des Ocean Design. Litho Enschedé)

2004 (3 Nov). Emperor Penguins. T **18** and similar vert designs. Multicoloured. Perf 13½×14.

89	45c. Type **18**	1·75	85
90	90c. Penguin Chick	3·25	1·60
91	$1.35 Penguin feeding Chick	3·75	2·00
92	$1.50 Two Penguins and Chick	3·75	2·50
93	$2 Group of Penguins	4·25	3·25
89/93 *Set of 5*		15·00	9·25

19 Dry Valleys (Craig Potton)   **20** Biologist, 1957–1958

(Des CommArts Design. Litho Wyatt & Wilson)

2005 (2 Nov). Photographs of Antarctica. T **19** and similar horiz designs. Multicoloured. Phosphor frame. Perf 13½.

94	45c. Type **19**	1·50	70
95	90c. Emperor Penguins (Andris Apse)	2·75	1·50
96	$1.35 Antarctic Fur Seal (Mark Mitchell)	3·00	2·25
97	$1.50 Hut of Captain Robert F. Scott (Colin Monteath)	3·50	2·75
98	$2 Antarctic Minke Whale (Kim Westerskov)	4·00	3·00
94/98 *Set of 5*		13·50	9·25

(Litho Southern Colour Print, Dunedin)

2006 (1 Nov). 50th Anniversary of New Zealand Antarctic Programme. T **20** and similar horiz designs. Multicoloured. Phosphorised paper. Perf 14.

99	45c. Type **20**	1·75	1·00
100	90c. Hydrologists, 1979–1980	3·00	2·00
101	$1.35 Geologist, 1984–1985	3·50	3·25
102	$1.50 Meteorologists, 1994–1995	3·75	4·00
103	$2 Marine biologist, 2004–2005	4·25	4·50
99/103 *Set of 5*		14·50	13·50

21 Beaver Aircraft   **22** Departure of *Nimrod* from Lyttelton

(Des Cue Design. Litho Southern Colour Print, Dunedin)

2007 (7 Nov). 50th Anniversary of Commonwealth Trans-Antarctic Expedition. T **21** and similar horiz designs, each greenish blue and olive-black. Phosphorised paper. Perf 14.

104	50c. Type **21**	1·75	1·00
105	$1 Harry Ayres and sledge	2·50	1·75
106	$1.50 Sled Dogs	3·50	3·50
107	$2 TE20 Ferguson tractor	3·75	4·00
108	$2.50 HMNZS *Endeavour*	4·75	5·00
104/108 *Set of 5*		14·50	13·50
MS109 120×80 mm. Nos. 107/108		9·00	9·00

(Des Cue Design. Litho Southern Colour Print)

2008 (5 Nov). Centenary of British Antarctic Expedition, 1907–1909. T **22** and similar horiz designs. Multicoloured. Phosphorised paper. Perf 13½.

110	50c. Type **22**	2·00	1·25
111	$1 Expedition hut, Cape Royds	2·75	2·00
112	$1.50 Arrol-Johnston car (first vehicle on Antarctica)	3·50	3·25
113	$2 Professor Edgeworth David, Douglas Mawson and Alistair Mackay, first to reach South Magnetic Pole, 16 January 1909	4·00	4·00
114	$2.50 Setting out for first ascent of Mount Erebus, 1908	4·50	5·00
110/114 *Set of 5*		15·00	14·00

23 Map of Antarctica   **24** Sperm Whale

(Des Inhouse Design. Litho Southern Colour Print)

2009 (25 Nov). 50th Anniversary of the Antarctic Treaty. T **23** and similar vert designs, each showing silhouettes in Antarctic landscape. Multicoloured. Perf 13×13½.

115	50c. Type **23**	1·60	1·00
116	$1 Penguins ('Antarctica shall be used for peaceful purposes only')	2·75	2·25
117	$1.80 Scientist ('Freedom of scientific investigation')	3·75	3·50
118	$2.30 Flags ('International co-operation in scientific investigation')	4·50	4·50
119	$2.80 Seal ('Preservation and conservation of living resources')	4·50	4·75
115/119 *Set of 5*		15·00	14·50

(Des Tim Garman. Litho Southern Colour Print)

2010 (17 Nov). Whales of the Southern Ocean. T **24** and similar horiz designs. Multicoloured. Phosphorised paper. Perf 14½.

120	60c. Type **24**	1·40	1·10
121	$1.20 Minke Whale	2·50	2·25
122	$1.90 Sei Whale	3·75	3·25
123	$2.40 Killer Whale	4·25	4·50
124	$2.90 Humpback Whale	4·50	4·75
120/124 *Set of 5*		14·50	14·50
MS125 160×85 mm. Nos. 120/124		16·00	16·00

25 Roald Engelbregt Gravning Amundsen and *Fram*

(Des Vertigo. Litho Southern Colour Print)

2011 (2 Nov). Race to the Pole. Centenary of the Amundsen and Scott Expeditions. T **25** and similar horiz designs. Multicoloured. Phosphorised paper. Perf 13½.

126	60c. Type **25**	1·75	1·10
127	$1.20 Amundsen triumphs	3·00	2·00
128	$1.90 Robert Falcon Scott and ship *Terra Nova*	4·00	3·50
129	$2.40 Scott's party and memorial cairn at their last camp	4·50	4·25
130	$2.90 Norwegian flag and Union Jack	6·50	6·00
126/130 *Set of 5*		18·00	15·00
MS131 161×91 mm. Nos. 126/130		18·00	15·00

(Litho)

2012 (14 Jan). Christchurch Philatelic Society Centennial Stamp and Postcard Exhibition. Sheet 130×90 mm. Multicoloured. Phosphorised paper. Perf 13½.

MS132 Nos. 128/129 .... 9·00   9·00

An uncut imperforate master sheet of 20×**MS**132 was donated by New Zealand Post to raise funds for the exhibition.

26 Mount Erebus

27 Antarctic Krill (*Euphausia superba*)

(Des Gregory Millen. Litho Southern Colour Print, New Zealand)

2012 (21 Nov). Landscapes. T **26** and similar horiz designs. Multicoloured. Phosphorised paper. Perf 13½×13.

133	70c. Type **26**	1·40	1·10
134	$1.40 Beardmore Glacier	2·50	2·25
135	$1.90 Lake Vanda	3·50	3·50
136	$2.40 Cape Adare	4·00	4·25
137	$2.90 Ross Ice Shelf	4·50	4·75
133/137 Set of 5		14·50	14·50
MS138 134×88 mm. Nos. 133/137		14·50	14·50

(Des Gregory Millen. Litho Southern Colour Print, New Zealand)

2013 (20 Nov). Antarctic Food Web. T **27** and similar horiz designs. Multicoloured. Perf 14.

139	70c. Type **27**	1·40	1·10
140	$1.40 Lesser Snow Petrel (*Pagodroma nivea*)	2·50	2·25
141	$1.90 Adélie Penguin (*Pygoscelis adeliae*)	3·50	3·50
142	$2.40 Crabeater Seal (*Lobodon carcinophaga*)	4·00	4·25
143	$2.90 Blue Whale (*Balaenoptera musculus*)	4·50	4·75
139/143 Set of 5		14·50	14·50
MS144 141×90 mm. Nos. 139/143		14·50	14·50

28 Emperor Penguin

(Litho Southern Colour Print)

2014 (19 Nov). Penguins of the Antarctic. T **28** and similar circular designs. Multicoloured. Phosphorised paper. Perf 14½.

145	80c. Type **28**	1·40	1·10
146	$1.40 Adélie Penguin	2·50	2·25
147	$2 Macaroni Penguin	3·50	3·50
148	$2.50 Gentoo Penguin	4·50	4·75
149	$3 Chinstrap Penguin	5·50	5·75
145/149 Set of 5		16·00	16·00
MS150 180×81 mm. Nos. 145/149		18·00	18·00

(Litho)

2014 (19 Nov). From Pole to Pole. Sheet 160×90 mm. Phosphorised paper. Perf 14½.

MS151 As No. 149		6·00	6·50

No. **MS**151 contains No. 149 and also a circular stamp-size label depicting a Polar Bear.

A similar sheet issued by Greenland on the same date contains the Polar Bear design as a Greenland stamp inscr 'KALAALLIT NUNAAT. GRØNLAND 2014 21.50' and a circular stamp-size label in the same design as No. 149 but without inscriptions.

29 Endurance

30 Stalked Crinoid (*Crinoidea*)

(Des Jonathan Grey. Litho Southern Colour Print)

2015 (4 Nov). Centenary of the Imperial Trans-Antarctic Expedition, 1914–1917. T **29** and similar horiz designs. Multicoloured. Phosphorised paper. Perf 14×14½.

152	80c. Type **29**	1·10	95
153	80c. Ocean Camp	1·10	95
154	$1.40 Elephant Island to South Georgia in the lifeboat *James Caird*	2·00	1·50
155	$2 The *Aurora*	2·75	2·75
156	$2.50 Laying the Depots	3·50	4·00
157	$3 Rescue of the Ross Sea Party	4·25	4·75
152/157 Set of 6		13·00	13·00
MS158 162×59 mm. Nos. 152/154		4·50	4·50
MS159 162×59 mm. Nos. 155/157		12·00	12·00

(Des Hannah Stancliffe-White. Litho Southern Colour Print, New Zealand)

2016 (16 Nov). Creatures of the Antarctic Sea Floor. T **30** and similar vert designs. Multicoloured. Phosphorised paper. Perf 14½×14.

160	$1 Type **30**	1·75	1·50
161	$1.80 Sea Star (*Odontaster validus*) (Asteroidea)	3·25	2·75
162	$2.20 Sponge (*Haliciona dancoi*) (Porifera)	4·00	4·25
163	$2.70 Hydroid (*Branchiocerianthus*) (Hydrozoa)	4·75	5·00
164	$3.30 Sea Spider (*Pycnogonida*)	6·00	6·25
160/164 Set of 5		18·00	18·00
MS165 183×100 mm. Nos. 160/164		20·00	21·00

31 Scott's Discovery Hut

(Des Sean Garwood (artist) and Jonathan Gray. Litho Southern Colour Print)

2017 (20 Sept). Historic Huts of the Ross Dependency. T **31** and similar square designs. Multicoloured. Phosphorised paper. Perf 14½.

166	$1 Type **31**	1·75	1·50
167	$2 Cognac ('Man's best friend'), preserved cabbage, kettle and wooden box of dog biscuits, Discovery Hut	3·50	3·50
168	$2.20 Shackleton's Nimrod Hut	4·00	4·25
169	$2.30 Stove ('Thank you Mrs Sam'), Nimrod Hut	4·25	4·50
170	$2.70 Scott's Terra Nova Hut	4·75	5·00
171	$3.30 Letter ('Dearest'), Terra Nova Hut	6·00	6·25
166/171 Set of 6		22·00	22·00
MS172 123×108 mm. Nos. 166/171		24·00	25·00

32 RNZAF Auster NZ1707 and Ship, 1956–1958

(Des Alan Hollows. Litho Southern Colour Print)

2018 (7 Nov). Aircraft. T **32** and similar horiz designs. Multicoloured. Phosphorised paper. Perf 14½×14.

173	$1.20 Type **32**	2·10	1·90
174	$1.20 RNZAF de Havilland Canada DHC-2 Beaver NZ6010	2·10	1·90
175	$1.20 RNZAF Lockheed C130 Hercules H series	2·10	1·90
176	$2.40 RNZAF Boeing 757	4·25	4·50
177	$3 Southern Lakes Helicopters AS350 B3 Squirrel	5·50	5·75
178	$3.60 Kenn Borek Air de Havilland Canada DHC6 Twin Otter	6·50	6·75
173/178 Set of 6		20·00	20·00
MS179 180×90 mm. Nos. 173/178		19·00	20·00

NEW ZEALAND Ross Dependency, Tokelau Islands

33 Carsten Borchgrevink

(Des Alan Hollows. Litho Southern Colour Print)

2019 (18 Sept). Cape Adare. T **33** and similar horiz designs. Multicoloured. Phosphorised paper. Perf 14½×14.
180		$1.30 Type **33**...................................	2·40	2·10
181		$1.30 Tin of fruitcake and interior of hut..........	2·40	2·10
182		$2.60 Bone-handled toothbrush and three men in hut..............................	4·75	5·00
183		$3.30 Primus stove outside hut and nesting Penguins........................	6·00	6·25
184		$4 Watercolour of Treecreeper found in hut and artist at work..................	7·25	7·50
180/184 Set of 5..			21·00	21·00
MS185 170×90 mm. Nos. 180/184............................			23·00	24·00

34 Aurora Australis (Winter) **35** Weddell Seal Pup, about 30 Days Old

(Des Cam Price. Litho Southern Colour Print)

2020 (7 Oct). Seasons of Scott Base. T **34** and similar horiz designs. Multicoloured. Phosphorised paper. Perf 13½.
186		$1.40 Type **34**..................................	2·50	2·00
187		$2.70 Sunrise (Spring).......................	4·75	5·00
188		$3.50 Sunset (Summer)....................	6·25	6·50
189		$4 Sunset (Autumn)........................	7·25	7·50
186/189 Set of 4..			19·00	19·00
MS190 150×90 mm. Nos. 186/189............................			21·00	22·00

Nos. 186/189 and the stamps within No. **MS**190 have had black thermochromic ink applied to them, giving a black finish with a fingerprint image. The images on the stamps are only revealed when heat is applied to them.

(Des Helcia Berryman, Mopsy Creative. Litho Southern Colour Print)

2021 (1 Sept). Megafauna. T **35** and similar vert designs. Multicoloured. Phosphorised paper. Perf 13×13½.
191		$1.50 Type **35**...................................	2·50	2·50
192		$2.80 Antarctic Minke Whale............	5·00	5·00
193		$3.60 South Polar Skua......................	6·25	6·50
194		$4.10 Emperor Penguin adult and chick...........	7·50	7·25
191/194 Set of 4..			18·00	18·00
MS195 150×89 mm. Nos. 191/194............................			22·00	22·00

TOKELAU ISLANDS

Formerly known as the Union Islands, and administered as part of the Gilbert and Ellice Islands Colony, Tokelau was transferred to New Zealand on 4 November 1925 and administered with Western Samoa. The Islands were finally incorporated in New Zealand on 1 January 1949 and became a dependency. The name Tokelau was officially adopted on 7 May 1946.

> Stamps of GILBERT AND ELLICE ISLANDS were used in Tokelau from February 1911 until June 1926 when they were replaced by those of SAMOA. These were current until 1948. The post office on Atafu opened in 1911, but the cancellations for the other two islands, Fakaofo and Nukunono, did not appear until 1926.

NEW ZEALAND ADMINISTRATION

1 Atafu Village and Map   **2** Nukunono Hut and Map

3 Fakaofo Village and Map

(Des J. Berry from photographs by T. T. C. Humphrey. Recess B.W.)

1948 (22 June). Types **1**/**3**. Wmk **98** of New Zealand (Mult N Z and Star). Perf 13½.
1	**1**	½d. red-brown and purple........................	15	1·00
2	**2**	1d. chestnut and green..............................	15	50
		w. Wmk inverted..	£275	
3	**3**	2d. green and ultramarine.........................	15	50
1/3 Set of 3...			40	1·75

Covers are known postmarked 16 June 1948, but this was in error for 16 July.

1953 (16 June*). Coronation. As No. 715 of New Zealand, but inscr 'TOKELAU ISLANDS'.
4	**164**	3d. brown...	1·25	2·00

* This is the date of issue in Tokelau. The stamps were released in New Zealand on 25 May.

(4)   (5)

1956 (27 Mar). No. 1 surch with T **4** by Govt Printer, Wellington.
5	**1**	1s. on ½d. red-brown and purple.........	75	1·25

1966 (8 Nov). Postal fiscal stamps of New Zealand (T **F6**), but without value, surch as T **5** by Govt Printer, Wellington. W **98** of New Zealand. Perf 14.
6		6d. light blue...	25	80
7		8d. light emerald......................................	25	80
8		2s. light pink...	30	80
6/8 Set of 3..			70	2·25

(New Currency. 100 cents = 1 New Zealand dollar)

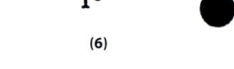

(6)

R. 7/1

Normal

On R. 7/1 of Nos. 12/15 the words 'TOKELAU' and 'ISLANDS' are ½ mm apart instead of 1½ mm.

1967 (4 Sept*)–**68**. Decimal currency.
(a) Nos. 1/3 surch in decimal currency as T **6** by Govt Printer, Wellington.
9		1c. on 1d. (No. 2).....................................	20	1·00
10		2c. on 2d. (No. 3).....................................	30	1·50
11		10c. on ½d. (No. 1)...................................	70	2·00

Tokelau Islands NEW ZEALAND

(b) Postal Fiscal stamps of New Zealand (T **F6**), but without value, surch as T **7** by Govt Printer, Wellington. W **98** of New Zealand (sideways). Perf 14 (line or comb).

12	**F6**	3c. reddish lilac	30	20
		a. Narrow setting	10·00	10·00
13		5c. light blue	30	20
		a. Narrow setting	10·00	10·00
		b. Pale blue (second setting) (18.9.68)	2·00	2·50
14		7c. light emerald	30	20
		a. Narrow setting	10·00	10·00
15		20c. light pink	30	30
		a. Narrow setting	10·00	10·00
9/15 Set of 7			2·25	4·75

* This is the date of issue in Tokelau. The stamps were released in New Zealand on 10 July.

In the second setting of the 5c. the words 'TOKELAU' and 'ISLANDS' are in thinner letters and almost 2 mm apart.

8 British Protectorate (1877)

(Des New Zealand PO artists from suggestions by Tokelau Administration. Litho B.W.)

1969 (8 Aug). History of Tokelau. T **8** and similar horiz designs. W **98** of New Zealand. Perf 13×12½.

16	5c. ultramarine, yellow and black	15	10
17	10c. vermilion, yellow and black	15	10
18	15c. green, yellow and black	20	15
19	20c. yellow-brown, yellow and black	25	15
16/19 Set of 4		65	45

Designs: 5c. T **8**; 10c. Annexed to Gilbert and Ellice Islands, 1916: 15c. New Zealand Administration, 1925; 20c. New Zealand Territory, 1948.

1969 (14 Nov*). Christmas. As T **301** of New Zealand, but inscr 'TOKELAU ISLANDS'. W **98** of New Zealand. Perf 13½×14½.

20	2c. multicoloured	10	15

* This is the date of issue in Tokelau. The stamps were released in New Zealand on 1 October.

1970 (15 Nov*). Christmas. As T **314** of New Zealand, but inscr 'TOKELAU ISLANDS'. Perf 12½.

21	2c. multicoloured	10	20

* This is the date of issue in Tokelau. The stamps were released in New Zealand on 1 October.

12 HMS *Dolphin*, 1765

(Des D. B. Stevenson. Litho B.W.)

1971 (9 Feb*). Discovery of Tokelau. T **12** and similar multicoloured designs. Perf 13½.

22	5c. Type **12**	35	20
23	10c. HMS *Pandora*, 1791	35	20
24	25c. *General Jackson* (American whaling ship), 1835 (horiz)	40	70
22/24 Set of 3		1·00	1·00

* This is the date of issue in Tokelau. The stamps were released in New Zealand on 9 December 1970.

13 Fan   **14** Windmill Pump

(Des Enid Hunter. Litho Harrison)

1971 (20 Oct). Various horiz designs as T **13** showing handicrafts. Multicoloured. Perf 14.

25	1c. Type **13**	15	20
26	2c. Handbag	15	30
27	3c. Basket	15	40
28	5c. Handbag	15	40
29	10c. Shopping bag	15	45
30	15c. Fishing box	20	1·00
31	20c. Canoe	20	1·10
32	25c. Fishing hooks	20	1·10
25/32 Set of 8		1·25	4·50

(Des A. G. Mitchell. Litho Questa)

1972 (6 Sept). 25th Anniversary of South Pacific Commission. T **14** and similar vert designs. Multicoloured. Perf 14×13½.

33	5c. Type **14**	15	30
34	10c. Community well	20	40
35	15c. Pest eradication	25	50
36	20c. Flags of member nations	50	60
33/36 Set of 4		1·00	1·60

On No. 35 'PACIFIC' is spelt 'PACFIC'.

15 Horny Coral   **16** Hump-back Cowrie

(Des Eileen Mayo. Litho B.W.)

1973 (12 Sept). Coral. T **15** and similar vert designs. Multicoloured. Perf 13.

37	3c. Type **15**	30	40
38	5c. Soft Coral	30	45
39	15c. Mushroom Coral	50	60
40	25c. Staghorn Coral	50	70
37/40 Set of 4		1·40	1·90

(Des G. F. Fuller. Litho Questa)

1974 (13 Nov). Shells of the Coral Reef. T **16** and similar horiz designs. Multicoloured. Perf 14.

41	3c. Type **16**	30	60
42	5c. Tiger Cowrie	30	60
43	15c. Mole Cowrie	50	80
44	25c. Eyed Cowrie	50	1·00
41/44 Set of 4		1·40	2·75

17 Moorish Idol   25c. 'a' for 'd' in 'Islands'; (R. 7/6)

(Des Eileen Mayo. Litho Questa)

1975 (19 Nov). Fish. T **17** and similar vert designs. Multicoloured. Perf 14.

45	5c. Type **17**	15	30
46	10c. Long-nosed Butterflyfish	15	30
47	15c. Lined Butterflyfish	20	40
48	25c. Lionfish ('Red Fire Fish')	20	60
	a. 'a' for 'd' in 'Islands'	6·00	
45/48 Set of 4		65	1·40

18 Canoe Building

(Des F. Paulo. Litho Questa)

1976 (27 Oct)–**81**. T **18** and similar multicoloured designs showing local life. Perf 14×13½ (9c. to $1) or 13½×14 (others)

49	1c. Type **18**	25	1·00
	a. Perf 14½×15 (15.7.81)	10	15
50	2c. Reef fishing	15	2·00

157

NEW ZEALAND Tokelau Islands

51	3c. Weaving preparation		15	75
	a. Perf 14½×15 (15.7.81)		10	15
52	5c. Umu (kitchen)		20	75
	a. Perf 14½×15 (15.7.81)		10	15
53	9c. Carving (vert)		10	1·00
	a. Perf 15×14½ (15.7.81)		15	15
54	20c. Husking Coconuts (vert)		15	60
	a. Perf 15×14½ (15.7.81)		15	20
55	50c. Wash day (vert)		20	70
	a. Perf 15×14½ (15.7.81)		20	20
56	$1 Meal time (vert)		35	2·00
	a. Perf 15×14½ (15.7.81)		30	30
49/56 Set of 8			1·40	8·00
49a/56a Set of 7			1·00	1·10

19 White Tern

20 Westminster Abbey

(Des F. Paulo. Litho Questa)

1977 (16 Nov). Birds of Tokelau. T **19** and similar horiz designs. Multicoloured. Perf 14½.

57	8c. Type **19**	25	20
58	10c. Ruddy Turnstone	30	25
59	15c. White-capped Noddy	35	35
60	30c. Common Noddy	40	55
57/60 Set of 4		1·10	1·25

(Des Eileen Mayo. Litho Questa)

1978 (28 June). 25th Anniversary of Coronation. T **20** and similar vert designs. Multicoloured. Perf 14.

61	8c. Type **20**	20	25
62	10c. King Edward's Chair	20	25
63	15c. Coronation regalia	30	40
64	30c. Queen Elizabeth II	50	65
61/64 Set of 4		1·10	1·40

21 Canoe Race

22 Rugby

(Des F. Paulo. Photo Heraclio Fournier)

1978 (8 Nov). Canoe Racing. T **21** and similar horiz designs showing races. Perf 13½×14.

65	8c. multicoloured	20	25
66	12c. multicoloured	20	30
67	15c. multicoloured	20	35
68	30c. multicoloured	30	60
65/68 Set of 4		80	1·40

(Des F. Paulo. Photo Heraclio Fournier)

1979 (7 Nov). Sports. T **22** and similar horiz designs. Multicoloured. Perf 13½.

69	10c. Type **22**	10	20
70	15c. Cricket	60	40
71	20c. Rugby (different)	20	30
72	30c. Cricket (different)	60	65
69/72 Set of 4		1·40	1·40

23 Surfing

24 Pole Vault

(Des F. Paulo. Litho J.W.)

1980 (5 Nov). Water Sports. T **23** and similar horiz designs. Multicoloured. Perf 13.

73	10c. Type **23**	10	10
74	20c. Surfing (different)	15	15
75	30c. Swimming	20	20
76	50c. Swimming (different)	25	25
73/76 Set of 4		60	65

(Des F. Paulo. Photo Heraclio Fournier)

1981 (4 Nov). Sports. T **24** and similar vert designs. Multicoloured. Perf 14×13½.

77	10c. Type **24**	10	10
78	20c. Volleyball	15	15
79	30c. Running	20	20
80	50c. Volleyball (different)	25	30
77/80 Set of 4		60	65

25 Wood-carving

26 Octopus Lure

(Des R. Conly. Litho Enschedé)

1982 (5 May). Handicrafts. T **25** and similar vert designs. Multicoloured. Perf 14×13½.

81	10s. Type **25**	10	15
82	22s. Bow-drilling sea shell	10	20
83	34s. Bowl finishing	15	30
84	60s. Basket weaving	25	60
81/84 Set of 4		55	1·10

(Des R. Conly. Litho Questa)

1982 (3 Nov). Fishing Methods. T **26** and similar vert designs. Multicoloured. Perf 14.

85	5s. Type **26**	10	10
86	18s. Multiple-hook fishing	15	15
87	23s. Ruvettus fishing	20	20
88	34s. Netting flying fish	20	25
89	63s. Noose fishing	25	35
90	75s. Bonito fishing	30	40
85/90 Set of 6		1·00	1·25

27 Outrigger Canoe

28 Javelin

(Des R. Conly. Litho Cambec Press, Melbourne)

1983 (4 May). Transport. T **27** and similar horiz designs. Multicoloured. Perf 13×13½.

91	5s. Type **27**	10	10
92	18s. Wooden whaleboat	10	15
93	23s. Aluminium whaleboat	10	15
94	34s. *Alia* (fishing catamaran)	15	20
95	63s. *Frysna* (freighter)	25	30
96	75s. Grumman MacKinnon G-21C Goose flying boat	30	40
91/96 Set of 6		85	1·10

(Des R. Conly. Litho Questa)

1983 (2 Nov). Traditional Pastimes. T **28** and similar horiz designs. Multicoloured. Perf 14.

97	5s. Type **28**	10	10
98	18s. String game	10	15
99	23s. Fire making	10	15
100	34s. Shell throwing	15	20
101	63s. Handball game	20	30
102	75s. Mass wrestling	25	40
97/102 Set of 6		70	1·10

Tokelau Islands NEW ZEALAND

29 Planting and Harvesting **30** Convict Tang ('Manini')

(Des R. Conly. Litho J.W.)

1984 (2 May). Copra Industry. T **29** and similar vert designs. Multicoloured. Perf 13½×13.

103	48s. Type **29**..	25	30
	a. Horiz strip of 5. Nos. 103/107	1·00	1·25
104	48s. Husking and splitting........................	25	30
105	48s. Drying...	25	30
106	48s. Bagging...	25	30
107	48s. Shipping..	25	30
103/107 Set of 5...		1·00	1·25

Nos. 103/107 were printed together, *se-tenant*, in horizontal strips of five throughout the sheet.

(Des R. Conly. Litho B.D.T.)

1984 (5 Dec). Fish. T **30** and similar horiz designs. Multicoloured. Perf 15×14.

108	1s. Type **30**..	10	10
109	2s. Flying Fish ('Hahave')..........................	10	10
110	5s. Surge Wrasse ('Uloulo')......................	15	10
111	9s. Unicornfish ('Ume ihu')......................	15	10
112	23s. Wrasse ('Lafilafi')................................	20	20
113	34s. Red Snapper ('Fagamea')...................	25	25
114	50s. Yellow-finned Tuna ('Kakahi')............	35	40
115	75s. Oilfish ('Palu po')................................	45	50
116	$1 Grey Shark ('Mokoha')........................	45	55
117	$2 Black Marlin ('Hakula')........................	70	80
108/117 Set of 10...		2·50	2·75

Examples of Nos. 108/117 are known postmarked at Nukunonu on 23 November 1984.

The 50s., No. 114, was sold at the STAMPEX 86 Stamp Exhibition, Adelaide, overprinted 'STAMPEX 86 4–10 AUGUST 1986' in three lines. These overprinted stamps were not available from post offices in Tokelau. Used examples come from dealers' stocks subsequently sent to the islands for cancellation.

31 *Ficus tinctoria* ('Mati') **32** Administration Centre, Atafu

(Des R. Conly. Litho Wyatt and Wilson Ltd, Christchurch, NZ)

1985 (26 June). Native Trees. T **31** and similar vert designs. Multicoloured. Perf 13.

118	5c. Type **31**...	10	10
119	18c. *Morinda citrifolia* ('Nonu').................	10	15
120	32c. Breadfruit Tree ('Ulu')........................	15	25
121	48c. *Pandanus tectorius* ('Fala').................	25	40
122	60c. *Cordia subcordata* ('Kanava')............	30	45
123	75c. Coconut Palm ('Niu')........................	35	55
118/123 Set of 6..		1·10	1·60

Nos. 118/123 were issued with matt, almost invisible, PVA gum.

(Des R. Conly. Litho Questa)

1985 (4 Dec). Tokelau Architecture (1st series). Public Buildings. T **32** and similar horiz designs. Multicoloured. Perf 14.

124	5c. Type **32**...	10	10
125	18c. Administration Centre, Nukunonu.........	15	15
126	32c. Administration Centre, Fakaofo............	15	20
127	48c. Congregational Church, Atafu.............	20	30
128	60c. Catholic Church, Nukunonu................	25	35
129	75c. Congregational Church, Fakaofo..........	25	40
124/129 Set of 6..		1·00	1·25

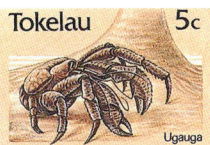

33 Atafu Hospital **34** Coconut Crab

(Des R. Conly. Litho Cambec Press, Melbourne)

1986 (7 May). Tokelau Architecture (2nd series). Hospitals and Schools. T **33** and similar horiz designs. Multicoloured. Perf 13½.

130	5c. Type **33**...	10	10
131	18c. St Joseph's Hospital, Nukunonu...........	15	15
132	32c. Fenuafala Hospital, Fakaofo................	15	20
133	48c. Matauala School, Atafu......................	20	30
134	60c. Matiti School, Nukunonu...................	25	40
135	75c. Fenuafala School, Fakaofo.................	25	50
130/135 Set of 6..		1·00	1·50

(Des R. Conly. Litho Questa)

1986 (3 Dec). Agricultural Livestock. T **34** and similar horiz designs. Multicoloured. Perf 14.

136	5c. Type **34**...	10	10
137	18c. Pigs..	10	15
138	32c. Chickens..	20	20
139	48c. Reef Hawksbill Turtle..........................	25	30
140	60c. Goats...	30	40
141	75c. Ducks..	35	55
136/141 Set of 6..		1·00	1·50

35 *Scaevola taccada* ('Gahu') **36** Javelin

(Des R. Conly. Litho Questa)

1987 (6 May). Tokelau Flora. T **35** and similar horiz designs. Multicoloured. Perf 14.

142	5c. Type **35**...	25	50
143	18c. *Hernandia nymphaeifolia* ('Puka')........	40	80
144	32c. *Pandanus tectorius* ('Higano').............	50	1·00
145	48c. *Gardenia taitensis* ('Tialetiale')............	55	1·25
146	60c. *Pemphis acidula* ('Gagie')..................	60	1·50
147	75c. *Guettarda speciosa* ('Puapua')............	70	1·75
142/147 Set of 6..		2·75	6·00

(Des F. Paulo. Litho Leigh-Mardon Ltd, Melbourne)

1987 (2 Dec). Tokelau Olympic Sports. T **36** and similar horiz designs. Multicoloured. Perf 14×14½.

148	5c. Type **36**...	15	20
149	18c. Shot put...	20	35
150	32c. Long jump...	30	40
151	48c. Hurdling..	35	60
152	60c. Sprinting..	40	1·00
153	75c. Wrestling...	55	1·10
148/153 Set of 6..		1·75	3·25

37 Small Boat Flotilla in Sydney Harbour **38** Island Maps and Ministerial Representatives

(Des and litho CPE Australia Ltd, Melbourne)

1988 (30 July). Bicentenary of Australian Settlement and Sydpex '88 National Stamp Exhibition, Sydney. T **37** and similar square designs. Multicoloured. Perf 13.

154	50c. Type **37**...	2·00	2·25
	a. Horiz strip of 5. Nos. 154/158	9·00	10·00
155	50c. Sailing ships and liners.......................	2·00	2·25
156	50c. Sydney skyline and Opera House.........	2·00	2·25
157	50c. Sydney Harbour Bridge.......................	2·00	2·25
158	50c. Sydney waterfront.............................	2·00	2·25
154/158 Set of 5..		9·00	10·00

NEW ZEALAND Tokelau Islands

Nos. 154/158 were printed together, *se-tenant*, in horizontal strips of five throughout the sheet, forming a composite aerial view of the re-enactment of First Fleet's arrival.

(Des F. Paulo. Litho Leigh-Mardon Ltd, Melbourne)

1988 (10 Aug). Political Development. T **38** and similar horiz designs. Multicoloured. Perf 14½.

159	5c. Type **38** (administration transferred to NZ Foreign Affairs Ministry, 1975)	40	60
160	18c. General Fono (island assembly) meeting, 1977	45	55
161	32c. Arms of New Zealand (first visit by New Zealand Prime Minister, 1985)	70	80
162	48c. UN logo (first visit by UN representative, 1976)	80	1·00
163	60c. Canoe and UN logo (first Tokelau delegation to UN, 1987)	1·00	1·40
164	75c. Secretary and NZ flag (first islander appointed as Official Secretary, 1987)	2·25	2·00
159/164 Set of 6		5·00	5·75

39 Three Wise Men in Canoe and Star

(Des F. Paulo. Litho Govt Ptg Office, Wellington)

1988 (7 Dec). Christmas. T **39** and similar horiz designs showing Christmas in Tokelau. Multicoloured. Perf 13½.

165	5c. Type **39**	20	35
166	20c. Tokelau Nativity	25	40
167	40c. Flight to Egypt by canoe	45	70
168	60c. Children's presents	50	80
169	70c. Christ child in Tokelauan basket	60	90
170	$1 Christmas parade	75	1·10
165/170 Set of 6		2·50	3·75

40 Launching Outrigger Canoe   **41** Basketwork

(Des F. Paulo. Litho Leigh-Mardon Ltd, Melbourne)

1989 (28 June). Food Gathering. T **40** and similar horiz designs. Multicoloured. Perf 14×14½.

171	50c. Type **40**	1·50	1·75
	a. Horiz strip of 3. Nos. 171/173	4·00	4·75
172	50c. Paddling canoe away from shore	1·50	1·75
173	50c. Fishing punt and sailing canoe	1·50	1·75
174	50c. Canoe on beach	1·50	1·75
	a. Horiz strip of 3. Nos. 174/176	4·00	4·75
175	50c. Loading Coconuts into canoe	1·50	1·75
176	50c. Tokelauans with produce	1·50	1·75
171/176 Set of 6		8·00	9·50

Nos. 171/173 and 174/176 were each printed together, *se-tenant*, in horizontal strips of three throughout the sheets, forming composite designs.

A $3 miniature sheet commemorating the 150th anniversary of the Penny Black and Stamp World London 90 International Stamp Exhibition exists, but was not issued or used by the New Zealand Post offices on the islands. Examples were subsequently offered to collectors in January 1994 (*Price £18 mint or used*).

(Des F. Paulo. Litho Leigh-Mardon Ltd, Melbourne)

1990 (2 May). Women's Handicrafts. T **41** and similar horiz designs. Multicoloured. Perf 14½.

177	5c. Type **41**	75	65
178	20c. Preparing cloth	1·25	1·10
179	40c. Tokelau fabrics	1·75	1·50
180	60c. Mat weaving	2·25	2·25
181	80c. Weaving palm fronds	3·00	3·25
182	$1 Basket making	3·25	3·50
177/182 Set of 6		11·00	11·00

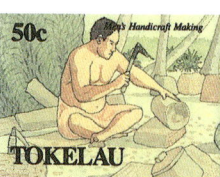 

42 Man with Adze and Wood Blocks   **43** Swimming

(Des F. Paulo. Litho Wyatt & Wilson, Christchurch)

1990 (1 Aug). Men's Handicrafts. T **42** and similar horiz designs. Multicoloured. Perf 13.

183	50c. Type **42**	2·00	2·25
	a. Horiz strip of 3. Nos. 183/185	5·50	5·50
184	50c. Making fishing boxes	2·00	2·25
185	50c. Fixing handles to fishing boxes	2·00	2·25
186	50c. Two men decorating fishing boxes	2·00	2·25
	a. Horiz strip of 3. Nos. 186/188	5·50	5·50
187	50c. Canoe building (two men)	2·00	2·25
188	50c. Canoe building (three men)	2·00	2·25
183/188 Set of 6		11·00	12·00

Nos. 183/185 and 186/188 were each printed together, *se-tenant*, in horizontal strips of three throughout the sheets, and have matt, almost invisible, gum.

Under the terms of the Tokelau Post Office Regulations which came into force on 1 March 1991 the responsibility for providing postage stamps for the islands passed from New Zealand Post to the Administrator of Tokelau, based at the Ministry of External Relations, Wellington.

(Des R. Roberts. Litho Southern Colour Print, Dunedin)

1992 (8 July). Olympic Games, Barcelona. T **43** and similar vert designs. Multicoloured. Perf 13½.

189	40c. Type **43**	50	50
190	60c. Long jump	70	80
191	$1 Volleyball	1·25	1·40
192	$1.80 Running	1·75	2·75
189/192 Set of 4		3·75	5·00

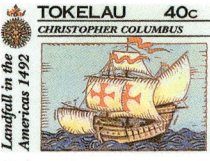 

44 Santa Maria   **45** Queen Elizabeth II in 1953

(Des R. Roberts. Litho Southern Colour Print, Dunedin)

1992 (18 Dec). 500th Anniversary of Discovery of America by Columbus. T **44** and similar horiz designs. Multicoloured. Perf 13½.

193	40c. Type **44**	75	75
194	60c. Christopher Columbus	1·00	1·10
195	$1.20 Fleet of Columbus	2·25	2·50
196	$1.80 Columbus landing in the New World	3·00	4·00
193/196 Set of 4		6·25	7·50

(Des M. Conly. Litho Southern Colour Print, Dunedin)

1993 (8 July). 40th Anniversary of Coronation. T **45** and similar horiz designs. Multicoloured. Perf 13½.

197	25c. Type **45**	50	55
198	40c. Prince Philip	60	70
199	$1 Queen Elizabeth II in 1993	1·00	1·10
200	$2 Queen Elizabeth II and Prince Philip	1·50	2·00
197/200 Set of 4		3·25	4·00

46 Bristle-thighed Curlew

(Des M. Conly. Litho Southern Colour Print, Dunedin)

1993 (15 Dec). Birds of Tokelau. T **46** and similar horiz designs. Multicoloured. Perf 13½.

201	25c. Type **46**	60	60
202	40c. Red-tailed Tropicbird	80	80
203	$1 Reef Heron	1·40	1·40

Tokelau Islands NEW ZEALAND

204	$2 Pacific Golden Plover	2·00	2·50
201/204 Set of 4		4·25	4·75

(Des M. Conly. Litho Southern Colour Print, Dunedin)

1994 (18 Feb). Hong Kong '94 International Stamp Exhibition. Multicoloured. Perf 14×14½.
MS205 125×100 mm. As Nos. 201/204 (sold at $5)............ 5·00 6·00

47 Great Egret ('White Heron')

(Des M. Conly. Litho Southern Colour Print, Dunedin)

1994 (16 Aug). Philakorea '94 International Stamp Exhibition, Seoul. Perf 12.
206	**47**	$2 multicoloured	2·50	3·25
MS207 110×76 mm. No. 206			4·50	4·50

48 Model Outrigger Canoe   **49** Fishing Pigs

(Des M. Conly. Litho Southern Colour Print, Dunedin)

1994 (19 Dec). Handicrafts. T **48** and similar horiz designs. Multicoloured. Perf 13½.
208	5c. Type **48**	10	10
209	25c. Plaited fan	20	25
210	40c. Plaited baskets	30	35
211	50c. Fishing box	35	40
212	80c. Water bottle	50	65
213	$1 Fishing hook	60	70
214	$2 Coconut gourds	1·10	1·25
215	$5 Shell necklace	2·25	3·50
208/215 Set of 8		4·75	6·50

(Des M. Conly. Litho Southern Colour Print, Dunedin)

1995 (3 Feb). Chinese New Year. Year of the Pig. Sheet 110×75 mm. Perf 14×14½.
MS218 **49** $5 multicoloured.. 6·00 7·50

1995 (3 Feb). PostX '95 National Stamp Exhibition, Auckland. No. MS218 optd with PostX '95 emblem on sheet margin in red.
MS219 **49** $5 multicoloured.. 13·00 13·00

50 Pacific Pigeon on Branch   **51** Long-nosed Butterflyfish

(Des Patricia Altman. Litho Southern Colour Print, Dunedin)

1995 (27 Apr). Endangered Species. Pacific Pigeon. T **50** and similar horiz designs. Multicoloured. Perf 13½.
220	25c. Type **50**	60	65
221	40c. On branch (different)	85	90
222	$1 On branch with berries	1·40	1·75
223	$2 Chick in nest	2·50	3·25
220/223 Set of 4		4·75	6·00

(Des R. Youmans. Litho Southern Colour Print, Dunedin)

1995 (1 Sept). Reef Fish. T **51** and similar horiz designs. Multicoloured. Perf 12.
224	25c. Type **51**	30	40
225	40c. Emperor Angelfish	40	55
226	$1 Moorish Idol	75	1·00
227	$2 Lined Butterflyfish	1·25	2·00
224/227 Set of 4		2·40	3·50
MS228 130×90 mm. $3 Lionfish (inscr 'Red Fire Fish') (39×34 mm)		2·00	3·50

No. MS228 includes the Singapore '95 International Stamp Exhibition logo on the sheet margin.

1995 (1 Sept). Singapore '95 International Stamp Exhibition. No. MS218 optd with exhibition emblem in red on sheet margin.
MS229 **49** $5 multicoloured.. 5·50 7·00

52 *Danaus plexippus*   **53** Hawksbill Turtle

(Des Patricia Altman. Litho Southern Colour Print, Dunedin)

1995 (16 Oct). Butterflies and Moths. T **52** and similar vert designs. Multicoloured. Perf 12.
230	25c. Type **52**	50	50
231	40c. *Precis villida samoensis*	70	70
232	$1 *Hypolimnas bolina*	1·25	1·75
233	$2 *Euploea lewenii*	2·00	3·00
230/233 Set of 4		4·00	5·50

(Des Patricia Altman. Litho Southern Colour Print, Dunedin)

1995 (27 Nov). Year of the Sea Turtle. T **53** and similar horiz designs. Multicoloured. Perf 12.
234	25c. Type **53**	55	55
235	40c. Leatherback Turtle	75	75
236	$1 Green Turtle	1·75	2·00
237	$2 Loggerhead Turtle	2·50	3·00
234/237 Set of 4		5·00	5·50
MS238 130×90 mm. $3 As $2 (50×40 mm)		4·00	5·50

54 Pacific Rat

(Des Patricia Altman. Litho Southern Colour Print, Dunedin)

1996 (19 Feb). Chinese New Year. Year of the Rat. Sheet 128×97 mm. Perf 12.
MS239 **54** $3 multicoloured.. 4·50 6·00

55 Queen Elizabeth II and Nukunonu   **56** Fraser's Dolphin

(Des D. Miller. Litho Enschedé)

1996 (22 Apr). 70th Birthday of Queen Elizabeth II. T **55** and similar vert designs, each incorporating a different photograph of the Queen. Multicoloured. Perf 13½.
240	40c. Type **55**	50	50
241	$1 Atafu at night	1·40	1·50
242	$1.25 Atafu	1·60	1·75
243	$2 Atafu village	2·00	2·50
240/243 Set of 4		5·00	5·75
MS244 64×66 mm. $3 Queen Elizabeth II		2·75	3·75

NEW ZEALAND Tokelau Islands

1996 (18 May). CHINA '96 9th Asian International Stamp Exhibition, Peking. No. **MS**239 optd with exhibition emblem on sheet margin in red.
MS245 128×97 mm. $3 Type **54**................................ 4·00 5·50

(Des R. Youmans. Litho Southern Colour Print, Dunedin)

1996 (15 July). Dolphins. T **56** and similar horiz designs. Multicoloured. Perf 14.
246	40c. Type **56**................................	1·00	1·00
247	$1 Common Dolphin................................	2·00	2·50
248	$1.25 Striped Dolphin................................	2·00	2·50
249	$2 Spotted Dolphin................................	3·25	3·50
246/249 Set of 4................................		7·50	8·50

57 Mole Cowrie **58** Ox

(Des Patricia Altman. Litho Southern Colour Print, Dunedin)

1996 (16 Oct). Sea Shells. T **57** and similar horiz designs. Multicoloured. Perf 12.
250	40c. Type **57**................................	60	60
251	$1 Humpback Cowrie................................	1·00	1·25
252	$1.25 Eyed Cowrie................................	1·00	1·50
253	$2 Tiger Cowrie................................	1·50	2·75
250/253 Set of 4................................		3·50	5·50

MS254 123×83 mm. $3 Humpback Cowrie (*different*) (50×40 mm)................................ 2·50 3·75

1996 (16 Oct). TAIPEI '96 Tenth Asian International Stamp Exhibition, Taiwan. No. **MS**239 optd with exhibition emblem on sheet margin in red.
MS255 128×97 mm. $3 Type **54**................................ 2·25 3·50

(Des Patricia Altman. Litho Southern Colour Print, Dunedin)

1997 (12 Feb). Chinese New Year. Year of the Ox. Sheet 120×78 mm. Perf 15×14½.
MS256 **58** $2 multicoloured................................ 2·50 3·25

1997 (12 Feb). HONG KONG '97 International Stamp Exhibition. No. **MS**256 optd with '**HONG KONG '97 STAMP EXHIBITION**' in gold on sheet margin.
MS257 120×78 mm. **58** $2 multicoloured................................ 3·00 3·50

1997 (29 May). Pacific '97 International Stamp Exhibition, San Francisco. No. **MS**256 optd with exhibition emblem in red on sheet margin.
MS258 120×78 mm. **58** $2 multicoloured................................ 2·25 3·25

59 Humpback Whale **60** Church by Lagoon

(Des Patricia Altman. Litho Southern Colour Print, Dunedin)

1997 (10 June). Humpback Whales. T **59** and similar horiz designs. Multicoloured. Perf 12.
259	40c. Type **59**................................	50	55
260	$1 Family of Humpback Whales...........	75	85
261	$1.25 Humpback Whale feeding............	1·00	1·50
262	$2 Humpback Whale and Calf............	1·50	2·50
259/262 Set of 4................................		3·25	4·75

MS263 135×87 mm. $3 Head of Humpback Whale........... 2·00 3·25

(Des R. Youmans. Litho Southern Colour Print, Dunedin)

1997 (17 Sept). 50th Anniversary of South Pacific Commission. T **60** and similar horiz designs showing views of Tokelau. Multicoloured. Perf 14.
264	40c. Type **60**................................	35	45
265	$1 Boy looking across lagoon	70	90
266	$1.25 Bungalow on small island...........	80	1·25
267	$2 Tokelau from the air...................	1·40	2·25
264/267 Set of 4................................		3·00	4·25

61 Gorgonian Coral and Emperor Angelfish **62** Tiger

(Des Patricia Altman. Litho Southern Colour Print, Dunedin)

1997 (20 Oct). Pacific Year of the Coral Reef. T **61** and similar horiz designs. Multicoloured. Perf 13½.
268	$1 Type **61**................................	75	1·00
	a. Horiz strip of 5. Nos. 268/272	3·25	4·50
269	$1 Soft Coral................................	75	1·00
270	$1 Mushroom Coral................................	75	1·00
271	$1 Staghorn Coral................................	75	1·00
272	$1 Staghorn Coral and Moorish Idols.........	75	1·00
268/272 Set of 5................................		3·25	4·50

Nos. 268/272 were printed together, *se-tenant*, in horizontal strips of five with the backgrounds forming a composite design.

(Des Patricia Altman. Litho Southern Colour Print, Dunedin)

1997 (13 Nov). Aupex '97 National Stamp Exhibition, Auckland. No. **MS**263 optd '**AUPEX'97 13–16 NOVEMBER NZ NATIONAL STAMP EXHIBITION**' on sheet margin in black. Perf 12.
MS273 135×87 mm. $3 Head of Humpback Whale.......... 2·00 3·00

(Des S. Chan. Litho Southern Colour Print, Dunedin)

1998 (28 Jan). Chinese New Year. Year of the Tiger. Sheet 130×95 mm. Perf 14×14½.
MS274 **62** $2 multicoloured................................ 1·75 2·50

62a Princess Diana **63** 1948 ½d. Atafu Village Stamp

(Des D. Miller. Litho Questa)

1998 (31 Mar). Diana, Princess of Wales Commemoration. T **62a** and similar vert designs. Multicoloured. Perf 14½×14.
275 $1 Type **62a**................................ 70 1·25
MS276 145×70 mm. $1 Wearing red polka-dot dress; $1 Wearing matching pink hat and jacket; $1 No. 275; $1 In pink and yellow jacket with flowers (*sold at $4+50c. charity premium*)................................ 1·50 2·75

(Des Sea Sky Design Studio. Litho Southern Colour Print, Dunedin)

1998 (22 June). 50th Anniversary of Tokelau Postage Stamps. Sheet 105×80 mm, containing T **63** and similar horiz designs. Multicoloured. Perf 14½.
MS277 $1 Type **63**; $1 1948 1d. Nukunono hut stamp; $1 1948 2d. Fakaofo village stamp............................ 3·50 4·00

64 *Oryctes rhinoceros* **65** *Ipomoea pes-caprae*

(Des Patricia Altman. Litho Southern Colour Print, Dunedin)

1998 (23 Aug). Beetles. T **64** and similar horiz designs. Multicoloured. Perf 14.
278	40c. Type **64**................................	70	80
279	$1 *Tribolium castaneum*................	1·40	1·50
280	$1.25 *Coccinella repanda*................	1·50	1·60

Tokelau Islands NEW ZEALAND

281	$2 *Amarygmus hydrophiloides*...........		2·25	3·00
278/281	Set of 4.................................		5·25	6·25
MS282	125×86 mm. $3 *Coccinella repanda* (*different*)......		2·50	3·25

(Des Patricia Altman. Litho Southern Colour Print, Dunedin)

1998 (18 Nov). Tropical Flowers. T **65** and similar horiz designs. Multicoloured. Perf 14.

283	40c. Type **65**...............................	30	50
284	$1 *Ipomoea littoralis*.....................	60	85
285	$1.25 *Scaevola taccada*................	70	1·10
286	$2 *Thespesia populnea*................	1·25	2·00
283/286	Set of 4...................................	2·50	4·00

66 Rabbit

(Des Stan Chan Graphics. Litho Southern Colour Print, Dunedin)

1999 (16 Feb). Chinese New Year. Year of the Rabbit. Sheet 105×70 mm. Perf 14.
MS287 **66** $3 multicoloured................................. 2·25 3·00

67 HMS *Pandora* (frigate)

1999 (19 Mar). Australia '99 International Stamp Exhibition, Melbourne. Sheet 119×80 mm. Perf 14.
MS288 **67** $3 multicoloured................................. 2·75 3·25

1999 (27 Apr). iBRA '99 International Stamp Exhibition, Nuremberg. No. MS287 optd with the iBRA logo on the sheet margin.
MS289 105×70 mm. **66** $3 multicoloured........................ 3·50 4·25

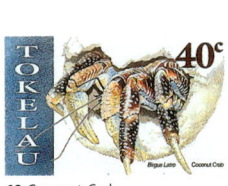 

68 Coconut Crab   **69** Lift-off

(Litho Southern Colour Print, Dunedin)

1999 (10 Aug). Pacific Crabs. T **68** and similar horiz designs. Multicoloured. Perf 14½.

290	40c. Type **68**...............................	40	40
291	$1 Ghost Crab.............................	85	95
292	$1.25 Land Hermit Crab................	1·00	1·40
293	$2 Purple Hermit Crab..................	1·60	2·25
290/293	Set of 4...................................	3·50	4·50
MS294	127×89 mm. $3 Ghost Crab (*different*)............	3·00	4·25

(Des N. Shewring. Litho Southern Colour Print, Dunedin)

1999 (31 Aug). 30th Anniversary of First Manned Landing on Moon. T **69** and similar vert designs. Multicoloured. Perf 13½.

295	25c. Type **69**..............................	40	40
296	50c. Rocket stage separation...............	60	60
297	75c. Aldrin deploying experiment...........	70	70
298	$1 Planting the flag.........................	85	85
299	$1.25 Separation of command module...........	1·00	1·25
300	$2 Recovery of astronauts..................	1·50	2·00
295/300	Set of 6...................................	4·50	5·25
MS301	90×65 mm. $3 Lunar module, Earth and Jupiter..	3·00	3·50

70 Black-naped Tern Chick and Egg   **71** Dragon

(Des Pat Altman. Litho Southern Colour Print, Dunedin)

1999 (31 Dec). Black-naped Tern. T **70** and similar horiz designs. Multicoloured. Perf 13½×14.

302	40c. Type **70**..............................	45	45
303	$1 Black-naped Tern perched on pebbles.	90	90
304	$1.25 Two Black-naped Terns................	1·10	1·10
305	$2 Two Black-naped Terns in flight..........	1·75	2·00
302/305	Set of 4...................................	3·75	4·00

(Litho Southern Colour Print, Dunedin)

2000 (5 Feb). Chinese New Year. Year of the Dragon. Sheet 105×70 mm. Perf 14.
MS306 **71** $3 multicoloured................................. 2·25 3·00

2000 (25 Mar). Bangkok 2000 World Youth Stamp Exhibition. No. MS306 optd on the margin with '**WORLD YOUTH STAMP EXHIBITION BANGKOK 2000**' in English and Thai. Perf 14.
MS307 105×70 mm. $3 Type **71**............................. 2·25 3·00

72 Nukunonu   **73** Queen Elizabeth the Queen Mother

(Litho Southern Colour Print, Dunedin)

2000 (22 May). The Stamp Show 2000 International Stamp Exhibition, London. Sheet 105×80 mm. Perf 14.
MS308 **72** $6 multicoloured................................. 3·75 5·00

2000 (7 July). EXPO 2000 World Stamp Exhibition, Anaheim, USA. No. MS301 optd '**WORLD STAMP EXPO 2000 7–16 JULY ANAHEIM–U.S.A.**' on sheet margin in silver.
MS309 90×65 mm. $3 Lunar module, Earth and Jupiter.. 3·00 4·00

(Litho Questa)

2000 (4 Aug). Queen Elizabeth the Queen Mother's 100th Birthday. T **73** and similar vert designs. Multicoloured. W w **14**. Perf 14½.

310	40c. Type **73**..............................	40	35
311	$1.20 Queen Mother waving...............	60	80
312	$1.80 Wearing diamond earrings and pearl necklace...........................	1·00	1·40
313	$3 Wearing blue hat and tartan scarf........	1·75	2·25
310/313	Set of 4...................................	3·25	4·25

74 *Gehyra oceanica*   **75** Snake

NEW ZEALAND Tokelau Islands

(Des Pat Altman. Litho Southern Colour Print, Dunedin)

2001 (1 Feb). Lizards. T **74** and similar horiz designs. Multicoloured. Perf 14.
314	40c. Type **74**	80	60
315	$1 *Lepidodactylus lugubris*	1·60	1·40
316	$1.25 *Gehyra mutilate*	1·75	1·75
317	$2 *Emoia cyanura*	2·75	2·75
314/317	Set of 4	6·25	5·75

(Litho Southern Colour Print, Dunedin)

2001 (1 Feb). Chinese New Year. Year of the Snake. Sheet 105×73 mm. Perf 14.
MS318 75 $3 multicoloured.................................. 3·50 4·00

2001 (1 Feb). Hong Kong 2001 Stamp Exhibition. No. **MS**318 optd '**HONG KONG 2001**' in English and Chinese on the sheet margin in gold.
MS319 105×73 mm. $3 Type **75**............... 3·50 4·00

76 Yellow and Orange Sea Horses **77** Atafu Island

(Des Patricia Altman. Litho Southern Colour Print, Dunedin)

2001 (23 Aug). Sea Horses. T **76** and similar vert designs. Multicoloured. Perf 14.
320	40c. Type **76**	50	50
321	$1 Baby Sea horses	80	80
322	$1.25 Pink Sea horse	1·10	1·10
323	$2 Yellow Sea horse	2·00	2·50
320/323	Set of 4	4·00	4·50
MS324	104×73 mm. $3 As No. 320	2·25	3·00

(Des W. Paterson and N. Thomson. Litho Southern Colour Print, Dunedin)

2001 (17 Nov). Island Views. T **77** and similar horiz designs. Multicoloured. Perf 14.
325	40c. Type **77**	60	60
326	$1 Fakaofo	1·00	1·25
327	$2 Sunrise over Nukunonu village	1·60	2·00
328	$2.50 Nukunonu beach	1·75	2·25
325/328	Set of 4	4·50	5·50

78 Princess Elizabeth and Lieutenant Philip Mountbatten, 1947 **79** Horse

(Des A. Robinson. Litho Questa)

2002 (6 Feb). Golden Jubilee. T **78** and similar designs. W w **14** (sideways). Perf 14½.
329	40c. agate, claret and gold	40	40
330	$1 multicoloured	60	70
331	$1.25 grey-black, claret and gold	70	90
332	$2 multicoloured	1·25	1·50
329/332	Set of 4	2·75	3·25
MS333	162×95 mm. Nos. 329/332 and $3 multicoloured. Perf 13½ ($3) or 14½ (others)	3·75	5·50

Designs: Horiz as T **78**—40c. T **78**; $1 Queen Elizabeth in mauve hat; $1.25, Princess Elizabeth holding Prince Charles, 1948; $2 Queen Elizabeth in Poland, 1996. Vert 38×51 mm—$3 Queen Elizabeth after Annigoni.

Designs as Nos. 329/332 in No. **MS**333 omit the gold frame around each stamp and the 'Golden Jubilee 1952–2002' inscription.

(Litho Southern Colour Print, Dunedin)

2002 (12 Feb). Chinese New Year. Year of the Horse. Sheet 105×70 mm. Perf 14.
MS334 79 $4 multicoloured.............................. 3·50 5·00

2002 (22 Feb). Stampex 2002 Stamp Exhibition, Hong Kong. No. **MS**334 optd '**STAMPEX 2002 HONG KONG 22–24 FEBRUARY 2002**' in gold on the sheet margin.
MS335 105×70 mm. $4 Type **79**............ 3·50 5·00

80 Pelagic Thresher Sharks

2002 (2 July). Endangered Species. Pelagic Thresher Shark. T **80** and similar horiz designs showing Sharks. Litho. Perf 14½.
336	40c. multicoloured	40	40
337	$1 multicoloured	70	90
338	$2 multicoloured	1·50	1·75
339	$2.50 multicoloured	1·60	2·25
336/339	Set of 4	3·75	4·75

80a Queen Elizabeth **81** HMNZS *Kaniere* (frigate), 1958–1959

(Des A. Robinson. Litho Questa)

2002 (5 Aug). Queen Elizabeth the Queen Mother Commemoration. T **80a** and similar vert designs. W w **14**. Perf 14½×14.
340	40c. black, gold and purple	50	40
341	$2 multicoloured	2·00	2·25
MS342	145×70 mm. $2.50 black and gold; $4 multicoloured. Wmk sideways	3·25	6·00

Designs: 40c. T **80a**; $2 Queen Mother wearing mauve hat and coat; $2.50, Wearing feathered hat and pearls; $4 Queen Mother smiling.

Designs in No. **MS**342 omit the '1900–2002' inscription and the coloured frame.

(Litho Southern Colour Print, Dunedin)

2002 (19 Dec). Royal New Zealand Navy Ships which have visited Tokelau. T **81** and similar horiz designs. Multicoloured. Perf 14.
343	40c. Type **81**	1·00	80
344	$1 HMNZS *Endeavour* (supply ship), 1990	1·75	1·75
345	$2 HMNZS *Wellington* (frigate), 1987, 1988, 1990	3·25	3·50
346	$2.50 HMNZS *Monowai* (survey ship), 1979, 1985, 1994	4·00	4·25
343/346	Set of 4	9·00	9·25

82 Ram **82a** Queen Elizabeth II with her Maids of Honour

(Des S. Chan. Litho Southern Colour Print, Dunedin)

2003 (3 Feb). Chinese New Year. Year of the Sheep. Sheet 105×70 mm. Perf 14.
MS347 82 $4 multicoloured.......................... 3·25 4·50

(Des Andrew Robinson. Litho D.L.R.)

2003 (2 June). 50th Anniversary of Coronation. T **82a** and similar horiz designs. Multicoloured. W w **14** (sideways). Perf 14×14½.
348	$2.50 Type **82a**	1·50	2·50
349	$4 Queen and Duke of Edinburgh	2·50	3·75
MS350	95×115 mm. $2.50, As No. 348; $4 As No. 349	4·00	5·50

Nos. 348/349 have scarlet frame; stamps from No. **MS**350 have no frame and country name in mauve panel.

Tokelau Islands **NEW ZEALAND**

83 Prince William at Polo Match and at Sighthill Community Education Centre, 2001

84 Shoreline with Palm Trees

(Des Andrew Robinson. Litho D.L.R.)

2003 (21 June). 21st Birthday of Prince William of Wales. T **83** and similar square designs. Multicoloured. W w **14** (sideways). Perf 14½.
351	$1.50 Type **83**	1·50	2·00
	a. Horiz pair. Nos. 351/352	3·25	5·00
352	$3 At Tidworth Polo Club, 2002 and at Highgrove, 2000	1·75	3·00

Nos. 351/352 were printed together, *se-tenant*, as horizontal pairs in sheets of ten (2×5) with enlarged illustrated left-hand margins.

2003 (13 Oct). Bangkok 2003 World Philatelic Exhibition. No. **MS**347 optd '**BANGKOK 2003**' in English and Thai in gold on the sheet margin.
MS353 105×70 mm. $4 Type **82** .... 3·25 4·00

(Litho Southern Colour Print, Dunedin)

2003 (7 Nov). Welpex 2003 National Stamp Exhibition, Wellington, New Zealand. Sheet 119×80 mm. Perf 14.
MS354 **84** $4 multicoloured .... 3·75 4·50

85 Chinese Character and Monkeys

86 Dawn at Atafu

(Litho Southern Colour Print)

2004 (22 Jan). Chinese New Year. Year of the Monkey. Sheet 105×71 mm. Perf 14.
MS355 **85** $4 bright red, black and gold .... 3·00 3·50

2004 (28 Jan). Hong Kong Stamp Exhibition. No. **MS**355 optd with '**2004 Hong Kong Stamp Expo**' in gold on the margin.
MS356 **85** $4 bright red, black and gold .... 3·00 3·50

(Des W. Paterton and Tracey Winiata. Litho Southern Colour Print, Dunedin)

2004 (30 June). Scenes. T **86** and similar horiz designs. Multicoloured. Perf 14.
357	40c. Type **86**	80	80
358	$1 Fishermen returning to Nukunonu	1·50	1·75
359	$2 Early evening at Fakaofo	2·50	3·50
360	$2.50 Beach scene, Atafu	3·00	4·00
357/360 Set of 4		7·00	9·00

(87)

88 Lesser Frigatebird

2004 (8 Aug). Commemoration of Visit by Prime Minister of New Zealand. No. **MS**354 optd as T **87** in silver with additional rectangular opt on top right of sheet margin.
MS361 **84** $4 multicoloured .... 4·00 5·50

(Des Pat Medearis Altman. Litho Southern Colour Print)

2004 (20 Dec). Lesser Frigatebird. T **88** and similar horiz designs. Multicoloured. Perf 14.
362	40c. Type **88**	1·00	80
363	$1 Birds in flight	1·75	1·75
364	$2 Two birds in nest	3·25	3·50
365	$2.50 Juvenile bird	4·00	4·25
362/365 Set of 4		9·00	9·25

89 Rooster

89a Pope John Paul II

2005 (9 Feb). Chinese New Year. Year of the Rooster. Sheet 115×75 mm. Perf 14.
MS366 **89** $4 bright vermilion, black and gold .... 7·00 7·50

2005 (21 Apr). Pacific Explorer World Stamp Exhibition. No. **MS**366 optd with Pacific Explorer logo in gold on the margin.
MS367 **89** $4 bright vermilion, black and gold .... 5·00 7·00

(Des Andrew Robinson. Litho D.L.R.)

2005 (18 Aug). Pope John Paul II Commemoration. T **89a**. Perf 14.
368 **89a** $1 $1 multicoloured .... 2·00 2·00

No. 368 was printed in sheetlets of eight stamps with an enlarged, illustrated right margin.

90 HMNZS *Te Kaha* and Launch

91 Leaping Dogs and Chinese Characters

(Litho Southern Colour Print, New Zealand)

2005 (15 Dec). HMNZS *Te Kaha* (frigate). T **90** and similar horiz designs. Multicoloured. Perf 14.
369	40c. Type **90**	1·25	1·00
370	$1 HMNZS *Te Kaha* offshore	2·00	1·75
371	$2 HMNZS *Te Kaha* at sunset	3·50	3·50
372	$2.50 Close up of HMNZS *Te Kaha*	4·25	4·50
369/372 Set of 4		10·00	10·00

(Des O. Bell. Litho Southern Colour Print, New Zealand)

2006 (29 Jan). Chinese New Year. Year of the Dog. Sheet 115×75 mm. Perf 14.
MS373 **91** vermilion, black and gold .... 6·00 7·00

92 Queen Elizabeth II

93 Fishing Pig

(Litho B.D.T.)

2006 (21 Apr). 80th Birthday of Queen Elizabeth II. T **93** and similar horiz designs. Multicoloured. Perf 14.
374	40c. Type **93**	1·00	85
375	$1 On wedding day	1·75	1·50
376	$2 Wearing tiara	3·25	3·25
377	$2.50 In close-up, wearing hat	3·50	3·75
374/377 Set of 4		8·50	8·50
MS378 144×75 mm. $2 As No. 375; $2.50 As No. 376		5·50	6·50

2006 (27 May). Washington 2006 International Stamp Exhibition. Sheet 144×85 mm containing Nos. 325/328. Perf 14.
MS379 144×85 mm. 40c. Type **77**; $1 Fakaofo; $2 Sunrise over Nukunonu Village; $2.50 Nukunonu beach .... 10·00 12·00

NEW ZEALAND Tokelau Islands

2006 (2 Nov). Kiwipex National Stamp Exhibition, Christchurch, New Zealand. No. **MS**378 optd '**National Stamp Exhibition, Christchurch, New Zealand**' in blue foil on the margin.
MS380 144×75 mm. $2 As No. 375 (optd 'KIWIPEX'); $2.50 As No. 376 (optd '2006')................. 7·00 7·00

2007 (18 Feb). Chinese New Year. Year of the Pig. Sheet 105×70 mm. Litho. Perf 14.
MS381 **93** $4 multicoloured............... 7·00 7·00

94 Pacific Golden Plover **95** Bicolour Angelfish (*Centropyge bicolor*)

(Des Owen Bell. Litho)

2007 (19 Oct). Endangered Species. Pacific Golden Plover (*Pluvialis fulva*). T **94** and similar horiz designs. Multicoloured. Litho. Perf 14.
382	40c. Type **94**..................	1·25	1·25
	a. Strip of 4. Nos. 382/385	11·00	11·00
383	$1 Head of Plover in breeding plumage	2·25	2·25
384	$2 On ground with wing outstretched (winter plumage)	4·00	4·00
385	$2.50 Pair in winter plumage	4·50	4·50
382/385 Set of 4		11·00	11·00

Nos. 382/385 were printed together, *se-tenant*, as horizontal and vertical strips of four stamps in sheetlets of 16, and also in separate sheets of 25.

(Des Owen Bell. Litho Southern Colour Print, New Zealand)

2007 (19 Dec). Marine Life. T **95** and similar horiz designs. Multicoloured. Perf 14½×14.
386	10c. Type **95**..................	55	55
	a. Sheetlet of 10. Nos. 386/395	27·00	27·00
387	20c. Staghorn Coral (*Acropora robusta*)	75	75
388	40c. Blacktip Reef Shark (*Carcharhinus melanopterus*)	1·10	1·10
389	50c. Seastar (*Linckia multiflora*)	1·25	1·25
390	$1 Porcupinefish (*Diodon hystrix*)	1·75	1·75
391	$1.50 Thorny Sea horse (*Hippocampus histrix*)	2·25	2·25
392	$2 Spotted Eagle Ray (*Aetobatis narinari*) ..	2·75	2·75
393	$2.50 Small Giant Clam (*Tridacna maxima*)	3·00	3·00
394	$5 Green Turtle (*Chelonia mydas*)	5·50	5·50
395	$10 Slate Pencil Urchin (*Heterocentrotus mammillatus*)	11·00	11·00
386/395 Set of 10		27·00	27·00

Nos. 386/395 were printed in separate sheets. They were also printed together, *se-tenant*, in sheetlets of ten.

96 Rat **97** Sir Edmund Hillary

(Des Stan Chan. Litho Southern Colour Print, New Zealand)

2008 (7 Feb). Chinese New Year. Year of the Rat. Sheet 105×70 mm. Perf 14.
MS396 **96** $4 multicoloured............... 6·00 7·00

(Litho Southern Colour Print, New Zealand)

2008 (5 Nov). Sir Edmund Hillary Commemoration. T **97** and similar multicoloured designs. Perf 14 (Nos. 397/400) or 13½ (No. **MS**401).
397	50c. Type **97**..................	90	1·00
398	$1 Hillary on Mount Everest (wearing checked shirt)...............	1·50	1·50
399	$2 Hillary on Mount Everest (wearing jacket)	2·50	2·75
400	$2.50 As older man	2·75	3·00
397/400 Set of 4		7·00	7·50
MS401 110×68 mm. $5 Hillary and Tenzing Norgay on summit of Mount Everest (*horiz*)...............		6·00	6·00

98 Houses on Seashore **99** Ox

(Litho Southern Colour Print, New Zealand)

2008 (7 Nov). Scenes of Tokelau. T **98** and similar horiz designs. Multicoloured. Perf 14 (Nos. 402/405) or 13½×13 (No. **MS**406).
402	50c. Type **98**..................	1·50	1·25
403	$1 Small boats off beach with Palm trees..	2·25	2·00
404	$2 Causeway lined with Palm trees............	3·75	4·00
405	$2.50 Houses at seashore	4·00	4·50
402/405 Set of 4		10·50	10·50
MS406 130×85 mm. $5 Landscape of tropical forest, beach and rocky islets...............		5·50	6·00

No. **MS**406 also commemorates Tarapex 2008 National Stamp Exhibition, New Plymouth, New Zealand.

(Litho)

2009 (26 Jan). Chinese New Year. Year of the Ox. Sheet 106×70 mm. Litho. Perf 13½.
MS407 **99** $4 multicoloured............... 7·50 7·50

100 Chile 1875 One Peso Coin **101** Tiger

(Litho)

2009 (22 Dec). Coins of the Pacific. T **100** and similar vert designs. Multicoloured. Litho. Multicoloured. Perf 14.
408	50c. Type **100**..................	1·00	1·00
409	$1 Great Britain 1911 one sovereign	1·75	1·75
410	$2 New Zealand 1950 half crown	3·25	3·25
411	$2.50 1997 Tokelau ten dollar	3·75	3·75
408/411 Set of 4		9·50	9·50
MS412 140×86 mm. Nos. 408/411...............		10·50	11·00

(Litho)

2010 (12 Feb). Chinese New Year. Year of the Tiger. Sheet 105×70 mm. Perf 13½.
MS413 **101** $4 multicoloured............... 13·00 13·00

2010 (8 May). London 2010 International Stamp Exhibition. No. **MS**412 inscr 'London 2010 Stamp Exhibition' in gold on lower left sheet margin. Perf 14.
MS414 140×86 mm. Nos. 408/411............... 9·50 9·50

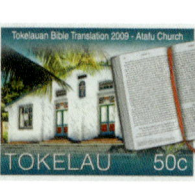 

102 Tokelauan Bible and Atafu Church **103** Rabbits feeding on Carrots

(Litho)

2010 (21 Sept). Tokelauan Bible Translation. T **102** and similar horiz designs. Multicoloured. Perf 13½.
415	50c. Type **102**..................	1·00	1·00
416	$1 Tokelauan Bible and Fakaofo Church	2·00	2·00
417	$2 Tokelauan Bible and Nukunonu Church	3·00	3·00

Tokelau Islands **NEW ZEALAND**

418	$2.50 Tokelauan Bibles		3·50	3·50
415/418 Set of 4			8·50	8·50

(Litho)

2011 (3 Feb). Chinese New Year. Year of the Rabbit. Sheet 105×71 mm. Perf 13½.
MS419 **103** $5 multicoloured..................... 12·00 12·00

104 Yellow-bellied Sea Snake **105** Prince William and Miss Catherine Middleton

(Litho)

2011 (25 Mar). Endangered Species. Yellow-bellied Sea Snake (*Pelamis platura*). T **104** and similar horiz designs. Multicoloured. Perf 13½×13.

420	50c. Type **104**	1·00	1·00
	a. Strip of 4. Nos. 420/423	9·50	9·50
421	$1 Sea Snake on sandy beach	2·00	2·00
422	$2 Sea Snake in sea	3·00	3·00
423	$2.50 Three Sea Snakes in sea	3·50	3·50
420/423 Set of 4		9·50	9·50

Nos. 420/423 were printed in ordinary sheets and also *se-tenant* as horizontal and vertical strips of four in sheetlets of 16.

(Litho B.D.T.)

2011 (29 Apr). Royal Wedding. Sheet 118×90 mm. W w **18** (sideways). Perf 14½×14.
MS424 **105** $6 multicoloured..................... 10·00 10·00

106 Christmas Tree **107** Gathering Coconuts

(Litho)

2011 (16 Nov). Christmas. T **106** and similar vert designs. Multicoloured. Phosphorised paper. Perf 13½.

425	40c. Type **106**	80	80
426	45c. Tree bauble	90	90
427	$1.40 Stocking	2·40	2·40
428	$2 Angel tree decoration	3·00	3·00
425/428 Set of 4		6·50	6·50

(Litho)

2012 (11 Apr). Scenic. T **107** and similar horiz designs. Multicoloured. Perf 13½.

429	10c. Type **107**	20	20
430	20c. Atoll with Palm trees and sandy beach	40	40
431	25c. Small offshore atoll with Palm trees and hut	50	50
432	40c. Divers in lagoon	80	80
433	45c. Sailing canoe off coast	90	90
434	50c. Beached canoes and church	1·00	1·00
435	$1 Sandy beach backed by Palm trees	2·00	2·00
436	$1.40 Angler and offshore atoll	2·40	2·40
437	$2 Palm forest and sandy beach	3·00	3·00
429/437 Set of 9		10·00	10·00

108 Queen Elizabeth II in Wellington, New Zealand, 1963 **109** Yellowfin Tuna

(Litho)

2012 (23 May). Diamond Jubilee. T **108** and similar horiz design. Multicoloured. Perf 13½.

438	$2 Type **108**	3·00	3·00
439	$3 Official New Zealand Portrait of Queen Elizabeth II, 2012	4·00	4·00
MS440 110×60 mm. Nos. 438/439		7·00	7·00

(Litho)

2012 (3 Oct). Fish of Tokelau. T **109** and similar horiz designs. Multicoloured. Perf 13½.

441	40c. Type **109**	1·00	1·00
442	45c. Ruby Snapper	1·00	1·00
443	$1.40 Wahoo	2·75	2·75
444	$2 Common Dolphinfish	3·50	3·50
441/444 Set of 4		7·50	7·50
MS445 110×90 mm. Nos. 441/444		8·00	8·00

110 Santa's Sleigh over Atafu **111** Queen Elizabeth II and Duke of Edinburgh waving from Buckingham Palace Balcony after Coronation, 2 June 1953

(Litho New Zealand Post)

2012 (21 Nov). Christmas. T **110** and similar vert designs. Multicoloured. Perf 13×13½.

446	45c. Type **110**	90	90
	a. Horiz strip of 3. Nos. 446/448	7·50	7·50
447	$2 Reindeer flying over Nukunonu	3·00	3·00
448	$3 Reindeer flying over Fakaofo	4·00	4·00
446/448 Set of 3		7·50	7·50
MS449 105×62 mm. Nos. 446/448		7·50	7·50

Nos. 446/448 were printed together, *se-tenant*, as horizontal strips of three stamps throughout the sheets.

(Litho New Zealand Post)

2013 (8 May). 60th Anniversary of the Coronation. T **111** and similar horiz design. Multicoloured. Perf 13½×13.

450	$2 Type **111**	3·00	3·00
451	$3 Coronation portrait of Royal family in Throne Room of Buckingham Palace, 1953	4·00	4·00
MS452 110×60 mm. Nos. 450/451		7·00	7·00

112 Blue Moon Butterfly (*Hypolimnas bolina pallescens*) (female) **113** Mary and Joseph on Road to Bethlehem

NEW ZEALAND Tokelau Islands

(Litho New Zealand Post)

2013 (7 Aug). Tokelau Butterflies. T **112** and similar horiz designs. Multicoloured. Perf 13½×13.

453	45c. Type **112**	1·25	1·25
454	$1 Blue Moon Butterfly (*Hypolimnas bolina pallescens*) (male)	2·50	2·50
455	$1.40 Common Crow (*Euploea lewinii bourkei*)	3·00	3·00
456	$3 Meadow Argus (*Junonia villida*)	4·50	4·50
453/456	*Set of 4*	10·00	10·00
MS457	100×85 mm. Nos. 453/456	10·00	11·00

(Litho New Zealand Post)

2013 (20 Nov). Christmas. T **113** and similar vert designs. Multicoloured. Perf 13×13½.

458	45c. Type **113**	90	90
459	$1.40 Nativity	2·40	2·40
460	$2 Shepherds	3·00	3·00
461	$3 Wise Men	4·00	4·00
458/461	*Set of 4*	9·25	9·25
MS462	135×63 mm. Nos. 458/461	9·75	9·75

114 Taulima (bracelets made from processed Pandanus leaf)   **115** Vakas

(Litho New Zealand Post)

2014 (23 Apr). Tokelau Weaving. T **114** and similar horiz designs. Multicoloured. Perf 13½.

463	45c. Type **114**	65	65
464	$1.40 Pupu (water holders made from a Coconut shell with wrapping of plaited Coconut husk fibres)	2·00	2·00
465	$2 Tapili (decorated fan made from young Coconut leaf and Coconut leaf midrib)	2·75	2·75
466	$3 Ato (basket made from synthetic materials)	4·25	4·25
463/466	*Set of 4*	8·75	8·75
MS467	191×60 mm. Nos. 463/466	9·50	9·50

(Litho New Zealand Post)

2014 (18 June). Tokelau Vaka (five man canoe constructed in segments). T **115** and similar vert designs. Multicoloured. Perf 13½.

468	45c. Type **115**	65	65
469	$1.40 Two men building vaka	2·00	2·00
470	$2 Paddling vaka towards shore	2·75	2·75
471	$3 Two fishermen coming ashore from vaka with catch	4·25	4·25
468/471	*Set of 4*	8·75	8·75
MS472	151×65 mm. Nos. 468/471	9·50	9·50

116 Mālō nī! (Hello)   **117** The Shepherds

(Litho New Zealand Post)

2014 (15 Oct). Tokelau Language Week. T **116** and similar horiz designs. Multicoloured. Perf 13½.

473	45c. Type **116**	65	65
474	$1.40 E ā mai koe? (How are you?)	2·00	2·00
475	$2 Ko ai tō agoa? (What is your name?)	2·75	2·75
476	$3 Tōfā la nī! (Farewell then)	4·25	4·25
473/476	*Set of 4*	8·75	8·75
MS477	Nos. 473/476	9·50	9·50

(Litho New Zealand Post)

2014 (10 Dec). Christmas. T **117** and similar vert designs. Multicoloured. Perf 13½.

478	45c. Type **117**	65	65
479	$2 Mary, Joseph and Jesus in manger	2·75	2·75
480	$3 Three Wise Men	4·25	4·25
478/480	*Set of 3*	7·00	7·00
MS481	113×54 mm. Nos. 478/480	7·50	7·50

118 Paddling for Atu (Skipjack)   **119** Ugauga (*Birgus latro*)

(Litho New Zealand Post)

2015 (7 Apr). Traditional Tokelau Fishing. T **118** and similar horiz designs. Multicoloured. Perf 13½.

482	45c. Type **118**	65	65
483	$1.40 Netting Manini (Convict Tang)	2·00	2·00
484	$2 Laulaufau (Moorish Idols) trap	2·75	2·75
485	$3 Noosing Pala (Wahoo)	4·25	4·25
482/485	*Set of 4*	8·75	8·75
MS486	90×70 mm. Nos. 482/485	9·50	9·50

(Litho New Zealand Post)

2015 (3 June). Tokelau Crabs. T **119** and similar horiz designs. Multicoloured. Perf 13½.

487	45c. Type **119**	65	65
488	$1.40 Tupa (*Cardisoma* sp.)	2·00	2·00
489	$2 Kaviki (*Ocypode* sp.)	2·75	2·75
490	$3 Kamakama (*Grapsus* sp.)	4·25	4·25
487/490	*Set of 4*	8·75	8·75
MS491	170×45 mm. Nos. 487/490	9·50	9·50

120 TAHI TE FALA (ONE PANDANUS TREE)   **121** Snowman made from Sand

(Des Hannah Stancliffe-White. Litho New Zealand Post)

2015 (13 Oct). Tokelau Language Week. T **120** and similar vert designs. Multicoloured. Perf 13½.

492	45c. Type **120**	65	65
	a. Sheetlet of 10. Nos. 492/501	12·50	12·50
493	45c. LUA IA TOLUMA (TWO TACKLE BOXES)	65	65
494	45c. TOLU IA MOTU (THREE ATOLLS)	65	65
495	45c. FA IA OLO (FOUR WICKETS)	65	65
496	45c. LIMA IA TUPA (FIVE CRABS)	65	65
497	$1.40 ONO IA LELEFUA (SIX BUTTERFLIES)	2·00	2·00
498	$1.40 FITU IA IKA (SEVEN FISH)	2·00	2·00
499	$1.40 VALU IA ILI (EIGHT FANS)	2·00	2·00
500	$1.40 IVA IA VAKA (NINE CANOES)	2·00	2·00
501	$1.40 HEFALU IA MATAU (TEN FISHHOOKS)	2·00	2·00
492/501	*Set of 10*	12·50	12·50
MS502	169×59 mm. Nos. 492/496	3·25	3·25
MS503	169×59 mm. Nos. 497/501	10·00	10·00

(Des Jonathan Gray. Litho New Zealand Post)

2015 (25 Nov). Christmas. Kilihimahi. T **121** and similar vert designs. Multicoloured. Perf 13½.

504	45c. Type **121**	65	65
505	$1.40 Christmas gifts under decorated Pandanus tree on beach	2·00	2·00
506	$2 Reindeer making sand Angels	2·75	2·75
507	$3 Santa lying on lounger on beach	4·25	4·25
504/507	*Set of 4*	8·75	8·75
MS508	136×56 mm. Nos. 504/507	9·50	9·50

Tokelau Islands NEW ZEALAND

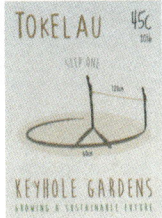 

122 Step One　　**123** Young Elizabeth with her Mother the Duchess of York

(Des Hannah Stancliffe-White. Litho Southern Colour Print, New Zealand)

2016 (6 Apr). Tokelau Keyhole Gardens. Growing a Sustainable Future. T **122** and similar vert designs. Multicoloured. Perf 13½.
MS509	210×100 mm. 45c. Type **122**; $1 Step Two; $1.40 Step Three; $2 Step Four; $3 Step Five Stages of garden growth.	12·00	12·00
MS510	180×48 mm. 45c. Type **122**; $1 Step Two; $1.40 Step Three; $2 Step Four; $3 Step Five.	11·00	11·00

No. **MS**509 has enlarged bottom margins describing the five steps of how to make a keyhole garden.
No. **MS**510 contains the same five designs but has smaller margins without the inscriptions.

(Des Hannah Stancliffe-White. Litho New Zealand Post)

2016 (4 May). 90th Birthday of Queen Elizabeth II. T **123** and similar vert designs. Multicoloured. Perf 13½.
511	45c. Type **123**	65	65
512	$1.40 Princess Elizabeth and Duke of Edinburgh with baby Prince Charles, 1948	2·00	2·00
513	$2 Queen Elizabeth and Duke of Edinburgh, 1972	2·75	2·75
514	$3 Queen Elizabeth II, 2010	4·25	4·25
511/514	Set of 4	8·75	8·75

124 MV *Mataliki*　　**125** Popo (Coconut)

(Des Hannah Stancliffe-White. Litho New Zealand Post)

2016 (3 Aug). Tokelau's New Ferry MV *Mataliki*. T **124** and similar square designs. Multicoloured. Perf 14½.
515	45c. Type **124**	75	75
516	$1.40 MV *Mataliki* sailing from Apia, Samoa	2·25	2·25
517	$2 MV *Mataliki* in Apia harbour	3·00	3·00
518	$3 Passengers transferring from MV *Mataliki* to Tokelau atoll by barge	4·50	4·50
515/518	Set of 4	9·50	9·50
MS519	154×57 mm. Nos. 515/518	10·00	11·00

(Des Richard Payne. Litho New Zealand Post)

2016 (5 Oct). Tokelau Language Week. T **125** and similar horiz designs. Multicoloured. Perf 13½.
520	45c. Type **125**	65	65
521	$1.40 Ugauga (Coconut Crab)	2·00	2·00
522	$2 Ika (fish)	2·75	2·75
523	$3 Fuāulu (Breadfruit)	4·25	4·25
520/523	Set of 4	8·75	8·75
MS524	100×88 mm. Nos. 520/523	9·50	9·50

126 Shepherd and Sheep　　**127** Bristle-thighed Curlew

(Des Hannah Stancliffe-White. Litho New Zealand Post)

2016 (7 Dec). Christmas. Kilihimahi. T **126** and similar vert designs. Multicoloured. Phosphorised paper. Perf 13×13½.
525	45c. Type **126**	65	65
526	$1.40 Mary, Joseph and baby Jesus in manger	2·00	2·00
527	$2 Three Wise Men	2·75	2·75
528	$3 Angel	4·25	4·25
525/528	Set of 4	8·75	8·75
MS529	129×58 mm. Nos. 525/528	9·50	9·50

(Des Jonathan Gray. Litho New Zealand Post)

2017 (1 Mar). Birds of Tokelau. T **127** and similar square designs. Multicoloured. Phosphorised paper. Perf 14.
530	45c. Type **127**	80	80
531	$1.40 Black Noddy	2·25	2·25
532	$2 Great Frigatebird	3·00	3·00
533	$3 Brown Booby	4·50	4·50
530/533	Set of 4	9·50	9·50
MS534	80×95 mm. Nos. 530/533	10·50	10·50

128 Common Mushroom Coral (*Fungia fungites*) (open)　　**129** Moth Skink (*Lipinia noctua*)

(Des Hannah Stancliffe-White. Litho New Zealand Post)

2017 (2 Aug). Endangered Species. Tokelau Corals. T **128** and similar horiz designs. Multicoloured. Phosphorised paper. Perf 13½.
535	45c. Type **128**	65	65
536	$1.40 Common Mushroom Coral (*Fungia fungites*) (closed)	2·00	2·00
537	$2 Polyps of Double-star Coral (*Diploastrea heliopora*)	2·75	2·75
538	$3 Double-star Coral (*Diploastrea heliopora*)	4·25	4·25
535/538	Set of 4	8·75	8·75
MS539	96×70 mm. Nos. 535/538	9·50	9·50

(Des Jonathan Gray. Litho New Zealand Post)

2017 (20 Sept). Reptiles of Tokelau. T **129** and similar horiz designs. Multicoloured. Phosphorised paper. Perf 13½.
540	45c. Type **129**	65	65
541	$1.40 Pelagic Gecko (*Nactus pelagicus*)	2·00	2·00
542	$2 Copper-tailed Skink (*Emoia cyanura*)	2·75	2·75
543	$3 Black Skink (*Emoia nigra*)	4·25	4·25
540/543	Set of 4	8·75	8·75
MS544	90×90 mm. Nos. 540/543	9·50	9·50

130 Princess Elizabeth and Prince Philip, May 1947　　**131** Angel

(Des Jonathan Gray. Litho New Zealand Post)

2017 (20 Nov). Platinum Wedding of Queen Elizabeth II and Duke of Edinburgh. T **130** and similar vert designs. Multicoloured. Phosphorised paper. Perf 13½.
545	45c. Type **130**	65	65
546	$1.40 Queen Elizabeth II, Duke of Edinburgh, Prince Charles, Princess Anne, Prince Andrew and Prince Edward, Buckingham Palace, 1972	2·00	2·00
547	$2 Queen Elizabeth II and Duke of Edinburgh on visit to Fiji, February 1977	2·75	2·75
548	$3 Queen Elizabeth II, Duke of Edinburgh, Prince Charles and Prince William at Clarence House for 50th anniversary of Coronation, 2003	4·25	4·25

NEW ZEALAND Tokelau Islands

545/548	*Set of* 4...	8·75	8·75
MS549	85×100 mm. Nos. 545/548............................	9·50	9·50

(Des Saint Andrew Matautia. Litho New Zealand Post)

2017 (6 Dec). *Christmas. Kilihimahi.* T **131** *and similar vert designs. Multicoloured. Phosphorised paper. Perf* 13½.

550	45c. Type **131**...	60	60
551	$1.40 Virgin Mary holding baby Jesus.........	1·75	1·75
552	$2 Three Wise Men with baby Jesus...........	2·50	2·50
553	$3 Baby Jesus in manger, two Lambs and Star of Bethlehem...........................	3·75	3·75
550/553	*Set of* 4...	7·75	7·75
MS554	80×100 mm. Nos. 550/553............................	8·50	8·50

132 Buildings and Seawall, Ocean Side of Nukunonu

133 Prince Harry and Meghan, Duchess of Sussex Riding in Carriage after their Wedding

(Des Saint Andrew Matautia. Litho New Zealand Post)

2018 (2 May). *Seawalls of Tokelau.* T **132** *and similar horiz designs. Multicoloured. Phosphorised paper. Perf* 13½×13.

555	45c. Type **132**...	60	60
556	$1.40 Houses and seawall facing Fakaofo Lagoon....................................	1·75	1·75
557	$2 House, seawall and Palm trees, ocean side of Fakaofo.............................	2·50	2·50
558	$3 Houses and seawall, Nukunonu............	3·75	3·75
555/558	*Set of* 4...	7·75	7·75
MS559	122×80 mm. Nos. 555/558............................	8·50	8·50

(Des Saint Andrew Matautia. Litho New Zealand Post)

2018 (21 May). *Royal Wedding.* T **133** *and similar vert designs. Multicoloured. Phosphorised paper. Perf* 13×13½.

560	45c. Type **133**...	65	65
561	$1.40 Prince Harry and Meghan, Duchess of Sussex kiss during Wedding ceremony	2·00	2·00
562	$2 Engagement photograph of Prince Harry and Ms Meghan Markle, Frogmore House, Windsor...................	2·75	2·75
563	$3 Engagement photograph of Prince Harry and Ms Meghan Markle, Kensington Palace (half length).........	4·25	4·25
560/563	*Set of* 4...	8·50	8·50
MS564	77×95 mm. Nos. 560/563............................	9·50	9·50

134 Atafu

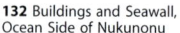

135 Taro

(Des Saint Andrew Matautia. Litho New Zealand Post)

2018 (5 Sept). *Tokelau from the Sky.* T **134** *and similar horiz designs. Multicoloured. Phosphorised paper. Perf* 13½×13.

565	45c. Type **134**...	65	65
566	$1.40 Fakaofo..	2·00	2·00
567	$2 Atafu. coral islet and reef.....................	2·75	2·75
568	$3 Nukunonu...	4·25	4·25
565/568	*Set of* 4...	8·50	8·50
MS569	100×79 mm. Nos. 565/568............................	9·50	9·50

(Des Saint Andrew Matautia. Litho New Zealand Post)

2019 (1 May). *Inati. Equal Portions.* T **135** *and similar vert designs. Multicoloured. Phosphorised paper. Perf* 13½.

570	45c. Type **135**...	65	65
571	$1.40 Breadfruit...	2·00	2·00
572	$2 Fish...	2·75	2·75
573	$3 Coconut...	4·25	4·25

570/573	*Set of* 4...	8·50	8·50
MS574	79×98 mm. Nos. 570/573............................	9·50	9·50

136 Saturn V on Launch Pad

137 Queen Victoria

(Des Saint Andrew Matautia. Litho New Zealand Post)

2019 (3 July). *50th Anniversary of First Manned Moon Landing.* T **136** *and similar vert designs. Multicoloured. Phosphorised paper. Perf* 13×13½.

575	45c. Type **136**...	65	65
576	$1.40 Launch of *Apollo* 11, 16 July 1969.....	2·00	2·00
577	$2 Astronaut Buzz Aldrin and Lunar Module *Eagle* on Moon........................	2·75	2·75
578	$3 Command Module with *Apollo* 11 crew and US Navy diver in inflatable after splashdown in Pacific Ocean, 24 July 1969..	4·25	4·25
575/578	*Set of* 4...	8·50	8·50
MS579	78×97 mm. Nos. 575/578............................	9·50	9·50

(Des Saint Andrew Matautia. Litho New Zealand Post)

2019 (16 Oct). *Birth Bicentenary of Queen Victoria.* T **137** *and similar vert designs. Multicoloured. Phosphorised paper. Perf* 13×13½.

580	45c. Type **137**...	65	65
581	$1.40 Queen Victoria (light background).....	2·00	2·00
582	$2 Queen Victoria and Prince Albert...........	2·75	2·75
583	$3 Queen Victoria (older)...........................	4·25	4·25
580/583	*Set of* 4...	8·50	8·50
MS584	131×50 mm. Nos. 580/583............................	9·50	9·50

138 Toluma with White Cross

139 Ili (fans)

(Des Saint Andrew Matautia. Litho New Zealand Post)

2019 (4 Dec). *Christmas. Tuluma (traditional wooden boxes).* T **138** *and similar vert designs. Multicoloured. Perf* 13×13½.

585	45c. Type **138**...	65	65
586	$1.40 Man with two tuluma......................	2·00	2·00
587	$2 Giving small tuluma as gift....................	2·75	2·75
588	$3 Hands holding tuluma...........................	4·25	4·25
585/588	*Set of* 4...	8·50	8·50
MS589	131×55 mm. Nos. 585/588............................	9·50	9·50

(Des Cam Price. Litho New Zealand Post)

2020 (16 Apr). *Tokelauan Weaving.* T **139** *and similar vert designs. Multicoloured. Phosphorised paper. Perf* 13½.

590	45c. Type **139**...	65	65
591	$1.40 Ato (woven basket)...........................	2·00	2·00
592	$2 Pupu (coconut shell containers in woven wrapping)..............................	2·75	2·75
593	$3 Titi (woman's garment worn around the waist)..	4·25	4·25
590/593	*Set of* 4...	8·50	8·50
MS594	150×70 mm. Nos. 590/593............................	9·50	9·50

Tokelau Islands, Cook Islands NEW ZEALAND

140 Angel Gabriel in Wave Form

(Des Cam Price. Litho New Zealand Post)

2020 (4 Nov). Christmas. Kilihimahi. T **140** and similar vert designs. Multicoloured. Phosphorised paper. Perf 13½.

595		45c. Type **140**	65	65
596		$1.40 Manger of Jesus on beach under palm tree and Star of Bethlehem	2·00	2·00
597		$2 Shepherds in the form of swimming turtles following the Star of Bethlehem	2·75	2·75
598		$3 Three Wise Men in the form of waves carrying a vaka (traditional canoe)	4·25	4·25
595/598 Set of 4			8·50	8·50
MS599 150×70 mm. Nos. 595/598			9·50	9·50

COOK ISLANDS

A British Protectorate was declared over this group of 15 islands by the local Vice-Consul on 20 September 1888.

Before the introduction of the Cook Islands Post Office, mail was forwarded via Auckland, New Zealand.

PRICES FOR STAMPS ON COVER TO 1945	
Nos. 1/4	from × 8
Nos. 5/74	from × 4
Nos. 75/145	from × 3

BRITISH PROTECTORATE

1   **2** Queen Makea Takau   **3** White Tern or Torea

(Des F. Moss. Typo Govt Printing Office, Wellington)

1892 (19 Apr). No wmk. Toned or white paper. Perf 12½.

1	**1**	1d. black	38·00	28·00
		a. Imperf between (vert pair)	£10000	
2		1½d. mauve	50·00	40·00
		a. Imperf (pair)	£17000	
3		2½d. blue	55·00	40·00
4		10d. carmine	£150	£150
1/4 Set of 4			£250	£225

Nos. 1/4 were printed in sheets of 60 (6×10) from plates constructed from a matrix of six slightly different types.

(Eng A. E. Cousins. Typo Govt Printing Office, Wellington)

1893 (28 July)–**1900**. W **12b** of New Zealand (N Z and Star wide apart) (sideways on T **3**).

(a) Perf 12×11½.

5	**2**	1d. brown	50·00	55·00
6		1d. blue (3.4.94)	13·00	2·00
		a. Perf 12×11½ and 12½ mixed	†	£2500
7		1½d. mauve	20·00	6·50
8		2½d. rose	55·00	25·00
		a. Rose-carmine	75·00	55·00
		ab. Perf 12×11½ and 12½ mixed	£3000	
9		5d. olive-black	23·00	18·00
10		10d. green	90·00	50·00
5/10 Set of 6			£225	£180

(b) Perf 11 (July 1896–1900).

11	**3**	½d. steel blue (1st setting) (11.99)	35·00	48·00
		a. Upper right 'd' omitted	£1500	
		b. Second setting	25·00	23·00
		ba. Deep blue (1900)	6·00	15·00
12	**2**	1d. blue	5·50	5·50
13		1d. deep brown/cream (4.99)	30·00	21·00
		a. Wmk sideways	£1800	
		b. Bistre-brown (1900)	30·00	23·00
14		1½d. deep lilac	20·00	7·00
		a. Deep mauve (1900)	14·00	7·00
15	**3**	2d. brown/thin toned (7.98)	19·00	7·50
		a. Deep brown (1900)	16·00	9·50
16	**2**	2½d. pale rose	55·00	45·00
		a. Deep rose (1900)	25·00	18·00
17		5d. olive-black	32·00	22·00
18	**3**	6d. purple/thin toned (7.98)	45·00	50·00
		a. Bright purple (1900)	25·00	30·00
19	**2**	10d. green	20·00	55·00
20	**3**	1s. red/thin toned (7.98)	65·00	85·00
		a. Deep carmine (1900)	55·00	60·00
11ba/20a Set of 10			£200	£200

Examples of the 1d., 1½d., 2½d. and 5d. perforated 11 and on laid paper are perforation trials.

On the first setting of the ½d. the face values are misplaced in each corner. As corrected in the second setting the face values are correctly positioned in each corner.

ONE HALF PENNY

(4)   **(5)**

1899 (24 Apr). No. 12 surch with T **4** by Govt Printer, Rarotonga.

21	**2**	½d. on 1d. blue	35·00	50·00
		a. Surch inverted	£850	£900
		b. Surch double	£1000	£1500

NEW ZEALAND TERRITORY

On 8 and 9 October 1900 the chiefs of all the main islands, except Aitutaki, ceded their territory to the British Crown. On 11 June 1901 all the islands, including Aitutaki, were transferred by Great Britain to New Zealand control.

1901 (8 Oct). No. 13 optd with T **5** by Govt Printer, Rarotonga.

22	**2**	1d. brown	£190	£160
		a. Crown inverted	£2250	£1700
		c. Optd with crown twice	£1600	£1600

1902. No wmk. Perf 11

(a) Medium white Cowan paper (February).

23	**3**	½d. blue-green	10·00	10·00
		a. Imperf horiz (vert pair)	£1300	
24	**2**	1d. dull rose	16·00	25·00

(b) Thick white Pirie paper (May).

25	**3**	½d. yellow-green	11·00	4·50
26	**2**	1d. rose-red	20·00	11·00
		a. Rose-lake	18·00	7·50
27		2½d. dull blue	15·00	22·00

> **NEW ZEALAND WATERMARKS**. In W **43** the wmk units are in vertical columns widely spaced and the sheet margins are unwatermarked or wmkd 'NEW ZEALAND POSTAGE' in large letters. In its sideways format it exists indiscriminately sideways, sideways inverted, sideways reversed and sideways inverted plus reversed, while the upright watermark exists both normal and inverted. Such variations are not listed.
> In W **98** the wmk units are arranged alternately in horizontal rows closely spaced and are continued into the sheet margins. Stamps with W **98** sideways show the star to the left of NZ, *as seen from the back*. Sideways inverted varieties have the star to the right, *as seen from the back*.

1902 (Sept). W **43** of New Zealand (single-lined NZ and Star, close together; sideways on T **2**). Perf 11.

28	**3**	½d. yellow-green	5·00	3·50
		a. Grey-green	30·00	70·00
29	**2**	1d. rose-pink	4·50	3·50
30		1½d. deep mauve	6·00	9·00
31	**3**	2d. deep brown	11·00	12·00
		a. No figures of value	£2250	£3500
		b. Perf 11×14	£2500	
32	**2**	2½d. deep blue	4·00	7·50
33		5d. olive-black	38·00	50·00
34	**3**	6d. purple	40·00	30·00
35	**2**	10d. green	60·00	£130
36	**3**	1s. carmine	65·00	£100
		a. Perf 11×14	£3000	
28/36 Set of 9			£200	£300

Stamps in T **3** were printed from a master plate with the value added by a series of separate duty plates. One sheet of the 2d. missed this second pass through the press and was issued without value.

NEW ZEALAND Cook Islands

1909–11. W **43** of New Zealand.
37	**3**	½d. green (Perf 14½×14) (1911)	13·00	9·00
38	**2**	1d. deep red (Perf 14)	45·00	35·00
		a. Wmk sideways (24.12.09)	14·00	2·50

For Nos. 37/38 the watermark is either upright or inverted. For No. 38a it is sideways, either with star to right or left of NZ.

1913–19. W **43** of New Zealand (sideways on T **3**). Chalk-surfaced paper.
39	**3**	½d. deep green (Perf 14) (1915)	11·00	15·00
		a. Wmk upright	15·00	25·00
40	**2**	1d. red (Perf 14) (7.13)	15·00	5·00
41		1d. red (Perf 14×14½) (1914)	12·00	6·00
42		1½d. deep mauve (Perf 14) (1915)	90·00	18·00
43		1½d. deep mauve (Perf 14×15) (1916)	22·00	5·00
44	**3**	2d. deep brown (Perf 15×14) (1919)	7·00	50·00
45	**2**	10d. green (Perf 14×15) (1918)	40·00	£130
46	**3**	1s. carmine (Perf 15×14) (1919)	35·00	£130
39/46 Set of 6			£110	£300

13 Huts at Arorangi   **14** Avarua Harbour

R. 2/8   R. 3/6   R. 5/2

Double derrick flaws

RAROTONGA

APA PENE

(8)

1919 (Apr–July). Stamps of New Zealand surch as T **8**.

*(a) T **53**. W **43**. De La Rue chalk-surfaced paper. Perf 14×15.*
47		1d. carmine (No. 405) (B.) (6.19)	2·00	6·00

*(b) T **60** (recess). W **43**. Cowan unsurfaced paper. Perf 14×13½.*
48		2½d. blue (No. 419) (R.) (6.19)	2·75	6·50
		a. Perf 14×14½	2·00	2·50
		b. Vert pair. Nos. 48/48a	20·00	50·00
49		3d. chocolate (No. 420) (B.)	4·00	8·00
		a. Perf 14×14½	4·00	4·50
		b. Vert pair. Nos. 49/49a	25·00	60·00
50		4d. bright violet (No. 422) (B.)	3·00	6·50
		a. Re-entry (Pl 20 R. 1/6)	60·00	
		b. Re-entry (Pl 20 R. 4/10)	60·00	
		c. Perf 14×14½	2·00	5·00
		d. Vert pair Nos. 50 and 50c	22·00	65·00
51		4½d. deep green (No. 423) (B.)	3·50	9·50
		a. Perf 14×14½	2·00	9·00
		b. Vert pair. Nos. 51/51a	25·00	75·00
52		6d. carmine (No. 425) (B.) (6.19)	4·25	8·50
		a. Perf 14×14½	2·00	6·00
		b. Vert pair. Nos. 52/52a	38·00	90·00
53		7½d. red-brown (No. 426) (B.)	2·25	7·50
54		9d. sage-green (No. 429) (R.)	5·00	15·00
		a. Perf 14×14½	3·50	15·00
		b. Vert pair. Nos. 54/54a	40·00	£120
55		1s. vermilion (No. 430) (B.) (6.19)	12·00	30·00
		a. Perf 14×14½	3·00	30·00
		b. Vert pair. Nos. 55/55a	50·00	£140

*(c) T **61** (typo). W **43**. De La Rue chalk-surfaced paper. Perf 14×15.*
56		½d. green (No. 435) (R.) (6.19)	55	1·00
57		1½d. orange-brown (No. 438) (R.) (6.19)	50	1·00
58		2d. yellow (No. 439) (R.)	2·25	2·50
59		3d. chocolate (No. 440) (B.) (7.19)	2·75	13·00
47/59 Set of 13			25·00	80·00

9 Captain Cook landing   **10** Wharf at Avarua

11 Captain Cook (Dance)   **12** Palm Tree

(Des, eng and recess Perkins Bacon & Co)

1920 (23 Aug). No wmk. Perf 14.
70	**9**	½d. black and green	4·50	28·00
71	**10**	1d. black and carmine-red	5·00	28·00
		a. Double derrick flaw (R. 2/8, 3/6 or 5/2)	13·00	
72	**11**	1½d. black and dull blue	10·00	9·50
73	**12**	3d. black and chocolate	3·00	6·00
74	**13**	6d. brown and yellow-orange	6·00	9·00
75	**14**	1s. black and violet	11·00	20·00
70/75 Set of 6			35·00	90·00

Examples of the 1d. and 1s. with centre inverted were not supplied to the Post Office (*Price £850 each, unused*).

RAROTONGA **RAROTONGA**

(15)   Trimmed overprint (R. 1/6 and R. 3/7)

1921 (Oct)–**23**. Postal Fiscal stamps as T **F4** of New Zealand optd with T **15**. W **43** (sideways). Chalk-surfaced 'De La Rue' paper. Perf 14½×14.
76		2s. deep blue (No. F111) (R.)	27·00	55·00
		a. Trimmed opt	£120	
		b. Carmine opt (1923)	£200	£225
		ba. Trimmed opt	£600	£650
		c. Optd on Jones chalk-surfaced paper	—	£650
77		2s.6d. grey-brown (No. F112) (B.)	20·00	50·00
		a. Trimmed opt	90·00	
78		5s. yellow-green (No. F115) (R.)	35·00	70·00
		a. Trimmed opt	£120	
79		10s. maroon (No. F120) (B.)	90·00	£140
		a. Trimmed opt	£275	
80		£1 rose-carmine (No. F123) (B.)	£150	£250
		a. Trimmed opt	£375	
76/80 Set of 5			£300	£500

For details of the Jones paper, see below No. 385 of New Zealand. See also Nos. 85/89.

16 Te Po, Rarotongan Chief   **17** Harbour, Rarotonga and Mount Ikurangi

(2½d. from a print; 4d. des A. H. Messenger. Plates by P.B. Recess Govt Ptg Office, Wellington)

1924–27. W **43** of New Zealand (sideways on 4d.). Perf 14.
81	**9**	½d. black and green (13.5.26)	6·00	10·00
82	**10**	1d. black and deep carmine (10.11.24)	8·00	4·00
		a. Double derrick flaw (R. 2/8, 3/6 or 5/2)	20·00	10·00
		x. Wmk reversed	£225	
83	**16**	2½d. red-brown and steel blue (15.10.27)	18·00	45·00
84	**17**	4d. green and violet (15.10.27)	30·00	18·00
81/84 Set of 4			55·00	70·00

Cook Islands NEW ZEALAND

1926 (Feb–May). As Nos. 76/80, but on thick, opaque white chalk-surfaced Cowan paper.

85	2s. blue (No. F131) (C.)	£200	£325
	a. Trimmed opt	£600	
86	2s.6d. deep grey-brown (No. F132) (B.)	95·00	£180
87	5s. yellow-green (No. F135) (R.) (5.26)	£110	£180
	a. Trimmed opt	£325	
88	10s. brown-red (No. F139) (B.) (5.26)	£140	£250
	a. Trimmed opt	£350	
89	£1 rose-pink (No. F142) (B.) (5.26)	£190	£375
	a. Trimmed opt	£550	
85/89 Set of 5		£650	£1200

1926 (Oct)–**28**. T **72** of New Zealand, overprinted with T **15**.

(a) Jones chalk-surfaced paper.

90	2s. deep blue (No. 466) (R.)	10·00	40·00
	w. Wmk inverted		

(b) Cowan thick, opaque chalk-surfaced paper.

91	2s. light blue (No. 469) (R.) (18.6.27)	19·00	40·00
92	3s. pale mauve (No. 470) (R.) (30.1.28)	18·00	50·00
90/92 Set of 3		42·00	£120

TWO PENCE COOK ISLANDS.
(18) (19)

1931 (1 Mar). Surch with T **18**. Perf 14.

(a) No wmk.

93	11	2d. on 1½d. black and blue (R.)	9·50	6·00

*(b) W **43** of New Zealand.*

94	11	2d. on 1½d. black and blue (R.)	4·75	12·00

1931 (12 Nov)–**32**. Postal Fiscal stamps as T **F6** of New Zealand. W **43**. Thick, opaque, white chalk-surfaced Cowan paper. Perf 14.

*(a) Optd with T **15**.*

95	2s.6d. deep brown (No. F147) (B.)	15·00	23·00
96	5s. green (No. F149) (R.)	28·00	55·00
97	10s. carmine-lake (No. F155) (B.)	42·00	£110
98	£1 pink (No. F158) (B.)	£120	£190

*(b) Optd with T **19** (3.32).*

98a	£3 green (No. F164) (R.)	£500	£900
98b	£5 indigo-blue (No. F168) (R.)	£300	£400

The £3 and £5 values were mainly used for fiscal purposes.

20 Captain Cook Landing   **21** Captain Cook

22 Double Maori Canoe   **23** Natives Working Cargo

24 Port of Avarua   **25** RMS *Monowai*

26 King George V

(Des L. C. Mitchell. Recess P.B.)

1932 (15 Mar–2 May). No wmk. Perf 13.

99	20	½d. black and deep green	4·00	17·00
		a. Perf 14	30·00	95·00
100	21	1d. black and lake	11·00	4·75
		a. Centre inverted	£8500	£8500
		b. Perf compound of 13 and 14	£225	£275
		c. Perf 14	16·00	32·00
101	22	2d. black and brown	3·50	9·00
		a. Perf 14	10·00	21·00
102	23	2½d. black and deep blue	28·00	60·00
		a. Perf 14	20·00	60·00
103	24	4d. black and bright blue	35·00	75·00
		a. Perf 14	14·00	60·00
		b. Perf 14×13	30·00	£110
		c. Perf compound of 14 and 13	75·00	£150
104	25	6d. black and orange	30·00	50·00
		a. Perf 14	6·00	18·00
105	26	1s. black and violet (Perf 14) (2.5)	24·00	25·00
99/105 Set of 7			75·00	£170

Nos. 100b and 103c come from sheets reperforated 14 on arrival at Wellington. No. 100b comes from the first vertical column of a sheet and has 14 at left and No. 103c from the third or fourth vertical column with 13 at left or right.

Other major errors exist on this issue, but these are not listed as they originated from printer's waste which appeared on the market in 1935. They include the ½d. in vertical pair, imperforate horizontally (*price* £425, *unused*), and the ½d. 2d. and 2½d. with centre inverted (*prices* ½d. £950, 2d. £500 *and* 2½d. £300, *unused*). Imperforate stamps are of proof status.

(Recess from P.B. plates at Govt Printing Office, Wellington)

1933–36. W **43** of New Zealand (Single NZ and Star). Perf 14.

106	20	½d. black and deep green	1·25	4·50
		w. Wmk inverted	£150	£120
107	21	1d. black and scarlet (1935)	1·50	2·25
		y. Wmk inverted and reversed	—	£350
108	22	2d. black and brown (1936)	1·50	50
		w. Wmk inverted	—	£425
109	23	2½d. black and deep blue	1·50	2·25
110	24	4d. black and bright blue	1·50	50
111	25	6d. black and orange-yellow (1936)	1·75	2·50
112	26	1s. black and violet (1936)	30·00	42·00
106/112 Set of 7			35·00	48·00

SILVER JUBILEE OF KING GEORGE V. 1910 - 1935.
(27)

B K E N
B K E N

Normal (top) and narrow (bottom) letters

1935 (7 May). Silver Jubilee. Optd at the Govt Printing Office, Wellington with T **27** (wider vertical spacing on 6d.). Colours changed. W **43** of New Zealand. Perf 14.

113	21	1d. red-brown and lake	1·00	1·40
		a. Narrow 'K' in 'KING'	2·25	5·50
		b. Narrow 'B' in 'JUBILEE'	20·00	22·00
114	23	2½d. dull and deep blue	4·50	3·50
		a. Narrow first 'E' in 'GEORGE'	6·00	6·00
115	25	6d. green and orange	12·00	7·00
		a. Narrow 'N' in KING'	20·00	20·00
113/115 Set of 3			16·00	10·50

All sheets of 80 (10×8) for the 1d. and 8×10 for the 2½d. and 6d.).

The narrow 'K' is on all stamps in column three, the three bottom stamps in column six and the top four and seventh stamps in column eight.

1936 (15 July)–**44**. Stamps of New Zealand optd with T **19**. W **43**. Perf 14.

*(a) T **72**. Cowan thick, opaque chalk-surfaced paper.*

116	2s. light blue (No. 469)	15·00	45·00
117	3s. pale mauve (No. 470)	16·00	75·00

*(b) T **F6**. Cowan thick, opaque chalk-surfaced paper.*

118	2s.6d. deep brown (No. F147)	48·00	£110
119	5s. green (No. F149) (R.)	50·00	£130
120	10s. carmine-lake (No. F155)	90·00	£250
121	£1 pink (No. F158)	£120	£275
118/121 Set of 4		£250	£700

*(c) T **F6**. Thin, hard, chalk-surfaced Wiggins Teape paper.*

122	2s.6d. dull brown (No. F170) (12.40)	£180	£170
123	5s. green (No. F172) (R.) (10.40)	£600	£500
123a	10s. pale carmine-lake (No. F177) (11.44)	£150	£225
123b	£3 green (No. F183) (R.) (20.4.48)	£450	£750
122/123b Set of 4		£1200	£1500

* Earliest known date.

NEW ZEALAND Cook Islands

COOK IS'DS. **IS'DS.**
(28)

Small second 'S' (R. 1/2 and R. 8/4, first printing, and R. 6/10, second printing)

1937 (1 June). Coronation. Nos. 599/601 of New Zealand (inscr '12th MAY 1937') optd with T **28**.

124		1d. carmine	75	80
	a.	Small second 'S'	16·00	18·00
125		2½d. Prussian blue	1·25	1·40
	a.	Small second 'S'	27·00	30·00
126		6d. red-orange	1·50	60
	a.	Small second 'S'	27·00	27·00
124/126 Set of 3			3·25	2·50

The Small second 'S' was corrected for the third printing.

29 King George VI

30 Native Village

31 Native Canoe

32 Tropical Landscape

(Des J. Berry (2s., 3s., and frame of 1s.). Eng B.W. Recess Govt Ptg. Office, Wellington)

1938 (2 May). W **43** of New Zealand. Perf 14.

127	**29**	1s. black and violet	9·00	14·00
128	**30**	2s. black and red-brown	22·00	15·00
		w. Wmk inverted		
129	**31**	3s. greenish blue and green	65·00	55·00
127/129 Set of 3			85·00	75·00

(Recess B.W.)

1940 (2 Sept). Surch as in T **32**. W **98** of New Zealand. Perf 13½×14.

130	**32**	3d. on 1½d. black and purple	75	60

T **32** was not issued without surcharge but archival examples exist (*Price, £250, unused*).

1943–54. Postal Fiscal stamps as T **F6** of New Zealand optd with T **19**. W **98**. Wiggins Teape chalk-surfaced paper. Perf 14.

131		2s.6d. dull brown (No. F193) (3.46)	£140	£150
		w. Wmk inverted (2.4.51)	55·00	55·00
132		5s. green (No. F195) (R.) (11.43)	19·00	45·00
		w. Wmk inverted (5.54)	65·00	70·00
133		10s. pale carmine-lake (No. F201) (10.48)	£110	£160
		w. Wmk inverted (10.51)	85·00	£120
134		£1 pink (No. F203) (11.47)	75·00	£130
		w. Wmk inverted (19.5.54)	£140	£200
135		£3 green (No. F208) (R.) (1946?)	£1700	£1800
		w. Wmk inverted (28.5.53)	75·00	£180
136		£5 indigo-blue (No. F211) (R.) (25.10.50)	£250	£500
		w. Wmk inverted (19.5.54)	£275	£450
131w/136w Set of 6			£550	£850

The £3 and £5 were mainly used for fiscal purposes.

(Recess Govt Ptg Office, Wellington)

1944–46. W **98** of New Zealand (sideways on ½d., 1d., 1s., and 2s.). Perf 14.

137	**20**	½d. black and deep green (11.44)	1·75	4·50
		w. Wmk sideways inverted	6·50	12·00
138	**21**	1d. black and scarlet (3.45)	2·00	3·50
		w. Wmk sideways inverted	9·00	4·25
		x. Wmk sideways reversed		
139	**22**	2d. black and brown (2.46)	5·00	21·00
140	**23**	2½d. black and deep blue (5.45)	2·00	5·00
141	**24**	4d. black and blue (4.44)	7·00	30·00
		y. Wmk inverted and reversed	42·00	80·00
142	**25**	6d. black and orange (6.44)	6·00	5·00
143	**29**	1s. black and violet (9.44)	6·00	6·00
144	**30**	2s. black and red-brown (8.45)	40·00	60·00
145	**31**	3s. greenish blue and green (6.45)	45·00	40·00
		w. Wmk inverted	£130	
137/145 Set of 9			£100	£160

The normal sideways watermark shows the star to the left of NZ *as seen from the back of the stamp*.

COOK ISLANDS
(33)

1946 (4 June). Peace. Nos. 668, 670, 674/675 of New Zealand optd with T **33** (reading up and down at sides on 2d.).

146		1d. green (Parliament House)	50	10
147		2d. purple (Royal Family) (B.)	50	50
148		6d. chocolate and vermilion (Coat of Arms, foundry and farm)	1·50	1·25
149		8d. black and carmine (St George) (B.)	1·00	1·25
146/149 Set of 4			3·25	2·75

34 Ngatangiia Channel, Rarotonga

35 Captain Cook and Map of Hervey Islands

36 Raratonga and Reverend John Williams

37 Aitutaki and Palm Trees

38 Rarotonga Airfield

39 Penrhyn Village

40 Native Hut

41 Map and Statue of Captain Cook

42 Native Hut and Palms

43 *Matua* (inter-island freighter)

Cook Islands, Aitutaki NEW ZEALAND

(Des J. Berry. Recess Waterlow)

1949 (1 Aug)–**61**. Types **34/43**. W **98** of New Zealand (sideways on shilling values). Perf 13½×13 (horiz) or 13×13½ (vert).

150	34	½d. violet and brown	10	1·75
151	35	1d. chestnut and green	3·00	3·75
152	36	2d. reddish brown and scarlet	2·00	3·75
153	37	3d. green and ultramarine	7·50	2·50
		aw. Wmk inverted	£100	
		b. Wmk sideways (white opaque paper) (22.5.61)	10·00	4·25
154	38	5d. emerald-green and violet	12·00	2·00
155	39	6d. black and carmine	5·50	3·00
156	40	8d. olive-green and orange	70	4·00
		w. Wmk inverted	£150	£100
157	41	1s. light blue and chocolate	5·00	4·00
158	42	2s. yellow-brown and carmine	7·50	15·00
		w. Wmk sideways inverted		
159	43	3s. light blue and bluish green	28·00	35·00
150/159 *Set of 10*			65·00	65·00

43a Queen Elizabeth II   (44)

(Des J. Berry. Photo Harrison)

1953 (25 May). Coronation. T **43a** and similar vert design. W **98**. Perf 14×14½.

160		3d. brown	2·50	1·00
161		6d. slate-grey	2·50	2·00

Designs: 3d. T **43a**; 6d. Westminster Abbey.

> **IMPERFORATE STAMPS.** Imperforate examples of many Cook Islands stamps formerly in the Islands' philatelic archives, were put on sale from mid-2013. These include Nos. 160/161 and numerous issues from 1966 onwards. Such material is outside the scope of this catalogue.

1960 (1 Apr). No. 154 surch with T **44**.

162		1s.6d. on 5d. emerald-green and violet	1·50	1·50

45 Tiare Maori   46 Fishing God   47 Frangipani

48 White Tern   49 Hibiscus

50 Long-tailed Tuna   51 Oranges   52 Queen Elizabeth II

53 Island Scene   54 Administration Centre, Mangaia

55 Rarotonga

(Des J. Berry. Recess (1s.6d.), litho (others) B.W.)

1963 (4 June). Types **45/55**. W **98** of New Zealand (sideways). Perf 13½×13 (1d., 2d., 8d.), 13×13½ (3d., 5d., 6d., 1s.) or 13½ (others).

163	45	1d. emerald-green and yellow	75	75
164	46	2d. brown-red and yellow	30	65
165	47	3d. yellow, yellow-green and reddish violet	70	75
166	48	5d. blue and black	7·00	2·25
167	49	6d. red, yellow and green	1·00	60
168	50	8d. black and blue	3·75	1·50
169	51	1s. orange-yellow and yellow-green	1·00	1·00
170	52	1s.6d. bluish violet	2·75	2·00
171	53	2s. bistre-brown and grey-blue	2·75	2·00
172	54	3s. black and yellow-green	2·00	3·75
173	55	5s. bistre-brown and blue	21·00	9·00
163/173 *Set of 11*			40·00	22·00

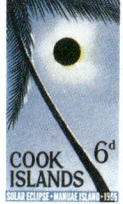 

56 Eclipse and Palm   57 NZ Ensign and Map

(Des L. C. Mitchell. Litho B.W.)

1965 (31 May). Solar Eclipse Observation, Manuae Island. W **98** of New Zealand. Perf 13½.

174	56	6d. black, yellow and light blue	20	10

The Cook Islands became a self-governing territory in free association with New Zealand on 16 September 1965.

AITUTAKI

> The island of Aitutaki, under British protection from 1888, was annexed by New Zealand on 11 June 1901.

NEW ZEALAND DEPENDENCY

Stamps of COOK ISLANDS were used in Aitutaki from 1892 until 1903.

PRICES FOR STAMPS ON COVER TO 1932	
Nos. 1/7	from × 4
Nos. 9/14	from × 3
Nos. 15/29	from × 4
Nos. 30/32	from × 6

Stamps of New Zealand overprinted or surcharged. For illustrations of watermarks and definitive types see New Zealand.

AITUTAKI.   Ava Pene.   Tai Pene.

(1)   (2) ½d.   (3) 1d.

NEW ZEALAND — Aitutaki, Penrhyn Island

Rua Pene Ma Te Ava.	Toru Pene.	Ono Pene.
(4) 2½d.	(5) 3d.	(6) 6d.

Tai Tiringi.
(7) 1s.

1903 (29 June)–**11**. Types **23**, **27/28**, **31**, **34** and **42** surch with T **1** at top and Types **2** to **7** at foot. Thin, hard Cowan paper. W **43**.

(a) Perf 14.

1	½d. green (No. 302) (R.)	4·75	7·50
2	1d. carmine (No. 303) (B.)	5·50	6·00
3	2½d. deep blue (No. 320a) (R.) (9.11)	8·00	19·00
	a. 'Ava' without stop	£150	£250
1/3 Set of 3		16·00	29·00

(b) Perf 11.

4	2½d. blue (No. 308) (R.)	20·00	13·00
5	3d. yellow-brown (No. 309) (B.)	18·00	18·00
6	6d. rose-red (No. 312a) (B.)	32·00	26·00
7	1s. bright red (No. 315a) (B.)	55·00	90·00
	a. 'Tiringi' without stop (R. 7/12)	£650	£950
	b. Orange-red	70·00	£110
	ba. 'Tiringi' without stop (R. 7/12)	£850	£1100
4/7 Set of 4		£110	£130

Nos. 1/2 and 4/7 were placed on sale in Auckland on 12 June 1903. There were four states of the overprint used for No. 3. On the first the 'no stop' variety (No. 3a) occurs on R. 6/8, on the second it appears on R. 1/4, 2/4 and 6/8, on the third on R. 5/8 and 6/8, and on the fourth all stops are present.

AITUTAKI.

Ono Pene.
(8)

1911–16. Types **51** and **53** surch with T **1** at top and T **2** or T **3** at foot and T **52** surch as T **8**. Perf 14×15 (½d., 1d.) or 14×14½ (others).

9	½d. green (No. 387) (R.) (9.11)	1·25	9·00
10	1d. carmine (No. 405) (B.) (2.13)	3·00	14·00
11	6d. carmine (No. 392) (B.) (23.5.16)	55·00	£140
12	1s. vermilion (No. 394) (B.) (9.14)	60·00	£160
9/12 Set of 4		£100	£300

1916–17. T **60** (recess) surch as T **8**. W **43**. Perf 14×13½.

13	6d. carmine (No. 425) (B.) (6.6.16)	9·00	50·00
	a. Perf 14×14½	7·50	35·00
	b. Vert pair. Nos. 13/13a	50·00	£200
14	1s. vermilion (No. 430) (B.) (3.17)	12·00	£100
	a. Perf 14×14½	15·00	£100
	ab. 'Tai' without dot (R. 8/9, 9/12, 10/12)	£225	£750
	ac. 'Tiringi' without dot on second 'i' (R. 8/12, 10/7)	£300	£850
	ad. 'Tiringi' without dot on third 'i' (R. 8/11)	£425	£1100
	b. Vert pair. Nos. 14/14a	£100	£450

1917–18. T **60** (recess) optd 'AITUTAKI' only, as in T **8**. W **43**. Perf 14×13½.

15	2½d. blue (No. 419) (R.) (12.18)	2·00	25·00
	a. Perf 14×14½	1·75	18·00
	b. Vert pair. Nos. 15/15a	30·00	£150
16	3d. chocolate (No. 420) (B.) (1.18)	1·75	40·00
	a. Perf 14×14½	1·50	32·00
	b. Vert pair. Nos. 16/16a	30·00	£180
17	6d. carmine (No. 425) (B.) (11.17)	6·00	28·00
	a. Perf 14×14½	4·75	25·00
	b. Vert pair. Nos. 17/17a	40·00	£160
18	1s. vermilion (No. 430) (B.) (11.17)	14·00	48·00
	a. Perf 14×14½	10·00	35·00
	b. Vert pair. Nos. 18/18a	65·00	£225
15/18 Set of 4		21·00	£120
15a/18a Set of 4		16·00	£100

1917–20. Types **53** and **61** (typo) optd 'AITUTAKI' only, as in T **8**. W **43**. Perf 14×15.

19	½d. green (No. 435) (R.) (2.20)	1·00	6·50
20	1d. carmine (No. 405) (B.) (5.20)	6·50	38·00
21	1½d. slate (No. 437) (R.) (11.17)	5·00	35·00
22	1½d. orange-brown (No. 438) (R.) (2.19)	90	7·50
23	3d. chocolate (No. 440) (B.) (6.19)	4·00	23·00
19/23 Set of 5		15·00	90·00

(Des and recess Perkins Bacon & Co)

1920 (23 Aug). Types **9/14** of Cook Islands, but inscr 'AITUTAKI'. No wmk. Perf 14.

24	½d. black and green	3·50	26·00
25	1d. black and dull carmine	3·50	17·00
	a. Double derrick flaw (R. 2/8, 3/6 or 5/2)	11·00	65·00
26	1½d. black and sepia	7·00	14·00
27	3d. black and deep blue	2·50	16·00
28	6d. red-brown and slate	6·00	16·00

29	1s. black and purple	10·00	16·00
24/29 Set of 6		28·00	95·00

Examples of the 6d. with centre inverted (*price £900, unused*) and the 1s. with frame printed double (*price £225, unused*) come from printer's waste and were not issued.

(Recess Govt Printing Office, Wellington)

1924–27. Types **9/10** and **16** of Cook Islands, but inscr 'AITUTAKI'. W **43** of New Zealand. Perf 14.

30	½d. black and green (5.27)	4·00	25·00
31	1d. black and deep carmine (10.24)	8·00	14·00
	a. Double derrick flaw (R. 2/8, 3/6 or 5/2)	20·00	35·00
32	2½d. black and dull blue (10.27)	12·00	85·00
30/32 Set of 3		22·00	£110

Cook Islands stamps superseded those of Aitutaki on 15 March 1932.

PENRHYN ISLAND

Stamps of the COOK ISLANDS were used on Penrhhyn Island from late 1901 until the issue of the surcharged stamps in May 1902.

PRICES FOR STAMPS ON COVER TO 1932

No.	1	from × 25
No.	3	—
Nos.	4/5	from × 25
Nos.	6/8	—
Nos.	9/10	from × 50
Nos.	11/13	—
Nos.	14/18	from × 2
Nos.	24/37	from × 3
Nos.	38/40	from × 5

NEW ZEALAND DEPENDENCY The island of Penrhyn, under British protection from 20 September 1888, was annexed by New Zealand on 11 June 1901.

Stamps of New Zealand overprinted or surcharged. For illustrations of New Zealand watermarks and definitive types see New Zealand.

PENRHYN ISLAND.	PENRHYN ISLAND.
½ PENI.	TAI PENI.
(1)	(2) 1d.

PENRHYN ISLAND.
2½ PENI.
(3)

1902 (5 May). Types **23**, **27** and **42** surch with Types **1**, **2** and **3**.

(a) Thick, soft Pirie paper. No wmk. Perf 11.

1	2½d. blue (No. 260) (R.)	16·00	16·00
	a. '½' and 'P' spaced (all stamps in 8th vert row)	32·00	35·00

*(b) Thin, hard Basted Mills paper. W **38** of New Zealand*
(i) Perf 11.

3	1d. carmine (No. 286) (Br.)	£850	£1200

(ii) Perf 14.

4	½d. green (No. 287) (R.)	1·00	14·00
	a. No stop after 'ISLAND'	£150	£325
5	1d. carmine (No. 288) (Br.)	3·25	28·00

(iii) Perf compound of 11 and 14.

6	1d. carmine (No. 290) (Br.)	£1500	£1400

(iv) Mixed perfs.

7	½d. green (No. 291) (R.)	£2500	
8	1d. carmine (No. 292) (Br.)	£3500	

*(c) Thin, hard Cowan paper. W **43** of New Zealand*
(i) Perf 14.

9	½d. green (No. 302) (R.)	4·75	16·00
	a. No stop after 'ISLAND' (R. 10/6)	£180	£375
10	1d. carmine (No. 303) (Br.)	1·25	10·00
	a. No stop after 'ISLAND' (R. 10/6)	60·00	£170

(ii) Perf compound of 11 and 14.

11	1d. carmine (No. 305) (B.)	£15000	

		(iii) Mixed perfs.		
12	½d. green (No. 306) (R.)		£2250	£2500
13	1d. carmine (No. 307) (B.)		£800	£1000

PENRHYN ISLAND. **Toru Pene.**
(4) (5) 3d.

Ono Pene. **Tahi Silingi.**
(6) 6d. (7) 1s.

1903 (28 Feb). Types **28**, **31** and **34** surch with name at top, T **4**, and values at foot, Types **5**/**7**. Thin, hard Cowan paper. W **43** (sideways) of New Zealand. Perf 11.

14	3d. yellow-brown (No. 309) (B.)	10·00	45·00
15	6d. rose-red (No. 312a) (B.)	16·00	50·00
16	1s. brown-red (No. 315) (B.)	60·00	60·00
	a. Bright red	45·00	45·00
	b. Orange-red	65·00	65·00
14/16a Set of 3		60·00	£120

1914 (May)–**15**. Types **51**/**52** surch with T **1** (½d.) or optd with T **4** at top and surch with Types **6**/**7** at foot.

19	½d. yellow-green (No. 387) (C.) (5.14)	80	12·00
	a. No stop after 'ISLAND'	25·00	£110
	b. No stop after 'PENI' (R. 3/17)	£110	£350
	c. Vermilion opt (1.15)	80	8·50
	ca. No stop after 'ISLAND'	10·00	75·00
	cb. No stop after 'PENI' (R. 3/5, 3/17)	55·00	£190
22	6d. carmine (No. 393) (B.) (8.14)	25·00	85·00
23	1s. vermilion (No. 394) (B.) (8.14)	55·00	£110
19/23 Set of 3		70·00	£180

The 'no stop after ISLAND' variety occurs on R. 1/4, 1/10, 1/16, 1/22, 6/4, 6/10, 6/16 and 6/22 of the carmine surcharge, No. 19, and on these positions plus R. 1/12, 1/24, 6/12 and 6/24 for the vermilion, No. 19c.

PENRHYN ISLAND. **PENRHYN ISLAND.**
Normal Narrow spacing

1917 (Nov)–**20**. Optd as T **4**.
*(a) T **60** (recess). W **43** of New Zealand. Perf 14×13½.*

24	2½d. blue (No. 419) (R.) (10.20)	3·00	20·00
	a. Perf 14×14½	2·00	13·00
	ab. No stop after 'ISLAND' (R. 10/8)	£190	£500
	b. Vert pair. Nos. 24/24a	45·00	£110
25	3d. chocolate (No. 420) (B.) (6.18)	12·00	70·00
	a. Perf 14×14½	9·50	70·00
	b. Vert pair. Nos. 25/25a	70·00	£275
26	6d. carmine (No. 425) (B.) (1.18)	8·00	26·00
	a. Perf 14×14½	5·00	21·00
	ab. No stop after 'ISLAND' (R. 10/8)	£450	£900
	b. Vert pair. Nos. 26/26a	55·00	£160
27	1s. vermilion (No. 430) (B.) (12.17)	15·00	45·00
	a. Perf 14×14½	12·00	35·00
	ab. No stop after 'ISLAND' (R. 10/8)	£550	£1000
	b. Vert pair. Nos. 27/27a	£100	£275
24/27 Set of 4		35·00	£140
24a/27a Set of 4		26·00	£120

*(b) T **61** (typo). W **43** of New Zealand. Perf 14×15.*

28	½d. green (No. 435) (R.) (2.20)	1·00	2·50
	a. No stop after 'ISLAND' (R. 2/24)	£150	£225
	b. Narrow spacing	7·50	17·00
29	1½d. slate (No. 437) (R.)	7·00	30·00
	a. Narrow spacing	18·00	65·00
30	1½d. orange-brown (No. 438) (R.) (2.19)	1·00	30·00
	a. Narrow spacing	7·50	65·00
31	3d. chocolate (No. 440) (B.) (6.19)	5·00	48·00
	a. Narrow spacing	17·00	£100
28/31 Set of 4		12·50	£100

The narrow spacing variety occurs on R. 1/5–8, 4/21–4, 7/5–8 and 9/21–4.

(Recess P.B.)

1920 (23 Aug). As Types **9**/**14** of Cook Islands, but inscr 'PENRHYN'. No wmk. Perf 14.

32	½d. black and emerald	1·50	25·00
	a. Part imperf block of 4	£1800	—
33	1d. black and deep red	1·50	17·00
	a. Double derrick flaw (R. 2/8, 3/6 or 5/2)	5·50	48·00
34	1½d. black and deep violet	9·00	19·00
35	3d. black and red	3·50	19·00
36	6d. red-brown and sepia	5·00	20·00
37	1s. black and slate-blue	15·00	28·00
32/37 Set of 6		32·00	£110

No. 32a comes from sheets on which two rows were imperforate between horizontally and the second row additionally imperforate vertically.

Examples of the ½d. and 1d. with centre inverted were not supplied to the Post Office (*Price* £1000 *each, unused*).

(Recess Govt Printing Office, Wellington)

1927–29. As Types **9**/**10** and **16** of Cook Islands, but inscr 'PENRHYN'. W **43**. Perf 14.

38	½d. black and green (5.29)	9·00	25·00
39	1d. black and deep carmine (14.3.28)	9·00	25·00
	a. Double derrick flaw (R. 2/8, 3/6 or 5/2)	20·00	70·00
40	2½d. red-brown and dull blue (10.27)	25·00	50·00
38/40 Set of 3		40·00	90·00

Cook Islands stamps superseded those of Penrhyn Island on 15 March 1932.

NIUE

Niue became a British Protectorate on 20 April 1900 and was transferred to New Zealand control on 11 June 1901. There was considerable local resentment at attempts to incorporate Niue into the Cook Islands and, in consequence, the island was recognised as a separate New Zealand dependency from 1902.

PRICES FOR STAMPS ON COVER TO 1945		
No.	1	from × 3
Nos.	2/5	from × 8
Nos.	6/7	—
Nos.	8/9	from × 30
Nos.	10/12	—
Nos.	13/31	from × 3
Nos.	32/37c	—
Nos.	38/47	from × 5
Nos.	48/49	—
Nos.	50	from × 15
Nos.	51/54	—
Nos.	55/61	from × 8
Nos.	62/68	from × 12
Nos.	69/71	from × 3
Nos.	72/74	from × 10
Nos.	75/78	from × 8
Nos.	79/88	—
Nos.	89/97	from × 2

NEW ZEALAND DEPENDENCY

Stamps of New Zealand overprinted

NIUE
(1)

1902 (4 Jan). Handstamped with T **1** in green or bluish green. Pirie paper. Wmk double-lined 'N Z' and Star, W **38** of New Zealand. Perf 11.

1	42	1d. carmine	£350	£325

A few overprints were made with a greenish violet ink. These occurred only in the first vertical row and part of the second row of the first sheet overprinted owing to violet ink having been applied to the pad (*Price* £1500 *unused*).

NIUE. **NIUE.** **NIUE.**
½ PENI. TAHA PENI. 2½ PENI.
(2) (3) 1d. (4)

1902 (4 Apr). Typeset surcharges. Types **2**, **3**, and **4**.
(i) Pirie paper. No wmk. Perf 11.

2	27	2½d. blue (R.)	3·00	6·50
		a. No stop after 'PENI'	30·00	65·00
		b. Surch double	£2500	

*(ii) Basted Mills paper. Wmk double-lined 'N Z' and Star, W **38** of New Zealand*
(a) Perf 14.

3	23	½d. green (R.)	7·50	10·00
		a. Spaced 'U' and 'E' (R. 3/3, 3/6, 8/3, 8/6)	25·00	38·00
		b. Surch inverted	£350	£600
		c. Surch double	£1200	
4	42	1d. carmine (B.)	50·00	55·00
		a. Spaced 'U' and 'E' (R. 3/3, 3/6, 8/6)	£190	£225
		b. No stop after 'PENI' (R. 9/3)	£500	£600
		c. Varieties a and b on same stamp (R. 8/3)	£500	£600

NEW ZEALAND — Niue

		(b) Perf 11×14.		
5	42	1d. carmine (B.)	2·25	4·50
		b. Spaced 'U' and 'E' (R. 3/3, 3/6, 8/6)	14·00	30·00
		c. No stop after 'PENI' (R. 9/3)	55·00	70·00
		d. Varieties b and c on same stamp (R. 8/3)	55·00	70·00
		(c) Mixed perfs.		
6	23	½d. green (R.)	£1900	
7	42	1d. carmine (B.)	£1000	

1902 (2 May). Typeset surcharges, Types **2**, **3**. Cowan paper. Wmk single-lined 'N Z' and Star, W **43** of New Zealand.

		(a) Perf 14.		
8	23	½d. green (R.)	2·50	2·00
		a. Spaced 'U' and 'E' (R. 3/3, 3/6, 8/3, 8/6)	9·50	13·00
9	42	1d. carmine (B.)	1·75	2·00
		a. Surch double	£1800	£2000
		b. Spaced 'U' and 'E' (R. 3/3, 3/6, 8/6)	15·00	25·00
		c. No stop after 'PENI' (R. 5/3, 7/3, 9/3, 10/3, 10/6)	10·00	19·00
		d. Varieties b and c on same stamp (R. 8/3)	55·00	95·00
		e. 'I' of 'NIUE' omitted (R. 6/5 from end of last ptg)	£1000	
		(b) Perf 14×11.		
10	23	½d. green (R.)		
		(c) Mixed perfs.		
11	23	½d. green (R.)	£1800	
12	42	1d. carmine (B.)	£200	£250
		a. Spaced 'U' and 'E' (R. 3/3, 3/6, 8/3, 8/6)	£600	
		b. No stop after 'PENI' (R. 5/3, 7/3, 9/3, 10/3, 10/6)	£550	

NIUE. Tolu e Pene.
(5)   (6) 3d.

Ono e Pene.   Taha e Silenl.
(7) 6d.   (8) 1s.

1903 (2 July). Optd with name at top, T **5**, and values at foot, Types **6/8**, in blue. W **43** of New Zealand (sideways). Perf 11.

13	28	3d. yellow-brown	11·00	5·00
14	31	6d. rose-red	16·00	12·00
15	34	1s. brown-red ('Tahae' joined)	£650	†
		a. Surch double, one albino	£850	†
16		1s. bright red	45·00	55·00
		a. Orange-red	45·00	55·00
13/16 Set of 3			65·00	65·00

No. 15/15a with 'Tahae' joined as one word comes from the small first printing, which was withdrawn when it was discovered that the absence of a space between 'Taha' and 'e' gave the meaning 'thief' rather than 'one'. One sheet had been sold in Auckland, but no supplies were ever sent to Niue. Other examples emanate from record sheets retained in New Zealand, later distributed in presentation sets.

NIUE. NIUE.
½ PENI.   2½ PENI.   NIUE.
(9)   (9a)   (10)

1911 (30 Nov). ½d. surch with T **9**, others optd at top as T **5** and values at foot as Types **7**, **8**. W **43** of New Zealand. Perf 14×15 (½d.) or 14×14½ (others).

17	51	½d. green (C.)	1·00	1·00
18	52	6d. carmine (B.)	2·25	7·00
19		1s. vermilion (B.)	7·00	48·00
17/19 Set of 3			9·00	50·00

1915 (Sept). Surch with T **9a**. W **43** of New Zealand. Perf 14.

20	27	2½d. deep blue (C.)	26·00	55·00

1917 (Aug). 1d. surch as T **3**, 3d. optd as T **5** with value as T **6**. W **43** of New Zealand.

21	53	1d. carmine (Perf 14×15) (Br.)	24·00	5·50
		a. No stop after 'PENI' (R. 10/16)	£850	
22	60	3d. chocolate (Perf 14×14½) (B.)	50·00	£110
		a. No stop after 'Pene' (R. 10/4)	£850	
		b. Perf 14×13½	65·00	£130
		c. Vert pair, Nos. 22/22b	£200	

1917–21. Optd with T **10**. W **43** of New Zealand.

		(a) Perf 14×15.		
23	61	½d. green (R.) (2.20)	70	3·50
24	53	1d. carmine (B.) (10.17)	10·00	17·00
		f. 'Q' flaw	£250	
25	61	1½d. slate (R.) (11.17)	1·25	3·00
26		1½d. orange-brown (R.) (2.19)	1·25	9·00
27		3d. chocolate (B.) (6.19)	1·60	38·00
		(b) Perf 14×13½.		
28	60	2½d. blue (R.) (10.20)	5·00	20·00
		a. Perf 14×14½	1·40	17·00
		ab. Opt double, one albino	£500	
		b. Vert pair, Nos. 28/28a	18·00	70·00
29		3d. chocolate (R.) (10.17)	4·50	3·00
		a. Perf 14×14½	1·75	3·00
		b. Vert pair, Nos. 29/29a	24·00	50·00
30		6d. carmine (B.) (8.21)	12·00	24·00
		a. Perf 14×14½	5·50	24·00
		b. Vert pair, Nos. 30/30a	32·00	£120
31		1s. vermilion (B.) (10.18)	18·00	42·00
		a. Perf 14×14½	6·00	30·00
		b. Vert pair, Nos. 31/31a	45·00	£130
23/31a Set of 9			25·00	£130

For illustration of No. 24f see above New Zealand No. 405.

1918–29. Postal Fiscal stamps as T **F4** of New Zealand optd with T **10**. W **43** of New Zealand (sideways).

		(i) Chalk-surfaced De La Rue paper		
		(a) Perf 14.		
32		5s. yellow-green (R.) (7.18)	£110	£130
		(b) Perf 14½×14, comb.		
33		2s. deep blue (R.) (9.18)	18·00	35·00
34		2s.6d. grey-brown (B.) (2.23)	25·00	55·00
35		5s. yellow-green (R.) (10.18)	28·00	65·00
36		10s. maroon (B.) (2.23)	£150	£190
37		£1 rose-carmine (B.) (2.23)	£180	£300
33/37 Set of 5			£350	£600

(ii) Thick, opaque, white chalk-surfaced Cowan paper. Perf 14½×14.

37a		5s. yellow-green (R.) (10.29)	30·00	65·00
37b		10s. brown-red (R.) (2.27)	95·00	£180
37c		£1 rose-pink (B.) (2.28)	£160	£300
37a/37c Set of 3			£250	£475

11 Landing of Captain Cook   **12** Landing of Captain Cook

1d. R.2/8   1d. R.3/6    1d. R5/2

Double derrick flaws

(Des, eng and recess P.B.)

1920 (23 Aug). T **11** and similar designs. No wmk. Perf 14.

38		½d. black and green	4·00	5·00
39		1d. black and dull carmine	2·50	1·25
		a. Double derrick flaw (R. 2/8, 3/6 or 5/2)	9·00	9·00
40		1½d. black and red	3·50	18·00
41		3d. black and blue	2·25	17·00
42		6d. red-brown and green	6·00	19·00
43		1s. black and sepia	8·50	20·00
38/43 Set of 6			24·00	70·00

Designs: ½d. T **11**. As Cook Islands Types **10/14** Vert—1d. Wharf at Avarua; 1½d. *Captain Cook* (Dance); 3d. Palm tree. Horiz—6d. Huts at Arorangi; 1s. Avarua Harbour.

Examples of the 6d. with inverted centre were not supplied to the Post Office (*Price*, £850, *unused*).

Niue NEW ZEALAND

1925–27. As Nos. 38/39 and new values. W **43** of New Zealand (sideways on 4d.) Perf 14.

44		½d. black and green (1927)	3·75	13·00
45		1d. black and deep carmine (1925)	1·75	1·00
	a.	Double derrick flaw (R. 2/8, 3/6 or 5/2)	5·50	4·75
46		2½d. black and blue (10.27)	7·00	16·00
47		4d. black and violet (10.27)	14·00	20·00
44/47 Set of 4			24·00	45·00

Designs: ½d. T **11**. As Cook Islands Types **16/17**: Vert—2½d. Te Po, Rarotongan chief. Horiz—4d. Harbour, Rarotonga, and Mount Ikurangi.

1927–28. Admiral type of New Zealand optd as T **10**. W **43** of New Zealand. Perf 14.

(a) Jones paper (wmk inverted).

48	**72**	2s. deep blue (2.27) (R.)	15·00	48·00

(b) Cowan paper.

49	**72**	2s. light blue (R.) (2.28)	18·00	35·00

1931 (1 Apr). No. 40 surch as T **18** of Cook Islands.

50		2d. on 1½d. black and red	5·50	2·00

1931 (12 Nov). Postal Fiscal stamps as T **F6** of New Zealand optd as T **10**. W **43** of New Zealand. Thick, opaque, chalk-surfaced Cowan paper. Perf 14.

51		2s.6d. deep brown (B.)	4·00	11·00
52		5s. green (R.)	35·00	70·00
53		10s. carmine-lake (B.)	42·00	£110
54		£1 pink (B.)	80·00	£160
51/54 Set of 4			£150	£325

See also Nos. 79/82 for different type of overprint.

(Des L. C. Mitchell. Recess P.B.)

1932 (16 Mar). T **12** and similar designs inscr 'NIUE' and 'COOK ISLANDS'. No wmk. Perf 13.

55		½d. black and emerald	14·00	26·00
	a.	Perf 13×14×13×13	£250	
56		1d. black and deep lake	1·00	1·25
57		2d. black and red-brown	8·00	5·50
	a.	Perf 14×13×13×13	£160	£200
58		2½d. black and slate-blue	8·00	85·00
59		4d. black and greenish blue	16·00	70·00
	a.	Perf 14	18·00	65·00
60		6d. black and orange-vermilion	3·50	2·50
61		1s. black and purple (Perf 14)	4·50	7·00
55/61 Set of 7			50·00	£170

Designs: ½d. T **12**. As Cook Islands Types **21/26** Vert—1d. Captain Cook; 1s. King George V. Horiz—2d. Double Maori canoe; 2½d. Islanders working cargo; 4d. Port of Avarua; 6d. RMS *Monowai*.

Examples of the 2½d. with inverted centre were not supplied to the Post Office. (*Price*, £300, *unused*).

Nos. 55a and 57a are mixed perforations, each having one side perforated 14 where the original perforation, 13, was inadequate.

(Recess from Perkins Bacon plates at Govt Ptg Office, Wellington, NZ)

1932 (May)–**36**. As Nos. 55/61, but W **43** of New Zealand. Perf 14.

62		½d. black and emerald (10.8.32)	50	3·50
63		1d. black and deep lake (10.8.32)	50	2·25
		w. Wmk inverted	50·00	
64		2d. black and yellow-brown (1.4.36)	1·25	1·75
		w. Wmk inverted	32·00	55·00
65		2½d. black and slate-blue	1·25	4·25
		w. Wmk inverted	50·00	
66		4d. black and greenish blue	2·25	4·25
		w. Wmk inverted	£160	
67		6d. black and red-orange (1.4.36)	2·00	75
68		1s. black and purple (1.4.36)	14·00	27·00
62/68 Set of 7			20·00	40·00

Imperforate proofs of No. 65 are known used on registered mail from Niue postmarked 30 August 1945 or 29 October 1945.

See also Nos. 89/97.

SILVER JUBILEE OF KING GEORGE V 1910-1935.

(13)

B K E N
B K E N

Normal (top) and narrow letters (bottom)

1935 (7 May). Silver Jubilee. Designs as Nos. 63, 65 and 67 (colours changed) optd with T **13** (wider vertical spacing on 6d.). W **43** of New Zealand. Perf 14.

69		1d. red-brown and lake	1·00	3·50
	a.	Narrow 'K' in 'KING'	5·00	9·00
	b.	Narrow 'B' in 'JUBILEE'	7·50	22·00
70		2½d. dull and deep blue (R.)	7·50	14·00
	a.	Narrow first 'E' in 'GEORGE'	12·00	20·00
71		6d. green and orange	11·00	11·00
	a.	Narrow 'N' in 'KING'	20·00	26·00
69/71 Set of 3			15·00	25·00

The narrow 'K' is on all stamps in column 3, the three bottom stamps in column 6 and the top four and seventh stamps in column 8.

The narrow 'B' is on all stamps in column 1, the top five stamps in column 6, the fifth, sixth and eighth stamps in column 8 and the fifth stamp in column 10.

The narrow 'E' is on all stamps in columns 4 and 8.

The narrow 'N' is on the top five stamps of columns 1 and 4, the bottom five stamps in column 5 and the top four and ninth stamps in column 10.

All sheets of 80 (10×8 for the 1d. and 8×10 for the 2½d. and 6d.).

Examples of No. 70 imperforate horizontally are from proof sheets not issued through the Post and Telegraph Department (*Price* £200 *for vert pair*).

NIUE **NIUE**

(14)   Short opt (R. 9/4)

1937 (13 May). Coronation. Nos. 599/601 of New Zealand optd with T **14**.

72		1d. carmine	30	10
	a.	Short opt	17·00	
73		2½d. Prussian blue	70	1·50
	a.	Short opt	18·00	
74		6d. red-orange	70	20
	a.	Short opt	18·00	
72/74 Set of 3			1·50	1·60

15 King George VI   **16** Tropical Landscape

1938 (2 May). T **15** and similar designs inscr 'NIUE COOK ISLANDS'. W **43** of New Zealand. Perf 14.

75		1s. black and violet	18·00	10·00
76		2s. black and red-brown	12·00	22·00
		w. Wmk inverted	£225	£350
77		3s. blue and yellowish green	35·00	26·00
75/77 Set of 3			60·00	50·00

Designs: 1s. T **15**. As Cook Islands Types **30/31** Vert—2s. Island village. Horiz—3s. Cook Islands canoe.

1940 (2 Sept). Unissued stamp surch as in T **16**. W **98** of New Zealand. Perf 13½×14.

78		3d. on 1½d. black and purple	75	75

T **16** was not issued without surcharge but archival examples exist. (*Price*, £200, *unused*).

NIUE.
(17)

1941–67. Postal Fiscal stamps as T **F6** of New Zealand with thin opt, T **17**. Perf 14.

(i) Thin, hard, chalk-surfaced Wiggins Teape paper with vertical mesh (1941–1943)

*(a) W **43** of New Zealand.*

79		2s.6d. deep brown (B.) (4.41)	£110	£120
80		5s. green (R.) (4.41)	£400	£400
81		10s. pale carmine-lake (B.) (6.42)	£140	£550
82		£1 pink (B.) (2.43?)	£200	£650
79/82 Set of 4			£750	£1500

*(b) W **98** of New Zealand (1942–1954).*

83		2s.6d. deep brown (B.) (3.45)	5·00	11·00
		w. Wmk inverted (11.51)	25·00	45·00
84		5s. green (R.) (11.44)	16·00	18·00
		w. Wmk inverted (19.5.54)	10·00	26·00
85		10s. carmine-lake (B.) (11.45)	60·00	£130
		w. Wmk inverted	75·00	£140
86		£1 pink (B.) (6.42)	75·00	85·00
83/86 Set of 4			£130	£225

NEW ZEALAND Niue

(ii) Unsurfaced Wiggins Teape paper with horizontal mesh.
W **98** of New Zealand (1957–1967).
87		2s.6d. deep brown (Perf 14×13½) (1.11.57)	18·00	12·00
88		5s. pale yellowish green (wmk sideways) (6.67)	16·00	75·00

No. 88 came from a late printing made to fill demands from Wellington, but no supplies were sent to Niue. It exists in both line and comb perf.

1944–46. As Nos. 62/67 and 75/77, but W **98** of New Zealand (sideways on ½d., 1d., 1s. and 2s.).
89	**12**	½d. black and emerald	50	6·00
90	–	1d. black and deep lake	1·00	4·50
91	–	2d. black and red-brown	14·00	14·00
92	–	2½d. black and slate-blue (1946)	60	3·50
93	–	4d. black and greenish blue	4·25	1·25
		y. Wmk inverted and reversed	25·00	25·00
94	–	6d. black and red-orange	2·25	1·75
95	**15**	1s. black and violet	3·00	2·00
96	–	2s. black and red-brown (1945)	12·00	6·50
97	–	3s. blue and yellowish green (1945)	20·00	14·00
89/97 *Set of 9*			50·00	48·00

1946 (4 June). Peace. Nos. 668, 670, 674/675 of New Zealand optd as T **17** without stop (twice, reading up and down on 2d.).
98		1d. green (Blk.)	75	25
99		2d. purple (B.)	75	25
100		6d. chocolate and vermilion (Blk.)	75	90
		a. Opt double, one albino	£550	
101		8d. black and carmine (B.)	75	90
98/101 *Set of 4*			2·75	2·00

Nos. 102/112 are vacant.

18 Map of Niue **19** HMS *Resolution* **20** Alofi Landing

20a Native Hut **21** Arch at Hikutavake  **21a** Alofi Bay

22 Spearing Fish **22a** Cave, Makefu **23** Bananas

24 Matapa Chasm

(Des J. Berry. Recess B.W.)

1950 (3 July). W **98** of New Zealand (sideways inverted on 1d., 2d., 3d., 4d., 6d. and 1s.). Perf 13½×14 (horiz) or 14×13½ (vert).
113	**18**	½d. orange and blue	20	2·25
114	**19**	1d. brown and blue-green	2·25	3·25
115	**20**	2d. black and carmine	1·25	3·25
116	**20a**	3d. blue and violet-blue	20	20
117	**21**	4d. olive-green and pale red-brown	20	20
118	**21a**	6d. green and brown-orange	1·00	1·25
119	**22**	9d. orange and brown	30	1·40
120	**22a**	1s. purple and black	30	20
		w. Wmk sideways		
121	**23**	2s. brown-orange and dull green	7·00	6·00
122	**24**	3s. blue and black	6·00	7·00
113/122 *Set of 10*			18·00	23·00

The normal sideways inverted watermark shows the tops of the stars pointing to the right, *as seen from the back of the stamp*.

1953 (25 May). Coronation. As Nos. 715 and 717 of New Zealand, but inscr 'NIUE'.
123		3d. brown	1·25	75
124		6d. slate-grey	1·50	75

(New Currency. 100 cents = 1 New Zealand dollar)

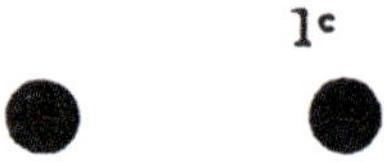

(25) **26**

1967 (10 July). Decimal currency.
*(a) No. 113/122 surch as T **25**.*
125		½c. on ½d. As Type **18**	10	20
126		1c. on 1d. As Type **19**	1·10	20
127		2c. on 2d. As Type **20**	10	20
128		2½c. on 3d. As Type **20a**	10	20
129		3c. on 4d. As Type **21**	10	20
130		5c. on 6d. As Type **21a**	10	20
131		8c. on 9d. As Type **22**	10	20
132		10c. on 1s. As Type **22a**	10	20
133		20c. on 2s. As Type **23**	35	2·00
134		30c. on 3s. As Type **24**	65	1·50
125/134 *Set of 10*			2·50	4·50

*(b) Arms type of New Zealand without value, surch as in T **26**. W **98** of New Zealand (sideways). Perf 14.*
135	**26**	25c. deep yellow-brown	30	55
		a. Rough perf 11	6·00	18·00
136		50c. pale yellowish green	70	80
		a. Rough perf 11	6·00	19·00
137		$1 magenta	45	1·25
		a. Rough perf 11	7·50	13·00
138		$2 light pink	50	2·00
		a. Rough perf 11	8·50	14·00
135/138 *Set of 4*			1·75	4·25
135a/138a *Set of 4*			25·00	55·00

The 25c., $1 and $2 perf 14 exist both line and comb perforated.
The 50c. is comb perforated only.
The perf 11 stamps resulted from an emergency measure in the course of printing.

1967 (3 Oct). Christmas. As T **278** of New Zealand, but inscr 'NIUE'. W **98** (sideways) of New Zealand. Perf 13½×14.
139		2½c. multicoloured	10	10
		w. Wmk sideways inverted	15	50

1969 (1 Oct). Christmas. As T **301** of New Zealand, but inscr 'NIUE'. W **98** of New Zealand. Perf 13½×14½.
140		2½c. multicoloured	10	10

27 'Pua' **37** Kalahimu

(Des Mrs K. W. Billings. Litho Enschedé)

1969 (27 Nov). T **27** and similar vert designs. Multicoloured. Perf 12½×13½.
141		½c. Type **27**	20	10
142		1c. Golden Shower	20	10
143		2c. Flamboyant	20	10
144		2½c. Frangipani	20	10
145		3c. Niue Crocus	20	10
146		5c. Hibiscus	20	10
147		8c. Passion Fruit	30	10
148		10c. Kampui	30	10
149		20c. Queen Elizabeth II (after Anthony Buckley)	1·00	1·75
150		30c. Tapeu Orchid	2·00	2·25
141/150 *Set of 10*			4·25	4·00

(Des G. F. Fuller. Photo Enschedé)

1970 (19 Aug). Indigenous Edible Crabs. T **37** and similar horiz designs. Multicoloured. Perf 13½×12½.
151		3c. Type **37**	10	10
152		5c. Kalavi	10	10

Niue, Samoa NEW ZEALAND

153	30c. Unga		30	25
151/153 Set of 3			45	40

1970 (1 Oct). Christmas. As T **314** of New Zealand, but inscr 'NIUE'.
154	2½c. multicoloured	10	10

38 Outrigger Canoe and Fokker F.27 Friendship Aircraft over Jungle

39 Polynesian Triller

(Des L. C. Mitchell. Litho B.W.)

1970 (9 Dec). Opening of Niue Airport. T **38** and similar horiz designs. Multicoloured. Perf 13½.
155	3c. Type **38**		10	20
156	5c. *Tofua II* (cargo liner) and Fokker F.27 Friendship over harbour		15	20
157	8c. Fokker F.27 Friendship over Airport		15	30
155/157 Set of 3			35	65

(Des A. G. Mitchell. Litho B.W.)

1971 (23 June). Birds. T **39** and similar horiz designs. Multicoloured. Perf 13½.
158	5c. Type **39**	15	35
159	10c. Purple-capped Fruit Dove	40	20
160	20c. Blue-crowned Lory	60	20
158/160 Set of 3		1·00	70

1971 (6 Oct). Christmas. As T **325** of New Zealand, but inscr 'Niue'.
161	3c. multicoloured	10	10

40 Niuean Boy

41 Octopus Lure

(Des L. C. Mitchell. Litho Harrison)

1971 (17 Nov). Niuean Portraits. T **40** and similar vert designs. Multicoloured. Perf 13×14.
162	4c. Type **40**	10	10
163	6c. Girl with garland	10	20
164	9c. Man	10	40
165	14c. Woman with garland	15	80
162/165 Set of 4		35	1·40

(Des A. G. Mitchell. Litho B.W.)

1972 (3 May). South Pacific Arts Festival, Fiji. T **41** and similar multicoloured designs. Perf 13½.
166	3c. Type **41**	10	10
167	5c. War weapons	15	15
168	10c. Sika throwing (*horiz*)	20	15
169	25c. Vivi dance (*horiz*)	30	25
166/169 Set of 4		65	55

42 Alofi Wharf

(Des A. G. Mitchell. Litho Questa)

1972 (6 Sept). 25th Anniversary of South Pacific Commission. T **42** and similar horiz designs. Multicoloured. Perf 14.
170	4c. Type **42**	10	10
171	5c. Medical Services	15	10
172	6c. Schoolchildren	15	10
173	18c. Dairy cattle	25	20
170/173 Set of 4		60	40

1972 (4 Oct). Christmas. As T **332** of New Zealand but inscr 'NIUE'.
174	3c. multicoloured	10	10

43 Silver Sweeper

44 *Large Flower Piece* (Jan Brueghel)

(Des G. F. Fuller. Litho Harrison)

1973 (27 June). Fish. T **43** and similar horiz designs. Multicoloured. Perf 14×13½.
175	8c. Type **43**	25	25
176	10c. Peacock Hind ('Loi')	25	30
177	15c. Yellow-edged Lyretail ('Malau')	30	40
178	20c. Ruby Snapper ('Palu')	30	45
175/178 Set of 4		1·00	1·25

(Des and litho Enschedé)

1973 (21 Nov). Christmas. T **44** and similar vert designs showing flower studies by the artists listed. Multicoloured. Perf 14×13½.
179	4c. Type **44**	10	10
180	5c. Bollongier	10	10
181	10c. Ruysch	20	20
179/181 Set of 3		30	30

45 Captain Cook and Bowsprit

210 Coconut Palm

(Des A. G. Mitchell. Litho Questa)

1974 (20 June). Bicentenary of Captain Cook's Visit. T **45** and similar horiz designs each showing Cook's portrait. Multicoloured. Perf 13½×14.
182	2c. Type **45**	20	20
183	3c. Niue landing place	20	20
184	8c. Map of Niue	20	30
185	20c. Ensign of 1774 and Administration Building	30	65
182/185 Set of 4		80	1·25

Niue became a self-governing territory in free association with New Zealand on 19 October 1974.

SAMOA

PRICES FOR STAMPS ON COVER TO 1945	
Nos. 1/20 are very rare used *on cover*.	
Nos. 21/40	from × 20
Nos. 41/48	from × 100
Nos. 49/51	—
No. 52	from × 20
Nos. 53/56	—
Nos. 57/64	from × 12
Nos. 65/70	from × 3
Nos. 71/97	from × 20
Nos. 101/109	from × 4
Nos. 110/114	—
Nos. 115/121	from × 4
Nos. 122/132	—
Nos. 134/164	from × 4
Nos. 165/176	—
Nos. 177/214	from × 2

NEW ZEALAND Samoa

INDEPENDENT KINGDOM OF SAMOA

The first postal service in Samoa was organised by C. L. Griffiths, who had earlier run the *Fiji Times* Express post in Suva. In both instances the principal purpose of the service was the distribution of newspapers of which Griffiths was the proprietor. The first issue of the *Samoa Times* (later the *Samoa Times and South Sea Gazette*) appeared on 6 October 1877 and the newspaper continued in weekly publication until 27 August 1881.

Mail from the Samoa Express post to addresses overseas was routed via New South Wales, New Zealand or USA and received additional franking with stamps of the receiving country on landing.

Cancellations, inscribed 'APIA SAMOA', did not arrive until 30 March 1878 so that examples of Nos. 1/9 used before that date were cancelled in manuscript with the date of despatch by the postmaster, W. E. Agar. The Samoa Express stamps may also be found cancelled at Fiji, Auckland and Sydney.

1

A 2nd State (Nos. 4/9)

B 3rd State (Nos. 10/19)

(Des H. H. Glover. Litho S. T. Leigh & Co, Sydney, New South Wales)

1877 (1 Oct)–**80**.

A. 1st state: white line above 'X' in 'EXPRESS' not broken. Perf 12½.

1	1	1d. ultramarine	£375	£275
2		3d. deep scarlet	£450	£250
3		6d. bright violet	£475	£250
		a. Pale lilac	£500	£250

B. 2nd state: white line above 'X' usually broken by a spot of colour, and dot between top of 'M' and 'O' of 'SAMOA'. Perf 12½ (1878–1879).

4	1	1d. ultramarine	£180	£250
5		3d. bright scarlet	£550	£650
6		6d. bright violet	£700	£700
7		1s. dull yellow	£325	£130
		b. Perf 12 (1879)	£110	£275
		c. Orange-yellow	£325	£130
8		2s. red-brown	£375	£600
		a. Chocolate	£400	£600
9		5s. green	£4000	£1300

C. 3rd state: line above 'X' repaired, dot merged with upper right serif of 'M' (1879)

(a) Perf 12½.

10	1	1d. ultramarine	£300	£120
11		3d. vermilion	£450	£200
12		6d. lilac	£550	£140
13		2s. brown	£400	£425
		a. Chocolate	£400	£425
14		5s. green	£2250	£800
		a. Line above 'X' not repaired (R. 2/3)	£3250	

(b) Perf 12.

15	1	1d. blue	40·00	£700
		a. Deep blue	45·00	
		b. Ultramarine	40·00	£700
16		3d. vermilion	70·00	£750
		a. Carmine-vermilion	70·00	
17		6d. bright violet	65·00	£500
		a. Deep violet	60·00	£500
18		2s. deep brown	£275	
19		5s. yellow-green	£600	
		a. Deep green	£800	
		b. Line above 'X' not repaired (R. 2/3)	£900	

D. 4th state: spot of colour under middle stroke of 'M'. Perf 12 (1880).

20	1	9d. orange-brown	80·00	£400

Originals exist imperf, but are not known used in this state.

On sheets of the 1d., 1st state, at least eight stamps have a stop after 'PENNY'. In the 2nd state, three stamps have the stop, and in the 3rd state, only one.

In the 1st state, all the stamps, 1d., 3d. and 6d., were in sheets of 20 (5×4) and also the 1d. in the 3rd state.

All values in the 2nd state, all values except the 1d. in the 3rd state and No. 20 were in sheets of ten (5×2).

As all sheets of all printings of the originals were imperf at the outer edges, the only stamps which can have perforations on all four sides are Nos. 1 to 3a, 10 and 15 to 15b, all other originals being imperf on one or two sides.

The perf 12 stamps, which gauge 11.8, are generally very rough but later the machine was repaired and the 1d., 3d. and 6d. are known with clean-cut perforations.

Remainders of the 1d., unissued 2d. rose, 6d. (in sheets of 21 (7×3), 3d., 9d., 5s. (in sheets of 12 (4×3)) and of the 1s. and 2s. (sheet format unknown) were found in the Samoan post office when the service closed down in 1881. The remainders are rare in complete sheets.

Reprints of all values, in sheets of 40 (8×5), were made after the originals had been withdrawn from sale. These are practically worthless.

The majority of both reprints and remainders are in the 4th state as the 9d. with the spot of colour under the middle stroke of the 'M', but a few stamps (both remainders and reprints) do not show this, while on some it is very faint.

There are six known types of forgery, one of which is rather dangerous, the others being crude.

The last mail despatch organised by the proprietors of the *Samoa Times* took place on 31 August 1881, although one cover is recorded postmarked 24 September 1881.

After the withdrawal of the *Samoa Times* service it would appear that the Apia municipality appointed a postmaster to continue the overseas post and from February 1882 the post office was located in the US consulate. Covers are known franked with USA or New Zealand stamps in Samoa, or routed via Fiji.

In December 1886 the municipal postmaster, John Davis, was appointed Postmaster of the Kingdom of Samoa by King Malietoa. Overseas mail sent via New Zealand was subsequently accepted without the addition of New Zealand stamps, although letters to the USA continued to require such franking until August 1891.

2 Palm Trees   **3** King Malietoa Laupepa   **4a** 6 mm

4b 7 mm   **4c** 4 mm

Samoa NEW ZEALAND

Description of Watermarks

(These are the same as W **12a**/W **12c** of New Zealand)

W **4a**. 6 mm between 'N Z' and star; broad irregular star; comparatively wide 'N'; 'N Z' 11½ mm wide, with horizontal mesh.

W **4b**. 7 mm between 'N Z' and star; narrower star; narrow 'N'; 'N Z' 10 mm wide, with vertical mesh.

W **4c**. 4 mm between 'N Z' and star; narrow star; wide 'N'; 'N Z' 11 mm wide, with vertical mesh.

(Des A. E. Cousins (T **3**). Dies eng W. R. Bock and A. E. Cousins (T **2**) or A. E. Cousins (T **3**). Typo Govt Ptg Office, Wellington)

1886–1900.

(i) W **4a**
(a) Perf 12½ (15 October–19 November 1886).

21	**2**	½d. purple-brown (5.11.86)	38·00	55·00
22		1d. yellow-green (5.11.86)	24·00	17·00
23		2d. dull orange (6.11.86)	50·00	18·00
24		4d. blue (19.11.86)	50·00	13·00
25		1s. rose-carmine (19.11.86)	65·00	14·00
		a. Bisected (2½d.) (on cover)*	†	£350
26		2s.6d. reddish lilac	65·00	75·00

(b) Perf 12×11½ (6 July–24 September 1887).

27	**2**	½d. purple-brown	70·00	85·00
28		1d. yellow-green	£110	38·00
29		2d. yellow	95·00	£140
30		4d. blue	£275	£225
31		6d. brown-lake (24.9.87)	50·00	21·00
32		1s. rose-carmine	—	£200
33		2s.6d. reddish lilac	£1500	

(ii) W **4c**. Perf 12×11½ (9 May 1890).

34	**2**	½d. purple-brown	80·00	45·00
35		1d. green	55·00	50·00
36		2d. brown-orange	80·00	50·00
37		4d. blue	£140	5·00
38		6d. brown-lake	£300	11·00
39		1s. rose-carmine	£350	16·00
		x. Wmk reversed	£600	£180
40		2s.6d. reddish lilac	£450	8·50

(iii) W **4b**
(a) Perf 12×11½ (9 May 1890–1892).

41	**2**	½d. pale purple-brown	8·50	8·00
		a. Blackish purple	9·00	8·00
42		1d. myrtle-green	40·00	2·50
		a. Green	40·00	2·50
		b. Yellow-green	40·00	2·50
43		2d. dull orange	50·00	1·75
		x. Wmk reversed	£190	£190
44	**3**	2½d. rose (22.11.92)	75·00	6·00
		a. Pale rose	75·00	6·00
45	**2**	4d. blue	£225	30·00
46		6d. brown-lake	£110	13·00
47		1s. rose-carmine	£250	6·00
48		2s.6d. slate-lilac	£325	13·00

(b) Perf 12½ (March 1891–1892).

49	**2**	½d. purple-brown		
50		1d. green		
51		2d. orange-yellow	—	£1500
52	**3**	2½d. rose (7.1.92)	42·00	4·50
53	**2**	4d. blue	£4500	£1500
54		6d. brown-purple	£4500	£2500
55		1s. rose-carmine	£1200	£1500
56		2s.6d. slate-lilac	£5000	

(c) Perf 11 (11 May 1895–1900).

57	**2**	½d. purple-brown	8·50	2·75
		a. Deep purple-brown	6·00	1·75
		b. Blackish purple (1900)	3·75	35·00
58		1d. green	15·00	2·25
		a. Bluish green (1897)	13·00	2·50
		b. Deep green (1900)	4·25	26·00
		c. Gummed both sides	—	†
		w. Wmk inverted	£750	£300
59		2d. pale yellow (11.5.95)	48·00	48·00
		a. Orange (20.1.96)	26·00	26·00
		b. Bright yellow (11.1.97)	19·00	13·00
		c. Pale ochre (5.8.97)	7·00	13·00
		d. Dull orange (1900)	9·00	
60	**3**	2½d. rose (9.7.95)	8·00	10·00
		a. Deep rose-carmine (1900)	3·00	42·00
61	**2**	4d. blue	20·00	12·00
		a. Deep blue (1900)	3·00	50·00
62		6d. brown-lake	22·00	3·00
		a. Brown-purple (1900)	1·75	60·00
63		1s. rose	20·00	3·75
		a. Dull rose-carmine/toned (5.98)	5·00	38·00
		b. Carmine (1900)	1·50	
64		2s.6d. purple	55·00	10·00
		a. Reddish lilac (wmk inverted) (1897)	20·00	15·00
		b. Deep purple/toned (wmk reversed) (17.5.98)		
		ba. Imperf between (vert pair)	4·75	11·00
		c. Slate-violet	£450	
			£120	

* Following a fire on 1 April 1895 which destroyed stocks of all stamps except the 1s. value perf 12½, this was bisected diagonally and used as a 2½d. stamp for overseas letters between 18 April and 22 May 1895, and was cancelled in blue. Fresh supplies of the 2½d. did not arrive until July 1895, although other values were available from 23 May.

Examples of the 1s. rose perforated 11, No. 63, were subsequently bisected and supplied cancelled-to-order by the post office to collectors, often with backdated cancellations. Most of these examples were bisected vertically and all were cancelled in black (*Price £7 on piece*).

The dates given relate to the earliest dates of printing in the various watermarks and perforations and not to issue dates. It is likely that first use was in March 1887 (Nos. 23/25) with other values following later in the year.

The perf 11 issues (including those later surcharged or overprinted), are very unevenly perforated owing to the large size of the pins. Evenly perforated copies are extremely hard to find.

For the 2½d. black, see Nos. 81/82 and for the ½d. green and 1d. red-brown, see Nos. 88/89.

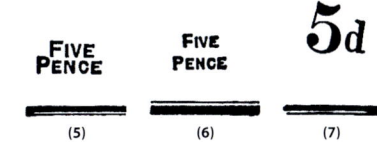

(5)   (6)   (7)

1893 (Nov–Dec). Handstamped singly, at Apia.

(a) In two operations.

65	**5**	5d. on 4d. blue (No. 37)	75·00	50·00
66		5d. on 4d. blue (No. 45)	65·00	£100
67	**6**	5d. on 4d. blue (No. 37)	£100	£110
68		5d. on 4d. blue (No. 45)	80·00	

(b) In three operations (December).

69	**7**	5d. on 4d. blue (No. 37) (R.)	45·00	38·00
70		5d. on 4d. blue (No. 45) (R.)	50·00	50·00

In Types **5** and **6** the bars obliterating the original value vary in length from 13½ mm to 16½ mm and can occur with either the thick bar over the thin one or vice versa. Examples can be found with the bars omitted. Double handstamps exist but we do not list them.

A surcharge as T **7** but with stop after 'd' is now considered to be a trial. It exists in black and in red. Where the 'd' was applied separately its position in relation to the '5' naturally varies.

(8)   (9)   (10)

The 'R' in T **10** indicates use for registration fee.

(Des and die eng A. E. Cousins. Typo New Zealand Govt Ptg Office)

1894 (26 Feb)–**1900**. W **4b** (sideways).

(a) Perf 11½×12.

71	**8**	5d. dull vermilion	40·00	3·50
		a. Dull red	40·00	3·75
		ab. Mixed perfs 11½×12 and 12½		

(b) Perf 11.

72	**8**	5d. dull red (1895)	50·00	14·00
		a. Deep red (1900)	6·00	24·00

No. 72 (like Nos. 71/71a) shows wmk sideways to left (*as seen from the back of the stamp*), whereas No. 72a shows wmk sideways to right.

1895 (28 Jan)–**1900**. W **4b**.

(i) Handstamped with T **9** or T **10**
(a) Perf 12×11½.

73	**2**	1½d. on 2d. dull orange (B.)	28·00	20·00
74		3d. on 2d. dull orange	55·00	24·00

(b) Perf 11 (6.95).

75	**2**	1½d. on 2d. orange (B.)	8·50	7·50
		a. Pair, one without handstamp	£650	
		b. Yellow	9·00	7·50
76		3d. on 2d. orange	9·50	16·00
		a. Yellow	11·00	16·00

(ii) Handstamped as T **9** or T **10**. Perf 11 (20 January 1896).

78	**2**	1½d. on 2d. orange-yellow (B.)	4·50	28·00
79		3d. on 2d. orange-yellow	6·00	50·00
		a. Imperf between (vert pair)	£700	
		b. Pair, one without handstamp		

NEW ZEALAND Samoa

*(iv) Surch typo as T **10**. Perf 11 (7 February 1900).*

| 80 | 2 | 3d. on 2d. deep red-orange (G.) | 2·50 | £130 |

In No. 78 the '2' has a serif and the handstamp is in pale greenish blue instead of deep blue. In No. 79 the 'R' is slightly narrower. In both instances the stamp is in a different shade.

A special printing in a distinctly different colour was made for No. 80 and the surcharge is in green.

Most of the handstamps exist double.

1896 (16 Jan). Printed in the wrong colour. W **4b**.

(a) Perf 10×11.

| 81 | 3 | 2½d. black | 3·25 | 3·50 |

(b) Perf 11.

| 82 | 3 | 2½d. black | 80·00 | 70·00 |
| | | a. Mixed perfs 10 and 11 | £425 | |

(11)   (12)

1898–99. W **4b**. Perf 11.

*(a) Handstamped as T **11** (10.98).*

| 83 | 2 | 2½d. on 1s. dull rose-carmine/*toned* | 50·00 | 50·00 |

*(b) Surch as T **11** (1899).*

84	2	2½d. on 1d. bluish green (R.)	75	3·00
		a. Surch inverted	£850	£425
85		2½d. on 1s. dull rose-carmine/*toned* (R.)	9·50	19·00
		a. Surch double	£400	
86		2½d. on 1s. dull rose-carmine/*toned* (Blk.)	15·00	13·00
		a. Surch double	£500	
87		2½d. on 2s.6d. deep purple/*toned* (wmk reversed)	15·00	27·00

Nos. 83/87 were produced to replace the 2½d. T **3**, showing King Malietou Laupepa, who died on 23 August 1898.

The typographed surcharge was applied in a setting of nine, giving seven types differing in the angle and length of the fractional line, the type of stop, etc.

1899 (18 July). Colours changed. W **4b**. Perf 11.

88		½d. dull blue-green	3·75	6·50
		a. Deep green	3·75	6·50
89		1d. deep red-brown	4·75	5·50

1899 (20 Sept)–**1900**. Provisional Government. New printings optd with T **12** (longer words and shorter letters on 5d.). W **4b**. Perf 11.

90	2	½d. dull blue-green (R.)	3·75	5·50
		a. Yellowish green (1900)	4·75	11·00
91		1d. chestnut (B.)	4·50	18·00
92		2d. dull orange (R.)	2·50	13·00
		a. Orange-yellow (1900)	5·00	15·00
93		4d. deep dull blue (B.)	70	32·00
94	8	5d. dull vermilion (B.)	3·75	16·00
		a. Red (1900)	5·50	16·00
95	2	6d. brown-lake (B.)	1·50	15·00
96		1s. rose-carmine (B.)	1·50	48·00
97		2s.6d. reddish purple (R.)	4·75	32·00
90/97	Set of 8		21·00	£150

The Samoan group of islands was partitioned on 1 March 1900. Western Samoa (Upolu, Savaii, Apolima and Manono) to Germany and Eastern Samoa (Tutuila, the Manu'a Island and Rose Island) to the United States. German issues of 1900–1914 will be found listed in the Stanley Gibbons *Germany Catalogue*, there were no US issues.

The Samoan Kingdom post office run by John Davis was suspended in March 1900.

GERMAN PROTECTORATE

A German postal agency opened at Apia on 21 September 1886. Unoverprinted German stamps were used from this date; prices given below are for the most common type of quoted postmark found on each stamp with cancellation before May 1900. Less common types and other Apia cancellations are worth more; cancellations from May 1900 are worth about 25% less than those before this date.

1886–1899. Stamps of Germany cancelled with circular postmark 'APIA/KAISERL DEUTSCHE/POSTAGENTUR' or other Apia postmarks

(a) Nos. 38b/38e (Numeral inscr 'DEUTSCHE REICHS-POST').

ZG1	7	2m. dull rose (4.1.89)	£12000
		a. Mauve (25.2.90)	£1800
		b. Deep claret (9.11.92)	£350
		c. Red-lilac (10.8.99)	£1900

(b) Nos. 39/44 (Numeral or Eagle inscr 'DEUTSCHE REICHS-POST').

ZG2	5	3pf. green (1890)	£1400
ZG3		5pf. mauve (19.12.87)	£550
ZG4	6	10pf. carmine (14.12.86)	£275
ZG5		20pf. pale blue (17.10.86)	£250
		a. Bright blue (1889)	£275
ZG6		25pf. deep chestnut (1890)	—
ZG7		50pf. pale grey-olive (1886)	£170
		a. Dull olive-green (1888)	£120
		b. Bronze green (1889)	£250

(c) Nos. 46/51 (Numeral or Eagle inscr 'REICHSPOST').

ZG8	8	3pf. brown (28.4.92)	£225
		a. Grey-brown (1892)	90·00
		b. Orange-brown (1899)	95·00
		c. Bistre-brown (1899)	95·00
ZG9		5pf. green (26.3.90)	£140
		a. Yellow-green (1891)	£140
ZG10	9	10pf. rose (29.3.90)	70·00
		a. Carmine (1894)	40·00
ZG11		20pf. ultramarine (24.6.90)	95·00
		a. Dull blue (1891)	70·00
ZG12		25pf. orange-yellow (14.9.92)	£650
		a. Orange (1894)	£475
ZG13		50pf. lake-brown (28.1.90)	£700
		a. Chocolate (1891)	80·00

Dates are those of earliest known use.

Nos. ZG5 and ZG7 with postmark 'APIA/DEUTSCHE/POSTDAMPFSCHIFFS-/AGENTUR' are priced the same as above; this postmark on other stamps is worth more than quoted prices.

The 2m. and Nos. ZG8/ZG13 were valid for postage until 30 September 1901.

(G1)

1900 (Apr). Stamps of Germany, 1889, optd with T **G1**

G1	8	3pf. grey-brown	13·00	18·00
G2		5pf. green	17·00	24·00
G3	9	10pf. carmine	13·00	24·00
G4		20pf. ultramarine	26·00	41·00
G5		25pf. orange	55·00	£110
G6		50pf. chocolate	55·00	£100
G1/G6	Set of 6		£160	£275

A   B

YACHT KEY TYPES. Types A and B, representing the ex-Kaiser's yacht *Hohenzollern*, were in use throughout the German colonies, inscribed with the name of the particular colony for which they were issued. Type A was printed in typography and Type B was recess-printed both by Imperial Printing Office, Berlin.

Perforations. Type A (low values) is perforated 14. In Type B (high values) there are three types of perforation, all measuring about 14½. They are distinguishable by the number of holes along the horizontal and down the vertical sides of the stamps, shown in the listings as (*a*) 26×17 holes.

1e Wmk Lozenges

Watermark. Some values listed on paper watermarked Lozenges were prepared for use and sold in Berlin, but owing to the war of 1914–1919 were not issued in the colonies

1900 (10 Dec)–**01**. No wmk

| G7 | A | 3pf. brown | 1·40 | 1·60 |
| G8 | | 5pf. green | 1·40 | 1·60 |

G9		10pf. carmine	1·40	1·60
G10		20pf. ultramarine	1·40	3·00
G11		25pf. black and red/*yellow*	1·60	17·00
G12		30pf. black and orange/*buff*	1·90	14·50
G13		40pf. black and carmine	1·90	17·00
G14		50pf. black and purple/*buff*	1·90	18·00
G15		80pf. black and carmine/*rose*	3·75	42·00
G16	B	1m. carmine (*a*) (1.01)	4·75	85·00
G17		2m. blue (*a*) (1.01)	6·50	£140
G18		3m. violet-black (*a*) (1.01)	11·00	£200
G19		5m. carmine and black (II) (*a*) (1.01)	£250	£700
G7/G19 *Set of 13*			£250	£1100
G7s/G19s Optd 'Specimen' *Set of 13*			£600	

The 2pf. grey in Type A is a proof.

1915–1919. Wmk Lozenges

G20	A	3pf. brown (1919)		1·40
G21		5pf. green (1919)		1·80
G22		10pf. carmine (1919)		1·80
G23	B	5m. carmine and black (II) (*a*)		65·00
		a. 25×17 holes (1919)		48·00

Nos. G20/G23a were only on sale in Berlin.

NEW ZEALAND OCCUPATION

The German Islands of Samoa surrendered to the New Zealand Expeditionary Force on 30 August 1914 and were administered by New Zealand until 1962.

G.R.I. **G.R.I.**

1 d. **1 Shillings.**

(13) (14)

SETTINGS. Nos. 101/109 were surcharged by a vertical setting of ten, repeated ten times across the sheet. Nos. 110/114 were from a horizontal setting of four repeated five times in the sheet.

Nos. 101b, 102a and 104a occurred on position 6. The error was corrected during the printing of No. 102.

Nos. 101c, 102c, 104d and 105b are from position 10.
Nos. 101d, 102e and 104b are from position 1.
No. 108b is from position 9.

(Surch by *Samoanische Zeitung*, Apia)

1914 (3 Sept). German Colonial issue (ship) (no wmk) inscr 'SAMOA' surch as T **13** or T **14** (mark values).

101		½d. on 3pf. brown	60·00	18·00
		a. Surch double	£750	£600
		b. No fraction bar	90·00	45·00
		c. Comma after 'I'	£700	£450
		d. '1' to left of '2' in '½'	85·00	42·00
102		½d. on 5pf. green	65·00	22·00
		a. No fraction bar	£140	60·00
		c. Comma after 'I'	£425	£180
		d. Surch double	£750	£600
		e. '1' to left of '2' in '½'	£110	45·00
103		1d. on 10pf. carmine	£100	40·00
		a. Surch double	£800	£650
104		2½d. on 20pf. ultramarine	60·00	14·00
		a. No fraction bar	95·00	42·00
		b. '1' to left of '2' in '½'	90·00	42·00
		c. Surch inverted	£1100	£1000
		d. Comma after 'I'	£550	£350
		e. Surch double	£750	£650
105		3d. on 25pf. black and red/*yellow*	80·00	40·00
		a. Surch double	£1100	£800
		b. Comma after 'I'	£5000	£1100
106		4d. on 30pf. black and orange/*buff*	£130	60·00
107		5d. on 40pf. black and carmine	£130	70·00
108		6d. on 50pf. black and purple/*buff*	65·00	35·00
		a. Surch double	£1100	£1000
		b. Inverted '9' for '6'	£180	£100
109		9d. on 80pf. black and carmine/*rose*	£200	£100
110		'1 Shillings' on 1m. carmine	£3250	£3500
111		'1 Shilling' on 1m. carmine	£11000	£7500
112		2s. on 2m. blue	£3500	£3250
113		3s. on 3m. violet-black	£1400	£1200
		a. Surch double	£10000	£11000
114		5s. on 5m. carmine and black	£1200	£1000
		a. Surch double	£13000	£15000

No. 108b is distinguishable from 108, as the 'd' and the '9' are not in a line, and the upper loop of the '9' turns downwards to the left.

UNAUTHORISED SURCHARGES. Examples of the 2d. on 20pf., 3d. on 30pf., 3d. on 40pf., 4d. on 40pf., 6d. on 80pf., 2s. on 3m. and 2s. on Marshall Islands 2m., together with a number of errors not listed above, were produced by the printer on stamps supplied by local collectors. These were not authorised by the New Zealand Military Administration.

SAMOA.

(15)

1914 (29 Sept)–**15**. Stamps of New Zealand. Types **53**, **51**, **52** and **27**, optd as T **15**, but opt only 14 mm long on all except 2½d. Wmk N Z and Star, W **43** of New Zealand.

115		½d. yellow green (R.) (Perf 14×15)	1·75	30
116		1d. carmine (B.) (Perf 14×15)	1·25	10
		a. 'Q' flaw	50·00	15·00
117		2d. mauve (R.) (Perf 14×14½) (10.14)	1·25	1·00
118		2½d. deep blue (R.) (Perf 14) (10.14)	2·25	1·75
		w. Wmk inverted		
119		6d. carmine (B.) (Perf 14×14½) (10.14)	2·00	2·00
		a. Perf 14×13½	17·00	23·00
		b. Vert pair. Nos. 119/119a (1915)	55·00	£100
		c. Pale carmine (Perf 14×14½)	11·00	10·00
121		1s. vermilion (B.) (Perf 14×14½) (10.14)	16·00	25·00
115/121 *Set of 6*			22·00	26·00

1914–24. Postal Fiscal stamps as T **F4** of New Zealand optd with T **15**. W **43** of New Zealand (sideways). Chalk-surfaced De La Rue paper.

(a) Perf 14 (November 1914–1917).

122		2s. blue (B.) (9.17)	£100	£100
123		2s.6d. grey-brown (B.) (9.17)	7·00	20·00
124		5s. yellow-green (R.)	27·00	12·00
125		10s. maroon (B.)	45·00	30·00
126		£1 rose-carmine (B.)	95·00	50·00

(b) Perf 14½×14, comb (1917–1924).

127		2s. deep blue (R.) (3.18)	8·50	5·50
128		2s.6d. grey-brown (B.) (10.24)	£425	£180
129		3s. purple (R.) (6.23)	16·00	65·00
130		5s. yellow-green (R.) (9.17)	32·00	17·00
131		10s. maroon (B.) (11.17)	85·00	48·00
132		£1 rose-carmine (B.) (3.18)	£110	70·00

We no longer list the £2 value as it is doubtful this was used for postal purposes.

See also Nos. 165/166e.

1916–19. King George V stamps of New Zealand optd as T **15**, but 14 mm long.

(a) Typo. Perf 14×15.

134	61	½d. yellow-green (R.)	1·25	1·25
135		1½d. slate (R.) (1917)	50	25
136		1½d. orange-brown (R.) (1919)	30	50
137		2d. yellow (R.) (14.2.18)	2·00	25
138		3d. chocolate (B.) (1919)	5·00	24·00

(b) Recess. Perf 14×13½.

139	60	2½d. blue (R.)	2·50	75
		a. Perf 14×14½	1·25	75
		b. Vert pair. Nos. 139/139a	17·00	27·00
140		3d. chocolate (B.) (1917)	65	1·75
		a. Perf 14×14½	65	1·00
		b. Vert pair. Nos. 140/140a	17·00	30·00
141		6d. carmine (B.) (5.5.17)	4·00	3·25
		a. Perf 14×14½	1·50	2·00
		b. Vert pair. Nos. 141/141a	19·00	40·00
142		1s. vermilion (B.)	7·50	1·50
		a. Perf 14×14½	7·50	9·00
		b. Vert pair. Nos. 142/142a	29·00	55·00
134/142 *Set of 9*			18·00	28·00

LEAGUE OF NATIONS MANDATE

Administered by New Zealand.

1920 (July). Victory. Nos. 453/458 of New Zealand optd as T **15**, but 14 mm long.

143		½d. green (R.)	9·00	19·00
144		1d. carmine (B.)	4·00	24·00
145		1½d. brown-orange (R.)	2·25	13·00
146		3d. chocolate (B.)	10·00	12·00
147		6d. violet (R.)	5·00	7·50
148		1s. orange-red (B.)	12·00	11·00
143/148 *Set of 6*			38·00	75·00

SILVER JUBILEE OF KING GEORGE V 1910 - 1935.

16 Native Hut (17)

NEW ZEALAND — Samoa

(Eng B.W. Recess-printed at Wellington, NZ)

1921 (23 Dec). W **43** of New Zealand.

(a) Perf 14×14½.

149	**16**	½d. green	6·50	22·00
150		1d. lake	11·00	2·00
151		1½d. chestnut	1·75	30·00
152		2d. yellow	3·00	3·25
149/152 Set of 4			20·00	50·00

(b) Perf 14×13½.

153	**16**	½d. green	4·00	1·75
154		1d. lake	7·00	20
155		1½d. chestnut	25·00	16·00
156		2d. yellow	14·00	80
157		2½d. grey-blue	1·75	12·00
158		3d. sepia	1·75	6·50
159		4d. violet	1·75	3·75
160		5d. light blue	1·75	9·50
161		6d. bright carmine	1·75	8·50
162		8d. red-brown	1·75	18·00
163		9d. olive-green	2·00	32·00
164		1s. vermilion	1·75	26·00
153/164 Set of 12			55·00	£120

1925–28. Postal Fiscal stamps as T **F4** of New Zealand optd with T **15**. W **43** of New Zealand (sideways). Perf 14½×14.

(a) Thick, opaque, white chalk-surfaced Cowan paper.

165	2s. blue (R.) (12.25)	£200	£225
166	2s.6d. deep grey-brown (B.) (10.28)	50·00	£110
166a	3s. mauve (R.) (9.25)	70·00	£120
166b	5s. yellow-green (R.) (11.26)	45·00	55·00
	ba. Opt at top of stamp	£2000	£2250
166c	10s. brown-red (B.) (12.25)	£200	£150
166d	£1 rose-pink (B.) (11.26)	£110	£120
165/166d Set of 6		£600	£700

(b) Thin, hard, chalk-surfaced Wiggins Teape paper.

166e	£1 rose-pink (B.) (1928)	£2750	£1200

1926–27. T **72** of New Zealand, optd with T **15**, in red.

(a) Jones paper.

167	2s. deep blue (11.26)	5·00	18·00
	w. Wmk inverted	—	27·00
168	3s. mauve (10.26)	29·00	50·00
	w. Wmk inverted	35·00	55·00

(b) Cowan paper.

169	2s. light blue (10.11.27)	6·00	45·00
170	3s. pale mauve (10.11.27)	60·00	£110

1932 (Aug). Postal Fiscal stamps as T **F6** of New Zealand optd with T **15**. W **43** of New Zealand. Thick, opaque, white chalk-surfaced Cowan paper. Perf 14.

171	2s.6d. deep brown (B.)	16·00	50·00
172	5s. green (R.)	26·00	55·00
173	10s. carmine-lake (B.)	55·00	£100
174	£1 pink (B.)	80·00	£150
175	£2 bright purple (R.)	£1100	
176	£5 indigo-blue (R.)	£2500	

The £2 and £5 values were primarily for fiscal use.

1935 (7 May). Silver Jubilee. Optd with T **17**. Perf 14×13½.

177	**16**	1d. lake	1·00	1·00
		a. Perf 14×14½	£100	£180
178		2½d. grey-blue	1·50	1·25
179		6d. bright carmine	4·50	8·50
177/179 Set of 3			6·50	10·00

18 Samoan Girl   **19** Apia   **20** River Scene

21 Chief and Wife   **22** Canoe and House   **23** R. L. Stevenson's Home *Vailima*

24 Stevenson's Tomb    **25** Lake Lanuto'o    **26** Falefa Falls

(Recess D.L.R.)

1935 (7 Aug). Types **18/26**. W **43** of New Zealand (N Z and Star). Perf 14×13½ (½d., 2½d., 2s., 3s.), 14 (2d.) or 13½×14 (others).

180	½d. green	10	50
	w. Wmk inverted	£100	
181	1d. black and carmine	10	10
	w. Wmk inverted	£100	
182	2d. black and orange	4·00	6·00
	aw. Wmk inverted	£250	£400
	b. Perf 13½×14	5·00	6·50
	bw. Wmk inverted		
183	2½d. black and blue	10	10
184	4d. slate and sepia	70	15
185	6d. bright magenta	50	25
186	1s. violet and brown	30	25
187	2s. green and purple-brown	2·00	2·00
188	3s. blue and brown-orange	6·00	6·00
180/188 Set of 9		12·50	14·00

See also Nos. 200/203.

WESTERN SAMOA.

(27)

1935–42. Postal Fiscal stamps as T **F6** of New Zealand optd with T **27**. W **43** of New Zealand. Perf 14.

(a) Thick, opaque chalk-surfaced Cowan paper (7.8.35).

189	2s.6d. deep brown (B.)	6·00	16·00
190	5s. green (B.)	26·00	42·00
191	10s. carmine-lake (B.)	70·00	90·00
192	£1 pink (B.)	60·00	£110
193	£2 bright purple (R.)	£160	£400
194	£5 indigo-blue (R.)	£225	£475

(b) Thin, hard chalk-surfaced Wiggins Teape paper (1941–1942).

194a	5s. green (B.) (6.42)	£180	£225
194b	10s. pale carmine-lake (B.) (6.41)	£150	£200
194c	£2 bright purple (R.) (2.42)	£550	£1000
194d	£5 indigo-blue (R.) (2.42)	£3000	£3750

The £2 and £5 values were primarily for fiscal use. A £10 deep blue (on Cowan paper) was also issued, and exists with postal cancellations.

See also Nos. 207/214.

28 Coastal Scene   **29** Map of Western Samoa

30 Samoan Dancing Party   **31** Robert Louis Stevenson

(Des J. Berry (1d. and 1½d.). L. C. Mitchell (2½d. and 7d.). Recess B.W.)

1939 (29 Aug). 25th Anniversary of New Zealand Control. Types **28/31**. W **98** of New Zealand. Perf 13½×14 or 14×13½ (7d.).

195	**28**	1d. olive-green and scarlet	1·00	40
196	**29**	1½d. light blue and red-brown	1·75	1·00
197	**30**	2½d. red-brown and blue	3·00	1·50
198	**31**	7d. violet and slate-green	8·00	6·00
195/198 Set of 4			12·00	8·00

32 Samoan Chief   **33** Apia Post Office

(Recess B.W.)

1940 (2 Sept). W **98** of New Zealand (Mult N Z and Star). Perf 14×13½.
199	**32**	3d. on 1½d. brown	75	20

T **32** was not issued without surcharge but archival examples exist (*Price*, £200 *unused*).

(T **33**. Des L. C. Mitchell. Recess B.W.)

1944–49. As Nos. 180, 182/183 and T **33**. W **98** of New Zealand (Mult N Z and Star) (sideways on 2½d.). Perf 14 or 13½×14 (5d.).
200	½d. green	30	24·00
202	2d. black and orange	4·00	9·00
203	2½d. black and blue (1948)	12·00	48·00
205	5d. sepia and blue (8.6.49)	4·00	2·25
200/205 *Set of 4*		18·00	75·00

SIDEWAYS WATERMARKS. For notes on the orientation of sideways watermarks, see above No. 577 of New Zealand.

1945–53. Postal Fiscal stamps as T **F6** of New Zealand optd with T **27**. W **98** of New Zealand. Thin hard, chalk-surfaced Wiggins Teape paper. Perf 14.
207	2s.6d. deep brown (B.) (6.45)	26·00	45·00
	w. Wmk inverted	42·00	60·00
208	5s. green (B.) (5.45)	21·00	15·00
	w. Wmk inverted	40·00	55·00
209	10s. carmine-lake (B.) (4.46)	20·00	18·00
	w. Wmk inverted	60·00	60·00
210	£1 pink (B.) (6.48)	£140	£200
211	30s. brown (8.48)	£200	£350
212	£2 bright purple (R.) (11.47)	£200	£300
	w. Wmk inverted	£600	£750
213	£3 green (8.48)	£300	£400
214	£5 indigo-blue (R.) (1946)	£425	£500
	w. Wmk inverted (5.53)	£425	£500
207/210 *Set of 4*		£180	£250

Values over £1 were mainly used for fiscal purposes.

WESTERN SAMOA
(34)

1946 (4 June). Peace Issue. Nos. 668, 670 and 674/675 of New Zealand optd with T **34** (reading up and down at sides on 2d.).
215	1d. green	60	40
	w. Wmk inverted	£225	
216	2d. purple (B.)	60	40
217	6d. chocolate and vermilion	60	40
218	8d. black and carmine (B.)	60	40
215/218 *Set of 4*		2·25	1·50

UNITED NATIONS TRUST TERRITORY
Administered by New Zealand.

35 Making Siapo Cloth   **36** Native Houses and Flags

37 Seal of Samoa   **38** Malifa Falls (wrongly inscribed 'Aleisa Falls')

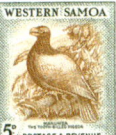

39 Tooth-billed Pigeon   **40** Bonito Fishing Canoe

41 Cacao Harvesting   **42** Thatching a Native Hut

43 Preparing Copra   **44** Samoan Chieftainess

1952 (10 Mar). Types **35/44**. W **98** of New Zealand (sideways inverted on 1s. and 3s.). Perf 13 (½d., 2d. and 1s.) or 13½ (others).
219	**35**	½d. claret and orange-brown	10	3·75
220	**36**	1d. olive-green and green	30	50
221	**37**	2d. carmine-red	30	10
222	**38**	3d. pale ultramarine and indigo	50	20
223	**39**	5d. brown and deep green	15·00	1·50
224	**40**	6d. pale ultramarine and rose-magenta	2·00	10
225	**41**	8d. carmine	1·50	30
226	**42**	1s. sepia and blue	1·50	10
227	**43**	2s. yellow-brown	1·50	25
228	**44**	3s. chocolate and brown-olive	6·00	3·50
219/228 *Set of 10*			26·00	10·00

1953 (25 May). Coronation. Designs as Nos. 715 and 717 of New Zealand, but inscr 'WESTERN SAMOA'.
229	2d. brown	2·25	1·00
230	6d. slate-grey	2·25	1·00

WESTERN SAMOA
(45)

1955 (14 Nov). Postal Fiscal stamps as T **F6** of New Zealand optd with T **45**. W **98** (inverted). Chalk-surfaced Wiggins, Teape paper. Perf 14.
232	5s. green (B.)	8·00	29·00
233	10s. carmine-lake (B.)	8·00	50·00
234	£1 pink (B.)	15·00	60·00
235	£2 bright purple (R.)	70·00	£160
232/235 *Set of 4*		90·00	£275

The £2 value was mainly used for fiscal purposes.

46 Native Houses and Flags   **47** Seal of Samoa

NEW ZEALAND Samoa, New Zealand Used Abroad

48 Map of Samoa and the Mace

(Recess B.W.)

1958 (21 Mar). Inauguration of Samoan Parliament. Types **46/48**. W **98** of New Zealand (sideways inverted). Perf 13½×13 (6d.) or 13½ (others).

236	**46**	4d. cerise	50	30
237	**47**	6d. deep reddish violet	50	30
238	**48**	1s. deep ultramarine	1·25	50
236/238 Set of 3			2·00	1·00

NEW ZEALAND USED ABROAD
GILBERT AND ELLICE ISLANDS

No organised postal service existed in the Gilbert and Ellice Islands before the introduction of stamp issues in January 1911. A New Zealand Postal Agency was, however, provided on Fanning Island, one of the Line Islands, primarily for the use of the staff of the Pacific Cable Board cable station which was established in 1902. The agency opened on 29 November 1902 and although Fanning Island became part of the Gilbert and Ellice Islands colony on 27 January 1916, continued to operate until replaced by a Protectorate post office on 14 February 1939. The cable station closed on 16 January 1964. Fanning Island is now known as Tabuaeran.

Z1

The following NEW ZEALAND stamps are known postmarked on Fanning Island with T **Z1** (in use from November 1902 until November 1936. The earliest known cover is postmarked 20 December 1902).

1882–1900 Q.V. (Perf 10) ½d. (No. 217) (Perf 11) ½d., 1d., 2d. (Nos. 236/238)
1898 Pictorials (no wmk) 1d., 2d., 2½d. (both), 9d. (Nos. 247/250, 260, 267)
1900 Pictorials (W **38**) ½d., 1½d., 2d. (Nos. 273, 275b, 276)
1901 1d. Universal (W **38**) (Nos. 278, 280)
1902 ½d. Mount Cook, 1d. Universal (no wmk) (Nos. 294/295)
1902 ½d. Pictorial, 1d. Universal (W **43**) (Nos. 302b, 303)
1902–1909 Pictorials (W **43**) 2d., 2½d., 3d., 4d., 5d., 6d., 8d., 9d., 1s., 2s., 5s. (Nos. 309/310, 312/317, 319/320, 322, 326, 328/329)
1907–1908 Pictorials (W **43**) 4d. (No. 379)
1908 1d. Universal (De La Rue paper) 1d. (No. 386)
1909–1912 King Edward VII (typo) ½d. (No. 387)
1909–1916 King Edward VII (recess) 2d., 3d., 4d., 5d., 6d., 8d., 1s. (Nos. 388/391, 393/396, 397/398)
1909–1926 1d. Dominion (W **43**) 1d. (Nos. 405, 410)
1915–1930 King George V (recess) 1½d., 2d. bright violet, 2½d., 3d., 4d. bright violet, 4½d., 5d., 6d., 7½d., 9d., 1s. (Nos. 416/417, 419/420, 422/426, 429/430)
1915–1934 King George V (typo) ½d., 1½d. (all 3), 2d., 3d. (Nos. 435/440, 446, 448/448b, 449/449b)
1915 WAR STAMP opt ½d. (No. 452)
1920 Victory 1d., 1½d. (Nos. 454/455)
1922 2d. on ½d. (No. 459)
1923–1925 Penny Postage 1d. (No. 460)
1925 Dunedin Exhibition ½d., 1d. (Nos. 463/464)
1926–1934 Admiral design 1d. (No. 468)
1935–1936 Pictorials ½d., 1d., 1½d., 2d., 4d., 6d., 8d., 1s. (Nos. 556, 557/557b, 558, 559, 562, 564/565, 567)
1935 Silver Jubilee ½d., 1d., 6d. (Nos. 573/575)
1936 Anzac ½d.+½d., 1d.+1d. (Nos. 591/592)
1915 3d. Official (No. O100)
1916 1½d. Official (No. O90)
1899 1d. Postage due (No. D10)
1913 2s. Postal fiscal (No. F111)

Z2

The following NEW ZEALAND stamps are known postmarked on Fanning Island with T **Z2** (in use from 7 December 1936 to 13 February 1939).

1935–1936 Pictorials (W **43**) 1d (No. 557)
1936–1939 Pictorials (W **98**) ½d., 1d., 1½d., 6d. (Nos. 577/579, 585)
1936 Anzac ½d.+½d., 1d.+1d. (Nos. 591/592)
1936 Chambers of Commerce Congress ½d., 1d. (Nos. 593/594)
1936 Health 1d.+1d. (No. 598)
1937 Coronation 1d., 2½d., 6d. (Nos. 599/601)
1938–1939 King George VI ½d., 1d., 1½d. (Nos. 603, 605, 607)

The schooner which carried the mail from Fanning Island also called at Washington Island, another of the Line group. Problems arose, however, as the authorities insisted that mail from Washington Island must first pass through the Fanning Island Postal Agency before being forwarded which resulted in considerable delays. Matters were resolved by the opening of a New Zealand Postal Agency on Washington Island which operated from 1 February 1921 until the Copra plantations were closed in early 1923. The postal agency was re-established on 15 May 1924, but finally closed on 30 March 1934. Covers from this second period occur with incorrectly dated postmarks. Manuscript markings on New Zealand Nos. 578, 599/600 and 692 are unofficial and were applied during the resettlement of the island between 1937 and 1948. Washington Island is now known as Teraina.

Z3

The following NEW ZEALAND stamps are known postmarked on Washington Island with T **Z3**.

1909–1916 King Edward VII 5d., 8d. (Nos. 402, 404b)
1915–1930 King George V (recess) 6d., 7½d., 8d., 9d., 1s. (Nos. 425/427, 429/430)
1915–1934 King George V (typo) ½d., 1½d., 2d., 3d. (Nos. 435, 438/439, 449)
1915 WAR STAMP opt ½d. (No. 452)
1920 Victory 1d., 1½d., 6d. (Nos. 454/455, 457)
1922 2d. on ½d. (No. 459)
1926–1934 Admiral design 1d. (No. 468/468a)

The above information is based on a special survey undertaken by members of the Kiribati & Tuvalu Philatelic Society and the Pacific Islands Study Circle, originally co-ordinated by Mr Michael Shaw.

PITCAIRN ISLANDS

In 1920 a regular mail service was introduced. As there were no stamps available, letters were allowed free postage as long as they carried a cachet, or manuscript endorsement, indicating their origin.

The New Zealand Government withdrew the free postage concession on 12 May 1926, but after representations from the islanders, opened a postal agency on Pitcairn using New Zealand stamps cancelled with T **Z1**. Some impressions of this postmark appear to show a double ring, but this is the result of heavy or uneven use of the handstamp. The postal agency operated from 7 June 1927 until 14 October 1940. The earlier New Zealand stamps are known cancelled with T **Z1**, but these were not supplied to the postal agency and their use is considered to be contrived.

> **PRICES.** Those quoted for Nos. Z1/Z72 and ZF1 are for examples showing a virtually complete strike of T **Z1**. Due to the size of the cancellation such examples will usually be *on piece*.

New Zealand Used Abroad NEW ZEALAND

Z1

Stamps of New Zealand cancelled with T **Z1**.

1915–29. King George V (Nos. 419, 422/426, 428/431 and 446/449).
Z1	½d. green	30·00
Z2	1½d. grey-slate	65·00
Z3	1½d. orange-brown	50·00
Z4	2d. yellow	48·00
Z5	2½d. blue	85·00
Z6	3d. chocolate	90·00
Z7	4d. bright violet	85·00
Z8	4½d. deep green	£120
Z9	5d. light blue	90·00
Z10	6d. carmine	£100
Z11	7½d. red-brown	£130
Z12	8d. red-brown	£170
Z13	9d. yellowish olive	£170
Z14	1s. vermilion	£160

1923. Map of New Zealand (No. 460).
Z14a	1d. carmine	£100

1925. Dunedin Exhibition (No. 464).
Z14b	½d. yellow-green/*green*	£150
Z14c	1d. carmine/*rose*	£120

1926–27. King George V in Field-Marshal's or Admiral's uniform (Nos. 468/469).
Z15	1d. rose-carmine	30·00
Z16	2s. light blue	£350

1929. Anti-Tuberculosis Fund (No. 544).
Z17	1d.+1d. scarlet	£160

1931. Air (Nos. 548/549).
Z18	3d. chocolate	£300
Z19	4d. blackish purple	£350

1932. Health (No. 552).
Z21	1d.+1d. carmine	£170

1935. Pictorials (Nos. 556/558 and 560/569). W **43**.
Z22	½d. bright green	65·00
Z23	1d. scarlet	40·00
Z24	1½d. red-brown	£100
Z26	2½d. chocolate and slate	85·00
Z27	3d. brown	£100
Z28	4d. black and sepia	£130
Z29	5d. ultramarine	£150
Z30	6d. scarlet	£130
Z31	8d. chocolate	£150
Z32	9d. scarlet and black	£150
Z33	1s. deep green	£130
Z34	2s. olive-green	£350
Z35	3s. chocolate and yellow-brown	£400

1935. Silver Jubilee (Nos. 573/575).
Z36	½d. green	50·00
Z37	1d. carmine	50·00
Z38	6d. red-orange	£100

1935. Health (No. 576).
Z39	1d.+1d. scarlet	75·00

1936. Pictorials (Nos. 577/582). W **98**.
Z40	½d. bright green	50·00
Z41	1d. scarlet	17·00
Z42	1½d. red-brown	85·00
Z43	2d. orange	70·00
Z44	2½d. chocolate and slate	75·00
Z45	3d. brown	80·00

1936. 21st Anniversary of Anzac Landing at Gallipoli (Nos. 591/592).
Z46	½d.+½d. green	50·00
Z47	1d.+1d. scarlet	50·00

1936. Congress of British Empire Chambers of Commerce (Nos. 593/597).
Z48	½d. emerald-green	48·00
Z49	1d. scarlet	48·00
Z50	2½d. blue	65·00
Z51	4d. violet	95·00
Z52	6d. red-brown	95·00

1936. Health (No. 598).
Z53	1d.+1d. scarlet	75·00

1937. Coronation (Nos. 599/601).
Z54	1d. carmine	40·00
Z55	2½d. Prussian blue	45·00
Z56	6d. red-orange	45·00

1937. Health (No. 602).
Z57	1d.+1d. scarlet	75·00

1938. King George VI (Nos. 603, 605, 607).
Z58	½d. green	75·00
Z59	1d. scarlet	75·00
Z60	1½d. purple-brown	85·00

1939. Health (Nos. 611/612).
Z60a	1d. on ½d. green	75·00
Z60b	2d. on 1d.+1d. scarlet	75·00

1940. Centenary of British Sovereignty (Nos. 613/622, 624/625).
Z61	½d. blue-green	38·00
Z62	1d. chocolate and scarlet	42·00
Z63	1½d. light blue and mauve	50·00
Z64	2d. blue-green and chocolate	45·00
Z65	2½d. blue-green and blue	50·00
Z66	3d. purple and carmine	50·00
Z67	4d. chocolate and lake	85·00
Z68	5d. pale blue and brown	95·00
Z69	6d. emerald-green and violet	95·00
Z70	7d. black and red	£130
Z71	9d. olive-green and orange	£130
Z72	1s. sage-green and deep green	£130

POSTAL FISCAL STAMPS

1932. Arms (No. F147).
ZF1	2s.6d. deep brown	£400

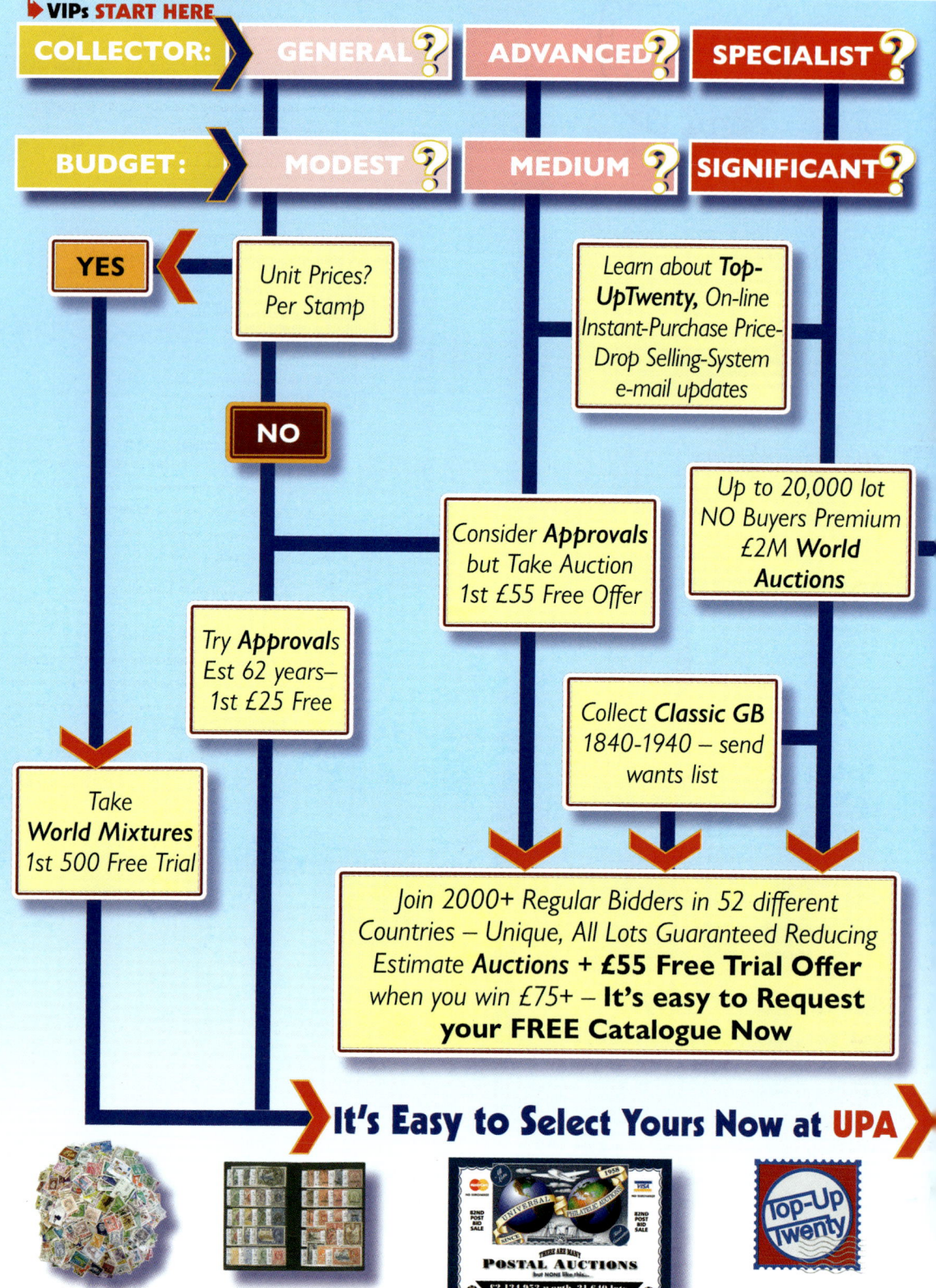

Sometimes Collectors Get a Raw Deal
Determine how You wish to be treated Here...

SELLING

Continuing Collecting?

YES → Yes – Cash / Part exchange/vendor options

NO ↓

Quality Sought – naturally

Contact Andrew Now or another member of his specialist Team to discuss the market/selling options:
andrew@upastampauctions.co.uk
☎ **01451 861111**

'money spent in the wrong way soon mounts up...'

Successful and enjoyable collecting depends upon understanding the relationship of your budget to your interest.

Offers and services can be confusing can't they, and money spent in the wrong way soon mounts up.

In philately, sometimes it is hard to decide which way to go. Your passion may exceed your resource, so just what may be best for you?

Often, it is not what you collect but how you collect

This is the reason why my team and I have devised this quick and easy philatelic route-map QUIZ which does not ask you what you collect – but helps you to determine by your answers just which type of collecting service may best suit you...

Presently you may find few philatelic companies other than UPA which can offer you integrated philatelic selling systems, but obviously once you determine which philatelic services best suit your collecting interest – you may have a clearer idea of which way is best to go – depending upon your levels of specialism and philatelic budget, of course

Check out our Philatelic QUIZ right now and see for yourself. To select your choice, visit our website or call my team

Dedicated to De-mystifying Philately

Andrew McGavin,
Veteran Philatelic Auctioneer
Philatelic Expert & Author
Managing Director Universal Philatelic Auctions (UPA)

Visit: www.UPAstampauctions.co.uk

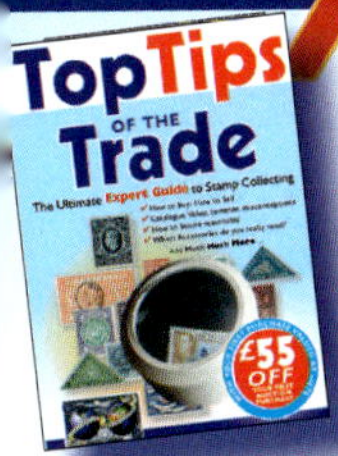

Fax: 01451 861297 ~ info@upastampauctions.co.uk ~ T: 01451 861111
Participate in this Philatelic Route-Map to Enjoyable Collecting.
Find UPA also on-line at www.top-uptwenty.co.uk
New Instant-Purchase Price-Drop Selling-System

SG New Zealand 2022

UPA VIP Series: 'Because' …

Philatelic Feelings…

A 'Must-Read' if You Don't Want to Burn Your Philatelic Budget …

Sometimes Collectors get a raw deal, don't they? For example, whilst on holiday, I remember my wife (a keen plant collector), once spent an extraordinary amount in the sum of £200 for some plants. She paid the bill and was just about to leave when she spotted the company's catalogue (price/stock list) which she hadn't seen. Being 200 miles away from home she asked if she might have one so that she could use their mail-order next time? Incredibly she was told the price of the company's pricelist was £5.

Naturally, she didn't buy one, nor did she ever do business with that company again – ALL for the sake of just £5 – that company lost the goodwill of a client who spent £200 on just one _first_ visit …

Similarly, some stamp companies are _extraordinarily_ mean. Sometimes auction catalogues are not supplied free, or buyer's premiums run at 20%+ levels _even upon company's own stock_, postage, packing and insurance may be added, scans/photocopies cost, moreover … not all auctions guarantee their lots – which is hard to understand when these days, so few collectors physically attend auctions in person.

At UPA, collectors really are **Very Important Philatelists** – that's right UPA VIP's, and you don't have to spend £200= to be charged £5 extra, or for that matter £40 extra buyer's premium. Indeed 'Buyer's Premium' sounds pretty special doesn't it, until you realise that it is you that is paying the premium, and what is it for?

Moreover, you don't have to spend or win £200 worth to be charged £5, or even charged £40 more on your 1st visit … at UPA, you will be joining more than 3,000 different collectors (and some dealers), who have spent £75+ and have been refunded back their 1st £55 FREE, so that they can test my company UPA, virtually for free, with no added buyer's premiums to pay, no extra charges for shipping and insurance, wherever you are in the world (light lots delivered UPA Loyalty Post-Free, naturally) …

Finally, your 20,000+ lot quarterly UPA auction catalogue is also FREE. That's 5,000 colour-corrected images and a catalogue that costs £60,000 just to print and post each auction. What is the secret formula that makes all this possible? The answer is **S C A L E**. More collectors bid in UPA auctions than any other auction in the UK (or most of the rest of the world, for that matter) … so, go on … it won't cost you even ONE penny, plus

It's so easy to collect Your Free Catalogue + 1st £55 FREE offer – **NOW! – simply GO to:**

upastampauctions.co.uk

or (UK collectors) telephone: 01451 861111

SG New Zealand 2022